Securities & Investment Institute Diploma

STUDY BOOK

Interpretation of Financial Statements

2009

In this 2009 edition

- A **user-friendly format** for easy navigation

- **Updated** on recent developments

- **Exam tips** to put you on the right track

- A **chapter roundup** and **test your knowledge** quiz at the end of each chapter

- A full **index**

APPROVED WORKBOOK

LEARNING MEDIA

Published February 2009

ISBN 9780 7517 7210 4

British Library Cataloguing-in-Publication Data
A catalogue record for this book
is available from the British Library

Published by

BPP Learning Media Ltd
BPP House, Aldine Place
London W12 8AA

www.bpp.com/learningmedia

Printed in Great Britain

Your learning materials, published by BPP Learning Media Ltd, are
printed on paper sourced from sustainable, managed forests.

£195.00

CONTENTS

1

Introduction to Financial Statements

INTRODUCTION

The purpose of this chapter is to introduce the general principles involved in preparing a set of accounts and the standard form and content of a set of accounts. You will not be asked to construct accounts in the exam, rather you need to be able to analyse or de-construct them. Fundamental to this analysis is an appreciation of the underlying principles involved.

CHAPTER CONTENTS

CHAPTER LEARNING OBJECTIVES

The syllabus area covered by this chapter is:

Accounting terminology and concepts

Accounting terminology and a knowledge of accounting concepts and conventions to include the statement of financial position, income statement, cash flow statement and notes to the accounts. An understanding of the distinction between capital and revenue, the valuation of assets for accounting purposes and the determination of profit and earnings per share on the nil, net and full distribution bases. An understanding of the significance of the statement of accounting policies in relation to the concept of a true and fair view.

1 PURPOSE OF FINANCIAL STATEMENTS

Exam tip

> This is very much an introductory section laying down some basic concepts and ideas that are expanded on in later chapters. An understanding of the ideas in this chapter provides an essential foundation for later. Exam questions are, however, rarely asked based on just these basic introductory ideas.

1.1 Introduction

In an historic context, company financial statements have usually been required for one of two main purposes.

1.1.1 Informing the shareholders

A company is owned by its shareholders. Frequently these shareholders are not involved in the management of the company and instead the company is managed by its directors. The financial statements are a means by which the company and its directors formally communicate to the owners of the company – the shareholders. The primary purpose of the financial statements is to help the shareholders understand how well the directors have performed in managing the company.

In the UK and US, the format of financial statements has been influenced by the information needs of shareholders.

1.1.2 Meeting tax laws

In other countries, such as France and Germany, where in the past equity markets have not been so well developed, companies have sought more debt finance. The banks, as the main finance providers, asked for more detailed information than normally found in the published financial statements.

For this reason the governmental tax authorities became the main users of financial statements, and so accounting followed legal tax rules in preference to providing commercially realistic information for shareholders.

These differing information needs resulted in significant differences between the accounting regulations in many countries.

More recently, the capital markets (providing finance for corporate activities) and the equity markets (for investors) have grown in size and global reach.

Consequently, and also following increased demands for information from groups other than shareholders, the use of published financial information has risen dramatically. This created demands for global accounting standards, which were addressed to a certain degree by many countries adopting International Accounting Standards. The Standards will be discussed in detail in Chapter 2.

This chapter, focuses on the principles of bookkeeping and the main elements of a set of financial statements.

1.1.3 Contents of financial statements

The contents of financial statements vary across countries, due to differences in accounting regulations. As financial statements are found in many different documents such as annual financial statements, merger and acquisition documents, and so on, the contents also vary, (depending on the requirements of the documents).

This exam is mainly based on the interpretation of financial statements produced by UK companies. The full contents of a UK annual report are discussed in Chapter 2. In this chapter, we focus only on the primary financial statements you expect to see published by a company, such as; Statement of Financial Position, Income Statement, and Statement of Cash Flows. The examiner could potentially ask about accounting regulations in the US – these are dealt with in Chapter 17.

These primary statements are described in the sections that follow. You should note that for accounting periods beginning on or after 1 January 2009, the international accounting standard that deals with the format of accounts IAS I has been revised. The changes are covered in a later chapter, Reporting Financial Performance. The updated standard introduces new names for the primary financial statements as follows:

- Statement of financial position (balance sheet)

- Statement of comprehensive income (income statement and statement of recognised income and expense)

- Statement of cash flow (cash flow statement)

2 STATEMENT OF FINANCIAL POSITION

2.1 Introduction

A statement of financial position is simply a list of all the company's assets and liabilities and their value at a particular point in time.

The statement of financial position states the assets and liabilities of an organisation at the end of its accounting period.
An accounting period is the period of time that the financial statements refer to. Normally this is a 12-month period, such as a calendar year but the accounting period can be longer or shorter, e.g. 6 months.

An asset is either something the company owns such as cash, buildings, equipment or intellectual property or something it is owed such as customer receivables.

A liability is anything that the company owes to other organisations or people and expects to have to pay over in the future. Liabilities are normally paid in cash but could be settled by other means.

In the UK, a simplified statement of financial position normally looks something like this.

Statement of financial position outline	(£'000)
Net Assets	
Assets	400
Liabilities	(150)
	250
Shareholders' Funds	
Share Capital	100
Reserves	150
	250

In the UK net assets are normally shown on the top of the statement of financial position and shareholders' funds at the bottom. Net assets are calculated as the assets minus liabilities. The liabilities are commonly shown in brackets to indicate a negative number as this is less confusing than using a minus sign.

The net assets in the top half of the statement of financial position show the financial position of the company. In the bottom half of the statement of financial position the shareholders' funds section demonstrates how the company achieved this position, i.e. either through shareholder investment or retained earnings. This is best illustrated with an example.

Example

Issue of shares for cash

If the company issues shares for cash and raises £100,000, the equation is in balance because the transaction is reflected as follows.

Impact on Net Assets	(£'000)
Cash up – a current asset	+100
	+100
Impact on Shareholders' Funds	
Ordinary Share Capital up	+100
	+100

The cash at bank represents the amount of money that the company has in its bank account at the statement of financial position date.

The share capital represents the funds invested in the company by its shareholders, i.e. money subscribed for shares.

It can be seen that the entries balance out against each other. This is shown as follows on the statement of financial position.

	Before (£'000)	Issue (£'000)	After (£'000)
Net Assets			
Current Assets			
Cash	–	+100	100
	–	+100	100
Shareholders' Funds			
Ordinary Share Capital	–	+100	100
	–	+100	100

The shareholders can see that the company's net worth of £100,000 (represented by £100,000 cash in the bank) was as a result of their investment. Therefore, it can be seen that the bottom half of the statement of financial position shows how the company came to be worth £100,000, whereas as the top half shows how those funds have been used, i.e. cash at bank.

This example also illustrates the fundamental concept underlying the preparation of the financial statements: the accounting equation.

2.2 Accounting equation

2.2.1 Introduction

If we look at the two statement of financial positions above we can see that the net assets equals shareholders' funds. This is not a coincidence, it is called the accounting equation and it always holds true for all statement of financial positions.

The accounting equation can be stated as

Formula to learn

> Net assets = Shareholders' funds

Statement of financial position Outline	(£'000)
Net Assets	
Assets	400
Liabilities	(150)
	250
Shareholders' Funds	
Share Capital	100
Reserves	150
	250

If we look at the statement of financial position above again we can see that we can extend the accounting equation as follows.

Formula to learn

> Assets − Liabilities = Share capital + Reserves

This equation can be rearranged as follows.

Formula to learn

> Assets = Liabilities + Share capital + Reserves

This is how a statement of financial position is structured in the US and sometimes internationally, with assets shown in the top half of the statement of financial position and liabilities and shareholders' funds shown in the bottom half of the statement of financial position. The financial position of the company is the same; the information is just presented in a different manner.

2.2.2 Double entry bookkeeping and the accounting equation

Accountants account for the transactions of the company using a special notation called double-entry bookkeeping, which is based on the accounting equation and the fundamental principle that each transaction has two sides or effects.

A transaction is anything the company does which affects its financial position such as buying an asset, paying its employees, taking out a loan or making a sale.

The notation is based on the principle that for each transaction there are two entries, a 'debit' entry and a 'credit' entry.

A **debit** entry represents an increase in an asset or a decrease in a liability. A **credit** entry represents an increase in a liability or shareholders' funds or a decrease in an asset.

From the Example (*Issue of shares for cash*) we can see that the double-entry bookkeeping is

Double Entry	(£'000)
DEBIT: Cash at bank	100
CREDIT: Share Capital	100

It can be seen that the total debits equal the total credits, which is the same as the accounting equation.

Formula to learn

> Debits = Credits

Therefore from the Example, it looks as though from the company's point of view that the debits are a good thing as they increase the assets of the company. However, most people associate the term 'debit' as being negative and the term 'credit' as being something positive. There is a simple explanation for this. When you receive your bank statement it is actually a statement written from the bank's point of view. Therefore, when you pay money into your account it appears to 'credit' the account, which is the bank stating that it has a liability to you as it owes you that money. Hence from the individual's point of view a bank deposit is a debit (asset) but from the bank's point of view it is a credit (liability).

It is worth trying to understand the basics of double-entry bookkeeping because it helps to explain some of the accounting entries for the more advanced topics discussed later.

2.2.3 Other transactions

Example

Borrowing from the bank

If the company borrowed £50,000 from the bank repayable in five years, the effect on the accounting equation is as follows.

Impact on Net Assets	(£'000)
Cash up	+50
Liabilities up	+(50)
	–
Impact on Shareholders' Funds	–

There is no change in the total net assets as the increase in assets has been matched by an increase in liabilities or shareholders' funds. The statement of financial position is as follows.

Net Assets	Before (£'000)	Loan (£'000)	After (£'000)
Current Assets			
Cash	100	+50	150
Liabilities	–	+(50)	(50)
	100	–	100
Shareholders' Funds			
Share Capital	100	–	100
	100	–	100

The double entry is as follows.

Double Entry	(£'000)
DEBIT: Cash	50
CREDIT: Liabilities	50

The increase in assets is a debit in the statement of financial position, whereas as increase in liabilities is a credit entry.

As both the entries are in the top half of the statement of financial position they cancel each other out.

Example

Buying equipment for cash

If the company uses £60,000 of cash to buy machinery for long-term use, i.e. a non-current asset, the equation is as follows.

Impact on Net Assets	(£'000)
Non-Current Assets up	+60
Cash down	−60
	−
Impact on Shareholders' Funds	−

Again, this does not affect the total net assets or shareholders' funds; we are simply exchanging one asset (cash) for another (the machinery). The statement of financial position is as follows.

Net Assets	Before (£'000)	Buy Equip (£'000)	After (£'000)
Non-Current Assets	−	+60	60
Current Assets			
Cash	150	−60	90
Liabilities	(50)		(50)
	100	−	100
Shareholders' Funds			
Share Capital	100		100
	100	−	100

Double Entry	£'000
DEBIT: Non-Current Assets	60
CREDIT: Cash	60

The plant and machinery is a non-current asset and therefore is shown as a debit – however, as all we have done is exchange one asset for another – the debit is cancelled out by a matching credit against cash.

Example

Buying goods for resale for cash

If the company now spends £20,000 cash to buy goods intended for resale the equation is as follows.

Impact on Net Assets	**(£'000)**
Inventory up	+20
Cash down	−20
	−
Impact on Shareholders' Funds	−

Once more we are simply exchanging one asset for another, with no impact on the total net assets or the shareholders' funds. The statement of financial position is as follows.

	Before	**Buy Inventory**	**After**
Net Assets	**(£'000)**	**(£'000)**	**(£'000)**
Non-Current Assets	60	−	60
Current Assets			
Inventory	−	+20	20
Cash	90	−20	70
Liabilities	(50)	−	(50)
	100	−	100
Shareholders' Funds			
Share Capital	100	−	100
	100	−	100

Double Entry	**(£'000)**
DEBIT: Inventory	20
CREDIT: Cash	20

The inventory is an asset and therefore is shown as a debit – however, as all we have done once again is exchange one asset for another – the debit is cancelled out by a matching credit against cash.

Example

Selling goods for cash

The company sells half of these goods for £19,000, i.e. goods that had cost £10,000 are being sold for £19,000. As a result, a profit of £9,000 is realised. The impact on the accounting equation is as follows.

Impact on Net Assets	**(£'000)**
Inventory down	−10
Cash up	+19
	+9
Impact on Shareholders' Funds	
Retained Earnings up	+9
	+9

And the statement of financial position is as follows.

Net Assets	Before (£'000)	Sell Inventory (£'000)	After (£'000)
Non-Current Assets	60	–	60
Current Assets			
Inventory	20	–10	10
Cash	70	+19	89
Liabilities	(50)	–	(50)
	100	+9	109
Shareholders' Funds			
Share Capital	100	–	100
Retained Earnings	–	+9	9
	100	+9	109

Double Entry	(£'000)
DEBIT: Cash	19
CREDIT: Inventory	10
CREDIT: Profit	9

The double entry for this transaction is slightly more complicated. When attempting to work out the double entry it is always best to start with cash entry (if relevant).

The cash has increased by £19,000 – the sales proceeds, so this will be the debit entry. As the total debits equal £19,000, the total credits must also total £19,000. We know that we have sold goods costing £10,000 so the value of inventory in the statement of financial position will fall by £10,000, leaving us needing a further credit of £9,000. This £9,000 represents the profit from the transaction.

In summary profits are credit entries in the statement of financial position.

As we can see from the statement of financial position above the accumulated profit or retained earnings is shown in the bottom half of the statement of financial position within shareholders' funds. The top half of the statement of financial position shows the increase in the company's assets. The net increase in the company's assets is £9,000 as we sold inventory for £19,000 that only cost £10,000.

Example

Selling goods on credit

If the company now sells the remaining goods (which cost £10,000) for £21,000 on credit, it generates a profit of £11,000. This profit is recognised immediately, we do *not* wait for the cash to be received. This concept is known as the accruals concept and is discussed later. The impact on the accounting equation is

Impact on Net Assets	(£'000)
Inventory down	–10
Accounts receivable	+21
	+11
Impact on Shareholders' Funds	
Retained Earnings up	+11
	+11

Accounts receivable are amounts owed to the company, amounts owed by a customer are known as trade receivables.

The statement of financial position reflects this change as

Net Assets	Before (£'000)	Sell Inventory (£'000)	After (£'000)
Non-Current Assets	60	–	60
Current Assets			
Inventory	10	–10	–
Accounts receivable	–	+21	21
Cash	89	–	89
Liabilities	(50)	–	(50)
	109	+11	120

Net Assets (cont.)	Before (£'000)	Sell Inventory (£'000)	After (£'000)
Shareholders' Funds			
Share Capital	100	–	100
Retained Earnings	9	+11	20
	109	+11	120

Double Entry	(£'000)
DEBIT: Accounts Receivable	21
CREDIT: Inventory	10
CREDIT: Profit	11

This transaction is different to the previous transactions as there is no cash involved. However, the company's assets have increased, as the company is owed money by its customers and this is shown as a debit entry.

In the UK accounts receivables used to be referred to as debtors; or more specifically trade debtors if the money was due from a customer.

The credit entries are as before.

Accruals

These transactions all illustrate one of the fundamental accounting principles, the **accruals or matching concept**. The concept requires revenue and the associated costs to be shown in the period they are earned or incurred. For instance, in the Example *Selling goods on credit*, the goods are sold on credit and the sale and resultant profit is accounted for in the current period, rather than the period in which the cash is received. This is known as accruals accounting and it will be examined further in the section on income statement (Section 1.3).

Example

Buying goods on credit

If the company buys £25,000 worth of goods, obtaining credit from the supplier, the impact on the accounting equation is as follows.

Impact on Net Assets	(£'000)
Inventory up	+25
Liabilities up	+(25)
	–
Impact on Shareholders' Funds	–

Which is reflected in the statement of financial position as

Net Assets	Before (£'000)	Buy Inventory (£'000)	After (£'000)
Non-Current Assets	60	–	60
Current Assets			
Inventory	–	+25	25
Accounts Receivable	21	–	21
Cash	89	–	89
Liabilities	(50)	+(25)	(75)
	120	–	120
Shareholders' Funds			
Share Capital	100	–	100
Retained Earnings	20	–	20
	120	–	120

Double Entry	(£'000)
DEBIT: Inventory	25
CREDIT: Liabilities – Trade Payables	25

The increase in assets (debit entry) is offset by an increase in liabilities (credit entry) in the top half of the statement of financial position. This has no effect on shareholders' funds – i.e. the amount invested in the company in terms of share capital and retained earnings.

Example

Paying for expenses

If the company pays the following expenses from cash

- Wages of £2,000
- Rent of £4,000
- Telephone bills of £1,000

i.e. £7,000 in total, the impact on the accounting equation is

Impact on Net Assets	(£'000)
Cash down	−7
	−7
Impact on Shareholders' Funds	
Expenses up (profits down)	−7
	−7

This is reflected in the statement of financial position as

Net Assets	Before (£'000)	Expenses (£'000)	After (£'000)
Non-Current Assets	60	–	60
Current Assets			
Inventory	25	–	25
Accounts Receivable	21	–	21
Cash	89	−7	82
Liabilities	(75)	–	(75)
	120	−7	113
Shareholders' Funds			
Share Capital	100	–	100
Retained Earnings	20	−7	13
	120	−7	113

Double Entry	(£'000)
DEBIT: Profits	7
CREDIT: Cash	7

As before, it is best to deal with the cash entry first of all. A cash payment is a credit entry because it represents a decrease in an asset. The opposite side – the expenses – must therefore be a debit entry. Expenses also represent a decrease in profits, which is shown as a debit.

Shareholders require a detailed breakdown of the performance of the company so movements in the retained profits between accounting periods are explained in the income statement. The income statement for the Examples on pages 8–11 looks like this.

Income Statement	(£'000)	(£'000)
Sales		40
Cost of sales		(20)
Gross profit		20
Expenses		(7)
Profit		13

The income statement is a detailed analysis of the entries to retained earnings.

The income statement will be analysed in more detail in Section 3.

2.2.4 Summary of this accounting equation illustration

We can see from the illustrations that each transaction impacts the statement of financial position and sometimes the income statement. The impact occurs in such a way however to keep the statement of financial position in balance.

At any point in time, and for each individual transaction, the accounting equation holds, i.e.

Net Assets = Shareholders' Funds

OR

Debits = Credits

2.3 Format and terminology

2.3.1 Format

The general format for a statement of financial position in the UK is prescribed in the Companies Act and can be illustrated by this extract from the interim financial statements of the Tomkins Group.

Tomkins Group
Consolidated statement of financial position as at 2 July 2005

	Notes	2005 (£m)	2004 (£m)
Non-current assets	1		
Goodwill	3	301.7	210.5
Other intangible assets	3	7.3	5.6
Property, plant and equipment	2	811.8	728.8
Investments in associates	4	4.1	3.7
Deferred tax assets	5	127.9	138.4
		1,252.8	1,087.0
Current assets	6		
Inventories		419.1	352.1
Trade and other receivables		599.3	546.2
Current tax recoverable		5.9	12.3
Investments		2.2	1.6
Cash and cash equivalents		165.2	168
		1,191.7	1,080.2
Assets held for sale		13.6	49
Total assets		2,458.1	2,216.2
Current liabilities	7/8		
Bank overdrafts		(27.3)	(20.0)
Bank and other loans		(10.7)	(10.0)
Unsecured loan notes		(0.3)	(0.3)
Obligations under finance leases		(1.6)	(2.9)
Trade and other payables		(413.3)	(368.6)
Current tax liabilities		(27.9)	(14.7)
Provisions	10	(39.2)	(37.2)
		(520.3)	(453.7)
Convertible cumulative preference shares		(297.9)	–
		(818.2)	(453.7)
Non-current liabilities	9		
Bank and other loans		(500.0)	(401.8)
Obligations under finance leases		(8.4)	(11.3)
Other payables		(7.3)	(7.4)
Post-employment benefit obligations		(273.8)	(313.6)
Deferred tax liabilities		(48.3)	(38.3)
Current tax liabilities		(130.7)	(168.1)

Tomkins Group
Consolidated statement of financial position as at 2 July 2005

	Notes	2005 (£m)	2004 (£m)
Provisions	10	(19.0)	(37.4)
Liabilities directly associated with assets held for sale		–	(13.2)
Total liabilities		(1,805.7)	(1,444.8)
Net assets		652.4	771.4
Capital and reserves			
Ordinary share capital	11	38.7	38.7
Share premium	12	95.4	93.9
Other reserves	13	458.8	432.6
Retained profits	14	17.0	170.3
Shareholders' funds – equity interests		609.9	394.9
Minority interest		42.5	39.3
Total equity		652.4	434.2
Convertible cumulative preference shares			337.2
		652.4	771.4

You will notice that the statement of financial position is shown for both this period end (2 July 2005) and the previous period end (3 July 2004) so that shareholders are able to compare the position of the company with the previous period.

In a set of financial statements, the **Notes** column contains a number, which gives a reference to the notes section of the financial statements, which provides further details about the item. We have changed the numbers to provide an overview of each of these items and further illustrations of accounting for basic transactions.

2.3.2 Terminology

Non-current assets

Non-current assets are assets acquired for continued use within the business and not for resale. These should be sub-classified into

- Intangibles, including goodwill.

- Property, plant and equipment (PPE).

- Investments such as interests in subsidiaries, associates, joint ventures and investments held for trade purposes.

Property, plant and equipment (PPE)

These are physical assets that are used within the business over a number of years with a view to deriving some benefit from their use, e.g. through their use in the manufacture of goods for resale.

PPE includes such items as

- Freehold land and buildings.
- Leasehold land and buildings.
- Plant and machinery.
- Motor vehicles.
- Fixtures and fittings.

Unless otherwise stated, PPE is shown in the balance at its net book value. This value is not an indication of the market value of the asset instead it is the cost of the asset less its accumulated depreciation.

Depreciation is the method by which the cost of using the asset is matched against its related benefit. It is an application of the accruals or matching concept.

This is best shown with an example.

Example

The Matching principle

In the Example *Buying equipment for cash* the company bought production machinery at a cost of £60,000. It expects, from previous experience, that it will last five years, after which time it will be sold for £5,000.

It will therefore cost the company £55,000 (£60,000 cost less £5,000 expected sale proceeds) to use the equipment over these five years.

Applying the matching concept, this £55,000 cost should be spread over the five years, i.e. an expense of £11,000 charged against the profit each year.

Impact on Net Assets	**(£'000)**
Depreciation provision up	−11
(PPE down)	−11
Impact on Shareholders' Funds	
Profits down – depreciation charge in the income statement	−11
	−11

The revised statement of financial position becomes

Net Assets	**Before (£'000)**	**Depreciation (£'000)**	**After (£'000)**
Non-Current Assets (PPE)	60	−11	49
Current Assets			
Inventory	25	–	25
Trade Receivables	21	–	21
Cash	82	–	82
Liabilities	(75)	–	(75)
	113	−11	102
Shareholders' Funds			
Ordinary Share Capital	100	–	100
Retained Earnings	13	−11	2
	113	−11	102

In the statement of financial position PPE is usually stated at net book value (NBV), i.e. cost less the accumulated depreciation provision.

Thus at the end of each of the next five years the PPE will be valued in the statement of financial position as follows.

	Year 1 (£'000)	**Year 2 (£'000)**	**Year 3 (£'000)**	**Year 4 (£'000)**	**Year 5 (£'000)**
Cost	60	60	60	60	60
Depreciation Provision	(11)	(22)	(33)	(44)	(55)
Net Book Value	49	38	27	16	5

The statement of financial position net book value of the equipment falls by £11,000 each year (as the amount is charged as an expense – depreciation) until in Year 5 it has dropped to the estimated sales proceeds of £5,000.

Depreciation spreads the cost of the asset less the residual value over the expected useful life. It follows from this that assets with indefinite lives need not be depreciated, e.g.

- Freehold land.
- Investment in shares.
- Certain intangibles, such as publishing rights and titles.

Intangible assets

Intangibles are literally assets without physical form.

They frequently represent intellectual property rights of the company that enable it to operate and generate profits in a way that competitors cannot.

The types of intangible assets that most frequently appear on the statement of financial position are

- Development expenditure.
- Patents, licences and trademarks.
- Publishing rights and titles.
- Goodwill.
- Brands.

Depreciation of intangible assets is normally referred to as amortisation.

2.3.3 Investments

Investments frequently represent long-term ownership of shares in other companies and are usually reported initially in the statement of financial position at historical cost.

Significant levels of shareholdings that have caused the investments to be classified as either a subsidiary or an associated undertaking require additional reporting regulations.

2.3.4 Deferred tax assets

Defered tax assets are one of the more complex issues in financial reporting. The assets are intangible in nature and represent a timing difference between the recognition of profits for accounting and tax purposes. This is discussed further in Chapter 14.

2.3.5 Current assets

Strictly speaking, these are all assets other than non-current assets, though perhaps the best description is that current assets are assets held for conversion into cash in the ordinary course of business. As we can see, current assets are sub-categorised into the following.

- **Inventory** – goods held available for sale.

- **Accounts receivable** – amounts owed to the company, perhaps as a result of selling goods on credit (often referred to as trade receivables).

- **Investments** – shares held in the short term with the intention of reselling, e.g. short-term speculative investments.

- **Cash** – either held physically or by a financial institution such as a bank.

Care should be taken when valuing current assets as they are valued at the lower of

- Cost.

  or

- Net realisable value (NRV), i.e. estimated selling price less any cost incurred in order to sell them.

Thus

- If the NRV exceeds cost the asset is valued at cost, i.e. no profit is anticipated.
- If the NRV is less than cost the asset is revalued down to NRV, i.e. a loss is recognised in the income statement.

Prepayments

In accordance with the accruals or matching concept, the income statement should include all income and expenses related to the full year of trading, and only that year. This may be different from the amounts actually paid in cash during the period, in which case it may be necessary to set up a prepayment.

Prepayments are a form of current asset – they are payments made before the statement of financial position date, which relate to the period after that date.

Example

Prepayments

In the Example *Paying for expenses* we paid rent of £4,000, which we charged to the income statement, which resulted in reduced profits.

However, if it is discovered that this payment relates to a two-year period and only £2,000 relates to this year, an adjustment will required to ensure that the costs charged to the income statement only relate to the current period.

As a result only the £2,000 relating to this year should be charged against the income statement for this year in accordance with the accruals or matching concept.

The remaining £2,000 is rent paid in advance for next year (a prepayment), which should be treated as an expense next year, again in accordance with the accruals concept.

The prepayment is treated as an asset, something owed to the company by someone (specifically the use of the premises without any further payments of rent).

We therefore need to

- Reduce the rent charge by £2,000 to recognise only that part of the payment that we have used (increasing profit).
- Set up a £2,000 asset (a prepayment).

The impact on the accounting equation is

Impact on Net Assets	**(£'000)**
Prepayments (Accounts Receivable) up	+2
	+2
Impact on Shareholders' Funds	
Expenses down (profits up)	+2
	+2

And the statement of financial position becomes

Net Assets	Before (£'000)	Depreciation (£'000)	After (£'000)
Non-Current Assets	49	–	49
Current Assets			
Inventory	25	–	25
Trade Receivables and Prepayments	21	+2	23
Cash	82	–	82
Liabilities	(75)		(75)
	102	+2	104
Shareholders' Funds			
Ordinary Share Capital	100	–	100
Retained Earnings	2	+2	4
	102	+2	104

The double entry is

Double Entry	(£'000)
DEBIT: Prepayments	2
CREDIT: Rent in the Income Statement	2

These entries are corrections because originally we charged retained profits with an expense of £4,000 when actually only £2,000 related to the year.

If we were aware from the beginning that the payment of rent related to more than one period then the double entry is as follows.

Double Entry	(£'000)
DEBIT: Prepayments	2
DEBIT: Retained Earnings	2
CREDIT: Cash	4

The net effect is the same.

2.3.6 Current liabilities

Current liabilities should fully reflect all liabilities payable within 12 months of the period end.

They include bank overdrafts and taxation payable within one year, as well as amounts owed to suppliers known as trade payables.

2.3.7 Accruals

These are not separately disclosed in the Tomkins financial statements – they are included within the *Trade and Other Payables* category.

An accrual is an amount due in respect of goods and services used during the year but not yet invoiced.

Example

Accruals

In the Example *Paying for expenses* the amount paid for the telephone (£1,000) relates to the first six months of the year. Since we have been using the telephone constantly throughout the year, it is reasonable to assume that we have incurred another £1,000 of telephone expense in the last six months. This is outstanding at the year-end because the invoice has not yet been received.

We therefore need to

- Charge an additional £1,000 expense to recognise its use (reducing profit).
- Set up a £1,000 liability (an accrual) for the invoice that has not yet been received.

The impact on the accounting equation for this will be as follows.

Impact on Net Assets	(£'000)
Accruals (Current Liabilities) up	+(1)
	−1
Impact on Shareholders' Funds	
Expenses up (profits down)	−1
	−1

And our statement of financial position after the accrual (and prepayment) becomes

	Before	Accrual	After
Net Assets	(£'000)	(£'000)	(£'000)
Non-Current Assets	49	−	49
Current Assets			
Inventory	25	−	25
Trade Receivables and Prepayments	23		23
Cash	82	−	82
Liabilities including Accruals	(75)	+1	(76)
	104	+1	103
Shareholders' Funds			
Ordinary Share Capital	100	−	100
Retained Earnings	4	−1	3
	104	−1	103

The double entry is as follows.

Double Entry	(£'000)
DEBIT: Electricity in the Income Statement	1
CREDIT: Accruals in the Current Liabilities	1

The debit entry increases the expenses in the income statement and reduces the profit. The credit entry in the statement of financial position shows that the company owes a further £1,000 at the year end.

Non-current liabilities

This will typically include such items as

- Long-term bank loans.
- Loan stock and debentures issued by the company.

Both must be repaid long term. It also includes any other known liabilities, such as trade payables that do not require settlement within the year.

2.3.8 Provisions

Provisions represent liabilities of uncertain amount and/or timing and generally relate to events that are significant, and perhaps unusual, where the degree of uncertainty is greater than is the case with a normal business accrual. An example of such a provision is the costs associated with the future demolition and site clearance of a factory closed down during the year.

The amounts are estimated because they are not yet certain and will not be until the process is completed in the future. Their value is therefore less reliable than items in liabilities such as bank loans where it is certain what is owed and when it is due for payment.

2.3.9 Ordinary share capital

This represents the total nominal value of the shares in issue at the year end, e.g. our company has in issue 100,000 shares, each with a £1 nominal value giving £100,000 share capital.

Under the Companies Act, UK companies have to ascribe a nominal or par value to each share. This represents

- The minimum value at which shares can be issued. The company is not allowed to issue shares at a price below the nominal value.

- The limits of the liability of the shareholder. If the company becomes insolvent, shareholders' liability is limited to any unpaid element of this nominal value.

2.3.10 Share premium account

Companies can issue shares at greater than their nominal value, i.e. at a premium.

Example

Share capital

If our company could raise £20,000 by issuing 5,000 new shares at a price of £4 each, then there is a premium of £3 on each share (full price of £4 less nominal value of £1).

Under the Companies Act, the company must record the issue of these shares by increasing the ordinary share capital by only the nominal value of the shares issued, i.e. £5,000. The premium of £15,000 must be added to the share premium account. The impact on the accounting equation is as follows.

Impact on Net Assets	**(£'000)**
Cash up	+20
	+20
Impact on Shareholders' Funds	
Share Capital up	+5
Share Premium Account up	+15
	+20

The effect on the statement of financial position is as follows.

	Before	**Issue**	**After**
Net Assets	**(£'000)**	**(£'000)**	**(£'000)**
Non-Current Assets	49	–	49
Current Assets:			
Inventory	25	–	25
Trade Payables	23	–	23
Cash	82	+20	102
Liabilities	(76)	–	(76)
	103	+20	123
Shareholders' Funds			
Ordinary Share Capital	100	+5	105
Share Premium Account	–	+15	15
Retained Earnings	3	–	3
	103	+20	123

The double entry is as follows.

Double Entry	(£'000)
DEBIT: Cash	20
CREDIT: Share Capital	5
CREDIT: Share Premium Account	15

2.3.11 Other reserves

Other reserves generally represent an apportionment or allocation of profits from the income statement. This is frequently done for the following reasons.

- To indicate that a certain element of profit is being retained for a specific reason.
- To indicate that a portion of profits will never be paid out as a dividend.
- To account for the treatment of unusual items such as a reserve arising on a merger.

Companies may also wish to revalue some or all of their assets in order to strengthen the statement of financial position and place a more up-to-date valuation on the assets.

When a company does revalue its property, plant and equipment upwards, it is unwise to treat this increase in shareholders' funds as part of the company's realised profits for the year. It has not been generated by the operational performance of the company and it is certainly not represented by cash. It is therefore, considered unrealised and non-distributable, i.e. the company cannot use the revaluation reserve to pay a dividend.

In this situation the increase in the net book value of the assets is reflected within shareholders' funds in the revaluation reserve.

Example

Revaluation of assets

If our company revalues its property, plant and equipment up to £52,000 at the year end from their net book value at that date of £49,000 (an increase of £3,000), the impact on the accounting equation will be

Impact on Net Assets	(£'000)
Non-Current Assets up	+3
	+3
Impact on Shareholders' Funds	
Revaluation Reserve up	+3
	+3

And our statement of financial position now becomes

Net Assets	Before (£'000)	Revalue (£'000)	After (£'000)
Non Current Assets	49	+3	52
Current Assets:			
Inventory	25	–	25
Trade Payables	23	–	23
Cash	102	–	102
Liabilities	(76)	–	(76)
	123	+3	126
Shareholders' Funds			
Ordinary Share Capital	105	–	105
Share Premium Account	15	–	15
Revaluation Reserve	–	+3	3
Retained Earnings	3	–	3
	123	+3	126

The double entry is as follows.

Double Entry	(£'000)
DEBIT: Non-Current Asset	3
CREDIT: Revaluation Reserve	3

2.3.12 Income statement

The retained earnings on the statement of financial position represent the **accumulated** profits made by the company since it started to trade, which have not been paid out as dividends or transferred to other reserves.

The separate income statement shows the impact of this year's trading activities on this accumulated figure. Any profits retained this year, which are detailed in the separate income statement, will be added to the accumulated retained earnings (or reserves) brought forward, giving the accumulated position at the end of the year. This could be viewed in a similar way to a bank or credit card statement, where the statement only shows the movements for the month, but these are added to the opening balance to arrive at the closing balance.

The statement of financial position figure represents the accumulated position since the company started trading, whereas the income statement details the movements for the year.

3 INCOME STATEMENT

3.1 Introduction

The income statement provides a detailed analysis of how the company has generated its profit or loss for the accounting period. It helps to explain why the statement of financial position has changed from one period to the next.

3.2 Format and Terminology

3.2.1 Format

We use as illustration the income statement of Tomkins Group financial statements.

Tomkins Group
Consolidated income statement for the year ended 2 July 2005

	Notes	2005 (£m)	2004 (£m)
Revenue	1	1,545.1	1,541.7
Cost of goods sold	2	(1,111.5)	(1,095.5)
Gross profit	3	433.6	446.2
Distribution costs		(157.3)	(169.3)
Administrative expenses	4	(127.9)	(121.4)
Share of trading profit of associates	4	0.5	0.2
Profit from operations before restructuring initiatives		148.9	155.7
Restructuring costs	5	(7.4)	(13.5)
(Loss)/profit for the period from discontinued operations	5	(0.7)	(1.8)
(Loss)/gain on disposals and on the exit of businesses	5	(1.1)	(4.3)
Profit from operations		139.7	136.1
Net interest payable	6	(17.3)	(17.3)
Profit before taxation		122.4	118.8
Tax	7	(22.4)	(32.8)
Profit for the period		100.0	86
Minority interests	8	(3.6)	(6.2)
Preference share dividends	9	–	(7.9)
Profit attributable to equity shareholders	10	96.4	71.9
Earnings basic – Ordinary share	11	12.50p	9.98p
Earnings diluted – Ordinary share	11	11.93p	4.83p

3.2.2 Terminology

The statement of financial position retained profit account (or retained earnings) helps explain why the company's financial position has changed, i.e. an increase in assets in the top half of the statement of financial position will be matched by an increase in the bottom half of the statement of financial position, such as retained earnings. The income statement provides a more detailed explanation of the items affecting the profit or loss for the period in question.

In line with the accruals or matching concept, income and expenses are recognised in retained earnings when earned, regardless of when paid. Any difference between the recognition of these items and the corresponding cash flow is reflected in a statement of financial position entry.

3.2.3 Revenue/Sales

The revenue or sales figure represents the total value of goods or services provided to customers during the accounting period either for cash or on credit. Goods or services provided that have been paid for will boost the company's cash accordingly. Those that have not been paid for at the year end result in a trade receivable on the statement of financial position at that date.

Example

Revenue

In our example company, the reported revenue figure will be £40,000, the sum total of the two sales achieved in the year (£19,000 + £21,000). Of this, £19,000 has been received as cash; the remaining £21,000 remains outstanding as a year-end trade receivable.

The double entry is as follows.

Cash sale

Double Entry	(£'000)
DEBIT: Cash	19
CREDIT: Retained Earnings	19

This is shown in the income statement as revenue.

Credit sale

Double Entry	(£'000)
DEBIT: Trade Receivables	21
CREDIT: Retained Earnings	21

3.2.4 Cost of goods sold / Cost of sales

The cost of sales represents the total cost to the business of the actual items sold. This should not be considered as all the goods purchased, since some of the goods that have been purchased may be unsold at the year end and remain in inventory at that date. These goods are charged against future years' profits (when sold) in accordance with the accruals concept.

During the year a company will have available for sale all the goods held at the start of the year (its opening inventory) plus all the goods bought throughout the year (its purchases). The goods sold will be the total available for sale less any goods not sold (its closing inventory at the year end).

The cost of sales can therefore be calculated as

Formula to learn

> Goods available for sale in year – Closing inventory (those unsold) = Cost of sales

OR

Formula to learn

> Opening inventory + Purchases – Closing inventory = Cost of sales

In a retail business, the cost of sales figure is simply the purchase cost of the goods that have been sold. In a manufacturing business, the cost of sales figure includes all direct manufacturing costs along with the purchase cost of any raw materials used in the manufacturing process. Hence, it includes such items as factory wages, factory depreciation, factory heat and light, and so on.

Example

Cost of sales

If the company is a retailer, the cost of sales could be established as

Cost of Goods Sold	£'000
Opening Inventory	–
Purchases	45
	45
Closing Inventory	(25)
	20

3.2.5 Gross profit

Gross profit is the difference between the value of the sales and the value of the cost of goods sold. One measure frequently used in determining the performance of the business is to consider its gross profit margin, which can be calculated as

Formula to learn

$$\text{Gross profit margin} = \frac{\text{Gross profit}}{\text{Revenue/Sales}} \times 100\%$$

Clearly the higher the margin for a particular level of operations, the higher the profit. However, this does not mean that low margins result in low profits. A number of businesses generate very healthy profits through selling very large numbers of items (achieving correspondingly large revenue) at low margins.

Example

Gross profit

For our example company the gross profit is £20,000 (£40,000 revenue less £20,000 cost of sales). As such, the gross profit margin is

Formula to learn

$$\text{Gross profit margin} = \frac{20,000}{40,000} \times 100\% = 50\%$$

3.2.6 Various operating costs

Operating costs include all other expenses incurred in generating the revenue for the period by way of administrative involvement and delivery/distribution. They will also include any depreciation charges or amortisation of intangible non-current assets.

Example

Operating costs

For our example company the operating costs charged against profits this year are

Operating Costs	£'000	Comments
Depreciation	11,000	Our depreciation charge for the year on the equipment we purchased was calculated as £11,000.
Wages	2,000	The amount paid in the year of £2,000 represents the full amount applicable to the year.
Rent	2,000	The £4,000 paid in the year relates to this year and next year, i.e. only £2,000 is charged against this year's profits, the other £2,000 is carried forward as a prepayment at this year end and will be charged against next year's profits.
Telephone	2,000	Only £1,000 has been paid in the year relating to a six-month period. We need to recognise the charge for a full 12 months by accruing an extra £1,000.
	17,000	

The double entry for the depreciation charge is

Double Entry	£'000
DEBIT: Retained Earnings – depreciation charge	11
CREDIT: Accumulated Depreciation – statement of financial position	11

The double entry for the wages is

Double Entry	£'000
DEBIT: Retained Earnings – expenses	2
CREDIT: Cash – statement of financial position	2

The double entry for rent is

Double Entry	£'000
DEBIT: Retained Earnings – expenses	2
DEBIT: Prepayments – statement of financial position	2
CREDIT: Cash – statement of financial position	4

The double entry for telephone is

Double Entry	£'000
DEBIT: Retained Earnings – expenses	2
CREDIT: Cash – statement of financial position	1
CREDIT: Accruals – current liabilities	1

3.2.7 Exceptional items

Exceptional items are unusual large items of income or expense arising during the year. Historically in UK accounts exceptional items were separately classified to highlight their one-off or unusual nature. Under International Financial Reporting Standards (IFRS) there is no specific definition of an exceptional item, however companies are still able to highlight expenses which they consider to be one-off in nature or unusual.

Removing such items from the normal ongoing costs and separately highlighting them makes it easier to see ratios and trends in the ongoing performance figures of the company that may otherwise be missed.

3.2.8 Interest

In common with most other business expenses, any interest payable reduces the company's profit before tax and hence taxable profit by the gross amount payable. For example, if a company has in issue £100,000 of 10% loan stock, then the interest charge in its income statement each year will be £10,000.

The double entry is the same as any other expense

Double Entry	(£'000)
DEBIT: Retained earnings – interest payable	10
CREDIT: Cash or interest accrual – statement of financial position	10

3.2.9 Taxation on profit on ordinary activities

The tax charge will be based on taxable profits for the accounting period. Taxable profits may be different from the profit before tax figure in the income statement, due to differences in how tax rules operate from accounting rules.

Accounting for tax will be discussed in more detail in Chapter 14.

3.2.10 Minority interests

The financial statements of the Tomkins Group represent the consolidated results of the parent company and subsidiaries. Not all of these subsidiary companies are wholly owned by the parent company. Therefore, some of the profits of the subsidiary companies belong to shareholders outside the Tomkins Group, these are known as minority interests. The deduction shows how much profit for the period belongs to these minority interests.

3.2.11 Dividends payable on equity interests

These represent the dividends paid out or declared to shareholders. Ordinary dividends are deducted from the retained profits in the statement of financial position when declared, normally after the end of the accounting period.

Most of the time companies pay out dividends that are less than their profits after tax, i.e. the dividend is being funded from this year's profits. A dividend which is more than this year's profits is known as an uncovered dividend. It is not essential for a dividend to be covered as it can be funded from retained profits.

In most cases, companies pay dividends in two stages.

- **Interim dividend paid** – this is paid out during the year based on the half year's performance.

- **Final dividend proposed** – this is paid to shareholders after the year end following the approval of the year end financial statements at the annual general meeting.

Companies may also have preference shareholders. If the preference shares are classified as liabilities then the dividend is deducted as part of the interest charge in the income statement. If the shares are considered to be equity the dividend is not deducted in the income statement.

3.2.12 Profit attributable to equity shareholders

This represents the profit attributable to the equity shareholders. If it is a loss, it represents how much of the previously retained profits of the business have been utilised this year in order to finance this year's activities.

Once the dividend has been deducted the figure is called a retained profit or loss.

This retained profit/(loss) goes to increase/(decrease) the statement of financial position retained profits figure and helps to explain the difference on this statement of financial position figure between the years.

3.2.13 Earnings per share (EPS)

This is a figure closely monitored by shareholders and analysts, who are looking for EPS to rise year-on-year. The earnings figure used is the total profits attributable to equity shareholders from the income statement after every cost has been accounted for (except ordinary dividend). The remaining profit figure therefore represents earnings belonging to the ordinary shareholders.

This earnings figure is then divided by the weighted average number of ordinary shares in issue during the year to obtain a figure of earnings generated on a per share basis.

Example

Our final income statement for our company (assuming zero tax) is

Income statement	(£'000)	(£'000)
Revenue		40
Cost of sales		(20)
Gross profit		20
Admin. and distribution expenses		
Depreciation	11	
Wages	2	
Rent	2	
Telephone	2	
		(17)
Profit before tax		3
Tax		–
Profit		3

From this we can see that the earnings available to pay a dividend to the ordinary shareholders are £3,000. If there were 100,000 shares in issue throughout the year, then the earnings per share figure is

Formula to learn

$$EPS = \frac{Earnings}{Number\ of\ shares}$$

$$EPS = \frac{£3,000}{100,000} = 3p$$

3.2.14 Capital and revenue expenditure

> You may be asked to distinguish between capital and revenue expenditure, e.g. Winter 2003, Question 6.

Capital expenditure

Capital expenditure is expenditure on acquiring or enhancing non-current assets such as intangibles and property, plant and equipment. As such the benefits will be derived from this expenditure over the remaining life of the asset. Hence, this expenditure is added to the value of non-current assets (is capitalised) on the statement of financial position and will subsequently be depreciated through the income statement.

Revenue expenditure

Revenue expenditure is expenditure incurred in

- Acquiring assets to be sold for conversion into cash, e.g. inventory.
- Manufacturing, selling, distributing goods, e.g. wages.
- Day-to-day administrative expenses, e.g. electricity, telephone.
- Maintenance of non current assets, e.g. repairs.

Revenue expenditure is charged directly against profits for the period to which it relates.

4 CASH FLOW

4.1 Introduction

4.1.1 Background

The statement of financial position and income statement are prepared on the accruals basis. They do not show how much cash the company has generated.

A company may be very profitable but almost bankrupt (unable to pay its liabilities as they fall due). This may appear a little strange, so let us examine this a little bit further.

4.1.2 Profit v Cash

Trade certainly causes cash to flow, for example when customers pay, or suppliers are paid. However, not all income statement items result in an immediate cash flow or even any cash flow at all. For example

- **Depreciation** – A cash flow occurs when the asset is purchased and when it is sold but not when it is depreciated.

- **Accrued expenses/purchases on credit** – Cash flows in relation to these items are when these amounts are actually paid which is after they have been charged against profits.

- **Sales on credit/prepaid expenses** – Cash flows are when these debts are settled which, again, differs from when they are taken into the income statement.

Cash also moves for other reasons, for example buying an asset or raising share capital/loans.

Since cash is such an important figure in determining the continuing existence of a company, we need a statement showing how the company's financial resources have been generated and have been used in order to highlight the liquidity position and trends of the company.

4.2 Format and terminology

4.2.1 Format

The illustration below shows the general format for a statement of cash flows as it appears in the financial statements of the Tomkins Group.

Tomkins Group
Consolidated statement of cash flows for the period 2 July 2005

	Notes	2005 (£m)	2004 (£m)
Operating activities			
Cash generated by operations		136.6	131.7
Income taxes paid		(34.4)	(31.9)
Income taxes received		6.0	11.9
Net cash inflow from trading activities	1	108.2	111.7
Investing activities			
Purchase of property, plant and equipment		(65.6)	(73.2)
Disposal of property, plant and equipment		11.3	3.0
Purchase of subsidiaries		(85.3)	–
Sale of subsidiaries, net of cash disposed		2.9	14.4
Dividends received from associates		0.3	0.1
Net cash outflow from investing activities	2	(136.4)	(55.7)
Financing activities			
Issue of ordinary share capital		1.4	1.1
Decrease in convertible cumulative preference shares		(0.7)	–
Increase in collateralised cash		(0.2)	–
Increase/(decrease) in debt		93.4	(1.1)
Capital element of finance lease rental payments		(2.7)	(1.8)
Interest element of finance lease rental payments		(0.3)	(0.5)
Purchase of own shares		(0.6)	(3.6)
Sale of own shares		2.9	–
Interest received		1.8	2.4
Interest paid		(12.4)	(9.1)
Equity dividend paid		(60.0)	(57.1)
Preference dividend paid		(8.1)	(7.9)
Investment by a minority shareholder		–	4.3
Dividend paid to a minority shareholder		(4.9)	(1.7)
Net cash inflow/(outflow) from financing activities	3	9.6	(75.0)
Net (decrease)/increase in cash and cash equivalents		(18.6)	(19.0)
Cash and cash equivalents at beginning of period		172.1	162.0
Currency translation differences		(15.6)	5.0
Cash and cash equivalents at end of period	4	137.9	148.0
Cash and cash equivalents comprise			
Cash and cash equivalents		165.2	168.0
Bank overdrafts		(27.3)	(20.0)
		137.9	148.0

4.2.2 Terminology

It can be seen that the statement of cash flows is sub-classified according to the activities that give rise to the cash flows, specifically

1. Net cash inflow from/absorbed by operating activities

Operating activities are the main revenue-producing activities of the company that are not investing or financing activities, so operating cash flows include cash received from customers and cash paid to suppliers and employees.

2. Investing activities

Investing activities are the acquisition and disposal of long-term assets and other investments that are not considered to be cash equivalents.

Normally, companies will also choose to include cash flows such as income from investments although it can be included in financing activities.

3. Financing activities

Financing activities are activities that alter the equity capital and borrowing structure of the enterprise.

This category includes a wide-range of cash flows such as the issue of ordinary share capital, interest payments and receipts and dividend payments. Interest payments and receipts can also be included within operating activities.

4. Cash and cash equivalents

This shows the overall movements in cash and cash equivalents during the period. Cash and cash equivalents comprise cash in hand and demand deposits, together with short-term, highly liquid investments that are readily convertible to a known amount of cash, and that are subject to an insignificant risk of changes in value.

Example

Cash

Let us consider our example company.

We know that the company was formed and hence had no cash at the start of the year, but at the end of the year it had £102,000 worth of cash on the statement of financial position, i.e. cash has increased by £102,000 over the year. This will be the figure we are trying to reconcile to, an increase in cash of £102,000.

Cash from operating activities

The cash from operations largely corresponds to the operating profit figure in the income statement and tends to be the hardest figure to determine. We will, therefore, consider all the items of income or expenditure that have contributed to this operating profit and establish their cash flow effects as follows.

	Income Statement (£'000)	Cash Flow (£'000)	Comments
Revenue	40	19	Amount received from sales (rest in trade receivables)
Cost of sales	(20)	(20)	Amount paid for goods purchased
Gross profit	20	(1)	
Expenses			
Depreciation	(11)	–	No cash payment
Wages	(2)	(2)	Amount paid in year = £2,000
Rent	(2)	(4)	Amount paid in year = £4,000
Telephone	(2)	(1)	Amount paid in year = £1,000
Operating profit	3	(8)	**Cash absorbed by operations**

Although we have generated a positive operating profit for the year, our operations have **absorbed** cash. This difference is largely accounted for by timing of cash flows from customers, and so on.

Statement of cash flows

We are now in a position to complete our statement of cash flows that is as follows.

Statement of cash flows	(£'000)
Net cash absorbed by operating activities	(8)
Investing activities	
Purchase of non-current asset	(60)
Financing activities	
Shares issued (£100,000 + £20,000)	120
Bank loan raised	50
Increase in cash and cash equivalents	102

Double entry

There is no double entry for the statement of cash flows as it presents the same information as in the income statement or statement of financial position, but shown in a different manner.

An easy way to remember if something affects the statement of cash flows is to think about the double entry. If one of the entries is debit or credit cash then there will be an entry in the statement of cash flows.

Also a debit entry will be a cash inflow because it increases the bank balance and a credit entry is a cash outflow because it decreases the bank balance.

CHAPTER ROUNDUP

You need to be familiar with and able to describe

- The purpose of financial statements.

- The format of financial statements and the terminology contained therein such as non-current assets, minority interest and so on.

- The accruals principle.

You need to appreciate the accounting equation and the impact of transactions, i.e.

- Net assets = shareholders' funds.

- For any transaction:

    - change in net assets = change in shareholders' funds

TEST YOUR KNOWLEDGE

Check your knowledge of the chapter here, without referring back to the text.

The following questions are to ensure that you have understood the idea of the accounting equation and the impact of transactions. They do not reflect the type of question you may see in the exam, but an appreciation of the ideas covered here is key to certain aspects covered later in this Study Book.

1.   Austen Limited was set up on January 1 2005 by its shareholders subscribing for 10,000 shares with a nominal value of £1 each at par. In addition, the company took out a bank loan of £15,000 at an interest rate of 10%. All interest due on the bank loan for the year had been paid in full. The purpose of the company was wholesale distribution of romantic novels. The company took out a lease on a shop and warehouse, paying 18 months rent of £7,200 in advance. It purchased fixtures and fittings costing £5,000 and a second-hand delivery van costing £6,000. It is anticipated that the fixtures and fittings will have a ten-year life and will be worth nothing at the end of the period. The van will be used for three years, after which it will be scrapped.

During the year, Austen Limited purchased inventories of books costing £90,000, of which it has paid for £70,000 by the end of the year. It sold books that had cost £80,000 for £200,000, but was still owed £30,000 of this money at the year end by customers. Sundry operating expenses paid for in the year came to £45,000. It was estimated that at the end of the year the company owed £2,000 for telephone charges and £3,000 for electricity charges not yet invoiced.

Requirements

Prepare the income statement for the year ended December 31 2005 and the statement of financial position as at December 31 2005 for Austen Limited.

2.   Shogun Limited was set up on July 1 2006 in order to sell kimonos and samurai swords to Western customers. Its shareholders subscribed for 20,000 £1 shares at par and the company took out a bank loan of £15,000 paying interest at a rate of 11% per annum, on a quarterly basis. The interest due on the bank loan had not been paid for the last quarter. The following information is relevant for the year ended June 30 2007.

(a)   The company made sales of £210,000 over the year. Of this total, £170,000 had been received as cash in the year.

(b)   The company made purchases of £150,000 during the year. Trade accounts payable at June 30 2007 came to £10,000. Inventories of goods at the year end were valued at £30,000.

(c)   The company took out a lease on office premises on July 1 2006, paying a rent deposit of £3,000 immediately and then paying monthly rent of £1,000 in arrears on the last day of each month, commencing July 31 2006. The company expanded later in the year and took out a lease on new warehouse premises on June 1 2007, paying three months rent in advance totalling £1,500.

(d)   The company purchased fixtures and fittings costing £6,000 with a three-year life and a car costing £12,000 with a four-year life. All assets are to be depreciated to a nil residual value.

(e)   Other operating expenses paid for in the year came to £40,000. In addition, there were unpaid electricity and telephone bills at the end of the year for £1,500.

Ignore any interest due on overdraft balances during the year.

Requirements

Prepare the statement of financial position as at June 30 2007 and the income statement for the year then ended for Shogun Limited.

3.   Miller Limited has been trading for several years in the business of selling holidays in the sun. It is now preparing its accounts for the year ended December 31 2006. The following information is relevant.

(a)   At the beginning of the year it had non-current assets with a cost of £30,000 and a net book value of £24,000. Accounts receivable were £35,000, inventories were worth £20,000, trade accounts payable were £15,000 and there were accruals for telephone bills of £500. There were no prepaid expenses at this date. The cash balance was £2,000. The company has a share capital of 5,000 £1 shares and the only reserve is retained earnings. It has no borrowings.

(b)   During the year the company made purchases of £200,000. It paid over £195,000 to suppliers in the year. Inventories at the year end had a cost of £32,000.

(c)   In the year the company made sales of £400,000 and had year-end accounts receivable of £37,000.

(d)   Rent bills totalling £28,000 were paid on premises on which the monthly rent was £2,000. Amounts paid in respect of telephone bills came to £2,500. At the year end, it was estimated that telephone charges totalling £600 should be accrued for.

(e)   Expenses paid for in the year, excluding rent and telephone, came to £50,000.

All non-current assets are depreciated over a ten-year period to a residual value of nil.

Requirements

Prepare the statement of financial position as at December 31 2006 and the income statement for the year then ended for Miller Limited.

4.   Picasso Limited is a new business set up on January 1 2006. The following transactions occurred in the year to December 31 2006.

(a)   The initial share issue raised £55,000 of share capital.

(b)   A long-term bank loan was taken out for £40,000.

(c)   Cash sales in the year were £36,000 and sales made on credit were £65,000.

(d)   Total purchases of £60,000 were made in the year, with trade accounts payable remaining at the year end of £35,000. Inventories at the end of the year were £10,000.

(e)   The rent bill for the year was £10,000 was paid in full.

(f)   The company's wage bill in the period was £25,000, but £3,750 was outstanding at the end of the period.

(g)   Cash paid in respect of utilities amounted to £1,700, including a payment of £300 relating to next year's rates.

(h)   Interest on the loan is calculated at a rate of 7% per annum and the due amount was paid in the year.

Fixtures and fittings of £15,000 were purchased in the year and are estimated to have a five-year life, with no residual value.

(j)   The auditors estimate they will charge £750 to prepare this year's accounts.

(k)   The tax charge for the year (fully paid in 2006) was £2,400.

Dividends are proposed to be paid of 50% of the profit after taxation for 2006.

Requirements

Prepare the income statement for the year ended December 31 2006 and the statement of financial position as at December 31 2006 for Picasso Limited.

5. (a) The following is an extract from the accounts of Allegra Limited.

	2005	2006
Non-current assets (net book value)	17,500	27,300

The depreciation charged in 2006's income statement amounted to £3,300. What was the net cash outflow in Allegra's statement of cash flows relating to the purchase of non-current assets in 2006?

(b) Allegra's income statement in 2006 showed sales revenue for the year of £43,000. If the accounts receivable in the 2005 statement of financial position amounted to £17,000 and the accounts receivable figure in 2006 was £19,000, what was the cash received from customers in 2006?

(c) Allegra's tax charge in the income statement was £9,000. If the tax liability in 2005's statement of financial position amounted to £1,500 and the tax paid in 2006 to the tax authorities was £7,000, what was the tax liability in 2006's statement of financial position?

(d) Allegra's 2006 statement of financial position shows an increase in accounts receivable from 2005 of £2,000.

Trade accounts payable have declined in the year by £5,500 and inventory levels have also declined by £900. If operating profit in 2006 was £25,000 and the depreciation expense in 2006 was £3,300 what is the operating cash flow of the business in 2006?

(e) Allegra's auditors have produced a series of adjustments to be put through the 2006 accounts. How would these adjustments be reflected in the financial statements:

- An additional £750 depreciation should be provided for.

- The audit fee of £430, relating to preparation of the 2006 accounts, (yet to be billed) has not been included in the financial statements.

- A bad debt of £800 should be written off.

- Non-current assets originally costing £1,000 have been impaired.

(f) What impact will the adjustments detailed in (d) above have on the company's year-end cash position?

TEST YOUR KNOWLEDGE: ANSWERS

1. Statement of financial position as at December 31 2006

	(£)	(£)	(£)
ASSETS			
Non-current assets	**Cost**	**Depreciation**	
Fixtures and fittings	5,000	(500)	4,500
Van	6,000	(2,000)	4,000
	11,000	(2,500)	**8,500**
Current assets			
Inventories(90,000 – 80,000)		10,000	
Receivables		30,000	
Prepaid expenses (6/18 × 7,200)		2,400	
Cash at bank and in hand (see working)		60,300	
		102,700	
TOTAL ASSETS			**111,200**
LIABILITIES			
Current liabilities			
Trade accounts payable(90,000 – 70,000)		(20,000)	
Accruals (2,000 + 3,000)		(5,000)	
		(25,000)	
Non-current liabilities			
Long-term loan		**(15,000)**	
TOTAL LIABILITIES			**(40,000)**
			71,200
NET ASSETS			
Share capital (10,000 × £1)			10,000
Retained earnings			61,200
EQUITY			**71,200**

Income statement for the year ended December 31 2006

	(£)	(£)
Revenue		**200,000**
Cost of sales		
Opening inventories	–	
Purchases	90,000	
	90,000	
Closing inventories (90,000 – 80,000)	(10,000)	
		(80,000)
Gross profit		**120,000**
Expenses		
Sundry operating expenses	(45,000)	
Rent $\left(\frac{12}{18} \times 7,200\right)$	(4,800)	
Depreciation $\left(5,000 \times \frac{1}{10} + 6,000 \times \frac{1}{3}\right)$	(2,500)	
Telephone and electricity (2,000 + 3,000)	(5,000)	
		(57,300)
Operating costs		**62,700**
Finance costs (10% × 15,000)		(1,500)
Profit before taxation		**61,200**

Cash Flow Working

	Inflows (£)	Outflows (£)
Sales (200,000 – 30,000)	170,000	–
Purchases (90,000 – 20,000)	–	70,000
Operating expenses	–	45,000
Rent	–	7,200
Interest	–	1,500
Non-current assets	–	11,000
Share issue	10,000	–
Loan received	15,000	–
	195,000	134,700
Increase in cash	*60,300*	

2. Statement of financial position as at June 30 2007

	(£)	(£)	(£)
ASSETS			
Non-current assets	Cost	Depreciation	
Fixtures and fittings	6,000	(2,000)	4,000
Van	12,000	(3,000)	9,000
	18,000	(5,000)	**13,000**
Current assets			
Inventories		30,000	
Receivables (210,000 − 170,000)		40,000	
Prepaid expenses $(3,000 + \frac{2}{3} \times 1,500)$		4,000	
			74,000
TOTAL ASSETS			**87,000**
LIABILITIES			
Current liabilities			
Bank overdraft *(see working)*		(10,737)	
Trade accounts payable		(10,000)	
Accruals $(1,500 + 11\% \times 1/4 \times 15,000)$		(1,913)	
		(22,650)	
Non-current liabilities			
Long-term loan		**(15,000)**	
TOTAL LIABILITIES			**(37,650)**
NET ASSETS			**49,350**
Share capital (20,000 × £1)			20,000
Retained earnings			29,350
EQUITY			**49,350**

Income statement for the year ended June 30 2007

	(£)	(£)
Revenue		**210,000**
Cost of sales		
Opening inventories	−	
Purchases	150,000	
	150,000	
Closing inventories	(30,000)	
		(120,000)
Gross profit		**90,000**
Expenses		
Sundry operating expenses	40,000	
Rent $\left(12,000 + 1,500 \times \frac{1}{3}\right)$	12,500	
Depreciation $\left(6,000 \times \frac{1}{3} + 12,000 \times \frac{1}{4}\right)$	5,000	
Telephone and electricity	1,500	(59,000)
Operating profit		**31,000**
Finance costs (11% × 15,000)		(1,650)
Profit before taxation		**29,350**

Cash Flow Working

	Inflows (£)	Outflows (£)
Sales	170,000	–
Purchases (150,000 – 10,000)	–	140,000
Operating expenses	–	40,000
Rent (3,000 + 12,000 + 1,500)	–	16,500
Interest ($\frac{3}{4}$ × 1,650)	–	1,237
Non-current assets	–	18,000
Share issue	20,000	–
Loan received	15,000	–
	205,000	215,737
Decrease in cash	*10,737*	

3. Statement of financial position as at December 31 2006

	(£)	(£)	(£)
ASSETS	Cost	Depreciation	
Non-current assets	30,000	(9,000)	21,000
Current assets			
Inventories		32,000	
Receivables		37,000	
Prepaid expenses (28 – 24)		4,000	
Cash at bank and in hand *(see working)*		124,500	
			197,500
TOTAL ASSETS			218,500
LIABILITIES			
Current liabilities			
Trade accounts payable (200 + 15 – 195)		(20,000)	
Accruals		(600)	
TOTAL LIABILITIES			(20,600)
NET ASSETS			197,900
Share capital (5,000 × £1)			5,000
Retained earnings *(see below)*			192,900
EQUITY			197,900

Income statement for the year ended December 31 2006

	(£)	(£)
Revenue		400,000
Cost of sales		
Opening inventories	20,000	
Purchases	200,000	
	220,000	
Closing inventories	(32,000)	
		(188,000)
Gross profit		212,000
Expenses		
Sundry operating expenses	50,000	
Rent (12 × £2,000)	24,000	
Depreciation (30,000 × $\frac{1}{10}$)	3,000	
Telephone (2,500 + 600 – 500)	2,600	
		(79,600)
Net profit		132,400

Cash Flow Working

	Inflows (£)	Outflows (£)
Sales (400,000 – 37,000 + 35,000)	398,000	–
Purchases	–	195,000
Operating expenses	–	50,000
Rent	–	28,000
Telephone	–	2,500
	398,000	275,500
Increase in cash	*122,500*	
Opening cash balance	*2,000*	
Closing cash balance	*124,500*	

Opening statement of financial position

	(£)
Non-current assets – Net Book Value	24,000
Inventories	20,000
Receivables	35,000
Cash	2,000
Trade accounts payable	(15,000)
Accruals	(500)
NET ASSETS	**65,500**
Share capital	5,000
Retained earnings (missing figure)	60,500
EQUITY	**65,500**

'Retained earnings' in the statement of financial position at 31 December 2006

At 1 January 2006	60,500
Net profit for 2006	132,400
At 31 December 2006	192,900

4. Statement of financial position

	(£)	(£)
ASSETS		
Non-current assets		
Fixtures and fittings (cost)		15,000
Accumulated depreciation		(3,000)
Net Book Value		12,000
Current assets		
Inventories	10,000	
Receivables	65,000	
Prepaid expenses	300	
Cash at bank and in hand *(see working)*	52,850	
		128,150
TOTAL ASSETS		**140,150**

	(£)	(£)
LIABILITIES		
Current liabilities		
Trade accounts payable	(35,000)	
Accruals *(3,750 + 750)*	(4,000)	
	(39,000)	
Non-current liabilities		
Long-term loan	(40,000)	
TOTAL LIABILITIES		**(79,000)**
		60,650
NET ASSETS		
Share capital		55,000
Retained earnings		5,650
EQUITY		**60,650**

Income statement

	(£)
Revenue	**101,000**
Cost of sales (60,000 – 10,000)	(50,000)
Gross profit	**51,000**
Expenses	
Rent	(10,000)
Wages	(25,000)
Utilities	(1,400)
Depreciation	(3,000)
Audit fee	(750)
Operating profit	**10,850**
Finance costs	(2,800)
Profit before taxation	**8,050**
Taxation	(2,400)
Profit after taxation	**5,650**

Cash Flow Working

	Inflows (£)	Outflows (£)
Share issue	55,000	
Bank loan	40,000	
Sales revenue	36,000	
Purchases		25,000
Rent		10,000
Wages		21,250
Utilities		1,700
Interest paid		2,800
Fixtures		15,000
Tax paid		2,400
Totals	131,000	78,150
Increase in cash	52,850	

Tutorial note

The proposed dividend of £2,825 (50% of profit after taxation for the year) is not recognised as a liability in the statement of financial position at the year end. IAS 10 requires that proposed dividends are treated as non-adjusting events arising after the statement of financial position date; they are not liabilities until declared by a resolution approved by shareholders at a general meeting. The proposed dividend will be disclosed in the 2006 financial statements but will not be recognised as a liability.

5. (a) The net cash outflow on the purchase of non-current assets amounts to £13,100.

    This can be computed by taking the movement in the net book value of the non-current assets, and adding back the depreciation expense for the year (27,300 − 17,500 + 3,300).

    (b)

Receivables: 2005	17,000
+ Sales	43,000
− Cash received from customers	(x)
=Receivables: 2006	19,000
Cash received from customers	= 17,000 + 43,000 − 19,000
	= £41,000

    (c)

Taxl iability: 2005	1,500
+ Tax expense	9,000
− Cash taxes paid	(7,000)
= Tax liability: 2006	x
Tax liability: 2006	= 1,500 + 9,000 − 7,000
	= £3,500

    (d)

Operating profit	25,000
+ Depreciation	3,300
− Increase in receivables	(2,000)
− Decrease in trade accounts payable	(5,500)
+ Decrease in inventories	900
= Cash flow from operations	£21,700

    (e) The adjustments would be reflected in the financial statements as follows.

    - Increase accumulated depreciation £750 (reduce assets); Depreciation expense £750 (reduce profit/equity).

    - Audit fee expense (operating cost) £430 (reduce profit/equity);Liabilities: accruals £430 (increase liabilities).

    - Reduce accounts receivable by £800 (reduce assets); Bad debt expense (operating cost) £800 (reduce profit/equity).

    - Reduce non current assets by £1,000; impairment expense (operating cost) £1,000 (reduce profit/equity).

    (f) The above adjustments have no effect on the company's cash position.

2 UK Generally Accepted Accounting Principles

INTRODUCTION

The last chapter introduced the broad form and content of a set of financial statements. This chapter builds up on the detailed requirements for the form and contents and the various sources of rules impacting on financial statements.

CHAPTER LEARNING OBJECTIVES

The syllabus areas covered by this chapter are

Interpretation of Financial Information

Elements of corporate securities

Understanding the relevance of all elements of corporate reports for financial analysis including Chairman's Statement and Directors' Report, Auditors' Report, Statement of Accounting Policies, cashflow statements and other qualitative information provided with the annual report and accounts, prospectuses, interim statements and merger documents.

Presentation of Financial Statements

Impact of statutory and non-statutory regulation on UK financial statements. An understanding of the effect on the presentation of financial statements of the Companies Acts and non-statutory regulations, including standards and other guidance issued by IASB and stock exchange requirements.

1 BACKGROUND AND HISTORY OF FINANCIAL REPORTING IN THE UK

Exam tip

> The exam focus concerns the application of accounting knowledge to the analysis of accounts. The areas covered by this chapter are more fact-based and consequently are rarely examined.

You will not be asked in detail about the history of financial reporting in the IFS exam. However, many aspects of the disclosure and presentation of financial statements in the UK, both at a detailed and general level, have undergone dramatic change in recent times. In order to put these changes into a wider context, therefore, it is useful to have a basic understanding of how Standards are created, and how the Standard-setting regime has developed over the years.

1.1 Generally Accepted Accounting Principles in the UK before 2005

The term 'Generally Accepted Accounting Principles' (GAAP) is often used to describe the various accounting and financial reporting rules with which companies in a given jurisdiction must comply. It is important to understand, however, that UK GAAP, for example, does not refer to one single set of rules, but is an umbrella term to describe the sometimes complex combination of different statutes (i.e. laws) and accounting regulations that UK companies must follow in presenting their financial statements.

For accounting periods beginning on or before 31 December 2004, UK GAAP entailed compliance with the following.

- The requirements of the Companies Act 1985, as amended by the Companies Act 1989 (see Section 5).

- For companies listed on the London Stock Exchange, the requirements of the *Listing Rules* (see Section 6).

- Financial Reporting Standards (FRSs) and other accounting regulations, as created or adopted by the UK's Accounting Standards Board (ASB).

The Accounting Standards Board was created in 1990 with the role of creating **Financial Reporting Standards**, specifying rules to be followed in dealing with specific transactions or aspects of accounting. Until 2005, the ASB had responsibility for setting all accounting standards relevant for companies reporting in the UK.

In addition to FRSs, other accounting rules created under UK GAAP were

- **UITF** (Urgent Issues Task Force) **Abstracts**, informing companies how to report specific issues on which no FRS or other accounting regulation was in place, or providing clarification on how a particular rule should be interpreted in particular scenarios.

- **Statements of Recommended Practice (SORPs)** giving recommendations on accounting practices for specific industries or sectors.

In addition, a number of rules created by the accounting profession prior to 1990, known as **Statements of Standard Accounting Practice (SSAPs)** were adopted by the ASB and continued to form part of UK GAAP, where there was no need for the standard to be replaced or updated by the ASB.

While FRSs, SORPs and SSAPs no longer form the basis of your syllabus for the IFS exam, you should be familiar with this terminology, as there will be specific instances where it is necessary to know how International Standards being used by companies today differ from those previously in force under UK GAAP, so that we can gain a complete understanding of the information presented in a company's financial statements.

1.2 Generally Accepted Accounting Principles in the UK since 2005

In June 2002, the European Union adopted a regulation requiring **listed** companies in Member States (including the UK) to prepare their group/consolidated financial statements using 'adopted International Accounting Standards' for accounting periods beginning **on or after 1 January 2005**.

As the exam will focus predominantly on the accounts of UK listed companies, it is therefore International Financial Reporting Standards (IFRSs) and their predecessors, International Accounting Standards (IASs), which now form the basis of the technical knowledge required for the IFS exam. We have therefore explored the background and conceptual framework of International Financial Reporting Standards in further detail below.

It should be noted that the requirement to comply with the Companies Act and the Listing Rules remains, although certain specific aspects of these pieces of regulation have been updated to ensure compatibility with IFRS. Therefore, IFRSs and IASs can be considered to have simply replaced UK Accounting Standards in the overall context of UK GAAP, as far as listed companies are concerned.

Companies listed on the Alternative Investment Market (AIM) were required to adopt IFRS for accounting periods beginning **on or after 1 January 2007**.

Unlisted companies can choose between UK IFRS and UK GAAP. UK FRSs (and other UK accounting rules) remains. However, a process of convergence has also been underway in recent years, whereby the ASB has replaced a number of previous UK standards with new standards identical to their international equivalents. This process is likely to continue, resulting in fewer material differences between UK and International Standards in the long term.

1.3 History of International Accounting Standards

The drive towards a single set of global accounting Standards began many years ago with the establishment of the International Accounting Standards Committee (IASC) in 1973. The IASC was created by the professional accounting bodies of Australia, Canada, France, Germany, Ireland, Japan, the Netherlands, the UK and the US and issued IAS 1 in 1975.

The IASC continued publishing Standards and garnering support from various bodies over the following years. It was not until 2000 that the move towards International Accounting Standards began to gather pace. Firstly, IOSCO (the International Organisation of Securities Commissions) recommended that its members allow multinational issuers to use IASC Standards in cross-border offerings and listings. Secondly, the European Union committed to using International Accounting Standards (IAS) for EU-listed companies by 2005. Furthermore, in May 2000, a new constitution was adopted under which the IASC was approved as an independent entity, henceforth delegating responsibility for standard-setting to a new body – the International Accounting Standards Board (IASB).

1.4 Objectives

Under the new constitution, the stated objectives of the IASC were

- To develop, in the public interest, a single set of high quality, understandable and enforceable global accounting standards that require high quality, transparent and comparable information in financial statements and other financial reporting to help participants in the world's capital markets (and other users) make informed economic decisions;

- To promote the use and rigorous application of those standards; and

- To bring about convergence of national accounting standards and international accounting standards to high quality solutions.

With respect to the first objective, the IASB was charged with delivering a complete set of standards for implementation in 2005, the adoption date for EU-listed companies.

During 2003, the IASB completed its improvements project – issuing major revisions to 14 existing International Accounting Standards (IASs) – and issued its first new standard, International Financial Reporting Standard 1 (IFRS 1).

With respect to the final aim, the IASB entered into the 'Norwalk Agreement' with the US standard-setting body, the Financial Accounting Standards Board (FASB). The agreement is aimed at converging US GAAP and International Standards over time.

2 FRAMEWORK FOR THE PREPARATION AND PRESENTATION OF FINANCIAL STATEMENTS

2.1 Aims of IASC Conceptual Framework

In July 1989, the IASC published a *Framework for the Preparation and Presentation of Financial Statements* to assist both those with the responsibility of setting standards, and those interpreting statements prepared in accordance with them.

The *Framework* lays out a conceptual basis for the characteristics and elements of financial statements as well as the recognition and measurement of items contained therein. The *Framework* is very similar to the *UK Statement of Principles for Financial Reporting*.

2.2 Objective of financial statements

The *Framework* suggests financial statements provide information about the financial position (through the statement of financial position), the performance (through an income statement) and changes in financial position (through a statement of cash flows and other reconciliations) of an enterprise. The financial statements also show the results of the stewardship of management, or the accountability of management for the resources entrusted to it.

While financial statements should provide, to a wide range of users, information that is useful in determining economic decisions, it is recognised that they do not contain all relevant information. Financial statements are only intended to portray the financial effects of past events, and do not necessarily provide non-financial information.

2.3 Underlying assumptions

The *Framework* suggests only two fundamental underlying assumptions inform the preparation of financial statements, namely

- **Accruals basis** – the effect of transactions and other events are reported in the period in which they occur or to which they relate.

- **Going concern** – financial statements are normally prepared on the basis that the enterprise has neither the need nor intention to liquidate, or curtail materially, the scale of its operations within the foreseeable future.

2.4 Qualitative characteristics of financial statements

Exam tip

This is the area most frequently examined from this section, e.g. Winter 2006 Question 7, Summer 2006 Question 6, Winter 2005 Question 5.

The *Framework* presents four characteristics of financial information as well as considering constraints upon such characteristics. The four characteristics are

- Understandability.
- Relevance.
- Reliability.
- Comparability.

2.4.1 Understandability

Financial information should be readily understood by a knowledgeable user of financial statements. However, complex information which is relevant to the decision-making needs of the users of financial statements should not be excluded on the grounds of complexity alone.

2.4.2 Relevance

Financial information is considered to be relevant where it would influence the assessment of economic decisions to be made by the user of financial statements. Relevance may relate to the evaluation of past, current or future events.

The relevance of information is affected by its **materiality**. Information may be material due to its nature or size. An item may be judged to be material if its omission or misstatement could influence the economic decisions based on the financial statements.

2.4.3 Reliability

Information will be reliable where it is free from material error or bias and can be depended upon by the user of financial statements. Reliable information is also asserted to have the following characteristics.

- **Faithful representation** – information must faithfully represent the transactions or other events it either purports to represent or might reasonably be expected to represent.

- **Substance over form** – faithful representation itself requires information to reflect the substance or economic reality of a transaction or event, not necessarily its legal form.

- **Neutrality** – reliable information will be free from bias.

- **Prudence** – in contending with the inevitable uncertainty surrounding events and circumstances, preparers of financial statements should exercise a degree of caution in the exercise of judgements needed to make estimates in conditions of uncertainty.

- **Completeness** – within the bounds of materiality and cost, information should be complete.

2.4.4 Comparability

Users of financial statements may wish to compare information regarding an enterprise through time and may wish to compare information regarding different enterprises. Consequently, the measurement, recording and display of the financial effects of similar transactions or events must be carried out in a consistent way throughout an enterprise and over time for that enterprise and in a consistent manner for different enterprises.

2.4.5 Constraints upon characteristics

The *Framework* acknowledges a balance between relevant, reliable information and certain constraints. Where producing reliable and relevant financial information may involve undue delay or excessive cost (with regard to potential benefit) professional judgement may be required to resolve such tensions.

2.5 The elements of financial statements

Financial statements portray the financial effects of transactions and other events by grouping them together according to their economic characteristics. These groupings form the elements of financial statements.

2.5.1 Financial position

The elements relating to the reporting of financial position are defined below.

- **Asset** – a resource controlled by the entity due to past events and from which future economic benefits are expected to flow.

- **Liability** – a present obligation of the enterprise arising from past events, the settlement of which is expected to result in an outflow of resources embodying economic benefits from the enterprise.

- **Equity** – the residual interest in the assets after deducting all liabilities.

2.5.2 Performance

Profit (or earnings) is the usual measure of performance. The elements which contribute to the calculation of profit are income and expenditure, as defined below.

- **Income** – increases in economic benefits during the accounting period in the form of inflows or enhancements of assets, or decreases in liabilities that result in increases in equity, other than those relating to contributions from equity participants.

- **Expenditure** – decreases in economic benefits during the accounting period in the form of outflows or depletions of assets or incurrences of liabilities that result in decreases in equity, other than those relating to distributions to equity participants.

2.6 Recognition of the elements of financial statements

Recognition of items within the financial statements of an enterprise constitutes their inclusion in the statement of financial position or income statement. They are included by means of words and a monetary amount which is incorporated in statement of financial position or income statement totals.

The *Framework* establishes two recognition criteria which must be met.

- It is **probable** that any future economic benefit associated with the item will flow to or from the enterprise.

- The item has a cost or value that can be **measured reliably**.

2.7 Measurement of the elements of financial statements

Measurement in financial statements refers to the manner in which the monetary amount which is to be recognised within the financial statements may be determined. There are various measurement approaches used for assets, liabilities, equity, income and expenses as outlined below.

- **Historic cost** – assets may be recorded at the cash or cash equivalent amount paid on their acquisition (for example, property, plant and equipment). Liabilities may be recorded at the amount of proceeds received in exchange for that obligation (such as recording of a loan).

- **Current cost** – assets may be carried at the cash or cash equivalent amount that would need to be paid if the asset were acquired currently (for example, derivatives which are being marked-to-market).

- **Realisable (settlement) values** – assets may be carried at the amount of cash or cash equivalents that could currently be obtained by selling the asset in an orderly disposal (for example, where the asset is written down to net realisable value as the result of an impairment review).

- **Present value** – assets may be carried at the discounted value of the expected future net cash inflows that the item is expected to generate in the normal course of business (for example, where an asset is written down to its value in use as a result of an impairment review).

2.8 Benchmark and allowed alternative treatment

Many of the old IASs permitted two accounting treatments for like transactions or events. One treatment is designated as the **benchmark treatment** (effectively the **preferred treatment**) and the other is known as the **alternative treatment**. However, as the standards are revised, many alternatives are being eliminated.

3 REGULATION OF FINANCIAL STATEMENTS

This section examines the regulations governing the financial statements prepared by a company in the UK. The regulations mentioned here apply to all financial statements, whether they are part of the annual accounts of a company or part of another document issued by the company, such as a prospectus or circular to shareholders.

As mentioned earlier, there are two sources of regulation in relation to a quoted company's financial statements other than accounting rules.

- Legal rules.
- Listing rules.

These are concerned with what should be disclosed in the financial statements.

4 LEGAL RULES

4.1 Introduction

A company is a business organisation created in law that is owned by its members or shareholders.

Generally, for listed companies and larger unlisted ones, the shareholders appoint directors to manage the company on their behalf, having little involvement in the day-to-day operations of the companies themselves.

The requirement for annual financial statements is from the Companies Act. The directors must report to the shareholders on the financial performance and position of the company.

The financial statements are, however, frequently used by other interested parties such as lenders, creditors, potential investors, tax authorities, the government, etc. to help them assess the returns they are receiving and the risks that they may face.

4.2 Consequences of incorporation

Upon incorporation a company becomes a separate legal entity, distinct from its owners/shareholders. This has three main implications.

4.2.1 Legal personality

Companies have a legal personality and existence separate from their owners. They can enter into contractual and other relationships with third parties through their directors/managers/employees without reference to the owners.

4.2.2 Unlimited life

A company's identity is unaffected by changes in ownership, hence they theoretically have unlimited lives.

4.2.3 Limited liability

Should a company become incapable of meeting its liabilities for any reason, the shareholders generally will not be personally liable. This contrasts with a sole trader or partnership where the owners of a business would have to meet the business liabilities from their own personal assets.

4.3 Legal requirement to prepare financial statements

The Companies Act 1985 (as amended by the Companies Act 1989) requires the directors of a company to produce financial statements, specifically a statement of financial position and an income statement (a profit and loss account), to be included in the annual accounts of the company.

Although it can be seen that the original requirement for financial statements was a part of the annual report and accounts, use of financial statements has widened considerably.

Listed companies in particular are required to publish financial statements within other documents according to Stock Exchange rules. These documents are discussed later in the chapter.

The financial statements prepared by the directors for the shareholders must

- Give a true and fair view (discussed in more detail below).
- Comply with the requirements of the Companies Acts.

Further legal regulations then deal with

- The formats for financial statements together with minimum disclosure requirements.
- Fundamental accounting principles.
- Valuation rules.
- Possible reporting exemptions.

We will now examine the true and fair view, fundamental accounting rules and valuation rules in more detail. The reporting exemptions for annual accounts are discussed later in the chapter in the section dealing specifically with annual accounts requirements.

4.4 True and fair view

4.4.1 Meaning of 'true and fair view'

One of the requirements of the Companies Act 1985 is that the financial statements should give a **true and fair view** of the performance of the company for the period and its financial position at the end of that period. The requirement to show a true and fair view **overrides all other requirements** in the preparation of financial statements, so what is a true and fair view?

True and fair is a fairly philosophical concept that changes over time as new rules and regulations are developed. However, generally speaking, we could define the terms as follows.

4.4.2 True

True is taken to refer to the accuracy of the figures contained in the financial statements, within the limitations of materiality and subjectivity in the valuation of various transactions, assets and liabilities.

The Companies Act refers to *a* true and fair view, not *the* true and fair view, indicating that the figures need only be substantially correct, not necessarily to-the-penny, and that anything that is immaterial in the context of the financial statements as a whole will not distort their truth.

4.4.3 Fair

Fair refers to the way in which material is presented. In assessing fairness we need to consider whether

- Correct emphasis has been placed on the more significant transactions.
- Sufficient information has been provided to enable the user to gain the correct impression of the performance and financial position of the company.

In summary, in order to give a true and fair view the information must be accurate and comprehensive, but only within acceptable limits.

4.4.4 Companies Act requirements

As noted above, the overriding requirement of the Companies Act 1985 is that the financial statements should give a true and fair view of the performance of the company for the period and its financial position at the end of that period.

A company may depart from the requirements of an accounting standard or companies legislation if it appears to the directors that an alternative treatment should be adopted in order to give a true and fair view.

If this is the case, then the Companies Act 1985 requires the directors to disclose the following in the financial statements.

- What the departure from accounting rules has been.
- The reasons for the departure.
- The effect of the departure.

The Act gives no elaboration on these requirements.

4.5 Fair presentation and compliance with IFRSs

It should be noted that under IFRSs there are similar but not quite the same requirements regarding the financial statements.

According to IAS 1 the financial statements must 'present fairly' the financial position, financial performance and cash flows of an entity. Fair presentation requires the faithful representation of the effects of transactions, other events and conditions in accordance with the definitions and recognition criteria for assets, liabilities, income and expenses set out in the *Framework*. The application of IFRSs with additional disclosures where necessary is presumed to result in financial statements that achieve a fair presentation.

IAS 1 requires that an entity whose financial statements comply with IFRSs makes an explicit and unreserved statement of such compliance in the notes.

IAS 1, however, acknowledges that, in extremely rare circumstances, management may conclude that compliance with an IFRS requirement would be so misleading that it would conflict with the objective of financial statements set out in the *Framework*. In such a case, the entity is required to depart from the IFRS requirement, with detailed disclosure of the nature, reasons and impact of the departure.

4.6 Fundamental accounting principles

The Companies Act sets out five fundamental accounting principles that must be used when preparing financial statements.

These principles are detailed below, with their definition and explanation as laid down in the Companies Act.

4.6.1 Going concern

The company shall be presumed to be carrying on business as a going concern.

4.6.2 Accruals

All income and charges relating to the financial year to which the accounts relate shall be taken into account, without regard to the date of receipt or payment.

4.6.3 Consistency

Accounting policies shall be applied consistently within the same accounts and from one financial year to the next.

4.6.4 Prudence

The amount of any item shall be determined on a prudent basis, in particular in relation to the following.

- Only profits realised at the statement of financial position date shall be included in the profit and loss account.
- All liabilities and losses that have arisen or are likely to arise in respect of the financial year to which the accounts relate or a previous financial year shall be taken into account.

4.6.5 No netting off

In determining the aggregate amount of any item, the amount of each individual asset or liability that falls to be taken into account, shall be determined separately.

4.6.6 Use of the Companies Act principles

The above principles should not be viewed in isolation as necessarily being fundamental throughout the financial reporting process. They must be placed within the context of the Framework for the Preparation and Presentation of Financial Statements, a document that did not exist at the time that the Companies Act principles were first enshrined in law.

As is discussed in the section of this chapter concerning accounting policies, it is only the going concern and accruals concepts that are considered fundamental to the entire financial reporting process.

4.7 Valuation rules

The Companies Act permits two alternative valuation methods.

- Historical cost accounting.
- Alternative valuation rules.

4.7.1 Historical cost accounting

Under the historical cost accounting rules, all assets, liabilities and items of income or expense must be evaluated in the financial statements based on their historical cost. Relating this to some of the categories of items in the financial statements, this rule should be applied as follows.

4.7.2 Fixed assets (non-current assets)

Fixed assets should be valued at purchase price or production cost less any provision for depreciation or permanent diminution in value. There should be no upward revaluation if we are strictly applying historical cost accounting rules.

All fixed assets with a limited useful economic life must be depreciated to their residual values on a systematic basis over that lifetime.

4.7.3 Current assets

Current assets should be valued at the lower of purchase price or production cost and net realisable value. This requirement is simply giving legal force to the regulations contained within accounting standards.

In determining the purchase price or production cost of either of the above items, the following should be considered.

4.7.4 Purchase price

The purchase price is the actual price paid plus import duties, transportation and handling costs and other directly attributable costs, less trade discounts, rebates, subsidies, i.e. the net overall amount paid to get the item to where it is to be used.

4.7.5 Production cost

The production cost must include the purchase price of any raw materials and consumables used, together with any other costs incurred which are directly attributable to the production of the asset. This will include manufacturing labour costs plus production overheads related to the production period.

Production costs may also include interest on capital borrowed to finance the production, to the extent that it accrues in respect of the period of production. It is not uncommon for interest to be capitalised in this way on major self-constructed fixed (non-current) assets such as buildings.

4.7.6 Alternative valuation rules

As an alternative to applying basic historical cost to the recording of any assets, liabilities, transactions and so on, the Companies Act permits certain of these assets to be revalued to market value or current cost, specifically

- Intangible fixed (non-current) assets, other than goodwill.
- Tangible fixed (non-current) assets.
- Fixed (non-current) asset investments.
- Stock (inventory).
- Other current assets.

Where the value of a fixed asset is based on an amount other than the historical cost, depreciation should be based on that revalued amount.

With regard to fixed asset investments, the directors may evaluate them at an amount considered appropriate, provided that the basis and reason for this evaluation are stated. This is a practical point to cover the possibility of investment in unquoted companies where no easy market value exists.

5 LISTING RULES

5.1 Introduction

Companies whose shares are listed on a recognised UK stock exchange (such as the London Stock Exchange) must comply with certain additional disclosure requirements laid out in the *Listing Rules*.

These rules are governed by the UKLA (UK Listing Authority) and cover a variety of documents published by companies, including annual accounts, interim accounts, merger documents and listing particulars. The contents of these documents, and the impact of the *Listing Rules* upon these documents, are discussed in more detail later in this chapter.

The Listing Rules also require that directors of listed companies comply with the provisions of the Combined Code on Corporate Governance. This is an area that is reported on in the annual accounts.

The rationale behind these rules is that listed companies, being owned largely by the public either individually or via institutional shareholdings, should have greater transparency and disclosure in their accounts.

In addition, the directors of listed companies must at all times be acting, and be seen to be acting, in the interests of the company and its shareholders.

5.2 Corporate governance

Traditionally, institutions in the UK have taken a back seat in management issues, preferring to leave management decisions to the directors they hired for the purpose. However, in recent years, notable corporate failures and the perception that directors may be improving their own pay and conditions at the expense of the shareholders has led to a greater awareness and willingness to participate in certain decisions.

Typically, institutions will still not wish to be involved in executive decision-making, but will be concerned with overall issues of relevance to them as shareholders and to their relationship with the directors.

These issues include

- Disapplication of pre-emption rights.

- Directors' remuneration and service contracts.

- Accountability of directors.

- The use of non-executive directors and audit committees.

- The role of institutional investors and the extent to which they should exert influence on a company and its management.

5.3 The Combined Code on corporate governance

A Combined Code on corporate governance has been published, derived from the recommendations of the Hampel, Greenbury and Cadbury committees concerning corporate governance. Companies are required to disclose in their annual report both how they have applied the principles of good governance and whether they have complied with the provisions of the code of best practice. In 2003, the Combined Code was updated to encompass the recommendations of the Higgs report, which looked at the role of non-executive directors, and the Smith Report, which considered audit committees.

The Combined Code is included as an appendage to the *Listing Rules*.

5.4 Implications for financial reporting

The Combined Code states that the principle of financial reporting should be the presentation of a balanced and understandable assessment of the company's position and prospects. This principle applies to interim reports and other public and regulatory reports, as well as to annual accounts.

Specific disclosures required by the Combined Code within the annual accounts have been detailed later in the chapter in the section on annual accounts requirements.

6 ANNUAL ACCOUNTS REQUIREMENTS

6.1 Responsibility for accounts preparation and audit

As discussed earlier, in the UK it is the directors' legal responsibility to prepare the financial statements for the shareholders and these must

- Give a true and fair view.
- Comply with the requirements of the Companies Act.

The financial statements form part of the annual accounts, which must then be sent to

- The members and debenture holders of the company (in an unabbreviated form).
- The Registrar of Companies (possibly in an abbreviated form).

The auditor is an independent third party appointed by the shareholders to give an opinion as to whether the directors have prepared financial statements that give a true and fair view and comply with the Companies Act. The auditors' report is also a legally required part of the annual report and accounts.

6.2 Format and contents of accounts

As a reminder, the accounts of listed companies in the UK must contain the following elements.

	Regulation		
	Companies Act	Listing Rules	FRS
Chairman's statement*			
Chief executive's review*			
Operating and financial review*			
Corporate governance and remuneration report		✓	
Directors' report	✓		
Auditors' report	✓		
Financial statements:			
Income statement	✓		
Statement of financial position	✓		
Statement of total recognised gains and losses			✓
Statement of cash flows			✓
Notes to the accounts	✓		
Accounting policies	✓		
(Figures for this year plus previous year's comparatives)	✓		
Five-year summary*			

*   It is not mandatory to include these items in the accounts of listed companies. However, listed companies will typically include them in their annual accounts.

We examined the primary financial statements in the previous chapter and we will be looking at the notes to the accounts throughout the remaining chapters. We will now consider the other elements of the annual accounts.

6.3 Listing Rules disclosure requirements – general disclosure

These Rules require that listed companies include in their annual report and accounts the following disclosures. Some of these disclosures would be made within the notes to the financial statements. Others would be contained in narrative sections of the annual accounts, for example, in the report on corporate governance.

Variations from Forecasts	Where the results of the company have differed materially from any published forecasts made by the company, an explanation must be included in the accounts for the period.
Allotments for Cash	Details of any issues of equity securities for cash, other than *pro rata* to the current shareholders.
Purchase of Own Shares	The accounts should disclose particulars of any shareholder's authority, of a purchase by the company, of his own shares (other than through the market or by tender or partial offer to all its shareholders). The accounts should also disclose particulars of the shareholders who have sold shares back to the company during the year.

Substantial Shareholdings	The financial statements should report particulars of any investors whose shareholding is substantial, i.e. exceeds 3% of the share capital of the company.
Waiver of Dividends	The accounts should disclose particulars of any arrangements under which shareholders have waived or agreed to waive any dividends.
Directors' Interests in Shares	The financial statements should show the interest of each director in the share capital of any member of the group, together with any options in respect of such shares. This statement should include details of any changes in that interest during the year.
Directors' Interests in Contracts	The accounts should disclose if the company has entered into any contracts in which any director had a material, personal interest.
Waiver of Emoluments	The accounts should disclose particulars of any arrangements under which a director has waived or agreed to waive any emoluments.
Related Party Transactions	The accounts should disclose any contract of significance between the company (or one of its subsidiaries) and a corporate substantial shareholder. A contract is considered to be significant where its value represents 1% or more of either – The net assets of the company in the case of capital expenditure; or – The total purchases, sales, payments or receipts for any revenue expenditure. A corporate substantial shareholder is one who has 30% or more of the voting power at general meetings, or who can control the composition of the majority of the board of directors of the company.
Related Party Service Contract	The accounts should disclose particulars of any contract for the provision of services to the company or any of its subsidiaries by a corporate substantial shareholder.
Interest Capitalised	The company must disclose the amount of any interest capitalised during the year as permitted under accounting rules.
Going Concern	The directors must make a statement that the business is a going concern, including supporting assumptions or qualifications as necessary.

6.4 Corporate governance/Directors' remuneration disclosures

Earlier in this chapter we discussed the importance of good corporate governance to listed companies and their directors, which has led to the Combined Code on Corporate Governance.

This section details the disclosures required on corporate governance and directors' remuneration in the annual accounts of listed companies.

6.5 Corporate governance

There must be a narrative statement in the annual report as to how the company has applied the principles of the Combined Code, providing an explanation that allows shareholders to evaluate how the principles have been applied.

The company must additionally state whether or not it has complied throughout the accounting period with the Combined Code on Corporate Governance.

Where a company complies with only part of the *Code* it must specify which paragraphs it has not complied with and why. Where a company has only complied for part of a period, it should state the period of, and the reason for, non-compliance.

6.6 Directors' remuneration report

The annual report should contain a report to the shareholders by the board, which must contain the following.

- A statement of the company's policy on executive directors' remuneration.

- The amount of each element of the remuneration package for each director, including benefits in kind, annual and deferred bonuses and compensation for loss of office.

- Information on share options for each director by name.

- Details of long-term incentive schemes (other than share option schemes already mentioned above), including interests of each director by name.

- Explanation and justification of any element of remuneration, other than basic salary, which is pensionable.

- Details of directors' service contracts with a notice period in excess of one year.

- The unexpired term of any service contract of a director proposed for election or re-election at the next AGM.

- Statement of company policy on granting of options or awards under employee share schemes.

- Details of defined benefit pension schemes, including for each director the accumulated accrued benefit under the scheme.

- Details of money purchase pension schemes, including details of the contributions made by the company in the period on behalf of each director.

6.7 Chairman's statement

This will usually be the first statement in a set of accounts, though it is not a legal requirement and there is no legally required form or content. Normally, they will comment on

- The overall trading conditions during the year and general outlook for the future.
- The performance achieved by each trading segment.
- Any special items of interest, e.g. new acquisitions or closures.
- The company's strategy and plans for the future.

The chairman's statement frequently includes some useful information that helps to explain information that is seen within the accounts, however, it must be noted that it is not audited and hence, there is no requirement that the comments made by the chairman must tie in or support the numbers presented in the financial statements. It is quite common for the chairman's statement to be little more than an advertising splash at the beginning of a set of accounts.

In addition to the chairman's statement, it is also common for listed companies to publish a chief executive's review. This tends to focus in more detail on historic performance and position, along with a discussion of future plans. Its inclusion could result in the chairman's statement being little more than a one-page introduction to the accounts, with little or no discussion of corporate performance or position.

BPP
LEARNING MEDIA

6.8 The Operating and Financial Review

The Operating and Financial Review is a narrative report prepared annually for shareholders, setting out the principal drivers of a company's performance both in the past and the future. It covers the issues seen as key to a company's performance – an account of its business, performance and strategy, a review of developments over the past year, and a description of the main risks. But it also covers prospects for the future and, where necessary, information about the environment, employees, customers or social and community issues where that information is important for an assessment of the company.

Whilst the inclusion of an Operating and Financial Review in the annual report is not mandatory, most major companies include it on a voluntary basis, and the ASB issued a statement of best practice in January 2006 recommending that they continue to do so.

6.9 Directors' report

6.9.1 Contents

Unlike the chairman's statement, there are a number of legally required elements to a directors' report, specifically

- A fair review of the developments during the year and position at the year end.

- Principal activities and any significant changes.

- Future developments in the business.

- Post-statement of financial position events.

- Research and development activities.

- Proposed dividends.

- Proposed transfers to reserves.

- Significant changes in fixed assets.

- Differences between book and market values of land and buildings if significant.

- Directors at any time during the period.

- Directors' interests in shares or debentures (including details of options granted or exercised, with comparatives at the start of the year or, if later, the date of appointment).

- Details regarding any of its own shares purchased by the company during the year, i.e. number, nominal value, consideration and reason.

- If the company has more than 250 employees.

  - The policy towards the disabled.
  - Action towards employee communication, consultation, involvement and awareness.

- Political and a charitable donations, detailing these two items separately if their totals together amount to more than £200, and giving the name of recipients for individual political donations in excess of £200.

- A statement regarding the reappointment of the auditors.

- The signature of director or company secretary.

Many of these disclosures are already provided elsewhere in the annual accounts and so a number of companies are now reducing the directors' report contents accordingly.

Example

Below we have illustrated an abbreviated Directors' Report extracted from the accounts of Boots Group plc.

Directors' report

The directors of Boots Group plc present their annual report to shareholders, together with the audited financial statements for the year ended 31 March 2005.

Principal activities

The Group's principal activities during the year were

Retailing of chemists' merchandise.

The provision of opticians' and other healthcare services.

The development, manufacture and marketing of healthcare and consumer products.

Further information on the Group's continuing activities is provided in the Operational Review.

Business review and future developments

A review of group activities during the year, research and development, and likely future developments are dealt with in the introduction, Chairman's Statement, Chief Executive's Review and Operational Review.

Group results

The Group profit and loss account for 2005 includes the following details.

	2005 (£m)	Restated[1] 2004 (£m)
Turnover (including share of joint ventures)	5,470.7	5,326.4
Profit on ordinary activities before exceptional items and taxation	481.3	543.5
Profit on ordinary activities before taxation	427.6	579.9

[1]   Restated on adoption of FRS 20 'Share-based payment' and UITF 38 'Accounting for ESOP trusts'.

Appropriations

The directors recommend the payment of a final dividend of 21.0p per share which, if approved by shareholders, will be paid on 5 August 2005 to shareholders registered on 3 June 2005. When added to the interim dividend of 9.1p paid on 21 January 2005, this makes a total dividend payment for the year of 30.1p per share (2004 29.8p per share. Payment of these dividends requires £216.6m (2004 £226.3m), leaving a profit of £85.8m (2004 £185.2m) retained in the business.

Group structure and operations

On 14 September 2004, Boots announced the exit from its Dentistry, Chiropody, Laser Eye Correction and Laser hair Removal businesses. The Chiropody and Laser Hair Removal businesses were closed. The Laser Eye Correction and Dentistry businesses were acquired by Optical Express Ltd on 10 November and 20 January respectively.

On 7 April 2005, Boots announced its intention to sell Boots Healthcare International and return a significant proportion of the proceeds to shareholders. An active programme to sell BHI is under way.

On 7 April 2005, Boots also announced the proposed sale and leaseback of 312 of its small stores. Proceeds from the transaction will be used to pay down short-term borrowings.

Share capital

Details of changes in the share capital are shown in note 23 to the financial statements.

At the AGM on 22 July 2004, shareholders authorised the company to make market purchases of its own ordinary shares of 25p each.

During the year, the company entered the market and purchased 45.4 million (2004 38.3 million) shares, which have subsequently been cancelled. This represented 6.2% (2004 4.9%) of the shares in issue at the end of the period, and the total cost was £300m (2004 £259.9m).

At the forthcoming annual general meeting on 21 July 2005, shareholders will be invited to renew the company's authority to make market purchases. The authority will be limited to the purchase of not more than 72,200,000 ordinary shares, being approximately 10% of the ordinary shares in issue at the date of this report; the maximum price payable to be no more than 5% above the average of the closing mid-market quotations for the five business days before the purchase, with the minimum price being the nominal value, exclusive of any expenses payable by the company.

Details of shares held by Boots Qualifying Employee Share Trust, Boots All Employee Share Ownership Plan and Boots ESOP Trust are shown in notes 21 and 22 to the financial statements.

Shareholders

As at 18 May 2005, the register maintained the company under Section 211 of the Companies Act 1985 contains the following notifications to the company.

Name of Shareholder	% of Issued Ordinary Share Capital Held
Franklin Resources Inc	4.0525%
Legal & General Investment Management	3.76%
Lazard Freres & Co	3.00%

Fixed assets

The directors are of the opinion that the market value of the group's properties at 31 March 2005 is 64.2% higher than that stated in the financial statements. It is not anticipated that any significant taxation will become payable on the revaluation surplus, as taxation gains on properties used for the purpose of the group's trade are expected to be deferred indefinitely or eliminated by capital losses.

Payment of suppliers

The Group is signatory of the Better Payment Practice Code (a copy of the code is available from www.payontime.co.uk). It is the policy of the Group to agree appropriate terms and conditions for its transactions with suppliers (by means ranging from standard written terms to individually negotiated contracts) and that payment should be made in accordance with those terms and conditions, provided that the supplier has also complied with them.

The number of days' purchases outstanding for the Group's UK operations at 31 March 2005 was 20 (2004 24 days). The company has no trade creditors.

People

The Group continues to involve its people in the decision-making process and communicates regularly with them during the year. Their involvement in the company's performance is encouraged with employee bonus and share schemes. The involvement extends to the Board of Boots Pensions Ltd, on which there are three employee representatives as well as a retired employee. The group's aim for all its people and applicants for employment is to fit the qualifications, aptitude and ability of each individual to the appropriate job, and to provide equal opportunity, regardless of sex, religion or ethnic origin. The Group does all that is practicable to meet its responsibility toward the employment and training of disabled people. Where an employee becomes disabled, every effort is made to provide continuity of employment in the same job or a suitable alternative.

Charitable and political donations

The group made cash donations for charitable purposes in the UK for the year of £1.65m (2004 £2.36m) being £0.23m for education, £0.05m for relief of financial hardship, and £1.37m for other charitable purposes (including health and economic development). The company made no political payments.

Directors

There were no changes to the Board during the year. Howard Dodd resigned from the Board on 18 May 2005.

Paul Bateman retires by rotation at the annual general meeting in accordance with article 87 of the company's articles of association and offers himself for reappointment. Jan Bennink also retires under article 87 but is not offering himself for reappointment.

The Chairman will recommend Mr Bateman's reappointment. Details of directors, their roles, responsibilities, achievements and significant external commitments are set out in the AGM notice, which is sent to shareholders with this report.

Information on service contracts and details of the interests of the directors and their families in the share capital of the company at 31 March 2005 are shown in the directors' remuneration report. Copies of the service contracts of executive directors and of the appointment letters of the Chairman and non-executive directors are available for inspection at the company's registered office during normal business hours and at the annual general meeting.

No director has a directorship in common or other significant links with any other director (except in the case of executive directors holding directorships of subsidiary companies of the company).

Auditors

Resolutions to reappoint KPMG Audit plc as auditors and to authorise the directors to determine their remuneration will be proposed at the annual general meeting.

By order of the Board

Michael Oliver

Secretary

18 May 2005

7 REPORTING EXEMPTIONS

7.1 Introduction

The Companies Act requires that complete sets of accounts be sent to the members and debenture holders, however, a company may, if it satisfies certain conditions, lodge abbreviated accounts with the Registrar. The idea behind this exemption is to provide a degree of commercial protection to the smaller company by limiting the amount of information it needs to disclose in its accounts, concealing it from its competitors.

The Companies Act defines two different sizes of company eligible to file abbreviated accounts, each of which has different reporting requirements.

- Small companies.
- Medium-sized companies.

7.2 Conditions

In order to qualify as either small or medium-sized, a company must satisfy (not exceed) two of the following three conditions.

	Must Not Exceed	
	Small	Medium-Sized
Turnover	£5,600,000	£22,800,000
Fixed and Current Assets	£2,800,000	£11,400,000
Average Number of Employees	50	250

In order to qualify as small or medium-sized in any accounting period other than its first, an entity must satisfy the criteria both in the current period and in the previous period.

7.3 Small companies

The exemptions available for a company that qualifies as a small company are that the profit and loss account and directors' report may be omitted. All that needs to be filed is an abbreviated statement of financial position together with the following detailed notes.

- Accounting policies.
- Debtors recoverable in more than one year.
- Creditors due after more than five years.
- Share capital and any allotments.
- The basis of translating any foreign currencies.
- Details of secured creditors.
- The ultimate holding company if applicable.
- Fixed asset movements in total.

These notes should all contain the same information as the usual statement of financial position notes.

7.4 Financial Reporting Standard for Smaller Entities

The ASB issued a Financial Reporting Standard for Smaller Entities in November 1997 (most recently revised in January 2007). The Standard simplifies existing FRSs for companies that qualify as 'small' under the Companies Act definition and includes the accounting requirements in the Companies Act.

The rules of this Standard are based on those of existing FRSs but with simpler valuation requirements and reduced disclosure requirements.

7.5 Medium-sized companies

There is only a very minor exemption for medium-sized companies in that they must file a full set of accounts (including the directors' report), but the profit and loss account can start with the gross profit figure rather than reporting turnover.

7.6 Both small and medium-sized companies

Where abbreviated accounts are filed with the registrar they must incorporate

- A statement by the directors that they have relied on exemptions for small or medium-sized companies.
- A report by the auditors stating that the abbreviated accounts have been properly prepared.

8 SUMMARY FINANCIAL STATEMENTS

8.1 Introduction

The Companies Act 1989 introduced provisions that, provided specific conditions are met, allow listed public companies to send summary financial statements to those of their members who wish to receive them instead of the full accounts.

The conditions that must be met in order to provide summary financial statements are as follows.

- The summary statements must be derived from the full accounts.

- The company must not be prohibited from sending summary financial statements by a provision in its Memorandum or Articles of Association.

- The company has ascertained that the shareholder wishes to receive summary financial statements either

    - As a result of an election by the shareholder in order to receive them

    or

    - A positive election to receive full statements has not been received having issued summary financial statements for the first time.

8.2 Contents

A directors' report giving details of

- A fair review of the development of the business during the year.
- Particulars of important events since the year end.
- Future developments.
- Names of all directors during the year.

A summarised profit and loss account that shows, with comparatives, the information contained in a normal profit and loss account excluding the details of any costs that are deducted from turnover to arrive at operating profit.

The summarised statement of financial position need only show the aggregate amounts for the main headings, specifically

- Fixed assets.
- Current assets (in total).
- Creditors (amounts falling due within one year).
- Creditors (amounts falling due after one year).
- Provisions for liabilities and charges.
- Capital and reserves.

It is not necessary to give a breakdown of these figures into their sub-components, e.g. the statement of financial position does not need to break down current assets into stock, debtors, investments and cash.

9 AUDITORS' REPORT

9.1 Introduction

Under the Companies Act 1985, every company was required to appoint an auditor or auditors at each annual general meeting, who is to hold office from the conclusion of that meeting until the conclusion of the next annual general meeting.

This legislation was modified in 1994, relaxing these requirements to a certain extent for smaller companies, the details of which we cover below.

9.2 Auditors' access to information

Under the Companies Act 1985, it is an offence for a director or company secretary to give false or misleading information to an auditor. In addition, auditors of holding companies have the right to obtain information about subsidiary companies that they do not audit themselves.

The auditor has the right of access at all times to the books and accounts of the company, and to require the officers of the company to provide such information and explanations as he believes necessary for the performance of his duties.

The auditor has the right to attend any general meetings and has the right to speak with regard to any matter that concerns him.

9.3 Scope of the audit

The auditor is required to report to the members as to whether, in his opinion, the accounts of the company give a true and fair view of the state of the company's affairs and its performance to the year end and comply with the Companies Act. This form of audit report will be considered an unqualified audit report.

If, however, he does not feel that he can express this positive opinion, then he must give a qualified report.

9.4 Reason for qualified audit reports

Qualified audit reports fall into two categories.

9.4.1 Limitation on the scope of the audit

Where there has been a limitation on the scope of the auditor's work that prevents him from obtaining sufficient evidence to give an unqualified opinion.

9.4.2 Disagreement

Where the auditor's opinion on the accounting treatment or disclosure of a matter conflicts with that disclosed in the financial statements the auditor must give an **adverse opinion**.

9.5 The importance of the qualification

The importance of the qualification also falls into two categories.

9.5.1 Material

Where the reader's view of the accounts in specifically stated parts would be altered by this limitation or disagreement.

9.5.2 Fundamental

The limitation or disagreement is so material as to render the whole accounts meaningless.

10 WORDING OF QUALIFIED AUDIT REPORTS

As a result, we have four possible styles of qualification, each of which will attract a slightly different wording in the auditor's report. The table below shows the form of wording that will be used when the auditor is stating his opinion.

	Limitation of Scope	Disagreement
Material	Give a true and fair view except for	Give a true and fair view except for
Fundamental	Unable to express an opinion (disclaimer of opinion)	Do not give a true and fair view (adverse opinion)

In all cases, the auditor will state what he is uncertain about or disagrees with.

10.1 Format

The audit report must

- Identify to whom the report is addressed.

- Identify the financial statements being audited.

- Contain a section covering the responsibilities of the

    - Auditor – to express an opinion.

    - Directors – to prepare the accounts and accept responsibility for their truth, fairness and compliance with the Companies Act.

- Indicate the basis of the auditor's opinion, i.e. the adherence to auditing standards, description of the audit process such as audit testing done and consideration of the appropriateness of accounting policies used.

- State that the auditor has planned and performed the audit in such a way as to obtain reasonable assurance that the financial statements are free from material error or misstatement, however, arising.

- Contain an audit opinion on the statement of financial position at the period end and the profit or loss and cash flows for the period.

Example

Independent auditors' report to the members of Boots Group plc

We have audited the financial statements. We have also audited the information in the directors' remuneration report that is described as having been audited.

This report is made solely to the company's members, as a body, in accordance with Section 235 of the Companies Act 1985. Our audit work has been undertaken so that we might state to the company's members those matters we are required to state to them in an auditors' report and for no other purpose. To the fullest extent permitted by law, we do not accept or assume responsibility to anyone other than the company and the company's members as a body, for our audit work, for this report, or for the opinions we have formed.

Respective responsibilities of directors and auditors

The directors are responsible for preparing the Annual Report and directors' remuneration report. This includes responsibility for preparing the financial statements in accordance with applicable United Kingdom law and accounting standards. Our responsibilities, as independent auditors, are established in the United Kingdom by statute, the Auditing Practices Board, the Listing Rules of the Financial Services Authority, and by our profession's ethical guidance.

We report to you our opinion as to whether the financial statements give a true and fair view and whether the financial statements and the part of the directors' remuneration report to be audited have been properly prepared in accordance with the Companies Act 1985. We also report to you if, in our opinion, the directors' report is not consistent with the financial statements, if we have not received all the information and explanations we require for our audit, or if information specified by law regarding directors' remuneration and transactions with the Group is not disclosed.

We review whether the corporate governance statement reflects the company's compliance with the nine provisions of the 2003 FRC Code specified for our review by the Listing Rules, and we report if it does not. We are not required to consider whether the Board's statements on internal control cover all risks and controls, or form an opinion on the effectiveness of the Group's corporate governance procedures or its risk and control procedures.

We read the other information contained in the Annual Report, including the corporate governance statement and the unaudited part of the directors' remuneration report, and consider whether it is consistent with the audited financial statements. We consider the implications for our report if we become aware of any apparent misstatements or material inconsistencies with the financial statements.

Basis of audit opinion

We conducted our audit in accordance with Auditing Standards issued by the Auditing Practices Board. An audit includes examination, on a test basis, of evidence relevant to the amounts and disclosures in the financial statements and the part of the directors' remuneration report to be audited. It also includes an assessment of the significant estimates and judgements made by the directors in the preparation of the financial statements, and of whether the accounting policies are appropriate to the Group's circumstances, consistently applied and adequately disclosed.

We planned and performed our audit so as to obtain all the information and explanations which we considered necessary in order to provide us with sufficient evidence to give reasonable assurance that the financial statements and the part of the directors' remuneration report to be audited are free from material misstatement, whether caused by fraud or other irregularity or error. In forming our opinion, we also evaluated the overall adequacy of the presentation of information in the financial statements and the part of the directors' remuneration report to be audited.

Opinion

In our opinion, the financial statements give a true and fair view of the state of affairs of the company and the Group as at 31 March 2005 and of the profit of the Group for the year then ended; and the financial statements and the part of the directors' remuneration report to be audited have been properly prepared in accordance with the Companies Act 1985.

KPMG Audit plc

Chartered Accountants

Registered Auditor

Birmingham

18 May 2005

10.2 Smaller company audits

In 1994, the Department of Trade and Industry (now the Department for Business, Enterprise and Regulatory Reform) issued regulations amending the Companies Act 1985 to exempt smaller companies from the requirement for an annual audit. Under this legislation, annual accounts are exempt the requirement for an audit if they satisfy certain conditions.

Subject to provisions permitting shareholders to require an audit, a company with turnover of not more than £5.6m for the financial year will be exempt from the requirement of an audit report in respect of a financial year if it meets the following conditions.

- It qualifies as a small company in relation to that year for the purposes of Section 246 of the Companies Act 1985.

- Its statement of financial position total for this year is not more than £2.8m.

- It was not at any time within that year

  - A parent company or a subsidiary undertaking.
  - A public company.
  - A banking or insurance company.

- Its statement of financial position contains specified disclosures.

The provison of not being part of a group will mean that small wholly owned subsidiaries will still need to have a statutory audit.

Directors of companies taking advantage of audit exemption will be required to state in the accounts that are filed at Companies House that

- The company is eligible to take advantage of audit exemption.

- No notice has been deposited by a member requiring an audit (see below).

- They are aware of their obligation to keep proper records and to prepare accounts that give a true and fair view of the company's position.

Any member or members holding at least 10% of the issued share capital of a company may, not later than one month before the end of a financial year, require that the company obtains an audit of its accounts for that year.

11 IAS 8 ACCOUNTING POLICIES, CHANGES IN ACCOUNTING ESTIMATES AND ERRORS

Before we leave this chapter and move on to looking at specific rules governing different transactions and scenarios, it is worth considering one accounting standard, IAS 8, in some detail.

IAS 8 *Accounting Policies, Changes in Accounting Estimates and Errors* describes how appropriate accounting policies should be selected, and how companies should deal with changes to their reported figures, resulting from the correction of errors or the implementation of new or alternative accounting treatments.

11.1 Definitions

Before we explore the detail of IAS 8, it is necessary to get to grips with some of the terminology used within it. The following definitions are given in IAS 8.

- **Accounting policies** are the specific principles, bases, conventions, rules and practices adopted by an entity in preparing and presenting financial statements.

- A **change in accounting estimate** is an adjustment of the carrying amount of an asset or a liability or the amount of the periodic consumption of an asset, that results from the assessment of the present status of, and expected future benefits and obligations associated with, assets and liabilities. Changes in accounting estimates result from new information or new developments and, accordingly, are not corrections of errors.

- **Prior period errors** are omissions from, and misstatements in, the entity's financial statements for one or more prior periods arising from a failure to use, or misuse of, reliable information that

  - Was available when financial statements for those periods were authorised for issue; and

  - Could reasonably be expected to have been obtained and taken into account in the preparation and presentation of those financial statements.

  Such errors include the effects of mathematical mistakes, mistakes in applying accounting policies, oversights or misinterpretations of facts, and fraud.

- **Retrospective application** is applying a new accounting policy to transactions, other events and conditions as if that policy had always been applied.

- **Retrospective restatement** is correcting the recognition, measurement and disclosure of amounts of elements of financial statements as if a prior period error had never occurred.

- **Prospective application** of a change in accounting policy and of recognising the effect of a change in an accounting estimate, respectively, are

  - Applying the new accounting policy to transactions, other events and conditions occurring after the date as at which the policy is changed; and

  - Recognising the effect of the change in the accounting estimate in the current and future periods affected by the change.

- **Impracticable**. Applying a requirement is impracticable when the entity cannot apply it after making every reasonable effort to do so. It is impracticable to apply a change in an accounting policy retrospectively or to make a retrospective restatement to correct an error if one of the following apply.

    - Retrospective application or retrospective restatement requires significant estimates of amounts and it is impossible to distinguish objectively information about those estimates that: provides evidence of circumstances that existed on the date(s) at which those amounts are to be recognised, measured or disclosed; and would have been available when the financial statements for that prior period were authorised for issue, from other information.

(IAS 8)

11.2 Accounting policies

Accounting policies are determined by **applying the relevant IFRS or IFRIC** and considering any relevant Implementation Guidance issued by the IASB for that IFRS/IFRIC.

Where there is no applicable IFRS or IFRIC management should use its **judgement** in developing and applying an accounting policy that results in information that is **relevant** and **reliable**. Management should refer to

- The requirements and guidance in IFRSs and IFRICs dealing with similar and related issues.

- The definitions, recognition criteria and measurement concepts for assets, liabilities and expenses in the *Framework*.

Management may also consider the most recent pronouncements of **other standard-setting bodies** that use a similar conceptual framework to develop standards, other accounting literature and accepted industry practices if these do not conflict with the sources above.

An entity must select and apply its accounting policies for a period **consistently** for similar transactions, other events and conditions, unless an IFRS or an IFRIC specifically requires or permits categorisation of items for which different policies may be appropriate. If an IFRS or an IFRIC requires or permits categorisation of items, an appropriate accounting policy must be selected and applied consistently to each category.

11.3 Changes in accounting policies

The same accounting policies are usually adopted from period to period, to allow users to analyse trends over time in profit, cash flows and financial position. **Changes in accounting policy will therefore be rare** and should be made only if required by one of three things.

- By statute.

- By an accounting standard-setting body.

- If the change will result in a more appropriate presentation of events or transactions in the financial statements of the entity.

The Standard highlights two types of event **which do not constitute changes in accounting policy**.

- Adopting an accounting policy for a **new type of transaction** or event not dealt with previously by the entity.

- Adopting a **new accounting policy** for a transaction or event which has not occurred in the past or which was not material.

In the case of tangible non-current assets, if a policy of revaluation is adopted for the first time then this is treated, not as a change of accounting policy under IAS 8, but as a revaluation under IAS 16 *Property, Plant and Equipment* (see Chapter 3). The following paragraphs do not therefore apply to a change in policy to adopt revaluations.

11.4 Treatment of a change in accounting policy

A change in accounting policy **must be applied retrospectively**. **Retrospective application** means that the new accounting policy is applied to transactions and events as if it had always been in use. In other words, at the earliest date such transactions or events occurred, the policy is applied from that date.

Prospective application is **no longer allowed** under the revised IAS 8 unless it is **impracticable** (see definitions) to determine the cumulative amount of charge.

11.5 Adoption of an IAS/IFRS

Where a new IAS or IFRS is adopted, IAS 8 requires any transitional provisions in the new IAS itself to be followed. If none are given in the IAS which is being adopted, then you should follow the general principles of IAS 8.

11.6 Other changes in accounting policy

IAS 8 requires **retrospective application**, *unless* it is **impracticable** to determine the cumulative amount of the change. Any resulting adjustment should be reported as an adjustment to the opening balance of retained earnings. Comparative information should be restated unless it is impracticable to do so.

This means that all comparative information must be restated **as if the new policy had always been in force**, with amounts relating to earlier periods reflected in an adjustment to opening reserves of the earliest period presented.

Prospective application is allowed only when it is impracticable to determine the cumulative effect of the change.

11.7 Disclosure

Certain **disclosures** are required when a change in accounting policy has a material effect on the current period or any prior period presented, or when it may have a material effect in subsequent periods.

- Reasons for the change.

- Amount of the adjustment for the current period and for each period presented.

- Amount of the adjustment relating to periods prior to those included in the comparative information.

- The fact that comparative information has been restated or that it is impracticable to do so.

An entity should also disclose information relevant to assessing the **impact of new IFRS** on the financial statements where these have **not yet come into force**.

11.8 Changes in accounting estimates

Estimates arise in relation to business activities because of the **uncertainties inherent within them**. Judgements are made based on the most up-to-date information and the use of such estimates is a necessary part of the preparation of financial statements. It does *not* undermine their reliability.
Here are some examples of accounting estimates.

- A bad debt provision.
- Useful lives of depreciable assets.
- Provision for obsolescence of inventory.

The rule here is that the **effect of a change in an accounting estimate** should be included in the determination of profit or loss in one of

- The period of the change, if the change affects that period only.
- The period of the change *and* future periods, if the change affects both.

Changes may occur in the circumstances which were in force at the time the estimate was calculated, or perhaps additional information or subsequent developments have come to light.

An example of a change in accounting estimate which affects only the **current period** is the bad debt estimate. However, a revision in the life over which an asset is depreciated would affect both the **current and future periods**, in the amount of the depreciation expense.

Reasonably enough, the effect of a change in an accounting estimate should be included in the **same income statement classification** as was used previously for the estimate. This rule helps to ensure **consistency** between the financial statements of different periods.

The **materiality** of the change is also relevant. The nature and amount of a change in an accounting estimate that has a material effect in the current period (or which is expected to have a material effect in subsequent periods) should be disclosed. If it is not possible to quantify the amount, this impracticability should be disclosed.

11.9 Errors

Errors discovered during a current period which **relate to a prior period** may arise through

- Mathematical mistakes.
- Mistakes in the application of accounting policies.
- Misinterpretation of facts.
- Oversights.
- Fraud.

Most of the time these errors can be **corrected through profit or loss for the current period**. Where they are material prior period errors, however, this is not appropriate.

11.10 Accounting treatment

Prior period errors: correct retrospectively. This involves

- Either restating the comparative amounts for the prior period(s) in which the error occurred; or

- When the error occurred before the earliest prior period presented, restating the opening balances of assets, liabilities and equity for that period

so that the financial statements are presented **as if the error had never occurred**.

Only where it is **impracticable** to determine the cumulative effect of an error on prior periods can an entity correct an error **prospectively**.

11.11 Prior period errors – disclosure

Various **disclosures** are required.

- **Nature** of the prior period error.
- For each prior period, to the extent practicable, the **amount** of the correction.

  - For each financial statement line item affected.
  - If IAS 33 applies, for basic and diluted earnings per share.

- The amount of the correction at the beginning of the earliest prior period presented.

- If retrospective restatement is impracticable for a particular prior period, the circumstances that led to the existence of that condition and a description of how and from when the error has been corrected. Subsequent periods need not repeat these disclosures.

Example

During 2006 Global discovered that certain items had been included in inventory at 31 December 2005, valued at £4.2m, which had in fact been sold before the year end. The following figures for 2005 (as reported) and 2006 (draft) are available.

	2005 (£'000)	2006 (draft) (£'000)
Sales	47,400	67,200
Cost of goods sold	(34,570)	(55,800)
Profit before taxation	12,830	11,400
Taxation	(3,880)	(3,400)
Profit	8,950	8,000

Reserves at 1 January 2005 were £13m. The cost of goods sold for 2006 includes the £4.2m error in opening inventory. The income tax rate was 30% for 2005 and 2006. No dividends have been declared or paid.

Solution

Income Statement	2005 (£'000)	2006 (£'000)
Sales	47,400	67,200
Cost of goods sold (W1)	(38,770)	(51,600)
Profit before tax	8,630	15,600
Taxation (W2)	(2,620)	(4,660)
Profit	6,010	10,940

Retained Earnings	2005 (£'000)	2006 (£'000)
Opening Retained Earnings		
As previously reported	13,000	21,950
Correction of prior period error (*4,200 – 1,260*)	–	(2,940)
As restated	13,000	19,010
Profit for year	6,010	10,940
Closing Retained Earnings	19,010	29,950

Workings

1. **Cost of goods sold**

	2005 (£'000)	2006 (£'000)
As stated in question	34,570	55,800
Inventory adjustment	4,200	(4,200)
	38,770	51,600

2.   **Taxation**

	2005 (£'000)	2006 (£'000)
As stated in question	3,880	3,400
Inventory adjustment (*4,200 × 30%*)	(1,260)	1,260
	2,620	4,660

APPENDIX

Glossary of accounting regulations

International Financial Reporting Standards (IFRSs)

IFRS 1 First-Time Adoption of International Financial Reporting Standards

IFRS 2 Share-Based Payment

IFRS 3 Business Combinations

IFRS 4 Insurance Contracts

IFRS 5 Non-Current Assets Held for Sale and Discontinued Operations

IFRS 6 Exploration for and Evaluation of Mineral Resources

IFRS 7 Financial Instruments: Disclosures

IFRS 8 Operating Segments

International Accounting Standards (IASs)

IAS 1 Presentation of Financial Statements

IAS 2 Inventories

IAS 7 Statement of cash flowss

IAS 8 Accounting Policies, Changes in Accounting Estimates and Errors

IAS 10 Events after the statement of financial position Date

IAS 11 Construction Contracts

IAS 12 Income Taxes

IAS 14 Segment Reporting

IAS 16 Property, Plant and Equipment

IAS 17 Leases

IAS 18 Revenue

IAS 19 Employee Benefits

IAS 20 Accounting for Government Grants and Disclosure of Government Assistance

IAS 21 The Effects of Changes in Foreign Exchange Rates

IAS 23 Borrowing Costs

IAS 24 Related Party Disclosures

IAS 26 Accounting and Reporting by Retirement Benefit Plans

IAS 27 Consolidated and Separate Financial Statements

IAS 28 Investments in Associates

IAS 29 Financial Reporting in Hyperinflationary Economies

IAS 31 Interests in Joint Ventures

IAS 32 Financial Instruments: Presentation

IAS 33 Earnings Per Share

IAS 34 Interim Financial Reporting

IAS 36 Impairment of Assets

IAS 37 Provisions, Contingent Liabilities and Contingent Assets

IAS 38 Intangible Assets

IAS 39 Financial Instruments: Recognition and Measurement

IAS 40 Investment Property

IAS 41 Agriculture

CHAPTER ROUNDUP

You need to be familiar with and able to describe

- The *Framework for the Preparation of Financial Statements*.

- Regulation and legal rules underlying financial statements.

- UK *Listing Rules*.

- Annual accounts requirements, especially corporate governance.

- Reporting exemptions.

- The role of the auditor.

Any of these areas could arise as a brief Section C question or, if topical, a more in-depth Section B discussion.

BPP)))
LEARNING MEDIA

TEST YOUR KNOWLEDGE

Check your knowledge of the chapter here, without referring back to the text.

1. (a) What is the nature of an expense? Explain with particular reference to the accruals concept. Discuss what is meant by a liability.

   (b) Costs may be recognised as either expenses or assets. Describe briefly the conceptual tensions which are involved in the treatment of costs.

2. (a) Explain why there is a need for regulation of financial information in the form of International Financial Reporting Standards.

   (b) What advantages are there to international harmonisation?

   (c) What are the barriers to international harmonisation?

3. (a) Who is responsible for preparing and issuing International Financial Reporting Standards?

   (b) What are the sources of accounting regulation for listed companies?

   (c) Distinguish between capital and revenue expenditure.

   (d) How are liabilities disclosed on the face of the statement of financial position?

   (e) What are the major required elements of the financial statements of a company under IFRS?

   (f) Who is responsible for the preparation of a company's annual accounts?

   (g) Who appoints the auditors of a company?

   (h) What do the acronyms IAS and IFRS stand for?

   (i) If there is a International Financial Reporting Standard in issue on a topic and the IASB issues an Exposure Draft of proposed amendments, which document should companies follow when preparing their accounts?

   (j) What are the key distinctions between a public limited company (plc) and a private limited company (Ltd)?

Test Your Knowledge: Answers

1. (a) **Nature of an expense**

An expense is incurred when a business contracts to purchase goods or accept services which will not constitute a resource for the future from which economic benefits can be expected to flow. In other words, an expense is a cost which is not classified as an asset to the business.

An **asset** is defined as a right or other access to **future economic benefits** controlled by an entity as a result of **past transactions or events**. A resource may be

- Physical (e.g. plant and equipment), or
- Intangible (e.g. patent and copyrights).

In either event, it is not the underlying item which is recognised in financial statements, but the fact that the item is able to generate economic benefits for the enterprise.

Without the ability to generate future economic benefits, an item such as plant and equipment would effectively be worthless scrap, and not an asset. In other words, the expenditure would be classified as of a **revenue** nature rather than **capital**. It would be written off against profit rather than **deferred**, the write-off becoming necessary as soon as the item ceased to be thought of as an asset.

In practice, some businesses might write off all items of capital expenditure costing below a **predetermined limit** on the basis of immateriality. This is done to minimise record keeping. In consequence, some expenditure that should be classified as assets is in fact expensed through the profit and loss account. Care needs to be exercised to ensure that when all the **individual elements** of capital items written off are **aggregated**, their **combined impact** does not constitute a **material misstatement**.

Illustrative example

The difference between an expense and an asset can best be illustrated via an example comparing the benefits to the business which arise from

- Expenditure on the annual audit.
- The purchase of three months worth of stationery, and
- The purchase of accounting software.

All three of the above examples give benefits. However, the audit will not generate future economic benefits (whatever the auditors may claim!) whereas the other two will. However, a large purchase of stationery is treated as an asset because it is really a **deferred expense** whereas software will be in place for a much longer period. The former is therefore treated as a **current asset** and the latter as a **non-current intangible fixed asset**.

Accruals concept

Application of the **accruals concept** requires that the **non-cash impact of transactions** and other events be reflected, as far as possible, in the financial statements of the accounting **period in which they occur** and not, for example, in the period any cash involved is received or paid. However, in **conditions of uncertainty**, more **confirmatory evidence** will be required to support the **recognition** of **assets or gain** as opposed to that required for the **recognition** of a **liability** or **loss**.

Hence, in practice, if in a given accounting period a business makes a sales of 100, then it should account for the costs of making all those sales, whether paid for yet or not. The expenses to be taken into account include overheads as well as direct costs.

In the above example, an audit fee is never payable in full until after the end of an accounting period. However, a company has an obligation at the end of each accounting period to have an audit. Therefore, the audit fee must be accrued as an expense of the period whose accounts are to be audited.

Inventories of stationery not used in an accounting period, if material, should not be treated as a charge to the income statement of that period. Instead, the expenditure should be **deferred** and accounted for in the next period.

The above involves the same principle which is applied in accounting for inventories of components, goods for resale etc. as assets at the end of an accounting period, if they are **expected** to be of **economic benefit** thereafter. However, where there is **uncertainty** regarding the likelihood of **future economic benefits**, the items involved must not be treated as deferred **expenses** (or assets), but as expenses of the **current period**.

Benefits are derived from non-current assets over **several accounting periods** but, in most cases, the expected economic life of the asset is limited. It is therefore argued that non-current assets should be **written off** over their **economic lives** in **proportion** to the **benefit derived** in **each period**.

The writing off process is called **depreciation** (or amortisation, in the case of an asset with a predetermined life, such as a patent or a leasehold). Depreciation is in keeping with the accruals concept to ensure that financial statements reflect the **non-cash impacts of transactions** in the **relevant accounting period**.

Meaning of liability

A liability may be defined as 'an entity's **obligation** to **transfer economic benefits** as a result of **past transactions** or events' The following are examples of liabilities.

(i)   **Trade payables**. These are liabilities to pay for goods or services that have been **received** or **supplied** and have been invoiced or formally agreed with the supplier.

(ii)   **Accruals**. These are liabilities to pay for goods or services that have been received or supplied but have **not been paid**, **invoiced or formally agreed** with the supplier, including amounts due to employees (for example, amounts relating to accrued holiday pay). Although it is **sometimes necessary to estimate** the amount or timing of accruals, the **uncertainty is generally much less than for provisions**.

(iii)   **Provisions**. An important point is the **distinction between liabilities and provisions**. Per IAS 37, a **provision is a liability of uncertain timing or amount** of expenditure required in settlement.

In practice, the terms accruals and provisions are sometimes used in confusion. Strictly, these terms should not be used interchangeably. Accruals should be reported as trade and other creditors, whereas provisions are reported separately.

(b) **Conceptual tensions**

There are several possible sources of conceptual tension in classifying costs as either expenses or assets.

(i) There is an obvious tension, touched on above, between the **accruals** and **prudence** concepts.

(ii) **Materiality** also restricts the full application of the accruals concept.

(iii) When the **going concern concept is not met**, there will be many costs which should be treated as expenses rather than assets, because the business no longer expects to continue in operational existence for the foreseeable future.

2. **International Financial Reporting Standards (IFRS)**

(a) The **users of financial information** – creditors, management, employees, business contacts, financial specialists, government and the general public – are entitled to this information about a business entity to a greater or lesser degree. However, the needs and expectations of these groups will vary.

The **preparers of the financial information** often find themselves in the position of having to reconcile the interests of different groups in the best way for the business entity. For example, while shareholders are looking for increased profits to support higher dividends, employees will expect higher wage increases; and yet, higher profits without corresponding higher tax allowances will result in a larger corporation (income) tax bill.

Without accounting standards to prescribe how certain transactions should be treated, preparers would be tempted to produce financial information which meets the expectations of the favoured user group. For example, creative accounting methods, such as off-statement of financial position finance were used to enhance a company's statement of financial position to make it more attractive to investors/lenders.

The **aim of accounting standards** is that they should **regulate financial information** in order that it shows the following characteristics.

(i) Objectivity.
(ii) Comparability.
(iii) Completeness.
(iv) Consistency.

(b) **Advantages of harmonisation**

The advantages of harmonisation will be based on the benefits to users and preparers of accounts.

(i) **Investors**, both individual and corporate, would like to be able to **compare** the financial results of different companies internationally as well as nationally in making investment decisions.

(ii) **Multinational companies** would benefit from harmonisation for many reasons, including the following.

(1) Better access would be gained to foreign investor funds.

(2) Management control would be improved, because harmonisation would aid internal communication of financial information.

(3) Appraisal of foreign entities for takeovers and mergers would be more straightforward.

(4) It would be easier to comply with the reporting requirements of an overseas stock exchange.

(5)   Preparation of group accounts would be easier.

(6)   A reduction in audit costs might be achieved.

(7)   Transfer of accounting staff across national borders would be easier.

(iii)   Governments of **developing countries** would save time and money if they could adopt international standards and, if these were used internally, governments of developing countries could attempt to control the activities of foreign multinational companies in their own countries. These companies could not 'hide' behind foreign accounting practices, which are difficult to understand.

(iv)   **Tax** authorities. It will be easier to calculate the tax liability of investors, including multinationals who receive income from **overseas sources**.

(v)   Regional economic groups usually promote trade within a specific geographical region. This would be aided by **common accounting practices** within the region.

(vi)   Large international accounting firms would benefit as accounting and auditing would be much **easier** if similar accounting practices existed throughout the world.

(c)   **Barriers to harmonisation**

(i)   **Different purposes of financial reporting**. In some countries, the purpose is solely for tax assessment while in others, it is for investor decision making.

(ii)   **Different legal systems**. These prevent the development of certain accounting practices and restrict the options available.

(iii)   **Different user groups**. Countries have different ideas about who the relevant user groups are and their respective importance. In the USA, investor and creditor groups are given prominence while in Europe, employees enjoy a higher profile.

(iv)   **Needs of developing countries**. Developing countries are obviously behind in the standard setting process and they need to develop the basic standards and principles already in place in most developed countries.

(v)   **Nationalism** is demonstrated in an unwillingness to accept another country's standard.

(vi)   **Cultural differences** result in objectives for accounting systems differing from country to country.

(vii)   **Unique circumstances**. Some countries may be experiencing unusual circumstances which affect all aspects of everyday life and impinge on the ability of companies to produce proper reports, for example hyperinflation, civil war, currency restriction and so on.

(viii)   The **lack of strong accountancy bodies**. Many countries do not have strong independent accountancy or business bodies, which would press for better standards and greater harmonisation.

3.   (a)   The International Accounting Standards Board (IASB).

    (b)   The law, largely the Companies Act 1985;

International Financial Reporting Standards (IFRS);

The Financial Services Authority, via the *Listing Rules*.

For accounting periods starting after 1 January 2005, listed companies must use IFRS when preparing their consolidated financial statements. The individual entity financial statements can either be prepared using IFRS or UK accounting standards, published by the Accounting Standards Board (ASB).

(c)   Capital expenditure represents the purchase of non-current assets or subsequent expenditure on non-current assets designed to enhance or improve their productive capacity. Revenue expenditure is expenditure designed to maintain the existing productive capacity of a non-current asset or expenditure not on non-current assets at all.

(d)   They are analysed between current liabilities (due within one year of the statement of financial position date) and non-current liabilities.

(e)   Statement of financial position, income statement, statement of cash flows, statement of changes in equity, accounting policies note, other notes to the above and comparative figures (one year) where appropriate. Note that a director's report is required in the annual report by company law, but strictly speaking it is not part of the financial statements. The same is true of the auditor's report. Neither the directors' report nor the auditor's report are required by IFRS.

(f)   The directors of the company.

(g)   The shareholders of the company.

(h)   International Accounting Standard and International Financial Reporting Standard.

(i)   Companies must apply current IFRS. An Exposure Draft (ED) is never compulsory and should not be followed.

(j)   Plcs are allowed to issue shares to the public whereas Ltds are not. Plcs must have an issued share capital of at least £50,000 of which at least £12,500, plus any share premium, must be paid up. In addition, regulation of plcs is generally stricter due to their right to issue shares to the public.

3

Non-Current Assets

INTRODUCTION

Non-current assets represent the long-term resources of business, resources that the business may call on over the coming years in order to trade effectively and efficiently.

There are several categories of non-current asset and we need to know

- What each one represents.

- Whether/how it is recognised in the financial statements.

At all times look out for accounting alternatives. You may be asked for the impact on the financial statements of selecting one alternative rather than another.

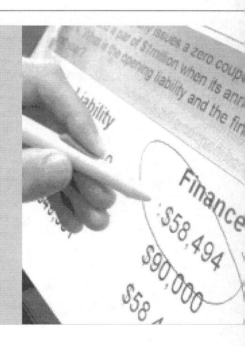

CHAPTER LEARNING OBJECTIVES

The syllabus areas covered by this chapter are

Interpretation of Financial Information

The effect of accounting practices

Understanding of the effect of accounting practices on the numbers most significant for investment decisions (profit, earnings per share, asset value etc).

Accounting terminology and concepts

Accounting terminology and a knowledge of accounting concepts and conventions to include the statement of financial position, income statement, statement of cash flows and notes to the accounts. An understanding of the distinction between capital and revenue, the valuation of assets for accounting purposes and the determination of profit and earnings share on the nil, net and full distribution bases. An understanding of significance of the statement of accounting policies in relation to the concept of a true and fair view.

Presentation of Financial Statements

Impact of statutory and non-statutory regulation on UK financial statements.

An understanding of the effect on the presentation of financial statements of the Companies Acts and non-statutory regulations, including standards and other guidance issued by IASB and stock exchange requirements.

In respect of non-current assets:

It is emphasised that the intention of the examination is to assess students' analytical and interpretative skills rather than their technical accounting ability. It is also expected that they should have an understanding of standard accounting practices and an awareness of matters currently under discussion.

1 INTRODUCTION

1.1 Definition of an asset

This is the first section with any real analytical contents and questions are frequently asked from the subjects covered.

The *Framework for the Preparation and Presentation of Financial Statements*, reviewed in detail in Chapter 2, provides a general definition of all assets as follows.

A resource controlled by the entity due to past events and from which future economic benefits are expected to flow.

Thus, an asset does not need to be owned by the business for it to be recognised, it merely needs to be **controlled**. In practice, this means that the business must have access to the future benefits from the asset's use (in the form of revenues and cash inflows) and be exposed to the risks of holding the asset (such as impairments in asset value through obsolescence, insurance costs and maintenance costs).

The other important feature of the definition is that the asset must have arisen as a result of a **past event**. This would normally be in the form of a transaction, such as the purchase of an item of machinery. However, some assets will be recognised as a result of events, such as the discovery of a new mineral deposit.

Assets such as intellectual skills (in the form of expert employees of a business), although recognised by the business as being valuable assets, will not normally be recognised in the financial statements. This is mainly because the asset has not arisen as a result of a past event of the business, but also due to the difficulty of placing a reliable monetary value on the asset.

1.2 Non-current assets

Non-current assets are assets acquired for continued use within the business. Non-current assets are not acquired for resale, rather they are acquired to help the business operate and generate profits for an extended period, e.g. through being used to manufacture units for sale.

Intangible non-current assets

Intangibles are literally assets without physical form.

They frequently represent intellectual property rights of the company, or abilities of its staff, that enable it to operate and generate profits in a way that competitors cannot.

The types of intangible assets that most frequently appear on the statement of financial position are as follows.

- Development expenditure.
- Patents, licences and trademarks.
- Publishing rights and titles.
- Goodwill.
- Brands.

Such assets may be incapable of being sold separately from the business as a whole, and are difficult to evaluate due to their nature, as discussed later.

1.2.1 Tangible non-current assets

Tangible assets are physical assets that are used within the business over a number of years with a view to deriving some benefit from this use, e.g. through their use in the manufacture of goods for resale.

Tangible assets include items such as the following.

- Freehold land and buildings.
- Leasehold land and buildings.
- Plant and machinery.
- Motor vehicles.
- Fixtures and fittings.
- Investment properties.

Example

Tomkins Group Interim Consolidated statement of financial position as at 2 July 2005	2 July 2005 (£m)	2 July 2004 (£m)
Non-current assets		
Goodwill	301.7	210.5
Other intangible assets	7.3	5.6
Property, plant and equipment	811.8	728.8
Interests in associates	4.1	3.7
Deferred tax assets	127.9	138.4
	1,252.8	1,087.0

Considerations

In order to understand the accounts and appreciate the impact of the use and accounting treatment of non-current assets, we need to consider the following.

- How they are valued on the statement of financial position (historical cost/valuation).
- How their use is recognised (depreciation of tangibles/amortisation of intangibles).
- What the accounts show (disclosure).
- Implications for analysis.

2 DEPRECIATION ACCOUNTING

Exam tip

> Questions are regularly asked on the idea of depreciation and the various depreciation bases in Section C, e.g. Winter 2006 Question 6, Summer 2004 Question 8.

> Where assets held by an entity have a **limited useful life** to that entity it is necessary to apportion the value of an asset used in a period against the revenue it has helped to create.

2.1 Non-current assets

If an asset's life extends over more than one accounting period and it contributes to earning profits over more than one period, it is a **non-current asset**.

With the exception of land held on freehold or very long leasehold, **every non-current asset eventually wears out over time**. Machines, cars and other vehicles, fixtures and fittings, and even buildings do not last for ever. When a business acquires a non-current asset, it will have some idea about how long its useful life will be, and it might decide what to do with it.

- Keep on using the non-current asset until it becomes **completely worn out**, useless, and worthless.

- **Sell off** the non-current asset at the end of its useful life, either by selling it as a second-hand item or as scrap.

Since a non-current asset has a cost, and a limited useful life, and its value eventually declines, it follows that a charge should be made in the income statement to reflect the use that is made of the asset by the business. This charge is called **depreciation**.

2.2 Scope

Depreciation accounting is governed by IAS 16 *Property, Plant and Equipment* which we will look at in Section 3 of this chapter. However, this section will deal with some of the IAS 16 definitions concerning depreciation.

- **Depreciation** is the result of systematic allocation of the depreciable amount of an asset over its estimated useful life. Depreciation for the accounting period is charged to net profit or loss for the period either directly or indirectly.

- **Depreciable assets** are assets which

  - Are expected to be used during more than one accounting period.

  - Have a limited useful life.

  - Are held by an entity for use in the production or supply of goods and services, for rental to others, or for administrative purposes.

- **Useful life** is one of two things.

  - The period over which a depreciable asset is expected to be used by the entity; or

  - The number of production or similar units expected to be obtained from the asset by the entity.

- **Depreciable amount** of a depreciable asset is the historical cost or other amount substituted for cost in the financial statements, less the estimated residual value.

(IAS 16)

An 'amount substituted for cost' will normally be a **current market value** after a revaluation has taken place.

2.3 Depreciation

IAS 16 requires the depreciable amount of a depreciable asset to be allocated on a **systematic basis** to each accounting period during the useful life of the asset. **Every part of an item of property, plant and equipment with a cost that is significant in relation to the total cost of the item must be depreciated separately**.

One way of defining depreciation is to describe it as a means of **spreading the cost** of a non-current asset over its useful life, and so matching the cost against the full period during which it earns profits for the business. Depreciation charges are an example of the application of the accruals principle in calculating profits.

There are situations where, over a period, an asset has **increased in value**, ie its current value is greater than the carrying value in the financial statements. You might think that in such situations it would not be necessary to depreciate the asset. The Standard states, however, that this is irrelevant, and that depreciation should still be charged to each accounting period, based on the depreciable amount, irrespective of a rise in value.

An entity is required to begin depreciating an item of property, plant and equipment when it is available for use and to continue depreciating it until it is derecognised even if it is idle during the period.

2.4 Useful life

The following factors should be considered when **estimating the useful life** of a depreciable asset.

- Expected physical wear and tear.
- Obsolescence.
- Legal or other limits on the use of the assets.

Once decided, the useful life should be **reviewed at least every financial year end** and depreciation rates adjusted for the current and future periods if expectations vary significantly from the original estimates. The effect of the change should be disclosed in the accounting period in which the change takes place.

The assessment of useful life requires **judgement** based on previous experience with similar assets or classes of asset. When a completely new type of asset is acquired (i.e. through technological advancement or through use in producing a brand new product or service) it is still necessary to estimate useful life, even though the exercise will be much more difficult.

The Standard also points out that the physical life of the asset might be longer than its useful life to the entity in question. One of the main factors to be taken into consideration is the **physical wear and tear** the asset is likely to endure. This will depend on various circumstances, including the number of shifts for which the asset will be used, the entity's repair and maintenance programme and so on. Other factors to be considered include obsolescence (due to technological advances / improvements in production / reduction in demand for the product or service produced by the asset) and legal restrictions, e.g. length of a related lease.

2.5 Residual value

In most cases the residual value of an asset is **likely to be immaterial**. If it is likely to be of any significant value, that value must be estimated at the date of purchase or any subsequent revaluation. The amount of residual value should be estimated based on the current situation with other similar assets, used in the same way, which are now at the end of their useful lives. Any expected costs of disposal should be offset against the gross residual value.

2.6 Depreciation methods

The depreciation method selected should be applied consistently from period to period unless altered circumstances justify a change. If the method *is* changed, the effect should be quantified and disclosed and the reason for the change should be stated. A change in method is a change in accounting estimate.

Various methods of allocating depreciation to accounting periods are available, but whichever is chosen must be applied **consistently** (as required by IAS 1), to ensure comparability from period to period. Change of method is not allowed simply because of the profitability situation of the entity.

You should be familiar with the various **accepted methods of allocating depreciation** and the relevant calculations and accounting treatments.

2.7 Calculation of depreciation

Exam tip

> You may be asked to do basic calculations on any of the bases illustrated below, e.g. Winter 2003, Question 5.

The calculation is to spread the cost less the residual value over the expected useful life of the asset by the method considered most appropriate with regard to the type of asset and its use in the business.

We consider four different methods below to illustrate the alternatives that the accounting profession has. We will illustrate each method based on the same example.

Example

A machine is bought at the cost of £100,000, it has an estimated useful life of five years and an estimated residual value of £25,000. What will be the statement of financial position value and income statement charge each year under each of the following methods?

- Straight-line.
- Reducing balance.
- Sum of the digits.
- Production units.

2.8 Straight-line method

Under the straight-line method, an equal amount of depreciation is charged each year so that the net book value of the asset diminishes steadily, on a straight-line basis. This method assumes that we get equal use (benefit) from the asset each year, hence we charge an equal cost each year. It is probably the most common method applied in practice.

Straight-line depreciation is sometimes quoted in accounts as being at a percentage on cost.

The depreciation charge for the year can be calculated as follows.

Formula to learn

$$\text{Depreciation} = \frac{\text{Cost} - \text{Residual value}}{\text{Expected useful life}}$$

Solution

From our example, the depreciation charge for each year would be

$$\text{Depreciation} = \frac{£100,000 - £25,000}{5 \text{ years}} = £15,000 \text{ p.a.}$$

This could be quoted in the accounting policies note as depreciation at 15% (£15,000/£100,000) on cost. The statement of financial position value and income statement charges are illustrated in the Table below.

	Year 1 (£'000)	Year 2 (£'000)	Year 3 (£'000)	Year 4 (£'000)	Year 5 (£'000)
Statement of financial position					
Cost	100	100	100	100	100
Depreciation provision	(15)	(30)	(45)	(60)	(75)
Net Book Value	85	70	55	40	25
Income Statement					
Depreciation charge	15	15	15	15	15

Double Entry	(£'000)
DEBIT: Profits	15
CREDIT: Depreciation provision	15

2.9 Reducing balance method

The reducing balance method apportions larger amounts of depreciation to the earlier years and lower amounts to the later years. The implication of applying this method is that a greater benefit is derived from the use of the asset in the earlier years than in the later ones.

The depreciation rate may be described in the accounting policies note as being a percentage on the opening net book value of the asset (last year's closing net book value), compared to the straight-line method where the depreciation percentage is on cost. That depreciation rate can be worked out by the following formula.

Formula to learn

$$\text{Depreciation} = 1 - \sqrt[n]{\frac{\text{Residual value}}{\text{Cost}}}$$

where
n = expected useful life of the asset

Solution

On the basis of the example above, we can calculate the depreciation rate as

$$\text{Depreciation rate} = 1 - \sqrt[n]{\frac{£25,000}{£100,000}}$$

Hence, our depreciation charge for any year would be 24.214% of the opening net book value for that year. Over the five-year period the statement of financial position net book values and income statement charges would appear as follows.

	Year 1 (£'000)	Year 2 (£'000)	Year 3 (£'000)	Year 4 (£'000)	Year 5 (£'000)
Statement of financial position					
Cost	100.0	100.0	100.0	100.0	100.0
Depreciation provision	(24.2)	(42.6)	(56.5)	(67.0)	(75.0)
Net Book Value c/f	75.8	57.4	43.5	33.0	25.0
Income Statement					
Depreciation charge	24.2	18.4	13.9	10.5	8.0
	$(100.0 \times 24.214\%)$	$(75.8 \times 24.214\%)$	$(57.4 \times 24.214\%)$	$(43.5 \times 24.214\%)$	$(33.0 \times 24.214\%)$

Clearly, applying this method charges higher depreciation and thus produces lower profits in the earlier years, but charges lower depreciation, hence higher profits in the later years.

2.10 Sum of the digits method

The sum of the digits method achieves a fairly similar result to the reducing balance method, but it is achieved by slightly different mechanics.

To use the sum of the digits method we need to do two things.

- Calculate the total accumulated depreciation that must be charged as

  Cost – Residual value = £100,000 – £25,000 = £75,000

- Ascertain the 'sum of the digits', by adding up the digits comprising the total number of years involved, i.e. for a five-year period, 5 + 4 + 3 + 2 + 1 = 15, hence we will divide the total accumulated depreciation charge into 15 units and apportion five units to the first year, four to the second, etc.

A quicker way of arriving at the same figure for the sum of digits is to use the formula

$$\text{Sum of digits} = \frac{n(n+1)}{2}$$

where n = the useful life of the asset in years.

Hence in our example

$$\text{Sum of digits} = \frac{5 \times 6}{2} = 15$$

Thus, each year's depreciation is calculated as

$$\text{Year 1: Depreciation} = \frac{5}{15} \times £75,000 = £25,000$$

$$\text{Year 2: Depreciation} = \frac{4}{15} \times £75,000 = £20,000$$

$$\text{Year 3: Depreciation} = \frac{3}{15} \times £75,000 = £15,000$$

$$\text{Year 4: Depreciation} = \frac{2}{15} \times £75,000 = £10,000$$

$$\text{Year 5: Depreciation} = \frac{1}{15} \times £75,000 = £5,000$$

The sum of the digits is used as the denominator and each individual digit is used as the numerator for the appropriate year, the larger digits being the earlier years.

Under this method, the statement of financial position and income statement figures will be as follows.

	Year 1 (£'000)	Year 2 (£'000)	Year 3 (£'000)	Year 4 (£'000)	Year 5 (£'000)
Statement of financial position					
Cost	100	100	100	100	100
Depreciation provision	(25)	(45)	(60)	(70)	(75)
Net Book Value c/f	75	55	40	30	25
Income statement					
Depreciation charge	25	20	15	10	5

As we can see, this produces a result similar to the reducing balance method and would, therefore, be most appropriate where the greatest benefit is derived in the earliest years.

2.11 Production units / Machine hour rate method

Under each of the above methods we have been measuring the life of the asset in terms of time or years. Under the production units method or machine hour rate, we measure the life of the asset in terms of units of production that can be achieved by the use of the asset or hours the machine can be operated.

This measure of life may be most appropriate in such situations as mining or quarrying where the total worth of the quarry land can be measured in the volume of, say, granite that can be mined.

To apply the method, we need to estimate the production units we are going to achieve each year, as well as in total, and our depreciation charge for any year will be the fraction of the total that is attributable to this year.

Solution

If we envisage that our production will be as follows.

Year 1:	1,200 units
Year 2:	1,600 units
Year 3:	1,700 units
Year 4:	1,600 units
Year 5:	1,400 units
Total:	7,500 units

Our total accumulated depreciation charge will be £75,000 (£100,000 cost less £25,000 residual value), then our depreciation charges will be as follows.

$$\text{Year 1: Depreciation} = \frac{1,200}{7,500} \times £75,000 = £12,000$$

$$\text{Year 2: Depreciation} = \frac{1,600}{7,500} \times £75,000 = £16,000$$

$$\text{Year 3: Depreciation} = \frac{1,700}{7,500} \times £75,000 = £17,000$$

$$\text{Year 4: Depreciation} = \frac{1,600}{7,500} \times £75,000 = £16,000$$

$$\text{Year 5: Depreciation} = \frac{1,400}{7,500} \times £75,000 = £14,000$$

Our statement of financial position and income statement figures will now look as follows.

	Year 1 (£'000)	Year 2 (£'000)	Year 3 (£'000)	Year 4 (£'000)	Year 5 (£'000)
Statement of financial position					
Cost	100	100	100	100	100
Depreciation provision	(12)	(28)	(45)	(61)	(75)
Net Book Value c/f	88	72	55	39	25
Income statement					
Depreciation charge	12	16	17	16	14

2.12 Depreciation dates

To truly apply the matching concept we should depreciate from the exact date of purchase to the exact date of sale.

Many companies, however, have a policy of applying a full year's depreciation in the year of purchase (regardless of the exact date of purchase within that year) and no depreciation in the year of disposal (regardless of the exact date of disposal in that year).

Clearly, this fails to apply matching for the specific asset concerned; however, if it is an asset that is being regularly replaced, such as a company car, then the overall depreciation charge approximates to what is required. In the year of disposal of the original asset (when there would be no depreciation on that item) we have instead a full year's depreciation on the replacement car. Hence we get a full year's charge each year on an ongoing basis – a fair charge each year when we are dealing with small assets that are regularly replaced.

This method would *not* be appropriate for significant or large non-current assets and would lead to distortions in reported profits and accounting ratios.

2.13 Disposals

When we dispose of a non-current asset and sell it for cash, it is highly unlikely that the amount we sell it for will exactly equal the residual value that we estimated when it was initially purchased. The question is, what do we do with this difference?

In basic terms, we are selling something at a price that is different from its value on the statement of financial position (its net book value). As a result, we will either be realising a profit (if we sell for more) or a loss (if we sell for less), just as we do when we deal with the sale of a unit of inventory. This profit will become part of the reported profit for the year.

The impact on the accounting equation for a disposal is

- Non-current assets down by NBV (net assets down).
- Cash up by amount received (net assets up).
- Profits up/down by difference.

Normally, the profit is simply netted off against that year's depreciation charge on other non-current assets. However, if it is a material figure, it will be separately disclosed in the income statement or in a note to the income statement.

Example

The above non-current asset is disposed of at the end of its five-year life, when it has a net book value of £25,000. Calculate the profit or loss on disposal if the cash received is

- £25,000
- £28,000
- £21,000

Solution

	(£)	(£)	(£)
Cash received	25,000	28,000	21,000
Net Book Value	(25,000)	(25,000)	(25,000)
Profit/(loss)	–	3,000	(4,000)

For each disposal amount, the double entry would be as follows.

Proceeds of £25,000

Double Entry	(£'000)
DEBIT: Cash	25
CREDIT: Non-Current Assets (NBV)	25

Proceeds of £28,000

Double Entry	(£'000)
DEBIT: Cash	28
CREDIT: Non-Current Assets (NBV)	25
CREDIT: Profit	3

Proceeds of £21,000

Double Entry	(£'000)
DEBIT: Cash	21
DEBIT: Profit	4
CREDIT: Non-Current Assets (NBV)	25

Example

A lorry bought for a business cost £17,000. It is expected to last for five years and then be sold for scrap for £2,000. Usage over the five years is expected to be

Year 1	200 days
Year 2	100 days
Year 3	100 days
Year 4	150 days
Year 5	40 days

Requirements

Work out the depreciation to be charged each year under

(a) The straight-line method.
(b) The reducing balance method (using a rate of 35%).
(c) The machine hour method.

Solution

(a) Under the straight-line method, depreciation for each of the five years is

$$\text{Annual depreciation} = \frac{£(17,000 - 2,000)}{5} = £3,000$$

(b) Under the reducing balance method, depreciation for each of the five years is

Year	Depreciation		
1	35% × £17,000	=	£5,950
2	35% × (£17,000 − £5,950) = 35% × £11,050	=	£3,868
3	35% × (£11,050 − £3,868) = 35% × £7,182	=	£2,514
4	35% × (£7,182 − £2,514) = 35% × £4,668	=	£1,634
5	Balance to bring book value down to £2,000 = £4,668 − £1,634 − £2,000	=	£1,034

(c)   Under the machine hour method, depreciation for each of the five years is calculated as follows.

Total usage (days) = 200 + 100 + 100 + 150 + 40 = 590 days

Depreciation per day = $\dfrac{£(17,000 - 2,000)}{590}$ = £25.42

Year	Usage (days)	Depreciation (£) (days × £25.42)
1	200	5,084.00
2	100	2,542.00
3	100	2,542.00
4	150	3,813.00
5	40	1,016.80
		14,997.80

NB: The answer does not come to exactly £15,000 because of the rounding carried out at the 'depreciation per day' stage of the calculation.

Example

(a)   What are the purposes of providing for depreciation?

(b)   In what circumstances is the reducing balance method more appropriate than the straight-line method? Give reasons for your answer.

Solution

(a)   The accounts of a business try to recognise that the cost of a non-current asset is gradually consumed as the asset wears out. This is done by gradually writing off the asset's cost in the income statement over several accounting periods. This process is known as depreciation, and is an example of the accruals assumption. IAS 16 *Property, Plant and Equipment* requires that depreciation should be allocated on a systematic basis to each accounting period during the useful life of the asset.

With regard to the accrual principle, it is fair that the profits should be reduced by the depreciation charge; this is not an arbitrary exercise. Depreciation is not, as is sometimes supposed, an attempt to set aside funds to purchase new non-current assets when required. Depreciation is not generally provided on freehold land because it does not 'wear out' (unless it is held for mining etc).

(b)   The reducing balance method of depreciation is used instead of the straight-line method when it is considered fair to allocate a greater proportion of the total depreciable amount to the earlier years and a lower proportion to the later years on the assumption that the benefits obtained by the business from using the asset decline over time.

In favour of this method it may be argued that it links the depreciation charge to the costs of maintaining and running the asset. In the early years these costs are low and the depreciation charge is high, while in later years this is reversed.

3   IAS 16 PROPERTY, PLANT AND EQUIPMENT

This Standard covers all aspects of accounting for property, plant and equipment. This represents the bulk of items which are **'tangible' non-current assets**. The Standard was revised in December 2003.

3.1 Scope

IAS 16 should be followed when accounting for property, plant and equipment *unless* another International Accounting Standard requires a **different treatment**.

IAS 16 **does not apply** to the following.

- Biological assets related to agricultural activity.
- Mineral rights and mineral reserves, such as oil, gas and other non-regenerative resources.

However, the Standard applies to property, plant and equipment used to develop these assets.

3.2 Definitions

The Standard gives a large number of definitions.

- Property, plant and equipment are tangible assets that

    - Are held for use in the production or supply of goods or services, for rental to others, or for administrative purposes; and

    - Are expected to be used during more than one period.

- **Cost** is the amount of cash or cash equivalents paid or the fair value of the other consideration given to acquire an asset at the time of its acquisition or construction.

- **Residual value** is the net amount which the entity expects to obtain for an asset at the end of its useful life after deducting the expected costs of disposal.

- **Entity specific value** is the present value of the cash flows an entity expects to arise from the continuing use of an asset and from its disposal at the end of its useful life, or expects to incur when settling a liability.

- **Fair value** is the amount for which an asset could be exchanged between knowledgeable, willing parties in an arm's length transaction.

- **Carrying amount** is the amount at which an asset is recognised in the statement of financial position after deducting any accumulated depreciation and accumulated impairment losses.

- An **impairment loss** is the amount by which the carrying amount of an asset exceeds its recoverable amount.

    (IAS 16)

3.3 Recognition

In this context, recognition simply means incorporation of the item in the business's accounts, in this case as a non-current asset. The recognition of property, plant and equipment depends on two criteria.

- It is probable that **future economic benefits** associated with the asset will flow to the entity.
- The cost of the asset to the entity can be **measured reliably**.

These recognition criteria apply to **subsequent expenditure** as well as costs incurred initially. There are no separate criteria for recognising subsequent expenditure.

Property, plant and equipment can represent **substantial amounts** in financial statements, affecting the presentation of the company's financial position (in the statement of financial position) and the profitability of the entity, through depreciation and also if an asset is wrongly classified as an expense and taken to the income statement.

3.3.1 First criterion: Future economic benefits

The **degree of certainty** attached to the flow of future economic benefits must be assessed. This should be based on the evidence available at the date of initial recognition (usually the date of purchase). The entity should thus be assured that it will receive the rewards attached to the asset and it will incur the associated risks, which will only generally be the case when the rewards and risks have actually passed to the entity. Until then, the asset should not be recognised.

3.3.2 Second criterion: Cost measured reliably

It is generally easy to measure the cost of an asset as the **transfer amount on purchase**, i.e. what was paid for it. **Self-constructed assets** can also be measured easily by adding together the purchase price of all the constituent parts (labour, material etc.) paid to external parties.

3.4 Separate items

Most of the time assets will be identified individually, but this will not be the case for **smaller items**, such as tools, dies and moulds, which are sometimes classified as inventory and written off as an expense.

Major components or spare parts, however, should be recognised as property, plant and equipment.

For very **large and specialised items**, an apparently single asset should be broken down into its composite parts. This occurs where the different parts have different useful lives and different depreciation rates are applied to each part, e.g. an aircraft, where the body and engines are separated as they have different useful lives.

3.5 Initial measurement

Once an item of property, plant and equipment qualifies for recognition as an asset, it will initially be **measured at cost**.

3.5.1 Components of cost

The Standard lists the components of the cost of an item of property, plant and equipment.

- **Purchase price**, less any trade discount or rebate.
- **Import duties** and non-refundable purchase taxes.
- **Directly attributable costs** of bringing the asset to working condition for its intended use, e.g.
    - Cost of site preparation.
    - Initial delivery and handling costs.
    - Installation costs.
    - Testing.
    - Professional fees (architects, engineers).
- Initial estimate of the unavoidable cost of dismantling and removing the asset and restoring the site on which it is located.

IAS 16 provides **additional guidance on directly attributable** costs included in the cost of an item of property, plant and equipment.

- These costs bring the asset to the location and working conditions necessary for it to be capable of operating in the manner intended by management, including those costs to test whether the asset is functioning properly.
- They are determined after deducting the net proceeds from selling any items produced when bringing the asset to its location and condition.

The revised Standard also states that income and related expenses of operations that are **incidental** to the construction or development of an item of property, plant and equipment should be recognised in the **income statement**.

The following costs **will not be part of the cost** of property, plant or equipment unless they can be attributed directly to the asset's acquisition, or bringing it into its working condition.

- Administration and other general overhead costs.
- Start-up and similar pre-production costs.
- Initial operating losses before the asset reaches planned performance.

All of these will be recognised as an **expense** rather than an asset.

3.6 Capitalisation of finance costs

The revised version of IAS 23 (effective for accounting periods beginning on or after 1 January 2009) requires the borrowing costs attributable to certain assets to be included as part of the asset cost – so called "capitalisation of interest". The idea here is that the carrying value of an asset on the statement of financial position should be a reflection of all relevant input costs to get the asset in working order. Finance costs are just as relevant as other more tangible costs such as raw materials and labour. The subsequent resale price of the asset (if applicable) will include compensation for all costs and the interest-inclusive valuation gives the most relevant information to the user of the financial statements.

To be capitalised, the interest costs must be **directly attributable** to the acquisition, construction or production of a **qualifying asset**.

- **Directly attributable** means those borrowing costs that would have been avoided if there had been no expenditure on the asset. This can be either specific borrowing relating to an asset or allocated central borrowing, to which a weighted average interest rate is applied.

- A **qualifying asset** is one which takes a substantial period of time to get ready for its intended use or sale. This will usually be a non current asset, such as property, plant and equipment but may also be inventory subject to a production process.

Capitalisation of borrowing costs is only permitted during periods in which the asset is being developed for use in the business or onward sale. Once the asset is complete and/or in use, further borrowing costs incurred should be expensed as usual through the income statement.

IAS 23 requires disclosure in the financial statements of the amount of borrowing costs capitalised in the period and the capitalisation rate used to determine the amount of borrowing costs eligible for capitalisation.

The analyst should consider capitalisation of interest when evaluating an entity's financial risk (See the subsequent chapter, Financial Statement Analysis Techniques). Care should be taken that financial ratios such as interest cover are adjusted to include all relevant interest accruing in the period, which may not be wholly reflected in the income statement.

3.7 Measurement subsequent to initial recognition

The Standard offers two possible treatments here, essentially a choice between keeping an asset recorded at **cost** or revaluing it to **fair value**.

- **Cost model.** Carry the asset at its cost less depreciation and any accumulated impairment loss.

- **Revaluation model.** Carry the asset at a revalued amount, being its fair value at the date of the revaluation less any subsequent accumulated depreciation and subsequent accumulated impairment losses. The revised IAS 16 makes clear that the **revaluation model is available only if the fair value of the item can be measured reliably**.

3.8 Revaluations

The **market value** of land and buildings usually represents fair value. Such valuations are usually carried out by professionally qualified valuers.

In the case of **plant and equipment**, fair value can also be taken as **market value**. Where a market value is not available, however, depreciated replacement cost should be used. There may be no market value where types of plant and equipment are sold only rarely or because of their specialised nature (i.e. they would normally only be sold as part of an ongoing business).

The frequency of valuation depends on the **volatility of the fair values** of individual items of property, plant and equipment. The more volatile the fair value, the more frequently revaluations should be carried out. Where the current fair value is very different from the carrying value then a revaluation should be carried out.

3.9 Which assets should be revalued?

Most importantly, when an item of property, plant and equipment is revalued, **the whole class of assets to which it belongs should be revalued**.

All the items within a class should be **revalued at the same time**, to prevent selective revaluation of certain assets and to avoid disclosing a mixture of costs and values from different dates in the financial statements. A rolling basis of revaluation is allowed if the revaluations are kept up-to-date and the revaluation of the whole class is completed in a short period of time.

3.10 Accounting treatment

How should any **increase in value** be treated when a revaluation takes place? The debit will be the increase in asset value in the statement of financial position, but what about the credit? IAS 16 requires the increase to be credited to a **revaluation surplus** (i.e. part of owners' equity), *unless* the increase is reversing a previous decrease which was recognised as an expense. To the extent that this offset is made, the increase is recognised as income; any excess is then taken to the revaluation surplus.

Example

Binkie Co. has an item of land carried in its books at £13,000. Two years ago a slump in land values led the company to reduce the carrying value from £15,000. This was taken as an expense in the income statement. There has been a surge in land prices in the current year, however, and the land is now worth £20,000.

Account for the revaluation in the current year.

Solution

The double entry is

Double Entry	(£)
DEBIT: Asset value (statement of financial position)	7,000
CREDIT: Income statement	2,000
CREDIT: Revaluation surplus	5,000

3.11 Revaluation downwards

The case is similar for a **decrease in value** on revaluation. Any decrease should be recognised as an expense, except where it offsets a previous increase taken as a revaluation surplus in owners' equity. Any decrease greater than the previous upwards increase in value must be taken as an expense in the income statement.

Example

Let us simply swap round the example given above. The original cost was £15,000, revalued upwards to £20,000 two years ago. The value has now fallen to £13,000.

Account for the decrease in value.

Solution

The double entry is

Double Entry	(£)
DEBIT: Revaluation surplus	5,000
DEBIT: Income Statement	2,000
CREDIT: Asset value (statement of financial position)	7,000

3.12 Depreciation and revalued assets

There is a further complication when a **revalued asset is being depreciated**. As we have seen, an upward revaluation means that the depreciation charge will increase as it must be based upon the revalued amount. Normally, a revaluation surplus is only realised when the asset is sold, but when it is being depreciated, part of that surplus is being realised as the asset is used. The amount of the surplus realised is the difference between depreciation charged on the revalued amount and the (lower) depreciation which would have been charged on the asset's original cost. **This amount can be transferred to retained (i.e. realised) earnings but *not* through the income statement**.

Example

Crinckle Co bought an asset for £10,000 at the beginning of 2005. It had a useful life of five years and an estimated residual value of nil. On 1 January 2007 the asset was revalued to £12,000. The expected useful life has remained unchanged (i.e. three years remain).

Account for the revaluation and state the treatment for depreciation from 2007 onwards.

Solution

On 1 January 2007 the carrying value of the asset is £10,000 − (2 × £10,000 ÷ 5) = £6,000. For the revaluation

Double Entry	(£)
DEBIT: Asset value (statement of financial position)	6,000
CREDIT: Revaluation surplus	6,000

The depreciation for the next three years will be £12,000 ÷ 3 = £4,000, compared to depreciation on cost of £10,000 ÷ 5 = £2,000. So each year, the extra £2,000 can be treated as part of the surplus which has become realised.

Double Entry	(£)
DEBIT: Revaluation surplus	2,000
CREDIT: Retained earnings	2,000

This is a movement on owners' equity only, not an item in the income statement.

3.13 Depreciation

The Standard states

- The **depreciable amount** of an item of property, plant and equipment should be allocated on a systematic basis over its useful life.

- The **depreciation method** used should reflect the pattern in which the asset's economic benefits are consumed by the entity.

- The **depreciation charge** for each period should be recognised as an expense unless it is included in the carrying amount of another asset.

Land and buildings are dealt with separately even when they are acquired together because land normally has an unlimited life and is therefore not depreciated. In contrast buildings do have a limited life and must be depreciated. Any increase in the value of land on which a building is standing will have no impact on the determination of the building's useful life.

Depreciation is usually treated as an **expense**, but not where it is absorbed by the entity in the process of producing other assets. For example, depreciation of plant and machinery can be incurred in the production of goods for sale (inventory items). In such circumstances, the depreciation is included in the cost of the new assets produced.

3.14 Review of useful life

A review of the **useful life** of property, plant and equipment should be carried out **at least at each financial year end** and the depreciation charge for the current and future periods should be adjusted if expectations have changed significantly from previous estimates. Changes are changes in accounting estimates and are accounted for prospectively as adjustments to future depreciation.

3.15 Review of depreciation method

The **depreciation method** should also be reviewed **at least at each financial year end** and, if there has been a significant change in the expected pattern of economic benefits from those assets, the method should be changed to suit this changed pattern. When such a change in depreciation method takes place the change should be accounted for as a **change in accounting estimate** and the depreciation charge for the current and future periods should be adjusted.

3.16 Impairment of asset values

An **impairment loss** should be treated in the same way as a **revaluation decrease** ie the decrease should be **recognised as an expense**. However, a revaluation decrease (or impairment loss) should be charged directly against any related revaluation surplus to the extent that the decrease does not exceed the amount held in the revaluation surplus in respect of that same asset.

A **reversal of an impairment** loss should be treated in the same way as a **revaluation increase**, ie a revaluation increase should be recognised as income to the extent that it reverses a revaluation decrease or an impairment loss of the same asset previously recognised as an expense.

3.17 Disclosure

The Standard has a long list of disclosure requirements, for each class of property, plant and equipment.

- **Measurement bases** for determining the gross carrying amount (if more than one, the gross carrying amount for that basis in each category).

- **Depreciation methods** used.

- **Useful lives** or depreciation rates used.

- **Gross carrying amount** and accumulated depreciation (aggregated with accumulated impairment losses) at the beginning and end of the period.

- **Reconciliation** of the carrying amount at the beginning and end of the period showing

    - Additions.
    - Disposals.
    - Acquisitions through business combinations.
    - Increases/decreases during the period from revaluations and from impairment losses.
    - Impairment losses recognised in the income statement.
    - Impairment losses reversed in the income statement.
    - Depreciation.
    - Net exchange differences (from translation of statements of foreign entity).
    - Any other movements.

The financial statements should also disclose the following.

- Any recoverable amounts of property, plant and equipment.
- Existence and amounts of **restrictions on title**, and items pledged as security for liabilities.
- Accounting policy for **the estimated costs of restoring the site**.
- Amount of expenditures on account of **items in the course of construction**.
- Amount of commitments to **acquisitions**.

Revalued assets require further disclosures.

- Basis used to revalue the assets.

- Effective date of the revaluation.

- Whether an independent valuer was involved.

- Nature of any indices used to determine replacement cost.

- Carrying amount of each class of property, plant and equipment that would have been included in the financial statements had the assets been carried at cost less accumulated depreciation and accumulated impairment losses.

- Revaluation surplus, indicating the movement for the period and any restrictions on the distribution of the balance to shareholders.

The Standard also **encourages disclosure** of additional information, which the users of financial statements may find useful.

- The carrying amount of temporarily idle property, plant and equipment.

- The gross carrying amount of any fully depreciated property, plant and equipment that is still in use.

- The carrying amount of property, plant and equipment retired from active use and held for disposal.

- The fair value of property, plant and equipment when this is materially different from the carrying amount.

Example

Roche Group Financial statements for year ended 31 December 2004
Property, plant and equipment: movements in carrying value of assets in millions of CHF.

	Land	Buildings and land improvements	Machinery and equipment	Construction in progress	2004 Total	2003 Total
Net book value						
At beginning of year	836	5,085	4,881	1,692	12,494	13,492
Disposals of businesses	(5)	(153)	(247)	(18)	(423)	(1,326)
Additions	182	118	828	1,229	2,357	2,265
Disposals	(4)	(57)	(113)	(18)	(192)	(244)
Transfers	36	584	751	(1,371)	–	–
Depreciation charge	–	(222)	(1,025)	–	(1,247)	(1,303)
Impairment charge	–	–	(8)	–	(8)	(4)
Currency translation effects	(53)	(232)	(210)	(78)	(573)	(386)
At end of year	992	5,123	4,857	1,436	12,408	12,494
At 31 December						
Cost	992	7,548	10,943	1,436	20,919	20,654
Accumulated depreciation	–	(2,425)	(6,086)	–	(8,511)	(8,160)
Net book value	992	5,123	4,857	1,436	12,408	12,494

The decrease in property, plant and equipment of 423 million Swiss francs from disposals of businesses consists of assets transferred with the business of 240 million Swiss francs and an impairment charge of 183 million Swiss francs (2003: 846 million Swiss francs).

Example

(a)   In a statement of financial position prepared in accordance with IAS 16, what does the net book value (carrying value) represent?

(b)   In a set of financial statements prepared in accordance with IAS 16, is it correct to say that the net book value (carrying value) figure in a statement of financial position cannot be greater than the market (net realisable) value of the partially used asset as at the statement of financial position date? Explain the reason for your answer.

Solution

(a)   In simple terms the net book value of an asset is the cost of an asset less the 'accumulated depreciation', that is all depreciation charged so far. It should be emphasised that the main purpose of charging depreciation is to ensure that profits are fairly reported. Thus depreciation is concerned with the income statement rather than the statement of financial position. In consequence the net book value figure in the statement of financial position can be quite arbitrary.

In particular, it does not necessarily bear any relation to the market value of an asset and is of little use for planning and decision making.

An obvious example of the disparity between net book value and market value is found in the case of buildings, which may be worth many time more than their net book value.

(b)   Net book value can in some circumstances be higher than market value (net realisable value). IAS 16 *Property, Plant and Equipment* states that the value of an asset cannot be greater than its 'recoverable amount'. However 'recoverable amount' as defined in IAS 16 is the amount recoverable from further use. This may be higher than the market value.

    This makes sense if you think of a specialised machine which could not fetch much on the secondhand market but which will produce goods which can be sold at a profit for many years.

3.18 Analysis problems

When undertaking analysis on a set of financial statements, two basic problems will arise as a result of any revaluations. They are

- Lack of consistency.
- Lack of comparability.

3.19 Lack of consistency

A policy of revaluation is an option that the directors have in preparing their annual statements. This clearly results in a lack of consistency between companies that revalue as a matter of policy and those that do not.

3.20 Lack of comparability

The policy of revaluation will lead to a lack of comparability, both year on year and with competitors.

Assets revalued this year will be held at new higher values than they were last year. Hence, all measurements will be based on this higher capital base and any ratios calculated on it will therefore be incomparable to previous years.

Similarly, if one company revalues its assets but a competitor does not, then comparisons of ratios concerning capital employed will prove difficult.

4   IAS 20 GOVERNMENT GRANTS

It is common for entities to receive government grants for various purposes (grants may be called subsidies, premiums, and so on). They may also receive other types of assistance which may be in many forms. The treatment of government grants is covered by IAS 20 *Accounting for Government Grants and Disclosure of Government Assistance* (SSAP 4 in the UK).

4.1 Scope

IAS 20 does *not* cover the following situations.

- Accounting for government grants in financial statements reflecting the effects of **changing prices**.
- Government assistance given in the form of '**tax breaks**'.
- Government acting as **part-owner** of the entity.

4.2 Definitions

These definitions are given by the Standard.

> - **Government**. Government, government agencies and similar bodies whether local, national or international.
>
> - **Government assistance**. Action by government designed to provide an economic benefit specific to an entity or range of entities qualifying under certain criteria.
>
> - **Government grants**. Assistance by government in the form of transfers of resources to an entity in return for past or future compliance with certain conditions relating to the operating activities of the entity. They exclude those forms of government assistance which cannot reasonably have a value placed upon them and transactions with government which cannot be distinguished from the normal trading transactions of the entity.
>
> - **Grants related to assets**. Government grants whose primary condition is that an entity qualifying for them should purchase, construct or otherwise acquire non-current assets. Subsidiary conditions may also be attached restricting the type or location of the assets or the periods during which they are to be acquired or held.
>
> - **Grants related to income**. Government grants other than those related to assets.
>
> - **Forgivable loans**. Loans of which the lender undertakes to waive repayment under certain prescribed conditions.
>
> - **Fair value**. The amount for which an asset could be exchanged, or a liability settled, between knowledgeable, willing parties in an arm's length transaction.

4.3 Accounting problems

You can see that there are many **different forms** of government assistance: both the type of assistance and the conditions attached to it will vary. Government assistance may have encouraged an entity to undertake something it otherwise would not have done.

How will the receipt of government assistance affect the financial statements?

- An appropriate method must be found to account for any **resources transferred**.

- The extent to which an entity has **benefited** from such assistance during the reporting period should be shown.

4.4 Recognition

An entity should not recognise government grants (including non-monetary grants at fair value) until it has **reasonable assurance** that

- The entity will comply with any **conditions** attached to the grant.
- The entity will **actually receive** the grant.

Even if the grant has been received, this does not prove that the conditions attached to it have been or will be fulfilled.

It makes no difference in the treatment of the grant whether it is received in cash or given as a reduction in a liability to government, i.e. the **manner of receipt is irrelevant**.

Any related **contingency** should be recognised under IAS 37 *Provisions, Contingent Liabilities and Contingent Assets*, once the grant has been recognised.

In the case of a **forgivable loan** (as defined above) from government, it should be treated in the same way as a government grant when it is reasonably assured that the entity will meet the relevant terms for forgiveness.

4.5 Possible methods of accounting

There are two methods which could be used to account for government grants, and the arguments for each are given in IAS 20.

- **Capital approach** – credit the grant directly to shareholders' interests.
- **Income approach** – the grant is credited to the income statement over one or more periods.

4.6 Capital approach

- The grants are a **financing device**, so should go through the statement of financial position. In the income statement they would simply offset the expenses which they are financing. No repayment is expected by the government, so the grants should be credited directly to shareholders' interests.

- Grants are **not earned**, they are incentives without related costs, so it would be wrong to take them to the income statement.

4.7 Income approach

- The grants are **not received from shareholders** so should not be credited directly to shareholders' interests.

- Grants are **not given or received for nothing**. They are earned by compliance with conditions and by meeting obligations. There are therefore associated costs with which the grant can be matched in the income statement as these costs are being compensated by the grant.

- Grants are an extension of **fiscal policies** and so as income taxes and other taxes are charged against income, so grants should be credited to income.

4.8 IAS 20 requirements

IAS 20 requires grants to be recognised under the **income approach**, i.e. grants are recognised as income over the relevant periods to match them with related costs which they have been received to compensate. This should be done on a systematic basis. **Grants should not, therefore, be credited directly to shareholders' interests**.

It would be against the accruals assumption to credit grants to income on a receipts basis, so a **systematic basis of matching** must be used. A receipts basis would only be acceptable if no other basis was available.

It will usually be easy to identify the **costs related to a government grant**, and thereby the period(s) in which the grant should be recognised as income, ie when the costs are incurred. Where grants are received in relation to a depreciating asset, the grant will be recognised over the periods in which the asset is depreciated *and* in the same proportions.

Example

Arturo Co receives a government grant representing 50% of the cost of a depreciating asset which costs £40,000. How will the grant be recognised if Arturo Co. depreciates the asset?

(a) Over four years straight line; or
(b) At 40% reducing balance?

The residual value is nil. The useful life is four years.

Solution

The grant should be recognised in the same proportion as the depreciation.

(a) *Straight line*

Year	Depreciation £)	Grant Income (£)
1	10,000	5,000
2	10,000	5,000
3	10,000	5,000
4	10,000	5,000

(b) *Reducing balance*

Year	Depreciation (£)	Grant Income (£)
1	16,000	8,000
2	9,600	4,800
3	5,760	2,880
4 (remainder)	8,640	4,320

4.9 Grants for non-depreciable assets

In the case of **grants for non-depreciable assets**, certain obligations may need to be fulfilled, in which case the grant should be recognised as income over the periods in which the cost of meeting the obligation is incurred. For example, if a piece of land is granted on condition that a building is erected on it, then the grant should be recognised as income over the building's life.

There may be a **series of conditions** attached to a grant, in the nature of a package of financial aid. An entity must take care to identify precisely those conditions which give rise to costs which in turn determine the periods over which the grant will be earned. When appropriate, the grant may be split and the parts allocated on different bases.

An entity may receive a grant as compensation for expenses or losses which it has **already incurred**. Alternatively, a grant may be given to an entity simply to provide immediate financial support where no future related costs are expected. In cases such as these, the grant received should be recognised as income of the period in which it becomes receivable.

4.10 Non-monetary government grants

A non-monetary asset may be transferred by government to an entity as a grant, for example a piece of land, or other resources. The **fair value** of such an asset is usually assessed and this is used to account for both the asset and the grant. Alternatively, both may be valued at a nominal amount.

4.11 Presentation of grants related to assets

There are two choices here for how government grants related to assets (including non-monetary grants at fair value) should be shown in the statement of financial position.

- Set up the grant as **deferred income.**
- **Deduct the grant** in arriving at the **carrying amount** of the asset.

These are considered to be acceptable alternatives and we can look at an example showing both.

Example

A company receives a 20% grant towards the cost of a new item of machinery, which cost £100,000. The machinery has an expected life of four years and a nil residual value. The expected profits of the company, before accounting for depreciation on the new machine or the grant, amount to £50,000 per annum in each year of the machinery's life.

Solution

The results of the company for the four years of the machine's life would be as follows.

(a)   *Reducing the cost of the asset*

	Year 1 (£)	Year 2 (£)	Year 3 (£)	Year 4 (£)	Total (£)
Profits					
Profit before depreciation	50,000	50,000	50,000	50,000	200,000
Depreciation*	20,000	20,000	20,000	20,000	80,000
Profit	30,000	30,000	30,000	30,000	120,000

*The depreciation charge on a straight-line basis, for each year, is ¼ of £(100,000 − 20,000) = £20,000.

Statement of financial position at year end (extract)

	(£)	(£)	(£)	(£)
Non-Current Asset at cost	80,000	80,000	80,000	80,000
Depreciation	20,000	40,000	60,000	80,000
Net Book Value	60,000	40,000	20,000	–

(b)   *Treating the grant as deferred income*

	Year 1 (£)	Year 2 (£)	Year 3 (£)	Year 4 (£)	Total (£)
Profits					
Profit before grant & dep'n	50,000	50,000	50,000	50,000	200,000
Depreciation	(25,000)	(25,000)	(25,000)	(25,000)	(100,000)
Grant	5,000	5,000	5,000	5,000	20,000
Profit	30,000	30,000	30,000	30,000	120,000

Statement of financial position at year end (extract)

	Year 1 (£)	Year 2 (£)	Year 3 (£)	Year 4 (£)
Non-Current Asset at cost	100,000	100,000	100,000	100,000
Depreciation	(25,000)	(50,000)	(75,000)	(100,000)
Net Book Value	75,000	50,000	25,000	–
Deferred income				
Government grant				
deferred income	15,000	10,000	5,000	–

Whichever of these methods is used, the **cash flows** in relation to the purchase of the asset and the receipt of the grant are often disclosed separately because of the significance of the movements in cash flow.

4.12 Presentation of grants related to income

These grants are a credit in the income statement, but there is a choice in the method of disclosure.

- Present as a **separate credit** or under a general heading, e.g. 'other income'.
- **Deduct from the related expense**.

Some would argue that offsetting income and expenses in the income statement is not good practice. Others would say that the expenses would not have been incurred had the grant not been available, so offsetting the two is acceptable. Although both methods are acceptable, disclosure of the grant may be necessary for a **proper understanding** of the financial statements, particularly the effect on any item of income or expense which is required to be separately disclosed.

4.13 Repayment of government grants

If a grant must be repaid it should be accounted for as a **revision of an accounting estimate** (see IAS 8).

- **Repayment of a grant related to income**: apply first against any unamortised deferred income set up in respect of the grant; any excess should be recognised immediately as an expense.

- **Repayment of a grant related to an asset**: increase the carrying amount of the asset or reduce the deferred income balance by the amount repayable. The cumulative additional depreciation that would have been recognised to date in the absence of the grant should be immediately recognised as an expense.

It is possible that the circumstances surrounding repayment may require a review of the **asset value** and an impairment of the new carrying amount of the asset.

4.14 Government assistance

Some forms of government assistance are excluded from the definition of government grants.

- Some forms of government assistance **cannot reasonably have a value placed on them**, e.g. free technical or marketing advice, provision of guarantees.

- There are transactions with government which **cannot be distinguished from the entity's normal trading transactions**, e.g. government procurement policy resulting in a portion of the entity's sales. Any segregation would be arbitrary.

Disclosure of such assistance may be necessary because of its significance; its nature, extent and duration should be disclosed. Loans at low or zero interest rates are a form of government assistance, but the imputation of interest does not fully quantify the benefit received.

4.15 Disclosure

Disclosure is required of the following.

- **Accounting policy** adopted, including method of presentation.
- **Nature and extent** of government grants recognised and other forms of assistance received.
- **Unfulfilled conditions and other contingencies** attached to recognised government assistance.

5 IAS 40 INVESTMENT PROPERTY

An entity may own land or a building **as an investment** rather than for use in the business. It may therefore generate cash flows largely independently of other assets which the entity holds.

5.1 Definitions

Consider the following definitions from IAS 40.

> **Investment property** is property (land or a building – or part of a building – or both) held (by the owner or by the lessee under a finance lease) to earn rentals or for capital appreciation or both, rather than for
>
> - Use in the production or supply of goods or services or for administrative purposes; or
> - Sale in the ordinary course of business.
>
> **Owner-occupied property** is property held by the owner (or by the lessee under a finance lease) for use in the production or supply of goods or services or for administrative purposes.
>
> **Fair value** is the amount for which an asset could be exchanged between knowledgeable, willing parties in an arm's length transaction.
>
> **Cost** is the amount of cash or cash equivalents paid or the fair value of other consideration given to acquire an asset at the time of its acquisition or construction.
>
> **Carrying amount** is the amount at which an asset is recognised in the statement of financial position.
>
> A property interest that is held by a lessee under an **operating lease** may be classified and accounted for as an **investment property** if, and only if, the property would otherwise meet the definition of an investment property and the lessee uses the IAS 40 **fair value model**. This classification is available on a property-by-property basis.

Examples of investment property include

- **Land held for long-term capital appreciation** rather than for short-term sale in the ordinary course of business.

- A **building** owned by the reporting entity (or held by the entity under a finance lease) and **leased out under an operating lease**.

Example

Rich Co. owns a piece of land. The directors have not yet decided whether to build a factory on it for use in its business or to keep it and sell it when its value has risen.

Would this be classified as an investment property under IAS 40?

Solution

Yes. If an entity has not determined that it will use the land either as an owner-occupied property or for short-term sale in the ordinary course of business, the land is considered to be held for capital appreciation.

5.2 IAS 40

IAS 40 *Investment Property* prescribes the accounting treatment for investment property and related disclosure requirements.

The Standard includes investment property held under a finance lease or leased out under an operating lease (see Chapter 12 for an explanation of these terms). However, the current IAS 40 does not deal with other matters covered in IAS 17 *Leases*.

You now know what an investment property *is* under IAS 40. Below are examples of items that are **not investment property**.

Type of non-investment property	Applicable IAS
Property intended for sale in the ordinary course of business	IAS 2 *Inventories*
Property being constructed or developed on behalf of third parties	IAS 11 *Construction Contracts*
Owner-occupied property	IAS 16 *Property, Plant and Equipment*
Property being constructed or developed for future use as investment property	IAS 16 until construction or development is complete, then treat as investment property

5.3 Recognition

Investment property should be recognised as an asset when **two conditions** are met.

- It is **probable** that the **future economic benefits** that are associated with the investment property will **flow to the entity**.

- The **cost** of the investment property can be **measured reliably**.

5.4 Initial measurement

An investment property should be measured initially at its **cost,** including transaction costs.

A property interest held under a lease and classified as an investment property shall be accounted for **as if it were a finance lease** (see Chapter 12). The asset is recognised at the lower of the fair value of the property and the present value of the minimum lease payments. An equivalent amount is recognised as a liability.

5.5 Measurement subsequent to initial recognition

IAS 40 requires an entity to **choose between two models**.

- **The fair value model**.
- **The cost model**.

Whatever policy it chooses should be applied to **all of its investment property**.

Where an entity chooses to classify a property held under an **operating lease** as an investment property, there is **no choice**. The **fair value model must be used** for **all the entity's investment property**, regardless of whether it is owned or leased.

5.6 Fair value model

- After initial recognition, an entity that chooses the **fair value model** should measure all of its investment property at fair value, except in the extremely rare cases where this cannot be measured reliably. In such cases it should apply the IAS 16 cost model.

- A gain or loss arising from a change in the fair value of an investment property should be recognised in profit or loss for the period in which it arises.

- The fair value of investment property should reflect market conditions at the statement of financial position date.

This was the first time that the IASB has allowed a fair value model for non-financial assets. This is not the same as a revaluation, where increases in carrying amount above a cost-based measure are recognised as revaluation surplus. Under the fair-value model all changes in fair value are recognised in the income statement.

5.7 What is fair value?

The Standard elaborates on **issues relating to fair value**.

- Fair value assumes that an arm's length transaction has taken place between '**knowledgeable, willing parties**', i.e. both buyer and seller are reasonably informed about the nature and characteristics of the investment property.

- A willing buyer is **motivated but not compelled** to buy. A willing seller is neither an over-eager nor a forced seller, nor one prepared to sell at any price or to hold out for a price not considered reasonable in the current market.

- **Fair value is not the same as 'value in use'** as defined in IAS 36 *Impairment of Assets*. Value in use reflects factors and knowledge specific to the entity, while fair value reflects factors and knowledge relevant to the market.

- In determining fair value an entity **should not double count assets**. For example, elevators or air conditioning are often an integral part of a building and should be included in the investment property, rather than recognised separately.

- In those rare cases where the **entity cannot determine the fair value of an investment property reliably**, the cost model in **IAS 16** must be applied until the investment property is disposed of. The **residual value must be assumed to be zero**.

5.8 Cost model

The cost model is the **cost model in IAS 16**. Investment property should be measured at **depreciated cost, less any accumulated impairment losses**. An entity that chooses the cost model should **disclose the fair value of its investment property**.

5.9 Changing models

Once the entity has chosen the fair value or cost model, it should apply it to all its investment property. It **should not change from one model to the other unless the change will result in a more appropriate presentation**. IAS 40 states that it is highly unlikely that a change from the fair value model to the cost model will result in a more appropriate presentation.

5.10 Disclosure requirements

These relate to

- Choice of fair value model or cost model.
- Whether property interests held as operating leases are included in investment property.
- Criteria for classification as investment property.
- Assumptions in determining fair value.
- Use of independent professional valuer (encouraged but not required).
- Rental income and expenses.
- Any restrictions or obligations.

5.11 Fair value model – additional disclosures

An entity that adopts this must also disclose a **reconciliation** of the carrying amount of the investment property at the beginning and end of the period.

5.12 Cost model – additional disclosures

These relate mainly to the depreciation method. In addition, an entity which adopts the cost model **must disclose the fair value** of the investment property.

6   INTANGIBLE NON-CURRENT ASSETS

Exam tip

Intangible assets represent the most frequently examined topic in this section, e.g. Winter 2006 Question 1, Summer 2005 Question 9, Winter 2004 Question 7.

6.1 Introduction

An intangible non-current asset is a non-current asset that is non-monetary in nature and without physical substance. Intangible non-current assets are of growing importance to many enterprises. Their non-physical nature, and the fact that many are unique assets based on intellectual property rights, give rise to particular problems concerning their recognition in the statement of financial position of an enterprise.

Problems arise from a clash of concepts, specifically

- The accruals concept – where the aim is to match costs against relevant income.
- The prudence concept – where assets should be valued at the lower of cost and the amount recoverable from their use.

Examples of intangibles that may appear on statement of financial positions are

- Development expenditure.
- Patents and trademarks.
- Publishing rights and titles.
- Goodwill.
- Brands.

The accruals concept would encourage the capitalisation of these costs and their amortisation (depreciation) to match against the income that they help generate.

The prudence concept would encourage the immediate writing off of these items due to their volatile nature. Intellectual property rights can be lost if the staff holding that intelligence is lost or if technology changes so fast as to make that intelligence outdated. Goodwill could be lost as quickly as a reputation is lost.

6.2 IAS 38 Intangible Assets

Intangible assets are defined by IAS 38 as non-monetary assets without physical substance.

6.3 The objectives of the Standard

- To establish the criteria for when an intangible asset may or should be **recognised**.
- To specify how intangible assets should be **measured**.
- To specify the **disclosure requirements** for intangible assets.

6.4 Scope

IAS 38 applies to all intangible assets with certain **exceptions**: deferred tax assets (IAS 12), leases that fall within the scope of IAS 17, financial assets, insurance contracts, assets arising from employee benefits (IAS 19), non-current assets held for sale (IFRS 5) and mineral rights and exploration and extraction costs for minerals etc. (although intangible assets used to develop or maintain these rights are covered by the Standard). It does *not* apply to goodwill acquired in a business combination, which is dealt with under IFRS 3 *Business Combinations*.

6.5 Definition of an intangible asset

The definition of an intangible asset is a key aspect of the Standard, because the rules for deciding whether or not an intangible asset may be **recognised** in the accounts of an entity are based on the definition of what an intangible asset is.

An **intangible asset** is an identifiable non-monetary asset without physical substance The asset must be

- Controlled by the entity as a result of events in the past; and
- Something from which the entity expects future economic benefits to flow.

Examples of items that might be considered as intangible assets include computer software, patents, copyrights, motion picture films, customer lists, franchises and fishing rights. An item should not be recognised as an intangible asset, however, unless it **fully meets the definition** in the Standard. The guidelines go into great detail on this matter.

6.6 Intangible asset: Must be identifiable

The distinguishing characteristic of other intangible assets is that they are '**identifiable**'. Goodwill is not an 'identifiable' asset. IAS 38 states that an asset is identifiable when it

- Is **separable**, i.e. is capable of being separated or divided from the entity and sold, licensed, transferred or exchanged; or
- Arises from **contractual or other legal rights**.

6.7 Intangible asset: Control by the entity

Another element of the definition of an intangible asset is that it must be under the control of the entity as a result of a past event. The entity must therefore be able to enjoy the future economic benefits from the asset, and prevent the access of others to those benefits. A **legally enforceable right** is evidence of such control, but is not always a *necessary* condition.

- Control over **technical knowledge or know-how** only exists if it is protected by a **legal right**.

- The skill of employees, arising out of the benefits of **training costs**, are most unlikely to be recognisable as an intangible asset, because an entity does not control the future actions of its staff.

- Similarly, **market share and customer loyalty** cannot normally be intangible assets, since an entity cannot control the actions of its customers.

6.8 Intangible asset: Expected future economic benefits

An item can only be recognised as an intangible asset if economic benefits are expected to flow in the future from ownership of the asset. Economic benefits may come from the **sale** of products or services, or from a **reduction in expenditures** (cost savings).

6.9 Initial recognition

An intangible asset, when recognised initially, must be measured at **cost**. It should be recognised if, and only if **both** the following occur.

- It is probable that the **future economic benefits** that are attributable to the asset will **flow to the entity**.

- The **cost can be measured reliably**.

Management has to exercise its judgement in assessing the degree of certainty attached to the flow of economic benefits to the entity. External evidence is best.

If an intangible asset is **acquired separately**, its cost can usually be measured reliably as its purchase price (including incidental costs of purchase such as legal fees, and any costs incurred in getting the asset ready for use).

When an intangible asset is acquired as **part of a business combination** (i.e. an acquisition or takeover), the cost of the intangible asset is its fair value at the date of the acquisition.

IFRS 3 explains that the fair value of intangible assets acquired in business combinations can normally be measured with sufficient reliability to be **recognised separately** from goodwill.

Quoted market prices in an active market provide the most reliable estimate of the fair value of an intangible asset. If no active market exists for an intangible asset, its fair value is the amount that the entity would have paid for the asset, at the acquisition date, in an arm's length transaction between knowledgeable and willing parties, on the basis of the best information available. In determining this amount, an entity should consider the outcome of recent transactions for similar assets. There are techniques for estimating the fair values of unique intangible assets (such as brand names) and these may be used to measure an intangible asset acquired in a business combination.

In accordance with IAS 20, intangible assets acquired by way of government grant and the grant itself may be recorded initially either at cost (which may be zero) or fair value.

6.10 Internally generated goodwill

Rule to learn: Internally generated goodwill may **not** be recognised as an **asset**.

The Standard deliberately precludes recognition of internally generated goodwill because it requires that, for initial recognition, the cost of the asset rather than its fair value should be capable of being measured reliably and that it should be identifiable and controlled. Thus you do not recognise an asset which is subjective and cannot be measured reliably.

7 RESEARCH AND DEVELOPMENT COSTS

Research and development may be examined in any section, e.g. Summer 2001, Question 3.

7.1 Research

Research activities by definition do not meet the criteria for recognition under IAS 38 (SSAP 13 in the UK). This is because, at the research stage of a project, it cannot be certain that future economic benefits will probably flow to the entity from the project. There is too much uncertainty about the likely success or otherwise of the project. **Research costs should therefore be written off as an expense as they are incurred**.

Examples of research costs are as follows.

- Activities aimed at obtaining new knowledge.

- The search for, evaluation and final selection of, applications of research findings or other knowledge.

- The search for alternatives for materials, devices, products, processes, systems or services.

- The formulation, design evaluation and final selection of possible alternatives for new or improved materials, devices, products, systems or services.

7.2 Development

Development costs **may qualify** for recognition as intangible assets provided that the following **strict criteria** can be demonstrated.

- The technical feasibility of completing the intangible asset so that it will be available for use or sale.

- Its intention to complete the intangible asset and use or sell it.

- Its ability to use or sell the intangible asset.

- How the intangible asset will generate probable future economic benefits. Among other things, the entity should demonstrate the existence of a market for the output of the intangible asset or the intangible asset itself or, if it is to be used internally, the usefulness of the intangible asset.

- Its ability to measure the expenditure attributable to the intangible asset during its development reliably.

7.3 Examples of development costs

In contrast with research costs development costs are incurred at a later stage in a project, and the probability of success should be more apparent. Examples of development costs include the following.

- The design, construction and testing of pre-production or pre-use prototypes and models.

- The design of tools, jigs, moulds and dies involving new technology.

- The design, construction and operation of a pilot plant that is not of a scale economically feasible for commercial production.

- The design, construction and testing of a chosen alternative for new or improved materials, devices, products, processes, systems or services.

7.4 Other internally generated intangible assets

The Standard **prohibits** the recognition of **internally generated brands**, **mastheads**, **publishing titles and customer lists** and similar items as intangible assets. These all fail to meet one or more (in some cases all) the definition and recognition criteria and in some cases are probably indistinguishable from internally generated goodwill.

7.5 Cost of an internally generated intangible asset

The costs allocated to an internally generated intangible asset should be only costs that can be **directly attributed** or allocated on a reasonable and consistent basis to creating, producing or preparing the asset for its intended use. The principles underlying the costs which may or may not be included are similar to those for other non-current assets and inventory.

The cost of an internally generated intangible asset is the sum of the **expenditure incurred from the date when** the intangible asset first **meets the recognition criteria**. If, as often happens, considerable costs have already been recognised as expenses before management could demonstrate that the criteria have been met, this earlier expenditure should not be retrospectively recognised at a later date as part of the cost of an intangible asset.

Example

Doug Co. is developing a new production process. During 2007, expenditure incurred was £100,000, of which £90,000 was incurred before 1 December 2007 and £10,000 between 1 December and 31 December 2007. Doug Co. can demonstrate that, at 1 December 2007, the production process met the criteria for recognition as an intangible asset. The recoverable amount of the know-how embodied in the process is estimated to be £50,000.

How should the expenditure be treated?

Solution

At the end of 2007, the production process is recognised as an intangible asset at a cost of £10,000. This is the expenditure incurred since the date when the recognition criteria were met, that is 1 December 2007. The £90,000 expenditure incurred before 1 December 2007 is expensed, because the recognition criteria were not met. It will never form part of the cost of the production process recognised in the statement of financial position.

8 ACCOUNTING TREATMENT OF INTANGIBLES

8.1 Recognition of an expense

All expenditure related to an intangible which does not meet the criteria for recognition either as an identifiable intangible asset or as goodwill arising on an acquisition should be **expensed as incurred**. The IAS gives examples of such expenditure.

- Start up costs.
- Training costs.
- Advertising costs.
- Business relocation costs.

Prepaid costs for services, for example advertising or marketing costs for campaigns that have been prepared but not launched, can still be recognised as a **prepayment**.

8.2 Measurement of intangible assets subsequent to initial recognition

The Standard allows two methods of valuation for intangible assets after they have been first recognised.

Applying the **cost model**, an intangible asset should be **carried at its cost**, less any accumulated amortisation and less any accumulated impairment losses.

The **revaluation model** allows an intangible asset to be carried at a revalued amount, which is its **fair value** at the date of revaluation, less any subsequent accumulated amortisation and any subsequent accumulated impairment losses.

- The fair value must be able to be measured reliably with reference to an **active market** in that type of asset.

- The **entire class** of intangible assets of that type must be revalued at the same time (to prevent selective revaluations).

- If an intangible asset in a class of revalued intangible assets cannot be revalued because there is **no active market** for this asset, the asset should be carried at its **cost less any accumulated amortisation and impairment losses**.

- Revaluations should be made with such **regularity** that the carrying amount does not differ from that which would be determined using fair value at the statement of financial position date.

> This treatment is **not** available for the **initial recognition** of intangible assets. This is because the cost of the asset must be measured initially at cost.

The guidelines state that there **will not usually be an active market** in an intangible asset; therefore the revaluation model will usually not be available. For example, although copyrights, publishing rights and film rights can be sold, each has a unique sale value. In such cases, revaluation to fair value would be inappropriate. A fair value might be obtainable however for assets such as fishing rights or quotas or taxi cab licences.

8.3 Treatment of revaluation

Where an intangible asset is revalued upwards to a fair value, the amount of the revaluation should be credited directly to equity under the heading of a **revaluation surplus**.

However, if a revaluation surplus is a **reversal of a revaluation decrease** that was previously charged against income, the increase can be recognised as income.

Where the carrying amount of an intangible asset is revalued downwards, the amount of the **downward revaluation** should be charged as an expense against income, unless the asset has previously been revalued upwards. A revaluation decrease should be first charged against any previous revaluation surplus in respect of that asset.

Example

An intangible asset is measured by a company at fair value. The asset was revalued by £400 in 2007, and there is a revaluation surplus of £400 in the statement of financial position. At the end of 2008, the asset is valued again, and a downward valuation of £500 is required.

Requirement

State the accounting treatment for the downward revaluation.

Solution

In this Example, the downward valuation of £500 can first be set against the revaluation surplus of £400. The revaluation surplus will be reduced to 0 and a charge of £100 made as an expense in the income statement of 2008.

8.4 Realisation of revaluation surplus

When the revaluation model is used, and an intangible asset is revalued upwards, the cumulative revaluation **surplus may be transferred to retained earnings** when the surplus is eventually realised. The surplus would be realised when the asset is disposed of. However, the surplus may also be realised over time as the **asset is used** by the entity. The amount of the surplus realised each year is the difference between the amortisation charge for the asset based on the revalued amount of the asset, and the amortisation that would be charged on the basis of the asset's historical cost. The realised surplus in such case should be transferred from revaluation surplus directly to retained earnings, and should not be taken through the income statement. This treatment is effectively the same as that for tangible assets which have been revalued.

8.5 Useful life

An entity should **assess** the useful life of an intangible asset, which may be **finite or indefinite**. An intangible asset has an indefinite useful life when there is **no foreseeable limit** to the period over which the asset is expected to generate net cash inflows for the entity.

Many factors are considered in determining the useful life of an intangible asset, including: expected usage; typical product life cycles; technical, technological, commercial or other types of obsolescence; the stability of the industry; expected actions by competitors; the level of maintenance expenditure required; and legal or similar limits on the use of the asset, such as the expiry dates of related leases. Computer software and many other intangible assets normally have short lives because they are susceptible to technological obsolescence. However, uncertainty does not justify choosing a life that is unrealistically short.

The useful life of an intangible asset that arises from **contractual or other legal rights** should not exceed the period of the rights, but may be shorter depending on the period over which the entity expects to use the asset.

8.6 Amortisation period and amortisation method

An intangible asset with a finite useful life should be amortised over its **expected useful life**.

- Amortisation should start when the asset is **available for use**.

- Amortisation should cease at the earlier of the date that the asset is classified **as held for sale** in accordance with IFRS 5 *Non-Current Assets Held for Sale and Discontinued Operations* and the date that the asset is **derecognised**.

- The amortisation method used should reflect the **pattern in which the asset's future economic benefits are consumed**. If such a pattern cannot be predicted reliably, the straight-line method should be used.

- The amortisation charge for each period should normally be recognised **in profit or loss**.

The **residual value** of an intangible asset with a finite useful life is **assumed to be zero** unless a third party is committed to buying the intangible asset at the end of its useful life or unless there is an active market for that type of asset (so that its expected residual value can be measured) and it is probable that there will be a market for the asset at the end of its useful life.

The amortisation period and the amortisation method used for an intangible asset with a finite useful life should be **reviewed at each financial year-end**.

8.7 Intangible assets with indefinite useful lives

An intangible asset with an indefinite useful life **should not be amortised**. (IAS 36 requires that such an asset is tested for impairment at least annually.)

The useful life of an intangible asset that is not being amortised should be **reviewed each year** to determine whether it is still appropriate to assess its useful life as indefinite. Reassessing the useful life of an intangible asset as finite rather than indefinite is an indicator that the asset may be impaired and therefore it should be tested for impairment.

Example

It may be difficult to establish the useful life of an intangible asset, and judgement will be needed. Consider how to determine the useful life of a **purchased** brand name.

Solution

Factors to consider would include the following.

- Legal protection of the brand name and the control of the entity over the (illegal) use by others of the brand name (i.e. control over pirating).
- Age of the brand name.
- Status or position of the brand in its particular market.
- Ability of the management of the entity to manage the brand name and to measure activities that support the brand name (e.g. advertising and PR activities).
- Stability and geographical spread of the market in which the branded products are sold.
- Pattern of benefits that the brand name is expected to generate over time.
- Intention of the entity to use and promote the brand name over time (as evidenced perhaps by a business plan in which there will be substantial expenditure to promote the brand name).

8.8 Disposals/Retirements of intangible assets

An intangible asset should be eliminated from the statement of financial position when it is disposed of or when there is no further expected economic benefit from its future use. On disposal the gain or loss arising from the **difference between the net disposal proceeds and the carrying amount** of the asset should be taken to the income statement as a gain or loss on disposal (i.e. treated as income or expense).

8.9 Disclosure requirements

The Standard has fairly extensive disclosure requirements for intangible assets. The financial statements should disclose the **accounting policies** for intangible assets that have been adopted.

For **each class of intangible asset**, disclosure is required of the following.

- The method of amortisation used.

- The useful life of the assets or the amortisation rate used.

- The gross carrying amount, the accumulated amortisation and the accumulated impairment losses as at the beginning and the end of the period.

- A reconciliation of the carrying amount as at the beginning and at the end of the period (additions, retirements/disposals, revaluations, impairment losses, impairment losses reversed, amortisation charge for the period, net exchange differences, other movements).

- The carrying amount of internally generated intangible assets.

The financial statements should also disclose the following.

- In the case of intangible assets that are assessed as having an indefinite useful life, the carrying amounts and the reasons supporting that assessment.

- For intangible assets acquired by way of a **government grant** and initially recognised at fair value, the **fair value initially recognised**, the **carrying amount**, and whether they are carried under the **cost model** or the **revaluation model** for subsequent remeasurements.

- The carrying amount, nature and remaining amortisation period of any intangible asset that is **material to the financial statements of the entity as a whole**.

- The existence (if any) and amounts of intangible assets whose **title is restricted** and of intangible assets that have been **pledged as security** for liabilities.

- The amount of any **commitments for the future acquisition of intangible assets**.

Where intangible assets are accounted for at revalued amounts, disclosure is required of the following.

- The **effective date of the revaluation** (by class of intangible assets).

- The **carrying amount** of revalued intangible assets.

- The carrying amount that would have been shown (by class of assets) **if the cost model had been used**, and the amount of amortisation that would have been charged.

- The amount of any **revaluation surplus** on intangible assets, as at the beginning and end of the period, and movements in the surplus during the year (and any restrictions on the distribution of the balance to shareholders).

The financial statements should also disclose the amount of research and development expenditure that have been charged as expenses of the period.

9 GOODWILL (IFRS 3)

Exam tip

Goodwill on acquisition frequently arises in the Section A case study. It is also examined in other sections, e.g. Summer 2001, Question 11.

Purchased goodwill arising on consolidation is retained in the statement of financial position as an intangible asset under IFRS 3 (FRS 10 in the UK). It must then be reviewed annually for impairment.

9.1 What is goodwill?

Goodwill is **created by good relationships** between a business and its customers.

- By building up a **reputation** (by word-of-mouth perhaps) for high quality products or high standards of service.

- By **responding promptly and helpfully** to queries and complaints from customers.

- Through the **personality of the staff** and their attitudes to customers.

The value of goodwill to a business might be **extremely significant**. However, goodwill is not usually valued in the accounts of a business at all, and we should not normally expect to find an amount for goodwill in its statement of financial position. For example, the welcoming smile of the bar staff may contribute more to a bar's profits than the fact that a new electronic cash register has recently been acquired. Even so, whereas the cash register will be recorded in the accounts as a non-current asset, the value of staff would be ignored for accounting purposes.

On reflection, we might agree with this omission of goodwill from the accounts of a business.

- The goodwill is **inherent** in the business but it has not been paid for, and it does not have an 'objective' value. We can guess at what such goodwill is worth, but such guesswork would be a matter of individual opinion, and not based on hard facts.

- Goodwill **changes** from day to day. One act of bad customer relations might damage goodwill and one act of good relations might improve it. Staff with a favourable personality might retire or leave, to be replaced by staff who need time to find their feet in the job, among other factors. Since goodwill is continually changing in value, it cannot realistically be recorded in the accounts of the business.

9.2 Purchased goodwill

There is one exception to the general rule that goodwill has no objective valuation. This is **when a business is purchased**. People wishing to set up in business have a choice of how to do it – they can either buy their own long-term assets and inventory and set up their business from scratch, or they can buy up an existing business from a proprietor willing to sell it. When a buyer purchases an existing business, he will have to purchase not only its long-term assets and inventory (and perhaps take over its accounts payable and receivable too) but also the goodwill of the business.

Purchased goodwill is recognised in the statement of financial position because it has been paid for. It has no physical substance, and so it is an **intangible non-current asset**.

9.3 How is the value of purchased goodwill decided?

When a business is sold, there is likely to be some purchased goodwill in the selling price. But **how is the amount of this purchased goodwill decided**?

This is not really a problem for accountants, who must simply record the goodwill in the accounts of the new business. The value of the goodwill is a **matter for the purchaser and seller to agree upon in fixing the purchase/sale price**. However, two methods of valuation are worth mentioning here.

- The seller and buyer agree on a price for the business **without specifically quantifying the goodwill**. The purchased goodwill will then be the difference between the price agreed and the value of the tangible net assets in the books of the new business.

- However, the calculation of goodwill often precedes the fixing of the purchase price and becomes a **central element of negotiation**. There are many ways of arriving at a value for goodwill and most of them are related to the profit record of the business in question.

No matter how goodwill is calculated within the total agreed purchase price, the goodwill shown by the purchaser in his accounts will be **the difference between the purchase consideration and his own valuation of the tangible net assets acquired**. If A values his tangible net assets at £40,000, goodwill is agreed at £21,000 and B agrees to pay £61,000 for the business but values the tangible net assets at only £38,000, then the goodwill in B's books will be £61,000 – £38,000 = £23,000.

9.4 IFRS 3 Business Combinations

IFRS 3 covers the accounting treatment of goodwill acquired in a business combination.

It is possible to define goodwill in different ways. The IFRS 3 definition of goodwill is different from the definition in IAS 22 which was the previous standard on business combinations. IFRS 3 emphasises benefits, rather than the method of calculation.

> - **Goodwill**. Future economic benefits arising from assets that are not capable of being individually identified and separately recognised. *(IFRS 3)*
>
> - **Goodwill**. Any excess of the cost of acquisition over the acquirer's interest in the fair value of the identifiable assets and liabilities acquired as at the date of the exchange transaction. *(IAS 22)*

Goodwill acquired in a business combination is **recognised as an asset** and is initially measured at **cost**. Cost is the excess of the cost of the combination over the acquirer's interest in the net fair value of the acquiree's identifiable assets, liabilities and contingent liabilities.

After initial recognition goodwill acquired in a business combination is measured **at cost less any accumulated impairment losses**. It is **not amortised**. Instead it is tested for impairment at least annually, in accordance with IAS 36 *Impairment of Assets* (see later in chapter).

Negative goodwill arises when the acquirer's interest in the net fair value of the acquiree's identifiable assets, liabilities and contingent liabilities exceeds the cost of the business combination. IFRS 3 refers to negative goodwill as the 'excess of acquirer's interest in the net fair value of acquiree's identifiable assets, liabilities and contingent liabilities over cost'.

Negative goodwill can arise as the result of **errors** in measuring the fair value of either the cost of the combination or the acquiree's identifiable net assets. It can also arise as the result of a **bargain purchase**.

Where there is negative goodwill, an entity should first **reassess** the amounts at which it has measured both the cost of the combination and the acquiree's identifiable net assets. This exercise should identify any errors.

Any negative goodwill remaining should be **recognised immediately in profit or loss** (that is, in the income statement).

IFRS 3 requires extensive **disclosures**. These include a **reconciliation** of the carrying amount of goodwill at the beginning and end of the period, showing separately

- The gross amount and accumulated impairment losses at the beginning of the period.
- Additional goodwill recognised during the period.
- Impairment losses recognised during the period.
- Net exchange differences arising during the period.
- The gross amount and accumulated impairment losses at the end of the period.

Example

What are the main characteristics of goodwill which distinguish it from other intangible non-current assets? To what extent do you consider that these characteristics should affect the accounting treatment of goodwill? State your reasons.

Solution

Goodwill may be distinguished from other intangible non-current assets by reference to the following characteristics.

- It is not an 'identifiable' asset, as defined in IAS 38.

- It is incapable of realisation separately from the business as a whole.

- Its value has no reliable or predictable relationship to any costs which may have been incurred.

- Its value arises from various intangible factors such as skilled employees, effective advertising or a strategic location. These indirect factors cannot be valued.

- The value of goodwill may fluctuate widely according to internal and external circumstances over relatively short periods of time.

- The assessment of the value of goodwill is highly subjective.

It could be argued that, because goodwill is so different from other intangible non-current assets it does not make sense to account for it in the same way. Thus the capitalisation and amortisation treatment would not be acceptable. Furthermore, because goodwill is so difficult to value, any valuation may be misleading, and it is best eliminated from the statement of financial position altogether. However, there are strong arguments for treating it like any other intangible non-current asset. This issue remains controversial.

10 IAS 36 IMPAIRMENT OF ASSETS

Exam tip

> Another regularly examined area, e.g. Winter 2006 Question 5, Summer 2006 Question 3.

> Impairment is determined by comparing the carrying amount of the asset with its recoverable amount.

There is an established principle that assets should not be carried at above their recoverable amount. An entity should write down the carrying value of an asset to its recoverable amount if the carrying value of an asset is not recoverable in full. IAS 36 (FRS 11 in the UK) was published in June 1998 and was revised in 2004. It puts in place a detailed methodology for carrying out impairment reviews and related accounting treatments and disclosures.

10.1 Scope

IAS 36 applies to all tangible, intangible and financial assets except inventories, assets arising from construction contracts, deferred tax assets, assets arising under IAS 19 *Employee Benefits* and financial assets within the scope of IAS 39 *Financial Instruments: Recognition and Measurement*. This is because those IASs already have rules for recognising and measuring impairment. Note also that IAS 36 does not apply to non-current assets held for sale, which are dealt with under IFRS 5 *Non-Current Assets Held for Sale and Discontinued Operations*.

10.2 Definitions

- **Impairment**: a fall in the value of an asset, so that its 'recoverable amount' is now less than its carrying value in the statement of financial position.

- **Carrying amount**: is the net value at which the asset is included in the statement of financial position (i.e. after deducting accumulated depreciation and any impairment losses).   *(IAS 36)*

10.3 Accounting issues

The basic principle underlying IAS 36 is relatively straightforward. If an asset's value in the accounts (its 'book value') is higher than its current value, measured as its 'recoverable amount', the asset is judged to have suffered an impairment loss. It should therefore be reduced in value, by the amount of the **impairment loss**. The amount of the impairment loss should be **written off against profit** immediately.

The main accounting issues to consider are therefore as follows.

- How is it possible to **identify when** an impairment loss may have occurred?
- How should the **recoverable amount** of the asset be measured?
- How should an 'impairment loss' be **reported in the accounts**?

10.4 Identifying a potentially impaired asset

An entity should assess at each statement of financial position date whether there are any indications of impairment to any assets. The concept of **materiality** applies, and only material impairment needs to be identified.

If there are indications of possible impairment, the entity is required to make a formal estimate of the **recoverable amount** of the assets concerned.

IAS 36 suggests how **indications of a possible impairment** of assets might be recognised. The suggestions are based largely on common sense.

- External sources of information
    - A fall in the asset's market value that is more significant than would normally be expected from passage of time or normal use.
    - A significant change in the technological, market, legal or economic environment of the business in which the assets are employed.
    - An increase in market interest rates or market rates of return on investments likely to affect the discount rate used in calculating value in use.
    - The carrying amount of the entity's net assets being more than its market capitalisation.
- **Internal sources of information**: evidence of obsolescence or physical damage, adverse changes in the use to which the asset is put, or the asset's economic performance.

Even if there are no indications of impairment, the following assets must **always** be tested for impairment annually.

- An intangible asset with an **indefinite useful life**.
- **Goodwill** acquired in a business combination.

10.5 Measuring the recoverable amount of the asset

What is an asset's recoverable amount?

The **recoverable amount of an asset** should be measured as the *higher* of

- The asset's fair value less costs to sell; and
- Its value in use. *(IAS 36)*

An asset's fair value less costs to sell is the amount net of selling costs that could be obtained from the sale of the asset. Selling costs include transaction costs, such as legal expenses.

- If there is **an active market** for the asset, the net selling price should be based on the **market value**, or on the price of recent transactions in similar assets.

- If there is **no active market** for the asset it might be possible to **estimate** a net selling price using best estimates of what 'knowledgeable, willing parties' might pay in an arm's length transaction.

Net selling price **cannot** be reduced, however, by including within selling costs any **restructuring or reorganisation expenses**, or any costs that have already been recognised in the accounts as liabilities.

The concept of 'value in use' is very important.

> The **value in use** of an asset is measured as the present value of estimated future cash flows (inflows minus outflows) generated by the asset, including its estimated net disposal value (if any) at the end of its expected useful life.

The cash flows used in the calculation should be **pre-tax cash flows** and a **pre-tax discount rate** should be applied to calculate the present value.

The calculation of **value in use** must reflect the following.

- An estimate of the **future cash flows** the entity expects to derive from the asset;
- Expectations about **possible variations** in the amount and timing of future cash flows;
- The **time value of money**;
- The price for bearing the **uncertainty** inherent in the asset; and
- **Other factors** that would be reflected in pricing future cash flows from the asset.

Calculating a value in use therefore calls for estimates of future cash flows, and the possibility exists that an entity might come up with **over-optimistic estimates** of cash flows. The IAS therefore states the following.

- Cash flow projections should be based on 'reasonable and supportable' assumptions.

- Projections of cash flows, normally up to a maximum period of five years, should be based on the most recent budgets or financial forecasts approved by management.

- Cash flow projections beyond this period should be obtained by extrapolating short-term projections, using either a steady or declining growth rate for each subsequent year (unless a rising growth rate can be justified). The long-term growth rate applied should not exceed the average long-term growth rate for the product, market, industry or country, unless a higher growth rate can be justified.

10.6 Recognition and measurement of an impairment loss

The rule for assets at historical cost is

> **Rule to learn**: If the recoverable amount of an asset is lower than the carrying amount, the carrying amount should be reduced by the difference (i.e. the impairment loss) which should be charged as an expense in the income statement.

The rule for assets held at a revalued amount (such as property revalued under IAS 16) is

> **Rule to learn**: The impairment loss is to be treated as a revaluation decrease under the relevant IAS.

In practice this means

- To the extent that there is a revaluation surplus held in respect of the asset, the impairment loss should be charged to revaluation surplus.
- Any excess should be charged to the income statement.

Example

An asset carried in the accounts based on historical cost has a net book value of £210,000 and an estimated remaining useful life of seven years. At that time, the net revenues expected to arise from its use (in present value terms) were £250,000. This asset is not impaired and should be carried in the statement of financial position at £210,000.

One year later, depreciation has reduced its net book value to £180,000 and its remaining useful life is six years. Unfortunately, now the market for our product has collapsed and the revenue that we can expect from using this asset (in present value terms) is now just £120,000. The fair value of the asset less costs to sell is just £95,000.

The asset has, therefore, suffered a diminution in value down from net book value to the higher of value in use and fair value less costs to sell. The fall in value is therefore £60,000 (£180,000 – £120,000) and our treatment now would be to immediately write off the diminution in value. The impact on our accounting equation for this adjustment is

- Credit non-current assets by £60,000 (net assets down).

- Debit profits by £60,000 (shareholders' funds down), the entire reduction being charged to the current year income statement.

We now have a non-current asset with a carrying amount of £120,000 and a remaining useful life of six years. We therefore need to revise the annual depreciation charge, which should, therefore, be £20,000 per annum (assuming straight-line depreciation) over the remaining six-year life.

10.7 Cash generating units

IAS 36 goes into detail about the important concept of cash generating units. As a basic rule, the recoverable amount of an asset should be calculated for the **asset individually**. However, there will be occasions when it is not possible to estimate such a value for an individual asset, particularly in the calculation of value in use. This is because cash inflows and outflows cannot be attributed to the individual asset.

If it is not possible to calculate the recoverable amount for an individual asset, the recoverable amount of the asset's cash generating unit should be measured instead.

> **A cash generating unit** is the smallest identifiable group of assets for which independent cash flows can be identified and measured.

Example

Minimart belongs to a retail store chain Maximart. Minimart makes all its retail purchases through Maximart's purchasing centre. Pricing, marketing, advertising and human resources policies (except for hiring Minimart's cashiers and salesmen) are decided by Maximart. Maximart also owns five other stores in the same city as Minimart (although in different neighbourhoods) and 20 other stores in other cities. All stores are managed in the same way as Minimart. Minimart and four other stores were purchased five years ago and goodwill was recognised.

What is the cash-generating unit for Minimart?

Solution

In identifying Minimart's cash-generating unit, an entity considers whether, for example

- Internal management reporting is organised to measure performance on a store-by-store basis.

- The business is run on a store-by-store profit basis or on a region/city basis.

All Maximart's stores are in different neighbourhoods and probably have different customer bases. So, although Minimart is managed at a corporate level, Minimart generates cash inflows that are largely independent from those of Maximart's other stores. Therefore, it is likely that Minimart is a cash-generating unit.

Example

Mighty Mag Publishing Co. owns 150 magazine titles of which 70 were purchased and 80 were self-created. The price paid for a purchased magazine title is recognised as an intangible asset. The costs of creating magazine titles and maintaining the existing titles are recognised as an expense when incurred. Cash inflows from direct sales and advertising are identifiable for each magazine title. Titles are managed by customer segments. The level of advertising income for a magazine title depends on the range of titles in the customer segment to which the magazine title relates. Management has a policy to abandon old titles before the end of their economic lives and replace them immediately with new titles for the same customer segment.

What is the cash-generating unit for an individual magazine title?

Solution

It is likely that the recoverable amount of an individual magazine title can be assessed. Even though the level of advertising income for a title is influenced, to a certain extent, by the other titles in the customer segment, cash inflows from direct sales and advertising are identifiable for each title. In addition, although titles are managed by customer segments, decisions to abandon titles are made on an individual title basis.

Therefore, it is likely that individual magazine titles generate cash inflows that are largely independent one from another and that each magazine title is a separate cash-generating unit.

10.8 Identification of cash generating units

If an active market exists for the output produced by the asset or a group of assets, this asset or group should be identified as a cash generating unit, even if some or all of the output is used internally.

Cash generating units should be identified consistently from period to period for the same type of asset unless a change is justified.

The group of net assets less liabilities that are considered for impairment should be the same as those considered in the calculation of the recoverable amount. (For the treatment of goodwill and corporate assets see below.)

Example

Fourways Co. is made up of four cash generating units. All four units are being tested for impairment.

- Property, plant and equipment and separate intangibles would be allocated to be cash generating units as far as possible.

- Current assets such as inventories, receivables and prepayments would be allocated to the relevant cash generating units.

- Liabilities (e.g. payables) would be deducted from the net assets of the relevant cash generating units.

- The net figure for each cash generating unit resulting from this exercise would be compared to the relevant recoverable amount, computed on the same basis.

10.9 Accounting treatment of an impairment loss

If, and only if, the recoverable amount of an asset is less than its carrying amount in the statement of financial position, an impairment loss has occurred. This loss should be **recognised immediately**.

- The asset's **carrying amount** should be reduced to its recoverable amount in the statement of financial position.

- The **impairment loss** should be recognised immediately in the income statement (unless the asset has been revalued in which case the loss is treated as a revaluation decrease; see earlier in chapter).

After reducing an asset to its recoverable amount, the **depreciation charge** on the asset should then be based on its new carrying amount, its estimated residual value (if any) and its estimated remaining useful life.

An impairment loss should be recognised for a **cash generating unit** if (and only if) the recoverable amount for the cash generating unit is less than the carrying amount in the statement of financial position for all the assets in the unit. When an impairment loss is recognised for a cash generating unit, the loss should be allocated between the assets in the unit in the following order.

- First, to any assets that are obviously damaged or destroyed.
- Next, to the **goodwill** allocated to the cash generating unit.
- Then to all other assets in the cash-generating unit, on a **_pro rata_ basis**.

In allocating an impairment loss, the carrying amount of an asset should not be reduced below the highest of

- Its fair value less costs to sell.
- Its value in use (if determinable).
- Zero.

Any remaining amount of an impairment loss should be recognised as a liability if required by other IASs.

Example

A company has acquired another business for £4.5m: tangible assets are valued at £4.0m and goodwill at £0.5m.

An asset with a carrying value of £1m is destroyed in a terrorist attack. The asset was not insured.
The loss of the asset, without insurance, has prompted the company to assess whether there has been an impairment of assets in the acquired business and what the amount of any such loss is.

The recoverable amount of the business (a single cash generating unit) is measured as £3.1m.

Solution

There has been an impairment loss of £1.4m (£4.5m – £3.1m).

The impairment loss will be recognised in the income statement. The loss will be allocated between the assets in the cash generating unit as follows.

A loss of £1m can be attributed directly to the uninsured asset that has been destroyed.

- The remaining loss of £0.4m should be allocated to goodwill.
- The carrying value of the assets will now be £3m for tangible assets and £0.1m for goodwill.

10.10 Reversal of an impairment loss

The annual assessment to determine whether there may have been some impairment should be **applied to all assets**, including assets that have already been impaired in the past.

In some cases, the recoverable amount of an asset that has previously been impaired might turn out to be **higher** than the asset's current carrying value. In other words, there might have been a reversal of some of the previous impairment loss.

- The reversal of the impairment loss should be **recognised immediately** as income in the income statement.

- The carrying amount of the asset should be increased to its **new recoverable amount**.

> An impairment loss recognised for an asset in prior years should be recovered if, and only if, there has been a change in the estimates used to determine the asset's recoverable amount since the last impairment loss was recognised.

The asset cannot be revalued to a carrying amount that is higher than its value would have been if the asset had not been impaired originally, i.e. its **depreciated carrying value** had the impairment not taken place. Depreciation of the asset should now be based on its new revalued amount, its estimated residual value (if any) and its estimated remaining useful life.

An exception to this rule is for **goodwill**. An impairment loss for goodwill must not be reversed in a subsequent period.

Example

A cash generating unit comprising a factory, plant and equipment etc and associated purchased goodwill becomes impaired because the product it makes is overtaken by a technologically more advanced model produced by a competitor. The recoverable amount of the cash generating unit falls to £60m, resulting in an impairment loss of £80m, allocated as follows.

	Carrying Amounts before Impairment (£m)	Carrying Amounts after Impairment (£m)
Goodwill	40	–
Patent (with no market value)	20	–
Tangible Non-Current Assets (market value £60m)	80	60
Total	140	60

After three years, the entity makes a technological breakthrough of its own, and the recoverable amount of the cash generating unit increases to £90m. The carrying amount of the tangible non-current assets had the impairment not occurred would have been £70m.

Required

Calculate the reversal of the impairment loss.

Solution

The reversal of the impairment loss is recognised to the extent that it increases the carrying amount of the tangible non-current assets to what it would have been had the impairment not taken place, i.e. a reversal of the impairment loss of £10m is recognised and the tangible non-current assets written back to £70m. Reversal of the impairment is not recognised in relation to the goodwill and patent because the effect of the external event that caused the original impairment has not reversed – the original product is still overtaken by a more advanced model.

10.11 Disclosure

IAS 36 calls for substantial disclosure about impairment of assets. The information to be disclosed includes the following.

- For each class of assets, the amount of **impairment losses recognised** and the amount of any **impairment losses recovered** (i.e. reversals of impairment losses).

- For each individual asset or cash generating unit that has suffered a **significant impairment loss**, details of the nature of the asset, the amount of the loss, the events that led to recognition of the loss, whether the recoverable amount is fair value less costs to sell or value in use, and if the recoverable amount is value in use, the basis on which this value was estimated (e.g. the discount rate applied).

CHAPTER ROUNDUP

You need to be able to discuss and undertake basic calculations in respect of

- Depreciation definitions

    - **Depreciation** is the result of systematic allocation of the depreciable amount of an asset over its estimated useful life. Depreciation for the accounting period is charged to net profit or loss for the period either directly or indirectly.

    - **Depreciable assets** are assets which

        - Are expected to be used during more than one accounting period.

        - Have a limited useful life.

        - Are held by an entity for use in the production or supply of goods and services, for rental to others, or for administrative purposes.

    - **Useful life** is one of two things.

        - The period over which a depreciable asset is expected to be used by the entity; or

        - The number of production or similar units expected to be obtained from the asset by the entity.

    - **Depreciable amount** of a depreciable asset is the historical cost or other amount substituted for cost in the financial statements, less the estimated residual value. *(IAS 16)*

- Depreciation calculations

    - Straight-line basis

        - $\text{Depreciation} = \dfrac{\text{Cost} - \text{Residual value}}{\text{Expected useful life}}$

    - Reducing balance basis

        - $\text{Depreciation} = 1 - \sqrt[n]{\dfrac{\text{Residual value}}{\text{Cost}}}$

    - Sum of digits basis

    - Reducing balance basis

- Disposal and profit disposal

- IAS 16 *Property, Plant and Equipment* definitions

    - **Property, plant and equipment** are tangible assets that

        - Are held for use in the production or supply of goods or services, for rental to others, or for administrative purposes; and

        - Are expected to be used during more than one period.

    - **Cost** is the amount of cash or cash equivalents paid or the fair value of the other consideration given to acquire an asset at the time of its acquisition or construction.

    - **Residual value** is the net amount which the entity expects to obtain for an asset at the end of its useful life after deducting the expected costs of disposal.

BPP
LEARNING MEDIA

- **Fair value** is the amount for which an asset could be exchanged between knowledgeable, willing parties in an arm's length transaction.

- **Carrying amount** is the amount at which an asset is recognised in the statement of financial position after deducting any accumulated depreciation and accumulated impairment losses.

- An **impairment loss** is the amount by which the carrying amount of an asset exceeds its recoverable amount.

  (IAS 16)

■ IAS 16 *Property, Plant and Equipment* requirements regarding

- Recognition of cost
- Revaluations
- Depreciation of revalued assets
- Impairments

■ IAS 20 *Government Grants* requirements regarding

- Methods

  - **Capital approach**: credit the grant directly to shareholders' interests.
  - **Income approach**: the grant is credited to the income statement over one or more periods.

- Grants for non-depreciable assets

■ IAS 40 *Investment Property* requirements regarding

- Definition of an investment property

  - **Investment property** is property (land or a building – or part of a building – or both) held (by the owner or by the lessee under a finance lease) to earn rentals or for capital appreciation or both, rather than for

    - Use in the production or supply of goods or services or for administrative purposes; or
    - Sale in the ordinary course of business.

  - **Owner-occupied property** is property held by the owner (or by the lessee under a finance lease) for use in the production or supply of goods or services or for administrative purposes.

  - **Fair value** is the amount for which an asset could be exchanged between knowledgeable, willing parties in an arm's length transaction.

  - **Cost** is the amount of cash or cash equivalents paid or the fair value of other consideration given to acquire an asset at the time of its acquisition or construction.

  - **Carrying amount** is the amount at which an asset is recognised in the statement of financial position.

  - A property interest that is held by a lessee under an **operating lease** may be classified and accounted for as an **investment property**, if and only if the property would otherwise meet the definition of an investment property and the lessee uses the IAS 40 **fair value model**. This classification is available on a property-by-property basis.

- Accounting treatment

■ Intangible assets and IAS 38

- Definition of intangibles

  - An **intangible asset** is an identifiable non-monetary asset without physical substance The asset must be

    - Controlled by the entity as a result of events in the past; and

- – Something from which the entity expects future economic benefits to flow.

- – Recognition of intangibles

  - – Internally generated goodwill may **not** be recognised as an **asset**.

- – The treatment of research and development costs

- – Accounting treatment and amortisation.

- ■ Goodwill and IFRS 3

  - – Definition
  - – Valuation

- ■ IAS 36 *Impairment of Assets*

  - – Definition

    - – Impairment: a fall in the value of an asset, so that its 'recoverable amount' is now less than its carrying value in the statement of financial position.

    - – Impairment is determined by comparing the carrying amount of the asset with its recoverable amount.

  - – Measurement

    - – **Carrying amount**: is the net value at which the asset is included in the statement of financial position (i.e. after deducting accumulated depreciation and any impairment losses).

    - – The **recoverable amount of an asset** should be measured as the *higher value* of

      - – The asset's fair value less costs to sell; and

      - – Its value in use.   *(IAS 36)*

    - – The **value in use** of an asset is measured as the present value of estimated future cash flows (inflows minus outflows) generated by the asset, including its estimated net disposal value (if any) at the end of its expected useful life.

  - – Recognition and measurement of an impairment loss

    - – If the recoverable amount of an asset is lower than the carrying amount, the carrying amount should be reduced by the difference (ie the impairment loss) which should be charged as an expense in the income statement.

    - – The impairment loss is to be treated as a revaluation decrease under the relevant IAS.

  - – Accounting treatment

TEST YOUR KNOWLEDGE

Check your knowledge of the chapter here, without referring back to the text.

1. (a) France Limited purchased a building for £50,000 on January 2 2001. It is depreciating the building on a straight-line basis over 50 years to a nil net book value. What will be the net book value as at December 31 2006?

    (b) France Limited decides to revalue the building to a value of £49,000 at December 31 2007. What will be the balance on the revaluation reserve at that date?

    (c) France Limited also decides to extend the useful life of the building by another ten years at December 31 2007. What will be the annual depreciation charge in subsequent years?

    (d) France Limited identifies at December 31 2008 that the building has suffered an impairment in value. Subsequent review determines that the market value of the building is now £36,000 and the value in use of the building is £38,000. Assuming that no depreciation has been charged yet for 2008, how will this impairment be accounted for in the financial statements for that year if the impairment has been caused by

    (i) A general slump in the property market?
    (ii) Identification of irreparable physical deterioration to the building?

    (e) Germany Limited buys a car for £15,000 on January 2 2005 and decides to depreciate it down to a net book value of around £2,000 over a four-year period. What is the net book value of the car as at December 31 2006 using

    (i) Straight-line depreciation?
    (ii) Reducing balance depreciation at an annual rate of 40%?

    (f) Assuming that Germany Limited has used straight-line depreciation, it is decided at December 31 2006 that the company will keep the car for another three years and then scrap it as worthless. What will be the annual depreciation charge in 2007?

    (g) Spain Limited buys some plant and machinery at a cost of £20,000 on April 3 2005. Its year end is December 31 each year. A full year's depreciation is charged in the accounting year in which assets are purchased, but nothing is charged in the year that they are sold. The machinery has an estimated useful life of nine years and an expected residual value at the end of its life of £2,000. What is the annual depreciation charge?

    (h) Spain Limited actually sells the plant and machinery on June 6 2007 for £6,000. What is the profit or loss on disposal of the machinery?

Non-Current Assets Quiz

2. (a) Name four different types of intangible asset.
    (b) After initial recognition of an intangible asset, is it possible to revalue it?
    (c) How are non-current assets defined under IFRS?
    (d) Name four types of non-current asset that are often not depreciated in a company's accounts.
    (e) What is the purpose of depreciation?
    (f) When must an impairment review normally be carried out?

3.   IAS 38 *Intangible Assets* defines the terms 'research' and 'development' in relation to internally generated intangible assets. The Standard also lays down rules which must be applied to the capitalisation of research and development expenditure.

Requirements

(a)   Distinguish between 'research' and 'development'.

(b)   Explain the criteria applied to research and development expenditure, according to IAS 38, to determine whether such costs should be expensed or capitalised.

4.   You are the management accountant of Historic Ltd. Historic Ltd makes up its financial statements to 30 September each year. The financial statements for the year ended 30 September 20X1 are currently being prepared. The directors have always included non-current assets under the historical cost convention. However, for the current year, they are considering revaluing some of the non-current assets. They obtained professional valuations as at 1 October 20X0 for the two properties owned by the company. Details of the valuations were as follows.

	Historical Cost NBV £'000	Existing Use Fair Value £'000	Open Market Value £'000
Property One	15,000	16,800	17,500
Property Two	14,000	12,000	12,500

No acquisitions or disposals of properties have taken place since 1 October 20X0 and none is expected in the near future. The buildings element of the two properties comprises 50% of both historical cost and the revalued amounts. Each property is reckoned to have a useful economic life to the company of 40 years from 1 October 20X0.

Given the results of the valuations, the directors propose to include Property One at its open market value in the financial statements for the year to 30 September 20X1. They wish to leave Property Two at its historical cost. They have no plans to revalue the other non-current assets of the company, which are plant and fixtures.

Requirements

(a)   State briefly the key arguments for and against including non-current assets at revalued amounts.

(b)   Evaluate the directors' proposal to revalue Property One as at 1 October 20X0 but to leave all other non-current assets at historical cost. Your answer should include reference to appropriate accounting standards.

(c)   The directors have decided to revalue the non-current assets of the company in accordance with their original wishes, amended where necessary to comply with appropriate accounting standards. Compute the net book value of each property as at 30 September 20X1. You should clearly explain where any differences on revaluation will be shown in the financial statements.

5.   What are the main characteristics of goodwill which distinguish it from other intangible assets? To what extent do you consider that these characteristics should affect the accounting treatment of goodwill?

State your reasons.

Test Your Knowledge: Answers

1. (a)

	(£)
Cost	50,000
Depreciation (6 years × £1,000)	(6,000)
Net book value at 31.12.2006	44,000

(b)

	(£)
Net book value at 31.12.07	43,000
Revalued amount	49,000
Revaluation surplus	6,000

(c)

	(£)
Revalued amount at 31.12.07	£49,000
Remaining useful life	53 years
Annual depreciation	£925

(d) The carrying amount of the building must be reduced to reflect the impairment. the amount of the impairment is £11,000, being the excess of the carrying amount of the asset (£49,000) over its 'recoverable amount' (£38,000). The asset's recoverable amount is the higher of its fair value less costs to sell (£36,000) and its value in use (£38,000).

The impairment would be accounted for as follows.

Non-current assets down by £11,000	(£49,000 NBV down to £38,000 recoverable amount)
Revaluation reserve down by £6,000 – disclosed in the statement of total recognised income and expense for the year	(Being the amount of the impairment loss represented by surpluses on previous revaluations of that same asset)
Profit of 2007 down £5,000	(Being the balance of the impairment loss)

(e) Straight line

	(£)
Cost	15,000
Depreciation (2 years × £3,250)	(6,500)
Net book value at 31.12.06	8,500

Annual depreciation = (15,000 – 2,000)/4 = £3,250

Reducing balance

	(£)
Cost	15,000
2005 depreciation (40% × 15,000)	(6,000)
Net book value at 31.12.05	9,000
2006 depreciation (40% × 9,000)	(3,600)
Net book value at 31.12.06	5,400

Note that, with reducing balance, there is no need to deduct the expected residual value from the original cost before applying the 40% factor. Applying the 40% factor to cost in Year 1 and net book value figures in future years will automatically reduce the net book value to the expected value in four years of £2,000.

(f)

	(£)
Net book value (see above)	£8,500
Remaining useful life	3 years
Scrap value	nil
Revised annual depreciation (8,500 × $\frac{1}{3}$)	£2,833

(g) Depreciation = (20,000 − 2,000)/9 = £2,000 per year

(h)

	(£)
Cost	20,000
Depreciation (2 years × £2,000)	(4,000)
Net book value	16,000
Sale proceeds	6,000
Less: NBV at date of sale	(16,000)
Loss on sale	(10,000)

2. Non-Current Assets Quiz

(a) Goodwill, brands, publishing rights and titles, patents, licenses, copyrights, computer software, development costs, customer lists and relationships.

(b) IAS 38 allows entities that have initially recognised an intangible asset to choose, as a matter of accounting policy, between the cost model and the revaluation model when subsequently measuring that asset.

If the revaluation model is chosen, the fair value of the asset must be determined by reference to an 'active market'. Active markets must meet all the following criteria.

(i) Items traded in the market are homogeneous.
(ii) Willing buyers and sellers can normally be found at any time.
(iii) Prices are available to the public.

In practice very few intangible assets meet the criteria; as a result most intangibles are accounted for under the cost model.

(c) IAS 1 defines a non-current asset as 'any asset other than a current asset'.

BPP LEARNING MEDIA

(d)   *Property, plant and machinery*

Land and investment properties (if accounted for under the fair value model).

Intangibles

Goodwill arising on a business combination and other intangibles with indefinite useful lives. An annual impairment review is required in these cases.

(e)   To allocate the cost of an asset to theincome statement, as an expense over the useful life of the asset. Depreciation is an application of the 'accruals' or 'matching concept'.

(f)   When there are indicators that the asset or assets in question have suffered impairment examples of such indicators are

- Evidence of obsolescence.
- Significant technological or economic change.
- Reduced profits or cash inflows from use of the assets.

In addition, annual impairment reviews must be carried outin relation to goodwill and other intangible assets that have indefinite useful lives.

3.   (a)   IAS 38 recognises two phases of research and development activity in relation to internally generated intangible assets.

(i)   **Research** is original and planned investigation undertaken with the prospect of gaining new scientific or technical knowledge and understanding.

(ii)   **Development** is the application of research findings or other knowledge to a plan or design for the production of new or substantially improved materials, devices, products, processes, systems or sevices before the start of commercial production or use.

(b)   Expenditure on research must be recognised as an expense in the period in which it is incurred. This reflects the fact that, at this stage, it cannot be demonstrated that an asset exists that will generate probable future economic benefits.

Development expenditure must be capitalised if and only if it satisfies all of the following conditions.

(i)   Technical feasibility of completing the intangible asset.

(ii)   Intention to complete the intangible asset and use or sell it.

(iii)   Ability to use or sell the intangible asset.

(iv)   How the intangible will generate probable future economic benefits.

(v)   Availability of adequate technical, financial and other resources to complete the development and to use or sell the intangible asset.

(vi)   Ability to measure reliably the expenditure attributable to the intangible asset during its development

4.   (a)   **Arguments for revaluing property, plant and equipment**

(i)   **Consistency and comparability** are important qualities of financial information. If all the assets in a particular class are revalued at the same time, there is consistency and comparability in the financial statements.

(ii)   Subsequent depreciation charges are a better reflection of the economic benefits consumed by such assets.

(iii)   Higher carrying values for tangible non-current assets have a **favourable effect** on the reporting entity's **capital gearing**.

(iv) **Relevance and reliability** are also commonly seen as desirable characteristics of financial information. Gross amounts for revalued assets are up to date, relevant and fairly reliable.

Arguments against revaluing property, plant and equipment.

(i) Carrying out revaluations is a **costly and time-consuming** exercise.

(ii) It may not be practical to carry out all revaluations at the same time. This can lead to **inconsistencies in reported carrying values**, particularly if the market for the assets is highly volatile.

(iii) The revaluation process is **subjective** and there is a danger that users will believe the statement of financial position is a statement of the worth of the reporting entity.

(iv) Upward revaluations lead to **higher depreciation charges** and therefore **lower reported profits**, with subsequent effects on financial performance measures such as ROCE.

(v) The above may mean that only some assets are revalued (even if this includes all of one class of non-current asset such as freehold properties). The resulting **financial statements may then be a hybrid of replacement** of fair value and historical cost.

(b) **Proposal to revalue Property One only**

The required treatment is governed byIAS 16 *Property, Plant and Equipment*. If the directors decide on a **policy of revaluing** property, plant and equipment, **all the assets in a particular class must be revalued**. These valuations must be **kept up-to-date**. IAS 16 does not specify the frequency of revaluations, only that they 'must be made with sufficient regularity to ensure that the carrying amount does not differ materially from fair value at the statement of financial position date'.

Valuations of land and buildings should usually be based on market-based evidence by appraisal that is normally undertaken by professionally qualified valuers. The directors cannot 'cherry pick' which properties they choose to revalue; the process must be consistent. They will need to report all revaluation gains and losses if they adopt a policy of revaluing properties. The **fall in value of Property Two will need to be recognised** as part of this policy.

Following IAS 16, it will be quite acceptable to retain the carrying values of other classes of property, plant and equipment (namely plant and fixtures) at their historical cost, less depreciation.

(c) **Net book values of revalued properties at 30 September 20X1**

	Property One (£'000)	Property Two (£'000)	Totals (£'000)
Historical cost net book value at 01.01.20X0	15,000	14,000	29,000
Revaluation gain	1,800		1,800
Revaluation loss/deficit		(2,000)	(2,000)
Gross value at 30.09.20X1	16,800	12,000	28,800
Depreciation to 30.09.20X1			
$(16,800 \times 50\% \times 1/40)$	210		
$(12,000 \times 50\% \times 1.40)$		150	360
Net book value at 30.09.20X1	16,590	11,850	28,440

The £1.8m **revaluation gain** on Property One should be credited to the non-distributable revaluation reserve. It should also be reported/recognised in the statement of **total recognised** income and expense for the year ended 30 September 20X1.

As Property Two has not been previously revalued, the £2m deficit should be reported / recognised in the income statement for the year ended 30 September 20X1. This is effectively an **impairment charge** or a reflection of the fact that depreciation over the property's previous years of use was understated.

5. An intangible asset (other than goodwill) is defined in IAS 38 as 'an identifiable non-monetary asset without physical substance'. An asset is identifiable when it

(a) Is separable, i.e. is capable of being separated or divided from the entity; or
(b) Arises from contractual or other legal rights.

Goodwill does not meet the above definition of an intangible asset because it is not identifiable. Goodwill is an **unidentifiable** non-monetary asset without physical substance. Goodwill can be either be purchased (e.g. in a business combination) or internally generated. In a business combination it represents a payment made by the acquirer in anticipation of future economic benefits from assets that are not capable of being individually identified and recognised separately; it is effectively a residual amount, ie a balancing figure. Internally generated goodwill arises from incurring expenditure that does not result in creating an intangible asset that can be identified and recognised in its own right.

The accounting treatment of goodwill follows from its characteristic of lack of identifiability.

(a) **Acquired in a business combination** – recognise initially in the consolidated financial statements at cost. Because it is not possible to estimate its useful economic life, do not amortise but test for impairment annually.

(b) **Internally generated** – do not recognise because it is not an identifiable resource controlled by the entity that can be measured reliably at cost.

The fundamental problem of accounting for goodwill is that it is often a valuable economic resource but is not recognised in financial statements as it often fails the test of what constitutes reliable measurement.

4

Current Assets

INTRODUCTION

The current assets of a business are the short-term resources that the business may call on in order to trade. A business will be seeking to turn these resources into cash in the short term, preferably at a profit.

There are several categories of current asset and we need to know

- What each one is

- How they are valued and reflected in the account

You will see that accounting rules do, at times, offer alternative treatments and you should ensure that you can contrast these alternatives and their impacts on financial statements and analysis.

CHAPTER LEARNING OBJECTIVES

The syllabus areas covered by this chapter are

Interpretation of Financial Information

The effect of accounting practices

Understanding of the effect of accounting practices on the numbers most significant for investment decisions (profit, earnings per share, asset value etc).

Accounting terminology and concepts

Accounting terminology and a knowledge of accounting concepts and conventions to include the statement of financial position, income statement, statement of cash flows and notes to the accounts. An understanding of the distinction between capital and revenue, the valuation of assets for accounting purposes and the determination of profit and earnings share on the nil, net and full distribution bases. An understanding of significance of the statement of accounting policies in relation to the concept of a true and fair view.

Presentation of Financial Statements

Impact of statutory and non-statutory regulation on UK financial statements.

An understanding of the effect on the presentation of financial statements of the Companies Acts and non-statutory regulations, including standards and other guidance issued by IASB and stock exchange requirements.

In respect of current assets:

It is emphasised that the intention of the examination is to assess students' analytical and interpretative skills rather than their technical accounting ability. It is also expected that they should have an understanding of standard accounting practices and an awareness of matters currently under discussion.

1 INTRODUCTION

1.1 Definition

IAS 1 defines current assets as cash, cash equivalents, assets held for collection, sale or consumption within the enterprises' normal operating cycle or assets held for trading with the next 12 months.

Example

Tomkins Group Interim Consolidated statement of financial position as at 2 July 2005	2 July 2005 (£m)	3 July 2004 (£m)
Current Assets		
Inventories	419.1	352.1
Trade and other receivables	599.3	546.2
Current tax recoverable	5.9	12.3
Investments	2.2	1.6
Cash and cash equivalents	165.2	168.0
	1,191.7	1,080.2

As we can see, current assets are sub-categorised and the main categories are

- **Inventories** – goods held available for sale.

- **Accounts receivable** – amounts owed to the company, perhaps as a result of selling goods on credit.

- **Investments (marketable securities)** – shares held in the short term with the intention of reselling, e.g. short-term speculative investments (see Chapter 11).

- **Cash and cash equivalents** – at bank or in hand, both sterling and foreign currencies (see Chapter 8).

We will consider each main category in turn, examining the supporting notes to the accounts to see what we will be provided with in the financial statements, and consider the accounting rules that are applied in evaluating these items.

1.2 General valuation rule

In valuing current assets generally, the accounting concept of prudence is applied, i.e. all current assets are valued at the lower of

- Cost.

- Net realisable value (NRV), i.e. estimated selling price less estimated costs of completion and estimated costs necessary to make the sale.

This provides a prudent valuation of our assets and profits, as

- If the NRV exceeds cost the asset is valued at cost, i.e. no profit is anticipated.
- If the NRV is less than cost the asset is revalued down to NRV, i.e. a loss is recognised.

1.3 Working capital cycle

Exam tip

> The idea of and analysis of the working capital cycle very regularly features in the exam, e.g. Summer 2006 Question 1, Summer 2004 Question 2, Winter 2003 Question 3.

Current assets include three of the four components of the **working capital cycle**, which is illustrated below. Consideration of the working capital cycle is important in the context of understanding the liquidity position of a company.

1.3.1 Diagrammatically

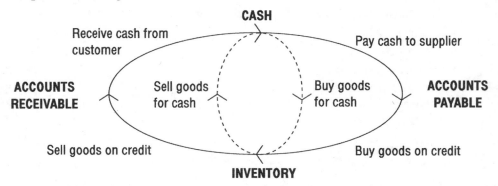

This diagram shows how cash is generated and used in the normal day-to-day operations of the business.

1.4 Value of working capital/Length of working capital cycle

1.4.1 Cash business

If we consider a business that simply buys and sells inventory for cash, then cash will be used to buy inventory and later, that inventory will be sold (hopefully at a higher price) realising a small amount of profit and a larger amount of cash (the inner dotted arrows on our working capital cycle).

In this situation, the time it takes to turn stock inventory into cash (say six weeks) will be the length of our working capital cycle. Clearly, however, we will need to have cash during this time to pay our staff salaries on a weekly basis and any other business expenses for those six weeks.

Therefore, the business must have sufficient financial resources to hold this inventory for six weeks and have cash to pay any other expenses if we are to continue trading. The total financial resources we need (inventory + cash) is our working capital requirement.

1.4.2 Sell on credit

If a company then starts to make sales on credit, the inventory asset will then be converted into a receivable asset of a higher value (since the asset is being sold at a profit). Later, say after three weeks, the receivable will pay up, converting into cash (the left-hand arrows above).

Clearly now the working capital cycle is longer. The time required to get our cash back is

- The six weeks it takes to sell the inventory.
- Plus three weeks required to convert the resultant receivable to cash.

The working capital cycle is now nine weeks long and the company must have sufficient financial resources to be able to afford to be without this cash for nine weeks, i.e. our Working capital requirement now = Inventory + Receivables + Cash.

1.4.3 Buy on credit

If, lastly, we can acquire our inventory on credit and do not have to pay for four weeks, then our working capital cycle reduces to five weeks (nine weeks – four weeks) and the amount of cash required to finance the day-to-day operations falls.

Our payables are effectively financing our inventory for four weeks free of charge. We only need to finance the last two weeks it will take to sell it and the three weeks it will take to recover the debt. In this final situation, our Working capital requirement = Inventory + Receivables + Cash – Payables.

1.5 Relevance

Different businesses have different working capital cycles and require different amounts of working capital depending on their operations. No one level of working capital could ever be considered as optimal for all businesses, hence it is impossible to say if a particular liquidity ratio is good or bad.

What we should always try to ensure with the working capital cycle is that the flow of cash is at a steady rate so that cash outflows are balanced by cash inflows. If we ever find we have a mismatch in this rate of flow of cash into and out of the business, then we may suffer liquidity problems.

Example

To illustrate this point, let us consider two different types of business at completely different ends of the working capital scale – a house builder and a supermarket.

House builder

A house builder may have a one-month credit period from his suppliers. However, the house builder will take quite some time to convert those raw materials (bricks and mortar) into finished goods (houses) that he can then sell.

It may take perhaps six months to build the houses on an estate and get them into a saleable condition. Even if these sales are then for cash, the builder will still need to find financing for five months' worth of purchases if business is continuous. If the sales are on credit terms, the situation gets even worse, i.e. the working capital requirements and the length of the working capital cycle grow.

In manufacturing businesses, there tends to be a long working capital cycle and correspondingly significant working capital requirement to finance the business for the number of months it may need to operate between when it has to pay for its supplies and when it receives money from its customers.

Supermarket

In a supermarket, inventory is acquired that will be sold within just a few days. The inventory will be sold for cash (very few people have an account with a supermarket). Hence, the conversion of the inventory asset into cash takes a very short time indeed.

This inventory in turn will have been acquired on credit, which may be quite long. We may therefore find that we are buying inventory on credit for which we do not have to pay for say 30 days, but that this inventory is being converted into cash within say, ten days.

Here, we have 20 days' interest free credit provided from our suppliers (we have cash in hand for 20 days that we owe to our suppliers but on which we pay no interest). The length of this working capital cycle is **minus** 20 days.

Therefore, so long as we are considered creditworthy, we need no financial resources at all to carry out our day-to-day operations, as they are wholly financed by our payables.

In Chapter 10, we will explain how we can use the information in the financial statements to calculate and interpret a company's working capital cycle.

2 IAS 2 INVENTORIES

2.1 Introduction

To determine the profit for the year we must match revenues and the cost of goods sold. This should not be thought of simply as all the goods purchased during the period since clearly some of the goods that have been purchased may be unsold at the year end and remain in inventory at that date. The costs of any unconsumed inventory must be carried forward and matched against future years' profits (when sold) in accordance with the accruals concept.

Example

The illustration below shows the accounting policies and the supporting note for inventory that tie back to the statement of financial position extract above.

Roche Group

Extracts from notes to the accounts as at 31 December 2004

Accounting policies

Inventories

Inventories are stated at the lower of cost or net realisable value. The cost of finished goods and work in process comprises raw materials, direct labour and other directly attributable costs and overheads based upon normal capacity of production facilities. Borrowing costs are not included. Cost is determined using the weighted average method. Net realisable value is the estimated selling price less cost to completion and selling expenses.

Statement of financial position notes

Inventories in millions of CHF	2004	2003
Raw materials and supplies	533	606
Work in process	621	590
Finished goods and intermediates	3,565	4,006
Less: provision for slow-moving obsolete inventory	(145)	(177)
Total inventories	4,574	5,025

2.2 IAS 2 (Revised) Inventories

IAS 2 was revised in December 2003. It lays out the required accounting treatment for inventories (sometimes called stocks) under the historical cost system. The major area of contention is the cost **value of inventory** to be recorded. This is recognised as an asset of the entity until the related revenues are recognised (i.e. the item is sold) at which point the inventory is recognised as an expense (i.e. cost of sales). Part or all of the cost of inventories may also be expensed if a write-down to **net realisable value** is necessary. The revised IAS also provides guidance on the cost formulae that are used to assign costs to inventories.

In other words, the fundamental accounting assumption of **accruals** requires costs to be matched with associated revenues. In order to achieve this, costs incurred for goods which remain unsold at the year end must be carried forward in the statement of financial position and matched against future revenues.

2.3 Definitions

The Standard gives the following important definitions.

- Inventories are assets
    - Held for sale in the ordinary course of business;
    - In the process of production for such sale; or
    - In the form of materials or supplies to be consumed in the production process or in the rendering of services.
- **Net realisable value** is the estimated selling price in the ordinary course of business less the estimated costs of completion and the estimated costs necessary to make the sale.
- **Fair value** is the amount for which an asset could be exchanged or a liability settled between knowledgeable, willing parties in an arm's length transaction. *(IAS 2)*

Inventories can **include** any of the following.

- **Goods purchased and held for resale**, e.g. goods held for sale by a retailer, or land and buildings held for resale.
- **Finished goods** produced.
- **Work in progress** being produced.
- Materials and supplies awaiting use in the production process (**raw materials**).

2.4 Measurement of Inventories

The Standard states that '**inventories should be measured at the lower of cost and net realisable value**'.

Exam tip	This is a very important rule and you will be expected to apply it in the exam.

2.5 Cost of inventories

The cost of inventories will consist of all costs of

- Purchase.
- Costs of conversion.
- Other costs incurred in bringing the inventories to their present location and condition.

2.5.1 Costs of purchase

The Standard lists the following as comprising the costs of purchase of inventories.

- Purchase price; plus
- Import duties and other taxes; plus
- Transport, handling and any other cost directly attributable to the acquisition of finished goods, services and materials; less
- Trade discounts, rebates and other similar amounts.

2.5.2 Costs of conversion

Costs of conversion of inventories consist of two main parts.

- Costs **directly related** to the units of production, e.g. direct materials, direct labour.

- Fixed and variable **production overheads** that are incurred in converting materials into finished goods, allocated on a systematic basis.

2.5.3 Other costs

Any other costs should only be recognised if they are incurred in bringing the inventories to their **present location and condition**.

The Standard lists types of cost which **would not be included** in cost of inventories. Instead, they should be recognised as an **expense** in the period they are incurred.

- **Abnormal amounts** of wasted materials, labour or other production costs.

- **Storage costs** (except costs which are necessary in the production process before a further production stage).

- **Administrative overheads** not incurred to bring inventories to their present location and conditions.

- **Selling costs**.

2.6 Net realisable value (NRV)

As a general rule assets should not be carried at amounts greater than those expected to be realised from their sale or use. In the case of inventories this amount could fall below cost when items are **damaged or become obsolete**, or where the **costs to completion have increased** in order to make the sale.

In fact we can identify the principal situations in which **NRV is likely to be less than cost**, i.e. where there has been

- An **increase in costs** or a **fall in selling price**.
- A **physical deterioration** in the condition of inventory.
- **Obsolescence** of products.
- A decision as part of the company's marketing strategy to manufacture and sell products at a **loss**.
- **Errors in production or purchasing**.

A write down of inventories would normally take place on an item by item basis, but similar or related items may be **grouped together**. This grouping together is acceptable for, say, items in the same product line, but it is not acceptable to write down inventories based on a whole classification (e.g. finished goods) or a whole business.

Example

A company undertakes the following transactions in this chronological order.

Buy/Sell	Number of Units	Price £	Value £
Buy	100	10	1,000
Sell	60	20	1,200
Buy	50	12	600
Sell	40	20	800
Buy	10	14	140

What is the closing value of inventory and the reported profit on these transactions?

Solution

Introduction

Regardless of how we value the inventory

- The total sales have been 100 units at £20, i.e. £2,000.
- The total number and cost of units acquired has been 160 units at £1,740.

As a result, the cost of 100 of the 160 units bought must be treated as the cost of sales, the rest of the cost being carried forward in inventory to be matched against revenues in the future when those goods are sold. But how do we split the cost of £1,740 associated with these 160 units?

What are the main possible bases for evaluating this inventory, and what will be the impact on our statement of financial position and reported profits of applying them?

FIFO

The first-in, first-out basis means literally what it says, i.e. the first units bought are the first ones sold. As a result, if we have any inventory at a particular point in time, it must represent the latest units purchased.

It can perhaps be visualised as a tube where items are put in at one end when they are bought, and taken out from the other end when they are sold. What is left in the tube will always be the last ones bought.

In our example, we have bought 160 units and only sold 100 and we therefore have 60 units left in inventory.

Under the FIFO basis, we would take these to be the last 60 purchased and evaluate them as follows.

Purchase	Number of Units	Unit Price (£)	Total (£)
Last but one	50	12	600
Latest	10	14	140
	60		740

Our reported profits could now be calculated as follows.

Income Statement	(£)	(£)
Revenue		2,000
Cost of sales		
Opening inventory	–	
Purchases (1,000 + 600 + 140)	1,740	
Less: Closing inventory	(740)	
		1,000
Profit		1,000

An obvious alternative here would be to say that the 100 units sold were the first 100 purchased and as such, cost £1,000. This can easily be done for this short example but would be less practical if there were many purchases and sales throughout the year. In this situation, it will be much more convenient to evaluate the few units that remain in inventory.

Simple weighted average

Under the simple weighted average method of evaluating units of inventory, units are not distinguished. Rather, an average cost for all units purchased in the period is calculated and all units either sold or held are evaluated at this amount, thus

$$\text{Simple average price} = \frac{£1,740}{160} = £10.875$$

Closing inventory value = £652.50 (60 × £10.875)

The reported profit under this basis of evaluating our inventory is

Income Statement	(£)	(£)
Revenue		2,000
Cost of sales		
Opening inventory	–	
Purchases (1,000 + 600 + 140)	1,740	
Less: Closing inventory	(653)	
		1,087
Profit		913

Moving weighted average

Under the moving weighted average method of evaluating units of inventory, units are not distinguished. Rather

- An ongoing average is calculated after each new addition to our inventory.
- This average is the amount at which all units sold and units held are evaluated.

Under the moving weighted average method we would evaluate the 60 units of inventory as follows.

	No. Units	Unit Price (£)	Value (£)	Moving Weighted Average (£)	Calculation of Average
Buy	100	10.00	1,000	10.00	£1,000 ÷ 100 units
Sell	(60)	10.00	(600)		
Balance	40	10.00	400		
Buy	50	12.00	600		
Balance	90		1,000	11.11	£1,000 ÷ 90 units
Sell	(40)	11.11	(444)		
Balance	50	11.11	556		
Buy	10	14.00	140		
Balance	60		696	11.60	£696 ÷ 60 units

The profits that result from this basis of evaluating our inventory are

Income Statement	(£)	(£)
Revenue		2,000
Cost of sales		
Opening inventory	–	
Purchases (1,000 + 600 + 140)	1,740	
Less: Closing inventory	(696)	
		1,044
Profit		956

2.6.1 Conclusion

Our different methods for evaluating inventory have given different inventory values and three different profit figures. You will note that in this example we are dealing with a situation of inflation, purchase prices having risen steadily from £10 to £14. In this situation, the FIFO valuation method gives the highest reported profits and inventory values, whilst the average method give lower values.

NB: An important relationship has been established here, that is the higher the value of the closing inventory, the higher the reported profits (increased net assets result in increased shareholders' funds).

Though the differences in profits and net assets have not been dramatic in this example, it does illustrate the point that the choice for accounting policies can impact on reported profits and the statement of financial position.

Exam tip

> This idea may be examined as a compare and contrast of the alternatives or as a question regarding the impact of an error in inventory valuation, e.g. Summer 2002, Question 6.

3 IAS 11 Construction Contracts

3.1 Introduction

Imagine that you are the accountant at a construction company. Your company is building a large tower block that will house offices, under a contract with an investment company. It will take three years to build the block and over that time you will obviously have to pay for building materials, wages of workers on the building, architects' fees and so on. You will receive periodic payments from the investment company at various predetermined stages of the construction. How do you decide, in each of the three years, **what to include as income and expenditure** for the contract in the income statement?

This is the problem tackled by IAS 11 *Construction Contracts*.

Example

A numerical example might help to illustrate the problem. Suppose that a contract is started on 1 January 2007, with an estimated completion date of 31 December 2008. The final contract price is £1,500,000. In the first year, to 31 December 2007

- Costs incurred amounted to £600,000.

- Half the work on the contract was completed.

- Certificates of work completed have been issued, to the value of £750,000. (*Note.* It is usual, in a construction contract, for a qualified person such as an architect or engineer to inspect the work completed, and if it is satisfactory, to issue certificates. This will then be the notification to the customer that progress payments are now due to the contractor. Progress payments are commonly the amount of valuation on the work certificates issued, minus a precautionary retention of 10%.)

■   It is estimated with reasonable certainty that further costs to completion in 2008 will be £600,000.

Required

What is the contract profit in 2007, and what entries would be made for the contract at 31 December 2007 if

(a)   Profits are deferred until the completion of the contract?

(b)   A proportion of the estimated revenue and profit is credited to the income statement in 2007?

Solution

(a)   If profits were deferred until the completion of the contract in 2008, the revenue and profit recognised on the contract in 2007 would be nil, and the value of work in progress on 31 December 2007 would be £600,000. IAS 11 takes the view that this policy is unreasonable, because in 2008, the total profit of £300,000 would be recorded. Since the contract revenues are earned throughout 2007 and 2008, a profit of nil in 2007 and £300,000 in 2008 would be contrary to the accruals concept of accounting.

(b)   **It is fairer to recognise revenue and profit throughout the duration of the contract.**

As at 31 December 2007 revenue of £750,000 should be matched with cost of sales of £600,000 in the income statement, leaving an attributable profit for 2007 of £150,000.

The only statement of financial position entry as at 31 December 2007 is a receivable of £750,000 recognising that the company is owed this amount for work done to date. No balance remains for work in progress, the whole £600,000 having been recognised in cost of sales.

3.2 What is a construction contract?

A contract which needs IAS 11 treatment does not have to last for a period of more than one year. The main point is that the contract activity **starts in one financial period and ends in another**, thus creating the problem: to which of two or more periods should contract income and costs be allocated? In fact the definition given in the IAS of a construction contract is very straightforward.

> A contract specifically negotiated for the construction of an asset or a combination of assets that are closely interrelated or interdependent in terms of their design, technology and function or their ultimate purpose or use.   *(IAS 11)*

Construction contracts may involve the building of one asset, e.g. a bridge, or a series of interrelated assets, e.g. an oil refinery. They may also include **rendering of services** (e.g. architects) or restoring or demolishing an asset.

3.3 Contract revenue

Contract revenue will be the **amount specified in the contract**, subject to variations in the contract work, incentive payments and claims *if* these will probably give rise to revenue and *if* they can be reliably measured. The result is that contract revenue is measured at the **fair value** of received or receivable revenue.

3.4 Contract costs

Contract costs consist of

- Costs relating **directly** to the contract.

- Costs attributable to general contract activity which can be **allocated** to the contract, such as insurance, cost of design and technical assistance not directly related to a specific contract and construction overheads.

- Any other costs which can be **charged to the customer** under the contract, which may include general administration costs and development costs.

3.5 Recognition of contract revenue and expenses

Revenue and costs associated with a contract should be recognised according to the stage of completion of the contract at the statement of financial position date, but *only when* the **outcome of the activity can be estimated reliably**. This is often known as the **percentage of completion method**. If a loss is predicted on a contract, then it should be recognised immediately.

The **percentage of completion method** is an application of the accruals assumption. Contract revenue is matched to the contract costs incurred in reaching the stage of completion, so revenue, costs and profit are attributed to the proportion of work completed.

We can **summarise** the treatment as follows.

- Recognise **contract revenue** as revenue in the accounting periods in which the work is performed.

- Recognise **contract costs** as an expense in the accounting period in which the work to which they relate is performed.

- Any **expected excess** of total contract costs over total contract revenue should be recognised as an expense immediately.

- The figure to appear in the statement of financial position either

  - Gross amount owed by customer; or
  - Gross amount due to customer.

- These are calculated as costs incurred plus recognised profits less recognised losses less progress billings.

3.6 Determining the stage of completion

How should you decide on the stage of completion of any contract? The Standard lists two methods.

- Surveys of work carried out (**work certified**).

- **The proportion that contract costs incurred** for work carried out to date bear to the estimated total contract costs.

4 ACCOUNTS RECEIVABLE

4.1 Introduction

The detail relating to receivables is contained in the accounts receivable note.

Roche Group

Extract from Notes to the Financial Statements as at 31 December 2004

Accounts receivable in millions of CHF	2004	2003
Trade accounts receivable	7,012	6,863
Notes receivable	143	283
Less: allowance for doubtful accounts	(374)	(372)
Total accounts receivable	6,781	6,774

Bad debt expense was 17 million Swiss francs (2003: 47 million Swiss francs).

4.2 Accounting treatment

In common with all other current assets, accounts receivable should be valued at the lower of cost and net realisable value. In the context of receivables

- Cost is the amount that we have invoiced.
- NRV equals the amount that we anticipate we will receive net of all recovery costs.

As with inventory, this comparison must be done on a line-by-line (receivable-by-receivable) basis. The question that arises in a normal commercial environment is, under what circumstances may what we receive be less than the amount invoiced? There are two possibilities.

- Our debtor has gone into liquidation and simply cannot pay.

- We have some dispute over the invoice, perhaps as a result of poor quality goods, and an amount may not be paid.

Each of these is accounted for in a slightly different way.

4.2.1 Bad debts

Where a company has gone into liquidation and definitely will not pay, then there is no point whatsoever in keeping any record of amounts owed from them on our statement of financial position. The amount should simply be extinguished and removed from the accounts – this bad debt is said to be written off. The effect on the accounting equation of writing-off a bad debt is

- Receivables down (net assets down), i.e. CREDIT receivables.
- Profits down (shareholders' funds down), i.e. DEBIT profit.

4.2.2 Doubtful debts

Where there is a dispute over an invoice, it would be prudent to anticipate that the disputed amount may not be recovered. However, we do not wish to write off the receivable account and forget the whole invoice outstanding completely. We do still have some hopes of recovery. We therefore reduce the value of the receivable down to the expected net realisable value by setting up a provision, just as a depreciation provision, reduces the cost of our non-current asset down to a net book value.

The impact on the accounting equation of making such provision is

- Provision for doubtful accounts up, hence receivables down (net assets down), i.e. CREDIT provision for doubtful accounts

- Bad debt expense up, hence profit down (shareholders' funds down), i.e. DEBIT profit.

NB: The figure shown in the statement of financial position will be net of this provision.

Example

A company has customers owing a total of £500,000, made up as follows.

Receivables	Owed (£'000)
A	30
B	70
Others	400
Total	500

Customer A has gone into liquidation and we have been informed by the receivers that there is no chance of receiving any of the amount outstanding.

Customer B is disputing one of the five invoices that we have issued on the basis that the goods did not arrive. The value of the invoice in dispute is £15,000. None of the other invoices are in dispute and therefore we will definitely receive the other £55,000 from this customer. What will happen to the £15,000 in dispute is currently uncertain.

In addition, our experience over the years has shown us that 2% of the invoices that we issue do not get paid due to customer bankruptcy/insolvency. We cannot highlight which particular receivables will not pay up, it is just our practical experience that shows this. We therefore anticipate that 2% of the other receivables of £400,000 will not pay.

How would these receivables be valued on the statement of financial position?

Solution

In relation to each of the receivables identified.

- Write-off £30,000 in relation to Receivable A as a bad debt reducing the listing of invoices outstanding down to the £470,000 that we hope we can recover.

- Make provisions against the other receivables for what we may not recover, specifically

  - £15,000 **specific provision** against Receivable B, i.e. a provision against a specific receivable.

  - £8,000 **general provision** against the other receivables (£400,000 × 2%), i.e. a provision against receivables in general.

Hence, we would evaluate the figure for the statement of financial position as follows.

Receivables	Owed	
	(£'000)	(£'000)
Receivables listing		
Receivable B		70
Others		400
		470
Allowances		
Specific	15	
General	8	
		(23)
		447

4.2.3 Bad debts and tax

From a tax viewpoint in the UK, the treatment of provisions is quite important, as

■ Specific provisions are treated as a tax allowable expense and will reduce our taxable profits for the year.

■ General provisions are not considered as an allowable expense, the expense will be allowed if the receivables do actually become bad.

Chapter Roundup

You need to be familiar with, able to describe and evaluate

- Current assets
  - Definitions
    - **Inventories** – goods held available for sale.
    - **Accounts receivable** – amounts owed to the company, perhaps as a result of selling goods on credit.
    - **Investments (marketable securities)** – shares held in the short term with the intention of reselling, e.g. short-term speculative investments.
    - **Cash and cash equivalents** – at bank or in hand, both sterling and foreign currencies.
  - Valuation = Lower of
    - Cost.
    - Net realisable value (NRV), i.e. estimated selling price less estimated costs of completion and estimated costs necessary to make the sale.

- Working capital cycle

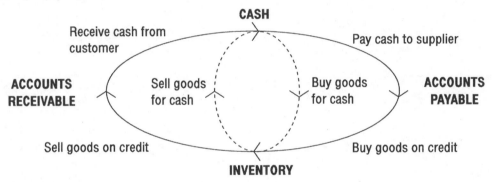

- IAS 2 *Inventories*
  - Definitions
    - Inventories are assets
      - Held for sale in the ordinary course of business;
      - In the process of production for such sale; or
      - In the form of materials or supplies to be consumed in the production process or in the rendering of services.
    - **Net realisable value** is the estimated selling price in the ordinary course of business less the estimated costs of completion and the estimated costs necessary to make the sale.
    - **Fair value** is the amount for which an asset could be exchanged or a liability settled between knowledgeable, willing parties in an arm's length transaction.   *(IAS 2)*

- Valuation methods

    - FIFO method
    - Simple weighted average method
    - Moving weighted average method

- IAS 11 *Construction Contracts*

    - Definition

        - A contract specifically negotiated for the construction of an asset or a combination of assets that are closely interrelated or interdependent in terms of their design, technology and function or their ultimate purpose or use. *(IAS 11)*

- Accounts receivable, bad debts and doubtful debts.

TEST YOUR KNOWLEDGE

Check your knowledge of the chapter here, without referring back to the text.

1. Inventory valuation

    The following inventories are owned by Funakoshi Limited at its year end.

Type	Costs incurred up to year end (£)	Future manufacturing costs (£)	Expected selling costs (£)	Expected sales price (£)
W	6,000	3,000	500	9,000
X	2,500	1,000	30	5,000
Y	10,000	–	300	9,000
Z	7,000	–	500	7,200

    Requirements

    Calculate the value at which inventories will be shown in Funakoshi Limited's statement of financial position as at its year end.

2. First In

    Egami Limited made the following purchases and sales of goods during the year ended June 30 2006.

Date	Units purchased	Purchase price per unit (£)	Units sold	Sales price per unit £
July 22 2005	3,000	5	–	–
August 5 2005	1,000	6	–	–
August 9 2005	–	–	1,500	12
September 30 2005	2,000	7	–	–
November 20 2005	–	–	2,500	12
January 9 2006	–	–	500	12
March 5 2006	5,000	8	–	–
May 3 2006	–	–	3,000	12
June 7 2006	500	9	–	–

    There were no opening inventories as at July 1 2005.

    Requirements

    (a) Calculate the cost of Egami Limited's closing inventories as at 30 June 2006, using the following methods of inventory valuation.

        (i)   First In First Out (FIFO).

        (ii)   Last in First Out (LIFO).

        (iii) Weighted average.

        (iv) Moving weighted average.

(b)   Present the income statement of Egami Limited for the year ended June 30 2006 under each of the four methods used above.

3.   Sampi

Sampi is a manufacturer of garden furniture. The company has consistently used FIFO (first in, first out) in valuing inventories, but it is interested to know the effect on its inventory valuation of using LIFO (last in, first out) and weighted average cost instead of FIFO.

At 28 February, the company had an inventory of 4,000 standard plastic tables, and has computed its value on each of the three bases as

Basis	Unit Cost (£)	Total Value (£)
FIFO	16	64,000
LIFO	12	48,000
Weighted average	13	52,000

During March, the movements on the inventory of tables were as follows.
Received from factory

Date	Number of Units	Production Cost per Unit (£)
8 March	3,800	15
22 March	6,000	18

Sales

Date	Number of Units
12 March	5,000
18 March	2,000
24 March	3,000
28 March	2,000

On a FIFO basis, the inventory at 31 March was £32,400.

Requirements

Compute what the value of the inventory at 31 March would be using

(a)   LIFO

(b)   Weighted average cost.

In arriving at the total inventory values, you should make calculations to two decimal places (where necessary) and deal with each inventory movement in date order.

4.   Current Assets Quiz

   (a)   Define the term 'current asset'.

   (b)   At what amount are inventories measured under IFRS where the cost model is used?

   (c)   Is the LIFO cost formula permitted for establishing the cost of inventories under IFRS?

   (d)   Distinguish between a bad debt and a doubtful debt.

   (e)   Would you expect a food retailer to have a current ratio of greater or less than one? Explain the reason for your answer.

   (f)   Which would give the greater value, the current ratio or the quick (acid test) ratio?

TEST YOUR KNOWLEDGE: ANSWERS

1.   Inventory valuation

Type	Cost at Year End (£)	NRV at Year End (£)	Valuation (£)
W	6,000	5,500	5,500
X	2,500	3,970	2,500
Y	10,000	8,700	8,700
Z	7,000	6,700	6,700
Total inventory valuation			*23,400*

Net realisable value represents the estimated selling price less estimated costs of completion and selling.

2.   First In

(a)   (i)   First In First Out

Since the first inventories bought are the first inventories sold, the last inventories purchased must be the items contained in closing inventories. The quick method of working out the FIFO valuation is to work backwards, as follows.

	Units
Total items purchased	11,500
Total items sold	(7,500)
Items in closing inventory	4,000

	Units	Price (£)	Value (£)
Jun 7 purchases	500	9.00	4,500
Mar 5 purchases	3,500	8.00	28,000
	4,000		32,500

(ii)   Last In First Out

There is no easy quick method of identifying inventories using the LIFO method. It is best to match each sale to a purchase on an individual basis following LIFO principles.

Purchases	Sale 9 Aug	Sale 20 Nov	Sale 9 Jan	Sale 3 May	Remaining units
3,000	(500)	(500)	(500)	–	1,500
1,000	(1,000)	–	–	–	–
2,000	–	(2,000)	–	–	–
5,000	–	–	–	(3,000)	2,000
500	–	–	–	–	500
					4,000

Purchases	Units	Price per Unit (£)	Value (£)
Jul 22	1,500	5.00	7,500
Mar 5	2,000	8.00	16,000
Jun 7	500	9.00	4,500
	4,000		28,000

(iii) Weighted average

Purchases	Units	Price per Unit (£)	Value
Jul 22	3,000	5.00	15,000
Aug 5	1,000	6.00	6,000
Sep 30	2,000	7.00	14,000
Mar 5	5,000	8.00	40,000
Jun 7	500	9.00	4,500
	11,500		79,500

The average price per unit is (79,500/11,500) £6.913 and the total value of closing inventories is (£6.913 × 4,000 units) £27,652.

(iv) Moving weighted average

With the moving weighted average approach, the average is recalculated after every transaction, as follows.

Purchases	Units	Price per Unit (£)	Value (£)
Jul 22 purchase	3,000	5.00	15,000
Aug 5 purchase	1,000	6.00	6,000
Average taken	4,000	5.25	21,000
Aug 9 sale	(1,500)	5.25	(7,875)
	2,500	5.25	13,125
Sep 30 purchase	2,000	7.00	14,000
Average taken	4,500	6.03	27,125
Nov 20 and Jan 9 sales	(3,000)	6.03	(18,090)
	1,500	6.03	9,035
Mar 5 purchase	5,000	8.00	40,000
Average taken	6,500	7.54	49,035
May 3 sale	(3,000)	7.54	(22,620)
	3,500	7.54	26,415
Jun 7	500	9.00	4,500
	4,000	7.73	30,915

The closing inventory valuation is therefore £30,915.

(b)   Income statements

	FIFO (£)	LIFO (£)	WA (£)	MWA (£)
Sales (7,500 × £12)	90,000	90,000	90,000	90,000
Cost of sales				
Opening inventory	–	–	–	–
Purchases	79,500	79,500	79,500	79,500
Closing inventory	(32,500)	(28,000)	(27,652)	(30,915)
	47,000	51,500	51,848	48,585
Profit	43,000	38,500	38,152	41,415

3.   Sampi

(a)   LIFO

Date	Narrative	No. of Units	Unit Cost (£)	Value (£)
28 Feb	Inventory b/f	4,000	12	48,000
8 Mar	Issues	3,800	15	57,000
12 Mar	Sale	(3,800)	15	(57,000)
		(1,200)	12	(14,400)
18 Mar	Sale	(2,000)	12	(24,000)
	Balance	800	12	9,600
22 Mar	Issues	6,000	18	108,000
24 Mar	Sale	(3,000)	18	(54,000)
28 Mar	Sale	(2,000)	18	(36,000)
28 Mar	Balance	1,000	18	18,000
		800	12	9,600
		1,800		27,600

(b)   Weighted average cost

Date	Narrative	No. of Units	Unit Cost (£)	Value (£)
28 Feb	Stock b/f	4,000	13.00	52,000
8 Mar	Issues	3,800	15.00	57,000
12 Mar	Sale	(5,000)	13.97	(69,850)
18 Mar	Sale	(2,000)	13.97	(27,940)
	Balance	800	14.01	11,210
22 Mar	Issues	6,000	18.00	108,000
24 Mar	Sale	(3,000)	17.53	(52,590)
28 Mar	Sale	(2,000)	17.53	(35,060)
28 Mar	Balance	1,800	17.53	31,560

4. (a) IAS 1 *Presentation of Financial Statements* states that an asset is classified as current when it satisfies any of the following.

    (i)   It is expected to be realised in, or is intended for sale or consumption in, the entity's normal operating cycle.

    (ii) It is held primarily for trading purposes.

    (ii) It is expected to be realised within 12 months after the statement of financial position date.

    (iv) It is cash or a cash equivalent.

    (b) They should be measured at the lower of cost and net realisable value.

    (c) IAS 2 *Inventories* was revised for accounting periods beginning on or after 1 January 2005. Since then LIFO has not been an acceptable cost formula under IFRS.

    (d) A bad debt is a debt that cannot be collected because the debtor has gone into receivership, for example.

    A doubtful debt is one which may be collected but, because there is a risk that it will not be due to a dispute with the customer, for example, it is considered prudent to make a provision against the debt. In addition, a company may make a general doubtful debt provision of, say, 2% of debtors to allow for the probability that a certain amount of debtors will not pay.

    (e) A food retailer typically sells goods for cash and therefore has no trade receivables. Goods are held in inventory for only a few days before being sold. However, suppliers may not be paid for a considerable period of time due to the purchasing power of food retailers. This means that trade accounts payable will exceed inventories. Since there are no trade account receivable and cash will be reinvested in non-current assets, the only major components of working capital are inventories and trade accounts payable. Therefore, the current ratio (current assets divided by current liabilities) will be less than one.

    (f) The current ratio is current assets divided by current liabilities. The acid test ratio is current assets less inventories divided by current liabilities. Therefore, the current ratio will give the greater value.

5 Liabilities

INTRODUCTION

Liabilities represents business obligations that will need to be satisfied at some future date. There are several categories of liability and we need to know

- What each one is.
- How they are valued and reflected in the accounts.

Historically, this area has been a major source of 'creative accounting' i.e. bending accounting rules in order to flatter the business. You need to be aware of this issue and how accounting rules have aimed to reduce this scope.

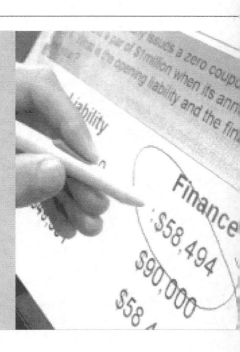

CHAPTER LEARNING OBJECTIVES

The syllabus areas covered by this section are

Interpretation of Financial Information

The effect of accounting practices

Understanding of the effect of accounting practices on the numbers most significant for investment decisions (profit, earnings per share, asset value etc).

Accounting Terminology and Concepts

Accounting terminology and a knowledge of accounting concepts and conventions to include the statement of financial position, income statement, statement of cash flows and notes to the accounts. An understanding of the distinction between capital and revenue, the valuation of assets for accounting purposes and the determination of profit and earnings share on the nil, net and full distribution bases. An understanding of significance of the statement of accounting policies in relation to the concept of a true and fair view.

Presentation of Financial Statements

Impact of statutory and non-statutory regulation on UK financial statements.

An understanding of the effect on the presentation of financial statements of the Companies Act and non-statutory regulations, including standards and other guidance issued by IASB and stock exchange requirements.

In respect of liabilities:

It is emphasised that the intention of the examination is to assess students' analytical and interpretative skills rather than their technical accounting ability. It is also expected that they should have an understanding of standard accounting practices and an awareness of matters currently under discussion.

1 INTRODUCTION

1.1 Definition of a liability

The *Framework for the Preparation and Presentation of Financial Statements* defines a liability as follows.

A present obligation arising from past events, the settlement of which is expected to result in an outflow of resources embodying economic benefits from the enterprise.

Fundamental to this definition is the existence of an **obligation**, thus ensuring that companies are not able to provide for future costs unless they are already obligated to incur those costs. This minimises the ability of the company to use provisioning as a means of smoothing profits over the years (as discussed below in the section on provisions).

A liability will normally have arisen as a result of a past transaction, e.g. the delivery to the company of raw materials that are as yet unpaid. However, it is possible for a liability to arise as a result of a past event. An example of this is the liability to restore the site of an opencast mine, which arises as soon as the land to be mined has been opened up for mining, i.e. at the commencement of the mining activities.

1.2 Scope of this chapter

In this chapter, we will look at the trading liabilities of a company, the rules regarding their treatment or valuation on the statement of financial position and their disclosure.

We are not considering the rules related to financing liabilities in this session, though the general valuation rules discussed here will still apply. Financing liabilities are dealt with in Chapter 6.

In common with the evaluation of current assets, the prudence concept needs to be applied when valuing liabilities. Prudence dictates that we should not anticipate any profits but we should always recognise liabilities or losses in full. That is to say that liabilities will be evaluated at the full liability that is likely to become payable.

1.3 Types of non-finance liabilities

There are three broad categories of liabilities.

1.3.1 Creditors or payables

Known amounts owed by the company, e.g. invoices received, bank overdrafts, and so on.

1.3.2 Accruals

Liabilities for which the timing of payment is generally known but the amount to be paid is uncertain. Accruals normally arise from routine transactions of the business, either of an operating or financing nature.

Examples of business expenses giving rise to accruals would be telephone and electricity bills, where an invoice covers a period of time that may not exactly coincide with the year end. We know that at the year end, we have used a certain amount of, say, electricity since the last bill was paid, but we have not received an invoice to the year-end date.

We therefore make our best estimate of how much it should be from the date of the last bill to the year end, to match the cost of power used in that period against the benefits we derive from its use.

The impact of an accrual on our accounting equation is

- Accruals up (net assets down), i.e. CREDIT accruals.

- Expense up/profits down (shareholders' funds down), i.e. DEBIT profit.

Example

A company's year end is the 31 December. Its last 'phone bill in the year covers the period up to 30 November. Each quarterly invoice for phone usage tends to be roughly £6,000. What amount should be accrued as of the 31 December?

Solution

Each quarter's bill is for £6,000, i.e. our telephone usage amounts to £2,000 per calendar month. Therefore, for the month of December we will probably have used £2,000 worth of telephone services and hence should acknowledge the expense and corresponding liability. However, we have not yet been billed (and probably will not be until the end of February), so we will set up an accrual. Our entry will be

CREDIT accruals up £2,000 (net assets down).
DEBIT telephone expense £2,000 (shareholders' funds down).

1.3.3 Provisions

A provision on a statement of financial position represents one of two things, though either way it results in a reduction of the net assets on the statement of financial position. A provision represents one of the following.

An amount to account for the reduction in the value of an asset (e.g. an accumulated depreciation provision reduces the cost of a non-current asset down to its net book value).

An estimate of a known but not exactly quantified liability arising from something outside of the normal trading activities of a company, e.g. pension provisions or provisions for costs that will be incurred as a result of say, a decision to close a factory.

2 TYPES OF PAYABLES

2.1 Trade payables

As noted above, payables represent known amounts owed by the company. Possibly the most common item to fall under this heading would be trade payables, which would be evaluated on the statement of financial position at the full face value of any valid invoices received in accordance with the prudence concept.

From this viewpoint there is very little problem in evaluating and accounting for trade payables. When an invoice is received, say for the purchase of goods for resale, the effect on the accounting equation is

- Inventory up (net assets up).
- Trade payables up (net assets down).

2.2 Value added tax

2.2.1 Introduction

In the UK sales tax is known as Value Added Tax (VAT).

VAT is a tax on the supply of goods and services that is eventually borne by the final customer, but which is collected at each stage of the production and distribution chain.

Companies add an amount of VAT to their sales, receiving the gross amount from their customers. Revenue is normally considered to be the net value of the sales invoices and the VAT element received must normally be paid over to HM Revenue and Customs on a quarterly basis.

The company also receives invoices from its suppliers that include VAT that they, in turn, must pay. The company can claim this element back from HM Revenue and Customs on a quarterly basis.

HM Revenue and Customs require a company to pay over the net of the VAT on sales and the VAT on supplies, i.e. effectively the VAT on the difference between the sales and the supplies. Looking at this another way, the VAT that must be paid represents tax on the value that has been added (the difference between the sales and supplies).

2.3 Accounting treatment

2.3.1 Revenue

Revenue in the income statement should be stated **excluding** VAT. Any VAT received from sales must be paid over to HM Revenue and Customs, i.e. it is *not* income for the company, rather the company is collecting it on behalf of the tax authorities.

2.3.2 Assets and expenses

Assets and expenses should be included in the statement of financial position and income statement **exclusive of VAT** in a similar fashion. Any VAT a company has paid on these items can be taken to reduce the amount that needs to be paid over to the tax authorities from VAT collected on turnover.

2.3.3 VAT liability/asset

The net amount of VAT due to, or from, the Revenue authorities should be included as part of non-current liabilities or non-current assets, but it will not normally require separate disclosure.

Example

A company buys a product for £100 plus VAT (£117.50) from a supplier and sells the product on for £160 plus VAT (£188.00). The ultimate customer has, therefore, paid £28 VAT (£160 × 17.5%), the VAT on the final invoice to him.

The Revenue authorities have, however, collected this £28 in two stages.

- £17.50 collected from the supplier based on its invoice of £100 plus VAT (£117.50).
- £10.50 collected from the company, which could be calculated as either

    - The difference between the £28 VAT charged on the sale and the £17.50 VAT on the purchases.

    - Tax on the added value of £60 (£160 − £100), which amounts to £60 × 17.5% = £10.50.

The company itself will report the following.

Income Statement Extract	(£'000)
Revenue	160
Cost of sales	100
Profit	60

Thus, it records all the transactions in its books (revenue and expenses, etc.) net of VAT.

If the £10.50 VAT has been paid over to HM Revenue and Customs (HMRC) before the year end, it will not appear at all in the accounts. If it remains unpaid at the year end, it will fall within current liabilities, since VAT is normally accounted for on a quarterly basis.

2.3.4 Exceptions and exemptions

Certain businesses do not have to charge VAT on some or all of their sales, e.g. sales of land and buildings, Post Office services, betting gaming and lotteries, non-profit making education. The consequence of this, however, may be that it cannot recover all of the VAT it pays over on its supplies (assets and expenses). As a result an element of irrecoverable VAT will arise, which should be treated as part of the cost of those assets or expenses.

Example

The following extract shows what items typically appear within the payables disclosure.

Tomkins Group Extract from Interim Accounts as at 2 July 2005	2 July 2005 (£m)	3 July 2004 (£m)
Current liabilities		
Trade payables	263.8	217.9
Other taxes and social security	14.2	16.2
Accruals and deferred income	117.9	113.5
Other payables	17.4	21.0
	413.3	368.6
Non-current liabilities		
Accruals and deferred income	0.6	4.5
Other payables	6.7	2.9
	7.3	7.4

3 IAS 37 AND PROVISIONS

3.1 Objective

IAS 37 *Provisions, Contingent Liabilities and Contingent Assets* aims to ensure that appropriate **recognition criteria** and **measurement bases** are applied to provisions, contingent liabilities and contingent assets and that **sufficient information** is disclosed in the **notes** to the financial statements to enable users to understand their nature, timing and amount.

3.2 Provisions

You will be familiar with provisions for depreciation from your earlier studies. The sorts of provisions addressed by IAS 37 are, however, rather different.

Before IAS 37, there was no accounting standard dealing with provisions. Companies wanting to show their results in the most favourable light used to make large 'one-off' provisions in years where a high level of underlying profits was generated. These provisions, often known as 'big bath' provisions, were then available to shield expenditure in future years when perhaps the underlying profits were not as good.

> In other words, provisions were used for profit smoothing. Profit smoothing is misleading.

The key aim of IAS 37 is to ensure that **provisions are made only** where there are valid grounds for them.

3.3 What is a provision?

IAS 37 views a provision as a liability.

> A **provision** is a **liability** of uncertain timing or amount.
>
> A **liability** is an obligation of an entity to transfer economic benefits as a result of past transactions or events.   *(IAS 37)*

The IAS distinguishes provisions from other liabilities such as trade payables and accruals. This is on the basis that for a provision there is **uncertainty** about the timing or amount of the future expenditure. While uncertainty is clearly present in the case of certain accruals the uncertainty is generally much less than for provisions.

3.4 Recognition

IAS 37 states that a provision should be **recognised** as a liability in the financial statements when

- An entity has a **present obligation** (legal or constructive) as a result of a past event.
- It is probable that a **transfer of economic benefits** will be required to settle the obligation.
- A **reliable estimate** can be made of the obligation.

3.5 Meaning of obligation

It is fairly clear what a legal obligation is. However, you may not know what is meant by a **constructive obligation**.

> IAS 37 defines a **constructive obligation** as
>
> 'An obligation that derives from an entity's actions where
>
> - By an established pattern of past practice, published policies or a sufficiently specific current statement the entity has indicated to other parties that it will accept certain responsibilities; and
>
> - As a result, the entity has created a valid expectation on the part of those other parties that it will discharge those responsibilities.'

Example

In which of the following circumstances might a provision be recognised?

(a) On 13 December 2007 the board of an entity decided to close down a division. The accounting date of the company is 31 December. Before 31 December 2007 the decision was not communicated to any of those affected and no other steps were taken to implement the decision.

(b) The board agreed a detailed closure plan on 20 December 2007 and details were given to customers and employees.

(c) A company is obliged to incur clean up costs for environmental damage (that has already been caused).

(d) A company intends to carry out future expenditure to operate in a particular way in the future.

Solution

(a) No provision would be recognised as the decision has not been communicated.

(b) A provision would be made in the 2007 financial statements.

(c) A provision for such costs is appropriate.

(d) No present obligation exists and under IAS 37 no provision would be appropriate. This is because the entity could avoid the future expenditure by its future actions, maybe by changing its method of operation.

3.6 Probable transfer of economic benefits

For the purpose of the IAS, a transfer of economic benefits is regarded as 'probable' if the event is more likely than not to occur. This appears to indicate a probability of more than 50%. However, the Standard makes it clear that where there are a number of similar obligations the probability should be based on considering the population as a whole, rather than one single item.

Example

If a company has entered into a warranty obligation then the probability of transfer of economic benefits may well be extremely small in respect of one specific item. However, when considering the population as a whole the probability of some transfer of economic benefits is quite likely to be much higher. If there is a greater than 50% probability of some transfer of economic benefits then a provision should be made for the expected amount.

3.7 Measurement of provisions

The amount recognised as a provision should be the best estimate of the expenditure required to settle the present obligation at the statement of financial position date.

The estimates will be determined by the judgement of the entity's management supplemented by the experience of similar transactions.

Allowance is made for **uncertainty**. Where the provision being measured involves a large population of items, the obligation is estimated by weighting all possible outcomes by their associated probabilities, i.e. **expected value**.

Where the effect of the **time value of money** is material, the amount of a provision should be the **present value** of the expenditure required to settle the obligation. An appropriate **discount** rate should be used.

The discount rate should be a **pre-tax rate** that reflects current market assessments of the time value of money. **The discount rate(s) should not reflect risks for which future cash flow estimates have been adjusted**.

Example

Parker Co. sells goods with a warranty under which customers are covered for the cost of repairs of any manufacturing defect that becomes apparent within the first six months of purchase. The company's past experience and future expectations indicate the following pattern of likely repairs.

Percentage of goods sold	Defects	Cost of repairs if all items suffered from these defects £m
75	None	–
20	Minor	1.0
5	Major	4.0

What is the expected cost of repairs?

Solution

The cost is found using 'expected values' (75% × £nil) + (20% × £1.0m) + (5% × £4.0m) = £400,000.

3.8 Changes in provisions

Provisions should be reviewed at each statement of financial position date and adjusted to reflect the current best estimate. If it is no longer probable that a transfer of economic benefits will be required to settle the obligation, the provision should be reversed.

3.9 Use of provisions

A provision should be used only for expenditures for which the provision was originally recognised. Setting expenditures against a provision that was originally recognised for another purpose would conceal the impact of two different events.

3.10 Future operating losses

Provisions should not be recognised for future operating losses. They do not meet the definition of a liability and the general recognition criteria set out in the Standard.

3.11 Onerous contracts

If an entity has a contract that is onerous, the present obligation under the contract **should be recognised and measured** as a provision. An example might be vacant leasehold property.

An **onerous contract** is a contract entered into with another party under which the unavoidable costs of fulfilling the terms of the contract exceed any revenues expected to be received from the goods or services supplied or purchased directly or indirectly under the contract and where the entity would have to compensate the other party if it did not fulfil the terms of the contract.

3.12 Examples of possible provisions

It is easier to see what IAS 37 is driving at if you look at examples of those items which are possible provisions under this Standard. Some of these we have already touched on.

- **Warranties**. These are argued to be genuine provisions as on past experience it is probable, i.e. more likely than not, that some claims will emerge. The provision must be estimated, however, on the basis of the class as a whole and not on individual claims. There is a clear legal obligation in this case.

- **Major repairs**. In the past it has been quite popular for companies to provide for expenditure on a major overhaul to be accrued gradually over the intervening years between overhauls. Under IAS 37 this is no longer possible as IAS 37 would argue that this is a mere intention to carry out repairs, not an obligation. The entity can always sell the asset in the meantime. The only solution is to treat major assets such as aircraft, ships, furnaces etc as a series of smaller assets where each part is depreciated over shorter lives. Thus any major overhaul may be argued to be replacement and therefore capital rather than revenue expenditure.

- **Self insurance**. A number of companies have created a provision for self insurance based on the expected cost of making good fire damage etc instead of paying premiums to an insurance company. Under IAS 37 this provision is no longer justifiable as the entity has no obligation until a fire or accident occurs. No obligation exists until that time.

- **Environmental contamination**. If the company has an environmental policy such that other parties would expect the company to clean up any contamination or if the company has broken current environmental legislation then a provision for environmental damage must be made.

- **Decommissioning or abandonment costs**. When an oil company initially purchases an oilfield it is put under a legal obligation to decommission the site at the end of its life. Prior to IAS 37 most oil companies set up the provision gradually over the life of the field so that no one year would be unduly burdened with the cost. IAS 37, however, insists that a legal obligation exists on the initial expenditure on the field and therefore a liability exists immediately. This would appear to result in a large charge to profit and loss in the first year of operation of the field. However, the IAS takes the view that the cost of purchasing the field in the first place is not only the cost of the field itself but also the costs of putting it right again. Thus all the costs of abandonment may be capitalised.

- **Restructuring**. This is considered in detail below.

3.13 Provisions for restructuring

One of the main purposes of IAS 37 was to target abuses of provisions for restructuring. Accordingly, IAS 37 lays down **strict criteria** to determine when such a provision can be made.

> IAS 37 defines a **restructuring** as a programme that is planned and is controlled by management and materially changes one of two things.
>
> - The scope of a business undertaken by an entity.
> - The manner in which that business is conducted.

The IAS gives the following **examples** of events that may fall under the definition of restructuring.

- The **sale or termination** of a line of business.

- The **closure of business locations** in a country or region or the **relocation** of business activities from one country or region to another.

- **Changes in management structure**, for example, the elimination of a layer of management.

- **Fundamental reorganisations** that have a material effect on the **nature and focus** of the entity's operations.

The question is whether or not an entity has an obligation – legal or constructive – at the statement of financial position date. For this to be the case

- An entity must have a **detailed formal plan** for the restructuring.

- It must have **raised a valid expectation** in those affected that it will carry out the restructuring by starting to implement that plan or announcing its main features to those affected by it.

> **A mere management decision is not normally sufficient**. Management decisions may sometimes trigger off recognition, but only if earlier events such as negotiations with employee representatives and other interested parties have been concluded subject only to management approval.

Where the restructuring involves the **sale of an operation** then IAS 37 states that no obligation arises until the entity has entered into a **binding sale agreement**. This is because until this has occurred the entity will be able to change its mind and withdraw from the sale even if its intentions have been announced publicly.

3.14 Costs to be included within a restructuring provision

The IAS states that a restructuring provision should include only the **direct expenditures** arising from the restructuring, which are those that are both

- **Necessarily entailed** by the restructuring; and
- Not associated with the **ongoing activities** of the entity.

The following costs should specifically **not** be included within a restructuring provision.

- **Retraining** or relocating continuing staff.
- **Marketing**.
- **Investment in new systems** and distribution networks.

3.15 Disclosure

Disclosures for provisions fall into two parts.

- Disclosure of details of the **change in carrying value** of a provision from the beginning to the end of the year.

- Disclosure of the **background** to the making of the provision and the uncertainties affecting its outcome.

4 CONTINGENT LIABILITIES AND CONTINGENT ASSETS

Exam tip

> This is the most frequently examined subject from this section, e.g. Winter 2005 Question 8, Winter 2002 Question 6.

4.1 Definition

Now you understand provisions it will be easier to understand contingent assets and liabilities.

IAS 37 defines a **contingent liability** as follows.

> - A possible obligation that arises from past events and whose existence will be confirmed only by the occurrence or non-occurrence of one or more uncertain future events not wholly within the entity's control; or
>
> - A present obligation that arises from past events but is not recognised because
>
>   - It is not probable that a transfer of economic benefits will be required to settle the obligation; or
>
>   - The amount of the obligation cannot be measured with sufficient reliability.

As a rule of thumb, probable means more than 50% likely. **If an obligation is probable, it is not a contingent liability** – instead, a **provision is needed**.

4.2 Treatment of contingent liabilities

Contingent liabilities **should not be recognised in financial statements** but they **should be disclosed**. The required disclosures are

- A brief description of the nature of the contingent liability.
- An estimate of its financial effect.
- An indication of the uncertainties that exist.
- The possibility of any reimbursement.

4.3 Contingent assets

IAS 37 defines a **contingent asset** as

> A possible asset that arises from past events and whose existence will be confirmed by the occurrence or non-occurrence of one or more uncertain future events not wholly within the entity's control.

A contingent asset must not be recognised. Only when the realisation of the related economic benefits is **virtually certain** should recognition take place. At that point, **the asset is no longer a contingent asset!**

4.4 Disclosure

4.4.1 Disclosure: Contingent liabilities

A **brief description** must be provided of all material contingent liabilities unless they are likely to be remote. In addition, provide

- An estimate of their **financial effect**.
- Details of **any uncertainties**.
- The possibility of any reimbursement.

4.4.2 Disclosure: Contingent assets

Contingent assets must only be disclosed in the notes if they are **probable**. In that case a brief description of the contingent asset should be provided along with an estimate of its likely financial effect.

4.5 'Let out'

IAS 37 permits reporting entities to avoid disclosure requirements relating to provisions, contingent liabilities and contingent assets if they would be expected to **seriously prejudice** the position of the entity in dispute with other parties. However, this should only be employed in **extremely rare** cases. Details of the general nature of the provision/contingencies must still be provided, together with an explanation of why it has not been disclosed.

4.6 Example of a provisions note

Tomkins Group

Extract from Interim Accounts as at 2 July 2005

	Restructuring Provisions (£m)	Other Provisions (£m)
At 1 January 2005	14.7	44.7
Foreign exchange translation	0.7	2.9
Subsidiaries acquired	–	0.3
Charge for the period	7.4	7.7
Reversal of provisions for disposal of operations	(4.1)	–
Utilised during the period	(8.5)	(7.6)
At 2 July 2005	10.2	48.0
Included in current liabilities	6.5	32.7
Included in non-current liabilities	3.7	15.3
	10.2	48.0

CHAPTER ROUNDUP

- You need to be familiar with, able to describe and evaluate

    - Liabilities

        - A present obligation arising from past events, the settlement of which is expected to result in an outflow of resources embodying economic benefits from the enterprise.

    - The three broad categories of

        - Creditors or payables.
        - Accruals.
        - Provisions.

- IAS 37 *Provisions and Contingent Liabilities*

    - Provision definitions

        - A **provision** is a **liability** of uncertain timing or amount.

        - A **liability** is an obligation of an entity to transfer economic benefits as a result of past transactions or events.   *(IAS 37)*

        - IAS 37 states that a provision should be **recognised** as a liability in the financial statements when

            - An entity has a **present obligation** (legal or constructive) as a result of a past event.

            - It is probable that a **transfer of economic benefits** will be required to settle the obligation.

            - A **reliable estimate** can be made of the obligation.

        - IAS 37 defines a **constructive obligation** as

        'An obligation that derives from an entity's actions where

            - By an established pattern of past practice, published policies or a sufficiently specific current statement the entity has indicated to other parties that it will accept certain responsibilities; and

            - As a result, the entity has created a valid expectation on the part of those other parties that it will discharge those responsibilities.'

        - The amount recognised as a provision should be the best estimate of the expenditure required to settle the present obligation at the statement of financial position date.

        - An **onerous contract** is a contract entered into with another party under which the unavoidable costs of fulfilling the terms of the contract exceed any revenues expected to be received from the goods or services supplied or purchased directly or indirectly under the contract and where the entity would have to compensate the other party if it did not fulfil the terms of the contract.

        - IAS 37 defines a **restructuring** as a programme that is planned and is controlled by management and materially changes one of two things.

            - The scope of a business undertaken by an entity.
            - The manner in which that business is conducted.

– Contingent liabilities

  – A possible obligation that arises from past events and whose existence will be confirmed only by the occurrence or non-occurrence of one or more uncertain future events not wholly within the entity's control; or

  – A present obligation that arises from past events but is not recognised because

    – It is not probable that a transfer of economic benefits will be required to settle the obligation; or

    – The amount of the obligation cannot be measured with sufficient reliability.

  – IAS 37 defines a **contingent asset** as

    – A possible asset that arises from past events and whose existence will be confirmed by the occurrence or non-occurrence of one or more uncertain future events not wholly within the entity's control.

TEST YOUR KNOWLEDGE

Check your knowledge of the chapter here, without referring back to the text.

1.   Smack Co.

During 2007 Smack Co. gives a guarantee of certain borrowings of Pony Co., whose financial condition at that time is sound. During 2008, the financial condition of Pony Co deteriorates and at 30 June 2008 Pony Co. files for protection from its creditors.

What accounting treatment is required

(a)   At 31 December 2007?
(b)   At 31 December 2008?

2.   Warren Co.

Warren Co. gives warranties at the time of sale to purchasers of its products. Under the terms of the warranty the manufacturer undertakes to make good, by repair or replacement, manufacturing defects that become apparent within a period of three years from the date of the sale. Should a provision be recognised?

3.   Callow Co.

After a wedding in 2007 ten people died, possibly as a result of food poisoning from products sold by Callow Co. Legal proceedings are started seeking damages from Callow but it disputes liability. Up to the date of approval of the financial statements for the year to 31 December 2007, Callow's lawyers advise that it is probable that it will not be found liable. However, when Callow prepares the financial statements for the year to 31 December 2008 its lawyers advise that, owing to developments in the case, it is probable that it will be found liable.

What is the required accounting treatment

(a)   At 31 December 2007?
(b)   At 31 December 2008?

TEST YOUR KNOWLEDGE: ANSWERS

1. Smack Co.

   (a) *At 31 December 2007*

   There is a present obligation as a result of a past obligating event. The obligating event is the giving of the guarantee, which gives rise to a legal obligation. However, at 31 December 2007 no transfer of economic benefits is probable in settlement of the obligation.

   No provision is recognised. The guarantee is disclosed as a contingent liability unless the probability of any transfer is regarded as remote.

   (b) *At 31 December 2008*

   As above, there is a present obligation as a result of a past obligating event, namely the giving of the guarantee.

   At 31 December 2008 it is probable that a transfer of economic benefits will be required to settle the obligation. A provision is therefore recognised for the best estimate of the obligation.

2. Warren Co.

   Warren Co. **cannot avoid** the cost of repairing or replacing all items of product that manifest manufacturing defects in respect of which warranties are given before the statement of financial position date, and a provision for the cost of this should therefore be made.

   Warren Co. is obliged to repair or replace items that fail within the entire warranty period. Therefore, in respect of **this year's sales**, the obligation provided for at the statement of financial position date should be the cost of making good items for which defects have been notified but not yet processed, **plus** an estimate of costs in respect of the other items sold for which there is sufficient evidence that manufacturing defects **will** manifest themselves during their remaining periods of warranty cover.

3. Callow Co.

   (a) *At 31 December 2007*

   On the basis of the evidence available when the financial statements were approved, there is no obligation as a result of past events. No provision is recognised. The matter is disclosed as a contingent liability unless the probability of any transfer is regarded as remote.

   (b) *At 31 December 2008*

   On the basis of the evidence available, there is a present obligation. A transfer of economic benefits in settlement is probable.

   A provision is recognised for the best estimate of the amount needed to settle the present obligation.

6

Company Financing

INTRODUCTION

Companies raise finance in one of two ways.

- Issuing shares – of which there are several classes.
- Borrowing – where there area a variety of methods and sources.

Each source of finance will need to be serviced in some way, i.e. the investors will be looking for a return, and may need to be repaid.

We need to know

- The characteristics of the various sources.
- The impact on the business and risks associated with each source.
- How the sources are serviced.
- Any rules and treatment regarding the repayment of those sources.

CHAPTER CONTENTS

CHAPTER LEARNING OBJECTIVES

The syllabus areas covered by this chapter are

Interpretation of Financial Information

The effect of accounting practices

Understanding of the effect of accounting practices on the numbers most significant for investment decisions (profit, earnings per share, asset value etc).

Accounting terminology and concepts

Accounting terminology and a knowledge of accounting concepts and conventions to include the statement of financial position, income statement, statement of cash flows and notes to the accounts. An understanding of the distinction between capital and revenue, the valuation of assets for accounting purposes and the determination of profit and earnings share on the nil, net and full distribution bases. An understanding of significance of the statement of accounting policies in relation to the concept of a true and fair view.

Presentation of Financial Statements

Impact of statutory and non-statutory regulation on UK financial statements.

An understanding of the effect on the presentation of financial statements of the Companies Act and non-statutory regulations, including standards and other guidance issued by IASB and stock exchange requirements.

In respect of financing:

It is emphasised that the intention of the examination is to assess students' analytical and interpretative skills rather than their technical accounting ability. It is also expected that they should have an understanding of standard accounting practices and an awareness of matters currently under discussion.

1 INTRODUCTION

1.1 Sources of finance

Businesses obtain finance from two main sources.

- Shareholders.
- Loan providers.

1.2 Shareholders

The shareholders' funds represent the total finance provided by the owners of the business.

Some of the shareholder finance is provided directly by the shareholders subscribing for new shares in the company.

The remaining shareholder finance represents increases in the value of the business. Some of this, the shareholders have allowed the business to keep in order to finance growth, i.e. retained profits or retained earnings. The rest, such as revaluation surpluses, represents increases in value that are required to be kept by the company and therefore could not be paid out to the shareholders in any case.

1.3 Loan providers

Loans fall broadly into three categories.

- **Debentures and unsecured loan stock**, which can be held by the general public and can be bought and sold in the same way as shares.

- **Loans** from banks and other financial institutions.

- **Bank overdrafts**.

1.4 Distinguishing characteristics

The characteristics that distinguish these sources are as follows.

- **Annual returns** – the dividends or interest that must be paid by the company on an ongoing basis.

- **Capital repayment** – any provisions relating to this one-off payment for the particular instrument.

- **Security** – any rights that the provider of finance has over various assets of the business.

- **Influence** – the voting rights or other influence that the provider of finance has and hence his ability to impact on the operations of the business.

- **Negotiability** – the ability of the holder of the financial instrument to trade the instrument and realise its value.

1.5 Raising finance

Organisations raise capital to finance the acquisition of assets that are required for a variety of purposes. Broadly speaking, non-current assets represent the long-term productive capacity of the business, while current assets are acquired for resale or conversion into cash during the ordinary course of business. Hence, the type of capital required to finance the asset varies with the nature of the asset concerned.

In general, assets that are to be held for a long period should be financed by stable, long-term sources of finance, whereas assets with short or unpredictable lives should be financed by a more flexible short-term source. For example, you do not finance the purchase of a holiday with a 25-year mortgage, nor do you finance the purchase of a house on a bank overdraft. The former would give a very short-term benefit but a long-term commitment over the next 25 years. The latter might result in an overdraft that has to be repaid at short notice when it may be difficult, if not impossible, to sell the house.

2 SHARE FINANCE

2.1 Introduction

A limited company is formed by a minimum of one person (two for a public limited company), lodging certain documents with the registrar of companies and the payment of the necessary fees. Of these documents the two most important are the Memorandum and Articles of Association.

2.2 Memorandum of Association

The Memorandum of Association is concerned with the relationship between the company and the outside world.

In relation to the financing of the company, the Memorandum of Association specifies two important factors.

2.2.1 Authorised share capital

The amount of share capital that can be issued by the company in total. Most companies do not issue shares up to the authorised share capital limit. Details of both the authorised share capital and the issued share capital must be included within the accounts.

2.2.2 Nominal value

The authorised share capital of any UK company is divided into shares of a fixed amount – a **nominal value**. This nominal value represents the maximum amount that any shareholder may be required to pay to the company. As a result, the nominal value places a limit on the liability of any shareholder.

When a company is initially formed, the nominal value might represent the fair value of the shares issued. Later, when profits have been generated and retained by the business, the market value of the shares is likely to have risen above this nominal value. The nominal value therefore has little relevance to an investor, except that

- Any unpaid element of the nominal value represents the limit on the investors' liability should the company become insolvent.

- Shares cannot be issued at a price below nominal value.

- When shares are issued at a price in excess of the nominal value, the difference must be taken to a share premium account, i.e. the share capital represents the nominal value of shares in issue and the share premium represents the premium received by the company on the issue of any shares at a higher price.

- The total nominal value of any investor's shares as a proportion of the total share capital (nominal value of shares in issue) will reflect the investor's proportion of ownership of the company.

2.3 Articles of Association

The Articles of Association are concerned with the internal operations of the company.

With regard to financing, the Articles of Association specify the procedure to be adopted should the company need to raise the authorised share capital limit to extend its ability to issue shares. This procedure usually requires a simple majority of votes of the Ordinary shareholders.

Having determined the authorised share capital, the directors of the company cannot issue new shares in excess of this limit, nor can they issue any form of securities that confer the rights to subscribe for shares, e.g. convertibles and warrants, if exercising these rights would involve issuing shares in excess of the limits.

2.4 Characteristics of shares

As we noted above, there are a number of distinguishing characteristics for the main sources of finance relating to the rights of the investor. For investment in shares, these rights are specified in the Articles of Association and are likely to vary with the different classes of shares. The characteristics of shares are now considered.

2.4.1 Annual returns

The regular return that a shareholder receives is dividends, i.e. a cash distribution out of the profits earned by the company after tax.

2.4.2 Capital repayment

Certain types of share capital, known as redeemable share capital, may be entitled to a repayment of capital by the company, however, most are not, except on the winding up of the company.

2.4.3 Security

A shareholder is somebody who has provided risk finance and, as such, there is no security on his investment provided by the company.

Where different categories of shares exist, however, there will be a strict order of repayment of shareholders or classes of shares on a winding up, hence the level of security for the shareholder depends on how far up that list he lies.

2.4.4 Influence

Shares frequently confer the right to vote at shareholders' meetings, and hence provide the ability to influence the conduct of the business. Certain factors are voted on by companies at each annual general meeting, for example, the appointment of directors and auditors. In addition, shareholders, as the owners, must always decide in the case of a takeover bid.

2.4.5 Negotiability

Generally, shares can be negotiated or sold on, but there may be some restrictions regarding whom they can be sold to.

The shares of listed companies can be freely traded on the Stock Exchange.

2.5 Types of company

The Companies Act specifies two types of company, specifically public limited companies and private companies.

2.5.1 Public limited companies (plc)

A public limited company is one

- That has a minimum issued share capital of £50,000 on which all the share premium and at least 25% of the nominal value have been paid up.

- Whose Memorandum of Association states that it is a public company.

- Which is correctly registered as public.

Such companies must have either 'plc' or 'Public Limited Company' at the end of their names and require a minimum of two members or shareholders.

Public companies are allowed to sell their shares to the public and are able to obtain a stock exchange listing, however, they do not have to be listed. The terminology here is sometimes confusing, as obtaining a listing is frequently referred to as 'going public'.

2.5.2 Private companies

All other companies are private companies and must have 'Limited' at the end of their names.

Private companies may place restrictions on who may be a shareholder, reducing the opportunity of any shareholder to sell his shares. They require a minimum of only one member or shareholder.

3 TYPES OF SHARES

Exam tip

> You may be asked to contrast ordinary shares and preference shares, e.g. Winter 2005 Question 7.

3.1 Introduction

We described shares above as risk finance, i.e. shareholders are the first investors to lose if the company fails. We also noted that the degree of risk can vary within the same company depending on the class of shares held. This risk can vary from little more than that of an unsecured lender, to a substantial, highly speculative risk. As we would expect, however, the prospect of reward/return usually vary accordingly.

The main types of shares in increasing order of risk (the order in which they rank in the event of a liquidation) are as follows.

- Preference shares.
- Ordinary shares.
- Deferred shares.
- Warrants to subscribe for shares.

We will review each of these in turn and consider the normal rights that they confer on the investor.

NB: These are only generalisations and the specifics for any individual company may be different. They are, however, always clearly spelt out in that company's Articles of Association.

3.2 Preference shares

3.2.1 General preference shares

A number of sub-categories of preference shares are frequently met in practice and each give different rights to the relevant shareholders. We will start with a general consideration of the rights that preference shares confer, then look at the sub-categories.

3.2.2 Annual returns

Preference shares carry a fixed rate of dividend, normally payable half yearly. This rate is fixed regardless of the levels of profit of the company.

As the name suggests, these shares receive preferential treatment by the company with regard to dividend distribution and capital repayment. In particular, no dividend may be paid on any other class of shares until the preference dividend has been paid for the year.

This does not, however, mean that a preference dividend must be declared. Preference shareholders are in an inferior position to lenders from this viewpoint since any loan interest must always be paid.

3.2.3 Capital repayment

In general there is no entitlement to any capital repayment from the company, though certain sub-categories do confer this right.

On a winding up, preference shareholders are generally only entitled to the repayment of the nominal value of their shares; they do not participate in any remaining profits.

3.2.4 Security

There is no specific security attached to preference shares.

3.2.5 Influence

When a preference dividend has not been declared for a given period (specified in the Articles of Association), preference shareholders usually become entitled to vote at shareholders' general meetings, along with ordinary shareholders. Normally, provided preference dividends are paid, preference shares do not carry any voting rights.

3.2.6 Negotiability

The general rules outlined above apply to preference shares.

3.3 Cumulative preference shares

If the dividend on a cumulative preference share is not paid in any one year, then it must be accumulated and paid later. That is, it should be accrued in the accounts even if the company cannot afford to pay it this year. This accumulated liability must be paid off in full in later years before any ordinary dividend can be paid.

3.4 Redeemable preference shares

These are shares that are repayable at a

- Predetermined price, which is normally quoted as being at a premium above their nominal value.
- At a predetermined date or dates.

As such, they represent a temporary source of financing for the company that will rank 'for dividends' for a short period of time and then be repaid.

3.5 Participating preference shares

As noted above, preference shares usually carry a fixed dividend, representing their full annual return entitlement. Participating preference shares will receive this fixed dividend and an additional dividend that is usually a proportion of any ordinary dividend declared. As such they participate more in the risks and rewards of ownership of the company.

3.6 Convertible preference shares

Up to the date of conversion, a convertible preference share offers the shareholder all the normal risks and returns associated with preference shares, i.e. fixed dividend returns and preferential rights to any capital repayment. On reaching the date of conversion, the shareholders will have the option of converting the preference shares into ordinary shares or taking a predetermined cash alternative.

3.7 Ordinary shares

In the same way as preference shares, a number of sub-categories of ordinary shares exist that confer slightly different rights on the shareholder. Again, we start with a general consideration of these rights, then look at some specific sub-categories.

Ordinary shares usually form the bulk of the share capital of the company. The ordinary shareholders are normally entitled to all profits remaining after tax and preference dividends have been deducted. These profits will either be paid out to them as a dividend or retained within the company increasing its value and hence generating capital growth in the value of their shares.

Let us consider the general characteristics of ordinary shares.

3.7.1 Annual returns

Ordinary shareholders are entitled to a dividend that will be proposed by the directors at each annual general meeting.

3.7.2 Capital repayment

Ordinary shareholders are not usually entitled to any capital repayment from the company. If they wish to realise their investment they must sell their shares to another investor.

3.7.3 Security

Ordinary shareholders are the first people to lose should a company become insolvent, i.e. they are the last people to be paid out if there are any financial resources left in the business in such a circumstance.

3.7.4 Influence

Ordinary shareholders are generally entitled to vote at general meetings, giving them control over the directors of the company and hence the operations of the business. It is usual for each ordinary share to carry one vote, i.e. the level of influence a particular investor has will be determined by the number of shares he holds.

However, these are just generalisations. Remember that for any particular company, it will be necessary to look to the Articles of Association to find out the specific rules for each ordinary share.

3.7.5 Negotiability

The general rules outlined above apply to ordinary shares.

3.8 Non-voting ordinary shares

When companies wish to raise finance from people other than the existing shareholders without diluting the control of the existing shareholders, they may issue non-voting shares.

These shares are identical in all respects to the ordinary shares except that they carry no voting rights (called N/V or A shares) or restricted voting rights (R/V shares).

Such shares offer no greater return (they receive the same ordinary dividend), though the shareholder faces a much higher risk since he cannot influence the operations of the company. As a result it is becoming increasingly difficult for companies to raise new capital by issuing non-voting shares.

Very few UK-listed companies have non-voting shares in issue. Young & Co., the London-based brewery and pub management group, is one of the few. The practice is more common in Continental Europe.

3.9 Redeemable ordinary shares

Companies are allowed to issue redeemable ordinary shares providing they also have shares in issue that are not redeemable (CA85 S159). The company may also purchase its own shares subject to satisfying a number of conditions, as we will see later.

3.10 Deferred shares

These are shares that do not rank for a dividend until a particular circumstance is satisfied, typically either

- Until the ordinary dividends have reached a predetermined level; or
- Until a specified period after the issue.

3.11 Warrants

Warrants are options issued by a company, which, if exercised will result in the company issuing new ordinary shares at the predetermined exercise price. The terms attached to a warrant will specify the exercise price and exercise period, i.e. when this option can be exercised.

Warrants are frequently attached to unsecured loan stock in order to make the issue more attractive. The stockholder then has the opportunity to convert their stock into shares at the predetermined exercise date.

4 ISSUING SHARES

Exam tip

> You are frequently asked questions, often involving some calculations, in relation to the various methods of issuing shares, e.g. Summer 2005 Question 5, Winter 2001 Question 2.

4.1 Introduction

There are four factors that control or limit a share issue by a company, specifically authorised share capital, nominal value, pre-emption rights and paid-up share capital.

4.2 Authorised share capital

As noted above, shares cannot be issued above the maximum authorised share capital as specified in the company's Memorandum of Association.

4.3 Nominal value

The Memorandum of Association also specifies the nominal value of each share. Shares cannot be issued at a price less than this nominal value (CA85 S100).

4.4 Pre-emption rights

Legally, the current shareholders of a company have prior rights to subscribe for any new issues of shares **for cash** before they can be offered to anyone else. These are called their **pre-emption rights**, and their purpose is to ensure that the level of influence or control that a shareholder has is not diluted by any issue without his prior knowledge and agreement.

The existence of pre-emption rights means that listed companies cannot issue equity shares, convertibles or warrants for cash other than to the current equity shareholders of the company except with their prior approval in a general meeting.

It is quite common to see the waiving of pre-emption rights as a proposed special resolution at the Annual General Meeting (AGM) of public companies. Shareholders can vote to forego their pre-emption rights for a period of up to five years (CA85 S95).

4.5 Paid-up share capital

Most companies issue shares fully paid, i.e. the new subscriber must pay the full nominal value and premium on those shares.

4.6 Methods of issuing shares

Subject to satisfying the above rules, there are a number of ways that a company can issue shares or change its share capital. We look at each method below, examining its impact on the following.

- The share capital of the company.
- The theoretical market price of the shares (Total value of business ÷ Number of shares).

Example

We will illustrate each idea by considering a company (ABC) that has one million £1 ordinary shares in issue at a current market price of £3, and that has the following summarised statement of financial position.

Summarised statement of financial position	(£'000)
Total assets	2,600
Share capital	1,000
Share premium	500
Retained earnings	500
	2,000
Liabilities	600
	2,600

The total market value of the business is currently £3m (1 million shares at £3 per share). This theoretical total value is known as the 'market capitalisation'.

4.7 Market price issue

If new shares are issued at their full market price, then the nominal value of the shares issued is added to the share capital and any premium on the issue is added to the share premium account.

Example

Suppose ABC issues 200,000 shares at the current market price of £3 per share. It has, therefore, raised £600,000 (200,000 × £3), which would be considered as £200,000 nominal value (200,000 × £1) and £400,000 share premium [200,000 × (£3 − £1)]. What would be the impact on the accounts and the share price?

Solution

Impact on the accounts

The impact on the accounts would be as follows.

	Before (£'000)	Issue (£'000)	After (£'000)
Total Assets	2,600	600	3,200
Share Capital	1,000	200	1,200
Share Premium	500	400	900
Retained Earnings	500	–	500
	2,000	600	2,600
Liabilities	600	–	600
	2,600		3,200

As we can see, shareholders' funds have increased by £600,000; total assets correspondingly increase by the £600,000 cash received.

Impact on the share price

Since the new shares are being issued at a price equal to the market price of the existing shares, there will theoretically be no impact on the share price. This can be seen by considering the number and value of shares in existence both before and after this new issue.

	Shares ('000)	Price (£)	Value (£'000)
Before	1,000	3.00	3,000
Full price issue	200	3.00	600
After	1,200		3,600

Hence, the share price after the issue is £3.00 (£3,600 ÷ 1,200 shares).

NB: This calculation gives the **theoretical** share price after the issue. The actual share price may be affected by a number of other factors, such as what the new finance is being used for, and so on. As a result, the actual share price may differ from this theoretical value.

4.8 Scrip / Bonus / Capitalisation issue

A scrip or bonus or capitalisation issue is an issue of new shares to the current shareholders at no cost, i.e. no new finance is raised. Hence, the value of total assets is unaltered and theoretically the total value of the business is unaltered. The purposes of undertaking a bonus issue may be to

- Reduce the market price of the shares and hence improve the marketability.
- Tidy up shareholders' funds by converting undistributable reserves into share capital.

The term capitalisation issue is perhaps most descriptive of the accounting adjustment undertaken, which increases the share capital at the expense of the reserves (typically share premium). Any reserve could be used to record an issue of this kind. However, if the retained earnings are capitalised, the company's capacity to distribute profits as dividends is reduced.

Example

ABC makes a 1 for 4 bonus issue, i.e. for every four shares currently in issue, one new share is issued. What is the impact on the accounts and the theoretical share price?

Solution

There are currently one million ordinary shares in issue, therefore our 1 for 4 bonus issue will result in a further 250,000 new shares being issued, taking the total up to 1,250,000 shares.

Impact on the accounts

	Before	Issue	After
	(£'000)	(£'000)	(£'000)
Total Assets	2,600	–	2,600
Share Capital	1,000	250	1,250
Share Premium	500	(250)	250
Retained Earnings	500	–	500
	2,000	–	2,000
Liabilities	600		600
	2,600		2,600

We can see from this that the total assets and shareholders' funds remain unaltered, and all we have done is reduce the share premium account and increase the share capital account.

We could have fully eliminated the share premium account completely by undertaking a 1 for 2 bonus issue that would have increased the share capital to £1.5m.

Impact on the share price

Again, to establish the theoretical impact on the share price, we need to consider the total market value of the business and the number of shares in issue as follows.

	Shares	Price	Value
	(£'000)	(£)	(£'000)
Before	1,000	3.00	3,000
Bonus issue	250	–	–
After	1,250		3,000

Hence, the theoretical share price after the issue is £2.40 (£3,000 ÷ 1,250 shares), though it may be higher if it improves the marketability of the shares.

4.9 Split

This reduction in the share price as a result of a bonus issue may have its advantages but it also has disadvantages. If share prices are falling, it may result in the price dropping below the nominal value, preventing us from raising finance by issuing more shares.

An alternative way of lowering the price per share but avoiding this problem is to undertake a split.

A split is achieved by dividing the existing share capital into a larger number of shares with a lower nominal value per share, though the total nominal value of all the shares will remain the same.

Example

ABC undertakes a split of its one million £1 ordinary shares into five million 20p ordinary shares. Please note that the nominal value of the shares is £1m both before and after the split.

What is the impact on the accounts and the theoretical share price?

Solution

Impact on the accounts

	Before	Issue	After
	(£'000)	(£'000)	(£'000)
Total Assets	2,600	–	2,600
Share Capital			
1m £1 ordinary shares	1,000	(1,000)	
5m 20p ordinary shares		1,000	1,000
Share Premium	500	–	500
Retained Earnings	500	–	500
	2,000	–	2,000
Liabilities	600	–	600
	2,600		2,600

We can see that from the company's viewpoint the accounts have hardly altered.

Impact on the share price

	Shares	Price	Value
	('000)	(£)	(£'000)
Before	1,000	3.00	3,000
Split issue	4,000	–	–
After	5,000		3,000

From this, we can see that the price per share will drop to 60p (£3,000 ÷ 5,000 shares). This is below the original nominal value of £1 per share, but is still considerably above the new nominal value of 20p per share. Hence, this will not cause any problems in issuing new shares.

4.10 Consolidation

A consolidation is the reverse of a split and has the reverse effect on the accounts and the price per share.

Example

ABC consolidates its one million £1 ordinary shares into 500,000 £2 Ordinary shares. What is the impact on the accounts and the market price per share?

Solution

Again, we can see that the share capital both before and after the consolidation is £1m.

Impact on the accounts

	Before (£'000)	Issue (£'000)	After (£'000)
Total Assets	2,600	–	2,600
Share Capital			
1m £1 ordinary shares	1,000	(1,000)	
500,000 £2 ordinary shares		1,000	1,000
Share Premium	500	–	500
Retained Earnings	500	–	500
	2,000	–	2,000
Liabilities	600	–	600
	2,600		2,600

Again, in commercial terms, the statement of financial position of ABC is unaltered. Its net assets and shareholders' funds remain at £2,000 and its share capital and reserves are unchanged.

Impact on the share price

No new finance has been raised, therefore there is no reason to believe that the total value of the business should be altered in any way. The theoretical impact on the share price is, therefore

	Shares ('000)	Price (£)	Value (£'000)
Before	1,000	3.00	3,000
Split issue	(500)	–	–
After	500		3,000

Therefore, new market price is £6 per share (£3,000 ÷ 500 shares).

4.11 Rights

A rights issue is an issue of new shares for cash to the existing shareholders in proportion to their existing holdings, at a discount to the current market price. Such an issue is an attractive way of raising new finance, since

There is no dilution of shareholders' interest, i.e. someone who held 20% of the shares before the issue will hold 20% after (assuming they take up their rights).

Shareholders who do not want to subscribe more cash and take up their rights can sell them, receiving cash as payment for the dilution of interest that he will suffer. This is referred to as selling the 'nil paid rights'.

The price at which shares are offered in a rights issue is invariably at a discount to the existing market price. This is necessary because of the fact that shareholders must be given at least 21 days to decide whether they will buy the new shares. The issue price must allow for possible falls in the market over the period.

In addition, rights issues are generally underwritten to cater for those individuals who do not want to exercise their rights, thus the company can be sure of raising all the finance it requires. Underwriting involves the company paying commission to financial institutions who undertake to subscribe for any new shares that existing shareholders do not take up.

Example

ABC makes a 1 for 5 rights issue at a price of £1.50 in order to raise £300,000.

What is the impact on the accounts, the theoretical market price per share after this issue and the value of the nil paid rights?

Solution

A 1 for 5 rights issue means that for every five shares previously in existence, one new share will be issued. In our example, one million shares were previously in issue, hence, 200,000 new shares will be issued at a price of £1.50 raising the £300,000 cash required.

Impact on the accounts

Since £1 ordinary shares are being issued at a price of £1.50, each share is being issued at a premium over its nominal value of 50p. Hence, the impact on the accounts will be as outlined below.

	Before (£'000)	Issue (£'000)	After (£'000)
Total Assets	2,600	300	2,900
Share Capital	1,000	200	1,200
Share Premium	500	100	600
Retained Earnings	500	–	500
	2,000	300	2,300
Liabilities	600	–	600
	2,600		2,900

Impact on the share price

Theoretically, the impact on the market value of the company will be that it will rise by £300,000 – the amount of cash raised. As a result, we can calculate the new share price as follows.

	Shares ('000)	Price (£)	Value (£'000)
Before	1,000	3.00	3,000
Rights issue	200	1.50	300
After	1,200		3,300

Therefore the new share price will theoretically be £2.75 (£3,300 ÷ 1,200 shares).

Value of nil paid rights

The right gives us the opportunity to buy a share for £1.50 that is likely to be worth £2.75. We should, therefore, be willing to pay £1.25 (£2.75 – £1.50) for the nil paid rights.

4.12 Placing

A placing is where shares are sold to selected investors in order to raise finance. This will clearly be in breach of the pre-emption rights of the existing shareholders, unless the company is currently wholly owned by the investor with whom we are placing the new shares.

As noted above, shareholders can vote by special resolution to forego their pre-emption rights for a period of up to five years (CA85 S95) for issues of shares for cash.

In terms of accounting and impact on market price per share, a placing is equivalent to an issue at full market price. However, it does offer the following advantages to a company.

- There is no possibility that the issue will not be fully subscribed.
- Costs and administration involved may be lower, in particular underwriting costs.
- The cash may be raised more quickly.
- The shareholder base may be broadened.

Clearly, the disadvantages are for the current shareholders whose interest/influence in the company will be diluted.

4.13 Vendor issues

Vendor consideration issues and vendor placings arise when a company issues shares as part of the purchase consideration for the acquisition of a subsidiary (shares in another company). As a result, the shares issued by the acquiring company are not being issued for cash and hence the pre-emption rights noted above do not apply.

4.13.1 Vendor consideration

A vendor consideration issue is where the vendor accepts shares in the acquiring company as consideration for his investment.

The impact on the accounts and the market price per share will be very similar to the market price issue except that the net assets will rise by the value of the investment, no cash being raised.

4.13.2 Vendor placing

A vendor placing is where the acquiring company wishes to pay by issuing new shares, but the vendor or seller wishes to receive cash.

To satisfy both parties, the acquiring company will issue the shares to the vendor in exchange for the investment. These shares are then placed with an institutional investor for cash, the vendor receiving the cash from that institution.

Stock exchange requirements dictate that this placing cannot be valued at a discount of more than 10% to the prevailing share price at the time of the placing.

4.14 Underwriting

Most share issues for cash are underwritten, whereby a third party (typically an investment bank) agrees to purchase any shares issued by the company that it is unable to sell to the market. The underwriter will charge a fee for this service, even if it is not required that the process be undertaken.

A share issue that is not underwritten may result in the company being unable to issue all the shares, and raise all the cash that it requires.

However, if the company undertakes a rights issue at a **deep discount to market value**, there may be less or no need for underwriting, saving the company some cost.

5 PURCHASING OWN SHARES

Exam tip

> Occasionally covered in the exam, e.g. Summer 2006 Question 1, Summer 2000 Question 2.

5.1 Introduction

Companies Act 1985 specifies the rules for a company repurchasing its own shares. Prior to 1 December 2003, any company repurchasing its own shares had to subsequently cancel them. From 1 December 2003, the rules have been reviewed to allow companies to buy back shares and, rather than cancel them, hold them as treasury shares. These treasury shares can then be sold for cash at a subsequent date. The maximum amount of shares that can be held in treasury is 10% of the issued share capital. Above this limit, the shares must be cancelled.

The following section first looks at the rationale and rules for companies buying back shares and then cancelling them. Then, we look at the rationale and rules for companies buying back shares and holding them as Treasury shares.

5.2 Why repurchase own shares?

One question that needs to be answered is why might a company wish to repurchase its own shares? In fact, there could be many possible reasons, such as

- Part of a capital reorganisation where the company wishes to repurchase preference shares and issue new equity shares.

- An employee share scheme where the company wishes to be able to buy back shares from employees when they leave the company.

- To pay surplus cash to shareholders as an alternative to dividends.

- To buy back unwanted share holdings in a private company that cannot be sold on the stock exchange.

- To provide an exit route for venture capitalists.

- To increase the share price and earnings per share (this will be achieved if the interest received on cash surpluses used to finance the repurchase is lower than the returns generated on the main operations of the company).

- To adjust the capital structure of the company by increasing the proportion of debt financing relative to shareholder funding.

5.3 Creditors' buffer

An important consideration for companies undertaking a share repurchase is maintenance of the creditors' buffer (share capital and undistributable reserves).

Since the accounting equation holds (Total asset = Shareholders' funds + Liabilities) the share capital plus undistributable reserves should be matched by a corresponding amount of total assets available to pay our liabilities.

The higher the value of this creditors' buffer, the greater the payables' security. Correspondingly, the lower the value of this creditors' buffer, the greater the risk to the provider of finance.

If the repurchase would result in the reduction of this creditors' buffer then a transfer must be made from the retained earnings (distributable reserves) to a capital redemption reserve (undistributable reserve) in order to maintain that buffer at its pre-repurchase level.

5.4 General rules

The following general rules apply to the repurchase.

- Shares repurchased must be fully paid prior to that date.

- Shares repurchased that are cancelled by the company result in a reduction to the nominal value of share capital.

- In order to maintain the creditors' buffer, the reduction in the share capital must be covered by either, or a combination of

    - The proceeds of the fresh issue that will add to the share capital and share premium (both part of the creditors' buffer).

    - The distributable reserves (from which a transfer to the capital redemption reserve may be made to maintain the buffer).

Example

ABC wishes to repurchase 200,000 shares from a particular shareholder at the current share price of £3.00. The repurchase will be financed from cash balances and the shares will subsequently be cancelled.

What will be the procedure and the impact on the accounting equation of each step?

Solution

Repurchase old shares

ABC is repurchasing 200,000 old shares at a price of £3 per share, hence the impact on the accounting equation will be

Double Entry	(£)
CREDIT: Cash down	600,000
DEBIT: Share capital down	200,000
DEBIT: Retained earnings down	400,000

Reducing the creditors' buffer by £200,000.

Maintain creditors' buffer

The net effect is that our creditors' buffer has been reduced by £200,000 and this now needs to be reinstated by transferring £200,000 from the retained earnings into a capital redemption reserve. The impact of this on the accounting equation will be

Double Entry	(£)
CREDIT: Capital redemption reserve up	200,000
DEBIT: Retained earnings down	200,000

Summary

The overall position is illustrated below.

	Before (£'000)	Repurchase (£'000)	Maintain Buffer (£'000)	After (£'000)
Total assets	2,600	(600)	–	2,000
Share capital	1,000	(200)	–	800
Share premium	500	–	–	500
Capital redemption reserve	–	–	200	200
Creditors' buffer	1,500	(200)	200	1,500
Retained earnings	800	(400)	(200)	200
	2,300	(600)	–	1,700
Liabilities	300	–	–	300
	2,600	(600)	–	2,000

This illustration shows that the creditors' buffer is being maintained at £1.5m following the repurchase. Also the repurchase itself (costing £600,000) has been financed from the distributable reserves (the retained earnings being reduced by £600,000).

5.5 Why repurchase own shares and hold as treasury shares?

It is possible to buy back shares and hold them as Treasury shares.

Reasons for holding shares as Treasury shares are as follows.

- These shares are available for subsequent sale for cash or transfer into an employee share scheme.

- Provides the company with greater flexibility in managing their share capital, leading to a reduction in the cost of funding for the company.

- The accounting treatment is such that the company has the potential to restore the distributable profits used when the shares are bought back. When the shares are sold out of Treasury, the sales price replenishes the distributable reserves up to the amount lost on their acquisition.

5.6 Accounting treatment

Example

ABC wishes to repurchase 200,000 shares at a price of £3. These shares represent less than 10% of the share capital of the company. The repurchase will be financed from cash balances, and the shares will be held as treasury shares. The shares will then be sold for £3.50 each at a later date.

What will be the procedure and impact on the accounting equation at each step?

Solution

Repurchase shares

Double Entry	(£)
CREDIT: Cash down	600,000
DEBIT: Retained earnings down	600,000

Hence, there is a reduction in the distributable reserves, the same as when shares are cancelled.

At this point the treasury shares must be shown as a deduction from equity according to IAS 32.

Subsequent sale

However, when the shares are subsequently sold, the distributable reserves can be replenished with the amount they were depleted on acquisition. Any surplus is shown in the share premium account.

Double Entry	(£)
DEBIT: Cash up	700,000
CREDIT: Retained earnings up	600,000
CREDIT: Share premium up	100,000

6 DIVIDENDS AND DISTRIBUTABLE PROFITS

Exam tip

Questions on dividends and distributable profits arise quite regularly, e.g. Winter 2006 Question 1.

6.1 Introduction

Dividends represent the amounts paid out, or proposed to be paid out, to shareholders by the company. They therefore represent one element of the total return generated by the company for the shareholders, the other being the appreciation in value of the shares held by the investor.

The level of dividend is recommended by the directors for approval by the shareholders at the annual general meeting.

Dividends may be paid in one of two forms.

- Normal cash dividend.
- Scrip dividend.

6.2 Payment of dividends

Most of the time companies pay out dividends that are less than their profits after tax, i.e. the dividend is being paid from this year's profits and is said to be covered. However, it is not essential for a dividend to be covered, it may be financed from previously retained profits.

In addition, in most cases UK-listed companies pay dividends in two stages.

- **Interim dividend paid** – this is usually paid out during the year based on the half-year's performance.
- **Final dividend proposed** – this is paid to shareholders following the approval of the year-end accounts at the annual general meeting.

We need to be aware of the impact, on both the company and the investor, of paying a dividend.

6.3 Normal cash dividend

A normal cash dividend is when the company distributes cash to its shareholders from the total retained profits. To establish the implications for the company and the investor we will consider the following example.

Example

Company viewpoint

A company has 100,000 ordinary shares in issue. The shareholders approve a dividend of 7.2 pence per share that is paid as a cash amount. What consequences arise for the company?

Investor's viewpoint

A shareholder who holds 100 shares will, therefore, receive a cash amount of £7.20 direct from the company. How much tax will be payable/recoverable on this amount, and what will be the net cash that the investor is left with after all taxes if the investor is

- A lower rate or basic rate taxpayer?
- A higher rate taxpayer?
- Tax exempt?

Solution

Company viewpoint

The amount deducted from equity in respect of dividends will be £7,200 (100,000 × 7.2p), which will also be the amount of cash paid directly to the shareholders.

Investor's viewpoint

Dividends received by investors represent a form of taxable income. The dividend received, however, has an attached tax credit, i.e. is deemed to be net of a certain rate of income tax. As a result, the investor must account for the difference between the tax payable at their relevant rate and the tax deemed to have been paid on the tax credit.

The tax rate payable on dividend income, and the tax credit attached to dividends is shown below.

Tax Status	(%)
Tax Rate	
Higher rate taxpayer	32.5
Basic or lower rate taxpayer	10
Tax exempt	0
Tax Credit	
Taxpayer and tax-exempt individuals	10

The UK tax authorities treat the shareholders as having received an amount of income net of 10% income tax, i.e. a **net dividend** of £7.20 from which income tax at a rate of 10% has already been deducted. So in our example, the £7.20 received represents 90% of the gross income or **gross dividend**.

Hence, the government treats the dividend as gross income of £8 (£7.20 × $^{100}/_{90}$) on which income tax of £0.80 has already been paid, when computing the individual's income tax position.

Lower rate and basic rate taxpayers

For the lower rate or basic rate taxpayer who will suffer tax at 10% on dividend income, no further tax liability will arise. The individual is deemed by HMRC to have received gross income of £8 but paid tax of

£0.80 as required. The net cash that this investor will be left with will be the £7.20 received directly from the company, as you would expect after paying 10% tax on £8 income.

Higher rate taxpayer

Higher rate taxpayers are liable to tax at the rate of 32.5% on dividend income. As 10% tax has already been deducted, they must pay an additional 22.5%. As a result, this investor will need to pay over to HMRC a further £1.80 (£8 × 22.5%), leaving him with net cash of £5.40 (£7.20 − £1.80), as you would expect after paying 32.5% tax on £8 income.

Tax-exempt individual

If the individual is tax exempt (a zero-rate taxpayer) the £0.80 tax that is deemed to have been suffered (paid) may not be reclaimed.

NB: The net position of a tax-exempt individual is therefore identical to that of a lower or basic rate taxpayer.

6.4 Scrip dividend

A scrip dividend is when the shareholders elect to receive bonus shares instead of a cash dividend. Frequently, the value of the bonus shares exceeds the value of the cash dividend (the scrip is enhanced) to encourage shareholders to take up this option. Again, we will consider the impact of such a dividend on both the company and the investor, as well as the reasons why each may or may not prefer this form of dividend.

Example

Company viewpoint

A company has 100,000 ordinary shares in issue. The shareholders approve a dividend of 7.2 pence per share with the option of taking one new share for every 25 held as a scrip alternative. The average mid-market value of the company's shares is £2.25 in the week before going ex-dividend. What consequences arise for the company and what are the advantages and disadvantages to the company of paying this type of dividend?

Investor's viewpoint

A shareholder who holds 100 shares will receive either

- £7.20 cash; or
- Four shares with a market value of £9.00.

Assuming that the shareholder elects to take the scrip, what are the tax consequences of this and its advantages and disadvantages to the shareholder?

Solution

Company viewpoint

The amount deducted from equity and set up as a proposed liability (provided that it was proposed before the year end) for dividends will be the cash dividend value of £7,200 (100,000 × 7.2p), regardless of whether any part is taken in the form of a scrip.

Advantages

The advantages to the company of paying a scrip dividend are

- Financial resources are retained in the business as no cash is paid out.
- Shareholders' funds will, therefore, be higher (since retained earnings will be higher) with a consequent positive impact on gearing.

Disadvantages

The disadvantages to the company of paying a scrip dividend are

- The expense involved in undertaking a share issue.
- The diluting effect that more shares have on the reported earnings per share figure.

Investor's viewpoint

There is the question as to how much income should be considered to have been received if the scrip has been enhanced as in the example above, i.e. has somebody who elects for the above scrip dividend received net income of £7.20 (the cash alternative) or £9.00 (the market value of the shares).

HMRC rules regarding the value of the income for tax purposes are that the value of a scrip dividend will be taken to be the value of the cash alternative unless the market value of the shares is significantly different (greater than 15% different) from this cash alternative, in which case the market value of the shares will be the value considered.

In our example above, the value of the shares received (£9.00) exceeds the net cash dividend alternative (£7.20) by 25%. Clearly, this would be classified as significantly different by HMRC and hence the investors would be deemed to have received a net dividend of £9.00.

Lower rate and basic rate taxpayers

A lower rate or basic rate taxpayer would be deemed to have received gross income of £10.00 ($£9 \times {}^{100}\!\!/_{90}$) on which income tax of £1.00 has already been paid, thus satisfying his full liability to income tax. This investor would, therefore, be able to retain the shares and suffer no further income tax liability as before.

Higher rate taxpayer

As for the basic rate taxpayer, the higher rate taxpayer would be deemed to have received income of £10.00 on which tax of £1.00 has already been paid. The higher rate taxpayer is due to pay tax at 32.5% on this gross income of £10.00, i.e. tax of £3.25 (£10.00 × 32.5%). As a result, this investor will need to pay over to HMRC a further £2.25 to fully satisfy his income tax liability as before.

Tax-exempt individual

The value of the shares received represents their gross income. Thus, a tax-free individual is in no better position than a basic rate taxpayer as regards the net income he receives from a scrip dividend.

Advantages to the investor

The advantages to the investor of receiving income in the form of a scrip dividend are

- Their stake in the company will be increased without suffering any transaction costs (assuming not everybody elects for the scrip dividend).
- The net income they receive may be greater, especially if the scrip is enhanced.

Disadvantages to the investor

- The disadvantages to the individual investor of receiving a scrip dividend are
- People taking the cash alternative will have their interest diluted.
- The increased number of shares may depress the share price.
- The investor may wish to receive cash income without having to sell these shares.
- Once an election is made the investor cannot change his mind and will, therefore, suffer if the share price falls.

6.5 Distributable profits

If a company wishes to pay a dividend, two conditions must be met.

6.5.1 Cash

The providers of finance will, naturally, require a return. However, this demand is only one of many placed on the financial resources of a company. When they recommend a dividend, the directors must consider the ongoing business requirements for these liquid funds.

If the company does not require the cash or cannot profitably use it, then it may as well return it to the shareholders. If, on the other hand, there are significant demands on this resource then the directors will need to carefully balance these demands.

6.5.2 Profits

The Companies Act 1985 states that a company can only pay dividends out of **distributable profits**, but what is the distinction between distributable profits and undistributable profits?

The definition of what is distributable differs for private and public companies, though both have the same starting point of looking at the retained earnings balance.

Retained earnings balance

The Companies Act states that only **realised profits** should be recorded in the retained earnings, that is profits treated as realised in accordance with generally accepted accounting principles, i.e. in accordance with accounting standards. Such profits represent the maximum that may be distributed by any company.

NB: To pay a dividend in one year does not require profits to have been generated this year, dividends may be paid from retained earnings. Thus, the accumulated balance on the retained earnings account represents the upper limit on the potentially distributable profits of a company, being the net of the accumulated realised profits and the accumulated realised losses.

6.6 Private companies

For private companies, this retained earnings balance represents the full legally distributable profit, i.e. they can pay out as a dividend all the realised profits less losses that have been accumulated.

6.7 Public companies

The difference for public companies is that the distributable profits may be restricted below this accumulated retained earnings balance if any unrealised losses have arisen, e.g. on a devaluation of investment properties resulting in a negative balance on the investment revaluation reserve in the UK.

The additional requirement for public companies is that the net assets of the company following the distribution should not be less than the share capital and positive undistributable reserves. Thus, public companies must retain (not distribute) sufficient realised profit to cover such unrealised losses.

Example

Two UK companies have the following summarised statement of financial positions.

	A (£)	B (£)
Net assets	10,000	60,000
Share Capital	2,000	12,000
Share Premium	1,000	15,000
Investment Revaluation Reserve	(500)	14,000
Retained Earnings	7,500	19,000
Shareholders' Funds	10,000	60,000

What are their distributable profits if they are

- Private companies?
- Public companies?

Solution

Company A

Private company

If Company A were a private company, the distributable profits would be the full £7,500 balance of retained earnings.

Public Company

If Company A were public, then it would need to ensure that its net assets after the distribution were at least equal to its share capital and positive undistributable reserves, i.e. the share premium account. As a result the company must have £3,000 (£2,000 + £1,000) of net assets following the distribution, and hence it can only distribute £7,000 (£10,000 – £3,000).

An alternative way of viewing this is that we must retain £500 profit to cover the unrealised loss on our investment properties, hence we can only distribute £7,000 (£7,500 – £500).

Company B

Private Company

If this is a private company, then the distributable profit would be the full retained earnings balance of £19,000.

Public Company

If Company B is a public company then, to satisfy the Companies Act requirements, it must hold £41,000 (£12,000 + £15,000 + £14,000) of net assets following the distribution. As a result, it can also distribute the full £19,000 retained earnings balance (£60,000 – £41,000).

Alternatively, there are no unrealised losses that need to be covered by distributable profits, therefore the full retained earnings balance is distributable.

7 RESERVES AND THEIR USES

Exam tip

You may be asked how the various reserves arise and how they are used, e.g. Summer 2004 Question 9

7.1 Introduction

The reserves of a business represent funding that has been provided by the shareholders. This finance will have been provided either directly or indirectly as follows.

- **Direct funding** in the share premium account, as a result of investors subscribing for new shares in the company at a premium to nominal value.

- **Indirect funding** in reserves such as the retained earnings, where the company has generated added value through its activities and has retained that value within the business to finance growth.

7.2 Profit and loss reserve or retained earnings

The profit and loss reserve or retained earnings represents the accumulated retained profits that have been generated since the company commenced trading, i.e. profits generated in those years and due to the shareholders but not distributed to the shareholders as a dividend.

The retained earnings are viewed as the distributable profits of the company (subject to our comments above regarding distributable profits) and are the source of any dividends paid in excess of the profits for the year.

It also represents a source of additional finance since profits that the shareholders allow the company to retain are enabling the company to increase its asset base.

7.3 Share premium account

A share premium account arises when shares are issued at a price in excess of their nominal value, i.e. at a premium. The nominal value of the shares is added to the share capital account, the premium must be added to the share premium account under CA85 S130.

Example

If a company could raise £20,000 by issuing 5,000 £1 ordinary shares at a price of £4 each, then there is a premium of £3 on each share (£4 − £1).

The impact on the accounting equation for this share issue is

	(£'000)
Impact on Net Assets	
DEBIT: Cash up	+20
	+20
Impact on Shareholders' Funds	
CREDIT: Share Capital up	+5
CREDIT: Share Premium Account up	+15
	+20

7.4 Uses of the share premium account

Having been created, the share premium account can only subsequently be reduced in five circumstances in the UK (without the Court's permission).

- To issue bonus shares.
- To write-off preliminary expenses.
- To write-off expenses incurred issuing shares or debentures.
- To provide for the discount on the issue of any debentures.
- To provide the premium on repayment of debentures.

The share premium account can never be reduced to pay dividends to the shareholders, it is one of the company's non-distributable reserves.

It therefore forms a part of the permanent financing of the business provided by the shareholders.

7.5 Revaluation reserve

7.5.1 Introduction

UK companies are permitted by the Companies Act to undertake the upward revaluation of all non-current assets other than goodwill, increasing net assets and shareholders' funds. Where a company does revalue its non-current assets upwards, that increase in the net assets must be reflected within shareholders' funds in the revaluation reserve.

This treatment is adopted, as it would be imprudent to treat this increase in shareholders' funds as part of the company's realised, distributable profits for the year. It has not been generated by the operational performance of the company and it is certainly not represented by cash.

Example

If a company revalues its non-current assets up to £250,000 at year end from their net book value of £170,000 (an increase of £80,000), the impact on the accounting equation will be

	(£'000)
Impact on Net Assets	
DEBIT: Non-Current Assets up	+80
	+80
Impact on Shareholders' Funds	
CREDIT: Revaluation Surplus up	+80
	+80

The revaluation reserve or surplus represents unrealised and non-distributable gains made by the company, i.e. the company cannot reduce the revaluation reserve to pay a dividend. It can, however, be reduced to make a bonus issue of shares.

This reserve also represents increased funding for the business. However, this is not normally as a result of the business adding value but rather a function of the fact that the value of certain assets, e.g. property, tends to appreciate with the passage of time.

7.6 Capital redemption reserve

The capital redemption reserve will arise when a company undertakes the repurchase of some of its own shares. The rules for this have been described above in Section 6.5. A transfer needs to be made from the profit and loss account to the capital redemption reserve in order to maintain the creditors' buffer (share capital plus undistributable reserves) – the capital redemption reserve is one of these undistributable reserves.

Since it is undistributable, it clearly cannot be used to pay dividends. The only use for a capital redemption reserve is to issue bonus shares. Its purpose, as stated above, is to maintain the permanent funding base of the company and thus ensure that the company has sufficient assets to pay its liabilities at any time.

7.7 Other reserves

Any other reserves represent an apportionment or allocation that has been made from retained earnings.

This is frequently done for the following reasons.

- To indicate that a certain element of profit is being retained for a specific reason by transferring it to a general reserve.

- To indicate that a portion of profits will never be paid out as a dividend, again by the transfer to a general reserve.

8 LOAN FINANCE

8.1 Introduction

Companies borrow in two basic ways.

- Formal loans from banks/issue of debt securities.

- Informal cost-free borrowing from trade payables where extended periods of credit are taken.

In this section, we are considering formal borrowings on which some interest is charged, and not the informal cost-free ones. The accounting treatment is discussed in more detail in Chapter 11, *Financial Instruments*.

8.2 Why borrow?

There are a number of advantages to borrowing over raising finance through the issue of shares, including the following.

- Interest is an allowable expense for tax purposes, i.e. a payment of interest will reduce the tax charge whereas a dividend payment will not.

- The interest paid will be independent of the levels of profitability of the company. If the operating profits rise while interest paid remains constant, then profit available to shareholders will rise more rapidly. This also has its downside however if profits fall.

- The costs of raising loan finance are much lower than those of raising share finance by issuing shares.

8.3 Risks of borrowing

The risks of borrowing are that interest must be paid before any dividends can be paid. If profits fall, dividends could be cut in the case of a company wholly financed by shares. However, if the company is financed by debt, then that interest must be paid regardless of the levels of profits, and if the company is unable to achieve this it may become insolvent. Having some debt is the capital structure is known as gearing.

Gearing therefore seems to bring some risk to a company. However, gearing does not cause risk of itself, rather gearing amplifies the basic risk inherent in the operations of the company. This is perhaps most clearly illustrated with an example.

Example

Consider the performance of two operationally identical (they generate the same profit before interest payable and tax) but differently financed companies, one geared and one ungeared (entirely equity financed).

We will assume that the geared company needs to pay interest of £30,000 p.a. and that the effective rate of tax for both companies is 30%. Interest is an allowable expense for tax purposes.

Given this information, we can work out the impact on the results of the two companies over a three-year period.

	Ungeared			Geared		
	Year 1 (£'000)	Year 2 (£'000)	Year 3 (£'000)	Year 1 (£'000)	Year 2 (£'000)	Year 3 (£'000)
Operating profit	50	100	150	50	100	150
Interest	–	–	–	(30)	(30)	(30)
Profit before tax	50	100	150	20	70	120
Tax at 30%	(15)	(30)	(45)	(6)	(21)	(36)
Profit after tax	35	70	105	14	49	84

Taking Year 2 as our starting point, we can see that operating profits either increase by 50% (up to Year 3's figure of £150,000) or decrease by 50% (down to Year 1's figure of £50,000) for both companies. After that point, however, the picture changes.

Ungeared company

What this example shows is that in the ungeared company the increase or decrease of 50% in operating profit is matched by an increase or decrease of 50% in profit after tax, which is available to the ordinary shareholders.

Hence, in an ungeared company the risk that the shareholders face will be equal to the risk inherent in the operating profit of the company itself.

Geared company

In the geared company, however, a 50% increase in operating profit results in a 71% increase in shareholders' returns (profits after tax rising from £49,000 to £84,000). Correspondingly a 50% decrease in operating profit results in a 71% decrease in profits for shareholders.

The shareholders face much more variable returns, i.e. a much higher risk. The variability of returns in operating profit has effectively been amplified by the fact that a fixed amount of interest must be removed.

Does gearing cause risk?

Clearly, however, if operating profit was constant at £100,000 we would be at no risk whatsoever, regardless of the level of gearing (so long as the interest payable was also less than £100,000). Hence, gearing and having to pay interest does not in itself cause risk. It does, however, amplify the variability of earnings when considering the variability of returns to shareholders (profit after tax).

8.4 Main characteristics

As a reminder, the main characteristics that distinguish the various sources of finance are as follows.

- **Annual returns** – the dividends or interest that must be paid by the company on an ongoing basis.

- **Capital repayment** – any provisions relating to this one-off payment for the particular instrument.

- **Security** – any rights that the provider of finance has over various assets of the business.

- **Influence** – the voting rights or other influence that the provider of finance has and hence his ability to impact on the operations of the business.

- **Negotiability** – the ability of the holder of the financial instrument to trade the instrument and realise its value.

Each of these factors will be specified in a loan agreement in the same way that they are specified for share finance in the Memorandum and Articles of Association.

8.5 Types of loan finance

A company's loan financing can be broadly split into three categories.

- Debentures and loan stock.
- Bank loans and loans from other financial institutions.
- Bank overdrafts.

These items will be recorded within liabilities on the statement of financial position. For the first two categories, a company should also disclose in its notes to the accounts the following.

- The rate of interest (return).
- The terms of repayment, including the date.
- Any security given.

8.6 Debentures and loan stock

Debentures and loan stock are written acknowledgement of debt that, as such, can often be traded. The word debenture is used when the lender is being furnished with some security by the borrower. When there is no security being provided the stock is referred to as loan stock or unsecured loan stock (ULS).

Within this general category of debentures and loan stock, there are a number of different types of stock with differing characteristics, however the general characteristics are as detailed below.

8.7 Annual returns

Most debentures and ULSs carry a fixed annual coupon (interest) rate that is payable half yearly.

The coupon rate shows the **gross** interest that the company will have to pay, which will be treated as an allowable expense for tax purposes.

8.8 Capital repayment

Repayment dates are normally determined at the outset. They will typically be either

- A fixed repayment date on which the company must repay the debt; or

- A repayment period during which the company must repay the debt, the exact timing being at the choice of the company within that period.

8.9 Security

Debentures will be secured by one or both of

- A fixed charge.
- A floating charge.

8.10 Fixed charge

A fixed charge is a charge over an identifiable asset of the company, the debenture deed will note the specific asset in question. Typically, a specific non-current asset, such as land or a freehold building will be used for this purpose as it can be readily identified and should not deteriorate substantially in value over the term of the debenture.

The commercial impact of having a fixed charge is that the company cannot sell the asset in question unless the debenture holder releases the charge. The debenture holder is unlikely to do this unless he is offered some equally good asset over which he can have an alternative charge.

If the company falls into arrears with its interest payment or defaults on its capital repayment, then the debenture holder can either

- Appoint a receiver and obtain income from the asset held under charge; or

- Take possession of the asset and sell it, using the proceeds to repay the debentures in full. Any excess proceeds will be returned to the company, any shortfall will become an unsecured liability of the company.

8.11 Floating charge

This is a general charge over the assets of the company that allows them to be freely traded (unlike a fixed charge) until such time as the charge **crystallises**, i.e. there is an arrears in interest payment or a default of capital repayment. When a charge crystallises it becomes fixed to the assets held at that time.

8.12 Consequences of charging assets

The security offered affects the order of payments on the liquidation of a company that would be as follows.

1. Liquidator.
2. Fixed charge holders.
3. Preferential creditors (government, employees).
4. Floating charge holders.
5. Unsecured creditors, i.e. ULS holders and other trade creditors.
6. Deferred creditors (holders of subordinated loans).
7. Preference shareholders.
8. Ordinary shareholders.

8.13 Influence

Debenture or loan stockholders do not automatically have any influence over the day-to-day operations of the company. However, they may influence it in the following ways.

- Certain clauses in any loan agreements may restrict the levels of gearing at which the company can operate thus restricting its ability to raise further debt finance.

- If there is a default then any charged assets can be seized.

- The loan agreement may include a clause which restricts the level of dividend payable during the loan period.

8.14 Negotiability

As noted above, being written acknowledgements of debt, debentures and loan stock are frequently negotiable, though not always.

8.15 Deep discounted/Zero-coupon bonds

A deep discounted security is one that pays a very low coupon compared to the prevailing interest rates but which was issued at a substantial discount from its par value or redemption price. The premium on redemption makes up for the low rate of interest over the term of the loan.

A zero-coupon bond is an extreme case of this, which pays no coupon interest at all throughout the life of the bond, the total return to the investor being the premium on redemption.

The cash flow benefit to the borrower of this low or zero coupon is obvious, however, the appropriate accounting treatment is not. Should we

- Recognise only the interest paid, which may be zero, in each year up to the year of redemption, then the redemption premium as an additional charge that year?

- Spread the total cost (total interest to be paid plus redemption premium) over the full period of the loan, arguably achieving better matching?

IAS 39 requires such bonds to be measured at amortised cost using the effective interest rate. Therefore the total cost (interest (if any) plus premium on redemption) is written off to the income statement over the life of the bond (see Chapter 11).

8.16 Convertible loan stock

This may be either unsecured loan stock or debentures that offer the option of conversion into Ordinary shares at the redemption date as an alternative to cash.

By offering apparently favourable conversion terms, companies have historically been able to issue this stock with relatively low coupon rates. The idea being that in a similar way to deep discounted securities, the low rate of interest will be made up for by a favourable return on redemption or conversion.

Under IAS 32 this is a compound instrument and must be split between its liability component and its equity component on the statement of financial position (see Chapter 11).

8.17 Eurobonds

The Eurobond market offers companies the opportunity to raise loan finance from overseas. A Eurobond is loan stock issued in a market other than a domestic one. Such stock may be denominated in sterling or any foreign currency, with loan terms typically between seven and ten years.

8.18 Bank loans and overdrafts

Bank loans and overdrafts arise when a specific amount is borrowed and must be repaid. Over the period of the loan or overdraft, the bank will charge interest, and the capital will be repaid either at regular intervals on an ongoing basis, or as a lump sum at the end of the loan term.

The specifics regarding interest payments, capital repayment and security are all included in the loan agreement. Such forms of finance are never negotiable, and any security arrangements are determined when the loan is agreed.

No accounting problems arise in relation to bank loans and overdrafts, which will appear in the accounts as follows.

- The capital outstanding on the loan will appear as a liability on the statement of financial position, split between what is payable within one year and what is payable after more than one year.

- The interest payable for the year will be included as a charge in the income statement whether paid in the year or not, any unpaid interest will be included as an accrual on the statement of financial position.

8.19 Disclosure example

Example

This extract illustrates the extensive debt disclosures required.

Roche Group

Extract from Notes to the Financial Statements as at 31 December 2004

Debt: recognised liabilities in millions of CHF	2004	2003
Debt instruments	6,472	10,579
Amounts due to banks and other financial institutions	1,643	3,666
Capitalised lease obligations	701	890
Other borrowings	144	152
Total debt	8,960	15,287
Reported as		
Long-term debt	6,947	10,246
Short-term debt	2,013	5041
Total debt	8,960	15,287

Roche Group

Extract from Notes to the Financial Statements as at 31 December 2004

Debt: repayment terms in millions of CHF	2004	2003
Within one year	2,013	5,041
Between one and two years	688	2,327
Between two and three years	2,297	493
Between three and four years	2,743	2,223
Between four and five years	568	3,010
More than five years	651	2,193
Total debt	8,960	15,287

The fair value of the debt instruments is 6.9 billion Swiss francs (2003: 11.6 billion Swiss francs) and the fair value of total debt is 9.4 billion Swiss francs (2003: 16.3 billion Swiss francs). This is calculated based upon the present value of the future cash flows on the instrument, discounted at a market rate of interest for instruments with similar credit status, cash flows and maturity periods.

There are no pledges on the Group's assets in connection with debt, except as noted below. The obligation arising from leases at Genentech is secured on property, plant and equipment which has a net book value of 502 million Swiss francs at 31 December 2004.

Amounts due to banks and other financial institutions

Interest rates on these amounts, which are primarily denominated in euros, average approximately 3.5% (2003: 3.4%). Repayment dates vary between one and four years. 683 million Swiss francs (2003: 1,571 million Swiss francs) are due within one year.

Debt Instruments Recognised Liabilities and Effective Interest Rates of Debt Instruments (in millions of CHF)	Effective interest rate	2004	2003
European medium-term note programme			
4% bonds due 9 October 2008, principal 750 million euros	4.16%	1,150	1,159
5.375% bonds due 29 August 2023, principal 250 million pounds sterling	5.46%	536	541
3.25 bonds due 2 October 2007, principal 750 million US dollars	3.28%	848	926
Swiss franc bonds			
'Rodeo' 1.75% due 20 March 2008, principal 1 billion Swiss francs	3.00%	969	956
US dollar bonds			
'Chamelon' 6.75% due 9 July 2009, principal 487 million US dollars (1 billion US dollar in 2003)	6.77%	561	1,229
Zero coupon US dollar exchangeable notes			
'LYONs III' due 6 May 2012, principal 3 billion US dollars in 2003	6.91%	–	2,136
'LYONs IV' due 19 January 2015, principal 1.506 billion US dollars in 2003	4.26%	–	1,171
'LYONs V' due 25 July 2021, principal 2.051 billion US dollars	4.14%	1,264	1,233
Japanese yen exchangeable bonds			
'Sumo' 0.25% due 25 March 2005, principal 104.6 billion Japanese yen	1.89%	1,123	1,186
Limited conversion preferred stock			
due 11 November 2004,	3.00%	–	2
Japanese yen convertible bonds issued by Chugai			
'Series 6 Chugai Pharmaceutical Unsecured Convertible Bonds' 1.05% due 30 September 2008, principal amount of 1.86 billion Japanese yen (3.44 billion Japanese yen in 2003)	1.05%	21	40
Total debt instruments		6,472	10,579
Weighted average effective interest rate		3.80%	4.65%

CHAPTER ROUNDUP

You need to be familiar with, able to describe and discuss the impact of

- Share finance

    - Memorandum of Association.
    - Articles of Association.

- Types of shares

    - Preference shares.
    - Ordinary shares.
    - Deferred shares.
    - Warrants to subscribe for shares.

- Impact of share issues on the accounts

    - Market price issue.
    - Bonus/scrip/capitalisation issue.
    - Split.
    - Consolidation.
    - Rights issue.

- Rules for a company purchasing its own shares

- Types of dividends and dividend payments

    - Cash dividend.
    - Scrip dividend.
    - Distributable profits.

- Reserves and their uses

    - Profit and loss.
    - Share premium.
    - Revaluation reserve.
    - Capital redemption reserve.
    - Other reserves.

- Loan or debt finance

    - Types.
    - Security.

TEST YOUR KNOWLEDGE

Check your knowledge of the chapter here, without referring back to the text.

1. Jolly plc

    The statement of financial position of Jolly plc, a quoted company, is as follows.

	(£m)	(£m)
Non-current assets		109
Current assets		30
Total assets		**411**
Current liabilities	(281)	
Non-current liabilities	(45)	
Total liabilities		**(326)**
Net assets		**85**
Share capital (50p nominal value)		30
Share premium account		20
Retained earnings		35
Equity		**85**

    The current share price of Jolly plc is £2.00.

    Consider each of the following parts separately from each other.

    (a)   Jolly plc decides to do a 1 for 3 bonus issue.
    (b)   Jolly plc decides to consolidate its shares so that two 50p shares become one £1 share.
    (c)   Jolly plc decides to do a 1 for 5 rights issue at a subscription price of £1.20.
    (d)   Jolly plc decides to do a public issue of 2 million shares for cash at a price of £2.00.

    Requirements

    For each of the above situations, show how Jolly plc's statement of financial position will appear after the transaction and calculate the theoretical effect of the transaction on the company's share price.

2.   Yamagata plc

The following is the statement of financial position of Yamagata plc, a quoted company.

	(£m)	(£m)
Non-current assets		398
Current assets		410
Total assets		**808**
Current liabilities	(296)	
Non-current liabilities	(200)	
Total liabilities		**(496)**
Net assets		**312**
Share capital (£1 shares)		100
Share premium		150
Retained earnings		62
Equity		**312**

Yamagata plc decides to repurchase 20 million shares at a price of £2.00 each. The repurchase will be funded by increasing the company's overdraft.

Requirements

(a)   Show how Yamagata plc's statement of financial position will appear after the repurchase.

(b)   What would be the maximum price which Yamagata plc would legally be allowed to pay when repurchasing the 20 million shares?

3.   Tall plc

You are the management accountant of Tall plc. The company is planning a number of acquisitions in 2010 and so, you are aware that additional funding will be needed. Today's date is 30 November 2009. The statement of financial position of the company at 30 September 2009 (the financial year end of Tall plc) showed the following balances.

	(£m)
Assets	425.5
Liabilities	(200.0)
Net assets	**225.5**
Equity share capital	100.0
Share premium account	35.8
Retained earnings	89.7
Equity	**225.5**

On 1 October 2009, Tall plc raised additional funding as follows.

(a)   Tall plc issued 15 million £1 bonds at par. The bonds pay no interest, but are redeemable on 1 October 2004 at £1.61 – the total payable on redemption being £24.15m. As an alternative to redemption, bondholders can elect to convert their holdings into £1 equity shares on the basis of one equity share for every bond held. The current price of a £1 share is £1.40 and it is reckoned that this will grow by at least 5% per annum for the next five years.

(b)   Tall plc issued 10 million £1 preference shares at £1.20 per share, incurring issue costs of £100,000. The preference shares carry no dividend and are redeemable on 1 October 2005 at £2.35 per share – the total payable on redemption being £23.5m.

Your assistant is unsure how to reflect the additional funding in the financial statements of Tall plc. He expresses the opinion that both of the new capital instruments should logically be reflected in the 'equity section of the statement of financial position. He justifies this as follows.

(a) The preference shares are legally shares and so, shareholders' funds is the appropriate place to present them.

(b) The bonds and the preference shares seem to have very similar terms of issue and it is quite likely that the bonds will *become* shares in five years' time, given the projected growth in the equity share price.

He has no idea how to show the finance costs of the instruments in the income statement. This is because he has never before encountered a financial instrument where no payments will be made to the holders of the instrument until the date of redemption.

Requirements

(a) Write a memorandum to your assistant which evaluates the comments he has made and explains the correct treatment where necessary. Your memorandum should refer to the provisions of relevant accounting standards.

(b) Prepare the relevant balances in the statement of financial position of Tall plc immediately after the issue of the bonds and the preference shares.

1.   Jolly plc

Note that Jolly plc has share capital with a nominal value of £30m, made up of shares with a nominal value of 50p each. This means that there are 60 million shares in issue.

(a)

	(£m)	(£m)	
Non-current assets		109	
Current assets		302	
Total assets		**411**	
Current liabilities	(281)		
Non-current liabilities	(45)		
Total liabilities		**(326)**	
Net assets		**85**	
Share capital (50p nominal value)		40	(+10) +20m shares
Share premium account		10	(−10)
Retained earnings		35	
EQUITY		**85**	

Impact on share price

	(£)
Before: 3 shares × £2.00 each	6.00
Bonus: 1 share	−
After: 4 shares	6.00

Price per share = £1.50 (£6/4)

(b)

	(£m)	(£m)	
Non-current assets		109	
Current assets		302	
Total assets		**411**	
Current liabilities	(281)		
Non-current liabilities	(45)		
Total liabilities		**(326)**	
Net assets		**85**	
Share capital (£1 nominal value)		30	30m shares
Share premium account		20	
Retained earnings		35	
Equity		**85**	

Impact on share price

	(£)
Before:2 shares × £2.00 each	4.00
After: 1 share	4.00

Price per share = £4.00 (£4/1)

(c)

	£m	(£m)	(£m)
Non-current assets		109	
Current assets		316	+14
Total assets		**425**	+14
Current liabilities	(281)		
Non-current liabilities	(45)		
Total liabilities		**(326)**	
Net assets		**99**	+14
Share capital (50p nominal value)		36	+6
Share premium account		28	+8
Retained earnings		35	
Equity		**99**	+14

The rights issue is for 12 million shares (60m/5) raising £14.4m (rounded down to £14m).

Impact on share price

Before:5 shares × £2.00 each	£10.00
Rights:1 share × £1.20	£1.20
After: 6 shares	£11.20

Price per share = £1.87 (£11.20/6)

(d)

	£m	(£m)	(£m)
Non-current assets		109	
Current assets		306	+4
Total assets		**415**	+4
Current liabilities	(281)		
Non-current liabilities	(45)		
Total liabilities		**(326)**	
Net assets		**89**	+4
Share capital (50p nominal value)		31	+1 (2m × 50p)
Share premium account		23	+3 (2m × 150p)
Retained earnings		35	
Equity		**89**	+4

Impact on share price

Since the issue is being made at the existing share price of £2.00, there will be no change in the share price after the issue.

2.   Yamagata plc

	£m	(£m)	(£m)
Non-current assets		398	
Current assets		410	
Total assets		808	
Current liabilities	(336)		– 40 (20m × £2)
Non-current liabilities	(200)		
Total liabilities		(536)	
Net assets		272	– 40
Share capital (£1 shares)		80	– 20 (20m × £1)
Share premium		150	
Capital redemption reserve		20	+20
Retained earnings		22	– 40
Equity		272	– 40

The whole of the repurchase must be funded out of distributable reserves, i.e. here, out of retained earnings. The maximum price will therefore be (£62m/20m shares) £3.10 per share. If this occurred, the overdraft would increase by £62m and retained earnings would fall by £62m to a nil balance.

3.   Tall plc

(a)

MEMORANDUM

To: Assistant Accountant

From: Management Accountant   **Date:** 10 October 2009

Treatment of Financial Instruments

The relevant accounting standards are IAS 32 and IAS 39.

IAS 32 deals with the presentation of financial instruments by issuers. It requires that financial instruments initially must be classified as financial liabilities or equity instruments according to commercial substance; where this conflicts with the legal form of the instrument, substance prevails. Determining substance requires careful analysis of the terms and conditions of the instruments.

(i)   **Convertible bond**

Holders of the bond have the option of either being repaid in cash or of converting their bonds into a fixed number of equity shares. IAS 32 classifies the convertible bond as a compound financial instrument and requires that the issuer must split the proceeds of issue (£15m) into liability and equity components.

The liability component must be calculated first. To do this it is necessary to establish the rate of interest at which the Tall could have borrowed £15m, given current market rates and Tall's credit rating and assuming that bondholders had no equity conversion option. By using this rate to discount the cash flows on the bond we fair value the liability component (say £11m). The equity component is the residual amount, £4m); it is simply the balancing figure.

Therefore the initial accounting entries for the convertible bond issue are:

Increase assets – cash	£15m
Increase non-current liabilities – convertible bond	£11m
Increase equity – other reserves	£4m

A finance cost must be charged in the income statement at the rate of interest initially used to split the issue proceeds; this reduces profit and increases the liability in the statement of financial position. As this bond pays no interest until redemption, there will be no interest cash outflows during the bond's life.

The total finance cost to be recognised will be the excess of the redemption amount (£24.15m) over the fair value of the liability component at the date of issue (say £11m)

(ii) Redeemable preference shares

The requirement to redeem the preference shares represents an obligation on Tall to transfer future economic benefits; ie in substance the preference shares are liabilities. Thus, they must be recorded in the non-current liabilities section of the statement of financial position.

Initially the liability will be measured at the proceeds of issue (£12m) less direct issue costs (£100,000). As the instrument is classified as a liability, the associated finance cost will be charged in the income statement. The total finance cost (amount payable on redemption £23.5m less net proceeds of issue £11.9m) must be allocated over the five-year period at a constant rate on the carrying amount – also known as the effective interest method.

(b)

Tall plc statement of financial position (extract)	(£'000)
Assets (425.5 + 15 + 11.9)	452,400
Liabilities (200 + 11 + 11.9)	(222,900)
Net assets	**229,500**
Equity share capital	100,000
Share premium account	37,700
Other reserves – convertible bond; equity component (+ 4)	4,000
Retained earnings	89,700
Equity	**229,500**

7

Reporting Financial Performance

INTRODUCTION

In order to fully understand the historical performance of a business and appreciate the risks that the business is exposed to it is essential to appreciate

- What classes or lines of business are undertaken.

- Where they are undertaken.

- How profitable they are.

- How this picture may have been distorted by the effects of acquisitions and disposals and so on.

This will help an investor form a view as to how sustainable they are.

This chapter introduces the rules relevant to the reporting of financial performance, making you aware of what you are seeing when you analyse a set of accounts.

CHAPTER CONTENTS

CHAPTER LEARNING OBJECTIVES

The syllabus areas covered by this chapter are

Interpretation of Financial Information

The effect of accounting practices

Understanding of the effect of accounting practices on the numbers most significant for investment decisions (profit, earnings per share, asset value etc).

Accounting Terminology and Concepts

Accounting terminology and a knowledge of accounting concepts and conventions to include the statement of financial position, income statement, statement of cash flows and notes to the accounts. An understanding of the distinction between capital and revenue, the valuation of assets for accounting purposes and the determination of profit and earnings share on the nil, net and full distribution bases. An understanding of significance of the statement of accounting policies in relation to the concept of a true and fair view.

Presentation of Financial Statements

Impact of statutory and non-statutory regulation on UK financial statements.

An understanding of the effect on the presentation of financial statements of the Companies Act and non-statutory regulations, including standards and other guidance issued by IASB and stock exchange requirements.

In respect of financial performance:

It is emphasised that the intention of the examination is to assess students' analytical and interpretative skills rather than their technical accounting ability. It is also expected that they should have an understanding of standard accounting practices and an awareness of matters currently under discussion.

1 ELEMENTS OF FINANCIAL PERFORMANCE

1.1 Introduction

The *Framework* issued by the IASB states that users of financial statements require information on three main financial areas in order to make economic decisions.

These areas are **financial performance, position and changes in financial position**. The information on financial position is provided mainly by the statement of financial position and changes in that position can be analysed by reviewing the statement of cash flows in conjunction with the other primary financial statements.

This chapter is concerned with identifying the financial **performance** of the company. The assessment of performance can be categorised into three discrete areas.

- **Trading performance** arising from the direct operations of the business. This element of financial performance is what gives rise to operational cash inflows, essential for the long-term survival of the business.

- **Financial performance**, being either returns generated on the company's financial assets (such as cash and short-term investments) or the expenses incurred on financing the operating assets (interest and finance charges on borrowings).

- **Other gains and losses** that although they are not related to either trading or financial performance, have impacted on the overall value of the business, e.g. revaluation gains or losses.

1.2 International Accounting Standards governing the reporting of financial performance

The IAS/IFRSs relating to the reporting of financial performance will all be considered in this chapter.

- IAS 1 – *Presentation of Financial Statements*
- IFRS 8 – *Operating Segments*
- IFRS 5 – *Non-Current Assets Held for Sale and Discontinued Operations*
- IAS 33 – *Earnings per Share*
- IAS 18 – *Revenue*
- IAS 10 – *Events after the Statement of financial position Date*
- IAS 24 – *Related Party Disclosures*

The purpose of these standards is to provide more information to the user to enable a better assessment of the performance of the company and the risks to which he is exposed. The intention is also to enable the estimation by the investor of future performance and risks.

1.3 Nature of gains and losses

Given the focus on principles, evident from many of the accounting requirements in this area, we have given the definitions of both gains and losses below.

- Gains are increases in ownership interest not resulting from owners' contributions.

- Losses are decreases in ownership interest not resulting from distributions to owners.

The above definitions are written so as to make clear that any transactions of the company with the owners (equity shareholders) of the company are not of the nature of gains and losses.

Therefore, the payment by the company of a dividend to the equity shareholders does not represent a loss – it is instead a **distribution to the owners**.

Payments to the company by the equity shareholders do not represent gains – they are instead **contributions from owners**.

These payments and receipts will be disclosed as part of the movements in shareholders' funds, an area that is discussed later in this chapter.

2 IAS 1 PRESENTATION OF FINANCIAL STATEMENTS

The IASN and the US Financial Accounting Standards Board (FASB) decided, as part of their convergence agenda, to review and harmonise the presentation of financial statements. In September 2007, the ASB published an amended version of IAS 1 which is compulsory for annual periods beginning on or after 1 January 2009.

IAS 1 gives substantial guidance on the form and content of published financial statements. The standard prescribes the basis of presentation, to ensure comparability between the financial statements of different entities.

For accounting periods beginning on or after 1 January 2009, IAS 1 states that all financial statements must contain:

- A statement of financial position (the statement of financial position)
- A statement of performance, titled 'comprehensive income' (the income statement and SORIE)
- A statement of cash flows (the cash flow statement)

The 2007 changes to IAS 1 have introduced new names for the financial statements as detailed above. The old names are shown in the brackets. Companies are permitted to continue with existing titles or adopt the new terminology. The new titles will be adopted in the accounting standards.

The performance statement includes all items of income and expenditure (including those shown directly in equity). Companies can choose to present this either as a single statement, a 'statement of comprehensive income' or in two statements, an 'income statement' and a 'statement of comprehensive income'. The first option is new and effectively combines the content of the income statement and the statement of recognised income and expense (SORIE). The second option is already followed by many preparers of IFRS accounts.

Whichever presentation method is chosen, the key point here is that all income and expenses must be shown in a performance statement and not included as part of a statement of changes in equity as permitted by the previous version of IAS 1.

Comments in this chapter relate mainly to the statement of comprehensive income as the statement of financial position is considered in detail in other chapters.

2.1 Reporting financial performance

The IASB has revised the requirements regarding the presentation of income and expenses but has allowed entities to retain a choice as to the format adopted. A single performance statement is the IAS 1 preferred presentation, principally because it is believed that there are no clear principles that can be used to separate income and expenses into two statements.

If entities decide to retain the two statement approach, other comprehensive income will continue to comprise those items of income and expense that are not recognised in profit or loss as required or permitted by other IFRSs. These items include:

- Changes in revaluation surplus (under IAS 16 Property, Plant and Equipment and IAS 38 Intangible Assets)

- Actuarial gains and losses on defined benefit plans recognised in accordance with IAS 19 Employee Benefits

- Gains and losses arising from translating the financial statements of a foreign operation (IAS 21)

- Gains and losses on revaluing available-for-sale financial assets (IAS 39); and

- The effective portion of gains and losses on hedging instruments in a cash flow hedge (IAS 39).

In addition to the single or dual performance statement approach, companies must present a statement of changes in equity. This reconciles changes in shareholders' equity in the opening and closing period. It will detail separately transactions with the shareholders, such as dividends paid, new share issues or share repurchases that will not have been included in the performance statement above. It will also include the total carried forward from the statement of comprehensive income.

Illustrative Examples

(1) Statement of comprehensive Income (single statement)

	2009 (£m)	2008 (£m)
Revenue	347.2	185.9
Cost of sales	(153.2)	(76.4)
Gross profit	194.0	109.5
Operating costs	(75.9)	(52.7)
Operating profit	118.1	56.8
Finance costs	(33.8)	(27.0)
Share of profits of associates	12.9	3.4
Profit before tax	97.2	33.2
Income taxes	(29.1)	(10.0)
Profit from continuing operations	68.1	23.2
Loss from discontinued operations	(9.6)	(1.9)
Profit for the year	**58.5**	**21.3**
Other comprehensive income:		
Loss on property revaluation	(31.0)	-
Exchange differences on translating foreign operations	1.5	(2.8)
Actuarial gain (loss) on defined benefit pension scheme	(7.9)	(2.6)
Share of other comprehensive income of associates	1.5	0.2
Income tax relating to components of other comprehensive income	7.2	1.3
Other comprehensive income for the year, net of tax	**(28.7)**	**(3.9)**
Total comprehensive income for the year	**29.8**	**17.4**

(2)   Statement of comprehensive Income (two statements)

Income statement

	2009 (£m)	2008 (£m)
Revenue	347.2	185.9
Cost of sales	(153.2)	(76.4)
Gross profit	194.0	109.5
Operating costs	(75.9)	(52.7)
Operating profit	118.1	56.8
Finance costs	(33.8)	(27.0)
Share of profits of associates	12.9	3.4
Profit before tax	97.2	33.2
Income taxes	(29.1)	(10.0)
Profit from continuing operations	68.1	23.2
Loss from discontinued operations	(9.6)	(1.9)
Profit for the year	**58.5**	**21.3**

Statement of comprehensive income

	2009 (£m)	2008 (£m)
Profit for the year	58.5	21.3
Other comprehensive income:		
Loss on property revaluation	(31.0)	-
Exchange differences on translating foreign operations	1.5	(2.8)
Actuarial gain (loss) on defined benefit pension scheme	(7.9)	(2.6)
Share of other comprehensive income of associates	1.5	0.2
Income tax relating to components of other comprehensive income	7.2	1.3
Other comprehensive income for the year, net of tax	**(28.7)**	**(3.9)**
Total comprehensive income for the year	**29.8**	**17.4**

(3)   Statement of changes in equity

	Share capital (£m)	Retained earnings (£m)	Revaluation surplus (£m)	Translation differences (£m)	Total (£m)
At 31.12.08	157.2	122.1	189.9	23.9	493.1
Changes in equity for 2009:					
Issue of share capital	50.0	-	-	-	50.0
Dividends	-	(22.2)	-	-	(22.2)
Total comprehensive income for the year	-	59.3*	(31.0)	1.5	29.8
At 31.12.09	207.2	159.2	158.9	25.4	550.7

The prior year comparative for 2008 should also be provided.

* For ease of illustration, all income tax relating to the comprehensive income has been allocated to retained earnings.

2.2 Income statement

IAS 1 offers **two possible formats** for the income statement, the difference between the two being the classification of expenses: by function or by nature.

2.3 Examples of income statements

XYZ Group
Income statement for the year ended 31 December 2005

Illustrating the classification of expenses by function	2005 (£'000)	2004 (£'000)
Revenue	X	X
Cost of sales	(X)	(X)
Gross profit	X	X
Other income	X	X
Distribution costs	(X)	(X)
Administrative expenses	(X)	(X)
Other expenses	(X)	(X)
Finance costs	(X)	(X)
Share of profit of associates	X	X
Profit before tax	X	X
Income tax expense	(X)	(X)
Profit for the period	X	X
Attributable to:		
Equity holders of the parent	X	X
Minority interest	X	X
	X	X

XYZ Group
Income statement for the year ended 31 December 2005

Illustrating the classification of expenses by nature	2005 (£'000)	2004 (£'000)
Revenue	X	X
Other operating income	X	X
Changes in inventories of finished goods and work in progress	(X)	X
Work performed by the enterprise and capitalised	X	X
Raw material and consumables used	(X)	(X)
Employee benefits expense	(X)	(X)
Depreciation and amortisation expense	(X)	(X)
Impairment of property, plant and equipment	(X)	(X)
Other expenses	(X)	(X)
Finance costs	(X)	(X)
Share of profit of associates	X	X
Profit before tax	X	X
Income tax expense	(X)	(X)
Profit for the period	X	X
Attributable to:		
Equity holders of the parent	X	X
Minority interest	X	X
	X	X

Example

Tomkins Group
Interim consolidated income statement for the six months ended 2 July 2005

	6 months ended 2 July 2005 (£m)	6 months ended 3 July 2004 (£m)	Year ended 1 January 2005 (£m)
Continuing operations			
Revenue	1,545.1	1,541.7	2,974.1
Cost of sales	(1,111.5)	(1,095.5)	(2,120.2)
Gross profit	433.6	446.2	853.9
Distribution costs	(157.3)	(169.3)	(333.5)
Administrative expenses	(127.9)	(121.4)	(216.9)
Share of results of associates	0.5	0.2	0.8
Profit from operations before restructuring initiatives	148.9	155.7	304.3
Restructuring costs	(7.4)	(13.5)	(20.5)
(Loss)/gain on disposals and on the	(1.1)	(4.3)	2.5
Profit from operations	140.4	137.9	286.3
Interest payable	(40.2)	(32.2)	(64.8)
Investment income	19.2	19.9	38.8
Other finance income	3.7	–	–
Profit before tax	123.1	125.6	260.3
Tax	(22.4)	(32.8)	(51.1)
Profit for the period from continuing operations	100.7	92.8	209.2
Discontinued operations			
(Loss)/profit for the period from discontinued operations	(0.7)	(1.8)	0.9
Profit for the period	100.0	91.0	210.1
Minority interests	(3.6)	(6.2)	(10.1)
Dividends payable on convertible cumulative preference shares	–	(7.9)	(15.6)
Profit for the period attributable to equity shareholders	96.4	76.9	184.4
Earnings per share			
Basic			
Continuing operations	12.59p	10.21p	23.81p
Discontinued operations	(0.09)p	(0.23)p	0.12p
Total operations	12.50p	(9.98)p	23.93p
Diluted			
Continuing operations	12.01p	9.89p	22.71p
Discontinued operations	(0.08)p	(0.21)p	0.10p
Total operations	11.93p	9.68p	22.81p
Dividends per ordinary share	5.07p	4.83p	12.60p

2.4 Information presented on the face of the income statement

The Standard lists the following as the **minimum** to be disclosed on the face of the income statement.

- Revenue.

- Finance costs.

- Share of profits and losses of associates and joint ventures accounted for using the equity method.

- Pre-tax gain or loss recognised on the disposal of assets or settlement of liabilities attributable to discontinued operations.

- Tax expense.

- Profit or loss.

The following items must be disclosed on the face of the income statement as allocations of profit or loss for the period.

- Profit or loss attributable to minority interest (see Chapter 9).
- Profit or loss attributable to equity holders of the parent.

Income and expense items can only be **offset** when, and only when

- It is permitted or required by an IFRS; or

- Gains, losses and related expenses arising from the same or similar transactions and events are immaterial, in which case they can be aggregated.

2.5 Information presented either on the face of the income statement or in the notes

An analysis of expenses must be shown either on the face of the income statement (as above, which is encouraged by the Standard) or by note, using a classification based on *either* the nature of the expenses or their function. This **sub-classification of expenses** indicates a range of components of financial performance; these may differ in terms of stability, potential for gain or loss and predictability.

2.6 Dividends

IAS 1 also requires disclosure of the amount of **dividends per share** (declared or proposed) for the period covered by the financial statements. This may be shown either on the face of the income statement or in the statement of changes in equity. It will usually tend to be shown in the statement of changes in equity.

3   IFRS 8 OPERATING SEGMENTS

Exam tip

Segmental reporting is often key to the Section A case study but the ideas are also examined in other sections, e.g. Winter 2006 Question 1, Winter 2001 Question 4, Summer 2001 Question 5.

3.1 Introduction

Businesses may operate in several areas (geographical or business type) with different

- Risks (market and exchange rate).
- Growth opportunities.
- Levels of profitability.

The purpose of IFRS 8 – *Operating segments* is to provide additional information to assist the user of the financial statements to appreciate more thoroughly the nature of the different activities undertaken by the enterprise. The analysis shows the contributions of the individual segments to the overall financial results of the enterprise and, as a result, enables the user to

- Appreciate more thoroughly the results and financial position of the company by permitting a better understanding of the company's past performance and thus a better assessment of its future prospects.

- Appreciate what impact any changes in the components of the business may have on the business as a whole.

IFRS 8 only applies to entitles whose equity or debt securities are publicly traded.

IFRS 8 is mandatory for annual financial statements for periods beginning on or after 1 January 2009. IFRS 8 is substantially similar to the US standard, SFAS 131 *Segment Disclosures*. IFRS 8 is part of the convergence project between the IASB and FASB.

IFRS 8 is based on what is called the 'management' approach. This requires that operating segments are identified on the basis of internal reports about components of the business that are regularly reviewed by the chief operating decision maker in order to allocate resources to segments and to assess performance. Segment reporting therefore is similar to looking over the shoulders of senior managers and seeing segment performance in the way that they review it.

3.2 Identifying operating segments

An operating segment is defined by IFRS 8 as one that:

- Engages in business activities from which the segment may earn revenues and incur expenses

- Has operating results which are regularly reviewed by the entity's chief operating decision maker in deciding resource allocations to segments and in assessing segment performance; and

- Has discrete financial information available.

This approach to identifying operating segments uses a "management" approach. Organisations are encouraged to look at their own internal financial reporting practices in deciding what is appropriate to disclose in the notes to the accounts. If an organisation has a matrix reporting structure, financial information may be reported by business and geographic split, but this is not required by IFRS 8.

Operating segments identified will include those segments that sell primarily or exclusively to other operating segments (ie reports mainly or wholly intra-group transactions).

The end result should give consistency between what is disclosed to the users of financial statements and what is reported to managers internally. It will provide greater consistency between what is included in the financial statements and what is shown elsewhere in the Annual Report, for example the management commentaries.

However IFRS 8 will also allow greater variations between companies as to the nature and the format of information reported, making comparison between businesses more problematic. Discretion exercised regarding what is reported will be limited by internal financial reporting practices.

3.3 Identifying reporting segments

Once operating segments have been identified, an entity needs to decide which operating segments meet the criteria to be classified as reportable segments. Reportable segments are the basis of the segmental disclosure note that is included in the financial statements of an entity.

Reportable segments are those which meet any one of the following quantitative thresholds:

- Revenue (external and intergroup) is 10% of more of total external and internal group revenue

- Reported profit or loss is 10% or more of

    – The combined profit of all operating segments that do not report a loss; or
    – The combined reported loss of all segments that report a loss

- Assets are 10% or more of combined assets of all operating segments.

'Profit' is not defined by IFRS 8 and will depend on the measure used internally by companies. This will usually be operating profit excluding exceptional items.

If an operating segment does not meet the 10% criteria, it may be combined into a separately reportable segment with other operating segments. This is acceptable as long as the segments share similar economic characteristics and operations.

The entity must disclose at least 75% of reported external revenue on a segmental basis as external revenue. This may necessitate including as a reportable segment, one or more operating segments which fall below the 10% threshold. Once 75% is reached, then all remaining segments should be aggregated into a segment called 'all other segments'. This 75% rule is to prevent entities from avoiding reporting some segmental information through bundling it up in an "other" category. It is deemed that 75% is the minimum level to provide useful information to the analyst.

3.4 Reporting segments: disclosure requirements

3.4.1 Description of segments

IFRS 8 requires identification of business segments based on a management approach. As such, the segmental information disclosed will vary company to company. To assist analysts in utilising this information, IFRS 8 requires companies to provided detailed information regarding the basis on which reportable segments have been identified (for example, is the structure based around products or geography or a matrix-type structure). This description should also include information on whether segments have been aggregated. The relevant discussion here will often be contained within the management narratives rather than the notes to the financial statements.

3.4.2 Financial information

Disclosure of amounts allocated to each segment should be based on amounts reported to the chief operating decision maker internally. This must include:

- Segment profit or loss (or cash flow); and
- Segment total assets.

Other segmental information must also be disclosed if it forms part of the internal financial reporting system. This includes:

- Revenues from external customers
- Inter-segment revenues
- Interest income
- Interest expense
- Depreciation and amortisation
- Unusual items
- Share of associates'/joint ventures' profits/losses
- Tax
- Material non-cash items
- Statement of financial position investments in associates/ joint ventures

- Capital expenditure
- Deferred tax assets
- Liabilities

The basis for calculating the segment profit/ loss is not prescribed by IFRS 8, other than that this should reflect management reporting practices. In addition, the company does not have to use the same accounting policies in computing the segmental revenue as that disclosed in the income statement.

Standard setters are aiming here to provide users of the accounts with relevant meaningful information at the expense perhaps of reliability and ease of comparability across different companies.

The standard does not require disclosure of segment liabilities unless they form part of the management reporting system. Many liabilities will be group obligations (for example, financing) and it may not thus be appropriate to allocate these on a segmental basis.

IFRS 8 requires disclosure of the difference between the segmentally reported profit/ loss and the total consolidated profit before tax figure disclosed in the income statement. This difference may include differences in accounting policy, interest charges and central costs. Generally, IFRS 8 requires that all totals provided in the segmental information note to be reconciled to the totals in the income statement.

4 IFRS 5 Non-Current Assets Held for Sale and Discontinued Operations

4.1 Introduction

The aim of IFRS 5 is that users of financial statements will be better able to make projections about the financial position, profits and cash flows. This is done by requiring assets 'held for sale' to be presented separately on the face of the statement of financial position and the results of discontinued operations to be presented separately in the income statement.

4.2 Classification of assets held for sale

A non-current asset (or disposal group) should be classified as **held for sale** if its carrying amount will be recovered **principally through a sale transaction** rather than **through continuing use**. A number of detailed criteria must be met

- The asset must be **available for immediate sale** in its present condition.
- Its sale must be **highly probable** (i.e. significantly more likely than not).

For the sale to be highly probable, the following must apply.

- Management must be **committed** to a plan to sell the asset.
- There must be an active programme to **locate a buyer**.
- The asset must be marketed for sale at a **price that is reasonable** in relation to its current fair value.
- The sale should be expected to take place **within one year** from the date of classification.
- It is unlikely that significant changes to the plan will be made or that the plan will be withdrawn.

4.3 Definitions

The following are key IFRS 5 definitions.

- **Fair value:** the amount for which an asset could be exchanged, or a liability settled, between knowledgeable, willing parties in an arm's length transaction.

- **Costs to sell:** the incremental costs directly attributable to the disposal of an asset (or disposal group), excluding finance costs and income tax expense.

- **Recoverable amount:** the higher of an asset's fair value less costs to sell and its value in use.

- **Value in use:** the present value of estimated future cash flows expected to arise from the continuing use of an asset and from its disposal at the end of its useful life.   *(IFRS 5)*

4.4 Measurement of assets held for sale

A non-current asset (or disposal group) that is held for sale should be measured at the **lower of** its **carrying amount** and **fair value less costs to sell**. Fair value less costs to sell is equivalent to net realisable value. If fair value less costs to sell is lower than the carrying value an impairment loss is recognised in the income statement.

4.5 Discontinued operations – Definitions

- **Discontinued operation**: a component of an entity that has either been disposed of, or is classified as held for sale, and

  - Represents a separate major line of business or geographical area of operations;

  - Is part of a single co-ordinated plan to dispose of a separate major line of business or geographical area of operations; or

  - Is a subsidiary acquired exclusively with a view to resale.

- **Component of an entity**: operations and cash flows that can be clearly distinguished, operationally and for financial reporting purposes, from the rest of the entity.

4.6 Presenting discontinued operations

An entity should **present and disclose information** that enables users of the financial statements to evaluate the financial effects of **discontinued operations** and disposals of non-current assets or disposal groups.

An entity should disclose a **single amount** on the **face of the income statement** comprising the total of

- The **post-tax profit or loss** of discontinued operations; and

- The post-tax gain or loss recognised on the **measurement to fair value less costs to sell** or on the disposal of the assets or disposal group(s) constituting the discontinued operation.

4.7 Analysis of discontinued operations figure

An entity should also disclose an **analysis** of this single amount into

- The revenue, expenses and pre-tax profit or loss of discontinued operations.

- The related income tax expense.

- The gain or loss recognised on the measurement to fair value less costs to sell or on the disposal of the assets of the discontinued operation.

- The related income tax expense.

This may be presented either on the face of the income statement or in the notes. If it is presented on the face of the income statement it should be presented in a section identified as relating to discontinued operations, i.e. separately from continuing operations. This analysis is not required where the discontinued operation is a newly acquired subsidiary that has been classified as held for sale.

Example

The following example is taken from the implementation guidance to IFRS 5. Profit for the period from discontinued operations would be analysed in the notes.

XYZ Group
Income Statement for the Year Ended 31 December 2005

	2005 (£'000)	2004 (£'000)
Continuing operations		
Revenue	X	X
Cost of sales	(X)	(X)
Gross profit	X	X
Other income	X	X
Distribution costs	(X)	(X)
Administrative expenses	(X)	(X)
Other expenses	(X)	(X)
Finance costs	(X)	(X)
Share of profit of associates	X	X
Profit before tax	X	X
Income tax expense	(X)	(X)
Profit for the period from continuing operations	X	X
Discontinued operations		
Profit for the period from discontinued operations	X	X
Profit for the period	X	X
Attributable to:		
Equity holders of the parent	X	X
Minority interest	X	X
	X	X

An alternative to this presentation would be to analyse the profit from discontinued operations in a separate column on the face of the income statement.

4.8 Presentation of a non-current asset or disposal group classified as held for sale

Non-current assets and disposal groups classified as held for sale should be **presented separately** from other assets in the statement of financial position. The liabilities of a disposal group should be presented separately from other liabilities in the statement of financial position.

- Assets and liabilities held for sale **should not be offset**.

- The **major classes** of assets and liabilities held for sale should be **separately disclosed** either on the face of the statement of financial position or in the notes.

5   IAS 33 EARNINGS PER SHARE

5.1 Basic Disclosure

IAS 33 – *Earnings Per Share*, requires all companies whose ordinary shares are publicly traded to disclose their earnings per share on the face of their income statement.

The detailed calculations involved in establishing the earnings per share figure are not included in this session, but in Chapter 10. However, IAS 33 requires the disclosure of the

- Basic earnings per share.
- Diluted earnings per share.

5.2 Additional EPS disclosure

Basic and fully diluted EPS are based on the profit/loss for ordinary shareholders.

As there is now greater disclosure and breakdown of performance in the income statement, it is possible to identify various alternative earnings figures from the information provided in the accounts, such as earnings excluding exceptional items or earnings based on ongoing activities (see below). IAS 33 therefore allows companies to disclose an **alternative EPS** of their choice on the face of the income statement, albeit no more prominently than the basic EPS figure.

Companies have mainly focused on alternative EPS figures that are more indicative of ongoing performance and/or which exclude one-off distorting items (such as those described above). The benefit to the analyst is that the alternative EPS is typically more indicative of ongoing trend performance, and therefore more appropriate when forecasting ahead, for example an EPS based on profit which does not include profit/loss on discontinued operations.

Whenever an alternative EPS is published, the company must be consistent year on year and publish the same alternative. The profit used for the alternative EPS must also be reconciled back to the appropriate profit line in the income statement.

6   IAS 18 REVENUE

Exam tip

You may well be asked about revenue recognition, e.g. Summer 2006, Question 7.

6.1 Introduction

IAS 18 governs the recognition of revenue in specific (common) types of transaction. Generally, recognition should be when it is probable that **future economic benefits** will flow to the enterprise and when these benefits can be **measured reliably**.

Income, as defined by the IASB's *Framework* document, includes both revenues and gains. Revenue is income arising in the ordinary course of an enterprise's activities and it may be called different names, such as sales, fees, interest, dividends or royalties.

6.2 Definitions

The following definitions are given in the Standard.

> **Revenue** is the gross inflow of economic benefits during the period arising in the course of the ordinary activities of an enterprise when those inflows result in increases in equity, other than increases relating to contributions from equity participants.
>
> **Fair value** is the amount for which an asset could be exchanged, or a liability settled, between knowledgeable, willing parties in an arm's length transaction. *(IAS 18)*

Revenue **does not include** sales taxes, value added taxes or goods and service taxes which are only collected for third parties, because these do not represent an economic benefit flowing to the entity.

6.3 Measurement of revenue

When a transaction takes place, the amount of revenue is usually decided by the **agreement of the buyer and seller**. The revenue is actually measured, however, as the **fair value of the consideration received**, which will take account of any trade discounts and volume rebates.

6.4 Sale of goods

Revenue from the sale of goods should only be recognised when *all* these conditions are satisfied.

- The enterprise has transferred the **significant risks and rewards** of ownership of the goods to the buyer.

- The enterprise has **no continuing managerial involvement** to the degree usually associated with ownership, and no longer has effective control over the goods sold.

- The amount of revenue can be **measured reliably**.

- It is probable that the **economic benefits** associated with the transaction will flow to the enterprise.

- The **costs incurred** in respect of the transaction can be measured reliably.

The transfer of risks and rewards can only be decided by examining each transaction. Mainly, the transfer occurs at the same time as either the **transfer of legal title**, or the **passing of possession** to the buyer - this is what happens when you buy something in a shop.

If **significant risks and rewards remain with the seller**, then the transaction is *not* a sale and revenue cannot be recognised, for example if the receipt of the revenue from a particular sale depends on the buyer receiving revenue from his own sale of the goods.

It is possible for the seller to retain only an **'insignificant' risk of ownership** and for the sale and revenue to be recognised. The main example here is where the seller retains title only to ensure collection of what is owed on the goods. This is a common commercial situation, and when it arises the revenue should be recognised on the date of sale.

6.5 Rendering of services

When the outcome of a transaction involving the rendering of services can be estimated reliably, the associated revenue should be recognised by reference to the **stage of completion of the transaction** at the statement of financial position date. The outcome of a transaction can be estimated reliably when *all* these conditions are satisfied.

- The amount of revenue can be **measured reliably**.

- It is probable that the **economic benefits** associated with the transaction will flow to the enterprise.

- The **stage of completion** of the transaction at the statement of financial position date can be measured reliably.

- The **costs incurred** for the transaction and the costs to complete the transaction can be measured reliably.

The parties to the transaction will normally have to agree the following before an enterprise can make reliable estimates.

- Each party's **enforceable rights** regarding the service to be provided and received by the parties.
- The **consideration** to be exchanged.
- The **manner and terms of settlement**.

There are various methods of determining the stage of completion of a transaction, but for practical purposes, when services are performed by an indeterminate number of acts over a period of time, revenue should be recognised on a **straight-line basis** over the period, unless there is evidence for the use of a more appropriate method. If one act is of more significance than the others, then the significant act should be carried out *before* revenue is recognised.

In uncertain situations, when the outcome of the transaction involving the rendering of services cannot be estimated reliably, the Standard recommends a **no loss/no gain approach**. Revenue is recognised only to the extent of the expenses recognised that are recoverable.

This is particularly likely during the **early stages of a transaction**, but it is still probable that the enterprise will recover the costs incurred. So the revenue recognised in such a period will be equal to the expenses incurred, with no profit.

Obviously, if the costs are not likely to be reimbursed, then they must be recognised as an expense immediately. **When the uncertainties cease to exist**, revenue should be recognised as laid out in the first paragraph of this section.

6.6 Interest, royalties and dividends

When others use the enterprise's assets yielding interest, royalties and dividends, the revenue should be recognised on the bases set out below when

- It is probable that the **economic benefits** associated with the transaction will flow to the enterprise; and

- The amount of the revenue can be **measured reliably**.

The revenue is recognised on the following bases.

- **Interest** is recognised on a time proportion basis that takes into account the effective yield on the asset.

- **Royalties** are recognised on an accruals basis in accordance with the substance of the relevant agreement.

- **Dividends** are recognised when the shareholder's right to receive payment is established.

7 IAS 10 EVENTS AFTER THE STATEMENT OF FINANCIAL POSITION DATE

7.1 Introduction

Events after the statement of financial position date are those events, both favourable and unfavourable, that occur between the statement of financial position and the date on which the financial statements are authorised for issue.

Events after the statement of financial position date fall into one of two categories.

- Adjusting events.
- Non-adjusting events.

These categories are outlined below.

Exam tip

> The distinction between these types of event may arise in Section C, e.g. Winter 2002, Question 9.

7.2 Adjusting events

7.2.1 Definition

> An **adjusting event** is an event that gives additional evidence of conditions existing at the statement of financial position date.

Examples of adjusting events would include

- **Non-current assets** – the determination of costs or proceeds related to assets sold prior to the year end.

- **Inventory** – evidence regarding the net realisable value of items of inventory.

- **Receivables** – evidence as to the recoverability of trade receivable accounts.

Accounting treatment

The accounts should be adjusted for any such **material** events.

7.3 Non-adjusting events

7.3.1 Definition

> Non-adjusting events are events concerning conditions that arose subsequent to the statement of financial position date.

Examples of non-adjusting events that may require disclosure include

- Mergers and significant acquisitions.
- Issues of shares and debentures.
- Changes in the rates of foreign exchange.
- Strikes.
- Opening new trading activities.
- Purchase or sale of non-current assets and investments and profits or losses arising therefrom.

Accounting treatment

All **material** non-adjusting events should be disclosed.

The disclosure required for these events is

- The nature of the event.
- The estimated financial effect.

7.4 Proposed dividends

An important aspect of IAS 10 is that if an equity dividend for a period is declared after the statement of financial position date but before the financial statements are approved, it should not be recognised as a liability but shown as a note in the financial statement.

8 IAS 24 RELATED PARTY DISCLOSURES

8.1 Introduction

In the absence of information to the contrary, it is assumed that a reporting entity has **independent discretionary power** over its resources and transactions and pursues its activities independently of the interests of its individual owners, managers and others. Transactions are presumed to have been undertaken on an **arm's length basis**, ie on terms such as could have obtained in a transaction with an external party, in which each side bargained knowledgeably and freely, unaffected by any relationship between them.

These assumptions may not be justified when **related party relationships** exist, because the requisite conditions for competitive, free market dealings may not be present. While the parties may endeavour to achieve arm's length bargaining the very nature of the relationship may preclude this occurring.

8.2 Objective

IAS 24 aims to ensure that financial statements contain the disclosures necessary to draw attention to the possibility that the reported financial position and results may have been affected by the existence of related parties and by material transactions with them. In other words, this is a Standard which is primarily concerned with **disclosure**.

8.3 Scope

The Standard requires disclosure of related party transactions and outstanding balances in the **separate financial statements** of a parent, venturer or investor presented in accordance with IAS 27 as well as in consolidated financial statements.

This is a **change** from the previous version of IAS 24, which did not require disclosure in the separate financial statements of a parent or wholly-owned subsidiary that are made available or published with consolidated financial statements for the group.

8.4 Definitions

The following important definitions are given by the Standard.

Related party. A party is related to an entity if

(a)   Directly, or indirectly through one or more intermediaries, it

–   Controls, is controlled by, or is under common control with, the entity (this includes parents, subsidiaries and fellow subsidiaries);

–   Has an interest in the entity that gives it significant influence over the entity; or

–   Has joint control over the entity.

(b)   It is an associate.

(c)   It is a joint venture in which the entity is a venturer.

(d)   It is a member of the key management personnel of the entity or its parent.

(e)   It is a close member of the family of any individual referred to in (a) or (d).

(f)   It is an entity that is controlled, jointly controlled or significantly influenced by; or for which significant voting power in such entity resides with, directly or indirectly, any individual referred to in (d) or (e).

(g)   It is a post-employment benefit plan for the benefit of employees of the entity, or of any entity that is a related party of the entity.

Related party transaction. A transfer of resources, services or obligations between related parties, regardless of whether a price is charged.

Control is the power to govern the financial and operating policies of an entity so as to obtain benefits from its activities.

Significant influence is the power to participate in the financial and operating policy decisions of an entity, but is not control over these policies. Significant influence may be gained by share ownership, statute or agreement.

Joint control is the contractually agreed sharing of control over an economic activity.

Key management personnel are those persons having authority and responsibility for planning, directing and controlling the activities of the entity, directly or indirectly, including any director (whether executive or otherwise) of that entity.

Close members of the family of an individual are those family members who may be expected to influence, or be influenced by, that individual in their dealings with the entity. They may include

■   The individual's domestic partner and children.

■   Children of the domestic partner.

■   Dependants of the individual or the domestic partner.   (IAS 24)

The most important point to remember here is that, when considering each possible related party relationship, attention must be paid to the **substance of the relationship, not merely the legal form**.

8.5 Not necessarily related

IAS 24 lists the following which are **not necessarily related parties**.

- **Two entities simply because they have a director or other key management in common** (notwithstanding the definition of related party above, although it is necessary to consider how that director would affect both entities).

- **Two venturers, simply because they share joint control over a joint venture**.

- Certain other bodies, simply as a result of their **role in normal business dealings** with the entity.
    - Providers of finance.
    - Trade unions.
    - Public utilities.
    - Government departments and agencies.

- **Any single customer, supplier, franchisor, distributor, or general agent** with whom the entity transacts a significant amount of business, simply by virtue of the resulting economic dependence.

8.6 Disclosure

As noted above, IAS 24 is almost entirely concerned with disclosure and its provisions are meant to **supplement** those disclosure requirements required by national company legislation and other IASs .

The Standard lists some **examples** of transactions that are disclosed if they are with a related party.

- Purchases or sales of goods (finished or unfinished).
- Purchases or sales of property and other assets.
- Rendering or receiving of services.
- Leases.
- Transfer of research and development.
- Transfers under licence agreements.
- Provision of finance (including loans and equity contributions in cash or in kind).
- Provision of guarantees and collateral security.
- Settlement of liabilities on behalf of the entity or by the entity on behalf of another party.

8.6.1 Parent and subsidiaries

Relationships between **parents and subsidiaries** must be **disclosed irrespective** of **whether** any **transactions** have **taken place between** the related parties. An entity must disclose the **name** of its **parent** and, if different, the **ultimate controlling party**. This will enable a reader of the financial statements to be able to form a view about the effects of a related party relationship on the reporting entity.

If neither the parent nor the ultimate controlling party produces financial statements available for public use, the name of the next most senior parent that does so shall also be disclosed.

8.6.2 Key management personnel

An entity should disclose **key management personnel compensation** in **total** and for **each** of the following **categories**.

- **Short-term employee benefits** (e.g., wages, salaries, social security contributions, paid annual leave and paid sick-leave, profit sharing and bonuses and non-monetary benefits such as medical care, housing, cars and free or subsidised goods or services);

- **Post-employment benefits** (e.g., pensions, other retirement benefits, life insurance and medical care);

- **Other long-term benefits** (e.g., long-service leave, sabbatical leave, long-term disability benefits and, if they are not payable within twelve months after the end of the period, profit sharing, bonuses and deferred compensation);

- Termination benefits; and

- **Equity compensation benefits**.

8.6.3 Related party transactions

Where **transactions have taken place** between related parties, the entity should disclose the **nature** of the related party relationships, as well as information about the **transactions and outstanding balances** necessary for an understanding of the potential effect of the relationship on the financial statements. As a minimum, disclosures must include

- The **amount of the transactions**.

- The **amount of outstanding balances** and their terms and conditions, including whether they are secured, and the nature of the consideration to be provided in settlement.

- Details of any guarantees given or received.

- Provisions for **doubtful debts** related to the amount of outstanding balances.

- The **expense** recognised during the period in respect of **bad or doubtful debts** due from related parties.

Example

Roche Holdings
Note from the Financial Statement for the Year Ended 31 December 2004

Controlling Shareholders

The share capital of Roche Holding Ltd, which is the Group's parent company, consists of 160,000,000 bearer shares. Based on information supplied by a shareholders' group with pooled voting rights, comprising Ms Vera Michalski-Hoffman, Ms Maja Hoffmann, Mr André Hoffman, Dr Andreas Oeri, Ms Sabine Duschmalé-Oeri, Ms Catherine Oeri, Ms Beatrice Oeri and Ms Maja Oeri, that group holds 80,020,000 shares as in the preceding year, which represents 50.01% of the issued shares. This figure does not include any shares without pooled voting rights that are held outside this group by individual members of the group.

Mr André Hoffman and Dr Andreas Oeri are members of the Board of Directors of Roche Holding Ltd and in this capacity receive an annual remuneration of 300 thousand Swiss francs. In addition Mr Hoffmann and Dr Oeri receive 20 thousand Swiss francs and 10 thousand Swiss francs respectively for their time and expenses related to their membership of Board committees. Until his retirement at the Annual General Meeting on 6 April 2004 Dr Fritz Gerber was a member of the above mentioned shareholders' group and was also a member of the Board of Directors of Roche Holding Limited. For the period until 6 April 2004 Dr Gerber received a remuneration of 75 thousand Swiss francs and a pension of 396 thousand Swiss francs.

There were no other transactions between the Group and the individual members of the above shareholders' group.

Subsidiary and Associated Companies

A listing of the major Group subsidiaries and associated companies is included in Note 41. Transactions between the parent company and its subsidiaries and between subsidiaries are eliminated on consolidation.

Transactions between the Group and its associated companies **in millions of CHF**	**2004**	**2003**
Income statement		
Income from the sale of goods or supply of services	–	4
Expenses for the purchase of goods or supply of services	–	(21)
Milestone and other upfront payments	–	(11)
Statement of financial position		
Trade accounts receivables	–	1
Trade accounts payable	–	–

Key Management Personnel

Members of the Board of Directors of Roche Holding Ltd receive an annual remuneration and payment for their time and expenses related to their membership of Board committees. Total payments to non-executive directors in 2004 for the remuneration and expenses were 3 million Swiss francs (2003: 3 million Swiss francs). Payment to Dr Franz B. Humer, who is also a member of the Executive Committee, are included in the figures for the Executive Committee below.

Members of the Executive Committee received total remuneration as shown in the table below.

Remuneration of members of the Executive Committee **in millions of CHF**	**2004**	**2003**
Salary	12	13
Bonuses	5	4
Total cash remuneration paid	17	17
Options awarded		
(equivalent number of non-voting equity securities)	147,815	226,482
Pension and social insurance contributions paid by the Group	8	6

As part of the Roche Performance Share Plan, members of the Executive Committee were awarded 193,418 non-voting equity securities with a fair value of 25 million Swiss francs in respect of the Group's performance in 2002-2004.

CHAPTER ROUNDUP

You need to be familiar with and able to describe

- Three discrete areas

    - **Trading performance** arising from the direct operations of the business. This element of financial performance is what gives rise to operational cash inflows, essential for the long-term survival of the business.

    - **Financial performance**, being either returns generated on the company's financial assets (such as cash and short-term investments) or the expenses incurred on financing the operating assets (interest and finance charges on borrowings).

    - **Other gains and losses** that although they are not related to either trading or financial performance, have impacted on the overall value of the business, e.g. revaluation gains or losses.

- IAS 1 *Presentation of Financial Statements*

- Changes in equity.

- IFRS 8 *Operating Segments*

    - Segments disclosed are based on the management reporting structure.

    - Differences may exist between information reported segmentally and the group income statement and statement of financial position totals.

    - Full reconciliations and explanations should be provided.

- IFRS 5 *Non-Current Assets Held for Resale*

    - A non-current asset (or disposal group) that is held for sale should be measured at the **lower of** its **carrying amount** and **fair value less costs to sell**. Fair value less costs to sell is equivalent to net realisable value.

    - **Fair value**: the amount for which an asset could be exchanged, or a liability settled, between knowledgeable, willing parties in an arm's length transaction.

    - **Costs to sell**: the incremental costs directly attributable to the disposal of an asset (or disposal group), excluding finance costs and income tax expense.

    - **Recoverable amount**: the higher of an asset's fair value less costs to sell and its value in use.

    - **Value in use**: the present value of estimated future cash flows expected to arise from the continuing use of an asset and from its disposal at the end of its useful life.

- IAS 33 *Earnings per Share*

- IAS 18 *Revenue*

    - **Revenue** is the gross inflow of economic benefits during the period arising in the course of the ordinary activities of an enterprise when those inflows result in increases in equity, other than increases relating to contributions from equity participants.

    - **Fair value** is the amount for which an asset could be exchanged, or a liability settled, between knowledgeable, willing parties in an arm's length transaction. *(IAS 18)*

- IAS 10 *Events After the Statement of Financial Position Date*
  - Adjusting.
  - Non-adjusting.

- IAS 24 *Related Party Disclosures*

TEST YOUR KNOWLEDGE

Check your knowledge of the chapter here, without referring back to the text.

1.   Fully define a reportable segment under IFRS 8.

2.   Define and describe the treatment of events after the statement of financial position date.

3.   Outline the required disclosures for related party transactions.

TEST YOUR KNOWLEDGE: ANSWERS

1.   See Section 4.

2.   See Section 8.

3.   See Paragraph 9.6.

8

Statement of Cash Flows

INTRODUCTION

Generating profits is essential to the long-term success of a business. Balancing cash inflows and outflows is equally central to the long-term survival of the business. For long-term survival, a business needs to be receiving cash at least as fast as it pays it out. Statement of cash flows show how a company is receiving in and paying out cash. They allow us to assess whether this balance exists for the company.

This section considers the rules underlying the preparation of statement of cash flows and the approach to analysis.

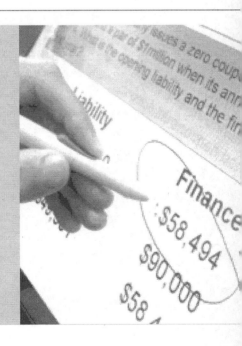

CHAPTER LEARNING OBJECTIVES

The syllabus areas covered by this chapter are

Interpretation of Financial Information

The effect of accounting practices

Understanding of the effect of accounting practices on the numbers most significant for investment decisions (profit, earnings per share, asset value etc).

Accounting Terminology and Concepts

Accounting terminology and a knowledge of accounting concepts and conventions to include the statement of financial position, income statement, statement of cash flows and notes to the accounts. An understanding of the distinction between capital and revenue, the valuation of assets for accounting purposes and the determination of profit and earnings share on the nil, net and full distribution bases. An understanding of significance of the statement of accounting policies in relation to the concept of a true and fair view.

Presentation of Financial Statements

Impact of statutory and non-statutory regulation on UK financial statements.

An understanding of the effect on the presentation of financial statements of the Companies Act and non-statutory regulations, including standards and other guidance issued by IASB and stock exchange requirements.

In respect of statement of cash flows:

It is emphasised that the intention of the examination is to assess students' analytical and interpretative skills rather than their technical accounting ability. It is also expected that they should have an understanding of standard accounting practices and an awareness of matters currently under discussion.

1 INTRODUCTION

1.1 Background

The statement of financial position and income statement are prepared on an accruals basis. They give no indication of the effects of the business' operations on its cash flows. It should always be noted that profits do not correspond exactly to cash. A company may be very profitable and have very high levels of net assets but at the same time, be almost bankrupt. This may appear a little strange, so let us examine this state of affairs a bit further.

1.2 Profit v Cash

Trade certainly causes cash to flow, for example when customers pay or suppliers are paid, therefore trade does impact on cash flows. However, not all income statement items result in an immediate cash flow or even any cash flow at all, for example

- **Depreciation** – the cash flow arises when the original non-current asset is purchased from the supplier, the income statement depreciation charge is *not* a cash flow.

- **Sales on credit/purchases on credit** – cash flows in relation to these items arise when the amounts are actually received/paid, which is after they have been credited/charged within the income statement.

- **Accrued expenses/prepaid expenses** – cash flows arise when these expenses are settled which, again, differs from when they are recognised in the income statement.

Cash also moves for other reasons, for example buying subsidiaries, raising share capital/loans, etc.

1.3 The need for a statement of cash flows

The following are all important advantages that come from the availability of cash flow information and justify the requirement for a statement of cash flows.

- Cash is highly relevant to a company's survival. Lenders foreclose due to inadequacies of cash to service debt.

- Many users, especially lenders, make their business decisions based on cash flow analysis.

- It may be possible to identify creative accounting through a comparison of cash flow with profits.

- The format of the statement of cash flows under IAS 7 assists analysis, enabling the analyst to identify the level of reinvestment, non-discretionary demands on the company, and so on.

2 IAS 7 STATEMENT OF CASH FLOWS

2.1 Objective of IAS 7

The aim of IAS 7 is to provide information to users of financial statements about the entity's **ability to generate cash and cash equivalents**, as well as indicating the cash needs of the entity. The statement of cash flows provides *historical* information about cash and cash equivalents, classifying cash flows between operating, investing and financing activities.

2.2 Scope

A statement of cash flows should be presented as an **integral part** of an entity's financial statements. All types of entity can provide useful information about cash flows as the need for cash is universal, whatever the nature of their revenue-producing activities. Therefore **all entities are required by the Standard to produce a statement of cash flows**.

2.3 Benefits of cash flow information

Exam tip

> The usefulness of statement of cash flows is a prime area for discussion questions, e.g. Summer 2001, Question 4.

The use of statement of cash flows is very much **in conjunction** with the rest of the financial statements. Users can gain further appreciation of the change in net assets, of the entity's financial position (liquidity and solvency) and the entity's ability to adapt to changing circumstances by affecting the amount and timing of cash flows. statement of cash flows **enhance comparability** as they are not affected by differing accounting policies used for the same type of transactions or events.

Cash flow information of a historical nature can be used as an indicator of the amount, timing and certainty of future cash flows. Past forecast cash flow information can be **checked for accuracy** as actual figures emerge. The relationship between profit and cash flows can be analysed as can changes in prices over time.

2.4 Definitions

The Standard gives the following definitions, the most important of which are **cash** and **cash equivalents**.

- **Cash** comprises cash on hand and demand deposits.

- **Cash equivalents** are short-term, highly liquid investments that are readily convertible to known amounts of cash and which are subject to an insignificant risk of changes in value.

- **Cash flows** are inflows and outflows of cash and cash equivalents.

- **Operating activities** are the principal revenue-producing activities of the entity and other activities that are not investing or financing activities.

- **Investing activities** are the acquisition and disposal of non-current assets and other investments not included in cash equivalents.

- **Financing activities** are activities that result in changes in the size and composition of the equity capital and borrowings of the entity.
  (IAS 7)

2.5 Cash and cash equivalents

Exam tip

> May be asked as a basic definition in Section C, e.g. Summer 2001, Question 9.

The Standard expands on the definition of cash equivalents: they are not held for investment or other long-term purposes, but rather to meet short-term cash commitments. To fulfil the above definition, an investment's **maturity date should normally be within three months from its acquisition date**. It would usually be the case then that equity investments (i.e. shares in other companies) are *not* cash equivalents. An exception would be where preferred shares were acquired with a very close maturity date.

Loans and other borrowings from banks are classified as investing activities. However, **bank overdrafts** are repayable on demand and are treated as part of an entity's total cash management system. In these circumstances an overdrawn balance will be included in cash and cash equivalents.

Movements between different types of cash and cash equivalent are not included in cash flows. The investment of surplus cash in cash equivalents is part of cash management, not part of operating, investing or financing activities.

2.6 Presentation of a statement of cash flows

IAS 7 requires the statement of cash flows to report cash flows during the period classified by **operating, investing and financing activities**.

Example

Tomkins Group Interim Consolidated statement of cash flows for the six months ended 2 July 2005	6 months ended 2 July 2005 (£m)	6 months ended 3 July 2004 (£m)
Operating activities		
Cash generated by operations	136.6	131.7
Income taxes paid	(34.4)	(31.9)
Income taxes received	6.0	11.9
Net cash inflow from operating activities	108.2	111.7
Investing activities		
Purchase of property, plant and equipment	(65.6)	(73.2)
Disposal of property, plant and equipment	11.3	3.0
Purchase of subsidiaries	(85.3)	–
Sale of subsidiaries, net of cash disposed	2.9	14.4
Dividends received from associates	0.3	0.1
Net cash outflow from investing activities	(136.4)	(55.7)
Financing activities		
Issue of Ordinary share capital	1.4	1.1
Decrease in convertible cumulative preference shares	(0.7)	–
Increase in collateralised cash	(0.2)	–
Increase/(decrease) in debt	93.4	(1.1)
Capital element of finance lease rental payments	(2.7)	(1.8)
Interest element of finance lease rental payments	(0.3)	(0.5)
Purchase of own shares	(0.6)	(3.6)
Sale of own shares	2.9	–
Interest received	1.8	2.4
Interest paid	(12.4)	(9.1)
Equity dividend paid	(60.0)	(57.1)
Preference dividend paid	(8.1)	(7.9)
Investment by a minority shareholder	–	4.3
Dividend paid to a minority shareholder	(4.9)	(1.7)
Net cash inflow/(outflow) from financing activities	9.6	(75.0)
Net (decrease)/increase in cash and cash equivalents	(18.6)	(19.0)
Cash and cash equivalents at beginning of period	172.1	162.0
Currency translation differences	(15.6)	5.0
Cash and cash equivalents at end of period	137.9	148.0

Cash and cash equivalents comprise:

Cash and cash equivalents	165.2	168.0
Bank overdrafts	(27.3)	(20.0)
	137.9	148.0

3 CASH FLOW CLASSIFICATION

3.1 Terminology

It can be seen that the statement of cash flows is sub-classified according to the activities that give rise to the cash flows. There are three classifications.

- Operating activities.
- Investing activities.
- Financing activities.

3.2 Net cash inflow from/Absorbed by operating activities

Exam tip

> You are regularly asked to reconcile between profits and cash in both Section B and Section C, e.g. Winter 2006 Question 3, Summer 2004 Question 2, Winter 2004 Question 5.

The net cash arising from operations, is the cash generated corresponding to the operating profit in the income statement. This figure will be calculated at the start of the statement of cash flows. What factors do we need to take into account in reconciling operating profit to cash arising from operations?

The answer turns out to be three types of transaction.

- Income or expenses that are not the direct result of any cash flow, e.g. depreciation or profits and losses on disposal of non-current assets.

- Provisions and expenditure incurred in respect of previously provided costs.

- Movements in working capital.

We will illustrate these points by building up a simple illustration.

Example

Cash-only business

If we had a cash-only business (i.e. hold no other assets) that generated cash sales of £5,000 and cash purchases (cost of sales) of £4,000, then its profit and cash from operations would both be £1,000. For this type of business, cash does correspond to profit.

Depreciation and profits on disposal

If this business owns a non-current asset bought some time ago that it is depreciating at £200 per annum, then the operating profit would now be reduced to £800, though the cash from operations is still £1,000, i.e. the reconciliation is

	(£)
Operating profit	800
Add: depreciation	200
Net cash generated by operations	1,000

Therefore, we need to **add** back any expenses deducted in arriving at the operating profit that do not cause cash to flow. Similarly, we would need to **deduct** any income that has not caused a direct cash inflow, such as profits on disposal.

Provisions

A provision can impact on the statement of cash flows in two ways.

- When it is set up.
- When the provided expenditure is paid.

Setting up a provision

The impact on the calculation of setting up a provision is identical to that for depreciation, in that it is an expense that does not result from a cash flow. Hence, in a year when provisions are set up, we will need to **add** these in to the operating profit. For example, if our company above made a restructuring provision of £100, then the operating profit would be reduced down to £700 and the calculation would become

		(£)
Operating profit		700
Add:	Depreciation		200
	Restructuring provision set up		100
Net cash generated by operations		1,000

Paying for previously provided costs

When we make a payment against previously provided expenses, this does *not* impact on this year's operating profit (it impacted when the provision was set up) but it clearly does reduce cash.

If our company had paid £50 this year against previously provided costs then our net cash from operations would be reduced to £950 without there being any impact on this year's operating profit, and our calculation would become

		(£)
Operating profit		700
Add:	Depreciation		200
	Restructuring provision set up		100
Less: previously provided cost paid		(50)
Net cash generated by operations		950

Thus, we need to **deduct** such items from the calculation.

Working capital items

Finally, if our sales had been on credit then we would not have received the £5,000 as cash and hence our cash absorbed by operations would be down £5,000 to (£4,050). The reconciliation would then be

	(£)
Operating profit	700
Add: Depreciation	200
Restructuring provision set up	100
Less: previously provided cost paid	(50)
	950
Less: increase in debtors	(5,000)
Net cash absorbed by operations	(4,050)

Thus, the increase in receivables must be **deducted**.

Thinking about this logically, if we increase non-cash working capital it must be at the expense of cash, all other things being equal, e.g. buying inventory for cash increases inventory but reduces cash. Hence, this same rule applies for all non-cash working capital items (inventory and payables).

An increase in inventory or receivables causes a **deduction**, an increase in payables an addition to this reconciliation.

Conclusion

To summarise

Item	Addition or Deduction
Depreciation/Profit on disposal	
Depreciation	Addition
Loss on disposal (like depreciation)	Addition
Profit on disposal	Deduction
Provision	
Set up	Addition
Utilised (paid for)	Deduction
Working capital	
Increase in inventory	Deduction
Increase in receivables	Deduction
Increase in payables	Addition

3.3 Investing activities

The cash flows classified under this heading show the extent of new investment in **assets which will generate future profit and cash flows**. The Standard gives the following examples of cash flows arising from investing activities.

- Cash payments to acquire property, plant and equipment, intangibles and other non-current assets, including those relating to capitalised development costs and self-constructed property, plant and equipment.

- Cash receipts from sales of property, plant and equipment, intangibles and other non-current assets.

- Cash payments to acquire shares or debentures of other entities.

- Cash receipts from sales of shares or debentures of other entities.

- Cash advances and loans made to other parties.

- Cash receipts from the repayment of advances and loans made to other parties.

3.4 Financing activities

This section of the statement of cash flows shows the share of cash which the entity's capital providers have claimed during the period. This is an indicator of **likely future interest and dividend payments**. The Standard gives the following examples of cash flows which might arise under this heading.

- Cash proceeds from issuing shares.

- Cash payments to owners to acquire or redeem the entity's shares.

- Cash proceeds from issuing debentures, loans, notes, bonds, mortgages and other short or long-term borrowings.

- Principal repayments of amounts borrowed under finance leases.

3.5 Reporting cash flows from operating activities

The Standard offers a choice of method for this part of the statement of cash flows.

- **Direct method:** disclose major classes of gross cash receipts and gross cash payments.

- **Indirect method**: net profit or loss is adjusted for the effects of transactions of a non-cash nature, any deferrals or accruals of past or future operating cash receipts or payments, and items of income or expense associated with investing or financing cash flows.

The **direct method is the preferred method** because it discloses information, not available elsewhere in the financial statements, which could be of use in estimating future cash flows.

3.6 Using the direct method

There are different ways in which the **information about gross cash receipts and payments** can be obtained. The most obvious way is simply to extract the information from the accounting records. This may be a laborious task, however, and the indirect method below may be easier.

Example

The illustration below shows how the net cash flow from operating activities might be calculated using the direct method.

Consolidated statement of cash flows for the Year Ended 31 December 2004

	Notes	2004 (£m)	2003 (£m)
Trading cash flows			
Receipts from customers	a	X	X
Payments to suppliers	b	(X)	(X)
Payments to and on behalf of employees	c	(X)	(X)
Other payments	d	(X)	(X)
Net cash inflow from operating activities		6,527	7,005

The remainder of the statement of cash flows would be exactly the same as that produced under the indirect method.

3.7 Explanation of line items

(a) Receipts from customers

This represents cash received from customers in payment of revenue amounts invoiced to those customers for goods and services supplied. The amount of cash received may not tie back to the revenue figure in the income statement, mainly because of increases and decreases in the level of receivables, but also due to bad debts being written off and not recovered in the cash figure.

(b) Payments to suppliers

This represents cash paid to suppliers for goods and services received that relate to the operational expenses of the business. The cash paid will not tie back to any figure or figures in the income statement directly, but will relate to elements of all the operational expense categories (e.g. cost of sales, distribution costs).

(c) Payments to and on behalf of employees

This represents cash paid relating to employment costs, covering items such as net wages and salaries, income tax, National Insurance and pension contributions. There will be timing differences for some items (e.g. income taxes) between recognition in income statement and the statement of cash flows. Other items, such as pension costs, will not reconcile due to accounting differences.

(d) Other payments

The main cash flow within this caption will be the payment of VAT collected by the company to HMRC in the UK.

Example of the direct method

The following income statement and statement of financial position information relates to Company XYZ and covers the period from 1 January to 31 December 2006.

	£'000
Sales	6,000
Purchases	4,200
Payments to and on behalf of employees	1,300
Opening receivables @ 1 January 2006	350
Closing receivables @ 31 December 2006	420
Opening payables @ 1 January 2006	270
Closing payables @ 31 December 2006	290

The numbers for the first section of the statement of cash flows for Company XYZ, using the direct method, would be calculated as follows.

	(£'000)
Cash received from customers	
Sales	6,000
Add: Opening receivables	350
Less: Closing receivables	(420)
Cash received	5,930
Cash paid to suppliers	
Purchases	4,200
Add: Opening payables	270
Less: Closing payables	(290)
Cash paid	4,180

Therefore, the first section of the statement of cash flows itself would appear as follows.

	£'000
Cash received from customers	5,930
Cash paid to suppliers	(4,180)
Cash paid to and on behalf of employees	(1,300)
Net cash inflow from operations	450

3.8 Interest and dividends

Cash flows from interest and dividends received and paid should each be **disclosed separately**. Each should be classified in a consistent manner from period to period as either operating, investing or financing activities.

Dividends paid by the entity can be classified in **one of two ways**.

- As a **financing cash flow**, showing the cost of obtaining financial resources.

- As a component of **cash flows from operating activities** so that users can assess the entity's ability to pay dividends out of operating cash flows.

3.9 Taxes on income

Cash flows arising from taxes on income should be **separately disclosed** and should be classified as cash flows from operating activities *unless* they can be specifically identified with financing and investing activities.

Taxation cash flows are often **difficult to match** to the originating underlying transaction, so most of the time all tax cash flows are classified as arising from operating activities.

3.10 Components of cash and cash equivalents

The components of cash and cash equivalents should be disclosed and a **reconciliation** should be presented, showing the amounts in the statement of cash flows reconciled with the equivalent items reported in the statement of financial position.

It is also necessary to disclose the **accounting policy** used in deciding the items included in cash and cash equivalents, in accordance with IAS 1 *Presentation of Financial Statements*, but also because of the wide range of cash management practices worldwide.

3.11 Other disclosures

All entities should disclose, together with a **commentary by management**, any other information likely to be of importance, for example

- Restrictions on the use of or access to any part of cash equivalents.

- The amount of undrawn borrowing facilities which are available.

- Cash flows which increased operating capacity compared to cash flows which merely maintained operating capacity.

- Cash flows arising from each reported industry and geographical segment.

4 ILLUSTRATION OF THE PREPARATION OF A STATEMENT OF CASH FLOWS

Example

A company starts trading on 1 April having received £1,800 subscribed for shares. It raises a bank loan of £1,200 on which interest is payable quarterly at an annual rate of 10% (first payment due on 30 June). It subsequently undertakes the following transactions to 30 June.

- Bought a non-current asset with a life of five years for £600.
- Bought 80 units of inventory for cash at £10 each.
- Sold 60 units on credit for £900 in total.
- Bought a further 20 units on credit at £10 each.

The rate of income tax for this company is 25%.

The income statement and statement of financial position to 30 June are given below.

Income statement

	(£)	(£)
Revenue		900
Cost of Sales		
Opening Inventory	–	
Purchases [(80 + 20) × £10]	1,000	
Closing Inventory [(80 + 20 – 60) × £10]	(400)	
		(600)
Gross Profit		300
Depreciation $\left(600 \div 5 \times \frac{3}{12}\right)$		(30)
Operating Profit		270
Interest $\left(£1,200 \times 10\% \times \frac{3}{12}\right)$		(30)
Profit before tax		240
Tax (£240 × 25%)		(60)
Profit		180

Statement of financial position

	(£)	(£)
Non-Current Assets		
Cost		600
Depreciation		(30)
NBV		570
Current Assets		
Inventory [(80 + 20 – 60) × £10]	400	
Receivables	900	
Cash (1,800 + 1,200 – 600 – 800 – 30)	1,570	
		2,870
		3,440

Share Capital		1,800
Retained Earnings		180
		1,980
Loan		1,200
Trade Payables (20 × £10)		200
Tax		60
		3,440

Requirement

Prepare the statement of cash flows.

Solution

Cash from operations

This is the first figure that we need to establish and, as we have already noted, corresponds to the operating profit figure in the income statement. It tends to be the hardest figure to calculate and understand, though as we mentioned above there are two alternative approaches.

Calculating the actual cash flows

We will consider all the items of income or expenditure that have contributed to this operating profit and establish their cash flow effects as follows.

	Income Statement (£)	Cash Flow (£)	Comments
Revenue	900	–	All the sales were on credit (shown in receivables)
Cost of Sales	(600)	(800)	Amount paid for goods purchased
Gross Profit	300	(800)	
Depreciation	(30)	–	No cash payment
Operating profit	270	(800)	**Cash absorbed by operations**

As we can see, although we have generated a positive operating profit of £270, our operations have **absorbed** £800 cash, emphasising that cash does not directly correspond to profits.

Operating profit to cash flow from operating activities

We could reconcile the two as follows.

Operating Profit to Net Cash from Operating Activities	(£)	**Comments**
Operating profit	270	
Add: Depreciation	30	Depreciation has reduced profits but not cash,
	300	therefore we need to add it back.
Increase in:		
Inventory	(400)	Any financial resources tied up in working capital must mean less cash, all other things being equal.
Receivables	(900)	
Payables	200	Having payables means that we have some assets that we have not paid for.
Net cash absorbed by operations	(800)	

Statement of cash flows for the three months ended 30 June	(£)	(£)
Cash flows from operating activities		
Operating profit	270	
Add: Depreciation	30	
Operating profit before working capital changes	300	
Increase in inventory	(400)	
Increase in receivables	(900)	
Increase in payables	200	
Cash generated from operations	(800)	
Interest paid	(30)	
Net cash used in operating activities		(830)
Cash flows from investing activities		
Purchase of non-current asset		(600)
Cash flows from financing activities		
Share capital issued	1,800	
Bank loan raised	1,200	
Net cash from financing activities		3,000
Increase in cash and cash equivalents		1,570
Cash and cash equivalents at start of period		–
Cash and cash equivalents at end of period		1,570

5 CASH FLOW ANALYSIS

5.1 Analysing the statement of cash flows

One of the objectives of statement of cash flows is to ensure that it is relatively easy to analyse the cash flow performance of a company. IAS 7 achieves this objective by requiring companies to adopt a standardised format which contains a wealth of useful information.

5.2 Cash flow from operations

When analysing cash flow from operations, it is important to understand how the cash flows have been generated and why they differ from the previous year. This can be done by looking at the reconciliation of operating profits to cash flow from operations. Reasons for changes in cash flow include the following.

- Changes in operating profits.
- Changes in working capital levels.

5.3 Changes in operating profits

The underlying profits of the business may have changed. The reasons for this will be apparent from the analysis of the income statement. For example, margins or volumes may have changed. Changes in volumes can be linked into other areas of the statement of cash flows, such as purchases of non-current assets and changes in levels of working capital in the business.

5.4 Changes in working capital levels

Even if profits have risen, cash flow may not benefit if there has been a significant increase in receivables over the year, or the company has built up its inventory to meet anticipated future demand.

It is often the case that, as businesses expand, they suffer a severe strain on their cash resources since they have to pay cash out up front, buying non-current assets and inventory, but only receive cash later after they make the sales and receive payments from their customers. This may only be a short-term problem as the cash flows from receivables are received. However, if a business does not have sufficient finance from shareholders and banks to cover the initial cash outflows, it may become insolvent. This is known as 'overtrading' and is a common cause of insolvency for start-up and small expanding companies.

Conversely, a business may suffer poor profits but still generate operating cash in the short term by squeezing working capital levels. For example, a company could take longer to pay its suppliers, reduce inventory levels and pressurise its customers to pay more quickly. In the short term, this will give improved cash flow. However, it will only give a one-off benefit to the company, since working capital cannot be squeezed indefinitely, and may result in higher cash outflows in future years, if working capital is restored to its previous levels. As a result, high cash flow due solely to falling working capital levels should not always be viewed as being good news for a company.

5.5 Non-cash items in profit

It has been shown above that, apart from working capital, there are various non-cash items in profit, such as depreciation and provisions. If a company has high depreciation charges, then its operating cash flow will be higher than its profits in the statement of cash flows. Note, however, that such a company must have high non-current assets and therefore some of this operating cash flow will need to be used to pay for replacement of non-current assets, covered in the investing activities section of the statement of cash flows.

5.6 Interest paid

The level of interest paid should be compared to the previous year and reasons for differences identified. This may be due to changes in interest rates or levels of borrowings over the year. If borrowings have increased, then the use of the borrowed funds should be identified. If borrowings have fallen, then the source of cash to repay the borrowings should be identified (these points are covered in more detail below).

The amount of interest paid should be compared to the interest charge in the income statement and explanations found for any significant differences. These may be due to the accruals concept. For example, where interest is paid annually on a bond, if it is issued one month into the year, then the income statement will show 11 months of interest charge accrued while no interest has yet been paid. Alternatively, the company may be capitalising interest as a non-current asset, rather than charging it as an expense in the income statement (this will be apparent from the interest note to the income statement). Another possibility is that the company has issued a zero-coupon bond, where interest is being charged to the income statement over the bond's life, but no interest is paid until redemption.

A comparison of interest paid and interest charged to the absolute level of borrowings in the statement of financial position is also useful. For example, if the interest paid/charged seems very low compared to the closing borrowings level, it may be that the borrowings were made very late in the year. This will be reinforced by looking at the opening borrowings, if they are significantly lower than the closing borrowings.

The company's level of gearing can be assessed by looking at the level of interest paid relative to the level of operating cash flow available to cover the interest.

The level of interest cover in cash terms can be assessed by calculating the following ratio, the result of which shows the number of times the interest payments could have been made out of operating cash flows. The higher this figure is, the less of a concern there would be about the ability of the company to service its debt.

$$\text{Interest in cash flow} = \frac{\text{Operating cash flow}}{\text{Interest paid}}$$

5.7 Preference dividends paid

Preference dividends paid are non-discretionary. The cash outflow should therefore be fairly constant year on year. An increase may indicate additional preference shares issued in the year, whereas a decrease could be from a redemption of existing shares or, more worryingly, be indicative of an inability to declare a dividend as a result of poor cash flow or insufficient profits.

5.8 Investment income

A company with high levels of investment income will presumably have high levels of surplus cash on its statement of financial position. While this means that the company is in a very strong financial position, whether or not it is effectively using the cash being generated should be considered. It may be that the business needs cash balances for the future or it may be that the company has insufficient investment opportunities that yield acceptable returns. In this case, there will be a case for returning surplus cash to shareholders to reinvest elsewhere.

5.9 Taxation

The level of tax paid should be considered in relation to the tax charge and the profits of the company. In doing this, the analyst will need to consider the source of the tax payments.

- Corporation tax in the UK, which will be based on the quarterly instalments per the tax regime.
- Overseas tax, which will depend on the overseas regimes in which the company is operating.

5.10 Capital expenditure and financial investment

The level of capital expenditure should be evaluated, to establish if the company is replacing its non-current assets and maintaining its level of underlying capital employed. A simple test here is to compare the depreciation charge with the level of capital expenditure. The idea is that the depreciation charge indicates the level of capital expenditure required to replace non-current assets and maintain the asset base, called maintenance capital expenditure.

For example, a company has non-current assets with a two-year life, which cost £1,000 each. The company has two assets and it replaces these in alternate years, i.e. it buys one new asset a year. The cost of buying the asset each year will be £1,000. This is the same as the annual depreciation charge for two assets of £1,000.

This simple idea has several limitations.

- Inflation is ignored.

- It is assumed that the depreciation charge and the capital expenditure relate to the same assets, whereas the company may be contracting one area of its business and expanding in another, or replacing existing expensive non-current assets with newer assets that are more efficient to operate (meaning we need less) but cheaper to buy.

The level of capital expenditure can also indicate whether a company has expanded its operations significantly over the year or is in a process of contraction. In either case, the reasons for this, the business areas in which it is occurring and the implications for the company need to be considered.

Cash flows from financial investment will indicate the extent to which the company is lending funds to other entities and whether those loans are being repaid. Large loans to other entities may be indicative of a long-term cash surplus, which could be better utilised by acquisitions or return of funds to shareholders.

5.11 Acquisitions and disposals

Purchase and sale of businesses will highlight several important issues.

- Acquisitions may indicate that the company is attempting to utilise a cash surplus in order to provide greater returns to shareholders. Alternatively, the company may be attempting to gear up its position where its current debt levels are considered too low.

- Disposals may be indicative of a strategy to release funds from non-core businesses in order to invest in growth within the main business areas. Alternatively, the company may be in urgent need of cash to bolster funds available for operations.

- The cash flows in this area need to be reviewed in conjunction with the financing section (to determine how acquisitions have been funded or disposals from sale used to reduce borrowing) and the purchase of non-current if funds from disposals have been used for financing organic growth.

5.12 Equity dividends paid

Dividends paid will link in closely to the profit performance of the company. If a company has increasing profits, it is likely that dividends per share will be increased. Notwithstanding this, it is often the case that companies may suffer falls in profits but maintain the dividend to avoid incurring the wrath of their shareholders, at least for the short term. The statement of cash flows can be used to assess whether the business has the underlying ability to generate cash to justify paying a dividend.

5.13 Financing activities

Having generated its operating cash flows and paid interest, dividends, tax and capital expenditure, a company will either have surplus cash or a deficit. Surplus cash will need to be utilised in some respect and a deficit will need to be financed. The financing activities section and the change in cash and cash equivalents will tell us how this has happened.

Surpluses may have been used to repay debt or complete a share repurchase operation, in which case, this will be apparent from the financing activities. Alternatively, they may have been used to increase cash balances or decrease overdrafts and short-term borrowings, which will be evident from the change in cash and cash equivalents. This can be determined from the statement of financial position.

Deficits may have been funded by an increase in borrowings, a share issue or a change in cash and cash equivalents. Each of these can be identified from the statement, as with the use of surpluses.

Even if the company has no significant surplus or deficit from its operations for the year, the financing and change in cash and cash equivalents may indicate a change in the source of finance, for example, short-term borrowings may have been repaid through a share issue or a long-term borrowing.

5.14 Discretionary and non-discretionary cash flows

The cash flows of a business can be categorised into those that are non-discretionary (i.e. which have to be made) and those that are discretionary. It is essential for the long-term health of a business that it is able to meet its non-discretionary requirements from its operating cash flows without having to raise funds from outside sources, such as shareholders or banks. If this is not the case, then the business does not have a long-term future.

5.15 Non-discretionary flows

It is difficult to define non-discretionary flows precisely. As always, there is an element of subjectivity and judgement that needs to be applied when analysing a company. The following are items that would typically be considered non-discretionary.

- Interest payments.
- Tax payments.
- Replacement capital expenditure.

In the short term, it is possible for a business to cut back on its replacement capital expenditure, at the risk of running down the business and reducing its competitive edge. This may be appropriate if the company is in serious financial difficulty and is unable to raise external finance to fund the expenditure. However, in such a situation where outside backers are unavailable it may be appropriate to call it a day anyway.

5.16 Discretionary flows

As with non-discretionary items, the classification of flows as discretionary is subject to discretion and judgement.

- Dividends.
- Expansionary capital expenditure.

In the long term, it is difficult for a business, particularly a listed company, not to pay dividends to shareholders since they will not be keen to finance a business without receiving any rewards. Therefore, although dividends can easily be cut in the short term, it is probably advisable to view them as being non-discretionary on a long-term basis.

5.17 Free cash flow

The purpose of the calculation of free cash flow is to identify the surplus cash flow that a company is generating. This free cash flow can then be used to evaluate a company. At a simplistic level, the current level of free cash flow can be compared to the value of the company, giving a multiple for comparison with other companies. At a more complex level, free cash flow can be forecast into the future and the present value of the free cash flow calculated, giving a valuation of the business.

5.18 The definition of free cash flow

The definition of free cash flow varies quite substantially between companies and analysts, largely because of what they are trying to achieve with their definition. As a result, it is not possible to be exhaustive when defining free cash flow and the various ways in which it may be calculated. We will, therefore, focus on two major categories of definitions – free cash flow to the enterprise and free cash flow to equity.

5.19 Enterprise cash flow

Enterprise cash flow represents the total cash flow generated by a business or enterprise that is available to service all providers of capital, including equity investors, preference share investors, debt investors and minority interests.

5.20 Equity cash flow

Equity cash flow represents the cash flow generated by a business that is available to service the providers of equity finance.

5.21 Which is most useful

Although it may seem more appropriate to focus on equity cash flow at first sight, since we are trying to assess the business from the point of view of its equity investors, enterprise cash flow has an important part to play in the analysis process. The reason for this is that it ignores the level of gearing and other related financial factors when analysing a business.

In addition, enterprise cash flow is a useful benchmark for comparisons across companies. Since many companies in different countries will have different gearing levels, even though they are in the same industry, it will not be easy to compare their businesses based on equity cash flows. A more appropriate comparison would be to look at multiples based on enterprise cash flow. For example, cash flow multiples based on turnover, research and development costs, number of locations, and so on. can be calculated and compared across the international sector.

In doing such multiple comparisons, care should be taken that you are comparing on a like-for-like basis. For example, a multiple based on sales to equity cash flow has limited meaning, since the turnover of the company is based on total finance, not just equity. A company could have a high level of sales relative to equity cash flow by being highly geared. Sales to enterprise cash flow is a much more meaningful ratio to calculate.

Conversely, comparing enterprise cash flow to profit after tax would not be very useful, since profit after tax is after the deduction of interest. A more meaningful comparison would be enterprise cash flow compared to profit after tax but before interest. In this case, the tax charge would be the tax charge assuming that there was no tax relief on the interest, i.e. the tax charge of an equivalent ungeared company.

5.22 Calculating equity free cash flow

If we wish to establish the free cash flow for equity, the analyst would aim to identify the surplus cash flow available after all other non-discretionary costs have been met. This could therefore be defined as follows.

	(£)
Net cash from operating activities	X
Less: interest payments	(X)
Less: tax payments	(X)
Less: capital expenditure	(X)
Less: preference dividends	(X)
Free cash flow for equity	X

Note that this is not the only possible definition of free cash flow for equity. However, it does aim to highlight the key issues to consider when calculating such a cash flow figure.

5.23 Calculating enterprise free cash flow

The free cash flow to the enterprise is often referred to as 'net operating cash flow' and it can be calculated in the following way.

	(£)
Net cash from operating activities	X
Less: tax payments	(X)
Less: capital expenditure	(X)
Free cash flow for the enterprise	X

The free cash flow is the total amount of cash the company generates after funding purchases of non-current assets and any required increases in working capital, assuming that there is no debt. As such, it represents the maximum amount that a company could pay out to all its investors, assuming that the company is ungeared and has no commitment to pay interest to debt investors.

CHAPTER ROUNDUP

You need to be familiar with and able to discuss

- The importance of cash and statement of cash flows.
- IAS 7 *Statement of Cash Flows* format.

You may be asked to do some basic cash flow calculations, in particular in relation to determining the cash flow operational activities, either by

- Reconciling from operating profits.
- Direct method.

You need to be able to analyse a given statement of cash flows to determine whether there appears to be risks to the business arising from how it controls cash.

TEST YOUR KNOWLEDGE

Check your knowledge of the chapter here, without referring back to the text.

1.   XYZ Ltd

XYZ Limited was set up by its shareholders subscribing on January 1 2006 for 60,000 £1 shares at par. In addition, a 12% bank loan (interest payable quarterly) of £70,000 was received. The company purchased non-current assets at a cost of £120,000 with a five-year life and nil residual value. In the year ended December 31 2005, XYZ Limited made sales of £950,000 and purchased goods costing £800,000. Other operating expenses, all of which were paid in the year, amounted to £120,000. Year-end trade receivables were £300,000, trade payables were £100,000 and closing inventories were £200,000. The charge for corporation tax is £90,000 and a final dividend of £50,000 has been proposed.

Requirements

Prepare the income statement and a statement of cash flows for the year ended December 31 200 for XYZ Limited.

2.   Saucy Apples Ltd

Using the information below, prepare a statement of cash flows for Saucy Apples Limited for the year ended December 31 2006.

Income Statement for the Year Ended December 31 2006	(£'000)
Revenue	1,450
Cost of sales	(900)
Gross profit	550
Distribution costs	(100)
Administrative expenses	(50)
Operating profit	400
Finance costs	(150)
Profit before taxation	250
Taxation	(100)
Profit for the period	150

Note

During the year a dividend of £50,000 was paid in cash. This represents the dividend proposed out of the profits of the year ended December 31 2005. The directors propose to pay a dividend of £60,000 out of the current period's profits. This will be considered for approval by shareholders at the AGM to be held in May 2007.

Statement of Financial Position as at December 31	2006 (£'000)	2005 (£'000)
Non-current assets		
Cost	1,100	950
Depreciation	390	330
	710	620
Current assets		
Inventories	80	60
Receivables	110	95
Cash at bank and in hand	30	20
	220	175
Total assets	**930**	**795**
Current liabilities		
Trade payables	(25)	(13)
Bank overdraft	(39)	(35)
Tax payable	(100)	(80)
	(164)	(128)
Non-current liabilities		
Loans	(300)	(351)
Total liabilities	**(464)**	**(479)**
Net assets	**466**	**316**
Share capital	200	150
Retained earnings	266	166
Equity	**466**	**316**

3.   Pavlova plc

(a)   The finance director of Pavlova plc has resigned suddenly and had only prepared an income statement and statement of financial position as set out below. As the only remaining accountant, you are required to prepare the statement of cash flows for the year ended December 31 2006.

(b)   Having prepared the statement of cash flows, you notice the following errors have been made in the accounts. What would be the impact on net assets, profits and cash if the following errors were adjusted for?

(i)   The depreciation charge for the year of £2,500,000 has been based on an incorrect useful economic life and should have been £3,000,000.

(ii)   The auditor's fees due of £1,000,000 has been omitted from the accounts altogether.

(iii)   The proposed dividend at the year end of £100,000 has not been entered in the accounts.

(iv)   A provision for restructuring costs of £2,500,000 has not been accounted for.

Statement of Financial Position as at December 31 2006	2006 (£'000)	2005 (£'000)
Non-current assets	14,400	12,900
Current assets		
Inventories	1,200	2,100
Trade receivables	5,700	5,500
Prepaid expenses	1,000	500
Cash and cash equivalents	3,700	1,000
	11,600	9,100
Total assets	**26,000**	**22,000**
Current liabilities		
Trade payables	(8,200)	(7,100)
Accruals	(2,000)	(1,000)
	(10,200)	(8,100)
Non-current liabilities		
Loan	(7,600)	(6,400)
Total liabilities	**(17,800)**	**(14,500)**
	8,200	**7,500**
Net assets		
Share capital	5,500	5,000
Retained earnings	2,700	2,500
Equity	**8,200**	**7,500**

Income Statement for the Year Ended December 31 2006	(£'000)	(£'000)
Revenue		20,500
Cost of sales		
Opening inventories	(2,100)	
Purchases	(9,600)	
	(11,700)	
Closing inventories	1,200	
		(10,500)
Gross profit		10,000
Other expenses		
Sundry operating expenses	(3,000)	
Rent	(2,300)	
Depreciation	(2,500)	
Telephone and electricity	(1,500)	
		(9,300)
Operating profit		700
Finance costs		(400)
Profit before taxation		300
Taxation		(100)
Profit for the period		200

TEST YOUR KNOWLEDGE: ANSWERS

1. XYZ Ltd

Income Statement for the Year Ended December 31 2006	(£)	(£)
Revenue		950,000
Cost of sales		
Purchases	800,000	
Closing inventories	(200,000)	
		(600,000)
Gross profit		350,000
Other operating expenses		(120,000)
Depreciation ($\frac{1}{5}$ × 120,000)		(24,000)
Operating profit		206,000
Finance costs (12% × 70,000)		(8,400)
Profit before taxation		197,600
Taxation		(90,000)
Profit for the period		107,600

(a) **Direct method**

Statement of Cash Flows for the Year Ended December 31 2006	Outflows (£)	Inflows (£)
Receipts from customers (950,000 – 300,000)	–	650,000
Payments to suppliers (800,000 – 100,000)	700,000	–
Operating expenses	120,000	–
Interest	8,400	–
Non-current assets	120,000	–
Share issue	–	60,000
Loan	–	70,000
	948,400	780,000
Net cash outflow	168,400	

(b) Indirect method

Statement of Cash Flows for the Year Ended December 31 2006	(£)	(£)
Operating profit		206,000
Depreciation		24,000
Increase in inventories	(200,000)	
Increase in receivables	(300,000)	
Increase in payables	100,000	
Operating cash flow		(400,000)
		(170,000)
Investing cash flows		
Non-current assets purchased		(120,000)
Financing cash flows		
Share issue	60,000	
Loans raised	70,000	
Interest paid	(8,400)	
		121,600
Decrease in cash and cash equivalents		(168,400)

Tutorial note

In this solution interest paid has been shown as a financing cash outflow. IAS 7 allows a choice between this approach and deducting interest paid as an operating cash outflow.

2. Saucy Apples Ltd

Statement of Cash Flows for the Year Ended December 31 2006	(£'000)	(£'000)
Net cash from operating activities		
Operating profit		400
Depreciation (390 – 330)		60
Increase in inventories (80 – 60)		(20)
Increase in receivables (110 – 95)		(15)
Increase in payables (25 – 13)		12
		437
Income taxes paid (last year's liability)		(80)
Net cash provided by operating activities		357
Investing activities		
Non-current assets purchased (1,100 – 950)		(150)
Financing activities		
Dividends paid	(50)	
Interest paid	(150)	
Proceeds of issue of shares	50	
Repayment of loans (351-300)	(51)	
		(201)
Increase in cash and cash equivalents		6
Represented by		
Increase in cash at bank (30 – 20)		10
Increase in overdraft (39 – 35)		(4)
		6

Tutorial note

This solution has classified interest paid as a financing cash outflow. IAS 7 allows interest paid to be treated as an operating cash outflow.

Similarly, this answer treats dividends paid as a financing item. IAS 7 also offers the possibility of reporting dividends paid as operating cash outflows.

3   Pavlova plc

(a)

Reconciliation of Operating Profit to Cash Flow from Operations	(£'000)
Operating profit	700
Add: Depreciation	2,500
Change in:	
Inventories (decrease)	900
Trade receivables (increase)	(200)
Trade payables (increase)	1,100
Prepaid expenses (increase)	(500)
Accruals (increase)	1,000
	5,500
Tax paid	(100)
	5,400

Statement of Cash Flows for the Year Ended December 31 2006	(£'000)
Cash flow from operations	5,400
Capital expenditure	(4,000)
Interest paid	(400)
Issue of shares	500
Loans raised	1,200
Increase in cash and cash equivalents	2,700

(b)   Impact of adjustments

Adjustment		Impact on Net Assets	Impact on Profits	Impact on Cash
(i)	Accumulated depreciation Up £500k			
	Expenses Up £500k	Down £500k	Down £500k	No impact
(ii)	Accruals Up £1,000k	Down	Down	
	Expenses Up £1,000k	£1,000k	£1,000k	No impact
(iii)	Proposed dividend not recognised as a current liability until declared by shareholders at AGM	No impact	No impact	No impact
(iv)	Provision Up £2,500k	Down	Down	No impact
	Expenses Up £2,500k	£2,500k	£2,500k	

BPP
LEARNING MEDIA

9

Investment and Group Accounting

INTRODUCTION

The vast majority of business in the UK are not individual companies, rather they are groups of companies managed to achieve a common objective. We therefore need to be able to analyse group accounts but in order to do this, we must understand how group accounts are constructed.

This chapter looks at the rules underlying the construction of a set of accounts and the factors to consider in their analysis.

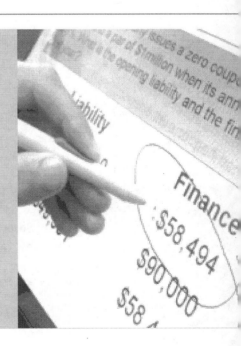

CHAPTER CONTENTS

The syllabus area covered by this chapter is

Interpretation of Financial Information

Group accounts

An understanding of the averages and limitations of presenting group accounts in the form of consolidated accounts.

1 INTRODUCTION

1.1 Investments

When a company buys shares in another company it is making an investment, the basic accounting treatment for which is outlined diagrammatically below.

Investments

When we invest, the impact on the accounting equation is

- Cash down (net assets down)
- Investment up (net assets up)
- Double entry

    DEBIT: Investment (asset)
    CREDIT: Cash

The investment is an asset, but what type?

Current Asset

Definition

Not a non-current asset investment, i.e.

- Speculative
- For the purpose of resale

Accounting treatment

- Statement of financial position at lower of cost and NRV

- IS: Dividends received = Income

Non-Current Asset

Definition

- Long term

- For continuing use, not intended for resale

Accounting treatment

- Statement of financial position at cost less provision for any permanent diminution in value

- IS: Dividends received = Income

The above treatment of current asset investments is appropriate as the interest is very similar to that of holding a unit of inventory for resale. The question is whether this treatment of non-current asset investments is appropriate for all the levels of investment?

1.2 Accounting treatment

It certainly seems appropriate for very low levels of investment of, say, one or two per cent of share capital of the company in which the investment is held. However, is it appropriate for higher levels of investment? Will this treatment give a fair presentation of the performance of a company and its position at the year-end for significant levels of investment? We will answer this with an example.

Example

A company (H) was formed ten years ago with the investment of £1,200 cash by the shareholders. Its statement of financial position today is

H's Statement of financial position	(£)
Investment in S	1,000
Other Non-Current Assets	800
Current Assets	1,000
	2,800
Liabilities	(200)
Net Assets	2,600
Share Capital	1,200
Retained Earnings	1,400
Shareholders' Funds	2,600

The £1,000 investment on the statement of financial position of H represents the cost of acquiring 100% of the shares in S, formed on the same day as H itself was set up. Neither H nor S has ever paid any dividends, hence, based on these accounts, the only return that the investors are aware of being generated from their initial £1,200 investment is the £1,400 profit in the books of H, not a very exciting return over ten years!

However, if we are now told that the statement of financial position of S is as follows, we see a different picture of how well the original £1,200 investment has been utilised.

S's Statement of financial position	(£)
Non-Current Assets	50,000
Current Assets	120,000
	170,000
Liabilities	(20,000)
Net Assets	150,000
Share Capital	1,000
Retained Earnings	149,000
Shareholders' Funds	150,000

As we can see, of the original £1,200 invested in H, £1,000 was immediately invested in S and that £1,000 has managed to generate £149,000 profit over the intervening years. The £1,400 profit we see in H's books is the profit that has been generated on the remaining £200 of the initial capital invested.

Since S has never paid any dividends to H (its shareholder), the shareholders of H have had no indication as to how their cash has been used. Since the directors of H control S through their 100% ownership of its shares and the shareholders of H have effectively financed S, does simply showing S being worth £1,000 in the books of H give a fair presentation of the state of affairs of H Limited at that date?

Clearly H's shareholders need more information. One possibility might be to provide them with the financial statements of all companies controlled by H and a commentary explaining the implications. If H had many subsidiaries, this would lead to information overload and shareholders would find it impossible to interpret.

1.3 Consolidated accounts / Group accounts

The chosen option has been to aggregate the financial statements of the parent company (also known as the holding company) with those of its subsidiaries into a single set of accounts referred to as either 'group' or 'consolidated' accounts. Group accounts do not reflect the legal position, as the group is not a legal entity, but they present the commercial reality (the substance). Since the parent company's directors control the operating and financial policy decisions taken by subsidiaries there is, in commercial reality, a single business managed by the parent company's board. It follows that there should also be a single set of financial statements for this entity. This is an important example of the accounting convention that prefers to reflect the (commercial) substance of a transaction where this conflicts with its (legal) form – 'substance over form'. Accountants believe that this approach is necessary if a fair presentation is to be given.

1.4 What are group accounts?

The individual financial statements of the parent and its subsidiaries are the starting point for the group accounts. However, these must be adjusted to remove the effects of transactions between them. These intra-group transactions typically include

- Loans between members of the group.
- Share capital of subsidiaries held by the parent.
- Purchase and sale of goods and/or services (including management charges).
- Interest and dividends paid and received within the group.

These transactions take place within the group and cannot be shown as assets, liabilities, income or expenditure in the group accounts that show that entity's relationship with the outside world.

1.5 Preparation of group accounts

Users of the accounts do not see what adjustments have been made to eliminate intra-group transactions – they are only shown the results of the process. There are three steps in preparing group accounts where the parent owns 100% of the share capital of a subsidiary.

1.   Eliminate intra-group transactions.
2.   Aggregate remaining assets, liabilities, income and expenses.
3.   Calculate group/consolidated retained earnings.

Where a subsidiary is partly owned, i.e. the parent has a controlling interest but does not own all the subsidiary's share capital, there is a fourth step.

4.   Calculate minority interests.

In this case, H owns 100% of the share capital of S and so there are no minority interests.

Example – Wholly-owned subsidiary

Statement of financial position	H (£)	S (£)
Investment in S (100%)	1,000	
Other Non-Current Assets	800	50,000
Net Current Assets	1,000	120,000
	2,800	170,000
Liabilities	(200)	(20,000)
Net Assets	2,600	150,000
Share Capital	1,200	1,000
Retained Earnings	1,400	149,000
Shareholders' Funds	2,600	150,000

- **Step 1** – Eliminate intra-group transactions

The investment asset in the statement of financial position of H represents the cost (£1,000) of acquiring 100% of S's share capital on its formation ten years ago. At that date, S had no retained earnings as it had not yet started to trade.

H's asset is matched by 100% of S's share capital. Share capital is in the nature of a liability owed by the company to its shareholders although it is not usually expected to be repaid. From the point of view of H and S combined (the group), H cannot own shares in itself and S cannot owe obligations to itself. The adjustment to eliminate these items is

Reduce investment in S	(CREDIT: Investment in S)	£1,000
Reduce share capital of S	(DEBIT: Share capital of S)	£1,000

A similar adjustment would be made if H had lent money to S: neither H's loan asset (debtor) nor S's loan liability (creditor) would be reported in the group statement of financial position.

- **Step 2** – Aggregate remaining assets and liabilities
- **Step 3** – Calculate group/consolidated retained earnings

Group retained earnings are made up of the parent company's retained earnings plus the group's share of any increase generated in the retained earnings of each subsidiary since it joined the group. In this case, the group's share is 100% and all the retained earnings (£149,000) of the subsidiary have been generated since H acquired its interest ten years ago, before S started to trade.

Thus, the group retained earnings are made up of

H		£1,400
S	100% × £149,000	£149,000
		£150,400

Group statement of financial position		(£)
Other Non-Current Assets	(800 + 50,000)	50,800
Current Assets	(1,000 + 120,000)	121,000
Liabilities	(200 + 20,000)	(20,200)
Net Assets		151,600
Share Capital		1,200
Retained Earnings	(1,400 + 149,000)	150,400
Shareholders' Funds		151,600

In a group statement of financial position, there is no asset 'investment in subsidiary'. It has been replaced by all of the subsidiary's assets and liabilities as if they were held by the parent itself. It therefore shows all of the assets and liabilities that are effectively under the control of the parent company's directors. The

BPP
LEARNING MEDIA

share capital that appears in a group statement of financial position is always the share capital of the parent company and the reserves show what the parent's retained earnings would have been if it had earned the profits on its own account, rather than operating through a subsidiary company.

1.6 Group accounts and parent company accounts

Exam tip

You may be asked to explain the differences between the company and group accounts, e.g. Summer 2004 Question 10.

Where a company has subsidiaries it is therefore required by law to prepare two sets of accounts for its shareholders.

- Individual company accounts of the parent company.
- Group accounts.

The parent company's accounts are relevant mainly for determining the maximum amount of dividend that the company can legally distribute (its distributable profits). The group accounts are used by investors and lenders for valuation, performance measurement and assessing risk.

Example – Partly-owned subsidiary

The previous Example (*wholly-owned subsidiary*) shows how the group statement of financial position is generated where the parent company acquired 100% of the subsidiary's share capital for £1,000 on the formation of the subsidiary.

This Example uses similar figures except for the fact that it is assumed that H acquired 70% of S's share capital at a cost of £700. Other investors contributed £300 for 30% of S's share capital. H's statement of financial position therefore records the investment in subsidiary at £700 and its net current assets will be £1,100, not £800, if it only spent £700 on buying shares in S.

Statement of financial position	H (£)	S (£)
Investment in S (70%)	700	
Other Non-current Assets	800	50,000
Net Current Assets	1,100	100,000
Net Assets	2,600	150,000
Share Capital	1,200	1,000
Retained Earnings	1,400	149,000
Shareholders' Funds	2,600	150,000

Step 1 – Eliminate intra-group transactions

Reduce investment in S	(DEBIT: Investment in S)	£700
Reduce share capital of S	(CREDIT: Share capital of S)	£700

This leaves £300 (30%) of the share capital of S, which is not owned by H but by other shareholders in S. These outside shareholders are known as minority shareholders and their proportion of the subsidiary's capital and retained earnings will be shown in the group statement of financial position as a separate caption after shareholders' funds.

Step 2 – Aggregate remaining assets and liabilities

An important principle of consolidation is that 100% of a subsidiary's assets and liabilities (£50,000 and £100,000) are reported in the group statement of financial position, even when, as is the case here, the parent does not own all the share capital of the subsidiary. The reason for this is that the group statement of financial position must show all the assets and liabilities over which the parent company's directors exercise control: whether H owns 100%, 70% or 51% of S's share capital, it is still able to direct the financial and operating policy decisions of S because it only needs a simple majority (more than 50%) of voting power to appoint and remove directors to/from the board of S. The group statement of financial position will report all the assets and liabilities of S with H's own and then show how much of S's net assets/shareholders' funds are financed by the minority shareholders in S.

2 MINORITY INTERESTS

Exam tip

You may be asked to define or calculate the value of minority interests in any section of the exam, e.g. Summer 2005 Question 8, Summer 2005 Question 2.

2.1 Introduction

If a parent company does not own all of the shares of the subsidiary but still controls it, the total assets and liabilities of the subsidiary are included in the consolidated statement of financial position. A proportion of the net assets of such subsidiaries in fact belongs to investors from outside the group (**minority interests**).

The net assets of a company are financed by share capital and retained earnings. The consolidation procedure for dealing with partly owned subsidiaries is to **calculate the proportion of ordinary shares, preference shares and retained earnings attributable to minority interests**.

We will now look at an example with a minority interest.

Example – Minority interests

P Co has owned 75% of the share capital of S Co since the date of S Co's incorporation. Their latest statement of financial position are given below.

P Co Statement of financial position	(£)	(£)
Non-Current Assets		
PPE	50,000	
30,000 £1 ordinary shares in S Co at cost	30,000	
		80,000
Current Assets		45,000
Current Liabilities		(20,000)
Net Assets		105,000
Equity and Liabilities		
Equity		
80,000 £1 ordinary shares	80,000	
Retained Earnings	25,000	
Shareholders' Funds		105,000

S Co Statement of financial position	(£)	(£)
Non-Current Assets		
PPE		35,000
Current Assets		35,000
Current Liabilities		(20,000)
		50,000
Net assets		
40,000 £1 ordinary shares	40,000	
Retained Earnings	10,000	
Shareholders' Funds		50,000

Requirement

Prepare the consolidated statement of financial position.

Solution

All of S Co's net assets are consolidated despite the fact that the company is only 75% owned.
The amount of net assets attributable to minority interests is calculated as follows.

	(£)
Minority share of share capital (25% × £40,000)	10,000
Minority share of retained earnings (25% × £10,000)	2,500
	12,500

Of S Co's share capital of £40,000, £10,000 is included in the figure for minority interest, while £30,000 is cancelled with P Co's asset 'investment in S Co'.

The consolidated statement of financial position can now be prepared.

P Group Consolidated Statement Of Financial Position	(£)	(£)
Non-Current Assets (50,000 + 35,000)		85,000
Current Assets (45,000 + 35,000)		80,000
Current Liabilities (20,000 + 20,000)		(40,000)
Net Assets		125,000
Share Capital (P only)	80,000	
Retained Earnings (25,000 + (75% × £10,000)	32,500	
		112,500
Minority Interest		12,500
		125,000

3 GOODWILL ARISING ON CONSOLIDATION

Exam tip

> You may be asked to calculate the goodwill arising from a given scenario, e.g. Summer 2001 Question 11.

In the Examples we have looked at so far the cost of shares acquired by the parent company has always been equal to the par value of those shares. This is seldom the case in practice and we must now consider some more complicated examples.

3.1 Accounting

To begin with, **we will examine the entries made by the parent company in its own statement of financial position when it acquires shares**.

When a company P Co wishes to **purchase shares** in a company S Co it must pay the previous owners of those shares. The most obvious form of payment would be in **cash**. Suppose P Co purchases all 40,000 £1 shares in S Co and pays £60,000 cash to the previous shareholders in consideration. The entries in P Co's books would be

Double Entry	(£)
DEBIT: Investment in S Co at cost	60,000
CREDIT: Bank	60,000

However, the previous shareholders might be prepared to accept some other form of consideration. For example, they might accept an agreed number of **shares** in P Co. P Co would then issue new shares in the agreed number and allot them to the former shareholders of S Co. This kind of deal might be attractive to P Co since it avoids the need for a heavy cash outlay. The former shareholders of S Co would retain an indirect interest in that company's profitability via their new holding in its parent company.

Continuing the Example, suppose the shareholders of S Co agreed to accept one £1 ordinary share in P Co for every two £1 ordinary shares in S Co. P Co would then need to issue and allot 20,000 new £1 shares. How would this transaction be recorded in the books of P Co?

The simplest method would be as follows.

Double Entry	(£)
DEBIT: Investment in S Co	20,000
CREDIT: Share capital	20,000

However, if the 40,000 £1 shares acquired in S Co are thought to have a value of £60,000 this would be misleading. The former shareholders of S Co have presumably agreed to accept 20,000 shares in P Co because they consider each of those shares to have a value of £3. This view of the matter suggests the following method of recording the transaction in P Co's books.

Double Entry	(£)
DEBIT: Investment in S Co	60,000
CREDIT: Share capital	20,000
CREDIT: Share premium account	40,000

The second method is the one which should normally be used in preparing consolidated accounts.

3.2 Goodwill on consolidation

The amount which P Co records in its books as the cost of its investment in S Co may be more or less than the book value of the assets it acquires. Suppose that S Co in the previous Example has no retained earnings and no liabilities, so that its share capital of £40,000 is balanced by tangible assets with a book value of £40,000. For simplicity, assume that the book value of S Co's assets is the same as their market or fair value.

Now when the directors of P Co agree to pay £60,000 for a 100% investment in S Co they must believe that, in addition to its tangible assets of £40,000, S Co must also have intangible assets worth £20,000. This amount of £20,000 paid over and above the value of the tangible assets acquired is called **goodwill arising on consolidation** (also sometimes called **premium on acquisition**).

Following the normal cancellation procedure the £40,000 share capital in S Co's statement of financial position could be cancelled against £40,000 of the 'investment in S Co' in the statement of financial position of P Co. This would leave a £20,000 debit uncancelled in the parent company's accounts and this £20,000 would appear in the consolidated statement of financial position under the caption 'Intangible non-current assets: goodwill arising on consolidation'.

3.3 Goodwill and pre-acquisition profits

Up to now we have assumed that S Co did not have any retained earnings when its shares were purchased by P Co. Assuming instead that S Co had earned profits of £8,000 in the period before acquisition, its statement of financial position just before the purchase would look as follows.

	(£)
PPE	48,000
Share Capital	40,000
Retained Earnings	8,000
	48,000

If P Co now purchases all the shares in S Co it will acquire total tangible assets worth £48,000 at a cost of £60,000. Clearly in this case S Co's intangible assets (goodwill) are being valued at £12,000. It should be apparent that any **retained earnings** earned by the subsidiary **prior to its acquisition** by the parent company must be **incorporated in the cancellation** process so as to arrive at a figure for goodwill arising on consolidation. In other words, not only S Co's share capital, but also its **pre-acquisition retained earnings**, must be cancelled against the asset 'investment in S Co' in the accounts of the parent company. The uncancelled balance of £12,000 appears in the consolidated statement of financial position.

The consequence of this is that **any pre-acquisition retained earnings of a subsidiary company are not aggregated with the parent company's retained earnings** in the consolidated statement of financial position. The figure of consolidated retained earnings comprises the retained earnings of the parent company plus the **post-acquisition retained earnings only of subsidiary companies**. The post-acquisition retained earnings are simply retained earnings now *less* retained earnings at acquisition.

Example

Sing Co acquired the ordinary shares of Wing Co on 31 March when the draft statement of financial position of each company were as follows.

Sing Co statement of financial position as at 31 March	(£)
Non-current Assets	
Investment in 50,000 shares in Wing Co at cost	80,000
Current Assets	40,000
Net Assets	120,000
Ordinary Shares	75,000
Retained Earnings	45,000
Shareholders' Funds	120,000

Wing Co statement of financial position as at 31 March	(£)
Net Assets	60,000
50,000 ordinary shares of £1 each	50,000
Retained Earnings	10,000
	60,000

Requirement

Prepare the consolidated statement of financial position as at 31 March.

Solution

The technique to adopt here is to produce a new working: 'Goodwill'. A proforma working is set out below.

Goodwill	(£)	(£)
Cost of investment		X
Share of net assets acquired as represented by:		
Ordinary share capital	X	
Share premium	X	
Retained earnings on acquisition	X	
Group share a%		(X)
		X
b% preferred shares		(X)
Goodwill		X

Applying this to our Example the working will look like this.

	(£)	(£)
Cost of investment		80,000
Share of net assets acquired as represented by:		
Ordinary share capital	50,000	
Retained earnings on acquisition	10,000	
	60,000	
Group share 100%		60,000
Goodwill		20,000

Sing Co consolidated statement of financial position as at 31 March	(£)
Non-Current assets: Goodwill arising on consolidation	20,000
Current Assets (40,000 + 60,000)	100,000
Net Assets	120,000
Ordinary Shares (Sing Co only)	75,000
Retained Earnings (Sing Co only – no post-acquisition retained earnings in Wing Co)	45,000
Shareholders' Funds	120,000

3.4 IFRS 3 Business Combinations

Goodwill arising on consolidation is one form of **purchased goodwill**, and is governed by IFRS 3.
As explained in an earlier chapter IFRS 3 requires that goodwill arising on consolidation should
be capitalised in the consolidated statement of financial position and **reviewed for impairment every year**.

3.5 Negative goodwill

Goodwill arising on consolidation is the difference between the cost of an acquisition and the value of the subsidiary's net assets acquired. This difference can be **negative**: the aggregate of the fair values of the separable net assets acquired may exceed what the parent company paid for them. The treatment of this 'negative goodwill' is

- An entity should first **re-assess** the amounts at which it has measured both the cost of the combination and the acquiree's identifiable net assets. This exercise should **identify any errors**.

- Any **negative goodwill remaining** should be **recognised immediately in profit or loss**, that is in the **income statement**.

4 INTRA-GROUP TRADING

4.1 Unrealised profit

Any receivable/payable balances outstanding between the companies are cancelled on consolidation. No further problem arises if all such intra-group transactions are undertaken at cost, without any mark-up for profit.

However, each company in a group is a separate trading entity and may wish to treat other group companies in the same way as any other customer. In this case, a company (say, A Co) may buy goods at one price and sell them at a higher price to another group company (B Co). The accounts of A Co will quite properly include the profit earned on sales to B Co; and similarly B Co's statement of financial position will include inventories at their cost to B Co, i.e. at the amount at which they were purchased from A Co.

This gives rise to two problems.

- Although A Co makes a profit as soon as it sells goods to B Co, the group does not make a sale or achieve a profit until an outside customer buys the goods from B Co.

- Any purchases from A Co which remain unsold by B Co at the year end will be included in B Co's inventory. Their statement of financial position value will be their cost to B Co, which is not the same as their cost to the group.

The objective of consolidated accounts is to present the financial position of several connected companies as that of a single entity, the group. This means that **in a consolidated statement of financial position the only profits recognised should be those earned by the group** in providing goods or services to outsiders; and similarly, inventory in the consolidated statement of financial position should be valued at cost to the group.

Example

Suppose that a holding company P Co buys goods for £1,600 and sells them to a wholly-owned subsidiary S Co for £2,000. The goods are in S Co's inventory at the year end and appear in S Co's statement of financial position at £2,000. In this case, P Co will record a profit of £400 in its individual accounts, but from the group's point of view the figures are

Cost	£1,600
External sales	nil
Closing inventory at cost	£1,600
Profit/loss	nil

If we add together the figures for retained earnings and inventory in the individual statement of financial positions of P Co and S Co the resulting figures for consolidated retained earnings and consolidated inventory will each be overstated by £400.

Solution

A **consolidation adjustment** is therefore necessary as follows.

Double Entry
DEBIT: Group reserves
CREDIT: Group inventory (statement of financial position)

with the amount of **profit unrealised** by the group.

Example

P Co acquired all the shares in S Co one year ago when the reserves of S Co stood at £10,000. Draft statement of financial positions for each company are as follows.

	P Co (£)	P Co (£)	S Co (£)	S Co (£)
Assets				
Non-Current Assets				
PPE	80,000			40,000
Investment in S Co at cost	46,000			
		126,000		
Current Assets		40,000		30,000
Current Liabilities		(21,000)		(18,000)
Net Assets		145,000		52,000
Ordinary shares of £1 each		100,000		30,000
Reserves		45,000		22,000
Shareholders' Funds		145,000		52,000

During the year P Co sold goods to S Co for £50,000, the profit to S Co being 20% of selling price. At the statement of financial position date, £15,000 of these goods remained unsold in the inventories of S Co. At the same date, P Co owed S Co £12,000 for goods bought and this debt is included in the trade payables of P Co and the receivables of S Co. The goodwill arising on consolidation has been impaired. The amount of the impairment is £1,500.

Requirement

Prepare a draft consolidated statement of financial position for P Co.

Solution

1. **Goodwill**

	(£)	(£)
Cost of investment		46,000
Share of net assets acquired as represented by		
Share capital	30,000	
Retained earnings	10,000	
	40,000	
Group share (100%)		40,000
Goodwill		6,000
Less: impairment loss		(1,500)
		4,500

2. **Retained Earnings**

	P Co (£)	S Co (£)
Retained earnings per question	45,000	22,000
Unrealised profit: 20% × £15,000	(3,000)	
	42,000	
Pre-acquisition retained earnings		(10,000)
		12,000
Share of S Co (post-acquisition)	12,000	
Goodwill impairment loss	(1,500)	
	52,500	

P Co consolidated statement of financial position	(£)	(£)
Non-Current Assets		
PPE	120,000	
Goodwill (6,000 − 1,500)	4,500	
		124,500
Current Assets (W1)		55,000
Current Liabilities (W2)		(27,000)
Net Assets		152,500
Ordinary Shares of £1 each	100,000	
Retained Earnings	52,500	
Shareholders' Funds		152,500

Workings

1. **Current Assets**

	(£)	(£)
In P Co's statement of financial position		40,000
In S Co's statement of financial position	30,000	
Less S Co's current account with P Co cancelled	12,000	
		18,000
		58,000
Less unrealised profit excluded from inventory valuation		3,000
		55,000

2. **Current Liabilities**

	(£)
In P Co's statement of financial position	21,000
Less P Co's current account with S Co cancelled	12,000
	9,000
In S Co's statement of financial position	18,000
	27,000

5 IFRS 3 AND FAIR VALUES IN ACQUISITION ACCOUNTING

Fair values are very important in calculating goodwill.

5.1 Goodwill

To understand the importance of fair values in the acquisition of a subsidiary consider the definition of **goodwill**.

> Any excess of the cost of the acquisition over the acquirer's interest in the fair value of the identifiable assets and liabilities acquired as at the date of the exchange transaction.

The **statement of financial position of a subsidiary company** at the date it is acquired may not be a guide to the fair value of its net assets. For example, the market value of a freehold building may have risen greatly since it was acquired, but it may appear in the statement of financial position at historical cost less accumulated depreciation.

5.2 What is fair value?

Fair value is defined as follows by IFRS 3 and various other Standards – it is an important definition.

> The amount for which an asset could be exchanged, or a liability settled, between knowledgeable, willing parties in an arm's length transaction.

5.2.1 Fair value adjustment calculations

Until now we have calculated goodwill as the difference between the cost of the investment and the **book value** of net assets acquired by the group. If this calculation is to comply with the definition above we must ensure that the book value of the subsidiary's net assets is the same as their **fair value**.

Example

P Co acquired 75% of the ordinary shares of S Co on 1 September 2005. At that date the fair value of S Co's non-current assets was £23,000 greater than their net book value, and the balance of retained earnings was £21,000. The statement of financial positions of both companies at 31 August 2006 are given below.

S Co has not incorporated any revaluation in its books of account.

P Co statement of financial position as at 31 August 2006	(£)
Non-Current Assets	
PPE	63,000
Investment in S Co at cost	51,000
	114,000
Current Assets	82,000
Current Liabilities	(20,000)
Net Assets	176,000
Ordinary shares of £1 each	80,000
Retained Earnings	96,000
Shareholders' Funds	176,000

S Co consolidated statement of financial position as at 31 December 2005	(£)
Non-Current Assets – PPE	28,000
Current Assets	43,000
Current Liabilities	(10,000)
Net Assets	61,000
Ordinary shares of £1 each	20,000
Retained Earnings	41,000
Shareholders' Funds	61,000

If S Co had revalued its non-current assets at 1 September 2005, an addition of £3,000 would have been made to the depreciation charged in the income statement for 2005/06.

Requirement

Prepare P Co's consolidated statement of financial position as at 31 August 2006.

Solution

S Co has not incorporated the revaluation in its draft statement of financial position. Before beginning the consolidation workings we must therefore adjust the company's balance of profits at the date of acquisition and at the statement of financial position date.

S Co Adjusted Balance of Accumulated Profits	(£)	(£)
Balance per accounts at 1 September 2005		21,000
Consolidation adjustment: revaluation surplus		23,000
∴ Pre-acquisition retained earnings for consolidation purposes		44,000
Profit for year ended 31 August 2006		
Per draft accounts £(41,000 – 21,000)	20,000	
Consolidation adjustment: increase in depreciation charge	(3,000)	
		17,000
Adjusted balance of retained earnings at 31 August 2006		61,000

In the consolidated statement of financial position, S Co's non-current assets will appear at their revalued amount: £(28,000 + 23,000 – 3,000) = £48,000. The consolidation workings can now be drawn up.

Workings

1. **Minority interest**

	(£)
Share capital (25% × £20,000)	5,000
Retained earnings (25% × £61,000)	15,250
	20,250

2. **Goodwill**

	(£)	(£)
Cost of investment		51,000
Share of net assets acquired as represented by		
Ordinary share capital	20,000	
Retained earnings	21,000	
Fair value adjustment	23,000	
	64,000	
Group share (75%)		48,000
Goodwill		3,000

3. **Retained earnings**

	P Co (£)	S Co (£)
Per question	96,000	41,000
Pre-acquisition retained earnings		(21,000)
Depreciation adjustment		(3,000)
Post acquisition S Co		17,000
Group share in S Co (£17,000 × 75%)	12,750	
Group retained earnings	108,750	

P Co consolidated statement of financial position as at 31 August 2006	(£)	(£)
Non-Current Assets: PPE (63,000 + 48,000)	111,000	
Goodwill (W2)	3,000	

P Co consolidated statement of financial position as at 31 August 2006	(£)	(£)
		114,000
Current Assets (82,000 + 43,000)		125,000
Current Liabilities (20,000 + 10,000)		(30,000)
Net Assets		209,000
Ordinary shares of £1 each	80,000	
Retained Earnings (W3)	108,750	
		188,750
Minority Interest (W1)		20,250
Shareholders' Funds		209,000

6 THE CONSOLIDATED INCOME STATEMENT

Exam tip

> Historically you have been asked to determine the impact of an acquisition on group performance in Section B, e.g. Winter 1999 Question 2, Winter 1997 Question 2.

As always, the source of the consolidated statement is the individual accounts of the separate companies in the group.

6.1 Consolidation procedure

The individual income statements are set out side by side and totalled to form the basis of the consolidated income statement.

Example

P Co acquired 75% of the ordinary shares of S Co on that company's incorporation in 2003. The summarised income statements of the two companies for the year ending 31 December 2006 are set out below.

	P Co (£)	S Co (£)
Sales revenue	75,000	38,000
Cost of sales	30,000	20,000
Gross profit	45,000	18,000
Administrative expenses	14,000	8,000
Profit before tax	31,000	10,000
Tax	10,000	2,000
Profit for the year	21,000	8,000
Retained earnings brought forward	87,000	17,000
Retained earnings carried forward	108,000	25,000

Requirement

Prepare the consolidated income statement and movement in retained earnings.

Solution

P Co Consolidated Income Statement for the Year Ended 31 December 2006	(£)
Sales revenue (75 + 38)	113,000
Cost of sales (30 + 20)	50,000
Gross profit	63,000
Administrative expenses (14 + 8)	22,000
Profit before tax	41,000
Tax (10 + 2)	12,000
Profit after tax	29,000
Minority interest (25% × £8,000)	2,000
Group profit for the year	27,000
Retained earnings brought forward	
(group share only: 87 + (17 × 75%))	99,750
Retained earnings carried forward	126,750

Note how the minority interest is dealt with.

- Down to the line '**profit after taxation**' the **whole** of S Co's results is included without reference to group share or minority share. A **one-line adjustment** is then inserted to deduct the minority's share of S Co's profit after taxation.

- The minority's share (£4,250) of S Co's retained earnings brought forward is **excluded**. This means that the carried forward figure of £126,750 is the figure which would appear in the statement of financial position for group retained earnings.

This last point may be clearer if we revert to our **statement of financial position technique** and construct the working for group retained earnings.

	(£)
Group reserves	
P Co	108,000
Share of S Co's post-acquisition retained reserves (75% × £25,000)	18,750
	126,750

The minority share of S Co's retained earnings comprises the minority interest in the £17,000 profits brought forward plus the minority interest (£2,000) in £8,000 retained earnings for the year.

Notice that a consolidated income statement **links up** with a consolidated statement of financial position exactly as in the case of an individual company's accounts: the figure of retained earnings carried forward at the bottom of the income statement appears as the figure for retained earnings in the statement of financial position. (*Note.* Under IAS 1 this would be shown as a movement in retained earnings; for convenience the retained earnings movements are shown here with the income statement.)

We will now look at the complications introduced by **inter-company trading** and **mid year acquisition** of the subsidiary.

6.2 Intra-group trading

Like the consolidated statement of financial position, the consolidated income statement should deal with the results of the group as those of a single entity. When one company in a group sells goods to another an identical amount is added to the sales revenue of the first company and to the cost of sales of the second. Yet as far as the entity's dealings with outsiders are concerned no sale has taken place.

The consolidated figures for sales revenue and cost of sales should represent **sales to**, and **purchases from, outsiders**. An adjustment is therefore necessary to reduce the sales revenue and cost of sales figures by the value of intra-group sales during the year.

We have also seen in an earlier chapter that any unrealised profits on intra-group trading should be excluded from the figure for group profits. This will occur whenever goods sold at a profit within the group remain in the inventory of the purchasing company at the year end. The best way to deal with this is to **calculate the unrealised profit on unsold inventories at the year end and reduce consolidated gross profit by this amount**. Cost of sales will be the balancing figure.

Example

Suppose in our earlier example that S Co had recorded sales of £5,000 to P Co during 2006. S Co had purchased these goods from outside suppliers at a cost of £3,000. One half of the goods remained in P Co's inventory at 31 December 2006. Prepare the revised consolidated income statement.

Solution

The consolidated income statement for the year ended 31 December 2006 would now be as follows.

	(£)
Sales revenue (75 + 38 − 5)	108,000
Cost of sales (balancing figure) or (30 + 20 − 5 + 1)	(46,000)
Gross profit (45 + 18 − 1*)	62,000
Administrative expenses	(22,000)
Profit before tax	40,000
Tax	(12,000)
Profit after tax	28,000
Minority interest (25% × (£8,000 − £1,000*))	(1,750)
Group profit for the year	26,250
Retained earnings brought forward	99,750
Retained earnings carried forward	126,000
*Unrealised profit: ½ × (£5,000 − £3,000)	

An adjustment will be made for the unrealised profit against the inventory figure in the consolidated statement of financial position, as explained earlier in the chapter.

6.3 Mid-year acquisition

As explained earlier, the figure for retained earnings at the bottom of the consolidated income statement must be the same as the figure for retained earnings in the consolidated statement of financial position. We have seen earlier in this chapter that retained earnings in the consolidated statement of financial position comprise

- The **whole of the parent company's** retained earnings.

- A **proportion of the subsidiary company's** retained earnings. The proportion is the **group's share of post-acquisition retained earnings** in the subsidiary. From the total retained earnings of the subsidiary we must therefore **exclude** both the **minority's share** of total retained earnings and the **group's share of pre-acquisition** retained earnings.

A similar procedure is necessary in the consolidated income statement if it is to link up with the consolidated statement of financial position. Previous Examples have shown how the minority share of profits is excluded in the income statement. Their share of profits for the year is deducted from profit after tax, while the figure for profits brought forward in the consolidation schedule includes only the group's proportion of the subsidiary's profits.

In the same way, if the subsidiary is **acquired during the accounting year**, it is therefore necessary to apportion its profit for the year between pre-acquisition and post-acquisition elements.

Example

P Co acquired 60% of the equity of S Co on 1 April 2005. The income statements of the two companies for the year ended 31 December 2005 are set out below.

	P Co (£)	S Co (£)	S Co ($^9/_{12}$) (£)
Sales Revenue	170,000	80,000	60,000
Cost of Sales	65,000	36,000	27,000
Gross Profit	105,000	44,000	33,000
Administrative Expenses	43,000	12,000	9,000
Profit before tax	62,000	32,000	24,000
Tax	23,000	8,000	6,000
Profit after tax	39,000	24,000	18,000
Dividends (paid 31 December)	12,000	6,000	
Retained Earnings brought forward	81,000	40,000	
Retained Earnings carried forward	108,000	58,000	

P Co has not yet accounted for the dividends received from S Co.

Requirement

Prepare the consolidated income statement and movements in retained earnings.

Solution

The shares in S Co were acquired three months into the year. Only the post-acquisition proportion (9/12ths) of S Co's income statement is included in the consolidated income statement. This is shown above for convenience.

P Co Consolidated Income Statement for the Year Ended 31 December 2005	(£)
Sales Revenue (170 + 60)	230,000
Cost of Sales (65 + 27)	92,000
Gross Profit	138,000
Administrative Expenses (43 + 9)	52,000
Profit before tax	86,000
Tax (23 + 6)	29,000
Profit after tax	57,000
Minority Interest (40% × £18,000)	7,200
Group Profit for the year	49,800
Retained Earnings brought forward*	81,000
Profit for the year	49,800
Dividends	(12,000)
Retained earnings carried forward	118,800

* All of S Co's profits brought forward are pre-acquisition.

CHAPTER ROUNDUP

You need to be familiar with and able to describe

- The purpose of group accounts.

- Minority interest.

- Goodwill and IFRS 3 – Fair values

    - **Goodwill**. Any excess of the cost of the acquisition over the acquirer's interest in the fair value of the identifiable assets and liabilities acquired as at the date of the exchange transaction.

    - **Fair value**. The amount for which an asset could be exchanged, or a liability settled, between knowledgeable, willing parties in an arm's length transaction.

- Intra-group trading.

- Impact of acquisitions and disposals on the

    - Statement of financial position.
    - Income statement (especially mid year).

TEST YOUR KNOWLEDGE

Check your knowledge of the chapter here, without referring back to the text.

1. Hibiya plc

    The statement of financial positions of Hibiya plc and Sendai plc as at December 31 2006 are as follows.

	Hibiya		Sendai	
	(£'000)	(£'000)	(£'000)	(£'000)
Other non-current assets		5,000		2,000
Investment in Sendai plc		1,000		–
		6,000		2,000
Current assets		4,000		3,000
Total assets		**10,000**		**5,000**
Current liabilities	(2,500)		(1,700)	
Non-current liabilities	(2,000)		(2,300)	
Total liabilities		**(4,500)**		**(4,000)**
Net assets		**5,500**		**1,000**
Share capital		2,000		300
Retained earnings		3,500		700
Equity		**5,500**		**1,000**

Hibiya plc has just acquired 100% of the share capital of Sendai plc for £1,000,000.

Requirement

Prepare the consolidated statement of financial position of the Hibiya group as at December 31 2006.

2. Hibiya plc Part 2

    The statement of financial positions of Hibiya plc and Sendai plc as at December 31 2006 are as follows.

	Hibiya		Sendai	
	£'000	£'000	£'000	£'000
Other non-current assets		5,000		2,000
Investment in Sendai plc		1,000		–
		6,000		2,000
Current assets		4,000		3,900
Total assets		**10,000**		**5,900**
Current liabilities	(2,500)		(1,900)	
Non-current liabilities	(2,000)		(2,000)	
Total liabilities		**(4,500)**		**(3,900)**
Net assets		**5,500**		**2,000**
Share capital		2,000		300
Retained earnings		3,500		1,700
Equity		**5,500**		**2,000**

Hibiya plc acquired 100% of Sendai plc on December 31 2005 for £1,000,000 when the retained earnings of Sendai plc were £700,000.

Requirement

Prepare the consolidated statement of financial position of the Hibiya group as at December 31 2006.

3.   Horenso plc

The statement of financial position of Horenso plc and Sarada plc as at December 31 2006 are as follows.

	Horenso (£'000)	Sarada (£'000)
Other non-current assets	2,000	1,000
Investment in Sarada plc	1,600	–
	3,600	1,000
Current assets	7,000	3,000
Total assets	**10,600**	**4,000**
Total liabilities	**(5,000)**	**(2,000)**
Net assets	**5,600**	**2,000**
Share capital	2,000	500
Retained earnings	3,600	1,500
Equity	**5,600**	**2,000**

Horenso plc has just bought 80% of the shares of Sarada plc for £1,600,000.

Requirement

Prepare the consolidated statement of financial position of the Horenso group as at December 31 2006.

4.   Horenso plc Part 2

The statement of financial position of Horenso plc and Sarada plc as at December 31 2006 are as follows.

	Horenso (£'000)	Sarada (£'000)
Other non-current assets	2,000	1,200
Investment in Sarada plc	1,600	–
	3,600	1,200
Current assets	7,000	3,700
Total assets	**10,600**	**4,900**
Total liabilities	**(5,000)**	**(2,100)**
Net assets	**5,600**	**2,800**
Share capital	2,000	500
Retained earnings	3,600	2,300
Equity	**5,600**	**2,800**

Horenso plc bought 80% of the shares of Sarada plc for £1,600,000 on December 31 2005 when Sarada plc's retained earnings were £1,500.

Requirement

Prepare the consolidated statement of financial position of the Horenso group as at December 31 2006.

5.   Holmes plc

The statement of financial position of Holmes plc and Sherlock plc as at June 30 2006 are as follows.

	Holmes (£'000)	Sherlock (£'000)
Other non-current assets	5,600	2,200
Investment in Sherlock plc	4,000	–
	9,600	2,200
Current assets	6,200	2,300
Total assets	**15,800**	**4,500**
Total liabilities	**(8,700)**	**(2,200)**
Net assets	**7,100**	**2,300**
Share capital	400	1,000
Share premium account	100	700
Retained earnings	6,600	600
Equity	**7,100**	**2,300**

Holmes plc has just acquired 100% of Sherlock plc's share capital for £4,000,000.

Requirements

Prepare the consolidated statement of financial position of the Holmes group as at June 30 2006. Assume that the amounts recorded above for the assets and liabilities of Sherlock plc represent their fair values at June 30 2006.

6.   Holmes plc Part 2

The statement of financial positions of Holmes plc and Sherlock plc as at June 30 2006 are as follows.

	Holmes (£'000)	Sherlock (£'000)
Other non-current assets	5,600	2,200
Investment in Sherlock plc	4,000	–
	9,600	2,200
Current assets	6,200	2,300
Total assets	**15,800**	**4,500**
Total liabilities	**(8,700)**	**(2,200)**
Net assets	**7,100**	**2,300**
Share capital	400	1,000
Share premium account	100	700
Retained earnings	6,600	600
Equity	**7,100**	**2,300**

Holmes plc has just acquired 80% of Sherlock plc's share capital for £4,000,000.

Requirements

Prepare the consolidated statement of financial position of the Holmes group as at June 30 2006.Assume that the amounts recorded above for the assets and liabilities of Sherlock plc represent their fair values at June 30 2006.

7.   Hard plc

Hard plc has owned 60% of Soft plc's share capital for ten years. Goodwill on the acquisition, which was previously being amortised over 20 years, was £400,000. In the year ended September 30 2006, under IFRS 3, goodwill is no longer being amortised; the annual impairment test indicates that the goodwill has been impaired by £10,000. The income statements of each individual company for the year ended September 30 2006 are as follows.

	Hard (£'000)	Soft (£'000)
Revenue *(Note)*	3,000	1,200
Cost of sales	(1,700)	(700)
Gross profit	1,300	500
Distribution costs	(150)	(50)
Administration expenses	(250)	(100)
Operating profit	900	350
Finance costs	(100)	–
Profit before taxation	800	350
Taxation	(300)	(100)
Profit for the period	500	250

Note

During the year, Soft plc sold goods to Hard plc for a total of £50,000. Hard plc had sold these outside the group by the end of the period.

Hard paid a dividend of £100,000 to its shareholders during the year ended September 30 2006.

Requirements

Prepare the consolidated income statement for the year ended September 30 in 2006 for the Hard group.

8.   Pappa plc

Pappa plc purchased 1,450,000 equity shares in Lima plc in 20X0, when other reserves of Lima plc stood at £400,000 and there were no retained earnings.

The statement of financial position of the two companies as at 31 December 20X4 are set out below.

	Pappa plc		Lima plc	
	(£'000)	(£'000)	(£'000)	(£'000)
Non-current assets				
Property plant and equipment				
Buildings	5,000		1,000	
Plant	3,396		543	
Vehicles	472		244	
		8,868		1,787
Financial asset				
Shares in Lima plc at cost		1,450		–
		10,318		1,787
Current assets				
Inventories	1,983		1,425	
Receivables	1,462		1,307	
Cash	25		16	
		3,470		2,748
TOTAL ASSETS		13,788		4,535
Current liabilities				
Borrowings	(1,456)		(840)	
Trade accounts payable	(887)		(1,077)	
Tax	(540)		(218)	
	(2,883)		(2,135)	
Non-current liabilities				
7% Notes	(4,000)			
9% Notes	–		(500)	
TOTAL LIABILITIES		(6,883)		(2,635)
NET ASSETS		6,905		1,900
Equity shares of 50p each		5,000		1,000
Share premium account		500		–
Other reserves		1,200		800
Retained earnings		205		100
EQUITY		6,905		1,900

At the statement of financial position date, the current account of Pappa plc with Lima plc was agreed at £23,000, owed by Lima plc. This account is included in the appropriate receivables and trade accounts payable balances shown above.

Requirements

(a)   Prepare a consolidated statement of financial position for the Pappa Lima Group at 31 December 20X4.

(b)   Show the alterations necessary to the group statement of financial position if the inter-company balance owed by Lima plc to Pappa plc represented an invoice for goods sold by Pappa to Lima at a mark-up of 15% on cost, and still unsold by Lima plc at 31 December 20X4.

Assume that the accounting policy is not to amortise goodwill and that it has not suffered any impairment.

TEST YOUR KNOWLEDGE: ANSWERS

1. Hibiya plc

Consolidated statement of financial position as at December 31 2006	(£'000)	(£'000)
Non-current assets (5,000 + 2,000)		7,000
Current assets (4,000 + 3,000)		7,000
Total assets		**14,000**
Current liabilities (2,500 + 1,700)	(4,200)	
Non-current liabilities (2,000 + 2,300)	(4,300)	
Total liabilities		**(8,500)**
Net assets		**5,500**
Share capital		2,000
Retained earnings		3,500
Equity		**5,500**

2. Hibiya Part 2

Consolidated statement of financial position as at December 31 2006	(£'000)	(£'000)
Non-current assets (5,000 + 2,000)		7,000
Current assets (4,000 + 3,900)		7,900
Total assets		**14,900**
Current liabilities (2,500 + 1,900)	(4,400)	
Non-current liabilities (2,000 + 1,900)	(4,000)	
Total liabilities		**(8,400)**
Net assets		**6,500**
Share capital		2,000
Retained earnings *(see below)*		4,500
Equity		6,500

Working

Retained Earnings at December 31 2006	(£'000)	(£'000)
Hibiya		3,500
Sendai	1,700	
Sendai's retained earnings at acquisition	(700)	
Increase in Sendai's retained earnings since acquisition		1,000
		4,500

3.   Horenso plc

Consolidated statement of financial position as at December 31 2006	(£'000)
Other non-current assets (2,000 + 1,000)	3,000
Current assets (7,000 + 3,000)	10,000
Total assets	**13,000**
Total liabilities (5,000 +2,000)	**(7,000)**
Net assets	**6,000**
Share capital	2,000
Retained earnings	3,600
	5,600
Minority interest (20% × {500 + 1,500})	400
Equity	**6,000**

4.   Horenso plc Part 2

Consolidated statement of financial position as at December 31 2006	(£'000)
Other non-current assets (2,000 + 1,200)	3,200
Current assets (7,000 +3,700)	10,700
Total assets	**13,900**
Total liabilities (5,000 +2,100)	**(7,100)**
Net assets	**6,800**
Share capital	2,000
Retained earnings *(see below)*	4,240
	6,240
Minority interest (20% × {500 + 2,300})	560
Equity	**6,800**

Working

Retained Earnings at December 31 2006	(£'000)	(£'000)
Horenso		3,600
Sarada	2,300	
Sarada's retained earnings at acquisition	(1,500)	
Increase in Sarada's retained earnings since acquisition	800	
Group's share of Sarada's increase in retained earnings since acquisition	× 80%	640
		4,240

5.   Holmes plc

Consolidated statement of financial position as at June 30 2006	(£'000)
Other non-current assets (5,600 + 2,200)	7,800
Goodwill *(see below)*	1,700
	9,500
Current assets (6,200 +2,300)	8,500
Total assets	**18,000**
Total liabilities (8,700 +2,200)	**(10,900)**
Net assets	**7,100**
Share capital	400
Share premium account	100
Retained earnings	6,600
Equity	**7,100**

Goodwill	(£'000)
Cost of investment in Sherlock	4,000
Fair value of net assets acquired	(2,300)
Goodwill	1,700

6.   Holmes plc Part 2

Consolidated statement of financial position as at June 30 2006	(£'000)
Other non-current assets (5,600 + 2,200)	7,800
Goodwill *(see below)*	2,160
	9,960
Current assets (6,200 +2,300)	8,500
Total assets	**18,460**
Total liabilities (8,700 + 2,200)	**(10,900)**
Net assets	**7,560**
Share capital	400
Share premium account	100
Retained earnings	6,600
	7,100
Minority interest (20% × {1,000 + 700 + 600})	460
Equity	**7,560**

Goodwill	(£'000)
Cost of investment in Sherlock	4,000
Fair value of net assets acquired (80% × 2,300)	(1,840)
Goodwill	2,160

7.   Hard plc

Consolidated income statement for the year ended September 30 2006	(£'000)
Revenue (3,000 + 1,200 – 50)	**4,150**
Cost of sales (1,700 + 700 – 50))	(2,350)
Gross profit	**1,800**
Distribution costs	(200)
Administration expenses	(350)
Impairment of goodwill	(10)
Operating profit	**1,240**
Finance costs	(100)
Profit before taxation	**1,140**
Taxation	(400)
Profit for the period	**740**
Attributable to:	
Equity holders of the parent	640
Minority interest (40% × 250)	100
	740

8.   Pappa plc

(a)

Pappa plc consolidated statement of financial position as at 31 December 20X4	(£'000)	(£'000)
Non-current assets		
Intangible assets		
Goodwill (W2)		435
Property plant and equipment		
Buildings	6,000	
Plant	3,939	
Vehicles	716	
		10,655
Current assets		11,090
Inventories	3,408	
Receivables (less £23,000 inter-company)	2,746	
Cash	41	
		6,195
TOTAL ASSETS		17,285
Current liabilities		
Borrowings	(2,296)	
Trade accounts payable (less £23,000 inter-company)	(1,941)	
Tax	(758)	
	(4,995)	
Non-current liabilities		
7% Notes	(4,000)	
9% Notes	(500)	
	(4,500)	
TOTAL LIABILITIES		**(9,495)**
NET ASSETS		**7,790**
Share capital		
Equity shares of 50p each		5,000.0
Share premium account		500.0
Other reserves (W4)		1,490.0
Retained earnings (W4)		277.5
Minority interests (W3)		2,267.5
		522.5
EQUITY		**7,790.0**

(b)   Pappa plc has made a profit of 15/115 × £23,000 = £3,000 on its sale of goods to Lima plc. Lima plc has not yet sold goods to an outside party and the profit is therefore unrealised as far as the group is concerned. The adjustment is necessary to reduce the balance of retained earnings, and the value of inventories by £3,000.

Workings

1.   Group structure

Pappa

$$\frac{1,450}{2,000} = 72.5\%$$

Lima

2.

Goodwill	(£'000)	(£'000)
Cost of investment		1,450
Net assets acquired		
Share capital	1,000	
Other reserves	400	
Retained earnings	–	
Net assets at acquisition	1,400	
	× 72.5%	
		(1,015)
Goodwill at acquisition/statement of financial position date		435

3.

Minority interest	(£'000)
Net assets financed by	
Share capital	1,000
Other reserves	800
Retained earnings	100
	1,900
	× 27.5%
	522.5

4.

Reserves	Pappa (£'000)	Lima (£'000)
Retained earnings	205	100
At 31 December 20X4		
At date of acquisition		–
Increase since acquisition		100
Share of increase since acquisition (100 × 72.5%)	72.5	
	277.5	
Other reserves		
At 31 December 20X4	1,200	800
At date of acquisition		(400)
Increase since acquisition		400
Share of increase since acquisition (400 × 72.5%)	290	
	1,490	

10

Financial Statement Analysis Techniques

INTRODUCTION

Core to this examination is the practical analysis of a published set of financial statements. The purpose of analysing a set of accounts is to again a view as to whether the business represents a good investment opportunity or not. In this respect we are trying to determine the returns a business is offering and the risks inherent in those returns arising as a result of how the business is trading and how it is financed.

The purpose of this section is to lead you through the ideas of analysis in order to enable you to apply those ideas to a practical example in the exam.

CHAPTER CONTENTS

The syllabus areas covered by this chapter are

Interpretation of Financial Information

Financial and accounting ratios

Analysis and interpretation of ratios. Understanding of the significance of the main financial and accounting ratios to investors. Presentation of findings in report form for the benefit of an investor.

Comparisons of accounting figures

Ability to compare, contrast and recognise the significance of accounting information for:

(a)   Companies in different industries.
(b)   Different companies within the same industry.
(c)   The same company over successive accounting periods.

In respect of financial statement analysis techniques:

It is emphasised that the intention of the examination is to assess student's analytical and interpretative skills rather than their technical accounting ability. It is also expected that they should have an understanding of standard accounting practices and an awareness of matters currently under discussion.

1   INTRODUCTION

Exam tip

It is absolutely essential that you are fully familiar with, able to calculate and able to comment on all the various ratios. Ratio calculations are central to **every sitting** and you can expect to be calculating and commenting on ratios in **every section** of the exam.

We do not comment any further in this chapter, but the exam relevance of the subject matter of this section cannot be understated.

1.1 Financial statements

The financial statements, being the income statement, the statement of financial position, the cash flow and all the associated notes, contain a vast amount of information. Sometimes it is very difficult to see the wood for the trees. The role of the analyst is to distil this information down into some usable form for his client.

The financial statements are primarily prepared for the shareholders. However, they may have several other users such as lenders, creditors, the government, tax authorities, and so on. Each of these will be looking to use the accounts to get some indication of the

■   Returns they are receiving.
■   Risks they are facing.

A number of fairly standard ratios have been developed to assist with this process.

1.2 Types of ratio

These ratios can be grouped under four headings.

Profitability	Measures to assess the trading or operating performance of the company, i.e. levels of trading profits generated and the effectiveness of the use of trading assets.
Liquidity	Measures to assess the trading risk of the company. This is the risk that, as a result of trading activities, the company may be unable to pay its suppliers as the debts fall due and cease to exist.
Investors' ratios	Measures to assess the returns to providers of finance, who may be either shareholders or lenders.
Gearing	Measures to assess the risks to the providers of finance due to the company's level of borrowing.

We can see that there are effectively two sides to a business – a trading side and the financing side. A company raises finance then uses this to enable it to trade. Our analysis will be used to measure the risks and returns on each side.

1.3 Statement of financial position

In order to undertake this analysis, we need to either mentally or physically rearrange the statement of financial position to show the information we want. The standard statement of financial position is prepared for the benefit of the shareholders. The top half of the statement of financial position shows the net assets or under IFRS total assets, the bottom the shareholders' funds and under IFRS total liabilities as well.

Rather than showing net assets and shareholders' funds as two sides of the statement of financial position, what we, as analysts really want is some kind of statement of financial position that shows the trading assets on one side and all the financing on the other. Effectively, we want to shift the non-current liabilities from the top of the statement of financial position onto the bottom of the statement of financial position.

Example

We have the following initial statement of financial position showing net assets and shareholders' funds.

Statement of financial position	£'000
Non-Current Assets	50
Current Assets	60
Non-Current Liabilities	(30)
Current Liabilities	(45)
Net Assets	35
Share Capital	12
Reserves	23
Shareholders' Funds	35

It would be useful to rearrange the statement of financial position to show the trading assets and how they are financed, i.e.

Rearranged statement of financial position	£'000	£'000
Non-Current Assets		50
Current Assets	60	
Current Liabilities	(45)	
Net Current Assets		15
Total Trading Assets		65
Share Capital		12
Reserves		23
Non-Current Liabilities		30
Total Financing		65

In practice, it will not normally be necessary to re-jig the statement of financial position in this way. However, it is very useful to try to picture it in this way as it ensures that no factors are ignored when considering either the trading assets or the financing. It also enables us to appreciate the effect of the accounting policies on various ratios.

1.4 Usefulness of ratios

Ratios are very convenient for summarising and presenting information. In general they are very easy to understand and they help to focus attention on the important aspects of business performance and risk (trading or financial).

A ratio is, however, **meaningless in isolation**. In order to be useful, a ratio must have some reasonable comparative, for example

- Prior year figures.
- Competitors' figures.
- Budget figures.

We can then review how we are doing compared with, say, the previous year. The ratio itself is not an answer, simply a means to an end. If all of our ratios this year are the same as they were last year, then our returns and risks for all interested parties are unaltered.

Ratios can be used to highlight trends over a number of years, which may not be so apparent from the figures themselves. These trends can then be used by the analyst's client to assess how the company is performing.

When using ratios to focus our attention for analysis purposes, we will essentially be looking for

- **Discontinuities**, i.e. large changes in the ratios from one year to the next, or large variances of the ratio against competitors or budgets. These, in all probability, will be highlighting some anomaly.

- **Trends** illustrated by the ratios over a period of time. These may be upward/downward trends in terms of returns being achieved, or the risks people face.

1.5 Link between users and the structure of accounts

Clearly, as analysts we need to identify who our client is and what their concerns are. The table below shows a summarised income statement and a summarised statement of financial position along with various possible users of the account; and in outline terms, illustrates which aspects of the accounts they will be most concerned with.

User/Interest	Income statement	Statement of financial position	Ratios
Managers/Employees	Revenue	Non-current assets	Profitability
■ Job security	(Operating costs)	Current assets	Liquidity
■ Pay rises		(Current liabilities)	
Lenders/Government	Operating profit	Trading assets	
■ Can company pay debts?	(Interest)	(Loans)	Liquidity
■ Is company paying correct tax?	Profit before tax	Net assets	Gearing
	(Tax)		
Investors	Profit after tax	Share capital	Gearing
■ Return on investment	(Dividends)	Reserves	Investors
■ Security of investment	Profit after dividends	Shareholders' funds	

Managers and employees would be interested in the availability and effectiveness of the use of assets, i.e.

- **Trading performance** – how effective the company has been at generating profits (concentrating on the breakdown of profits and profitability ratios).

- **Trading position** – what resources the company has available for the purposes of trade (concentrating on the build up of the statement of financial position assets and liquidity ratios).

Investors and lenders would be interested in the breakdown and servicing of financing, i.e.

- **Financial performance** – how effective the company has been in generating a return to its providers of finance (concentrating on the levels of interest and dividends and related investors' ratios).

- **Financial position** – how the company is financed (concentrating on the financial build up on the statement of financial position).

This table should only be considered as a general overview or starting point for analysis. It is not a hard and fast rule by which you should feel constrained. When considering an investor's ratio, such as earnings per share, it may be necessary to analyse profitability in detail, i.e. analysis should never be compartmentalised as the table above may indicate. Again, this table provides just a starting point based on who the stakeholder is.

1.6 Definition of ratios

Other than earnings per share, there is **no strict definition of any ratio**. What we describe below are fairly standard ratios, but how certain elements should be treated may be open to some debate. It is your job as the analyst to determine the best way to deal with these items, although the most important factor is that you are **consistent in how you treat them** from one year to another or from one company to another.

For example, in our rearrangement of the statement of financial position into trading assets and financing, how should a bank overdraft be treated? Is the bank overdraft part of the trading resources of the organisation or is it part of the long-term financing?

A bank overdraft may arise because our receivables are slow at paying this month, whereas we have paid our suppliers, in which case it would be a trading liability. On the other hand it may be something that we have had for many years helping finance all our operations, in which case it should be viewed as financing. If we are looking at figures for a company over a number of years, it may be possible to highlight the general level of overdraft that is always there and may be considered long-term financing with any excess overdraft above that amount being considered as a trading liability. However, if we were just comparing this year to last, we would not have the information to do this.

There is simply no right answer to this question, but do not become concerned. The ratio can be worked out treating it as a trading liability and then reworked treating it as financing to see what trends are shown.

We will run through each of these categories of ratios, illustrating them with an example taken from the company details at the end of this session.

2 PROFITABILITY RATIOS

The aim of profitability ratios is to measure the underlying profitability of the business itself regardless of how it is financed. Perhaps the best starting point is a calculation of return on capital employed (ROCE).

2.1 Return on capital employed

2.1.1 Basic calculation

The return on capital employed is calculated as

Formula to learn

$$\text{ROCE} = \frac{\text{Profit from operations} + \text{Interest receivable and other income receivable}}{\text{Capital employed}} \times 100\%$$

Considerations

This profit figure can be viewed as operating profit plus interest receivable and income from other investments, i.e. the profits that management has generated from the resources it has available. It is specifically before interest payable since that will clearly be dependent on the financing of the business – the larger the loans, the larger the interest payable.

The capital employed figure is the total trading assets (or total financing since they are equal) that we identified earlier in the session when we rearranged the statement of financial position. Based on this, capital employed can be calculated from the financing side as

Formula to learn

Capital employed = Shareholders' funds + Non-current liabilities + Borrowings in current liabilities

or from the trading side as

Formula to learn

Capital employed = Total assets − Current liabilities
(excluding borrowings in current liabilities, such as overdrafts, finance lease obligations)

NB: We have treated the overdraft as financing here, this is the most consistent treatment of overdrafts for this ratio. However, we may treat them differently for other ratios.

Example

The Example uses information from the illustration financial statements included at the end of this chapter, Section 9.

After exceptional items

$$ROCE = \frac{6,484 + 62 + 303}{33,041 + 4,445 + 137 + 16,942} \times 100\%$$

$$ROCE = \frac{6,849}{54,565} \times 100\%$$

$$ROCE = 12.6\%$$

Before exceptional items (included in administration costs)

$$ROCE = \frac{6,849 + 3,192}{54,565} \times 100\%$$

$$ROCE = 18.4\%$$

For this Example, we have calculated the capital employed as shareholders' funds, including minority interest, non-current liabilities and the bank overdraft and finance lease liabilities. We have done this since these two liabilities are being treated as part of the financing of the company, not the trading assets.

The ratio can be calculated either before or after 'exceptional items'. These are items which are one-off in nature, such as restructuring cots or profit and losses on disposal of an asset. Ratios calculated on a pre-exceptional basis can be more useful for analysing trends. However, the analyst needs to consider if the exceptional item is actually a one-off item or a regular feature of the income statement.

2.1.2 Potential problems

Ideally, it would be best to use the average capital employed as our aim is to match the profits generated throughout the year to the capital or assets that have been used to generate them, or the total financing of the business.

It is unlikely that this information will be available, and normally the calculation would be based on year-end figures. This can lead to some **major distortions in our ratios**, especially if there have been large changes in capital employed during the year, i.e. from the acquisition of a subsidiary or the raising of funds near the year end.

2.1.3 Analysis points

Having established our return on capital employed, we now need to consider what may have caused any change from one year to the next. This is caused by one of two factors.

- Changes in profit margin.
- Changes in turnover volumes.

We have standard ratios to assess these two items. The following diagram illustrates how we can disaggregate the return on capital employed ratio into its component parts.

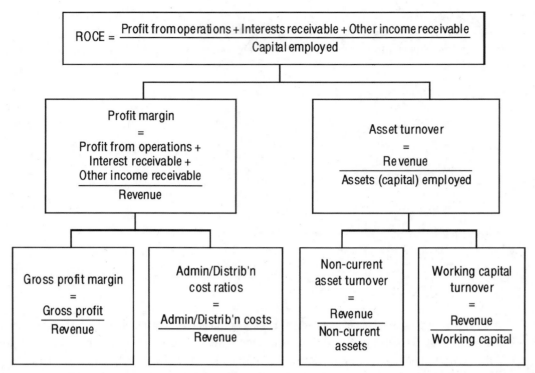

From our above definitions, we can see that if we multiply the profit margin by the asset turnover, we will get back to the return on capital employed since the revenue figures will cancel. We will now consider each of these ratios in more detail.

2.2 Profit margins

A profit margin is a measure of the profit achieved per £1 sale generated.

<table>
<tr><td>**Formula to learn**</td><td>$$\text{Profit margin} = \frac{\text{Profits}}{\text{Revenue}} \times 100\%$$</td></tr>
</table>

Considerations

From our diagram above we have taken profit as profit from operations and other income. This ensures that the ratios exactly 'interlock'. However, this brings with it the problem that not all elements of this profit as defined here have any relationship to the levels of revenue. For example, this profit is stated after

- Interest receivable.
- Income from non-current asset investments.
- Share of profits of associated undertakings.

None of the above three are related to revenue. In some cases it might be better, therefore, particularly if examining the profit margin in isolation, to use the operating profit figure only. However, we will continue using our 'full' PBIT figure for now.

Example

Again, using information contained in our illustration financial statements at the end of this chapter.

$$\text{Profit margin} = \frac{£6,849 \text{ (see ROCE above)}}{£135,761} \times 100\%$$

$$\text{Profit margin} = 5.0\%$$

2.2.1 Analysis points

Once we have calculated this ratio, we need to make something meaningful out of it. When doing this, it is important to consider the causes and possible consequences, not just the numbers.

If profit margins are up it may appear to be good news – higher levels of profits. However, these higher profits may mean that the company loses customer loyalty if they perceive that they are being exploited. Alternatively, high prices may attract competitors into the field, in which case the company may lose a substantial amount of market share.

Conversely, margins going down may normally be perceived as bad news. However, it may be as a consequence of a policy of penetration pricing; or it may be that the company is incurring high development costs and future years' profitability will be that much higher as a result.

2.3 Asset turnover

The asset turnover ratio assesses the effectiveness of the use of the trading assets available.

Formula to learn

$$\text{Asset turnover} = \frac{\text{Revenue}}{\text{Assets (capital) employed}}$$

2.3.1 Considerations

To make these ratios exactly interlock, as in the diagram above, we would need to take all the capital employed as being the denominator in this calculation. However, again, some assets bear no relationship to turnover whatsoever, e.g.

- Investment in associated undertakings.
- Short-term investments.

It may therefore be more appropriate to take just those trading assets that have contributed to turnover.

Example

Using information from our illustration financial statements (Section 9)

$$\text{Asset turnover} = \frac{\text{£135,761}}{\text{£54,565 (see ROCE above)}}$$

Asset turnover = 2.49×

2.3.2 Potential problems

Again a problem with this ratio, in common with the problem of return on capital employed, is that we are comparing a full year's transactions (revenue) to a year-end statement of financial position figure (assets employed). Unless this year-end figure is representative of the assets employed throughout the year, we will not exactly be comparing like with like and there may be some distortions.

For example, if the company buys a subsidiary or raises new finance close to the year end, then the year-end assets employed would be substantially higher than the general level throughout the year.

Another problem is the impact of accounting policies. If, for example, non-current assets are revalued this year then this will have two effects.

- Profits will be down due to increased depreciation charges.
- Capital assets employed will be up due to the increase in non-current asset NBVs.

The result will be that our return on capital employed and asset turnover figures will be reduced, although the effectiveness of our trade, in truth, may be unaltered. It is very difficult to remove these distorting effects. It is probably more convenient to calculate the ratios but to note any distortions.

2.3.3 Analysis points

Again, when considering this ratio, it may be tempting just to state the obvious – but take care. We should **consider the causes**, not just the numbers.

Considering just the numbers, it would be tempting to believe that increased asset turnover is a positive thing. However, it may arise from

- Overtrading, which would result in liquidity problems.
- A deterioration of the capital base, i.e. sales are not rising, rather the asset base is falling.

As the diagram above illustrates, this ratio may be further sub-analysed into, for example, working capital turnover and non-current asset turnover; each of which may be an appropriate ratio for a particular sort of industry. Non-current asset turnover may be an appropriate ratio in a capital-intensive industry where a large amount of the capital of the business is tied up in non-current assets. The analyst needs to decide which ratios to use and how to use them.

2.4 Operational gearing

The operational gearing ratio gives the percentage change in profits per 1% change in revenue, which may be calculated as

Formula to learn

$$\text{Operational gearing ratio} = \frac{\text{Revenue} - \text{Variable costs}}{\text{Profit}}$$

2.4.1 Considerations

This ratio is a measure of operational risk, i.e. risk to the operating profit figure, and is assessing the levels of variable and fixed operating costs in the business. Variable costs are costs whose level varies directly with the level of output, hence if sales increase/(decrease) then variable costs increase/(decrease), e.g. raw material costs. Fixed costs are costs whose level remains constant regardless of output levels, e.g. rent, rates, depreciation.

The greater the level of fixed costs in the business, the **greater the variation in the profit figure** as a result of revenue changes.

Example

A company sells its product for £10 per unit, has variable costs of £6 per unit and fixed costs of £15,000 per annum. The normal level of output is 10,000 units p.a., but if output levels vary, we will see the following.

Output (Units)	8,000	10,000	13,000
	£'000	£'000	£'000
Revenue	80	100	130
Variable costs	(48)	(60)	(78)
	32	40	52
Fixed costs	(15)	(15)	(15)
Profit before tax	17	25	37

The operational gearing calculated at the normal output level of 10,000 units is

$$\text{Operational gearing ratio} = \frac{100-60}{25} = 1.6 \times$$

What we can see is that a 20% fall in revenue (down to 8,000 units from 10,000) results in a 32% (20% × 1.6) fall in profits, a fall of £8,000 (25,000 × 32%) from £25,000 to £17,000.

Similarly, a 30% increase in revenue (up to 13,000 units from 10,000) results in a 48% (30% × 1.6) increase in profits, a rise of £12,000 (25,000 × 48%) from £25,000 to £37,000.

What this ratio is considering is the levels of profit generated by the company before (the top line) and after (the bottom line) suffering the fixed costs.

2.4.2 Potential problems and analysis points

The difficulty that we have in applying this idea in the analysis of the accounts of a company is that the accounts do not reveal the extent of the fixed and variable costs. An income statement by function of expense breaks down the operating costs into cost of sales, distribution costs and administrative expenses. Within each of these headings there may be an element of variable costs and an element of fixed costs. An income statement analyses the expenses in a manner that may enable this ratio to be calculated, however, this is still doubtful.

Operational gearing is more a factor to consider given the nature of the business, rather than a statistic that can be calculated. For example, capital intensive businesses will suffer from high fixed costs due to the depreciation of their non-current assets.

3 Liquidity Ratios

3.1 Introduction

There are two main sources of information relating to the liquidity position of a company.

- The statement of financial position.
- The following liquidity ratios.

The ratios we look at below aim to establish one of two things.

- Do we have the resources to meet our liabilities in hard cash terms?
- Are we realising those resources quickly enough to pay off the liabilities as they fall due?

As we will see, some of these ratios are rather blunt tools but they are useful for showing trends and are frequently used in loan agreements.

3.2 Current ratio

The purpose of this ratio is to see whether the current assets recoverable within one year are sufficient to cover the liabilities that fall due within one year.

Formula to learn

$$\text{Current ratio} = \frac{\text{Current assets}}{\text{Current liabilities}}$$

Example

Using information from our illustration at the end of this chapter (Section 9)

$$\text{Current ratio} = \frac{£57,653}{£43,666}$$

Current ratio = 1.32x

3.2.1 Potential problems and analysis points

Other practical problems when calculating or using this ratio are as follows.

- **Overdrafts** will be included within current liabilities but are frequently payable after more than one year in practice. Banks frequently allow companies to extend overdrafts for several years.

- **Realisation of inventory** – inventory is contained within current assets and is therefore almost automatically assumed to be realisable within one year, but this may not necessarily be the case. Unlike receivables there will be no note anywhere indicating the recoverability or likely time scale for the realisation of inventories.

- This ratio completely ignores the **timing of cash flows** within the period. In theory it could be possible that all the liabilities are payable now and all the assets are recoverable in 12 months' time. Although in total terms they match, in actual cash flow terms they do not.

3.3 Quick ratio

The quick ratio is an adaptation of the current ratio designed to remove the problem of inventory.

Formula to learn

$$\text{Quick ratio} = \frac{\text{Current assets} - \text{Inventory}}{\text{Current liabilities}}$$

3.3.1 Considerations

The quick ratio considers just the readily realisable assets (cash, investments and receivables) and whether they are sufficient to cover the short-term liabilities of the business. Being a modification of the current ratio, it suffers from the same problems, excluding realisability of inventory.

Example

Using information from our illustration at the end of this chapter (Section 9)

$$\text{Quick ratio} = \frac{£57,653 \text{ (see above)} - £19,420}{£43,666}$$

$$\text{Quick ratio} = \frac{£38,233}{£43,666}$$

$$\text{Quick ratio} = 0.88x$$

Our company has a quick ratio of less than one. This does not mean that it is insolvent and unable to pay off its liabilities. However, depending on the type of business, it may be a sign of liquidity problems.

The current and quick ratios will be influenced by the sector in which the company operates. For example, a supermarket group may have a current and quick ratio of less than one. Supermarkets usually have very low receivables because most customers pay for their goods immediately. Inventory is normally kept at low levels by using a just-in-time system, which delivers the inventory shortly before the sale. This results in low levels of current assets compared to current liabilities, which in turn gives rise to low current and quick ratios.

3.4 Inventory turnover

This measure gives an indication of how quickly we are selling our inventory.

Formula to learn

$$\text{Inventory turnover} = \frac{\text{Cost of sales}}{\text{Inventory}}$$

The cost of sales figure shows the total cost value of the goods sold in the year. The inventory figure shows the total cost value of the goods still held at the year end. This ratio therefore shows how many times during a year we can expect to sell our normal holding of inventory. For example, if this ratio was 6, then it takes us two months to sell our inventory on average; if the ratio was 12 it takes us one month, and so on.

3.4.1 Considerations

Within any business the ideal is to hold no inventory whatsoever, i.e. any item arrives from our supplier exactly at the time the customer walks in through the door to buy it, so they can specifically be matched one to another and the company need not hold any inventory at all. However, this is unlikely to be the case in practice.

In practice, companies will need to hold inventory on the shelves for customers to select, but they have got to make sure they do not hold too much inventory. Holding too much inventory will tie up much of the company's resources in goods for resale, and may lead to high insurance costs and high inventory obsolescence. Similarly, too little inventory will mean that customers cannot be served and may choose to go elsewhere. There needs to be a good balance somewhere in between.

Example

Using information from our illustration financial statements at the end of this chapter (Section 9)

$$\text{Inventory turnover} = \frac{£83,604}{£19,420}$$

Inventory turnover = 4.31×

3.4.2 Potential problems

This ratio, in common with others, is comparing a full year's transactions (cost of sales) to a year-end balance that may not be representative of the levels of inventory throughout the year. This would especially be the case in a business with seasonal demand and hence seasonal inventory levels.

Depending on the information provided in the income statement, it may not be possible to establish a cost of sales figure. Unfortunately not all companies separately identify cost of sales. Hence, in this situation, it is acceptable to use the revenue figure in place of the cost of sales. Clearly, this will distort the ratio. However, it is changes or trends that are important in analysis, not the value of the ratio itself.

3.4.3 Analysis points

Inventory turnover indicates the amount of inventory we are holding in terms of the time it may take to realise it, and any movement in this ratio from one year to the next may indicate whether we are tending to hold too much or too little inventory.

As we have already pointed out, the ideal amount of inventory and the inventory turnover rate are dependent on the business circumstances. For example

- A supermarket would expect a very high inventory turnover for its milk – perhaps as high as 365×.

- A whisky distiller whose inventory takes several years to mature would expect an inventory turnover rate of say 0.1×.

Hence, we should always consider the nature of the business.

However, care needs to be taken in stating what the ratio is showing. For example, an increased inventory turnover may naively be considered fairly good, and viewed as confirming increased levels of revenue. However, it may be a result of holding very low levels of inventory, which, as we have just noted, may be commercially bad.

3.5 Receivables' collection period

This measure gives an indication of how quickly we are realising our trade receivables, i.e. turning them into cash.

Formula to learn

$$\text{Receivables' collection period} = \frac{\text{Trade receivables}}{\text{Revenue}} \times 365 \text{ days}$$

3.5.1 Considerations

Assuming all sales are made on credit, the revenue figure will represent the total invoiced sales in the year, the trade receivables' figure will represent the unpaid invoices at the year end. Hence, receivables over revenue shows the proportion of the year's sales that have not been paid for, i.e. the credit period we are offering.

Example

Using information from our illustration financial statements at the end of the chapter (Section 9)

$$\text{Receivables' collection period} = \frac{£21,753}{£135,761} \times 365 \text{ days}$$

Receivables' collection period = 58.5 days

3.5.2 Potential problems and analysis points

Again, the problem with this ratio is that we are comparing the year-end balance (receivables) to a year's transactions (revenue), which could lead to some distortions if, for some reason, these figures are not representative.

For example, if sales are very seasonal, they may peak at one time in the year and reach a low point at another time in the year. We would expect our receivables to be correspondingly high at one point in the year and low at another point in the year. The revenue figure would be the sum total of all the sales in the year, regardless of the seasonal nature. Clearly, however, we would show substantially different receivables' collection periods if our year end was when we had a high receivables' figure or when we had a low receivables' figure.

3.6 Payables' payment period

This measure shows how quickly we are settling our liabilities.

Formula to learn

$$\text{Payables' payment period} = \frac{\text{Trade payables}}{\text{Cost of sales}} \times 365 \text{ days}$$

3.6.1 Considerations

This ratio, in a very similar way to the receivables' collection period, measures the amount of credit we are taking from our suppliers. To be a worthwhile and valid comparison, we really need to try to compare invoiced payables to invoiced costs. Remember, however, that in a manufacturing business the cost of sales may include such things as wages and salaries of the production staff, which will distort the ratio unless care is taken.

Example

Using information from our illustration financial statements at the end of this chapter (Section 9)

$$\text{Payables' payment period} = \frac{£18,702}{£83,604} \times 365 \text{ days}$$

Payables' payment period = 81.6 days

3.6.2 Potential problems and analysis points

The problems with the use of this ratio are identical to those identified for the receivables' collection period above.

3.7 Working capital cycle

The previous three ratios are really looking at the speed of cash flow around the working capital cycle.

■ The **inventory turnover ratio** shows how quickly inventory is being turned into a sale (receivables).

■ The **receivables' collection period** shows how quickly those receivables are being turned into cash (in days).

■ The **payables' payment period** shows the time scale over which we have to pay off our suppliers.

An organisation should always look to **maintain a balance** in these areas. In particular, between the collection period for receivables and the payment period for payables, assuming they are of a similar scale.

If we are forced by our customers to increase the credit period we offer, we must endeavour to increase the credit period we can get from our suppliers in turn. Otherwise, we will find ourselves with a cash flow problem, since we will have to settle our liabilities without having the cash available to do so.

This is quite a frequent problem for businesses that fall into the liquidity trap. Such businesses, in an effort to boost sales, may extend credit terms to their customers. This has the effect of increasing the sales as anticipated. However, it causes the mismatch of the cash flows in from receivables and out to payables, and subsequent liquidity problems may arise.

4 FINANCIAL GEARING

4.1 Introduction

These ratios consider the build up of the financing side of the capital employed equation and address the relationships between

■ Interest bearing borrowed capital on which the return must be paid.
■ Shareholders' capital on which the return is optional.

4.2 Financial gearing and risk

It is generally accepted that high levels of gearing imply high financial risks for the company, but why is this the case? Let us consider this with two examples.

Example 1

Consider an individual who buys a £32,000 house with a £30,000 mortgage and £2,000 of his own cash, then subsequently sells it in five years time for

(a) **£64,000 (i.e. the price has doubled – a 100% increase)**

Here the individual is walking away with a £32,000 profit on effectively a £2,000 investment – a 1,600% return.

(b) **£16,000 (i.e. the price has halved – a 50% decrease)**

Here, the individual has lost £16,000 on his £2,000 investment – an 800% loss.

The scale of the profits and losses is significantly greater than the change in the house price. If risk is viewed as the variability of returns, we can see that the risk to the investor is much greater than the basic risk in house prices.

Example 2

A company has interest payable of £30,000 per annum. In three different years, it generates three different levels of operating profits as shown below.

	Year 1 (£'000)	Year 2 (£'000)	Year 3 (£'000)
Operating profits	50	100	150
Interest	(30)	(30)	(30)
Profit before tax	20	70	120

We can see from the above that when operating profits fluctuate 50% up or down from their normal level of £100,000, the profit before tax fluctuates by 71.43% from its normal level, i.e. profits before tax are **significantly more volatile** than operating profits themselves, and this volatility increases as the interest charge (or gearing) rises.

NB: Financial gearing is not necessarily introducing risk in itself. Financial gearing is augmenting or amplifying the risk inherent in the basic operations. If our operating profit did not vary from £100,000, the profit figure before tax would always be £70,000. If there is no risk in operating profit, there is no risk in the profit before tax introduced by the gearing.

The level of gearing does, however, amplify the effect of changes in operating profit on changes in profit before tax. Work out for yourself what the variability would be if the interest paid each year was £40,000 (answer +/– 83.33%).

Standard gearing ratios are calculated by either looking at the proportions of the financial build up on the statement of financial position, or the expenses in the income statement.

4.3 Investors' debt to equity ratio

This is a relationship that our shareholders would consider as a measure of the risk to their dividends.

$$\text{Debt to equity} = \frac{\text{Interest bearing loans} + \text{Preference share capital}}{\text{Equity shareholders' funds}} \times 100\%$$

4.3.1 Considerations

We consider only interest-bearing debt since this is what is causing the risk to profit before tax, hence ultimately the profits after tax and amounts available for payment as dividends to our shareholders.

Example

Using information from our illustration financial statements at the end of this chapter,

$$\text{Debt to equity} = \frac{16,942 + 137 + 1,356 + 1,016 + 837}{32,138 - 837} \times 100\%$$

$$\text{Debt to equity} = \frac{20,288}{31,301} \times 100\%$$

$$\text{Debt to equity} = 64.8\%$$

4.3.2 Potential problems

Bank overdrafts

You would need to consider how to treat bank overdrafts. Should they be treated as part of interest-bearing loans, or excluded from this calculation altogether? Once again, there is no one right answer to this question. Rather, it is for the analyst to determine the nature of the overdraft – long-term financing used by the company or a short-term trading anomaly.

Accounting policies

The statement of financial position gearing in particular can be greatly influenced by the **accounting policies**. For example, if we revalue non-current assets upwards then our shareholders' funds will rise (since we will be increasing the revaluation surplus) but there will be no change in our debt figure, hence our gearing ratio will fall. If we consider the impact of this on our interest cover (see below), however, a larger value of non-current assets will result in a larger depreciation figure in subsequent years. Hence, a lower operating profit and therefore a lower interest cover in subsequent years. Therefore, if a policy of revaluation is adopted in a year it will distort both the statement of financial position and income statement ratios compared to the previous years.

Convertibles

How should convertibles be treated in our gearing ratio? Is a convertible debt or should we consider it as equity if we believe it likely to convert? Once again, there is no right answer, although in the statement of financial position convertibles will be shown as part equity and part liability. No ratio is specifically defined except EPS. It is down to you, the analyst, to decide the best treatment for a particular item.

If you believe the convertible is likely to convert (the conversion terms are favourable to the investor) then it maybe better treated as equity. However, interest on such debt does have to be paid in the near term and thus, it may be more conservative and prudent to treat it as debt.

Analysis points

"Is there an optimal gearing ratio?" is a question frequently asked. The answer is no, not a general one, but certainly the level of gearing a business can stand can be determined in some way. As our Example above shows, if there is no variability in operating profit, then financial gearing is of no consequence whatsoever.

Financial gearing is only a factor to consider if operating profits do vary, in which case **financial gearing amplifies that variation**. Therefore, in very safe businesses such as utilities, with steady levels of earnings, they can stand a much higher level of gearing than in a very volatile industry, such as high technology businesses.

As with all ratios, again, the most important thing is not the absolute value but the trend that we are seeing. Are we seeing a trend of improving gearing or a trend of deteriorating gearing?

4.4 Net debt to equity ratio

This is an alternative to the above which takes account of the cash that a business may also hold which could be used to repay debt.

Formula to learn

$$\text{Net debt to equity} = \frac{\text{Debt as above} - \text{Cash and current asset investments}}{\text{Equity shareholders' funds}} \times 100\%$$

4.4.1 Considerations

We should consider the ability of the company to use the cash it has available to repay debt. For example, it may be that some of the cash we hold is cash received on account from customers that we cannot use for the repayment of debts in general.

Example

$$\text{Net debt to equity} = \frac{20,288 \text{ (as above)} - 6,425 - 3,926}{31,301} \times 100\%$$

$$\text{Net debt to equity} = \frac{9,937}{31,301} \times 100\%$$

$$\text{Net debt to equity} = 31.7\%$$

4.5 Lenders' debt to equity ratio

This is a relationship that our unsecured lenders would consider as a measure of the risk to their returns.

Formula to learn

$$\text{Lenders' debt to equity} = \frac{\substack{\text{Total borrowings} \\ \text{(including non-interest bearing debt)}}}{\substack{\text{Total shareholders' funds} \\ \text{(including preference shares)}}} \times 100\%$$

Considerations

Here, total debt equals debt as defined above plus non-interest-bearing debt, i.e. we consider all obligations to pay all liabilities. This is therefore useful to lenders, who are just one of the many creditors of a company, all of whom need to be paid off.

Example

$$\text{Lenders' debt to equity} = \frac{43,666 + 4,445}{32,138} \times 100\%$$

$$\text{Lenders' debt to equity} = \frac{48,111}{32,138} \times 100\%$$

$$\text{Lenders' debt to equity} = 149.7\%$$

4.5.1 Potential problems and analysis points

The same problems arise in the context of this ratio as with the debt to equity ratio above.

4.6 Interest cover

This ratio considers gearing from the viewpoint of the income statement.

Formula to
learn

$$\text{Interest cover} = \frac{\text{Profit from operations} + \text{Interest receivables} + \text{Other income receivables}}{\text{Interest payable}}$$

4.6.1 Considerations

The interest cover gives a measure of the ability of the company to pay the fixed interest on borrowings out of its profits for the year. Clearly, the higher the level of interest cover, the less risk there is to either shareholders or lenders. However, again there is no optimal level.

Example

$$\text{Interest cover} = \frac{£6,849 \text{ (see ROCE above)}}{£3,176}$$

Interest cover = 2.16×

4.6.2 Potential problems and analysis points

As above for debt to equity ratios.

4.7 Asset cover (or capital cover)

In the same way that lenders are concerned about the interest cover, they may also be concerned over the safety of the loan itself as demonstrated by the assets available to repay it. The asset cover is calculated as

Formula to
learn

$$\text{Asset cover} = \frac{\text{Total assets} - \text{Current liabilities}}{\text{Loans payable}}$$

4.7.1 Considerations

If there are a number of loans with different priorities of repayment in a winding up, the asset cover is calculated for each of them in priority order on a cumulative basis.

Example

In order of priority, our debt can be analysed as

Debt	Value (£'000)	Cumulative (£'000)
Finance lease (secured on asset)	1,153	1,153
Unsecured loans and bank overdraft	18,298	19,451

Our total assets less current liabilities excluding current instalments due on loans and finance leases is £81,152 − 43,666 + £16,942 + £137 = £54,565.

Hence, asset covers are

Finance lease = 54,565 ÷ 1,153 = 47.3×

Loans = 54,565 ÷ 19,451 = 2.81×

5 EARNINGS PER SHARE

5.1 Investors' ratios

Investors want a good return, either as income now or capital growth, or some combination of both, plus security of their investment. Investors' ratios are designed to consider these factors. One of the key investor ratios is earnings per share.

5.2 Earnings per share

The calculation of earnings per share is specified in IAS 33 – *Earnings per Share* (FRS 22 in the UK).

Earnings per share (EPS) is the one ratio for which there are some rules regarding its calculation. These are laid out in IAS 33, which basically defines the EPS as

Formula to learn

$$EPS = \frac{\text{Net profit/loss attributable to ordinary shareholders}}{\text{Weighted average number of ordinary shares outstanding during the period}}$$

5.2.1 Considerations

What the Standard does is define each of these terms and what adjustments should be made to them under certain circumstances, such as the issue of shares during the year. It also details disclosure requirements.

5.3 Earnings

Earnings represent the profit available to pay out to the ordinary shareholders, i.e. after all deductions excluding ordinary dividends.

Example

$$EPS = \frac{£2,301 - £84}{17,925 \text{ shares}}$$

$$EPS = \frac{£2,217}{17,925}$$

$$EPS = 12.37p$$

5.4 Number of shares

5.4.1 Introduction

The number of shares is the number of equity shares in issue. So long as there have been no changes in the number of shares during the year, no problems will arise. However, if there have been any issues of shares, some adjustment will be required.

The purpose of the adjustments will be

- To ensure the ratio for the current year is valid by comparing the full year's earnings to the representative number of shares in issue during the year, not simply the number of shares in issue at the year end, which may be distorted by an issue near to year end.

- To ensure that previous years' earnings per share figures have been calculated on a similar basis, and thus ensure that they are comparable to this year's earnings per share figure, i.e. we may need to restate previous years' EPS figures.

Each possible circumstance is outlined below.

5.5 Full price issue

When shares are issued at full value part way through the year, then the new finance raised at that point is available to generate new profits from that point in the year. Hence, the level of earnings and number of shares will rise from the date the shares are issued.

To ensure we make a like-for-like comparison in the earnings per share calculation, we will need to compare the earnings for the year to a representative number of shares throughout the year, rather than simply the year-end number. This representative number is the **weighted average number of shares** in issue during the year.

For a full price issue **no adjustment to prior years' figures** is required since the shares were not in issue and will have had no impact on previous years.

Example

Earnings

Profit attributable to the group = £2,217 as used above.

Number of shares

If the company issued three million shares on 31 August (year end 31 December), then the weighted average number of shares is

Dates	Total Number	Time Apportion	Weighted Average
1 Jan–31 Aug	14,925	$\times \dfrac{8}{12}$	9,950
31 Aug issue	3,000		
1 Sept–31 Dec	17,925	$\times \dfrac{4}{12}$	5,975
			15,925

EPS

$$\text{EPS} = \frac{£2,217}{15,925}$$

$$\text{EPS} = 13.92p$$

The comparative EPS would remain unaltered.

5.6 Issue to acquire a subsidiary

When we issue shares as part of the purchase consideration to acquire a subsidiary, the treatment is exactly the same as a full price issue.

From the date we acquire the subsidiary, we will start to consolidate into the group accounts the profit of the subsidiary, i.e. from the date of acquisition group earnings will rise by the earnings generated by the subsidiary. We therefore want to take the number of shares as having risen from that date also; i.e. we need to take the **weighted average number of shares**.

5.7 Bonus issues and share splits

When we make a bonus issue, we are not actually altering the operating assets of the business at all; all we are doing is restructuring shareholders' funds.

A bonus issue does not raise any new cash and therefore will not generate any new earnings. The bonus issue has the effect of increasing share capital and reducing reserves, i.e. restructuring shareholders' funds, but causes no change in the total shareholders' funds or total net assets. From an operational viewpoint, these bonus shares may as well have been issued at the same time as the underlying shares on which they are now being 'paid'.

This last point really gives an indication of the treatment where there is a bonus issue. Specifically we backdate the bonus and pretend that those **shares had always been in issue**. As a result an adjustment will be required to the number of shares previously in issue by use of the bonus fraction, which is

Formula to learn

$$\text{Bonus fraction} = \frac{\text{Number of shares after the issue}}{\text{Number of shares before the issue}}$$

Example

Earnings

Profit attributable to the group = £2,217 as used above.

Number of shares

On 1 January, the company had 14,340 shares in issue. It made a 1 for 4 bonus issue on 31 August (year end 31 December), the bonus fraction being

$$\text{Bonus fraction} = \frac{5}{4}$$

since one new share is issued for every four currently in issue. The calculation of the weighted average is as follows.

Dates	Total Number	Bonus Fraction	Time Apportion	Weighted Average
1 Jan–31 Aug	14,340	$\times \dfrac{5}{4}$	$\times \dfrac{8}{12}$	11,950
31 Aug issue	3,585			
1 Sept–31 Dec	17,925		$\times \dfrac{4}{12}$	5,975
				17,925

You will notice that the number of shares that we arrive at is, in fact, the year-end number and this calculation proves to be unnecessary. It has been included here to illustrate an idea we will come back to when we consider a rights issue.

A quicker method of doing the calculations in the circumstance of a bonus issue is to simply take the year-end number of shares.

EPS

$$EPS = \frac{£2,217}{17,925}$$

$$EPS = 12.37p$$

In addition, we would need to **update last year's original EPS** of 12.43p in the Example to make it appear to have been based on 17,925 shares rather than the 14,340 actually in issue (i.e. we need to scale the EPS down – spread the same earnings over more shares).

We can do this by multiplying last year's EPS by the inverse of the bonus fraction $\left(\text{i.e. } \dfrac{1}{\text{Bonus fraction}} \right)$, sometimes referred to as the adjustment factor, giving a comparative EPS of

$$EPS \text{ (comparative)} = 12.43 \times \frac{4}{5} = 9.94p$$

5.8 Rights issue

Rights issues are typically made at a discount to the full market price. The purpose of a rights issue is to raise some new finance in order to undertake a project, hence, from the date of the issue we can imagine that earnings will rise. This is similar to the full price issue situation.

However, the increase in earnings will be less than it would have been had we made a full price issue since less cash is raised per share. We can consider a rights issue at a discount, as getting somebody to pay the full price for a proportion of the shares and then giving away the rest, i.e. we can consider the rights issue as being the equivalent of

- Part of the issue being at the full price.
- Part of the issue being a bonus.

As such, we would need to apply both the above ideas to the issue, specifically

- We need to calculate the weighted average number of shares this year for the full price issue element.
- We need to backdate the bonus element and revise the prior year figures.

We therefore need a method to split the full issue into those two components. Fortunately, we can calculate the bonus element by use of a simple formula.

Formula to learn

$$\text{Bonus fraction} = \frac{\text{Actual price before the issue (cum-rights price)}}{\text{Theoretical price after issue (ex-rights price)}}$$

We will firstly show how to calculate these figures, then why this formula actually works.

Example

Earnings

Profit attributable to the group = £2,217 as used above.

Number of shares

On 1 January, the company had 14,340 shares in issue. It made a 1 for 4 rights issue at a price of £1.20 on 31 August (the full share price on that date is £2.20). The bonus fraction for this can be calculated as follows.

	Number of Shares	Price (£)	Value (£)
Before	4	2.20	8.80
Issue	1	1.20	1.20
After	5		10.00

Hence, the theoretical ex-rights price (price after the issue) is £2.00 (£10.00 ÷ 5 shares), giving a bonus fraction of

$$\text{Bonus fraction} = \frac{2.20}{2.00} = 1.1$$

From this, we can calculate the appropriate number of shares (backdating the bonus element) as

Dates	Total Number	Bonus Fraction	Time Apportion	Weighted Average
1 Jan–31 Aug	14,340	$\times \dfrac{2.20}{2.00}$	$\times \dfrac{8}{12}$	10,516
31 Aug issue	3,585			
1 Sept–31 Dec	17,925		$\times \dfrac{4}{12}$	5,975
				16,491

EPS

$$\text{EPS} = \frac{£2,217}{16,491}$$

$$\text{EPS} = 13.44\text{p}$$

Again here, we would need to update last year's EPS to make it appear to have been based on a larger number of shares due to the bonus element of the issue. We do this by multiplying last year's EPS by the inverse of the bonus fraction $\left(\text{i.e. } \dfrac{1}{\text{Bonus fraction}} \right)$; again this is sometimes referred to as the adjustment factor, giving a comparative EPS of

$$\text{EPS (comparative)} = 12.43 \times \frac{2.00}{2.20} = 11.30\text{p}$$

Proof of bonus fraction

By taking the bonus fraction as 1.1, we are stating that the rights issue is the equivalent of a 1 for 10 bonus issue plus a full price issue for the remainder of the shares.

Considering an individual who held 40 shares before the rights issue, this would mean taking a bonus of four shares and paying the full price for six (taking his year end holding up to 50 shares as would be the case following the 1 for 4 rights issue). We will show that the share price under this alternative is the same as we calculated above and hence the two are equivalent.

	Number of Shares	Price (£)	Value (£)
Held	40	2.20	88.00
Bonus	4	–	–
	44		88.00*
Full price	6	2.00*	12.00
New holding	50		100.00

* Following the bonus element of the issue, our share price falls to £2.00 (£88 ÷ 44 shares), which must be the price for the full price element of the issue.

We can see from this that our shareholder is in exactly the same position following either the rights issue or the bonus issue plus the issue at full price. Specifically, he holds 50 shares worth £2.00 each. The two are therefore equivalent and our bonus fraction applies.

5.9 Post-statement of financial position events

The basic EPS is required to be altered to incorporate the effect of certain share issues on the number of ordinary shares where the issue occurs between the statement of financial position date and the date on which the accounts are approved.

Where the company undertakes a bonus issue, share split or consolidation, or where there is a bonus element to another issue (e.g. rights issue) the number of shares must include the extra shares now in issue after the event.

In the case of an issue that impacts on earnings, such as a rights issue, only those shares that have no earnings impact should be included in the EPS calculation. For a rights issue, this would be just the 'bonus' element.

5.10 Alternative measures of earnings

5.10.1 Maintainable earnings

Earnings per share is widely used as a performance measure from the point of view of equity shareholders. It is also the denominator in the Price/Earnings ratio (see Paragraph 6.2 of this chapter). An Accounting Standard (IAS 33) regulates how earnings per share must be calculated and disclosed in financial statements. It aims to ensure that calculations and disclosures are consistent across companies.

Basic EPS takes account of *all* transactions that have affected the profit or loss for the period. Financial analysts and other users of the financial statements may not find the IAS 33 published figures ideal for their purposes. For example, the current period's results may reflect some unusual one-off transactions. If EPS is being measured to monitor the trend in shareholders' profits, the trend will be distorted by including the non-recurring item in one period. Similarly inter-company comparisons may be distorted. If EPS is to be used for calculating and comparing Price/Earnings multiples it makes sense to adjust for one-offs. The point is that users would like to know the extent to which profits are derived from a business's core operating activities and are maintainable or likely to recur. In principle, this is about establishing those earnings that are of the highest quality and therefore most valuable to investors. Published EPS per IAS 33 cannot do this job, nor does it claim to.

IAS 33 recognises that companies may want to disclose additional measures of EPS and allows them to do so providing that these are

- Presented in the notes to the accounts, not on the face of the income statement.
- Reconciled to the basic and diluted figures per IAS 33.

This leaves preparers with scope to come up with different (and usually higher) EPS non-GAAP measures, frequently described as 'underlying EPS' or something similar. However, by definition these need not be calculated consistently between companies. This leaves individual users to develop their own measures of EPS; arguably that is what analysts are paid to do. The point is that no single measure of EPS can be the correct figure for all purposes and for all users.

Maintainable EPS is the holy grail and, so far, has proved unattainable. What has been developed is 'headline' earnings.

5.10.2 Headline earnings

Since 1992 Price/Earnings ratios appearing daily in the *Financial Times* (FT) have been calculated using 'headline' earnings. The concept was developed by the Institute of Investment Management and Research (IIMR), the professional body for investment analysts in the UK. In 2000 the IIMR merged with another body and became the UK Society of Investment Professionals (UKSIP) and it changed its name to the CFA Society of the UK in 2008.

Headline earnings was a measure of **trading** performance and involved making more or less standardised adjustments to published figures, thereby reducing the amount of subjective judgements involved.

The calculation was intended to be

- Robust.
- Derived from information readily available in the accounts.
- Objective (i.e. no scope for subjective judgments by the preparers of the financial statements).

The following items were **included** as trading items.

- All trading profits and losses, whether normal or abnormal.
- Profits or losses on operations discontinued in the period (until date of discontinuance).
- Profits or losses on disposals of investments acquired with the intention of resale.
- Pension costs relating to continuing activities.

Headline earnings **excluded** the following as capital items.

- Profits or losses on disposal of non-current assets/investments.
- Profits or losses on the disposal of businesses/subsidiaries.
- Provisions for losses on discontinuance of businesses.
- Bid defence costs.
- Profits or losses on reorganisation/redemption of long-term debt.
- Goodwill amortisation.
- Prior year adjustments.
- Any tax or minority interest attributable to any of the above adjustments.

Headline earnings did not have to be disclosed in UK financial statements.

Since 1995 the same calculation has been required in South Africa as part of the listing requirements on the Johannesburg Stock Exchange (JSE). Listed companies must disclose a per share figure (Headline Earnings Per Share or HEPS).

The method of calculation had to be revisited as a result of the fact that South African and UK companies were required to adopt IFRS. The revision (issued in July 2007) was a joint project between UKSIP (now CFA Institute of the UK) and various South African bodies, including the South African Institute of Chartered Accountants.

The original headline earnings distinguished between changes in value of capital items and trading items. The revised measure adopts the approach of excluding from the calculation all remeasurements produced under IFRS, except for those affecting the current assets and liabilities. The principles underlying both the old and the new are identical.

5.11 Diluted earnings per share

The purpose of publishing the diluted earnings per share figure is to warn shareholders of potential future changes in the earnings per share figure as a result of events that have already happened. There are two possible factors that could cause a diluted earnings per share to arise.

- Convertible loan stock or convertible preference shares in issue.
- Options or warrants in issue.

Each of these circumstances may potentially result in more shares being issued and ranking for a dividend in future years, hence leading to a dilution of the current earnings per share.

The diluted EPS figure, although a theoretical calculation based on assumptions about the future, is considered of such importance to the reader of the accounts that its **calculation and disclosure is required** by IAS 33 – *Earnings Per Share* (FRS 22 in the UK).

5.11.1 Calculation

To calculate diluted earnings per share, we take the basic earnings and the basic number of shares and make suitable adjustments to account for the changes that will occur if and when the new shares are issued.

5.12 Convertible preference shares and convertible loan stock

When we have convertibles in issue (either loan stock or preference shares) the holder of this stock has, at their option, the opportunity to convert into ordinary shares, hence the number of ordinary shares will be increased if the conversion option is taken up.

Often the number of shares into which convertibles may convert will change with time. Generally speaking, the number of shares that a bond holder can convert into will fall the longer the bond is held, as it is anticipated that the share price will rise over that time.

To warn current shareholders of the maximum possible diluting effect of any conversion of any loan stock or convertible preference shares in existence at the year end, we will calculate the number of ordinary shares to be issued based on the maximum possible number they could convert into in the future.

Conversion will also affect the earnings figure. With any convertible loan stock we will currently be paying interest, with any convertible preference shares we will currently be paying a preference dividend. If we bear in mind that the earnings figure is profit after tax, after minority interest, and after preference dividends, then we can see that the adjustments required will be as follows.

5.13 Earnings

For loan stock, add to earnings the after corporation tax interest charge that will no longer be suffered once conversion takes place. Currently, the profit before tax is reduced by the interest payment and the tax charge is also reduced as the interest charge attracts tax relief. This net reduction in profit will no longer occur, hence we need to add the net figure back.

For preference shares, when the preference shares convert we will no longer pay the preference dividend, hence we need to add the preference dividend currently payable to the basic earnings.

5.14 Number of shares

Add to the basic number of shares the greatest number of equity shares that may be issued in the future upon conversion of the loan stock or convertible preference shares in issue at the year end.

Example

The debt financing of the company at the year end includes £500,000 10% convertible loan stock, which was issued on 30 June this year. The terms of conversion for every £100 nominal value of loan stock are

31 December this year	120
31 December next year	115
31 December in two years	110

Assume corporation tax at the rate of 30%.

Earnings

	(£'000)	(£'000)
Basic earnings		2,217
Dilution		
Interest saved $\left(£500,000 \times 10\% \times \dfrac{6}{12} \right)$	25	
Tax (£25,000 × 30%)	(8)	
		17
Diluted earnings		2,234

Number of shares

Since the £500,000 of convertible loan stock is in issue at this year end, we know that these stockholders have not taken the option of converting to 120 shares. The best option that remains for them is to convert to 115 shares, resulting in a further 575,000 shares being issued, hence

	Number
Basic number	17,925
Dilution $\left(575 \times \dfrac{6}{12} \right)$	288
Diluted number	18,213

EPS

$$\text{Basic EPS} = \frac{£2,217}{17,925} = 12.37p$$

$$\text{Diluted EPS} = \frac{£2,234}{18,213} = 12.27p$$

The dilution is only assumed to occur for half a year, since the convertibles were only issued six months into the year. In subsequent years, the dilution calculation would assume dilution for the whole year.

5.15 Options and warrants

When a company has options or warrants in issue, it specifies a number of shares that a person can take up and the price at which they can exercise the option. The calculation of diluted earnings per share will assume exercise of the warrants or options. The assumed proceeds on exercise should be treated as having been received from the issue of shares at fair value. The difference between the number of shares issued and the number of shares that would have been issued at fair value is treated as an issue of shares for no consideration.

Fair value of the shares should be based on the **average price of the shares** over the year.

Since any shares issued at fair value would also cause an increase in earnings, they are excluded from the diluted calculation on the basis that any increase in earnings would counterbalance the increase in shares, causing no change to earnings per share.

The shares issued for free will be added to the weighted average of shares from the basic calculation.

5.16 Earnings

There will be no change to earnings in the diluted calculation.

5.17 Number of shares

Add to the basic number of shares the number of shares that would be issued on exercise of the warrants or options less the number of shares that would be issued at fair value, given the proceeds on exercise.

Example

Assume that the company has options in issue to subscribe for one million new shares at £1.20 per share. The average share price over the year has been £2.00.

Earnings

Earnings are left unchanged at £2,217,000.

Number of shares

On the assumed exercise of the options, the company would receive £1.2m. Using the average share price over the year, this would imply the issue of 600,000 shares at fair value. This indicates that, when the shares are being issued, 600,000 are being issued at a fair price and 400,000 are being issued for free.

	Number
Basic number	17,925
New shares issued	1,000
Shares that would have been issued at fair value	(600)
Diluted number	18,325

EPS

$$\text{Basic EPS} = \frac{£2,217}{17,925} = 12.37p$$

$$\text{Diluted EPS} = \frac{£2,217}{18,325} = 12.10p$$

5.18 Disclosure

IAS 33 requires the disclosure of basic and diluted earnings per share on the face of the income statement, both for net profit or loss for the period and profit or loss for continuing operations.

Any additional information, such as alternative methods of calculating the EPS, can only be disclosed by way of a note to the accounts.

A note needs to be included in the accounts detailing the basis upon which the calculations are done, specifically the earnings figure used and the number of shares figure used within the calculation, both for this year and the comparative year.

6 OTHER INVESTMENT RATIOS

6.1 Return on equity

The return on equity ratio is calculated as follows.

Formula to
learn

$$\text{Return on equity} = \frac{\text{Earnings attributable to ordinary shareholders}}{\text{Equity shareholders' funds}} \times 100\%$$

6.1.1 Considerations

The return on equity ratio measures the percentage return that the company is generating on the book (or statement of financial position) value of equity shareholders' funds invested in the business.

It is, therefore, a measure assessing profitability from the viewpoint of the owners of the business (the shareholders) and thus the return measure used in the ratio is the same as the earnings figure used in calculating EPS. The equity shareholders' funds figure used will consist of ordinary share capital plus the reserves of the business.

Example

If we take the earnings figure used in the EPS calculation together with the shareholders' funds figure excluding preference share capital and minority interest, the calculation will be as follows.

$$\text{Return on equity} = \frac{2,217}{31,301} \times 100 = 7.1\%$$

6.1.2 Potential problems

This ratio suffers, in the same way as EPS, from one-off gains and losses introducing volatility into the earnings figure. For trend analysis, therefore, it may be better to strip out the post-tax impact of gains and losses recognised in the income statement that are considered to be non-recurring.

The measurement of earnings and shareholders' funds is distorted by accounting policy choices (such as revaluations and recognition of development costs as an intangible asset) and therefore reduces comparability between different companies.

6.1.3 Analysis Points

Shareholders are looking for a rising trend of returns on equity in order to provide them with increasing levels of dividend income and/or growth in the share price.

Returns across different companies in the same sector can be compared but it should be noted that this ratio does *not* produce a yield or return on investment measure. To obtain such a number, it would be necessary to use the market value of equity as opposed to the book value (as used to calculate earnings yield).

6.2 Price/Earnings ratio (P/E)

The Price/Earnings ratio is calculated as follows.

$$\text{Price/Earnings} = \frac{\text{Current market price per share}}{\text{Earnings per share}}$$

6.2.1 Considerations

The P/E ratio expresses the number of years of earnings represented by the current market price.

Example

If we take our current share price as £2.20 and our EPS figure as 12.37p, then the P/E ratio is

$$\text{Price/Earnings} = \frac{220}{12.37}$$

$$\text{Price/Earnings} = 17.78x$$

6.2.2 Potential problems

The P/E ratio is **difficult to use in isolation** as a result of accounting choices distorting the profit measurement basis for different companies, even those operating in the same sectors. In addition, the globalisation of many industries now requires comparisons on a cross-border basis between companies reporting under different GAAP regimes. The resultant variability in reported profits can be huge and the resultant P/E comparisons would be virtually meaningless.

In order to overcome these problems, various other measures of earnings are used by both analysts and increasingly companies, to measure and analyse profit performance. These are discussed in more detail below.

6.2.3 Analysis points

The significance of a P/E ratio can only be judged in relation to the ratios of other companies in the same type of business. If the median P/E ratio for an industry sector was 8, then a ratio of 12 for a particular company would suggest that the shares of that company were in great demand possibly because a rapid growth of earnings was expected. A low ratio, say 4 for example, would indicate a company not greatly favoured by investors, which probably has poor growth prospects.

6.3 Enterprise value multiples

The following earnings multiples measuring corporate performance are used frequently by analysts as an **alternative to the P/E ratio**.

$$\text{Enterprise value to EBIT} = \frac{\text{Enterprise value}}{\text{Earnings before interest and tax}}$$

$$\text{Enterprise value to EBITDA} = \frac{\text{Enterprise value}}{\text{Earnings before interest, tax, depreciation and amortisation}}$$

$$\text{Enterprise value to sales} = \frac{\text{Enterprise value}}{\text{Revenue}}$$

6.3.1 Considerations

These earnings multiples work in the same way as the P/E ratio, in that they compare an historic earnings or revenue figure to the market value of the business. Thus, the higher the multiple the more growth expectation is factored into market values and the more positively the company is viewed in relation to its peers.

However, the market value used in these ratios is not the market value of equity, which is used for the P/E ratio. Instead, the **enterprise value** (EV) is used, which is the market value of equity plus the market value of net debt (in other words, the value of the business to all providers of finance).

The rationale for using the EV is that this is a figure that is not distorted by the gearing of the business, and therefore can be used to more directly compare companies with different financing strategies. Therefore, while the P/E ratio focuses only on earnings available to equity shareholders, EV multiples look at earnings available to all finance providers, being earnings before all dividends and before interest payments.

It is possible to use different earnings figures in the multiple, depending on which potential distorting factors need to be removed. Tax, for example, is distorted by the tax rules and rates in the countries in which profits are generated. Earnings performance is therefore distorted by the countries in which a company operates, making global comparisons more difficult. Thus, earnings figures used in EV multiples tend to be pre-tax.

It is also possible for companies to apply different rules on depreciation and amortisation of tangible and intangible non-current assets respectively, depending on the GAAP regime under which they report.

Therefore, many analysts and companies are turning to measures of **earnings before interest and tax (EBIT)** or **before interest, tax, depreciation and amortisation (EBITDA)**. These measures are therefore used for the following reasons.

- To eliminate distortions caused by different financing structures, tax regimes, depreciation mechanisms and amortisation periods.

- To facilitate cross-border comparisons.

- To obtain an earnings figure that is closer to a cash measure (after adjustment for two major non-cash expenses, depreciation and amortisation).

- To calculate meaningful multiples for companies in high growth sectors, such as telecommunications and technology, where traditional P/E measures are not able to be calculated due to the businesses currently being loss-making.

There is a further measure, **EV to sales**, that is used mainly for companies in the technology sector (especially Internet businesses), where they are at the early stages of growth and thus any form of profit figure tends to be relatively meaningless. By using sales, or revenue, as the historic measure of performance, all distortions to profit are stripped out. In addition, the calculation of sales will be very similar across almost all major reporting regimes.

Example

Assume that there is a charge of £14,500,000 for depreciation and £8,250,000 for amortisation included within the operating costs and that the book value of debt as stated on the statement of financial position is equivalent to its market value. The current share price is £2.20, making the market value of equity £39,435,000 (£2.20 × 17.925m shares).

Enterprise value is therefore calculated as follows.

	(£'000)
Market value of equity	39,435
Market value of debt (= book value)	19,451
Less: Cash and liquid investments	(10,351)
Enterprise value	48,535

$$\text{Enterprise value to EBIT} = \frac{48,535}{3,673 + 3,176 - 303} = 7.4\times$$

$$\text{Enterprise value to EBITDA} = \frac{48,535}{3,673 + 3,176 - 303 + 14,500 + 8,250} = 1.7\times$$

$$\text{Enterprise value to sales} = \frac{48,535}{135,761} = 0.4\times$$

6.3.2 Potential problems

The following problems may arise when using EV multiples.

- It may appear that a company with a high EV multiple is successful and profitable, when in fact at the post-tax level it may be loss-making.

- EBITDA as a measure ignores important real costs associated with running a business. Both depreciation and amortisation represent assets being used up in the business and ignoring them both can lead to misleading results. Tax is also a real cost and a cash outflow for companies.

- EV to sales is a measure that can be influenced by companies entering into barter transactions with the intention of increasing the sales figure, reducing the size of the multiple and thus appearing to be better value (or alternatively prompting an upward rerating of the share price).

6.3.3 Analysis points

EV multiples should be analysed in the same way as P/E multiples, to compare different companies within the same sector. Therefore, the same comments can be made, and conclusions drawn, as were discussed for the P/E ratio.

6.4 Earnings yield

The earnings yield expresses the most recent earnings per share as a percentage of the current market price as follows.

Formula to learn

$$\text{Earnings yield} = \frac{\text{Earnings per share}}{\text{Current market price per share}} \times 100\%$$

Example

$$\text{Earnings yield} = \frac{12.37}{220} \times 100\%$$

$$\text{Earnings yield} = 5.62\%$$

6.4.1 Analysis points

The earnings yield is **almost the inverse of the P/E ratio**, hence similar comments apply. If the median earnings yield for an industry sector was 10%, then a yield of only 6% for a particular company would suggest that the shares of that company were in great demand possibly because a rapid growth of earnings was expected. A higher yield, say 18% for example, would indicate a company not greatly favoured by investors which probably has poor growth prospects.

In practice, the earnings yield is used less frequently than the P/E ratio.

6.5 Dividend yield

The dividend yield of an ordinary share is calculated as follows.

Formula to learn

$$\text{Dividend yield} = \frac{\text{Dividend per share}}{\text{Current market price per share}} \times 100\%$$

Example

$$\text{Dividend yield} = \frac{6.25}{220} \times 100\%$$

$$\text{Dividend yield} = 2.84\%$$

6.5.1 Analysis points

A high dividend yield implies that the company is paying reasonable levels of income but not particularly highly regarded for its growth prospects and *vice versa*. If the figures show a high yield then the share price is relatively low, implying that the main factor attracting shareholders to the company is the reasonably high current level of income. Investors who believe that the company has good growth prospects would buy the share, driving the price up and reducing the yield.

It is therefore also true that companies with high P/E ratios tend to have low dividend yields and *vice versa*.

6.6 Dividend cover

Dividend cover is used as an attempt to assess the likelihood of the existing dividend being maintained. The dividend cover is calculated as follows.

$$\text{Dividend cover} = \frac{\text{Earnings per share}}{\text{Net dividend per share}}$$

Example

$$\text{Dividend cover} = \frac{12.37}{6.25}$$

$$\text{Dividend cover} = 1.98\times$$

6.6.1 Analysis points

An unusually high dividend cover implies that the company is retaining the majority of its earnings, presumably with the intention of reinvesting to generate growth.

A company may alternatively pay a larger dividend than the year's earnings, in which case it is drawing on past reserves and is said to be paying an uncovered dividend.

6.7 Net asset value / Net assets per share

The net asset value or net assets per share is calculated as

$$\text{Net asset value} = \frac{\text{Net assets attributable to ordinary shareholders}}{\text{Number of ordinary shares in issue}}$$

6.7.1 Considerations

The net asset value represents the 'intrinsic' worth of the shares in terms of the net assets that support that value. This could show an unrealistically low figure in terms of current worth if a strict policy of historical cost accounting has been applied. The shareholder may be more interested in the asset values if the company adopts a policy of revaluation.

Example

$$\text{Net asset value} = \frac{£32,138 - £837}{17,925}$$

$$\text{Net asset value} = \frac{£31,301}{17,925}$$

$$\text{Net asset value} = £1.75$$

Note that the net assets figure is after deducting those due to the preference shareholders.

6.7.2 Analysis points

While the company continues to trade, the net assets per share might be considerably higher or lower than the market value of those shares. This is because investors do not think that all of the assets will be sold and they are basing the value of the company on its ability to generate returns using those assets. The 'asset backing' tends to become more significant in the event of a potential takeover. It is also of regular concern to property companies and investment trusts.

7 ANALYSIS CONSIDERATIONS

7.1 Introduction

Ratios are useful tools for highlighting areas of concern in accounts. With the exclusion of the earnings per share figures none of the ratios we have described above have hard and fast definitions, hence there is no right answer to a question such as 'what is the return on capital employed?' It could depend on how you treat bank overdrafts, and so on as discussed earlier in the chapter.

Despite this, ratios do provide a useful tool. We can calculate the ratios and with the aid of useful comparatives that are essential for this process, we can look for trends or discontinuities from one year to the next.

Always remember, however, that the **ratio is not the answer in itself**, simply a tool to help us identify important factors. Once we have found a problem or point of concern, we need to look behind the ratio to find why we are seeing this.

For example, has the return on capital employed gone up because the return has gone up or because the capital employed has gone down? They clearly imply different things about the company.

When carrying out an analysis exercise there are a number of factors we need to consider.

7.2 Who is the information for?

We need to satisfy the requirements of our clients and hence concentrate on those areas that are of concern to them. If, for example, our client is a shareholder, then we would probably concentrate initially on the investors' ratios.

However, we should never adopt a blinkered approach to analysis. When looking at an investors' ratio we may consider, for example, the earnings per share figure. The earnings per share figure clearly depends on the profits and the number of shares. If the earnings per share figure is changed because profits have changed, we may well wish to go and consider further the profitability of the business. Hence our client tells us the starting point for our analysis, but we should be prepared to be taken off in different directions depending on what we find being highlighted by the ratios we initially consider.

7.3 Practical circumstances

In order to appreciate and understand the trends and ratios we are seeing, we need to consider the **practical circumstances of the business**.

7.4 Profitability

How did the business make its profits? Is it a 'stack 'em high, sell 'em fast', high volume, low margin retailer or is it a high margin, low turnover business, such as a jeweller?

What is the nature of the earnings and the dependency of those earnings on economic factors such as exchange rates, general state of the economy, recession, etc. For example, supermarkets largely provide necessities, hence in a recession we would expect their profits to remain fairly level. However, for luxury car manufacturers, we would expect their profits to decline substantially in a recession as demand for their goods drops.

7.5 Liquidity

In considering the liquidity of the business under consideration we should try to imagine its working capital cycle. We should try to picture in our minds what we expect to see or what we can see as the norm by considering the working capital cycle of the peer group. In this way we will be in a decent position to comment on what we are actually finding in the company under consideration.

7.6 Accounting policies

The **accounting policies adopted** by any company can significantly impact on its ratios.

If we revalue non-current assets, then our depreciation charge will be higher. Hence, profits will be lower, but on the statement of financial position, more non-current assets means a higher capital employed figure. Hence, our return on capital employed will be reduced (lower profits divided by higher capital employed).

If we are comparing two companies, one that does revalue non-current assets and one that does not, or if we are comparing one company to a previous year when we have revalued non-current assets in between, then we would expect to see a distortion between the ratios as a result of this accounting policy.

7.7 Window dressing

Window dressing techniques incorporate some dubious financing methods, hence they are worthy of consideration here.

Window dressing transactions are **transactions intended to mislead the user** of the accounts. We outline below two basic window dressing transaction types.

7.8 Circular transactions

In a circular transaction, Company A sells goods to Company B who in turn sells them back to Company A. The purpose of undertaking these transactions is simply to boost reported revenue, which in turn would boost such measures as asset turnover, distorting the view of the user as to the effectiveness of the management of the company.

Clearly, such a transaction is totally fictitious. It is likely that the transactions would have to be disclosed as a result of the rules in IAS 24 *Related Party Disclosures*, assuming that the two companies are in some way connected.

7.9 Bed and breakfast transactions

A bed and breakfast transaction is very much like a circular transaction that is undertaken over a year end, i.e. Company A sells to Company B before the year end, then repurchases after the year end. This will not only boost Company A's revenue for the year but also their reported profits if the goods have been sold at a profit.

Again, the transaction is totally fictitious and only designed to mislead the user of the account. As above, the transactions are likely to be disclosed as being with a related party.

7.10 Possible distorting effects

When calculating any ratios we should always try to look for **possible distorting effects** that impact on our analysis. Factors to consider would be as follows.

7.11 Comparing a full year's transactions to year end balances

One of the biggest possible distortions that is only tackled in the earnings per share calculation as a matter of course, is that we compare a full year's worth of transactions to a year-end statement of financial position figure with a number of the ratios. What we really should be doing is comparing a full year's transaction to a representative balance throughout the year. For example, ideally we should compare the full year's profits to a representative amount of capital employed to get return on capital employed.

When analysing a set of financial statements, it is highly unlikely that you will be able to calculate the representative amount of capital employed throughout the year, hence you may only be able to work out the return on capital employed based on start of the year or end of the year capital employed figures.

The problem is not only confined to return on capital employed, it is true for any ratio that compares a full year's transaction to a year-end figure, for example receivables' collection period, payables' payment period or inventory turnover rate. Hence, these ratios can be distorted by such things as

- **Subsidiary acquired near year end** – profits up only from the date of acquisition, capital up at the year end by the full amount.

- **Funds raised near year end** – capital employed higher, return increased by only a small amount based upon what the funds have managed to generate in the short period of time to year end.

- **Seasonal sale** – the receivables' collection period compares the year-end receivables to the year's sales. If sales are seasonal in nature then, depending on when the year end is, the receivables may be very significant or very small compared to the year's revenue.

7.12 Comparing like with like

All of our ratios should endeavour to **compare like-with-like**. For example, when considering the payables' payment period, we should try to compare the invoiced payables to the invoiced cost of sales. When calculating profit margins, we should compare the profit to the revenue that has generated that profit.

We should, therefore, always be looking for factors that cause any distortions in these ratios. For example, income from associated undertakings boosts the profits before tax, however, it has no revenue implications and therefore a simple calculation of profit margins based on profits before tax and revenue will incorporate a distorting effect.

The method of equity accounting for associates on the statement of financial position will similarly distort any asset turnover calculation, since this particular element of capital employed does not contribute to revenue. When considering any ratio the aim should always be to compare like-with-like.

7.13 Ability to realise assets

When considering any ratios, in particular liquidity, it may be very difficult for us to get any indication as to the **potential ability to realise assets**.

7.13.1 Cash

We would normally assume that we can get hold of any cash immediately. However, it is quite possible that a company may have significant amounts of cash held overseas that it cannot remit to the UK for certain reasons particular to the country concerned. Alternatively, a proportion of the cash a company is in possession of may not be freely available for its own use to repay debts. For example, a manufacturer may have received cash in advance that can only be used to fund a specific project and is not available to settle other debts.

7.13.2 Inventory

Inventory is shown on the statement of financial position under the heading current assets, which leads to the reasonable assumption that it is likely to be converted into cash within 12 months. However, this may not always be the case. In such industries as high technology or fashion, inventory may become unsaleable very rapidly. The financial statements give no indication as to what the inventory is, to enable you to assess any potential problems regarding realisation.

8 OTHER TOOLS OF INTERPRETATION

8.1 Introduction

In addition to ratios, there are a number of other tools of interpretation, specifically

- Trend statements.
- Common size statements.
- Multivariate analysis.

8.2 Trend statements

Trend statements are more commonly prepared for income statement information, by choosing one year as the base year and expressing similar items of other years as a percentage of that base year.

Example

We are given the following five-year summary information for a company.

	2004 (£'000)	2005 (£'000)	2006 (£'000)	2007 (£'000)	2008 (£'000)
Revenue	800	880	1,040	1,280	1,600
Gross profit	90	100	110	150	190
Profit before tax	40	46	52	90	130
Dividends	4	5	6	9	15

We may prepare a trend statement for these five years with the 2004 figures taken as 100% as follows.

	2004 (%)	2005 (%)	2006 (%)	2007 (%)	2008 (%)
Revenue	100	110	130	160	200
Gross profit	100	111	128	167	211
Profit before tax	100	115	130	225	325
Dividends	100	125	150	225	375

This is a useful approach when analysing performance from the five-year summary as it provides a convenient way of presenting data for a large number of years, and can be helpful in highlighting trends. In the above example, we can see that as revenue doubles, profit before tax more than trebles, indicating a reasonable degree of fixed costs since they have not increased in line with the increase in revenue.

Alternatively, when presented with data in this form it is sometimes useful if we recompute each individual year's movement as compared with the previous year.

Example

We are presented with the following trend data for the sales of two companies, A and B, over a five-year period.

	2004 (%)	2005 (%)	2006 (%)	2007 (%)	2008 (%)
A	100	110	130	160	200
B	100	150	210	240	250

If we restate this data in terms of the **increase** in sales achieved by each company we would show

	2005	2006	2007	2008
A	+10%	+18%	+23%	+25%
B	+50%	+40%	+15%	+4%

The trend statement indicated that, to each year, it would be correct to state that Company B had expanded sales more rapidly than Company A since 2004. On the other hand, the data on the increase in sales each year indicate that the rate of increase in sales is on the rise for Company A and on the decline for Company B, with the former company now increasing sales at a much faster rate.

Thus, both types of analysis can give us a useful insight when we are analysing performance over a number of years.

8.3 Common size statements

A common size statement expresses the amounts of successive years as a proportion of one figure in the accounts. Such statements are normally prepared in relation to the statement of financial position, relating each amount to the statement of financial position totals.

Example

We are provided with the following data in relation to a company.

	2004 (£'000)	2005 (£'000)	2006 (£'000)	2007 (£'000)	2008 (£'000)
Total assets					
Non-current assets	180	240	250	280	310
Current assets	175	185	220	300	370
	225	295	330	421	501
Financing					
Share capital	100	100	100	150	150
Reserves	50	79	110	166	241
Shareholders' funds	150	179	210	316	391
Loans	60	100	100	80	80
Current liabilities	145	146	160	184	209
	355	425	470	580	680

From which, we can prepare the following common size statement taking each figure as a percentage of total assets.

	2004 (%)	2005 (%)	2006 (%)	2007 (%)	2008 (%)
Trading assets					
Non-current assets	51	56	53	48	46
Current assets	49	44	47	52	54
	100	100	100	100	100
Financing					
Share capital	28	24	21	26	22
Reserves	14	18	23	28	35
Shareholders' funds	42	42	44	54	57
Loans	17	24	21	14	12
Current liabilities	41	34	35	32	31
	100	100	100	100	100

This is a valuable tool for identifying changes in the way in which assets employed are financed and the breakdown of the assets employed.

In this Example, we can now more readily identify the relative decline in the level of non-current assets and the impact on gearing of the raising of a loan in 2005 and the issue of shares, which is partly used to repay the loans in 2007.

8.4 Statement of financial positions

The statement of financial position is in itself a potentially valuable aid in the interpretation of accounts. This statement is a reanalysis of the data given in the income statement and statement of financial position, designed to give a view of the flow of cash through the business.

IAS 7 requires most limited companies to present a statement of financial position in a standard format. This format can provide some very useful input to any analysis we do as it closely ties in with the four main analysis areas we have been highlighting, as follows.

Analysis Area	Cash Flow Heading
Trading performance	Operating activities
Financial performance	Investing activities
Financial position	Financing activities

For example, the financing activities cash flows can help us identify causes for any changes in the gearing position of the company as it details all the finance raised and repaid in one place.

It will also be possible to make a year-on-year or cross-company cash flow comparison by using a common size statement of financial position.

8.5 Z-scores

One way of using ratios is to identify several ratios that reflect on a particular aspect of a business and produce a single, combined, 'multivariate' ratio that represents some kind of weighted average.

Most research in this field has focused on identifying liquidity problems, using ratios to identify companies that will have problems in meeting their obligations.

Z scores are frequently examined, for example summer 2008. In past questions, the examiner has provided the Z score formula and required students to apply the formula to a given set of accounts to assess the likelihood of bankruptcy. It is not therefore necessary to learn the formula or the conclusions, but you should familiarise yourself with how to calculate the ratios and be able to apply the Z score formula in a given scenario

One example of multivariate ratio analysis is the 'Z score' system. This is a composite ratio calculation derived by Altman (1983) which is designed to assess the solvency of a particular company. Depending on the number calculated by the formula, its 'Z score', a conclusion could be reached on the likelihood of bankruptcy. Altman's Z score is worked out as follows:

$$Z = 0.717A + 0.847B + 3.11C + 0.420D + 0.998E$$

Each of the letters in the formula represents a different financial ratio:

A = net working capital/ total assets
B = retained earnings/ total assets
C = earnings before interest and tax (EBIT)/ total assets
D = shareholders' equity/ total liabilities
E = sales/ total assets

The results can be interpreted as follows:

Z score < 1.20; bankruptcy is predicted
Z score > 1.20 but < 2.90; the position is unclear (ie a grey area)
Z score > 2.90; the company is safe with no risk of bankruptcy

The ratios A to E are deemed to provide an insight into a company's solvency.

Net working capital/ total assets: working capital is calculated by deducting current liabilities from current assets. The higher this ratio is, the greater the working capital, and thus the greater the statement of financial position liquidity. The current ratio or quick ratio gives a similar measure of liquidity. High statement of financial position liquidity lowers the bankruptcy risk.

Retained earnings/ total assets: the higher the level of retained earnings, the greater the 'creditors' buffer' and thus the lower the bankruptcy risk.

EBIT/ total assets: an indicator of profitability and efficiency. Making a reasonable return should make a business more able to meet the demand of creditors. Altman accords this ratio the highest weighting in his formula. A profitable business is more likely to survive going forward.

Shareholders' equity/ total liabilities: how does the shareholders' investment in the company compare to the amount owed by the business? The greater the proportion of shareholders' equity, the lower the bankruptcy risk.

Sales/ total assets: this is the asset turnover ratio, which is a measure of efficiency. Are the assets of the business productive in generating revenue? Higher capital efficiency lowers bankruptcy risk.

Example

The following is extracted from the accounts of Whiskey plc:

	2008 (£m)	2009 (£m)
Revenue	123	220
Profit before interest and tax	24	43
Working capital	48	72
Total assets	135	155
Total liabilities	97	123
Retained earnings	25	27
Shareholders equity	60	52

Calculate and interpret the Z score for Whiskey plc in 2008 and 2009.

Solution

	Weights	2008	2009
Net working capital/ total assets	0.72	0.36	0.46
Retained earnings/ total assets	0.85	0.19	0.17
Earnings before interest and tax/ total assets	3.11	0.18	0.28
Shareholders' equity/ total liabilities	0.42	0.62	0.42
Sales/ total assets	1.0	0.91	1.42
Z score		**2.15**	**2.94**

The Z score indicates that the company's financial position has changed from showing a possible bankruptcy risk in 2008 to no forecast risk of bankruptcy based on 2009's results. This improvement has been driven by a significant improvement in the efficiency of the business, with higher levels of revenue and profit being generated from the asset base. This is demonstrated by the increases in the asset turnover ratio (sales/ total assets) and in EBIT/ total assets ratio.

8.6 Summary

Any analysis should consist of the following points.

- What we have seen, stating the obvious, the limitations of our analysis and any further information needed.

- The possible causes of what we have seen, again stating the obvious possible causes but also thinking more broadly and trying to imagine alternative possible causes that are not highlighted by the accounts.

- Any impact of accounting policies or other distorting effects.

■   The implications for the future.

Therefore, we need to build up from the factual details of the past, through possible causes of the past, to speculation of the implications for the future.

9   ILLUSTRATIVE FINANCIAL STATEMENTS

Example

Statement of financial position as at 31 December	(£'000)	(£'000)
Non-Current Assets		
Intangible		3,926
Property, Plant and Equipment (PPE)		18,731
Investments		842
		23,499
Current Assets		
Inventory	19,420	
Trade Receivables	21,753	
Other Receivables	6,129	
Investments	3,926	
Cash	6,425	
		57,653
Total Assets		81,152
Non-Current Liabilities		
Loans	(1,356)	
Finance Leases	(1,016)	
Deferred Tax	(1,484)	
Provision for reorganisation costs	(589)	
		4,445
Current liabilities		
Bank Overdraft	(16,942)	
Finance Lease Obligation	(137)	
Trade Payables	(18,702)	
Tax	(1,625)	
Others	(6,260)	
		(43,666)
Net Assets		33,041
£1 Ordinary shares		17,925
Preference shares		837
Share Premium		2,455
Revaluation Reserve		2,681
Retained Earnings		8,240
		32,138
Minority Interest		903
Shareholders' Funds		33,041

Income Statement for the Period Ended 31 December	(£'000)
Revenue	135,761
Cost of sales	(83,604)
Gross profit	52,157
Distribution costs	(22,961)
Administration costs	(22,712)
Profit from operations	6,484
Income from associate	62
Interest receivable	303
Interest payable	(3,176)
Profit before taxation	3,673
Tax	(1,164)
Profit after taxation	2,509
Minority interest	(208)
Preference share dividends	(84)
Profit attributable to the group	2,217
Dividends	
Ordinary	1,120
Earnings per share	12.37p
Dividend per share	6.25p

Last year, the earnings per share was quoted as 12.43p. Included in administration costs is an exceptional expense of £3,192,000.

CHAPTER ROUNDUP

You need to be aware of the uses and limitations of ratios.

You need to be able to calculate and comment on

- **Profitability ratios**

    ROCE $= \dfrac{\text{Profit from operations} + \text{Interest receivable and other income receivable}}{\text{Capital employed}} \times 100\%$

    Profit margins $= \dfrac{\text{Profits}}{\text{Revenue}} \times 100\%$

    Asset turnover $= \dfrac{\text{Revenue}}{\text{Assets (capital) employed}}$

    Operational gearing ratio $= \dfrac{\text{Revenue} - \text{Variable costs}}{\text{Profit}}$

- **Liquidity ratios**

    Current ratio $= \dfrac{\text{Current assets}}{\text{Current liabilities}}$

    Quick ratio $= \dfrac{\text{Current assets} - \text{Inventory}}{\text{Current liabilities}}$

    Inventory turnover $= \dfrac{\text{Cost of sales}}{\text{Inventory}}$

    Receivables' collection period $= \dfrac{\text{Trade receivables}}{\text{Revenue}} \times 365 \text{ days}$

    Payables' payment period $= \dfrac{\text{Trade payables}}{\text{Cost of sales}} \times 365 \text{ days}$

- **Financial gearing**

    Debt to equity $= \dfrac{\text{Interest bearing loans} + \text{Preference share capital}}{\text{Equity shareholders' funds}} \times 100\%$

    Net debt to equity $= \dfrac{\text{Debt as above} - \text{Cash and current asset investments}}{\text{Equity shareholders' funds}} \times 100\%$

    Lenders' debt to equity $= \dfrac{\text{Total borrowings (including non-interest bearing debt)}}{\text{Total shareholders' funds (including preference shares)}} \times 100\%$

    Interest cover $= \dfrac{\text{Profit from operations} + \text{Interest Receivables} + \text{Other income receivables}}{\text{Interest payable}}$

    Asset cover $= \dfrac{\text{Total assets} - \text{Current liabilities}}{\text{Loans payable}}$

■ **Investors' ratios and EPS**

$$\text{EPS} = \frac{\text{Net profit/loss attributable to ordinary shareholders}}{\text{Weighted average number of ordinary shares outstanding during the period}}$$

$$\text{Bonus fraction} = \frac{\text{Number of shares after the issue}}{\text{Number of shares before the issue}}$$

$$\text{Bonus fraction} = \frac{\text{Actual price before the issue (cum-rights price)}}{\text{Theoretical price after issue (ex-rights price)}}$$

$$\text{Return on equity} = \frac{\text{Earnings attributable to ordinary shareholders}}{\text{Equity shareholders' funds}} \times 100\%$$

$$\text{Price/Earnings} = \frac{\text{Current market price per share}}{\text{Earnings per share}}$$

$$\text{Enterprise value to EBIT} = \frac{\text{Enterprise value}}{\text{Earnings before interest and tax}}$$

$$\text{Enterprise value to EBITDA} = \frac{\text{Enterprise value}}{\text{Earnings before interest, tax, depreciation and amortisation}}$$

$$\text{Enterprise value to sales} = \frac{\text{Enterprise value}}{\text{Revenue}}$$

$$\text{Earnings yield} = \frac{\text{Earnings per share}}{\text{Current market price per share}} \times 100\%$$

$$\text{Dividend yield} = \frac{\text{Dividend per share}}{\text{Current market price per share}} \times 100\%$$

$$\text{Dividend cover} = \frac{\text{Earnings per share}}{\text{Net dividend per share}}$$

$$\text{Net asset value} = \frac{\text{Net assets attributable to ordinary shareholders}}{\text{Number of ordiary shares in issue}}$$

You need to be familiar with and able to apply the other tools of analysis.

TEST YOUR KNOWLEDGE

Check your knowledge of the chapter here, without referring back to the text.

1. Financial analysis

    The following five-year summary relates to Wandafood Products plc, and is based on financial statements.

			20X5	20X4	20X3	20X2	20X1
Financial ratios							
Profitability							
Margin	Operating profit / Revenue	%	7.8	7.5	7.0	7.2	7.3
Return on capital employed	PBIT / Capital employed	%	16.3	17.6	16.2	18.2	18.3
Interest and dividend cover							
Interest cover	PBIT / Net finance charges	times	2.9	4.8	5.1	6.5	3.6
Dividend cover	Earnings per ordinary share / Dividend per ordinary share	times	2.7	2.6	2.1	2.5	3.1
Debt to equity ratios							
	Net borrowings / Shareholders' funds	%	65.9	61.3	48.3	10.8	36.5
	Net borrowings / Shareholders' funds + Minority interests	%	59.3	55.5	44.0	10.1	33.9
Liquidity ratios							
Quick ratio	Current assets − Inventories / Current liabilities	%	74.3	73.3	78.8	113.8	93.4
Current ratio	Current assets / Current liabilities	%	133.6	130.3	142.2	178.9	174.7
Asset ratios							
Operating asset turnover	Revenue / Capital employed	times	2.1	2.4	2.3	2.5	2.5
Working capital turnover	Revenue / Working capital	times	8.6	8.0	7.0	7.4	6.2

		20X5	20X4	20X3	20X2	20X1
Per share						
Earnings per share						
Pre-tax basis	p	23.62	21.25	17.96	17.72	15.06
Net basis	p	15.65	13.60	10.98	11.32	12.18
Dividend per share	p	5.90	5.40	4.90	4.60	4.10
Net assets per share	p	102.10	89.22	85.95	85.79	78.11

Requirements

Prepare a report on the company, clearly interpreting and evaluating the information given.

2. Ratios

What will be the impact on return on capital employed and earnings per share of the following changes in a set of accounts?

(a) Revaluation of property plant and equipment.
(b) Increasing the useful life of a non-current asset.
(c) Capitalisation of development costs.
(d) Treating a lease as a finance lease rather than an operating lease.

3. Ratios Part 2

The summarised financial statements of a manufacturing company are shown below.

Income Statements

	Year Ended 31 March 2005		Year Ended 31 March 2006	
	(£'000)	(£'000)	(£'000)	(£'000)
Revenue		3,200		4,000
Cost of sales				
Opening inventory	800		300	
Purchases	1,800		3,200	
	2,600		3,500	
Less: Closing inventory	300		500	
		(2,300)		(3,000)
Gross profit		900		1,000
Other operating expenses		(400)		(450)
Finance costs		(100)		(200)
Profit for the period		400		350

Statement of financial position

	Year Ended 31 March 2005		Year Ended 31 March 2006	
	(£'000)	(£'000)	(£'000)	(£'000)
Non-current assets		1,970		4,000
Current assets				
Inventory	300		500	
Trade receivables	600		800	
Prepaid expenses	60		70	
Cash	50		10	
		1,010		1,380
Total assets		**2,980**		**5,380**
Current liabilities				
Trade payables	(380)		(1,400)	
Accruals	(50)		(80)	
		(430)		(1,480)
Non-current liabilities				
10% debentures		(1,000)		(2,000)
Total liabilities		**(1,430)**		**(3,480)**
		1,550		1,900
Net assets				
Share capital		600		600
Share premium account		200		200
Retained earnings		750		1,100
Equity		**1,500**		**1,900**

Requirements

(a) Compute the following five ratios for each of the two years.

  (i) Return on capital employed.
  (ii) Current ratio.
  (iii) Inventory turnover (using closing figures).
  (iv) Number of days' purchases in trade payables.

(b) Comment briefly on the changes in the company's results and position between the two years, as shown by the movements in these ratios, mentioning possible causes for the changes.

4. MBC plc

The following figures have been extracted from the published accounts of MBC plc at 31 October 2006.

	(£m)
Ordinary share capital	30
Share premium	3
Reserves	5
Equity	**38**
Liabilities	
6% debentures	10

The profit (after tax of £1m) for the year to 31 October 2006 was £4m and dividends paid amounted to £0.5m. The company is considering raising a further £10m in the next financial year to finance research and development.

Requirements

(a)   State the formula for, and calculate, the company's gearing ratio.

(b)   State the formula for, and calculate, the company's return on capital employed (ROCE).

(c)   Discuss the different effects on gearing and ROCE of raising the additional £10m by the issue of shares or by the issue of debentures.

5.   Harris plc

Harris plc had 3 million £1 ordinary shares and 1 million £1 12% preference shares in issue as at January 1 2006. The preference shares are classified as liabilities in the statement of financial position. On May 1 2006, it issued
1 million £1 ordinary shares for cash at full market value. The profit and dividends of Harris for the years ended December 31 are as follows.

	2006	2005
	(£'000)	(£'000)
Profit after taxation	380	180
Dividends for the year		
Ordinary	100	90
Preference	120	120
	220	210

Requirement

Calculate the earnings per share figures that will be presented in Harris plc's accounts for the year ended December 31 2006.

6.   Tweed plc

Tweed plc has 5 million equity shares in issue as at December 31 2006. On September 30 2006, it issued 2 million equity shares as part consideration to acquire a subsidiary company. Tweed's profit and dividends for the year ended December 31 are as follows.

	2006	2005
	(£000)	(£000)
Profit after taxation	950	990
Equity dividends paid	150	110

Requirement

Show the earnings per share figures that will appear in Tweed plc's accounts for the year ended December 31 2006.

7.   Scrip plc

Scrip plc had 3,000,000 50p ordinary shares in issue as at September 30 2005. On February 28 2006, it made a scrip issue of 1,000,000 shares. Its profit after taxation figure for the year ended September 30 2006 is £500,000 and the ordinary dividends paid and proposed for the year totalled £150,000. Last year's earnings per share figure was 10p.

Requirement

Show the earnings per share figures that will be disclosed in the accounts for the year ended September 30 2006.

8. Bonus plc

    Bonus plc had profits before dividends of £250,000 for the year ended March 31 2006. Its share capital as at March 31 2005 comprised 2,000,000 ordinary shares of 50p each and 100,000 5% preference shares of £1 each. During the year ended March 31 2005, the following changes occurred in the capital structure.

    (a)   50,000 7% £1 preference shares were issued at par for cash on April 1 2005.

    (b)   A 1 for 4 bonus issue of ordinary shares on January 31 2006.

    The earnings per share figure for the year ended March 31 2005 in the 2005 accounts was quoted as 7p per share.

    Requirement

    What will be the earnings per share figures presented in the 2006 accounts?

9. Rights plc

    Rights plc has earnings for the year ended December 31 2006 of £550,000. At January 1 2006, it had 7 million shares in issue with a nominal value of 10p each. On May 1 2006, it made a 1 for 5 rights issue at a subscription price of 20p. The cum rights price of the shares immediately before they were declared ex rights was 80p a share.

    The earnings per share figure for 2005 in last year's accounts was 6p per share.

    Requirement

    What will be the earnings per share figures presented in the 2006 accounts?

10. Lefts plc

    Lefts plc's loss and dividends for the year ended September 30 2006 were as follows.

	(£)
Loss after taxation	(50,000)
Dividends	
Ordinary	100,000
Preference	500,000
	650,000

    The following is an extract from the statement of financial position as at September 30 2005.

	(£)
Share capital	
Ordinary shares with a nominal value of 25p each	3,000,000
Non-current liabilities	
5% preference shares with a nominal value of £1 each	10,000,000

    In the year ended September 30 2006, Lefts plc made a 1 for 4 rights issue for ordinary shares at a subscription price of £1 on December 31 2005. The cum rights price of the shares immediately before they were declared ex rights was £1.30.

    The earnings per share figure for the year ended September 30 2005 was 1p per share.

    Requirement

    What will be the earnings per share figures presented in the 2006 accounts?

11.   Convertibles plc

The earnings figure for Convertibles plc for the year ended December 31 2006 is £700,000. The company has a weighted average of shares in issue during the year of 8,000,000.

In addition, the company has £3,000,000 of 8% convertible debt in issue with the following conversion terms per £100 of nominal value.

September 30 2007   120 shares

September 30 2008   110 shares

September 30 2009   100 shares

The corporation tax rate is 30%.

Requirement

What will be the earnings per share figures presented in the 2006 accounts?

12.   Royal Warrants plc

Royal Warrants plc's profits and dividends for the year ended September 30 2006 are as follows.

	(£)
Profit after taxation	750,000
Dividends	
Ordinary	100,000
Preference	150,000
	250,000

The company has 6,000,000 ordinary shares and 1,000,000 preference shares in issue. The preference shares are not redeemable and Royal Warrants plc has complete discretion as to whether it pays the preference dividend; accordingly the preference shares are classified as equity in the statement of financial position.

In addition, there are 3 million warrants in issue to subscribe for shares at a price of £1.50 each. The average share price over the year was £1.80. The earnings per share figure in last year's accounts was 9p.

Requirement

What earnings per share figures will be required to be disclosed in the 2006 accounts?

13.   Working capital ratios

The following are extracts from the financial statements of Cadbury plc.

	Last year (£m)	This year (£m)
Inventories *(Note 1)*	332	328
Receivables *(Note 2)*	579	554
Financial assets	262	118
Cash at bank and in hand	85	63
	1,258	1,063
Current liabilities *(Note 3)*	1,033	962
Net current assets	225	101
Revenue	3,232	3,146
Cost of sales	1,736	1,738
Gross profit	1,496	1,408
Note 1		
Raw materials and consumables	118	119
Work in progress	21	22
Finished goods and goods for resale	193	187
	332	328
Note 2		
Trade accounts receivable	429	395
Other accounts receivable	150	159
	579	554
Note 3		
Trade accounts payable	262	260
Other current liabilities, including borrowings	771	702
	1,033	962

Requirements

(a)   Calculate the following ratios for Cadbury plc for both years.

      (i)   Inventory turnover.
      (ii)   Receivables collection period.
      (iii)   Suppliers payment period.
      (iv)   Current ratio.
      (v)   Quick (acid test) ratio.

(b)   Comment briefly on your results.

TEST YOUR KNOWLEDGE: ANSWERS

1.   Financial analysis

   Wandafood Products – Five-Year Summary: 20X1 to 20X5

   Prepared by: An Accountant

   Date: 28 February 20X6

   ### Introduction

   This report discusses the trends shown in the five-year summary prepared from the published accounts for the five years ended 31 December 20X5. It also considers how price changes over that period may have limited the usefulness of the historical cost data provided.

   ### Profitability

   The net profit margin has remained fairly constant, although it dropped in 20X3. Asset turnover has decreased over the five years, pulling back a little in 20X4. Return on capital employed, the primary ratio produced by combining these two secondary ratios, has therefore decreased over the period but was at its lowest in 20X3.

   These findings seem to indicate that assets are not being used more efficiently and that this has caused the decrease in return on capital employed. Inflation may be responsible for increases in revenue, which would mask even worse decreases in efficiency.

   ### Interest and Dividend Cover

   Interest cover improved markedly between 20X1 and 20X2, falling back a little in 20X3 and 20X4, but now below the 20X1 level, indicating increases in debt and/or interest rates. Dividend cover, however, after dropping below 20X1 levels for three years, has now recovered some lost ground. In both cases, cover was adequate, even at the lowest points; however, since there has been a substantial increase in gearing, interest cover ought to be watched carefully. Profits may be available to cover interest and dividends, but this must be matched by good cash flow.

   ### Debt to Equity

   Debt:equity fell in 20X2 but has steadily increased until, in 20X5, it was almost double its 20X1 level. Minority interests appear to have remained a relatively insignificant element in the group's funding. It is more likely that debt has increased than that equity has decreased (for example, because of a purchase or redemption of own shares). Interest cover has fallen in line with this increase in borrowing as a proportion of long-term capital.

   ### Liquidity

   Both the current and the quick ratios have declined over the period, although in 20X2, they both improved. However, they have been fairly constant between 20X3 and 20X5 and are quite high, although comments on the adequacy of these ratios are of very limited utility in the absence of information about the company's activities and industry averages.

   The reduction may have been planned to reduce the costs involved in maintaining high levels of inventory and allowing generous credit to customers. From the differential between the quick and current ratios, it would seem that inventory is a significant asset here. However, current liabilities must not be allowed to increase to the extent that current assets (and especially liquid assets) are insufficient to cover them, as this can lead to a liquidity crisis. Worsening liquidity ratios can be an indicator of overtrading, but this

BPP
LEARNING MEDIA

most often arises when expansion is funded from short-term borrowings whereas, here, new long-term capital in the form of debt appears to have been found.

Because working capital has fallen in size, it is now being used more efficiently, generating more sales from a reduced base. It would seem likely, given the slight fall in asset turnover, that non-current asset turnover has worsened considerably and that the improvement in working capital turnover has compensated for this in calculating total asset turnover. It may be that long-term borrowings have financed capital expenditure which has not yet affected operations (an increase in the amount of non-current assets would decrease non-current asset turnover if turnover did not increase correspondingly).

Investors' ratios

Earnings, dividends and net assets per share have all increased over the period. There has therefore been no need to increase dividends regardless of fluctuations in earnings.

The increase in net assets per share seems to indicate either that retained profits and borrowings have been used to increase capital expenditure or (less likely) that assets have been revalued each year.

Inflation

Historical cost accounts do not show the effect on the group's operating capacity of rising prices over a period. The modest increases in EPS and dividend do not suggest that profit has increased sufficiently to compensate for more than a very low level of inflation. It is also possible that the value of assets is understated so that ROCE and asset turnover measures are all understated. The underlying trends in real terms may be very much worse than those shown in historical cost terms.

Conclusion

The group would appear, from this superficial analysis, to be a steady performer but not expanding fast. This may be an advantage in times of recession: debt is probably not so high as to cause liquidity problems nor have shareholders come to expect a high payout ratio. However, inflation may be eroding its profits. The possible recent expansion of non-current assets may help it to grow in future, as will its improved working capital management.

2.   Ratios

	Impact on earnings per share	Impact on profit before interest	Impact on capital employed	Impact on return on capital employed
Revaluation of PPE	Higher depreciation therefore lower earnings EPS falls	Higher depreciation therefore lower profit before tax	Higher asset values increases capital employed	Lower ROCE
Increasing asset's useful life	Lower depreciation gives higher earnings EPS rises	Higher profit before interest	Higher capital employed since lower depreciation gives higher net book value	Uncertain
Capitalisation of development costs	Higher earnings due to lower expenses EPS rises	Higher profit before interest	Higher capital employed due to higher assets	Uncertain

	Impact on earnings per share	Impact on profit before interest	Impact on capital employed	Impact on return on capital employed
Finance lease	Uncertain effect Earnings increase due to the elimination of rental expenses but decrease due to the inclusion of depreciation and interest	Higher profit before interest probably, since finance lease expense will partly be finance charges	Higher capital employed due to the inclusion of a non-current asset financed by long-term obligations probably	Uncertain

3.　Ratios Part 2

(a)　(i)　ROCE

	2006	2005
$\dfrac{\text{PBIT}}{\text{Capital employed}}$	$\dfrac{550}{3,900}$	$\dfrac{500}{2,550}$
	= 14.1%	= 19.6%

(ii)　Current ratio

	2006	2005
$\dfrac{\text{Current assets}}{\text{Current liabilities}}$	$\dfrac{1,380}{1,480}$	$\dfrac{1,010}{430}$
	= 0.93:1	= 2.35:1

(iii)　Inventory turnover

	2005	2004
$\dfrac{\text{Cost of sales}}{\text{Closing inventory}}$	$\dfrac{3,000}{500}$	$\dfrac{2,300}{300}$
	= 6 times	= 7.67 times

(iv)　Supplier payment days

	2005	2004
$\dfrac{\text{Trade payables}}{\text{Purchases}} \times 365$	$\dfrac{1,400}{3,200} \times 365$	$\dfrac{380}{1,800} \times 365$
	= 160 days	= 77 days

(b)　All the ratios have declined from 2005 to 2006.

ROCE has decreased from 19.6% to 14.1%. Although sales revenue has increased by 25% over 2004, gross profit margin has dropped from 28.1% to 25.0%. This implies that increased sales have been driven by price reductions. This would account for the drop in ROCE.

The current ratio has slipped to less than one, which could indicate liquidity problems. When this is taken with the fact that supplier payment days have more than doubled, this is cause for concern Suppliers' goodwill is being pushed to the limit by taking over five months to pay. There has been a big increase in non-current assets over the year and it is reasonable to assume that money due to suppliers has been used to finance this non-current asset purchase.

Inventory turnover has slightly decreased. This can arise from a decrease in revenue. However, as closing inventory has increased over 2005, it could also indicate a large purchase near the year end.

4.   MBC plc

(a)   Gearing $= \dfrac{\text{Debt}}{\text{Equity}}$

$= \dfrac{10}{38} \times 100\%$

$= 26.3\%$

(b)   ROCE $= \dfrac{\text{Profit before interest and tax}}{\text{Capital employed}} \times 100\%$

$= \dfrac{5.6 \text{ (W1)}}{48 \text{ (W2)}} \times 100\%$

$= 11.7\%$

Workings

1.   Profit before interest and tax

	(£m)
Profit before interest and tax (balancing figure)	5.6
Interest (10 × 6%)	0.6
Tax	1.0
Profit after tax	4.0

2.   Average capital employed

	(£m)
Equity and debt	48.0

(c)   (i)   **Gearing**

If £10m is raised by the issue of shares the effect on the gearing ratio will be to reduce it. This is because the equity will increase but the amount of debt will not.

i.e. $\dfrac{10}{48} \times 100\% = 20.8\%$

However, if the capital is raised by the issue of debentures, the effect on the gearing ratio will be to increase it. This is because while equity will remain unchanged, the amount of debt will increase proportionately more.

i.e. $\dfrac{20}{48} \times 100\% = 34.5\%$

(ii)   **ROCE**

With the £10m of new capital raised, capital employed will increase to 58 reducing ROCE.

i.e. $\dfrac{5.6}{58} \times 100\% = 9.7\%$

If debentures were issued additional interest would be payable. However, this would have no effect on ROCE as profit is taken before charges for interest and tax. Therefore, ROCE would be reduced to the same extent as if equity were raised.

i.e. $\dfrac{5.6}{58} \times 100\% = 9.7\%$

---

5.   Harris plc

Summary of the year

2006 Weighted Average Number of Shares	('000)
4 months: 3m × 4/12	1,000
8 months: 4m × 8/12	2,667
	3,667

Earnings	2006	2005
	(£'000)	(£'000)
Profit after taxation	380	180
Number of shares ('000)	3,667	3,000
Earnings per share	*10.4p*	*6.0p*

Tutorial note

As the preference shares are classified as liabilities in the statement of financial position, the preference dividends of £120,000 will already have been deducted in the income statement in arriving at the profit for the year. Earnings are based on profit after taxation and preference dividends but before dividends on ordinary shares.

---

6.   Tweed plc

Summary of the year

		9 months		3 months	
	1 Jan		30 Sep		31 Dec
	3m shares		+2m		5m shares

2006 Weighted Average Number of Shares	('000)
9 months: 3m × 9/12	2,250
3 months: 5m × 3/12	1,250
	3,500

Earnings	2006 (£'000)	2005 (£'000)
Profit after taxation	950	990
Number of shares ('000)	3,500	3,000
Earnings per share	*27.1p*	*33.0p*

7. Scrip plc

2006 Earnings Per Share	(£'000)
Earnings	500
Number of shares ('000)	4,000
Earnings per share	*12.5p*

2006 Comparative Figure for Inclusion in 2006 Accounts	
Original EPS in 2005 accounts	10.0p
Adjustment factor = $\dfrac{\text{No. of shares before bonus}}{\text{No. of shares after bonus}}$ =	3/4
Restated EPS (10.0p × 3/4)	*7.5p*

8. Bonus plc

2006 Earnings Per Share	(£)
Profit before dividends	250,000
Preference dividends	
100,000 × 5%	(5,000)
50,000 × 7%	(3,500)
Earnings	241,500
Number of ordinary shares (2,000 × 5/4)	2,500,000
Earnings per share	*9.7p*

2006 Comparative Figure for Inclusion in 2006 Accounts	
Original EPS in 2005 accounts	7.0p
Adjustment factor = $\dfrac{\text{No. of shares before bonus}}{\text{No. of shares after bonus}}$ =	4/5
Restated EPS (7.0p × 4/5)	*5.6p*

9.   Rights plc

Summary of the year

                    4 months   8 months

         1 Jan   **1 May**   31 Dec
         └─────────────┴──────────────────┘
       7m shares   1 for 5 rights   8.4m shares

Stage 1 – Compute the Theoretical Ex-Rights Price

	Number	Price (p)	Value (p)
Before – cum rights	5	80	400
Issue – 1 for 5 @ 20p	1	20	20
After – ex-rights	6		420

The theoretical ex-rights price is 70p per share (420p/6 shares).

Tutorial note

The relationship between the cum rights price (80p) and theoretical ex-rights price (70p) arises from the bonus element in the rights issue. The bonus element must be taken account of in calculating the weighted-average **number** of shares for the current period's earnings per share figure and to adjust the previously reported earnings **per share** for the comparative period.

When adjusting the number of shares to be included in the current period's weighted average number of shares, we need to scale up the shares in issue for the period of four months before the rights issue by the **bonus fraction**.

$$\frac{\text{Cum rights price}}{\text{Theoretical ex-rights price}} \quad \frac{80}{70}$$

This is equivalent to a bonus issue of one new share for every seven already held.

When restating previously reported earnings per share figures, it is necessary to scale down earnings per share by the **adjustment factor**.

$$\frac{\text{Theoretical ex-rights price}}{\text{Cum rights price}} \quad \frac{70}{80}$$

This is the adjustment required for a 1 for 7 bonus issue.

Stage 2 – Weighted-Average Calculation for 2006

	('000)
4 months: $(7m \times 80/70) \times 4/12$	2,667
8 months: $8.4m \times 8/12$	5,600
	8,267

Stage 3 – Earnings Per Share Calculation for 2006

$550/8,267 = 6.7p$

Stage 4 – Restate 2005 Earnings Per Share to Reflect Bonus Element of Rights Issue

Original EPS in 2005 accounts	6.0p
Adjustment factor	$\dfrac{70}{80}$
Restated EPS (6.0p × 70/80)	*5.3p*

10.   Lefts plc

Stage 1 – Compute the Theoretical Ex-Rights Price

	Number	Price (p)	Value (p)
Before – cum rights	4	130	520
Issue – 1 for 4 @ 100p	1	100	100
After – ex-rights	5		620

The theoretical ex-rights price is 124p per share (620p/5 shares).

Tutorial note

The relationship between the cum rights price (130p) and theoretical ex-rights price (124p) arises from the bonus element in the rights issue. The bonus element must be taken account of in calculating the weighted-average **number** of shares for the current period's earnings per share figure and to adjust the previously reported earnings **per share** for the comparative period.

When adjusting the number of shares to be included in the current period's weighted average number of shares, we need to scale up the shares in issue for the period of four months before the rights issue by the **bonus fraction**.

$$\frac{\text{Cum rights price}}{\text{Theoretical ex-rights price}} \quad \frac{130}{124}$$

This equivalent to a bonus issue of 6 for every 124 held.

When restating previously reported earnings per share figures it is necessary to scale down earnings per share by the **adjustment factor**.

$$\frac{\text{Theoretical ex-rights price}}{\text{Cum rights price}} \quad \frac{124}{130}$$

This is the adjustment required for a 6 for 124 bonus issue.

Stage 2 – Weighted Average Calculation for 2006

	('000)
3 months: (12,000 × 130/124) × 3/12	3,145
9 months: 15,000 × 9/12	11,250
	14,395

Stage 3 – Earnings Per Share Calculation for 2006

	(£)
Loss after taxation	(50,000)
Number of ordinary shares ('000)	14,395
Loss per share	*(0.3p)*

Tutorial note

As the preference shares are classified as liabilities, the preference dividend of £500,000 will already have been charged as an expense in arriving at the loss after tax for the year.

Stage 4 – Restate 2005 Earnings Per Share to Reflect Bonus Element of Rights Issue

Original EPS in 2005 accounts	1.0p
Adjustment factor	124/130
Restated EPS (1.0p × 124/130)	*0.9p*

11. Convertibles plc

Basic calculation

Basic earnings per share = £700,000/8million = 8.8p

Diluted calculation

	('000)
Number of shares per basic	8,000
Add: notional conversion at 120 shares per £100	3,600
	11,600

	(£'000)	(£'000)
Basic earnings		700
Add: Post-tax savings on interest		
Gross interest (8% × £3,000)	240	
Tax relief lost (30% × 240)	(72)	
		168
		868

Diluted earnings per share = £868,000/11.6million = 7.5p

12. Royal Warrants plc

Basic calculation

	(£)
Profit after taxation	750,000
Preference dividends	(150,000)
Earnings	600,000
Number of ordinary shares ('000)	6,000
Earnings per share	*10.0p*
2005 comparative figure	*9.0p*

Diluted calculation

	('000)
Number of shares per basic	6,000
Add: notional exercise of warrants	3,000
Less: Shares unused at fair value	
(3,000 × 150 ÷ 180)	(2,500)
	6,500

	(£'000)
Basic earnings	600

Diluted earnings per share = £600,000/6.5 million = 9.2p

13. Working capital ratios

Inventory turnover

Last year:	1,736/332	5.2×
This year:	1,738/328	5.3×

Cost of sales has stayed virtually the same over the year but inventory levels have fallen slightly, leading to an increase in inventory turnover. This should lead to reduced costs and should therefore be good for the business through increased efficiency in use of assets. There is a risk, however, that if inventory levels are too low then sales will suffer as a result of stockouts.

Receivables collection period

Last year:	429/3,232 × 365	48 days
This year:	395/3,146 × 365	46 days

Trade accounts receivable have fallen relatively more than sales indicating an improvement in the time taken to collect from customers. Trade accounts receivable consist of retail outfits of various sizes. The fall in trade accounts receivable indicates improved efficiency in use of assets, as with the fall in inventory turnover. Due to the high demand for Cadbury products by the final customer, it is unlikely that this will affect Cadbury's sales revenue adversely at all.

Suppliers payment period

Last year:	262/1,736 × 365	55 days
This year:	260/1,738 × 365	55 days

'Suppliers payment period has remained fairly constant over the period. The length of time taken to pay suppliers is around ten days longer than that for customers to pay Cadbury. This indicates good working capital management since it means that, after allowing for the time it takes to make and sell inventories, the company is out of pocket for a smaller period of time.

Current ratio

Last year:	1,258/1,033	1.2×
This year:	1,063/962	1.1×

The overall fall in the levels of current assets and current liabilities has resulted in a slightly lower current ratio. Traditionally, manufacturers will have current ratios of above one due to the need to hold inventories and give a reasonable amount of credit to customers. In Cadbury's case, the high level of short-term borrowings and other current liabilities tends to reduce the current ratio. Without more details about the company it is difficult to say whether this level of short-term debt is appropriate. Overall, the current ratio indicates that Cadbury has few problems.

Quick ratio

Last year:	(1,258 – 332)/1,033	0.9×
This year:	(1,063 – 328)/962	0.8×

The same comments generally apply to the quick ratio as the current ratio.

General comments

Without more details about the remainder of Cadbury's financial statements, it is difficult to draw conclusions from the above details. In addition, ratios, such as inventory turnover, which compare an income statement figure with a statement of financial position figure, are liable to distortions if the statement of financial position is not representative of the company's financial position over the year. Nevertheless, it appears that while revenue and activity levels have stagnated over the year, active control of working capital levels has resulted in reduced costs and increased efficiency in use of assets.

11

Financial Instruments

INTRODUCTION

Company financing was introduced in detail in an earlier chapter, however shares and loans are not the only financial instruments the company may have some involvement with. The major concern here is derivatives such as futures or options which may have little or no historic cost but may expose a business to significant risk. It is likely however, that a business will use such instruments to control risk.

We need to appreciate how such instruments may be used by a business, how they will be reflected in the accounts and how they impact on the business risks return profile.

BPP
LEARNING MEDIA

CHAPTER LEARNING OBJECTIVES

The syllabus areas are covered by this chapter are

Interpretation of Financial Information

The effect of accounting practices

Understanding of the effect of accounting practices on the numbers most significant for investment decisions (profit, earnings per share, asset value etc).

Characteristics of corporate securities

A knowledge of the main classes of securities issued in the UK and the other member states of the EU and the major international markets. An ability to compare and contrast different types of security.

Classes of securities

Implications of different classes of security upon a company's gearing.

Accounting Terminology and Concepts

Accounting terminology and a knowledge of accounting concepts and conventions to include the statement of financial position, income statement, statement of cash flows and notes to the accounts. An understanding of the distinction between capital and revenue, the valuation of assets for accounting purposes and the determination of profit and earnings share on the nil, net and full distribution bases. An understanding of significance of the statement of accounting policies in relation to the concept of a true and fair view.

Presentation of Financial Statements

Impact of statutory and non-statutory regulation on UK financial statements.

An understanding of the effect on the presentation of financial statements of the Companies Act and non-statutory regulations, including standards and other guidance issued by IASB and stock exchange requirements.

In the context of financial instruments:

It is emphasised that the intention of the examination is to assess student's analytical and interpretative skills rather than their technical accounting ability. It is also expected that they should have an understanding of standard accounting practices and an awareness of matters currently under discussion.

1 FINANCIAL INSTRUMENTS

Financial instruments can be very complex, particularly derivative instruments.

1.1 Introduction

If you read the financial press you will probably be aware of **rapid international expansion** in the use of financial instruments in recent years. These vary from straightforward, traditional instruments, e.g. bonds, through to various forms of so-called 'derivative instruments', such as futures, options, swaps and so on.

The three Standards used for accounting for financial instruments are

- IAS 32 *Financial Instruments: Presentation,* which deals with

    - The classification of financial instruments between liabilities and equity.
    - Presentation of certain compound instruments.

- IAS 39 *Financial Instruments: Recognition and Measurement,* which deals with

    - Recognition and derecognition.
    - The measurement of financial instruments.
    - Hedge accounting.

- IFRS 7 *Financial Instruments: Disclosures,* which deals with

    - Disclosures which were originally required by IAS 32.
    - Some additional disclosures.

1.2 Definitions

The most important definitions are common to all three Standards.

- **Financial instrument**. Any contract that gives rise to both a financial asset of one entity and a financial liability or equity instrument of another entity.

- **Financial asset**. Any asset that is

    - Cash.

    - An equity instrument of another entity.

    - A contractual right to receive cash or another financial asset from another entity; or to exchange financial instruments with another entity under conditions that are potentially favourable to the entity.

    - A contract that will or may be settled in the entity's own equity instruments and is

        - A non-derivative for which the entity is or may be obliged to receive a variable number of the entity's own equity instruments; or

        - A derivative that will or may be settled other than by the exchange of a fixed amount of cash or another financial asset for a fixed number of the entity's own equity instruments.

- **Financial liability**. Any liability that is

    - A contractual obligation

        - To deliver cash or another financial asset to another entity; or

        - To exchange financial instruments with another entity under conditions that are potentially unfavourable; or

- A contract that will or may be settled in the entity's own equity instruments and is

  - A non-derivative for which the entity is or may be obliged to deliver a variable number of the entity's own equity instruments; or

  - A derivative that will or may be settled other than by the exchange of a fixed amount of cash or another financial asset for a fixed number of the entity's own equity instruments.

- **Equity instrument**. Any contract that evidences a residual interest in the assets of an entity after deducting all of its liabilities.

- **Fair value** is the amount for which an asset could be exchanged, or a liability settled, between knowledgeable, willing parties in an arm's length transaction.

- **Derivative**. A financial instrument or other contract with all three of the following characteristics:

  - Its value changes in response to the change in a specified interest rate, financial instrument price, commodity price, foreign exchange rate, index of prices or rates, credit rating or credit index, or other variable (sometimes called the 'underlying');

  - It requires no initial net investment or an initial net investment that is smaller than would be required for other types of contracts that would be expected to have a similar response to changes in market factors.

  - It is settled at a future date. *(IAS 32 and IAS 39)*

1.3 Clarification

We should clarify some points arising from these definitions. Firstly, one or two terms above should be defined.

- A '**contract**' need not be in writing, but it must comprise an agreement that has 'clear economic consequences' and which the parties to it cannot avoid, usually because the agreement is enforceable in law.

- An '**entity**' here could be an individual, partnership, incorporated body or government agency.

The definitions of **financial assets** and **financial liabilities** may seem rather circular, referring as they do to the terms financial asset and financial instrument. The point is that there may be a chain of contractual rights and obligations, but it will lead ultimately to the receipt or payment of cash *or* the acquisition or issue of an equity instrument.

1.4 Examples

Examples of **financial assets** include

- Trade receivables.
- Options.
- Shares (when held as an investment).

Examples of **financial liabilities** include

- Trade payables.
- Debenture loans payable.
- Redeemable preference (non-equity) shares.
- Forward contracts standing at a loss.

As we have already noted, financial instruments include both of the following.

- **Primary instruments**: e.g. receivables, payables and equity securities.
- **Derivative instruments**: e.g. financial options, futures and forwards, interest rate swaps and currency swaps.

IAS 32 makes it clear that the following items are *not* financial instruments.

- **Physical assets**, e.g inventories, property, plant and equipment, leased assets and **intangible assets** (patents, trademarks etc).
- **Prepaid expenses**, deferred revenue and most warranty obligations.
- Liabilities or assets that are **not contractual** in nature.
- Contractual rights/obligations that **do not involve transfer of a financial asset**, e.g. commodity futures contracts.

Example

Can you give the reasons why physical assets and prepaid expenses do not qualify as financial instruments?

Solution

Refer to the definitions of financial assets and liabilities given above.

- **Physical assets**: control of these creates an opportunity to generate an inflow of cash or other assets, but it does not give rise to a present right to receive cash or other financial assets.
- **Prepaid expenses**, etc: the future economic benefit is the receipt of goods/services rather than the right to receive cash or other financial assets.

Contingent rights and obligations meet the definition of financial assets and financial liabilities respectively, even though many do not qualify for recognition in financial statements. This is because the contractual rights or obligations exist because of a past transaction or event (e.g. assumption of a guarantee).

1.5 Derivatives

A **derivative** is a financial instrument that **derives** its value from the price or rate of an underlying item. Common **examples** of derivatives include the following.

- **Forward contracts**: agreements to buy or sell an asset at a fixed price at a fixed future date.
- **Futures contracts**: similar to forward contracts except that contracts are standardised and traded on an exchange.
- **Options**: rights (but not obligations) for the option holder to exercise at a pre-determined price; the option writer loses out if the option is exercised.
- **Swaps**: agreements to exchange one set of cash flows for another (normally interest rate or currency swaps).

The nature of derivatives often gives rise to **particular problems**. The **value** of a derivative (and the amount at which it is eventually settled) depends on **movements** in an underlying item (such as an exchange rate). This means that settlement of a derivative can lead to a very different result from the one originally envisaged. A company which has derivatives is exposed to **uncertainty and risk** (potential for gain or loss) and this can have a very material effect on its financial performance, financial position and cash flows.

Yet because a derivative contract normally has **little or no initial cost**, under traditional accounting it **may not be recognised** in the financial statements at all. Alternatively it may be recognised at an amount which bears no relation to its current value. This is clearly **misleading** and leaves users of the financial statements unaware of the **level of risk** that the company faces. IASs 32 and 39 were developed in order to correct this situation.

2 PRESENTATION OF FINANCIAL INSTRUMENTS

The objective of IAS 32 is

'to enhance financial statement users' understanding of the significance of on-balance-sheet and off-balance-sheet financial instruments to an entity's financial position, performance and cash flows.'

2.1 Scope

IAS 32 should be applied in the presentation of **all types of financial instruments**, whether recognised or unrecognised.

Certain items are **excluded** for example subsidiaries, associates and joint ventures, pensions and insurance contracts.

2.2 Liabilities and equity

The main thrust of IAS 32 here is that financial instruments should be presented according to their **substance**, **not merely their legal form**. In particular, entities which issue financial instruments should classify them (or their component parts) as **either financial liabilities, or equity**.

The classification of a financial instrument as a liability or as equity depends on the following.

- The substance of the contractual arrangement on initial recognition.
- The definitions of a financial liability and an equity instrument.

2.3 Liability or equity

How should a **financial liability be distinguished from an equity instrument**? The critical feature of a **liability** is an **obligation** to transfer economic benefits. Therefore, a financial instrument is a financial liability if there is a **contractual obligation** on the issuer either to deliver cash or another financial asset to the holder or to exchange another financial instrument with the holder under potentially unfavourable conditions to the issuer.

The financial liability exists **regardless of the way in which the contractual obligation will be settled**. The issuer's ability to satisfy an obligation may be restricted, e.g. by lack of access to foreign currency, but this is irrelevant as it does not remove the issuer's obligation or the holder's right under the instrument.

Where the above critical feature is *not* met, then the financial instrument is an **equity instrument**. IAS 32 explains that although the holder of an equity instrument may be entitled to a *pro rata* share of any distributions out of equity, the issuer does *not* have a contractual obligation to make such a distribution.

2.4 Preferred/preference shares

You have been asked to discuss this area in Section C, e.g. Winter 2004, Question 8.

Although substance and legal form are often **consistent with each other**, this is not always the case. In particular, a financial instrument may have the legal form of equity, but in substance it is in fact a liability. Other instruments may combine features of both equity instruments and financial liabilities.

For example, entities may issue **preferred shares** which must be **redeemed** by the issuer for a fixed (or determinable) amount at a fixed (or determinable) future date. Alternatively, the holder may have the right to require the issuer to redeem the shares at or after a certain date for a fixed amount. In such cases, the issuer has an **obligation**. Therefore the instrument is a **financial liability** and should be classified as such.

The classification of the financial instrument is made when it is **first recognised** and this classification will continue until the financial instrument is removed from the entity's statement of financial position.

2.5 Compound financial instruments

Some financial instruments contain both a liability and an equity element. In such cases, IAS 32 requires the component parts of the instrument to be **classified separately**, according to the substance of the contractual arrangement and the definitions of a financial liability and an equity instrument.

One of the most common types of compound instrument is **convertible debt**. This creates a primary financial liability of the issuer and grants an option to the holder of the instrument to convert it into an equity instrument (usually ordinary shares) of the issuer. This is the economic equivalent of the issue of conventional debt plus a warrant to acquire shares in the future.

Although in theory there are several possible ways of calculating the split, IAS 32 requires the following method.

- Calculate the value for the liability component.

- Deduct this from the instrument as a whole to leave a residual value for the equity component.

The reasoning behind this approach is that an entity's equity is its residual interest in its assets after deducting all its liabilities.

The **sum of the carrying amounts** assigned to liability and equity will always be equal to the carrying amount that would be ascribed to the instrument **as a whole**.

The valuation of the liability element is based on the calculation of the value of a bond without the conversion elements. For example, if a convertible bond is issued for $2m, and an equivalent non-convertible bond would be priced at $1.85m – the equity element would be deemed to be $0.15m.

The split between the liability and equity components remains the same throughout the term of the instrument, even if there are changes in the **likelihood of the option being exercised**. This is because it is not always possible to predict how a holder will behave. The issuer continues to have an obligation to make future payments until conversion, maturity of the instrument or some other relevant transaction takes place.

2.6 Interest, dividends, losses and gains

As well as looking at statement of financial position presentation, IAS 32 considers how financial instruments affect the income statement (and movements in equity). The treatment varies according to whether interest, dividends, losses or gains relate to a financial liability or an equity instrument.

- Interest, dividends, losses and gains relating to a financial instrument (or component part) classified as a **financial liability** should be recognised as **income or expense** in the income statement.

- Distributions to holders of a financial instrument classified as an **equity instrument** should be **debited directly to equity** by the issuer.

- **Transaction costs** of an equity transaction shall be accounted for as a **deduction from equity** (unless they are directly attributable to the acquisition of a business, in which case they are accounted for under IFRS 3).

3 RECOGNITION OF FINANCIAL INSTRUMENTS

> IAS 39 *Financial Instruments: Recognition and Measurement* establishes principles for recognising and measuring financial assets and financial liabilities.

3.1 Scope

IAS 39 applies to **all entities** and to **all types of financial instruments except** those specifically excluded, for example investments in subsidiaries, associates and joint ventures.

3.2 Initial recognition

A financial asset or financial liability should be recognised on the statement of financial position when the reporting entity becomes a party to the contractual provisions of the instrument.

> An important consequence of this is that all derivatives should be recognised on the statement of financial position.

Notice that this is **different** from the recognition criteria in the *Framework* and in most other Standards. Items are normally recognised when there is a probable inflow or outflow of resources and the item has a cost or value that can be measured reliably.

Example

An entity has entered into two separate contracts.

(a)   A firm commitment (an order) to buy a specific quantity of iron.

(b)   A forward contract to buy a specific quantity of iron at a specified price on a specified date.

Contract (a) is a **normal trading contract**. The entity does not recognise a liability for the iron until the goods have actually been delivered. (Note that this contract is not a financial instrument because it involves a physical asset, rather than a financial asset.)

Contract (b) is a **financial instrument**. Under IAS 39, the entity recognises a financial liability (an obligation to deliver cash) on the **commitment date**, rather than waiting for the closing date in which the exchange takes place.

Note that planned future transactions, no matter how likely, are not assets and liabilities of an entity – the entity has not yet become a party to the contract.

3.3 Derecognition

Derecognition is the removal of a previously recognised financial instrument from the statement of financial position.

An entity should derecognise a **financial asset** when

- The **contractual rights** to the cash flows from the financial asset **expire**; or

- It **transfers substantially all the risks and rewards of ownership** of the financial asset to another party.

3.4 Substance over form

The principle here is that of **substance over form**.

An entity should derecognise a **financial liability** when it is **extinguished** – i.e. when the obligation specified in the contract is discharged or cancelled or expires.

It is possible for only **part** of a financial asset or liability to be derecognised. This is allowed if the part comprises

- Only specifically identified cash flows; or

- Only a fully proportionate (*pro rata*) share of the total cash flows.

For example, if an entity holds a bond it has the right to two separate sets of cash inflows: those relating to the principal and those relating to the interest. It could sell the right to receive the interest to another party while retaining the right to receive the principal.

Where only part of a financial asset is derecognised, the carrying amount of the asset should be allocated between the part retained and the part transferred based on their relative fair values on the date of transfer. A gain or loss should be recognised based on the proceeds for the portion transferred.

4 MEASUREMENT OF FINANCIAL INSTRUMENTS

All financial assets should be initially measured at cost.

4.1 Initial measurement

Exam tip

You may be asked about valuation rules, e.g. Summer 2006, Question 9.

Financial instruments are initially measured at the **fair value** of the consideration given or received (ie, **cost**) **plus** (in most cases) **transaction costs** that are **directly attributable** to the acquisition or issue of the financial instrument.

The **exception** to this rule is where a financial instrument is designated as **at fair value through profit or loss** (this term is explained below). In this case, **transaction costs** are **not** added to fair value at initial recognition but are expensed in the income statement of the period.

The fair value of the consideration is normally the transaction price or market price. If market prices are not reliable, the fair value may be **estimated** using a valuation technique (for example, by discounting cash flows).

4.2 Subsequent measurement

For the purposes of measuring a financial asset held subsequent to initial recognition, IAS 39 classifies financial assets into four categories defined here.

A **financial asset or liability at fair value through profit or loss** meets either of the following conditions.

- It is classified as held for trading. A financial instrument is classified as held for trading if it is:

  - Acquired or incurred principally for the purpose of selling or repurchasing it in the near term.

  - Part of a portfolio of identified financial instruments that are managed together and for which there is evidence of a recent actual pattern of short-term profit-taking.

  - A derivative (unless it is a designated and effective hedging instrument).

- Upon initial recognition it is designated by the entity as at fair value through profit or loss. Any financial instrument may be so designated when it is initially recognised except for investments in equity instruments that do not have a quoted market price in an active market and whose fair value cannot be reliably measured.

Held-to-maturity investments are non-derivative financial assets with fixed or determinable payments and fixed maturity that an entity has the positive intent and ability to hold to maturity other than:

- Those that the entity upon initial recognition designates as at fair value through profit or loss.

- Those that the entity designates as available for sale.

- Those that meet the definition of loans and receivables.

Loans and receivables are non-derivative financial assets with fixed or determinable payments that are not quoted in an active market, other than

- Those that the entity intends to sell immediately or in the near term, which should be classified as held for trading and those that the entity upon initial recognition designates as at fair value through profit or loss.

- Those that the entity upon initial recognition designates as available-for-sale.

- Those for which the holder may not recover substantially all of the initial investment, other than because of credit deterioration, which shall be classified as available for sale.

An interest acquired in a pool of assets that are not loans or receivables (for example, an interest in a mutual fund or a similar fund) is not a loan or a receivable.

Available-for-sale financial assets are those financial assets that are not

- Loans and receivables originated by the entity.

- Held-to-maturity investments.

- Financial assets at fair value through profit or loss.   *(IAS 39)*

After initial recognition, all financial assets should be **remeasured to fair value**, without any deduction for transaction costs that may be incurred on sale or other disposal, except for

- Loans and receivables.

- Held-to-maturity investments.

- Investments in equity instruments that do not have a quoted market price in an active market and whose fair value cannot be reliably measured and derivatives that are linked to and must be settled by delivery of such unquoted equity instruments.

Loans and receivables and **held to maturity investments** should be measured at **amortised cost** using the **effective interest method**.

Definitions

- **Amortised cost of a financial asset or financial liability** is the amount at which the financial asset or liability is measured at initial recognition minus principal repayments, plus or minus the cumulative amortisation of any difference between that initial amount and the maturity amount, and minus any write-down (directly or through the use of an allowance account) for impairment or uncollectability.

- The **effective interest method** is a method of calculating the amortised cost of a financial instrument and of allocating the interest income or interest expense over the relevant period.

- The **effective interest rate** is the rate that exactly discounts estimated future cash payments or receipts through the expected life of the financial instrument to the net carrying amount.

(IAS 39)

Example

On 1 January 2006 Abacus Co purchases a debt instrument for its fair value of $1,000. The debt instrument is due to mature on 31 December 2010. The instrument has a principal amount of $1,250 and the instrument carries fixed interest at 4.72% that is paid annually. Assume that the instrument is classified as a held-to-maturity financial asset.

How should Abacus Co account for the debt instrument over its five-year term?

Solution

Abacus Co will receive interest of $59 (1,250 × 4.72%) each year and $1,250 when the instrument matures.

Abacus must allocate the discount of $250 and the interest receivable over the five-year term at a constant rate on the carrying amount of the debt. To do this, it must apply the effective interest rate of 10%.

The following table shows the allocation over the years

Year	Amortised cost at beginning of year ($)	Income statement: Interest income for year (@10%) ($)	Interest received during year (cash inflow) ($)	Amortised cost at end of year ($)
2006	1,000	100	(59)	1,041
2007	1,041	104	(59)	1,086
2008	1,086	109	(59)	1,136
2009	1,136	113	(59)	1,190
2010	1,190	119	(1,250+59)	–

Each year the carrying amount of the financial asset is increased by the interest income for the year and reduced by the interest actually received during the year.

4.3 Classification

There is a certain amount of flexibility in that *any* financial instrument can be designated as at fair value through profit or loss. However, this is a **once and for all choice** and has to be made on initial recognition. Once a financial instrument has been classified in this way it **cannot be reclassified**, even if it would otherwise be possible to measure it at cost or amortised cost.

In contrast, it is quite difficult for an entity *not* to remeasure financial instruments to fair value.

> Note that derivatives *must* be remeasured to fair value. This is because it would be misleading to measure them at cost.

For a financial instrument to be held to maturity it must meet several extremely narrow criteria. The entity must have a **positive intent** and a **demonstrated ability** to hold the investment to maturity. These conditions are not met if

- The entity intends to hold the financial asset for an undefined period.

- The entity stands ready to sell the financial asset in response to changes in interest rates or risks, liquidity needs and similar factors (unless these situations could not possibly have been reasonably anticipated).

- The issuer has the right to settle the financial asset at an amount significantly below its amortised cost (because this right will almost certainly be exercised).

- It does not have the financial resources available to continue to finance the investment until maturity.

- It is subject to an existing legal or other constraint that could frustrate its intention to hold the financial asset to maturity.

An **equity** instrument cannot meet the criteria for classification as held-to-maturity as it does not have a fixed maturity.

There is a **penalty** for selling or reclassifying a 'held-to-maturity' investment other than in certain very tightly defined circumstances. If this has occurred during the **current** financial year or during the **two preceding** financial years *no* financial asset can be classified as held-to-maturity.

If an entity can no longer hold an investment to maturity, it is no longer appropriate to use amortised cost and the asset must be re-measured to fair value. *All* remaining held-to-maturity investments must also be re-measured to fair value and classified as available-for-sale (see above).

4.4 Subsequent measurement of financial liabilities

Exam tip

> You may be asked to do some basic calculation in these areas, e.g. Winter 2003, Question 8.

After initial recognition, all financial liabilities should be measured at **amortised cost**, with the exception of financial liabilities at fair value through profit or loss (including most derivatives). These should be measured at **fair value**, but where the fair value **is not capable of reliable measurement**, they should be measured at **cost**.

Example

Galaxy Co issues a bond for £503,778 on 1 January 2007. No interest is payable on the bond, but it will be held to maturity and redeemed on 31 December 2009 for £600,000. The bond has *not* been designated as at fair value through profit or loss.

Requirement

Calculate the charge to the income statement of Galaxy Co for the year ended 31 December 2007 and the balance outstanding at 31 December 2007.

Solution

The bond is a 'deep discount' bond and is a financial liability of Galaxy Co. It is measured at amortised cost. Although there is no interest as such, the difference between the initial cost of the bond and the price at which it will be redeemed is a finance cost. This must be allocated over the term of the bond at a constant rate on the carrying amount.

To calculate amortised cost we need to calculate the effective interest rate of the bond:

$$\frac{600,000}{503,778} = 1.191 \text{ over three years. } \sqrt[3]{1.191} = 1.06 \text{ per annum.}$$

Therefore the effective interest rate is 6%.

The charge to the income statement for the year ended 31 December 2007 is £30,226 (503,778 × 6%)

The balance outstanding at 31 December 2007 is £534,004 (503,778 + 30,226)

4.5 Gains and losses

- Instruments at **fair value through profit or loss**: gains and losses are recognised **in profit or loss** (i.e. in the income statement).

- **Available-for-sale** financial assets: gains and losses are recognised **directly in equity** through the statement of changes in equity. When the asset is derecognised the cumulative gain or loss previously recognised in equity should be recognised in profit and loss.

- Financial instruments carried at **amortised cost**: gains and losses are recognised **in profit and loss** as a result of the amortisation process and when the asset is derecognised.

- Financial assets and financial liabilities that are **hedged items**: special rules apply (see next section).

4.6 Impairment and uncollectability of financial assets

At each statement of financial position date, an entity should assess whether there is any objective evidence that a financial asset or group of assets is impaired.

Where there is objective evidence of impairment, the entity should **determine the amount** of any impairment loss.

4.7 Financial assets carried at amortised cost

The impairment loss is the **difference** between the asset's **carrying amount** and its **recoverable amount**. The asset's recoverable amount is the present value of estimated future cash flows, discounted at the financial instrument's **original** effective interest rate.

The amount of the loss should be **recognised in profit or loss.**

If the impairment loss decreases at a later date (and the decrease relates to an event occurring *after* the impairment was recognised) the reversal is recognised in profit or loss. The carrying amount of the asset must not exceed the original amortised cost.

4.8 Financial assets carried at cost

Unquoted equity instruments are carried at cost if their fair value cannot be reliably measured. The impairment loss is the difference between the asset's **carrying amount** and the **present value of estimated future cash flows**, discounted at the current market rate of return for a similar financial instrument. Such impairment losses cannot be reversed.

4.9 Available-for-sale financial assets

Available-for-sale financial assets are carried at fair value and gains and losses are recognised directly in equity. Any impairment loss on an available-for-sale financial asset should be **removed from equity** and **recognised in net profit or loss for the period** even though the financial asset has not been derecognised.

The impairment loss is the difference between its **acquisition cost** (net of any principal repayment and amortisation) and **current fair value** (for equity instruments) or recoverable amount (for debt instruments), less any impairment loss on that asset previously recognised in profit or loss.

Impairment losses relating to equity instruments cannot be reversed. Impairment losses relating to debt instruments may be reversed if, in a later period, the fair value of the instrument increases and the increase can be objectively related to an event occurring after the loss was recognised.

5 HEDGING

Exam tip

> Hedge accounting is a prime area for exam questions, e.g. Winter 2006, Question 8.

IAS 39 **permits hedge accounting** where there is a **designated hedging relationship** between a hedging instrument and a hedged item. It is **prohibited otherwise**.

> **Hedging**, for accounting purposes, means designating one or more hedging instruments so that their change in fair value is offset, in whole or in part, by the change in fair value or cash flows of a hedged item.
>
> A **hedged item** is an asset, liability, firm commitment, or highly probable forecast future transaction that
>
> - Exposes the entity to risk of changes in fair value or changes in future cash flows; and that
> - Is designated as being hedged.
>
> A **hedging instrument** is a designated derivative or (in limited circumstances) another financial asset or liability whose fair value or cash flows are expected to offset changes in the fair value or cash flows of a designated hedged item. (A non-derivative financial asset or liability may be designated as a hedging instrument for hedge accounting purposes only if it hedges the risk of changes in foreign currency exchange rates.)
>
> **Hedge effectiveness** is the degree to which changes in the fair value or cash flows of the hedged item attributable to a hedged risk are offset by changes in the fair value or cash flows of the hedging instrument.
>
> *(IAS 39)*

In simple terms, entities **hedge** to **reduce** their **exposure to risk** and uncertainty, such as changes in prices, interest rates or foreign exchange rates. Hedge accounting recognises hedging relationships by allowing (for example) losses on a hedged item to be offset against gains on a hedging instrument.

5.1 Hedge accounting

Hedging usually involves acquiring a derivative (the hedging instrument) whose fair value or cash flows are expected to move in the opposite direction to those of the position being hedged (the hedged item). The intention is to mitigate some or all of the risk of that position.

Hedge accounting involves deferring gains and losses on the hedge so that they can be matched in the income statement in the same period(s) as those of the position hedged.

Under IAS 39, hedge accounting is only permitted if

- The hedging relationship is designated and documented at the outset.
- The hedge is effective and can be measured and tested for effectiveness on an ongoing basis.

The following example provides an illustration of a successful hedging relationship.

Example

A company raises £100m through the issue of a five-year 8% bond. It also takes out a five-year matching interest rate swap under which it will receive fixed rates of 8% and pay floating rates, effectively making this floating rate financing.

Actual interest rates and corresponding current values of the debt and swap are as follows.

	Year 1	Year 2	Year 3	Year 4	Year 5
Interest rate	6%	11%	15%	10%	10%
Value of debt (£m)	(107)	(93)	(89)	(98)	(100)
Value of swap (£m)	7	(7)	(11)	(2)	nil

The market values have been calculated by discounting the expected future cash payments at the specified rate.

What will be disclosed in the accounts over the next five years in relation to this?

Solution

Assets and liabilities

	Year 1	Year 2	Year 3	Year 4	Year 5
	(£m)	(£m)	(£m)	(£m)	(£m)
Swap	7	(7)	(11)	(2)	–
Borrowings	(107)	(93)	(89)	(98)	(100)
	(100)	(100)	(100)	(100)	(100)

Income statement – reported profits

	Year 1	Year 2	Year 3	Year 4	Year 5
	(£m)	(£m)	(£m)	(£m)	(£m)
Interest charge	(8)	(8)	(8)	(8)	(8)
Swap receipt/(payment)	2	(3)	(7)	(2)	(2)
	(6)	(11)	(15)	(10)	(10)

Hence, the expense charged in the income statement is the floating interest rate that we have swapped into.

Changes in equity

	Year 1 (£m)	Year 2 (£m)	Year 3 (£m)	Year 4 (£m)	Year 5 (£m)
Gain/(loss) on debt	(7)	14	4	(9)	(2)
Gain/(loss) on swap	7	(14)	(4)	9	2

The net effect of the above entries is the same as for a floating rate borrowing. This reflects the fact that the swap has effectively converted the borrowing from fixed to floating. The income statement shows a floating interest expense.

Showing both financial instruments at current values produces a zero net gain/loss each year in reserves because any gain/loss on the borrowing is exactly offset by any loss/gain on the swap.

5.2 Types of hedging relationship

The Standard identifies three types of hedging relationship.

> **Fair value hedge**: a hedge of the exposure to changes in the fair value of a recognised asset or liability, or an identified portion of such an asset or liability, that is attributable to a particular risk and could affect profit or loss.
>
> **Cash flow hedge**: a hedge of the exposure to variability in cash flows that
>
> - Is attributable to a particular risk associated with a recognised asset or liability (such as all or some future interest payments on variable rate debt) or a highly probable forecast transaction (such as an anticipated purchase or sale); and that
>
> - Could affect profit or loss.
>
> **Hedge of a net investment in a foreign operation**: IAS 21 defines a net investment in a foreign operation as the amount of the reporting entity's interest in the net assets of that operation. *(IAS 39)*

5.3 Conditions for hedge accounting

Before a hedging relationship qualifies for hedge accounting, **all** of the following **conditions** must be met.

- The hedging relationship must be **designated at its inception as a hedge** based on the entity's risk management objective and strategy. There must be formal documentation (including identification of the hedged item, the hedging instrument, the nature of the risk that is to be hedged and how the entity will assess the hedging instrument's effectiveness in offsetting the exposure to changes in the hedged item's fair value or cash flows attributable to the hedged risk).

- The hedge is expected to be **highly effective** in achieving offsetting changes in fair value or cash flows attributable to the hedged risk. (Note: the hedge need not necessarily be *fully* effective.)

- For **cash flow hedges**, a **forecast transaction** that is the subject of the hedge must be **highly probable** and must present an exposure to variations in cash flows that could ultimately affect profit or loss.

- The effectiveness of the hedge can be **measured reliably**.

- The hedge is **assessed** on an ongoing basis (annually) and has been **effective during the reporting period**.

5.4 Fair value hedges – accounting treatment

The **gain or loss** resulting from **re-measuring** the hedging instrument at fair value is **recognised in profit or loss**.

The gain or loss on the hedged item attributable to the hedged risk should **adjust the carrying amount** of the hedged item and be **recognised in profit or loss**.

5.5 Cash flow hedges – accounting treatment

The portion of the gain or loss on the hedging instrument that is determined to be an **effective** hedge shall be **recognised directly in equity** through the statement of changes in equity (see our earlier Example).

The **ineffective portion** of the gain or loss on the hedging instrument should be **recognised in profit or loss**.

When a hedging transaction results in the recognition of an asset or liability, changes in the value of the hedging instrument recognised in equity either

- Are adjusted against the carrying value of the asset or liability; or
- Affect the income statement at the same time as the hedged item (for example, through depreciation or sale).

5.6 Hedges of a net investment in a foreign operation – accounting treatment

These hedges are accounted for **in a similar way to cash flow hedges**.

- The effective portion of the gain or loss on the hedging instrument is recognised directly in equity through the statement of changes in equity.
- The ineffective portion is recognised in profit and loss.

On disposal of the foreign operation, gains and losses on the hedging instrument that have been taken to equity are 'recycled' and recognised in profit or loss.

6 DISCLOSURE OF FINANCIAL INSTRUMENTS

6.1 Introduction

When IAS 32 was issued one of its main purposes was to provide full and useful disclosure relating to financial instruments.

In August 2005, however, IFRS 7 *Finanacial Instruments: Disclosure* was issued and IAS 32 was renamed *Financial Instruments: Presentation*. IFRS 7 is effective for annual periods beginning on or after 1 January 2007 with earlier application encouraged and applies to all financial instruments other than those covered by another more specific standards such as interest in subsidiaries, associates and joint ventures, post-employment benefits, share-based payment and insurance contracts.

6.2 Disclosures required

An entity must group its financial instruments into classes of similar instruments and, where disclosures are required, make disclosures by class.

The two main categories of disclosures required by IFRS 7 are

- Information about the significance of financial instruments.
- Information about the nature and extent of risks arising from financial instruments.

6.3 Information about the significance of financial instruments – statement of financial position

Disclosure should be made for each of the following categories.

- Financial assets measured at fair value through profit and loss, showing separately those held for trading those designated at initial recognition.

- Held to maturity investments.

- Loans and receivables.

- Available for sale assets.

- Financial liabilities at fair value through profit and loss, showing separately those held for trading and those designated at initial recognition.

- Financial liabilities measured at amortised cost.

The disclosures required include

- For financial assets and liabilities designated to be measured at fair value through profit and loss disclosures about credit risk and market risk and changes in fair value.

- Reclassifications of financial instruments from fair value to amortised cost or *vice versa*.

- Disclosures about derecognitions, including transfers of financial assets for which derecognition accounting is not permitted by IAS 39.

6.4 Information about the significance of financial instruments – income statement and equity

Disclosure should be made of income, expense, gains and losses, with separate disclosure of gain and losses from

- Financial assets measured at fair value through profit and loss, showing separately those held for trading and those designated at initial recognition.

- Held to maturity investments.

- Loans and receivables.

- Available for sale assets.

- Financial liabilities measured at fair value through profit and loss, showing separately those held for trading and those designated at initial recognition.

- Financial liabilities measured at amortised cost.

Disclosure should also be made of

- Interest income and interest expense for those financial instruments that are not measured at fair value through profit and loss.

- Fee income and expense.

- Amount of impairment losses on financial assets.

- Interest income on impaired financial assets.

6.5 Information about the significance of financial instruments – other disclosures

- Accounting policies for financial instruments.

- Information about hedge accounting including

    - Description of each hedge, hedging instrument and fair values of those instruments and nature of risks being hedged.

    - For cash flow hedges, the periods in which the cash flows are expected to occur, when they are expected to enter into the determination of profit or loss, and a description of any forecast used but which is no longer expected to occur.

    - If a gain or loss on a hedging instrument in a cash flow hedge has been recognised directly in equity, an entity should disclose the amount recognised in equity, the amount removed from equity to profit and loss, and the amount removed from equity during the period and included in the initial measurement of the acquisition cost or other carrying amount of a non-financial liability in a hedged, highly probable forecast transaction.

    - For fair value hedges information about the fair value changes of the hedging instrument and the hedged item.

    - Hedge ineffectiveness recognised in profit and loss (separately for cash flow hedges and hedges of a net investment in a foreign operation).

    - Information about the fair values of each class of financial asset and financial liability.

6.6 Nature and extent of exposure to risks arising from financial instruments – qualitative disclosures

The qualitative disclosures describe

- Risk exposure for each type of financial instrument.
- Management's objectives, policies and processes for managing those risks.
- Change from the prior period.

6.7 Nature and extent of exposure to risks arising from financial instruments – quantitative disclosures

The quantitative disclosures provide information about the extent to which the entity is exposed to risk, based on information provided internally to the entity's key management personnel. These disclosures include

- Summary quantitative date about exposure to each risk at the reporting date.
- Disclosures about credit risk, liquidity risk and market risk (see below).
- Concentration of risk.

6.8 Credit risk disclosures

- Maximum amount of exposure, description of collateral, information about credit quality of financial assets.

- Analytical disclosures for financial assets that are past due or impaired.

- Information about collateral or other credit enhancements obtained or called.

6.9 Liquidity risk

- Maturity analysis of financial liabilities.
- Description of approach to risk management.

6.10 Market risk

Market risk is the risk that the fair value or cash flows of a financial instrument will fluctuate due to changes in market prices. Market risk reflects interest rate risk, currency risk and other price risks.

Disclosures include

- A sensitivity analysis of each type of market risk to which the entity is exposed.

- A sensitivity analysis for management purposes that reflects interdependencies of more than one component of market risk (for instance interest risk and foreign currency risk combined – it may disclose that analysis rather than a separate sensitivity analysis for each type of market risk.

6.11 IAS 1 Amendments

At the same time as the publication of IFRS 7 the IASB published an amendment to IAS 1. The amendment introduces the requirement for all entities to disclose

- The entity's objective, policies and processes for managing capital.
- Quantitative data about what the entity regards as capital.
- Whether the entity has complied with any capital requirements.
- If it has not complied, the consequences of non-compliance.

These disclosures about the level of an entity's capital and how it manages capital are important factors for users to consider in assessing the risk profile of an entity.

Example

The extract below is from the accounting policy note for the Roche Group detailing the types of risks it faces and how those risks are managed. Bear in mind, however, that this was published under IAS 32 not IFRS 7.

Roche Group
Extract from Notes to the Financial Statement, Year Ended 31 December 2004

Financial Risk Management

The Group is exposed to various financial risks arising from the Group's underlying operations and corporate finance activities. The financial risks the Group is exposed to are predominantly related to changes in foreign exchange rates, interest rates, equity prices as well as the creditworthiness and the solvency of the Group's counterparties.

The Group's subsidiaries Genentech and Chugai have their own treasury operations. These have operational independence, while working within a financial risk management framework that is consistent with the rest of the Group. More information on their financial risks is available in the annual reports of Chugai and Genentech.

Financial risk management within the Group is governed by policies and guidelines approved by senior management. These policies and guidelines cover foreign exchange risk, interest rate risk, market risk, credit risk and liquidity risk. Group policies and guidelines also cover areas such as cash management, investment of excess funds and the raising of short- and long-term debt. The compliance with the policies and guidelines is overseen by segregated functions within the Group.

The objective of financial risk management is to contain, where deemed appropriate, exposures in the various types of financial risks mentioned above in order to limit negative impact on the Group's financial income and statement of financial position.

The Group actively measures, monitors and manages its financial risk exposures by various functions pursuant to segregation of duties principles.

In accordance with the financial risk policies the Group manages its market risk exposures, when deemed appropriate, through the use of financial instruments such as derivatives. It is the Group's policy and practice not to enter into derivatives transactions for trading or speculative purposes nor purposes unrelated to the underlying business.

Foreign Exchange Risk

The Group operates across the world and is exposed to movements in foreign currencies affecting its net income and financial position, as expressed in Swiss francs. The Group actively monitors its currency exposures, and when appropriate, enters into transactions with the aim of preserving the value of assets, commitments and anticipated transactions. The Group uses forward contracts, foreign exchange options and cross-currency swaps to hedge certain committed and anticipated foreign exchange flows, financing transactions as well as net investments.

Transaction Exposure arises because the amount of local currency paid or received for transactions denominated in foreign currencies may vary due to changes in exchange rates. For many Group companies income will be primarily in the local currency. A significant amount of expenditure, especially for purchase of goods for resale and interest on and repayment of loans will be in foreign currencies. Similarly, transaction exposure arises on net balances of monetary assets held in foreign currencies. At local level, the Group companies manage this exposure, if necessary by means of financial instruments such as options and forward contracts. In addition, Group Treasury monitors total worldwide exposure with the help of comprehensive data received on a monthly basis.

Translation Exposure arises from the consolidation of the foreign currency denominated financial statements of the Group's foreign subsidiaries. The effect on the Group's consolidated equity is shown as a currency translation movement. The Group partially hedges net investments in foreign currencies by taking foreign currency loans or issuing foreign currency denominated debt instruments. Major translation exposures are monitored on a regular basis.

A significant part of the Group's cash outflows for research, development, production and administration is denominated in Swiss francs, while a much smaller proportion of the Group's cash inflows are Swiss franc denominated. As a result, an increase in the value of the Swiss franc relative to other currencies has an adverse impact on consolidated net income. Similarly, a relative fall in the value of the Swiss franc has a favourable effect on results published in Swiss francs.

Interest Rate Risk

Interest rate risk arises from movements in interest rates which could have effects on the Group's net income or financial position. Changes in interest rates cause variations in interest income and expenses and in interest bearing assets and liabilities. In addition, they can affect the market value of certain financial assets, liabilities and instruments as described in the following section on market risk. The interest rates on the Group's major debt instruments are fixed, as described in Note 32. The Group uses interest rate derivatives to manage its interest rate risk.

Market Risk of Financial Assets

Changes in the market value of certain financial assets and derivative instruments can affect the net income or financial position of the Group. Financial long-term assets are held for strategic purposes and marketable securities are held for fund management purposes. The risk of loss in value is managed by reviews prior to investing and continuous monitoring of the performance of investments and changes in their risk profile.

Investments in equities, bonds, debentures and other fixed income instruments are entered into on the basis of guidelines with regard to liquidity and credit rating.

Credit Risk

Credit risk arises from the possibility that the counter-party to a transaction may be unable or unwilling to meet their obligations causing a financial loss to the Group. Trade receivables are subject to a policy of active risk management focusing on the assessment of country risk, credit availability, ongoing credit evaluation and account monitoring procedures. There are no significant concentrations within trade receivables of counter-party credit risk, due to the Group's large number of customers and their wide geographical spread. For some credit exposures in critical countries, the Group has entered into respective credit insurance. Country risk limits and exposures are continuously monitored. The exposure of other financial assets to credit risk is controlled by setting a policy for limiting credit exposure to high-quality counterparties, regular reviews of credit ratings, and setting defined limits for each individual counter-party. Where appropriate to reduce exposure, netting agreements under an ISDA (International Swaps and Derivatives Association) master agreement are signed with the respective counter-parties. The maximum exposure to credit risk resulting from financial activities, without considering netting agreements, is equal to the carrying amount of financial assets. The credit exposure is diversified amongst different counter-parties.

Liquidity Risk

Group companies need to have sufficient availability of cash to meet their obligations. Individual companies are responsible for their own cash management, including the short-term investment of cash surpluses and the raising of loans to cover cash deficits, subject to guidance by the Group and, in certain cases, to approval at Group level. The Group maintains sufficient reserves of cash and readily realisable marketable securities to meet its liquidity requirements at all times. In addition, the strong international creditworthiness of the Group allows it to make efficient use of international capital markets for financing purposes.

Fair Values

Fair value is the amount for which a financial asset, liability or instrument could be exchanged between knowledgeable and willing parties in an arm's length transaction. It is determined by reference to quoted market prices or by the use of established estimation techniques such as option pricing models and estimated discounted values of cash flows. The fair values at the statement of financial position date are approximately in line with their reported carrying values unless specifically mentioned in the Notes to the Consolidated Financial Statements.

Financial Assets

Financial assets, principally investments, including marketable securities, are classified as either 'Held-for-trading', 'Available-for-sale', 'Held-to-maturity' or 'Originated by the Group'. Held-for-trading financial assets are acquired principally to generate profit from short-term fluctuations in price. Held-to-maturity financial assets are securities with a fixed maturity that the Group has the intent and ability to hold until maturity. Financial assets originated by the Group are loans and other long-term financial assets created by the Group or acquired from the issuer in a primary market. All other financial assets are considered as available-for-sale.

All financial assets are initially recorded at cost, including transaction costs. All purchases and sales are recognised on the settlement date. Held-for-trading financial assets are subsequently carried at fair value, with all changes in fair value recorded as financial income in the period in which they arise. Held-to-maturity financial assets are subsequently carried at amortised cost using the effective interest rate method. Available-for-sale financial assets are subsequently carried at fair value, with all unrealised changes in fair value recorded in equity. When the available-for-sale financial assets are sold, impaired or otherwise disposed of, the cumulative gains and losses previously recognised in equity are included in financial income for the current period. Financial assets originated by the Group are subsequently carried at amortised cost.

Financial assets are assessed for possible impairment at each statement of financial position date. An impairment charge is recorded where there is objective evidence of impairment, such as where the issuer is in bankruptcy, default or other significant financial difficulty. Any available-for-sale financial assets that have a market value of more than 25% below their original cost, net of any previous impairment, for a sustained six-month period will be considered as impaired. Any decreases in the market price of less than 25% of original cost, net of any previous impairment, or for less than a sustained six-month period are not by themselves considered as objective evidence of impairment, and such movements in fair value are recorded in equity until there is objective evidence of impairment or until the asset is sold or otherwise disposed of. For financial assets carried at amortised cost, any impairment charge is the difference between the carrying value and the recoverable amount, being calculated using estimated future cash flows discounted using the original effective interest rate. For available-for-sale financial assets, any impairment charge is the amount currently carried in equity for the difference between the original cost, net of any previous impairment, and the fair value.

Derivatives

All derivative financial instruments are initially recorded at cost, including transaction costs. Derivatives are subsequently carried at fair value. Apart from those derivatives designated as qualifying cash flow hedging instruments (see below), all changes in fair value are recorded as financial income in the period in which they arise. Embedded derivatives are recognised separately if not closely related to the host contract.

Hedging

For the purposes of hedge accounting, hedging relationships may be of three types. Fair value hedges are hedges of particular risks that may change the fair value of a recognised asset or liability. Cash flow hedges are hedges of particular risks that may change the amount or timing of future cash flows. Hedges of net investment in a foreign entity are hedges of particular risks that may change the carrying value of the net assets of a foreign entity.

To qualify for hedge accounting the hedging relationship must meet several strict conditions on documentation, probability of occurrence, hedge effectiveness and reliability of measurement. If these conditions are not met, then the relationship does not qualify for hedge accounting. In this case the hedging instrument and the hedged item are reported independently as if there were no hedging relationship. In particular any derivatives are reported at fair value, with changes in fair value included in financial income.

For qualifying fair value hedges, the hedging instrument is recorded at fair value and the hedged item is recorded at its previous carrying value, adjusted for any changes in fair value that are attributable to the hedged risk. Any changes in the fair values are reported in financial income.

For qualifying cash flow hedges, the hedging instrument is recorded at fair value. The portion of any change in fair value that is an effective hedge is included in equity, and any remaining ineffective portion is reported in financial income. If the hedging relationship is the hedge of a firm commitment or highly probable forecasted transaction, the cumulative changes of fair value of the hedging instrument that have been recorded in equity are included in the initial carrying value of the asset or liability at the time it is recognised. For all other qualifying cash flow hedges, the cumulative changes of fair value of the hedging instrument that have been recorded in equity are included in financial income at the time when the forecasted transaction affects net income.

For qualifying hedges of net investment in a foreign entity, the hedging instrument is recorded at fair value. The portion of any change in fair value that is an effective hedge is included in equity. Any remaining ineffective portion is recorded in financial income where the hedging instrument is a derivative and in equity in other cases. If the entity is disposed of, then the cumulative changes of fair value of the hedging instrument that have been recorded in equity are included in financial income at the time of the disposal.

Derivative Financial Instruments

In appropriate circumstances the Group uses derivative financial instruments as part of its risk management and trading strategies. This is discussed in Note 2. Derivative financial instruments are carried at fair value. The methods used for determining fair value are described in Note 1.

Derivative financial instruments in millions of CHF	Assets		Liabilities	
	2004	**2003**	**2004**	**2003**
Foreign currency derivatives				
Forward exchange contracts and swaps	85	167	(99)	(98)
Other	1	4	(4)	–
Interest rate derivatives				
Swaps	22	12	(6)	(42)
Other	–	–	–	–
Other derivatives	43	174	(61)	(8)
Total derivatives financial instruments	151	357	(170)	(148)

Hedge Accounting

The Group's accounting policy on hedge accounting, which is described in Note 1, requires that to qualify for hedge accounting the hedging relationship must meet several strict conditions on documentation, probability of occurrence, hedge effectiveness and reliability of measurement.

As described in Note 2, the Group has financial risk management policies, which cover foreign exchange risk, interest rate risk, market risk, credit risk and liquidity risk. When deemed appropriate, certain of the above risks are altered through the use of derivatives. While many of these transactions can be considered as hedges in economic terms, if the required conditions are not met, then the relationship does not qualify for hedge accounting. In this case the hedging instrument and the hedged item are reported independently as if there were no hedging relationship, which means that any derivatives are reported at fair value, with changes in fair value included in financial income.

The Group generally limits the use of hedge accounting to certain significant transactions. Consequently as at 31 December 2004 the Group has no fair value hedges, cash flow hedges or hedges of net investment in a foreign entity that meet the strict requirements to qualify for hedge accounting, apart from those described below.

The Group has hedged some of its fixed term debt instruments with interest rate swaps. As at 31 December 2004 such instruments, which are designated and qualify as fair value hedges, are recorded in the statement of financial position with a fair value of 15 million Swiss francs.

Genentech has non-US dollar cash flows from future royalty income and development expenses expected over the next one to five years. To hedge part of this transaction exposure Genentech enters into derivative financial instruments such as options and forward contracts. Genentech has equity investments in various biotechnology companies that are subject to a greater risk of market fluctuation than the stock market in general. To manage part of this exposure Genentech enters into derivative financial instruments such as zero cost collars and forward contracts. As at 31 December 2004 such instruments, which are designated and qualify for hedge accounting, are recorded in the statement of financial position with a fair value of 25 million Swiss francs. These matters are also described in Genentech's annual report and quarterly SEC filings.

Movements on the fair value reserve for designated cash flow hedges are included in Note 36.

CHAPTER ROUNDUP

You need to be familiar with the following definitions.

- **Financial instrument**. Any contract that gives rise to both a financial asset of one entity and a financial liability or equity instrument of another entity.

- **Financial asset**. Any asset that is
  - Cash.
  - An equity instrument of another entity.
  - A contractual right to receive cash or another financial asset from another entity; or to exchange financial instruments with another entity under conditions that are potentially favourable to the entity.
  - A contract that will or may be settled in the entity's own equity instruments and is
    - A non-derivative for which the entity is or may be obliged to receive a variable number of the entity's own equity instruments; or
    - A derivative that will or may be settled other than by the exchange of a fixed amount of cash or another financial asset for a fixed number of the entity's own equity instruments.

- **Financial liability**. Any liability that is
  - A contractual obligation
    - To deliver cash or another financial asset to another entity; or
    - To exchange financial instruments with another entity under conditions that are potentially unfavourable; or
  - A contract that will or may be settled in the entity's own equity instruments and is
    - A non-derivative for which the entity is or may be obliged to deliver a variable number of the entity's own equity instruments; or
    - A derivative that will or may be settled other than by the exchange of a fixed amount of cash or another financial asset for a fixed number of the entity's own equity instruments.

- **Equity instrument**. Any contract that evidences a residual interest in the assets of an entity after deducting all of its liabilities.

- **Fair value** is the amount for which an asset could be exchanged, or a liability settled, between knowledgeable, willing parties in an arm's length transaction.

- **Derivative**. A financial instrument or other contract with all three of the following characteristics:
  - Its value changes in response to the change in a specified interest rate, financial instrument price, commodity price, foreign exchange rate, index of prices or rates, credit rating or credit index, or other variable (sometimes called the 'underlying');
  - It requires no initial net investment or an initial net investment that is smaller than would be required for other types of contracts that would be expected to have a similar response to changes in market factors;
  - It is settled at a future date. *(IAS 32 and IAS 39)*

You need to be aware of the major classes of derivatives.

- **Forward contracts**: agreements to buy or sell an asset at a fixed price at a fixed future date.

- **Futures contracts**: similar to forward contracts except that contracts are standardised and traded on an exchange.

- **Options**: rights (but not obligations) for the option holder to exercise at a pre-determined price; the option writer loses out if the option is exercised.

- **Swaps**: agreements to swap one set of cash flows for another (normally interest rate or currency swaps).

You need to be familiar with

- IAS 32 *Financial Instruments: Presentation*

- IAS 39 *Financial Instruments: Recognition and Measurements*

  - All financial assets should be initially measured at cost.

  - After initial recognition, all financial assets should be **remeasured to fair value**, without any deduction for transaction costs that may be incurred on sale or other disposal, except for

    - Loans and receivables.

    - Held to maturity investments.

    - Investments in equity instruments that do not have a quoted market price in an active market and whose fair value cannot be reliably measured and derivatives that are linked to and must be settled by delivery of such unquoted equity instruments.

  - **Loans and receivables** and **held to maturity investments** should be measured at **amortised cost** using the **effective interest method**.

  - Recognition of gains/losses.

  - Hedging purpose and rules.

TEST YOUR KNOWLEDGE

Check your knowledge of the chapter here, without referring back to the text.

1. Financial instruments

    Two Standards have been published by the IASB to deal with the complex area of financial instruments.

    (a) IAS 32 *Financial Instruments: Disclosure and Presentation*.
    (b) IAS 39 *Financial Instruments: Recognition and Measurement*.

    Requirements

    (a) Define a 'derivative'.
    (b) Summarise the requirements of

        (i)   IAS 32.
        (ii) IAS 39.

2. Financial instruments Part 2

    Standard-setters have been struggling for several years with the practical issues of the disclosure and measurement of financial instruments. The IASB has issued two financial reporting Standards on the subject, IAS 39 *Financial Instruments: Recognition and Measurement* and IAS 32 *Financial Instruments: Disclosure and Presentation*. The dynamic nature of international financial markets has resulted in the widespread use of a variety of financial instruments, and present accounting rules struggle to deal effectively with the impact and risks of such instruments.

    Requirements

    (a) Discuss the concerns about the accounting practices used for financial instruments which led to demand for an Accounting Standard.

    (b) Explain why regulations dealing with disclosure alone are unlikely to solve the problem of accounting for financial instruments in financial statements.

TEST YOUR KNOWLEDGE: ANSWERS

1.   Financial instruments

   (a)   IAS 39 defines a **derivative** as a financial instrument

      (i)   Whose value changes in response to the change in a specified interest rate, security price, commodity price, foreign exchange rate, index of prices or rates, a credit rating or credit index, or similar variable (sometimes called the 'underlying');

      (ii)   That requires no initial net investment or little initial net investment relative to other types of contracts that have a similar response to changes in market conditions;

      (iii)   That is settled at a future date.

   (b)   (i)   IAS 32

         The presentation Standard, IAS 32, prescribes certain requirements for presentation of **on-statement of financial position financial instruments** and identifies the **information** that should be **disclosed about both** on-statement of financial position (**recognised**) and off-statement of financial position (**unrecognised**) financial instruments. The presentation Standard deals with the classification of financial instruments between liabilities and equity, the classification of related interest, dividends, losses and gains, and the circumstances in which financial assets and financial liabilities should be offset. It also deals with information about factors that affect the amount, timing and certainty of an entity's future cash flows relating to financial instruments and the accounting policies applied to the instruments. In addition, IAS 32 requires disclosure of information about the **nature** and **extent** of an entity's use of **financial instruments**, the **business purpose** that they serve, the **risks** associated with them and **management's policies** for **controlling** those **risks**. The disclosure requirements of IAS 32 will be removed and replaced by IFRS 7 for periods beginning on or after 1 January 2007.

      (ii)   IAS 39

         Under the measurement requirements of this Standard, all financial assets and liabilities should initially be measured at cost, which is the fair value of the consideration given or received to acquire the financial asset or liability (plus certain hedging gains and losses).

         Subsequent to initial recognition, all financial assets should be remeasured to **fair value**, **except** for the following.

         (1)   **Loans and receivables** (assets with fixed or determinable payments that are not quoted in an active market).

         (2)   Other **non-current maturity investments**, such as debt securities and mandatory redeemable preferred shares, that the entity intends and is able to **hold to maturity** ('held to maturity investments').

         (3)   **Financial assets** whose **fair value cannot be reliably measured** (limited to some equity instruments with no quoted market price and some derivatives that are linked to and must be settled by delivery of such unquoted equity instruments).

         Loans and receivables and held to maturity investments are measured at amortised cost. Financial assets whose fair value cannot be reliably measured are measured at cost.

After acquisition, most financial liabilities should be measured at original recorded amount less principal repayments and amortisation ('amortised cost'). Only liabilities at fair value through profit or loss (including derivatives and liabilities held for trading) should be remeasured to fair value.

An entity can opt to measure certain financial instruments at fair value, except for equity instruments that do not have a quoted market price and whose fair value cannot be reliably measured, by designating it as 'at fair value through profit or loss' when it is initially recognised. Once a financial instrument has been classified in this way, it cannot be reclassified. Derivatives must always be measured at fair value.

Where financial assets and liabilities are remeasured to fair value, gains and losses should be treated as follows.

(1)   Gains and losses on instruments at fair value through profit or loss should be included in profit or loss for the period.

(2)   Gains and losses on available-for-sale financial assets should be recognised directly in equity until the asset is disposed of, at which time the cumulative gain or loss previously recognised in equity should be included in profit and loss for the period.

IAS 39 establishes conditions for determining when **control** over a financial asset or liability has been **transferred to another party**.

Hedging, for accounting purposes, means **designating** a **derivative or** (in limited circumstances) a **non-derivative financial instrument** as an **offset**, in whole or in part, to the **change** in **fair value** or **cash flows** of a hedged item. A hedged item can be an **asset, liability, firm commitment**, or **forecasted future transaction** that is exposed to risk of change in value or changes in future cash flows. Hedge accounting **recognises** the **offsetting effects** on **profit or loss symmetrically**. **Hedge accounting** is permitted under FRS 26 in certain circumstances, provided that the **hedging relationship** is **clearly defined**, measurable, and **actually effective**.

2.   Financial instruments Part 2

Accounting practices used for financial instruments

(a)   The concerns were

(1)   The growth and **complexity** of financial instruments has increased dramatically in recent years.

(2)   Companies tend to use a range of instruments to transform and **manage risk**.

(3)   Accounting standards did not deal adequately with the growth of these complex capital instruments.

(4)   Many derivatives are **not recognised** in the statement of financial position because they have **no cost** and the financial statements use the **historic cost concept**.

(5)   Derivatives may expose an entity to **significant risks**.

(6)   Financial assets are **often recognised at depreciated historic cost**, even where market values differ considerably.

(7)   **Unrealised gains and losses** arising from value changes in financial instruments are **often ignored**. Unrealised losses are often ignored where an instrument is regarded as a hedge. IAS 39 regulates this question.

(8)   Companies have tended to **vary** the **timing** of **profit recognition** on instruments in order to engage in **profit smoothing**.

(9)   Circumstances can change rapidly because of volatile capital markets, and undisclosed risks can increase dramatically.

(b)   **Effectiveness of regulations**.

Disclosure of an entity's risk in relation to financial instruments is an important element of accounting for instruments and IAS 32 *Financial Instruments: Disclosure and Presentation* deals with this issue.

As well as disclosure and presentation, **measurement issues must also be considered**. It is important that a company knows when to derecognise a financial instrument. The use of **current values** is a **critical measurement issue**. In addition, there are issues of impairment to consider. IAS 39 *Financial Instruments: Recognition and Measurement* has been issued to deal with these problems.

12

Reporting the Substance of Transactions

INTRODUCTION

Historically, one of the most significant problems for the analyst was creative accounting, i.e. the selection of permitted accounting treatments with the specific intention distorting the picture of the company that is reflected by the accounts.

This chapter considers rules that have been developed in order to limit as far as possible the scope that businesses have to potentially mislead investors through this creative accounting.

CHAPTER CONTENTS

CHAPTER LEARNING OBJECTIVES

The syllabus areas covered by this chapter are

Interpretation of Financial Information

The effect of accounting practices

Understanding of the effect of accounting practices on the numbers most significant for investment decisions (profit, earnings per share, asset value etc).

Accounting Terminology and Concepts

Accounting terminology and a knowledge of accounting concepts and conventions to include the statement of financial position, income statement, statement of cash flows and notes to the accounts. An understanding of the distinction between capital and revenue, the valuation of assets for accounting purposes and the determination of profit and earnings share on the nil, net and full distribution bases. An understanding of significance of the statement of accounting policies in relation to the concept of a true and fair view.

Presentation of Financial Statements

Impact of statutory and non-statutory regulation on UK financial statements.

An understanding of the effect on the presentation of financial statements of the Companies Acts and non-statutory regulations, including standards and other guidance issued by IASB and stock exchange requirements.

In the context of reporting the substance of financial objectives:

It is emphasised that the intention of the examination is to assess student's analytical and interpretative skills rather than their technical accounting ability. It is also expected that they should have an understanding of standard accounting practices and an awareness of matters currently under discussion.

1 INTRODUCTION

Exam tip

This area has been examined in Section B, of Summer 2002, Question 3.

1.1 Problem transactions

In the past, many companies have attempted to acquire or use assets in such a way that the financing for those assets was not recognised on the statement of financial position. The resultant asset and liability figures did not realistically represent the value of assets or debt being used within the business.

This type of activity is known as **off-statement of financial position financing** – the financing of the activities of the company while keeping some or all of the finance off the statement of financial position. The process was normally achieved by structuring a legal arrangement such that the company could argue that in law the debt was not theirs. Some common examples of such problem transactions are as follows.

- **Leases**, whereby the company would acquire the use of an asset on a lease. The terms of the lease were such that the company did not legally own the lease but was able to make use of the asset. As the asset did not legally belong to the company, it was argued that it should not be shown on the statement of financial position. If it had been required to be shown, the corresponding liability to repay the leasing company would also have been required to be shown.

- **Sale and repurchase arrangements**, whereby the company sold an asset or assets but then had the option to repurchase them at a later date. Typically, the company still had the use of these assets and/or access to any excess revenues that the assets may generate. However, as they had been legally sold, the asset was simply replaced by cash proceeds.

- **Consignment inventory**, whereby a company would receive inventory from a supplier or manufacturer that would legally belong to the supplier but would be available for the company to sell. As the inventory was only on consignment, it was argued that it should not be shown in the statement of financial position of the company holding the inventory. Therefore, the company would also not be required to recognise the liability to pay for the inventory.

- **Linked arrangements**, such as debt factoring, where the company would sell the rights to economic benefit from certain assets (in the case of debt factoring, the rights from trade receivables) but would still retain some risk. In these situations, although the company has received cash for the assets sold, some or all of the cash should be shown as a liability if there may be a requirement to repay it. However, the argument given was that as the assets had legally been sold, the cash received simply represented sale proceeds.

- **Securitisation of assets**, commonly achieved through the sale of an asset or asset portfolio to an unrelated company (often called a Special Purpose Vehicle or SPV). The company would be able to raise cash from the 'sale' of the asset to the SPV and could continue to have use of excess revenues from the asset through a separate agreement.

1.2 Fundamental principles

The *Framework*, issued by the IASB, states that information contained in the financial statements should be **relevant and reliable**.

One of the key features of reliable information is that it accords with the **commercial reality or substance** of the circumstances. Thus the *Framework* effectively elevates this concept to the status of a fundamental principle that is required to be followed in the financial statements.

This concept, of **commercial substance over legal form**, forms the basis for the treatment of leases and other problematic transactions.

2 IAS 17 LEASES

A finance lease is a means of acquiring the long-term use of an asset whereas an operating lease is a short-term rental agreement.

2.1 What is a lease?

Where goods are acquired other than on immediate cash terms, arrangements have to be made in respect of the future payments on those goods. In the simplest case of **credit sales**, the purchaser is allowed a period of time (say one month) to settle the outstanding amount and the normal accounting procedure in respect of receivables/payables will be adopted. However, in recent years there has been considerable growth in leasing agreements (some types of lease are called **hire purchase agreements** in some countries).

IAS 17 *Leases* standardises the accounting treatment and disclosure of assets held under lease.

In a leasing transaction there is a **contract** between the lessor and the lessee for the hire of an asset. The lessor retains legal ownership but conveys to the lessee the right to use the asset for an agreed period of time in return for specified rentals. IAS 17 defines a lease and recognises two types.

2.2 Definitions

> - **Lease**. An agreement whereby the lessor conveys to the lessee in return for a payment or series of payments the right to use an asset for an agreed period of time.
>
> - **Finance lease**. A lease that transfers substantially all the risks and rewards incidental to ownership of an asset. Title may or may not eventually be transferred.
>
> - **Operating lease**. A lease other than a finance lease.   *(IAS 17)*

A **finance lease** may be a **hire purchase agreement**. (The difference is that under a hire purchase agreement the customer eventually, after paying an agreed number of instalments, becomes entitled to exercise an option to purchase the asset. Under other leasing agreements, ownership remains forever with the lessor.)

To expand on the definition above, a finance lease should be presumed if at the inception of a lease the **present value of the minimum lease payments** is approximately equal to the **fair value of the leased asset**.

The present value should be calculated by using the **interest rate implicit in the lease**.

- **Minimum lease payments**. The payments over the lease term that the lessee is or can be required to make, excluding contingent rent, costs for services and taxes to be paid by and be reimbursed to the lessor, together with

    - For a lessee, any amounts guaranteed by the lessee or by a party related to the lessee.

    - For a lessor, any residual value guaranteed to the lessor by one of the following.

        - The lessee.

        - A party related to the lessee.

        - An independent third party financially capable of meeting this guarantee.

    However, if the lessee has the option to purchase the asset at a price which is expected to be sufficiently lower than fair value at the date the option becomes exercisable for it to be reasonably certain, at the inception of the lease, that the option will be exercised, the minimum lease payments comprise the minimum payments payable over the lease term to the expected date of exercise of this purchase option and the payment required to exercise it.

- **Interest rate implicit in the lease**

    The discount rate that, at the inception of the lease, causes the aggregate present value of

    - The minimum lease payments; and
    - The unguaranteed residual value

    to be equal to the sum of

    - The fair value of the leased asset; and
    - Any initial direct costs of the lessor.

2.3 Accounting for leases: lessees and lessors

Operating leases do not really pose an accounting problem. The lessee pays amounts periodically to the lessor and these are **charged to the income statement** on a straight-line basis over the term of the lease.

The double entry is as follows.

DEBIT   Income statement (operating costs)

CREDIT   Cash

For assets held under **finance leases** (including hire purchase) this accounting treatment would not reflect the commercial reality of the situation.

A **lessee** may use a finance lease to fund the 'acquisition' of a major asset which he will then use in his business, perhaps for many years. **The substance of the transaction is that he has acquired a non-current asset**, and this is reflected in the accounting treatment prescribed by IAS 17, even though in law the lessee may never become the owner of the asset.

The revised IAS 17 states that when classifying a lease of **land and buildings** the **land** element is normally classified as an **operating lease unless title passes to the lessee** at the end of the contract.

2.4 Accounting treatment – statement of financial position

IAS 17 requires that, when an asset is the subject of a **finance lease**, **lessor and lessee should account for the transaction as though it were a credit sale**. In the lessee's books therefore

DEBIT   Asset account

CREDIT   Lessor (liability) account

The amount to be recorded in this way is the **lower of** the **fair value** of the leased asset and the **present value** of the **minimum lease payments**.

IAS 17 states that it is not appropriate to show liabilities for leased assets as deductions from the leased assets. A distinction should be made between **current and non-current** lease liabilities, if the entity makes this distinction for other liabilities.

The asset should be **depreciated** (on the bases set out in IAS 16 and IAS 38) over the shorter of

- The lease term.
- The asset's useful life.

2.5 Apportionment of rental payments

When the lessee makes a rental payment under a finance lease it will comprise two elements.

- An **interest charge** on the finance provided by the lessor. This proportion of each payment is interest payable in the income statement of the lessee.

- A repayment of part of the **capital cost** of the asset. In the lessee's books this proportion of each rental payment must be debited to reduce the outstanding liability.

The accounting problem is to decide what proportion of each instalment paid by the lessee represents interest, and what proportion represents a repayment of the capital advanced by the lessor. There are two apportionment methods you may encounter.

- **Actuarial method**.
- **Sum-of-the-digits method**.

Example

On 1 January, a company acquires an asset with a cash price of £255,000 under a lease. The terms of the lease are that five six-monthly instalments of £60,000 are to be paid in arrears, i.e. a total of £300,000 must be paid. In addition, we can extend the lease to a full four years and will probably do so, as we believe the asset will continue to be useful to us for that time.

The rent for this secondary period is negligible.

How will this be reflected in the accounts of the company for the next four years?

NB: The rate of interest implicit in the lease is 5.7% per instalment.

Solution

Classification – Finance/Operating lease

The present value of the minimum lease payments is approximately equal to the fair value of the asset so we will assume this is a finance lease.

Value Capitalised

We will base the value capitalised on the cash price of £255,000. The impact on the accounting equation on 1 January will be

- Non-current assets up £255,000. (**Debit**: Non current assets)
- Liabilities up £255,000 (representing the finance lease liability now payable). (**Credit**: liabilities)

Lease Term

Primary term – for finance charge allocation

In this Example, we have a primary lease term of 2½ years and should therefore allocate the total finance charge over this period. The total finance charge is the difference between the total amount being paid and the capitalised value of the asset (which equals the initial value of the loan). In this example, the total finance charge is £45,000 (£300,000 – £255,000).

Full lease term – for depreciation

The full lease term in this Example is four years, the period over which we can, and are expected to want to use the asset. This, therefore, represents the time over which we should depreciate the asset, i.e. our annual depreciation charge should be £63,750 (£255,000 ÷ 4 years) assuming straight-line depreciation.

Over the next four years, this asset will appear on the statement of financial position as follows.

Non-Current Assets	Year 1 (£'000)	Year 2 (£'000)	Year 3 (£'000)	Year 4 (£'000)
Cost	255.00	255.00	255.00	255.00
Depreciation	(63.75)	(127.50)	(191.25)	(255.00)
Net Book Value	191.25	127.50	63.75	–

Analysis of payments

Remember that the idea is that we calculate how much of the finance charge is allocated to each payment by one of two methods.

- The actuarial method.
- The sum-of-digits method.

We will illustrate both to show that they show substantially similar results.

Actuarial method

Using the rate of interest implicit in the lease of 5.7% per instalment we can calculate the following repayment schedule.

Period	Lease Liability b/f (£'000)	Finance Charge at 5.7% (£'000)	Paid (£'000)	Difference (Capital Repaid) (£'000)	Lease Liability c/f (£'000)
Year 1					
1 Jan–30 June	255.0	14.5	(60.0)	45.5	209.5
1 July–31 Dec	209.5	11.9	(60.0)	48.1	161.4
Year 2					
1 Jan–30 June	161.4	9.2	(60.0)	50.8	110.6
1 July–31 Dec	110.6	6.3	(60.0)	53.7	56.9
Year 3					
1 Jan–30 June	56.9	3.1	(60.0)	56.9	–
		45.0	300.0	255.0	

We can see from this that over the primary term of 2½ years, £300,000 is paid in total, which we can split into £45,000 total finance charge and £255,000 capital repaid, as we wanted.

Looking down this table we can see that the loan balance outstanding at the end of Year 1 is £161,400. Looking further down the table, we can see that £56,900 is still outstanding at the end of Year 2 and that the liability is cleared during Year 3. These, therefore, represent our full year-end liabilities at those dates.

What we need to do is split these balances between amounts current and non-current liabilities.

Liabilities	Year 1 (£'000)	Year 2 (£'000)	Year 3 (£'000)	Year 4 (£'000)
Current	104.50	56.90	–	–
Non-current	56.90	–	–	–
Total liability	161.40	56.90	–	–

Sum-of-Digits Method

To utilise this alternative method we firstly need to add up the digits corresponding to the number of payments we are making, i.e. 5 + 4 + 3 + 2 + 1 = 15. We will then use this to allocate the total finance charge of £45,000 as follows.

Alternatively the sum of digits can be calculated using the following formula.

$$\frac{n(n+1)}{2}$$

where 'n' is the number of instalments. Therefore, in our Example

$$\frac{5(5+1)}{2} = 15$$

Payment	Finance Charge	(£'000)
1	5/15 × 45,000	15
2	4/15 × 45,000	12
3	3/15 × 45,000	9
4	2/15 × 45,000	6
5	1/15 × 45,000	3

Hence, our repayment schedule on this basis looks as follows.

Period	Lease Creditor b/f (£'000)	Finance Charge (£'000)	Paid (£'000)	Difference (Capital Repaid) (£'000)	Lease Creditor c/f (£'000)
Year 1					
1 Jan–30 June	255	15	(60)	45	210
1 July–31 Dec	210	12	(60)	48	162
Year 2					
1 Jan–30 June	162	9	(60)	51	111
1 July–31 Dec	111	6	(60)	54	57
Year 3					
1 Jan–30 June	57	3	(60)	57	–
		45	300	255	

As we can see, the figures are substantially similar to those calculated under the actuarial method, with a liability at the end of Year 1 of £162,000, compared to £161,400 under the actuarial method.

We can also see that the finance charge for this year is very similar under both methods, being £27,000 (£15,000 + £12,000) under the sum-of-digits method and £26,400 (£14,500 + £11,900) under the actuarial method.

Solution

Using the actuarial method, we can produce the following extract from the statement of financial position and income statement.

Statement of financial positions

Non-Current Assets	Year 1 (£'000)	Year 2 (£'000)	Year 3 (£'000)	Year 4 (£'000)
Cost	255.00	255.00	255.00	255.00
Depreciation	(63.75)	(127.50)	(191.25)	(255.00)
Net Book Value	191.25	127.50	63.75	0.00
Liabilities:				
Current	104.50	56.90	–	–
Non-Current	56.90	–	–	–
Total Liability	161.40	56.90	–	–

Income statements

	Year 1 (£'000)	Year 2 (£'000)	Year 3 (£'000)	Year 4 (£'000)
Depreciation	63.75	63.75	63.75	63.75
Finance lease charges	26.40	15.50	3.10	–
	90.15	79.25	66.85	63.75

2.5.1 Analysis points

A number of accounting ratios are impacted upon as a result of treating a lease as a finance lease rather than an operating lease. Let us consider a few of the more important ratios as illustration.

Return on capital employed

Treating the lease as a finance lease results in a non-current asset being added to the trading assets and a finance lease liability being added to the loans. As a result, the capital employed will be larger and hence the return on capital employed may be lower than would be the case were we accounting for the lease as an operating lease.

Gearing

There will be no change in shareholders' funds as a result of acquiring this asset, however, there will be an increase in the level of borrowings as the finance lease liability is added to the debt. As a result, gearing will apparently be higher.

Interest cover

Since the finance lease charges will be added to the interest payable in the income statement, the interest cover is liable to be reduced.

Current / Quick ratios

Part of the finance lease liability will be recorded within current liabilities. There will be no corresponding increase in the current assets, thus the current and quick ratios will both be reduced, deteriorating the apparent liquidity position of the company.

2.6 Accounting for operating leases

The substance of an operating lease is that the risks and rewards of ownership remain with the lessor and therefore the lessee is simply hiring the equipment as opposed to effectively 'acquiring' it.

The accounting treatment for operating leases is simply to treat the full rent as an expense as incurred, with any rent paid in advance or in arrears appearing as a statement of financial position prepayment (current asset) or accrual (current liability) respectively.

2.7 Disclosure requirements for finance leases

IAS 17 (revised) requires the following disclosures by lessees in respect of finance leases.

- The **net carrying amount** at the statement of financial position date for each class of asset.

- A **reconciliation** between the total of minimum lease payments at the statement of financial position date, and their present value. In addition, an entity should disclose the total of minimum lease payments at the statement of financial position date, and their present value, for each of the following periods.

  - Not later than one year.

  - Later than one year and not later than five years.

  - Later than five years.

- **Contingent rents** recognised in income for the period.

- Total of **future minimum sublease payments** expected to be received under non-cancellable subleases at the statement of financial position date.

- A **general description** of the lessee's significant leasing arrangements including, but not limited to, the following.

  - The basis on which contingent rent payments are determined.

  - The existence and terms of renewal or purchase options and escalation clauses.

  - Restrictions imposed by lease arrangements, such as those concerning dividends, additional debt, and further leasing.

IAS 17 encourages (but does not require) further disclosures, as appropriate.

2.8 Disclosure requirements for operating leases

For **operating leases** the disclosures are as follows.

- The total of future minimum lease payments under non-cancellable operating leases for each of the following periods.

  - Not later than one year.
  - Later than one year and not later than five years.
  - Later than five years.

- The total of future minimum sublease payments expected to be received under non-cancellable subleases at the statement of financial position date.

- Lease and sublease payments recognised in income for the period, with separate amounts for minimum lease payments, contingent rents, and sublease payments.

- A general description of the lessee's significant leasing arrangements including, but not limited to, the following.

  - The basis on which contingent rent payments are determined.

  - The existence and terms of renewal or purchase options and escalation clauses.

  - Restrictions imposed by lease arrangements, such as those concerning dividends, additional debt, and further leasing.

3 OFF-STATEMENT OF FINANCIAL POSITION FINANCE EXPLAINED

3.1 Introduction

> **Off-statement of financial position finance** is the funding or refinancing of a company's operations in such a way that, under legal requirements and accounting rules, some or all of the finance may not be shown on its statement of financial position.

'Off-statement of financial position transactions' are transactions which meet the above objective. These transactions may involve the **removal of assets** from the statement of financial position, as well as liabilities, and they are also likely to have a significant impact on the income statement.

3.2 Why off-statement of financial position finance exists

Why might company managers wish to enter into such transactions?

■ In some countries, companies traditionally have a lower level of gearing than companies in other countries. Off-statement of financial position finance is used to **keep gearing low**, probably because of the views of analysts and brokers.

■ A company may need to keep its gearing down in order to stay within the terms of **loan covenants** imposed by lenders.

■ A quoted company with high borrowings is often expected (by analysts and others) to declare a **rights issue** in order to reduce gearing. This has an adverse effect on a company's share price and so off-statement of financial position financing is used to reduce gearing *and* the expectation of a rights issue.

■ Analysts' short-term views are a problem for companies **developing assets** which are not producing income during the development stage. Such companies will match the borrowings associated with such developing assets, along with the assets themselves, off-statement of financial position.

They are brought back on statement of financial position once income is being generated by the assets. This process keeps return on capital employed higher than it would have been during the development stage.

■ In the past, groups of companies have excluded **subsidiaries** from consolidation in an off-statement of financial position transaction because they carry out completely different types of business and have different characteristics. The usual example is a leasing company (in say a retail group) which has a high level of gearing.

You can see from this brief list of reasons that the overriding motivation is to avoid **misinterpretation**. In other words, the company does not trust the analysts or other users to understand the reasons for a transaction and so avoids any effect such transactions might have by taking them off-statement of financial position. Unfortunately, the position of the company is then misstated and the user of the accounts is misled.

You must understand that not all forms of 'off-statement of financial position finance' are undertaken for cosmetic or accounting reasons. Some transactions are carried out to **limit or isolate risk**, to reduce interest costs and so on. In other words, these transactions are in the best interests of the company, not merely a cosmetic repackaging of figures which would normally appear in the statement of financial position.

3.3 The off-statement of financial position finance problem

The result of the use of increasingly sophisticated off-statement of financial position finance transactions is a situation where the users of financial statements do not have a proper or clear view of the state of the company's affairs. The disclosures required by national company law and accounting standards did not in the past provide sufficient rules for disclosure of off-statement of financial position finance transactions and so very little of the true nature of the transaction was exposed.

Whatever the purpose of such transactions, insufficient disclosure creates a problem. This problem has been debated over the years by the accountancy profession and other interested parties and some progress has been made (see the later sections of this chapter). However, company collapses during recessions have often revealed much higher borrowings than originally thought, because part of the borrowing was off-statement of financial position.

The main argument used for banning off-statement of financial position finance is that the true **substance** of the transactions should be shown, not merely the **legal form**, particularly when it is exacerbated by poor disclosure.

4 SUBSTANCE OVER FORM

4.1 Introduction

> **Substance over form.** The principle that transactions and other events are accounted for and presented in accordance with their substance and economic reality and not merely their legal form. *(Framework)*

This is a very important concept. It is used to **determine the accounting treatment** in financial statements through accounting standards and so prevent off-statement of financial position transactions. The following paragraphs give examples of where the principle of substance over form is enforced in various accounting standards.

4.2 IAS 17 Leases

In IAS 17, there is an explicit requirement that if the lessor transfers substantially all the **risks and rewards of ownership** to the lessee then, even though the legal title has not necessarily passed, the item being leased should be shown as an asset in the statement of financial position of the lessee and the amount due to the lessor should be shown as a liability.

4.3 IAS 24 Related Party Disclosures

IAS 24 requires financial statements to disclose fully any material transactions undertaken with a related party by the reporting entity, **regardless of any price charged**.

4.4 IAS 11 Construction Contracts

In IAS 11 there is a requirement to account for **attributable profits** on construction contracts under the accruals convention. However, there may be a problem with realisation, since it is arguable whether we should account for profit which, although attributable to the work done, may not have yet been invoiced to the customer. It is argued that the convention of substance over form is applied to justify ignoring the strict legal position.

4.5 IAS 27 Consolidated and Separate Financial Statements

This is perhaps the most important area of off-statement of financial position finance which has been prevented by the application of the substance over form concept. The use of **quasi-subsidiaries** was very common in the 1980s.

These may be defined as follows.

> A **quasi-subsidiary** of a reporting entity is a company, trust, partnership or other vehicle that, though not fulfilling the definition of a subsidiary, is directly or indirectly controlled by the reporting entity and gives rise to benefits for that entity that are in substance no different from those that would arise were the vehicle a subsidiary.

The main off-statement of financial position transactions involving quasi-subsidiaries were as follows.

- **Sale of assets**. The sale of assets to a quasi-subsidiary was carried out to remove the associated borrowings from the statement of financial position and so reduce gearing, or perhaps so that the company could credit a profit in such a transaction. The asset could then be rented back to the vendor company under an operating lease (no capitalisation required by the lessee).

- **Purchase of companies or assets**. One reason for such a purchase through a quasi-subsidiary is if the acquired entity is expected to make losses in the near future. Post-acquisition losses can be avoided by postponing the date of acquisition to the date the holding company acquires the purchase from the quasi-subsidiary.

- **Business activities conducted outside the group**. Such a subsidiary might have been excluded through a quasi-subsidiary or not consolidated under an excuse of 'dissimilar activities'. Exclusion from consolidation might be undertaken because the activities are high risk and have high gearing.

IAS 27 contains a definition of a subsidiary based on **control** rather than just ownership rights, thus substantially reducing the effectiveness of this method of off-statement of financial position finance. IAS 27 defines control of another entity as

> **Control** is the power to govern the financial and operating policies of an entity so as to obtain benefits from its activities. *(IAS 27)*

The IAS goes on to state that control exists when

- The parent has a **majority of the voting rights** in the subsidiary (possibly **by agreement** with other members); or

- The parent can appoint or remove a **majority of the board** of the subsidiary; or

- The parent can **direct the operating and financial policies** through a statute or agreement; or

- The parent can cast the **majority of votes** at a board meeting of directors (or equivalent).

The main effects of this definition on the use of quasi-subsidiaries were as follows.

- The use of 'voting rights' rather than 'equity shares' prevents the use of **company structures** which give the benefits of ownership to one class of shareholder without the appearance of doing so, e.g. a company has 100 'A' shares with 10 votes each and 900 'B' shares with one vote each.

- The right to appoint or remove a majority of the board now means those directors who control a majority of the voting rights at board meetings. This prevents control through **differential voting rights** at board meetings.

IAS 27 therefore **curtailed drastically** the use of quasi-subsidiaries for off-statement of financial position finance. More complex schemes are likely to be curtailed by the IASB's *Framework* and by various other Standards (see below).

4.6 Creative accounting

You may also hear the term **creative accounting** used in the context of reporting the substance of transactions. This can be defined simply as the manipulation of figures for a desired result. Remember, however, that it is very rare for a company, its directors or employees to manipulate results for the purpose of fraud. The major consideration is usually the effect the results will have on the company's share price. Some areas open to abuse (although some of these loopholes have been closed) are given below and you should by now understand how these can distort a company results.

- Income recognition and cut-off.
- Impairment of purchased goodwill.
- Manipulation of reserves.
- Revaluations and depreciation.
- Changes in accounting policy.

5 THE IASB FRAMEWORK AND SUBSTANCE OVER FORM

5.1 Introduction

The IASB *Framework* states that accounting for items according to substance and economic reality and not merely legal form is a key determinant of reliable information.

- For the majority of transactions there is **no difference** between the two and therefore no conflict arises.

- For other transactions **substance and form diverge** and the choice of treatment can give different results due to non-recognition of an asset or liability even though benefits or obligations result.

Full disclosure is not enough: all transactions must be **accounted for** correctly, with full disclosure of related details as necessary to give the user of accounts a full understanding of the transactions.

5.2 Basic principles

How does the *Framework* enforce the substance over form rule? Its main method is to define the elements of financial statements and therefore to give rules for their recognition. The key considerations are whether a transaction has **given rise to new assets and liabilities**, and whether it has **changed any existing assets and liabilities**.

The characteristics of transactions whose substance is not readily apparent are as follows.

- The **legal title** to an item is separated from the ability to enjoy the principal benefits, and the exposure to the main risks associated with it.

- The transaction is **linked to one or more others** so that the commercial effect of the transaction cannot be understood without reference to the complete series.

- The transaction includes **one or more options**, under such terms that it makes it highly likely that the option(s) will be exercised.

5.3 Definitions

These are perhaps the most important definitions.

- An **asset** is a resource controlled by the entity as a result of past events and from which future economic benefits are expected to flow to the entity.

- A **liability** is a present obligation of the entity arising from past events, the settlement of which is expected to result in an outflow from the entity of resources embodying economic benefits.

(Framework)

Identification of **who has the risks** relating to an asset will generally indicate **who has the benefits** and hence **who has the asset**. If an entity is in certain circumstances unable to avoid an **outflow of benefits**, this will provide evidence that it has a liability.

The definitions given in the IASB *Framework* of income and expenses are not as important as those of assets and liabilities. This is because income and expenses are **described in terms of changes in assets and liabilities**, i.e. they are secondary definitions.

- **Income** is increases in economic benefits during the accounting period in the form of inflows or enhancements of assets or decreases of liabilities that result in increases in equity, other than those relating to contributions from equity participants.

- **Expenses** are decreases in economic benefits during the accounting period in the form of outflows or depletions of assets or incurrences of liabilities that result in decreases in equity, other than those relating to distributions to equity participants. *(Framework)*

The real importance, then, is the way the *Framework* defines assets and liabilities. This forces entities to acknowledge their assets and liabilities regardless of the legal status.

It is not sufficient, however, that the asset or liability fulfils the above definitions; it must also satisfy **recognition criteria** in order to be shown in an entity's accounts.

5.4 Recognition

Recognition is the process of incorporating in the statement of financial position or income statement an item that meets the definition of an element and satisfies the criteria for recognition set out below. It involves the depiction of the item in words and by a monetary amount and the inclusion of that amount in the statement of financial position or income statement totals.

The next key question is deciding **when** something which satisfies the definition of an asset or liability has to be recognised in the statement of financial position. Where a transaction results in an item that meets the definition of an asset or liability, that item should be recognised in the statement of financial position if

- It is **probable that a future inflow or outflow** of benefit to or from the entity will occur; and
- The item can be **measured at a monetary amount with sufficient reliability**.

This effectively prevents entities abusing the definitions of the elements by recognising items that are vague in terms of likelihood of occurrence and measurability. If this were not in force, entities could **manipulate the financial statements** in various ways, e.g. recognising assets when the likely future economic benefits cannot yet be determined.

Probability is assessed based on the situation at the statement of financial position date. For example, it is usually expected that some customers of an entity will not pay what they owe. The expected level of non-payment is based on past experience and the receivables asset is reduced by a percentage (the general bad debt provision).

Measurement must be reliable, but it does not preclude the use of **reasonable estimates**, which is an essential part of the financial statement preparation.

Even if something does not qualify for recognition now, it may meet the criteria **at a later date**.

6 COMMON FORMS OF OFF-STATEMENT OF FINANCIAL POSITION FINANCE

> How does the theory of the *Framework* **apply in practice**, to real transactions? The rest of this section looks at some complex transactions that occur frequently in practice.

6.1 Consignment inventory

Consignment inventory is an arrangement where inventory is held by one party (say a distributor) but is owned by another party (for example, a manufacturer or a finance company). Consignment inventory is common in the motor industry and is similar to goods sold on a 'sale or return' basis.

To identify the correct treatment, it is necessary to identify the point at which the distributor or dealer acquired the benefits of the asset (the inventory) rather than the point at which legal title was acquired. If the manufacturer has the right to require the return of the inventory, and if that right is likely to be exercised, then the inventory is *not* an asset of the dealer. If the dealer is rarely required to return the inventory, then this part of the transaction will have little commercial effect in practice and should be ignored for accounting purposes. The potential liability would need to be disclosed in the accounts.

6.1.1 Summary of indications of asset status

The following analysis summarises the range of possibilities in such a transaction.

Indications that the inventory is *not an asset* of the dealer at delivery	Indications that the inventory *is an asset* of the dealer at delivery
Manufacturer can require dealer to **return inventory** (or transfer inventory to another dealer) without compensation.	Manufacturer cannot require dealer to **return or transfer inventory**.
Penalty paid by the dealer to prevent returns/transfers of inventory at the manufacturer's request.	**Financial incentives** given to persuade dealer to transfer inventory at manufacturer's request.
Dealer has unfettered **right to return inventory** to the manufacturer without penalty and actually exercises the right in practice.	Dealer has **no right to return inventory** or is commercially compelled not to exercise its right of return.
Manufacturer bears **obsolescence risk**, e.g. Obsolete inventory is returned to the manufacturer without penalty; or Financial incentives given by manufacturer to prevent inventory being returned to it (eg on a model change or if it becomes obsolete).	Dealer bears **obsolescence risk**, e.g. Penalty charged if dealer returns inventory to manufacturer; or Obsolete inventory cannot be returned to the manufacturer and no compensation is paid by manufacturer for losses due to obsolescence.

Indications that the inventory is *not an asset* of the dealer at delivery	Indications that the inventory *is an asset* of the dealer at delivery
Inventory **transfer price** charged by manufacturer is based on manufacturer's list price at date of transfer of legal title.	Inventory **transfer price** charged by manufacturer is based on manufacturer's list price at date of delivery.
Manufacturer bears **slow movement risk**, e.g. transfer price set independently of time for which dealer holds inventory, and there is no deposit.	Dealer bears **slow movement risk**, e.g. Dealer is effectively charged interest as transfer price or other payments to manufacturer vary with time for which dealer holds inventory; or Dealer makes a substantial interest-free deposit that varies with the levels of inventory held.

6.1.2 Required accounting

The following apply where it is concluded that the inventory **is in substance an asset** of the dealer.

- The inventory should be recognised as such on the dealer's statement of financial position, together with a corresponding liability to the manufacturer.

- Any deposit should be deducted from the liability and the excess classified as a trade payable.

Where it is concluded that the inventory is **not in substance an asset** of the dealer, the following apply.

- The inventory should not be included on the dealer's statement of financial position until the transfer of risks and rewards has crystallised.

- Any deposit should be included under 'other receivables'.

Example

Daley Motors Co owns a number of car dealerships throughout a geographical area. The terms of the arrangement between the dealerships and the manufacturer are as follows.

(a) Legal title passes when the cars are either used by Daley Co for demonstration purposes or sold to a third party.

(b) The dealer has the right to return vehicles to the manufacturer without penalty. (Daley Co has rarely exercised this right in the past.)

(c) The transfer price is based on the manufacturer's list price at the date of delivery.

(d) Daley Co makes a substantial interest-free deposit based on the number of cars held.

Should the asset and liability be recognised by Daley Co at the date of delivery?

Solution

(a) Legal form is irrelevant.

(b) Yes: only because rarely exercised (otherwise 'no').

(c) Yes.

(d) Yes: the dealership is effectively forgoing the interest which could be earned on the cash sum.

Overall it can be seen that the asset and liability should be recognised at the date of delivery.

6.2 Sale and repurchase agreements

These are arrangements under which the company sells an asset to another person on terms that allow the company to **repurchase the asset** in certain circumstances. A common example is the sale and repurchase of maturing whisky inventories. The key question is whether the transaction is a **straightforward sale**, or whether it is, in effect, a **secured loan**. It is necessary to look at the arrangement to determine who has the rights to the economic benefits that the asset generates, and the terms on which the asset is to be repurchased.

If the seller has the right to the benefits of the **use of the asset**, and the repurchase terms are such that the **repurchase is likely** to take place, the transaction should be accounted for as a **loan**.

6.2.1 Summary of indications of the sale of the asset

The following summary is helpful.

Indications of *sale* of original asset to buyer (nevertheless, the seller may retain a different asset)	Indications of *no sale* of original asset to buyer (secured loan)
	Sale price does not equal **market value** at date of sale.
No commitment for **seller to repurchase** asset, e.g. call option where there is a real possibility the option will fail to be exercised.	Commitment for **seller to repurchase** asset, e.g. Put and call option with the same exercise price. Either a put or a call option with no genuine commercial possibility that the option will fail to be exercised; or Seller requires asset back to use in its business, or asset is in effect the only source of seller's future sales.
Risk of **changes in asset value** borne by buyer such that buyer does not receive solely a lender's return, e.g. both sale and repurchase price equal market value at date of sale/repurchase.	Risk of **changes in asset value** borne by seller such that buyer receives solely a lender's return, e.g. Repurchase price equals sale price plus costs plus interest. Original purchase price adjusted retrospectively to pass variations in the value of the asset to the seller. Seller provides residual value guarantee to buyer or subordinated debt to protect buyer from falls in the value of the asset.
Nature of the asset is such that it will be used over the life of the agreement, and seller has no rights to **determine its use**. Seller has no rights to determine asset's development or future sale.	Seller retains right to **determine asset's use**, development or sale, or rights to profits therefrom.

6.2.2 Required accounting

Where the substance of the transaction is that of a **secured loan**

- The seller should continue to recognise the original asset and record the proceeds received from the buyer as a liability.

- Interest, however designated, should be accrued.

- The carrying amount of the asset should be reviewed for impairment and written down if necessary.

Where the transaction is a **sale and leaseback** under a finance lease, then no profit should be recognised on entering in to the arrangement and no adjustment made to the carrying value of the asset. As stated in IAS 17, this represents the substance of the transactions, namely the raising of finance secured on an asset that continues to be held and that is not disposed of.

Where the **seller has a new asset or liability** (e.g. merely a call option to repurchase the original asset), it should recognise or disclose that new asset or liability on a prudent basis in accordance with the provisions of IAS 37. In particular, the seller should recognise (and not merely disclose) a liability for any kind of unconditional obligation it has entered into. Where doubts exist regarding the amount of any gain or loss arising, full provision should be made for any expected loss; but recognition of any gain, to the extent that it is in doubt, should be deferred until it is realised.

Example

A construction company, Mecanto Co, agrees to sell to Hamlows Bank some of the land within its landbank. The terms of the sale are as follows.

(a)   The sales price is to be at open market value.

(b)   Mecanto Co has the right to develop the land on the basis that it will pay all the outgoings on the land plus an annual fee of 5% of the purchase price.

(c)   Mecanto has the option to buy back the land at any time within the next five years. The repurchase price is based on

- Original purchase price.
- Expenses relating to the purchase.
- An interest charge of base rate + 2%.
- Less amounts received from Mecanto by Hamlows.

(d)   At the end of five years Hamlows Bank may offer the land for sale generally. Any shortfall on the proceeds relative to the agreed purchase price agreed with Mecanto has to be settled by Mecanto in cash.

Should the asset continue to be recognised by Mecanto Co and the sales proceeds treated as a loan?

Solution

(a)   No: the sales price is as for an arm's length transaction.

(b)   Yes: Mecanto has control over the asset.

Yes: Mecanto has to pay a fee based on cash received.

(c)   Yes: interest is charged on the proceeds paid by Mecanto.

Yes: the repurchase price is based on the lender's return

(d)   Yes: options ensure that Mecanto bears all the risk (both favourable and unfavourable) of changes in the market value of the land.

The asset should continue to be recognised and the sales proceeds treated as a loan.

6.3 Factoring of receivables/debts

Where debts or receivables are factored, the original creditor **sells the debts to the factor**. The sales price may be fixed at the outset or may be adjusted later. It is also common for the factor to offer a credit facility that allows the seller to draw upon a proportion of the amounts owed.

In order to determine the correct accounting treatment it is necessary to consider whether the benefit of the debts has been passed on to the factor, or whether the factor is, in effect, providing a loan on the security of the receivables balances. If the seller has to **pay interest** on the difference between the amounts advanced to him and the amounts that the factor has received, and if the seller bears the **risks of non-payment** by the receivable, then the indications would be that the transaction is, in effect, a loan. Depending on the circumstances, either a linked presentation or separate presentation may be appropriate.

6.3.1 Summary of indications of appropriate treatment

The following is a summary of indicators of the appropriate treatment.

Indications the debts are *not an asset* of the seller	Indications that the debts are an *asset* of the seller
Transfer is for a single non-returnable fixed sum.	Finance cost varies with speed of collection of debts, e.g. By adjustment to consideration for original transfer; or Subsequent transfers priced to recover costs of earlier transfers.
There is no recourse to the seller for losses.	There is full recourse to the seller for losses.
Factor is paid all amounts received from the factored debts (and no more). Seller has no rights to further sums from the factor.	Seller is required to repay amounts received from the factor on or before a set date, regardless of timing or amounts of collections from debtors.

6.3.2 Required accounting

Where the seller has retained no significant benefits and risks relating to the receivables and has no obligation to repay amounts received from the factors, the receivables should be removed from its statement of financial position and no liability shown in respect of the proceeds received from the factor. A profit or loss should be recognised, calculated as the difference between the carrying amount of the receivables and the proceeds received.

Example

If trade receivables of £100m are sold for £98m without recourse the following accounting entries would happen.

Reduce trade receivables	£100m **(Credit)**
Increase cash flow	£ 98m **(Debit)**
Increase expenses in income statement	£ 2m **(Debit)**

Where the seller does retain significant benefits and risks, a gross asset (equivalent in amount to the gross amount of the receivables) should be shown on the statement of financial position of the seller within assets, and a corresponding liability in respect of the proceeds received from the factor should be shown within liabilities. The interest element of the factor's charges should be recognised as it accrues and included in the income statement with other interest charges. Other factoring costs should be similarly accrued and included in the income statement within the appropriate caption.

Example

If the trade receivables are sold for £100m with full recourse, the following accounting entries would happen.

Increase cash	£100m (Debit)
Increase liabilities	£100m (Credit)

6.4 Securitised assets

Securitisation is very common in the financial services industry, and the assets that are most commonly securitised are mortgages and credit card accounts, although hire purchase loans, trade receivables and even property and inventories are sometimes securitised. **Blocks of assets** are thus financed, rather than the company's general business.

The normal procedure is for the assets to be transferred by the person who held them (the originator) to a special purpose company (the issuer) in exchange for cash. The issuer will use the proceeds of an issue of debentures or loan notes to pay for the assets. The shares in the issuer are usually held by a third party so that it does not need to be consolidated. The issuer will usually have a very small share capital, and so most of the risk will be borne by the people who lent it the money through the debentures to pay for the assets. For this reason there is usually some form of insurance taken out on the assets to give some security for the lenders.

6.4.1 Summary of indications as to accounting treatment

The following is a summary of indications of the appropriate treatment.

Indications that the securitised assets are *not assets* of the originator	Indications that the securitised assets are *assets* of the originator
Originator's individual financial statements	
Transaction price is arm's length price for an outright sale.	Transaction price is not arm's length price for an outright sale.
Transfer is for a single, non-returnable fixed sum.	Proceeds received are returnable, or there is a provision whereby the originator may keep the securitised assets on repayment of the loan notes or re-acquire them.
There is no recourse to the originator for losses.	There is or may be full recourse to the originator for losses, e.g. Originator's directors are unable or unwilling to state that it is not obliged to fund any losses. Noteholders have not agreed in writing that they will seek repayment only from funds generated by the securitised assets.

Indications that the securitised assets are *not* assets of the originator	Indications that the securitised assets are *assets* of the originator
Originator's consolidated financial statements	
Issuer is owned by an independent third party that made a substantial capital investment, has control of the issuer, and has the benefits and risks of its net assets.	Issuer is a subsidiary or quasi-subsidiary of the originator.

6.4.2 Required accounting: originator's financial statements

Where the originator has retained no significant benefits and risks relating to the securitised assets and has no obligation to repay the proceeds of the note issue, the asset should be removed from its statement of financial position, and no liability shown in respect of the proceeds of the note issue. A profit or loss should be recognised, calculated as the difference between the carrying amount of the assets and the proceeds received.

Where the originator has retained significant benefits and risks, a gross asset (equal in amount to the gross amount of the securitised assets) should be shown on the statement of financial position of the originator within assets, and a corresponding liability in respect of the proceeds of the note issue shown within liabilities. No gain or loss should be recognised at the time the securitisation is entered into (unless adjustment to the carrying value of the asset independent of the securitisation is required).

6.4.3 Required accounting: issuer's financial statements

The requirements set out in the paragraphs above for the originator's individual financial statements also apply to the issuer's financial statements. In most cases the issuer will be required to show the gross amounts, as explained above.

6.5 Loan transfers

These are arrangements where a loan is transferred to a transferee from an original lender. This will usually be done by the **assignment of rights and obligations** by the lender, or the **creation of a new agreement** between the borrower and the transferee. The same principles apply to loan transfers as to debt factoring and securitised assets.

6.5.1 Summary of indications of appropriate treatment

The indications may be summarised as follows.

Indications that the loan is *off* the lender's statement of financial position	Indications that the loan is *on* the lender's statement of financial position
Transfer is for a single, non-returnable fixed sum.	The proceeds received are returnable in the event of losses occurring on the loans.
There is no recourse to the lender for losses from any cause.	There is full recourse to the lender for losses.
Transferee is paid all amounts received from the loans (and no more), as and when received. Lender has no rights to further sums from the loans or the transferee.	Lender is required to repay amounts received from the transferee on or before a set date, regardless of the timing or amount of payments by the borrowers.

6.5.2 Required accounting

Where the lender has retained no significant benefits and risks relating to the loans and has no obligation to repay the transferee, the loans should be removed from its statement of financial position and no liability shown in respect of the amounts received from the transferee. A profit or loss may arise for the lender. Where the profit or loss is realised in cash it should be recognised, calculated as the difference between the carrying amount of the loans and the cash proceeds received. Where, however, the lender's profit or loss is not realised in cash and there are doubts as to its amount, full provision should be made for any expected loss but recognition of any gain, to the extent it is in doubt, should be deferred until cash has been received.

Where the lender has retained significant rights and benefits, a gross asset (equivalent in amount to the gross amount of the loans) should be shown on the statement of financial position of the lender within assets, and a corresponding liability in respect of the amounts received from the transferee should be shown within liabilities. No gain or loss should be recognised at the time of the transfer (unless adjustment to the carrying value of the loan independent of the transfer is required).

CHAPTER ROUNDUP

You need to be familiar with, able to describe and perform basic calculations in respect of

- IAS 17 *Leases*

    - **Lease**. An agreement whereby the lessor conveys to the lessee in return for a payment or series of payments the right to use an asset for an agreed period of time.

    - **Finance lease**. A lease that transfers substantially all the risks and rewards incidental to ownership of an asset. Title may or may not eventually be transferred.

    - **Operating lease**. A lease other than a finance lease.   *(IAS 17)*

    - To expand on the definition above, a finance lease should be presumed if at the inception of a lease the **present value of the minimum lease payments** is approximately equal to the **fair value of the leased asset**.

    - The present value should be calculated by using the **interest rate implicit in the lease**.

    - **Minimum lease payments**. The payments over the lease term that the lessee is or can be required to make, excluding contingent rent, costs for services and taxes to be paid by and be reimbursed to the lessor, together with

        - For a lessee, any amounts guaranteed by the lessee or by a party related to the lessee.

        - For a lessor, any residual value guaranteed to the lessor by one of the following.

            - The lessee.

            - A party related to the lessee.

            - An independent third party financially capable of meeting this guarantee.

        However, if the lessee has the option to purchase the asset at a price which is expected to be sufficiently lower than fair value at the date the option becomes exercisable for it to be reasonably certain, at the inception of the lease, that the option will be exercised, the minimum lease payments comprise the minimum payments payable over the lease term to the expected date of exercise of this purchase option and the payment required to exercise it.

    - **Interest rate implicit in the lease**

        The discount rate that, at the inception of the lease, causes the aggregate present value of

        - The minimum lease payments; and

        - The unguaranteed residual value

        to be equal to the sum of

        - The fair value of the leased asset; and

        - Any initial direct costs of the lessor.

- Off-statement of financial position finance treatment

    - Consignment inventory
    - Sale and repurchase agreement
    - Debt factoring
    - Asset securitisation

- Substance over form

    - **Substance over form**. The principle that transactions and other events are accounted for and presented in accordance with their substance and economic reality and not merely their legal form.

        (Framework)

- Definitions

    - An **asset** is a resource controlled by the entity as a result of past events and from which future economic benefits are expected to flow to the entity.

    - A **liability** is a present obligation of the entity arising from past events, the settlement of which is expected to result in an outflow from the entity of resources embodying economic benefits.

        (Framework)

    - **Income** is increases in economic benefits during the accounting period in the form of inflows or enhancements of assets or decreases of liabilities that result in increases in equity, other than those relating to contributions from equity participants.

    - **Expenses** are decreases in economic benefits during the accounting period in the form of outflows or depletions of assets or incurrences of liabilities that result in decreases in equity, other than those relating to distributions to equity participants. *(Framework)*

TEST YOUR KNOWLEDGE

Check your knowledge of the Chapter here, without referring back to the text.

1   Lease calculations

(a)   Jimbob Limited leased an asset on a three-year lease, agreeing to make annual payments in arrears of £100,000. The lease commenced on April 1 2007 and payments are due on March 31 each year thereafter. The interest rate implicit in the lease is 15% and the asset could have been bought on April 1 2007 for £230,000.

Requirement

Calculate the depreciation charge and finance cost to be shown in the income statement for the year ended March 31 2008 and the non-current asset and leasing liability to be shown in the statement of financial position as at that date.

(b)   Bimble Limited took out a four-year lease on an asset on July 1 2007, making a down payment of £50,000 and agreeing to make four subsequent instalments on June 30 each year. The lease expires on June 30 2011. The asset could have been purchased on July 1 2007 for £200,000. The interest rate implicit in the lease is 12%.

Requirement

What depreciation charge and finance cost will be shown in the income statement for the year ended June 30 2008?

2.   Operafin Ltd

Extracts from Operafin Limited's accounts for the year ended December 31 2007 are as follows.

	(£)
Revenue	**5,000,000**
Operating costs	(3,000,000)
Operating profit	**2,000,000**
Finance costs	(500,000)
Profit before taxation	**1,500,000**

Included in the above figure is a rental payment on a 30-year lease for leasehold buildings of £380,000 taken out on January 2 2007. The lease terms are that rentals of £380,000 should be paid annually in arrears for the whole of the lease term. The leasehold could have been purchased at a cost on that date of £3.5m. The company's accountant has been advised that in fact the lease should have been treated as a finance lease with an implicit cost of 10% per annum.

Requirements

Restate the accounts to reflect the implications of the finance lease treatment both for the statement of financial position and the income statement.

3.   Hire purchase

On 1 January 20X7, Cuthbert bought a machine costing £20,000 on hire purchase. He paid a deposit of £6,000 on 1 January 20X7 and he also agreed to pay two annual instalments of £5,828 on 31 December in each year, and a final instalment of £5,831 on 31 December 20X9.

The implied rate of interest in the agreement was 12%. This rate of interest is to be applied to the amount outstanding in the hire purchase loan account at the beginning of the year.

The machine is to be depreciated on a straight-line basis over five years on the assumption that it will have no residual value at the end of that time.

Requirements

(a)   Write up the hire purchase loan account for each of the three years to 31 December 20X7, 20X8 and 20X9.

(b)   Show the statement of financial position extracts for the year as at 31 December 20X7, 20X8 and 20X9 respectively for the following items.

(i)   Machine at cost.

(ii)   Accumulated depreciation on the machine.

(iii)   Non-current liabilities: obligations under hire purchase contract.

(iv)   Current liabilities: obligations under hire purchase contract.

TEST YOUR KNOWLEDGE: ANSWERS

1. Lease calculations

    (a)   Statement of financial position

		(£)
Non-current asset	– cost	230,000
	– depreciation (230 × 1/3)	(76,667)
	– net book value	153,333
Loan	– balance at April 1 2007	230,000
	– interest for year at 15%	34,500
	– repayment	(100,000)
Loan balance disclosed in the year-end statement of financial position –		164,500
obligations under finance leases		

    Income statement

Depreciation	(76,667)
Finance charge on finance leases	(34,500)

    (b)   Depreciation charge

Cost	£200,000
Useful life	4 years
Annual depreciation	£50,000

    Finance charge

Cost of asset	200,000
Less: Down payment made	(50,000)
Loan balance as at July 1 2007	150,000
Interest at 12% for the year ended June 30 2008	18,000

2.   Operafin Limited

Statement of financial position

There is currently nothing on the statement of financial position. The non-current asset and obligations under finance leases must be shown.

	(£)	(£)
Non-current asset		
Cost		3,500,000
Depreciation (3,500,000 × 1/30)		(116,667)
Net book value shown in the statement of financial position		
as part of non-current assets		3,383,333
Obligations under finance leases		
Balance at January 2 2007	(3,500,000)	
Annual interest @ 10%	(350,000)	
Repayment made during the year	380,000	
Obligation shown in the statement of financial position as part of liabilities		(3,470,000)
Alteration to net assets due to inclusion of asset and liability		(86,667)

Income Statement

		(£)
Revenue		5,000,000
Operating costs		
As previously stated	(3,000,000)	
Add back to profit: lease rental payment	380,000	
Deduct from profit: depreciation on the leased asset	(116,667)	
		(2,736,667)
Operating profit		2,263,333
Finance costs		
As previously stated	(500,000)	
Deduct from profit: finance charges on lease	(350,000)	
		(850,000)
Restated profit before taxation		1,413,333

3.   Hire purchase

    (a)

	(£)
Cost	20,000
Less: Deposit	(6,000)
Amount outstanding at beginning of 20X7	14,000
Interest for 20X7 (£14,000 × 12%)	1,680
Less: Annual instalment at 31.12.20X7	(5,828)
Balance at 01.01.20X8	9,852
Interest for 20X8 (£9,852 × 12%)	1,182
Less: Annual instalment at 31.12.20X8	(5,828)
Balance at 01.01.20X9	5,206
Interest for 20X9 (£5,206 × 12%)	625
Less: Annual instalment	(5,831)
	NIL

(b)   **Extracts from statement of financial position at 31 December**

	20X7	20X8	20X9
Non-current assets			
Cost	20,000	20,000	20,000
Less: Accumulated depreciation	(4,000)	(8,000)	(12,000)
	16,000	12,000	8,000
Current liabilities			
Obligations under hire purchase contract (see Working)	(4,646)	(5,206)	–
Non-current liabilities	(5,206)	–	–

Working

	(£)
Total liability at 01.01.20X8 [from (a) above]	9,852
Less: Non-current liability (i.e. balance at 01.01.20X9)	(5,206)
Current liability	4,646

13

Employment Costs

INTRODUCTION

Typically, one of the biggest costs a business faces are employment costs. This covers both wages and salaries and benefits such as pensions and healthcare plans.

The accounting treatment for many of these costs is fairly logical and straight forward, however the treatment of pensions is a more difficult area. The ability of a company to service its pension obligations must never be overlooked and we examine in this section how these should be accounted for. We also consider the treatment of share-based payments.

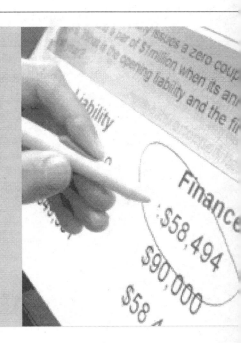

CHAPTER CONTENTS

BPP LEARNING MEDIA

CHAPTER LEARNING OBJECTIVES

The syllabus areas covered by this section are

Interpretation of Financial Information

The effect of accounting practices

Understanding of the effect of accounting practices on the numbers most significant for investment decisions (profit, earnings per share, asset value etc).

Accounting Terminology and Concepts

Accounting terminology and a knowledge of accounting concepts and conventions to include the statement of financial position, income statement, statement of cash flows and notes to the accounts. An understanding of the distinction between capital and revenue, the valuation of assets for accounting purposes and the determination of profit and earnings share on the nil, net and full distribution bases. An understanding of significance of the statement of accounting policies in relation to the concept of a true and fair view.

Presentation of Financial Statements

Impact of statutory and non-statutory regulation on UK financial statements.

An understanding of the effect on the presentation of financial statements of the Companies Act and non-statutory regulations, including standards and other guidance issued by IASB and stock exchange requirements.

In the respect of employment costs:

It is emphasised that the intention of the examination is to assess student's analytical and interpretative skills rather than their technical accounting ability. It is also expected that they should have an understanding of standard accounting practices and an awareness of matters currently under discussion.

1 IAS 19 EMPLOYEE BENEFITS

1.1 Introduction

IAS 19 (revised) *Employee Benefits* covers **all employee benefit costs**, except share-based payment, which are dealt with in IFRS 2. Before we look at IAS 19, we should consider the nature of employee benefit costs and why there is an accounting problem which must be addressed by a Standard.

1.2 The conceptual nature of employee benefit costs

When a company or other entity employs a new worker, that worker will be offered a **package of pay and benefits.** Some of these will be short-term and the employee will receive the benefit at about the same time as he or she earns it, for example basic pay, overtime etc. Other employee benefits are **deferred**, the main example being retirement benefits (i.e. a pension).

The cost of these deferred employee benefits to the employer can be viewed in various ways. They could be described as **deferred salary** to the employee. Alternatively, they are a **deduction** from the employee's true gross salary, used as a tax-efficient means of saving.

1.3 Accounting for employee benefit costs

Accounting for **short-term employee benefit costs**, such as salary, tends to be quite straightforward, because they are simply recognised as an expense in the employer's financial statements of the current period.

Accounting for the cost of **deferred employee benefits** is much more difficult. This is because of the large amounts involved, as well as the long time scale, complicated estimates and uncertainties. In the past, entities accounted for these benefits simply by charging the income statements of the employing entity on the basis of actual payments made. This led to substantial variations in reported profits of these entities and disclosure of information on these costs was usually sparse.

1.4 IAS 19 Employee Benefits

IAS 19 is intended to prescribe the following.

- When the cost of employee benefits should be **recognised as a liability or an expense**.
- The **amount** of the liability or expense that should be recognised.

As a basic rule, the Standard states the following.

- A **liability** should be recognised when an employee has provided a service in exchange for benefits to be received by the employee at some time in the future.

- An **expense** should be recognised when the entity enjoys the economic benefits from a service provided by an employee regardless of when the employee received or will receive the benefits from providing the service.

The basic problem is therefore fairly straightforward. An entity will often enjoy the **economic benefits** from the services provided by its employees in advance of the employees receiving all the employment benefits from the work they have done, for example they will not receive pension benefits until after they retire.

1.5 Categories of employee benefits

The Standard recognises four categories of employee benefits, and proposes a different accounting treatment for each. These four categories are as follows.

1. **Short-term benefits** including

    –   Wages and salaries.
    –   Social security contributions.
    –   Paid annual leave.
    –   Paid sick leave.
    –   Paid maternity/paternity leave.
    –   Profit shares and bonuses paid within 12 months of the year end.
    –   Paid jury service.
    –   Paid military service.
    –   Non-monetary benefits, medical care, cars, free goods.

2. **Post-employment benefits**, e.g. pensions and post-employment medical care.

3. **Other long-term benefits**, e.g. profit shares, bonuses or deferred compensation payable later than 12 months after the year end, sabbatical leave, long-service benefits.

4. **Termination benefits**, e.g. early retirement payments and redundancy payments.

Benefits may be paid to the employees themselves, to their dependants (spouses, children, etc) or to third parties.

1.6 Definitions

IAS 19 uses many definitions. They are grouped together here, but you should refer back to them as necessary as you work through the rest of this chapter.

Employee benefits are all forms of consideration given by an entity in exchange for service rendered by employees.

Short-term employee benefits are employee benefits (other than termination benefits) which fall due wholly within 12 months after the end of the period in which the employees render the related service.

Post-employment benefits are employee benefits (other than termination benefits) which are payable after the completion of employment.

Post-employment benefit plans are formal or informal arrangements under which an entity provides post-employment benefits for one or more employees.

Defined contribution plans are post-employment benefit plans under which an entity pays fixed contributions into a separate entity (a fund) and will have no legal or constructive obligation to pay further contributions if the fund does not hold sufficient assets to pay all employee benefits relating to employee service in the current and prior periods.

Defined benefit plans are post-employment benefit plans other than defined contribution plans.

Multi-employer plans are defined contribution plans (other than state plans) or defined benefit plans (other than state plans) that

- Pool the assets contributed by various entities that are not under common control.

- Use those assets to provide benefits to employees of more than one entity, on the basis that contribution and benefit levels are determined without regard to the identity of the entity that employs the employees concerned.

Other long-term employee benefits are employee benefits (other than post-employment benefits and termination benefits) which do not fall due wholly within 12 months after the end of the period in which the employees render the related service.

Termination benefits are employee benefits payable as a result of either

- An entity's decision to terminate an employee's employment before the normal retirement date; or
- An employee's decision to accept voluntary redundancy in exchange for those benefits.

Vested employee benefits are employee benefits that are not conditional on future employment.

The **present value of a defined benefit** obligation is the present value, without deducting any plan assets, of expected future payments required to settle the obligation resulting from employee service in the current and prior periods.

Current service cost is the increase in the present value of the defined benefit obligation resulting from employee service in the current period.

Interest cost is the increase during a period in the present value of a defined benefit obligation which arises because the benefits are one period closer to settlement.

Plan assets comprise

- Assets held by a long-term employee benefit fund.
- Qualifying insurance policies.

Assets held by a long-term employee benefit fund are assets (other than non-transferable financial instruments issued by the reporting entity) that

- Are held by an entity (a fund) that is legally separate from the reporting entity and exists solely to pay or fund employee benefits.

- Are available to be used only to pay or fund employee benefits, are not available to the reporting entity's own creditors (even in bankruptcy), and cannot be returned to the reporting entity, unless either

    - The remaining assets of the fund are sufficient to meet all the related employee benefit obligations of the plan or the reporting entity; or

    - The assets are returned to the reporting entity to reimburse it for employee benefits already paid.

The **return on plan assets** is interest, dividends and other revenue derived from the plan assets, together with realised and unrealised gains or losses on the plan assets, less any cost of administering the plan and less any tax payable by the plan itself.

Actuarial gains and losses comprise

- Experience adjustments (the effects of differences between the previous actuarial assumptions and what has actually occurred), and

- The effects of changes in actuarial assumptions.

Past service cost is the increase in the present value of the defined benefit obligation for employee service in prior periods, resulting in the current period from the introduction of, or changes to, post-employment benefits or other long-term employee benefits. Past service cost may be either positive (where benefits are introduced or improved) or negative (where existing benefits are reduced).

(IAS 19)

2 SHORT-TERM EMPLOYEE BENEFITS

2.1 Recognition and measurement

Accounting for short-term employee benefits is fairly straightforward, because there are **no actuarial assumptions** to be made, and there is **no requirement to discount** future benefits (because they are all, by definition, payable no later than 12 months after the end of the accounting period and consequently the effect of the time value of money is insignificant).

The rules for short-term benefits are essentially an application of **basic accounting principles and practice**.

- **Unpaid short-term employee benefits** as at the end of an accounting period should be recognised as an accrued expense. Any short-term benefits **paid in advance** should be recognised as a prepayment (to the extent that it will lead to, e.g. a reduction in future payments or a cash refund).

- The **cost of short-term employee benefits** should be recognised as an **expense** in the period when the economic benefit is given, as employment costs (except insofar as employment costs may be included within the cost of an asset, e.g. property, plant and equipment and consequently the effect of the time value of money is insignificant).

When a short-term employee benefit is paid the double entry is

– DEBIT: Retained earnings (expenses)
– CREDIT: Cash

If a short-term employee benefit is owed at the year end an accrual needs to be set up.

– DEBIT: Retained earnings
– CREDIT: Current liabilities (accruals)

2.2 Profit sharing or bonus plans

Profit shares or bonuses payable within 12 months after the end of the accounting period should be recognised as an expected cost when the entity has a **present obligation to pay it**, i.e. when the employer has no real option but to pay it. This will usually be when the employer recognises the profit or other performance achievement to which the profit share or bonus relates.

3 POST-EMPLOYMENT BENEFITS

3.1 Introduction

Many employers provide post-employment benefits for their employees after they have stopped working. **Pension schemes** are the most obvious example, but an employer might provide post-employment death benefits to the dependants of former employees, or post-employment medical care.

3.2 Types of post-employment benefit schemes

Post-employment benefit schemes are often referred to as '**plans**'. The 'plan' receives regular contributions from the employer (and sometimes from current employees as well) and the money is invested in assets, such as stocks and shares and other investments. The post-employment benefits are paid out of the income from the plan assets (dividends, interest) or from money from the sale of some plan assets.

There are two types or categories of post-employment benefit plan, as given in the definitions in Section 1.6 above.

- **Defined contribution plans**. With such plans, the employer (and possibly current employees too) pay regular contributions into the plan of a given or 'defined' amount each year. The contributions are invested, and the size of the post-employment benefits paid to former employees depends on how well or how badly the plan's investments perform. If the investments perform well, the plan will be able to afford higher benefits than if the investments performed less well.

- **Defined benefit plans**. With these plans, the size of the post-employment benefits is determined in advance, i.e. the benefits are 'defined'. The employer (and possibly current employees too) pay contributions into the plan, and the contributions are invested. The size of the contributions is set at an amount that is expected to earn enough investment returns to meet the obligation to pay the post-employment benefits. If, however, it becomes apparent that the assets in the fund are insufficient, the employer will be required to make additional contributions into the plan to make up the expected shortfall. On the other hand, if the fund's assets appear to be larger than they need to be, and in excess of what is required to pay the post-employment benefits, the employer may be allowed to take a 'contribution holiday' (i.e. stop paying in contributions for a while).

It is important to make a clear distinction between the following.

- **Funding** a defined benefit plan, i.e. paying contributions into the plan.
- **Accounting for** the cost of funding a defined benefit plan.

4 DEFINED CONTRIBUTION PLANS

4.1 Accounting

Accounting for payments into defined contribution plans is straightforward.

- The **obligation** is determined by the amount paid into the plan in each period.

- There are no actuarial assumptions to make.

- If the obligation to pay contributions is settled in the current period (or at least no later than 12 months after the end of the current period) there is **no requirement for discounting**.

4.2 IAS 19 requirements

IAS 19 requires the following.

- **Contributions** to a defined contribution plan should be recognised as an **expense** in the period they are payable (except to the extent that labour costs may be included within the cost of assets).

- Any liability for **unpaid contributions** that are due as at the end of the period should be recognised as a **liability** (accrued expense).

- Any **excess contributions** paid should be recognised as an asset (prepaid expense), but only to the extent that the prepayment will lead to, e.g. a reduction in future payments or a cash refund.

4.3 Disclosure requirements

- A **description** of the plan.
- The amount recognised as an **expense** in the period.

5 DEFINED BENEFIT PLANS

Exam tip

> Defined benefit schemes represent the most frequently examined area of employment costs and may arise in any section, e.g. Winter 2004 Question 2, Summer 2003 Question 3, Winter 2001 Question 6.

5.1 Accounting problems

Accounting for defined benefit plans is much more complex. The complexity of accounting for defined benefit plans stems largely from the following factors.

- The future benefits (arising from employee service in the current or prior years) **cannot be estimated exactly**, but whatever they are, the employer will have to pay them, and the liability should therefore be recognised now. To estimate these future obligations, it is necessary to use **actuarial assumptions**.

- The obligations payable in future years should be valued, by discounting, on a **present value** basis. This is because the obligations may be settled in many years' time.

- If actuarial assumptions change, the amount of required contributions to the fund will change, and there may be **actuarial gains or losses**. A contribution into a fund in any period is not necessarily the total for that period, due to actuarial gains or losses.

5.2 Outline of the method

An outline of the method used for an employer to account for the expenses and obligation of a defined benefit plan is given below. The stages will be explained in more detail later.

Step 1   **Actuarial assumptions** should be used to make a reliable estimate of the amount of future benefits employees have earned from service in relation to the current and prior years. Assumptions include, for example, assumptions about employee turnover, mortality rates, future increases in salaries (if these will affect the eventual size of future benefits such as pension payments).

Step 2   These **future benefits** should be attributed to service performed by employees in the current period, and in prior periods, using the **Projected Unit Credit Method**. This gives a total present value of future benefit obligations arising from past and current periods of service.

Step 3   The **fair value** of any plan assets should be established.

Step 4   The size of any **actuarial gains or losses** should be determined, and the amount of these that will be recognised.

Step 5   If the benefits payable under the plan have been improved, the **extra cost arising from past service** should be determined.

Step 6   If the **benefits payable** under the plan have been reduced or cancelled, the resulting gain should be determined.

5.3 The projected unit credit method

With this method, it is assumed that each period of service by an employee gives rise to an **additional unit of future benefits**. The present value of that unit of future benefits can be calculated, and attributed to the period in which the service is given. The units, each measured separately, build up to the overall obligation. The accumulated present value of (discounted) future benefits will incur interest over time, and an interest expense should be recognised.

5.4 Interest cost

The interest cost in the income statement is the **present value of the defined benefit obligation** as at the start of the year multiplied by the discount rate.

Note that the interest charge is *not* the opening statement of financial position liability multiplied by the discount rate, because the liability is stated after deducting the market value of the plan assets and after making certain other adjustments, for example for actuarial gains or losses. Interest is the **obligation** multiplied by the discount rate.

5.5 The statement of financial position

In the statement of financial position, the amount recognised as a **defined benefit liability** (which may be a negative amount, i.e. an asset) should be the total of the following.

- The present value of the defined obligation at the statement of financial position date; plus

- Any actuarial gains or minus any actuarial losses that have not yet been recognised; minus

- Any past service cost not yet recognised (if any); minus

- The fair value of the assets of the plan as at the statement of financial position date (if there are any) out of which the future obligations to current and past employees will be directly settled.

If this total is a **negative amount**, there is a statement of financial position asset and this should be shown in the statement of financial position as the **lower** of (a) and (b) below.

(a)   The figure as calculated above.

(b)   The total of the present values of

- Any unrecognised actuarial losses and past service costs.
- Any refunds expected from the plan.
- Any reductions in future contributions to the plan because of the surplus.

5.6 The income statement

The **expense** that should be recognised in the income statement for post-employment benefits in a defined benefit plan is the total of the following.

- The **current service cost**.
- **Interest**.
- The **expected return on any plan assets**.
- The actuarial gains or losses, to the extent that they are recognised.
- **Past service cost** to the extent that it is recognised.
- The effect of any **curtailments** or **settlements**.

5.7 Actuarial assumptions

Actuarial assumptions are needed **to estimate the size of the future (post-employment) benefits** that will be payable under a defined benefit scheme. The main categories of actuarial assumptions are as follows.

- **Demographic assumptions** are about mortality rates before and after retirement, the rate of employee turnover, early retirement, claim rates under medical plans for former employees, and so on.

- **Financial assumptions** are the discount rate to apply, the expected return on plan assets, future salary levels (allowing for seniority and promotion as well as inflation) and the future rate of increase in medical costs (not just inflationary cost rises, but also cost rises specific to medical treatments and to medical treatments required given the expectations of longer average life expectancy).

5.8 Actuarial gains or losses

Actuarial gains or losses arise because of the following.

- **Actual events** (e.g. employee turnover, salary increases) differ from the actuarial assumptions that were made to estimate the defined benefit obligations.

- **Actuarial assumptions are revised** (e.g. a different discount rate is used, or a different assumption is made about future employee turnover, salary rises, mortality rates, and so on)

- **Actual returns on plan assets** differ from expected returns

Since actuarial assumptions are rarely going to be exact, some actuarial gains or losses are inevitable. The standard suggests that, given the inevitability of actuarial gains or losses, they **need not be recognised unless they appear 'significant'**. They are not sufficient to warrant recognition if they fall within a tolerable range or 'corridor'.

The Standard requires the following.

- An entity should, as a **general rule**, recognise actuarial gains and losses as an item of income or expense (income statement), and as part of the deferred benefit liability (statement of financial position).

- However, only a portion of such actuarial gains or losses (as calculated above) should be recognised if the **net cumulative actuarial gains/losses exceed** the greater of

  - 10% of the present value of the defined benefit obligation (ie before deducting plan assets); and

  - 10% of the fair value of the plan assets.

The excess calculated under above should be **divided by the expected average remaining working lives of participating employees** and this gives the portion of actuarial gains and losses to be recognised.

IAS 19 allows, however, any systematic method to be adopted if it results in **faster recognition** of actuarial gains and losses. The same basis must be applied to both gains and losses and applied consistently between periods.

5.9 Immediate recognition – amendment to IAS 19

In December 2004, the IASB issued an amendment to IAS 19. This allows an entity to **recognise actuarial gains and losses immediately** in the period in which it arises, outside profit and loss. These gains and losses need to be presented in the **statement of recognised income and expense**. This statement would be compulsory for entities recognising actuarial gains and losses in reserves. If the entity adopts this approach, it must do so

- For all of its defined benefits plans.
- For all of its actuarial gains and losses.

This makes IAS 19 more convergent with the UK Standard, FRS 17. Most UK companies have adopted this approach.

In addition, the amendment requires **improved disclosures**, including many also required by FRS 17, and slightly eases the methods whereby the amounts recognised in the consolidated financial statements have to be allocated to individual group companies for the purposes of their own reporting under IFRSs.

5.10 Past service cost

A past service cost arises when an entity either introduces a defined benefits plan or **improves the benefits payable** under an existing plan. As a result, the entity has taken on additional obligations that it has not hitherto provided for. For example, an employer might decide to introduce a medical benefits scheme for former employees. This will create a new defined benefit obligation, that has not yet been provided for. How should this obligation be accounted for?

A past service cost may be in respect of either **current employees or past employees**. IAS 19 has introduced a different accounting treatment for past service costs, according to whether they relate to **current employees or past employees**.

- For **current employees**, the past service cost should be recognised as part of the defined benefit liability in the statement of financial position. For the income statement, the past service cost should be amortised on a straight-line basis over the average period until the benefits become vested.

- For **past employees** (if the change affects them) the past service cost should be recognised in full immediately the plan is introduced or improved (i.e. because they are immediately 'vested'), as part of the defined benefit liability and as an expense (in full) to the financial period.

Example

Watkins Co operates a pension plan that provides a pension of 2% of final salary for every year of service and the benefits become vested after five years' service. On 1 January 20X6 Watkins Co improved the pension to 2.5% of final salary for every year of service starting from 1 January 20X2.

At the date of improvement, the present value of the additional benefits for service from 1 January 20X2 to 1 January 20X6 is as follows.

	(£m)
Employees with more than 5 years' service at 1/11/20X6	300
Employees with less than 5 years' service at 1/11/20X6	
(average period until vesting = 3 years)	240
	540

Requirement

State the correct accounting treatment for past service costs.

Solution

Watkins Co should recognise £300m immediately, because these benefits are already vested. £240m should be recognised on a straight-line basis over three years from 1 January 20X6.

5.11 Plan assets

The contributions paid into a plan by the employer (and employees) are invested, and the plan builds up assets in the form of stocks and shares, etc. The **fair value of these plan assets** are deducted from the defined benefits obligation, in calculating the statement of financial position liability. This makes sense, because the employer is not liable to the defined benefits scheme to the extent that the assets of the fund are sufficient to meet those obligations.

5.12 Return on plan assets

It is also necessary to recognise the distinction between:

- The **expected return** on the plan assets, which is an actuarial assumption; and
- The **actual return** made by the plan assets in a financial period.

The **expected return** on the plan assets is a component element in the income statement, not the actual returns. The **difference between the expected return and the actual return** may also be included in the income statement, but within the actuarial gains or losses. This difference must only be recognised if the actuarial gains or losses are outside the 10% corridor for these gains or losses, otherwise they will not be included in the expense item because they are not regarded as significant.

Example

At 1 January 2007 the fair value of the assets of a defined benefit plan were valued at £1m. Net cumulative actuarial gains and losses were £76,000.

On 31 December 2007, the plan received contributions from the employer of £490,000 and paid out benefits of £190,000.

After these transactions, the fair value of the plan's assets at 31 December 2007 were £1.5m. The present value of the defined benefit obligation was £1,479,200 and actuarial losses on the obligation for 2007 were £6,000.

The expected return on the plan assets (net of investment transaction costs) is 8% per annum.

The reporting entity made the following estimates at 1 January 2007, based on market prices at that date.

	(%)
Dividend/interest income (after tax payable by fund)	9.25
Realised and unrealised gains (after tax) on plan assets	2.00
Administration costs	(1.00)
	10.25

Requirement

Calculate the expected and actual return on plan assets, calculate any actuarial gain or loss and state the required accounting.

Solution

The expected and actual return for 2007 are as follows.

	(£)
Return on £1m held for 12 months at 10.25%	102,500
Return on net contributions £(490,000 – 190,000) = £300,000 for 6 months at 5% (i.e. 10.25% annually compounded every 6 months)	15,000
Expected return on plan assets	117,500

	(£)
Fair value of plan assets at 31/12/2007	1,500,000
Less fair value of plan assets at 1/1/2007	(1,000,000)
Less contributions received	(490,000)
Add benefits paid	190,000
Actual return on plan assets	200,000

Actuarial gain = (200,000 – 117,500) = £82,500.

∴ Cumulative net unrecognised actuarial gains = (76,000 + 82,500 – 6,000) = £152,500.

The limits of the corridor are set at the greater of

- 10% × £1,500,000 = £150,000; and
- 10% × £1,479,200 = £147,920.

In 2007 the entity should recognise an actuarial gain of (152,500 – 150,000) = £2,500, divided by the expected average remaining working life of the relevant employees.

For 2007, the expected return on plan assets will be based on market expectations at 1/1/2007 for returns over the entire life of the obligation.

The following accounting treatment is required.

- In the **income statement**, an expected return on fund assets of £117,500 will be recognised, together with an actuarial gain of £2,500 divided by the expected average remaining useful life of the employees.

- In the **statement of financial position**, the defined benefit liability will adjust the defined benefit obligation as at
31 December 2007. The unrecognised actuarial gain (i.e. the gain within the 10% corridor) should be added, and the market value of the plan assets as at that date should be subtracted.

Alternatively the actuarial gain of £152,500 could be recognised in the statement of recognised income and expense.

5.13 Presentation and disclosure

The Standard states that an entity **should not offset** an asset relating to one plan against a liability relating to a different plan, unless the entity has a legally enforceable right of offset and intends to use it.

A reporting entity should disclose the following information about post-retirement defined benefit plans.

- **Accounting policy** for recognising actuarial gains and losses.
- **General description** of the type of plan.
- **Reconciliation** of the assets and liabilities recognised in the statement of financial position, showing the following as a minimum.
    - Present value at the statement of financial position date of defined benefit obligations that are wholly unfunded.
    - Present value (before deducting the fair value of plan assets) at the statement of financial position date of defined benefit obligations that are wholly or partly funded.
    - Fair value of any plan assets at the statement of financial position date.
    - Net actuarial gains or losses not recognised in the statement of financial position.

- Past service cost not yet recognised in the statement of financial position.

- Any amount not recognised as an asset, because of the limit.

- Amounts recognised in the statement of financial position.

■ Amounts included in the **fair value** of plan assets for

- Each category of the reporting entity's own financial instruments; and

- Any property occupied by, or other assets used by, the reporting entity:

■ Reconciliation showing the movements during the period in the net liability (or asset) recognised in the **statement of financial position**.

■ Total expense recognised in the **income statement** for each of the following, and the line item(s) of the income statement in which they are included.

- Current service cost.
- Interest cost.
- Expected return on plan assets.
- Actuarial gains and losses.
- Past service cost.
- Effect of any curtailment or settlement.

■ Actual return on plan assets.

■ Principal actuarial assumptions used as at the statement of financial position date, including, where applicable

- Discount rates.

- Expected rates of return on any plan assets for the periods presented in the financial statements.

- Expected rates of salary increases (and of changes in an index or other variable specified in the formal or constructive terms of a plan as the basis for future benefit increases).

- Medical cost trend rates.

- Any other material actuarial assumptions used.

Disclose each actuarial assumption in **absolute terms** (e.g. as an absolute percentage) and not just as a margin between different percentages or other variables.

Example

These disclosure requirements are extensive and are illustrated below.

Roche Group
Extract from Notes to the Financial Statement, Year Ended 31 December 2004

Employee remuneration in millions of CHF	2004	2003
Wages and salaries	6,290	6,494
Social security costs	769	777
Post-employment benefits: defined benefit plans	532	469
Post-employment benefits: defined contribution plans	146	117
Other employee benefits	362	397
Total employees' remuneration	8,099	8,254

The charges for employee benefits are included in the relevant expenditure line by function. The number of employees at the year-end was 64,703 (2003: 65,357). Other employee benefits consist mainly of life insurance schemes and certain other insurance schemes providing medical cover as well as long and short-term disability benefits.

Pensions and Other Post-Employment Benefits

Most employees are covered by retirement benefit plans sponsored by Group companies. The nature of such plans varies according to legal regulations, fiscal requirements and economic conditions of the countries in which the employees are employed. The major plans are defined benefit plans, the largest of which are located in Switzerland, the United States, Germany, the United Kingdom and Japan. Other post-employment benefits consist mostly of post-retirement healthcare and life insurance schemes, principally in the United States. Plans are usually funded by payments from the Group and by employees to trusts independent of the Group's finances. Where a plan is unfunded, notably for the major defined benefit plans in Germany, a liability for the obligation is recorded in the Group's statement of financial position.

Defined benefit plans: expenses recognised in millions of CHF	2004	2003
Current service cost	331	351
Interest cost	598	584
Expected return on plan assets	(599)	(602)
Net actuarial (gains) losses recognised	175	109
Past service cost	32	4
(Gains) losses on curtailment	(5)	23
Total included in employees' remuneration	532	469

The actual return on plan assets was 848 million Swiss francs (2003: 815 million Swiss francs).

In December 2004 the Group paid an additional contribution of 150 million Swiss francs into one of its Swiss post-employment defined benefit plans. This payment is included in 'contributions paid' in the table below and is accounted for as part of the recognised surplus on funded pension plans in the Group's consolidated financial statements in 2004. Thereafter it will be included in the actuarial calculation of the Group's pension expenses and balances.

Defined benefit plans: movements in recognised net asset (liability) in millions of CHF	2004	2003
At beginning of year	(1,206)	(1,165)
Disetronic	–	(7)
Consumer health (OTC) business	20	–
Vitamins and Fine Chemicals business	–	242
Total expenses included in employee's remuneration (as above)	(532)	(469)
Contributions paid	571	340
Benefits paid (unfunded plans)	91	94
Currency translation effects and other	(111)	(241)
At end of year (as below)	(1,167)	(1,206)

Defined benefit plans: amounts recognised in statement of financial position in millions of CHF	2004	2003
Funded plans		
Actuarial present value of funded obligations due to past and present employees	(10,233)	(9,785)
Plan assets held in trust at fair value	9,922	9,490
Plan assets in excess (deficit) of actuarial present value of funded obligations	(311)	(295)
Unrecognised actuarial (gains) losses	1,752	1,459
Unrecognised past service costs	(57)	(27)
Net recognised asset (liability) for funded obligations due to past and present employees	1,384	1,191
Unfunded plans		
Actuarial present value of funded obligations due to past and present employees	(2,731)	(2,626)
Unrecognised actuarial (gains) losses	169	233
Unrecognised past service costs	11	(4)
Recognised (liability) for actuarial present value of unfounded obligations due to past and present employees	(2,551)	(2,397)
Total recognised asset (liability) for funded and unfunded obligations due to past and present employees	(1,167)	(1,206)
Reported as		
– Surplus recognised as long-term asset	1,577	1,549
– Deficit recognised as non-current liability	(2,744)	(2,755)
Total net asset (liability) recognised	(1,167)	(1,206)

6 IFRS 2 SHARE-BASED PAYMENT

Exam tip

> Share option schemes are regularly examined in all three sections, e.g. Summer 2005 Question 1, Summer 2004 Question 4, Winter 2001 Question 5.

6.1 Background

Transactions whereby entities purchase goods or services from other parties, such as suppliers and employees, by issuing shares or share options to those parties are increasingly common. Companies whose shares or share options are regarded as a valuable 'currency' commonly use share-based payment to obtain employee and professional services.

The increasing use of share-based payment has raised questions about the accounting treatment of such transactions in company financial statements.

Share options are often granted to employees at an exercise price that is equal or higher than the market price of the shares at the date the option is granted. Consequently the options have no intrinsic value and so no transaction is recorded in the financial statements. This leads to an anomaly – if a company pays its employees in cash an expense is recognised in the income statement but if the payment is in share options, no expense is recognised.

6.2 Objective and scope of IFRS 2

IFRS 2 requires an entity to **reflect the effects of share-based payment transactions** in its profit or loss and financial position.

IFRS 2 applies to all share-based payment transactions. There are three types.

- **Equity-settled share-based payment transactions**, in which the entity receives goods or services in exchange for equity instruments of the entity (including shares or share options).

- **Cash-settled share-based payment transactions**, in which the entity receives goods or services in exchange for amounts of cash that are based on the price (or value) of the entity's shares or other equity instruments of the entity.

- Transactions in which the entity receives or acquires goods or services and either the entity or the supplier has a **choice** as to whether the entity settles the transaction in cash (or other assets) or by issuing equity instruments.

Certain transactions are **outside the scope** of the IFRS.

- Transactions with employees and others in their capacity as a holder of equity instruments of the entity (for example, where an employee receives additional shares in a rights issue to all shareholders).

- The issue of equity instruments in exchange for control of another entity in a business combination.

6.3 Definitions

Share-based payment transaction. A transaction in which the entity receives goods or services as consideration for equity instruments of the entity (including shares or share options), or acquires goods or services by incurring liabilities to the supplier of those goods or services for amounts that are based on the price of the entity's shares or other equity instruments of the entity.

Share-based payment arrangement. An agreement between the entity and another party (including an employee) to enter into a share-based payment transaction, which thereby entitles the other party to receive cash or other assets of the entity for amounts that are based on the price of the entity's shares or other equity instruments of the entity, or to receive equity instruments of the entity, provided the specified vesting conditions, if any, are met.

Equity instrument. A contract that evidences a residual interest in the assets of an entity after deducting all of its liabilities.

Equity instrument granted. The right (conditional or unconditional) to an equity instrument of the entity conferred by the entity on another party, under a share-based payment arrangement.

Share option. A contract that gives the holder the right, but not the obligation, to subscribe to the entity's shares at a fixed or determinable price for a specified period of time.

Fair value. The amount for which an asset could be exchanged, a liability settled, or an equity instrument granted could be exchanged, between knowledgeable, willing parties in an arm's length transaction.

Grant date. The date at which the entity and another party (including an employee) agree to a share-based payment arrangement, being when the entity and the other party have a shared understanding of the terms and conditions of the arrangement. At grant date the entity confers on the other party (the counterparty) the right to cash, other assets, or equity instruments of the entity, provided the specified vesting conditions, if any, are met. If that agreement is subject to an approval process (for example, by shareholders), grant date is the date when that approval is obtained.

Intrinsic value. The difference between the fair value of the shares to which the counterparty has the (conditional or unconditional) right to subscribe or which it has the right to receive, and the price (if any) the other party is (or will be) required to pay for those shares. For example, a share option with an exercise price of $15 on a share with a fair value of $20, has an intrinsic value of $5.

Measurement date. The date at which the fair value of the equity instruments granted is measured. For transactions with employees and others providing similar services, the measurement date is grant date. For transactions with parties other than employees (and those providing similar services), the measurement date is the date the entity obtains the goods or the counterparty renders service.

Vest. To become an entitlement. Under a share-based payment arrangement, a counterparty's right to receive cash, other assets, or equity instruments of the entity vests upon satisfaction of any specified vesting conditions.

Vesting conditions. The conditions that must be satisfied for the counterparty to become entitled to receive cash, other assets or equity instruments of the entity, under a share-based payment arrangement. Vesting conditions include service conditions, which require the other party to complete a specified period of service, and performance conditions, which require specified performance targets to be met (such as a specified increase in the entity's profit over a specified period of time).

Vesting period. The period during which all the specified vesting conditions of a share-based payment arrangement are to be satisfied.

6.4 Recognition: the basic principle

An entity should **recognise goods or services received or acquired in a share-based payment transaction when it obtains the goods or as the services are received.** Goods or services received or acquired in a share-based payment transaction **should be recognised as expenses unless they qualify for recognition as assets**. For example, services are normally recognised as expenses (because they are normally rendered immediately), while goods are recognised as assets.

If the goods or services were received or acquired in an **equity-settled** share-based payment transaction the entity should recognise **a corresponding increase in equity** (reserves).

If the goods or services were received or acquired in a **cash-settled** share-based payment transaction the entity should recognise a **liability**.

6.5 Equity-settled share-based payment transactions

6.5.1 Measurement

The issue here is how to measure the 'cost' of the goods and services received and the equity instruments (e.g. the share options) granted in return.

The general principle in IFRS 2 is that when an entity recognises the goods or services received and the corresponding increase in equity, it should measure these at the **fair value of the goods or services received**. Where the transaction is with **parties other than employees**, there is a rebuttable presumption that the fair value of the goods or services received can be estimated reliably.

If the fair value of the goods or services received cannot be measured reliably, the entity should measure their value by reference to the **fair value of the equity instruments granted**.

Where the transaction is with a party other than an employee fair value should be measured at the date the entity obtains the goods or the counterparty renders service.

Where shares, share options or other equity instruments are granted to **employees** as part of their remuneration package, it is not normally possible to measure directly the services received. For this reason, the entity should measure the fair value of the employee services received by reference to the **fair value of the equity instruments granted**. The fair value of those equity instruments should be measured at **grant date**.

6.5.2 Determining the fair value of equity instruments granted

Where a transaction is measured by reference to the fair value of the equity instruments granted, fair value is based on **market prices** if available, taking into account the terms and conditions upon which those equity instruments were granted.

If market prices are not available, the entity should estimate the fair value of the equity instruments granted using a **valuation technique**.

6.5.3 Transactions in which services are received

The issue here is **when** to recognise the transaction. When equity instruments are granted they may vest immediately, but often the counterparty must first meet specified conditions. For example, an employee may have to complete a specified period of service. This means that the effect of the transaction normally has to be allocated over more than one accounting period.

If the equity instruments granted **vest immediately** (i.e. the counterparty is not required to complete a specified period of service before becoming unconditionally entitled to the equity instruments) it is presumed that the services have already been received (in the absence of evidence to the contrary). The entity should **recognise the services received in full**, with a corresponding increase in equity, **on the grant date**.

If the equity instruments granted do not vest until the counterparty completes a specified period of service, the entity should account for those services **as they are rendered** by the counterparty during the vesting period. For example, if an employee is granted share options on condition that he or she completes three years' service, then the services to be rendered by the employee as consideration for the share options will be received in the future, over that three-year vesting period.

The entity should recognise an amount for the goods or services received during the vesting period based on the **best available estimate** of the **number of equity instruments expected to vest**. It should **revise** that estimate if subsequent information indicates that the number of equity instruments expected to vest differs from previous estimates. On **vesting date**, the entity should revise the estimate to **equal the number of equity instruments that actually vest**.

Once the goods and services received and the corresponding increase in equity have been recognised, the entity should make no subsequent adjustment to total equity after vesting date.

6.6 Cash-settled share-based payment transactions

Examples of this type of transaction include

- **Share appreciation rights** granted to employees: the employees become entitled to a future cash payment (rather than an equity instrument), based on the increase in the entity's share price from a specified level over a specified period of time; or

- An entity might grant to its employees a right to receive a future cash payment by granting to them a **right to shares that are redeemable**.

The basic principle is that the entity measures the goods or services acquired and the liability incurred at the **fair value of the liability**.

The entity should **remeasure** the fair value of the liability **at each reporting date** until the liability is settled **and at the date of settlement**. Any **changes** in fair value are recognised in **profit or loss** for the period (i.e. the income statement).

The entity should recognise the services received, and a liability to pay for those services, **as the employees render service**. For example, if share appreciation rights do not vest until the employees have completed a specified period of service, the entity should recognise the services received and the related liability, over that period.

6.7 Disclosures

IFRS 2 requires entities to disclose information that enables users of the financial statements to understand the **nature and extent** of share-based payment **arrangements that existed during the period**.

- A **description** of each type of share-based payment arrangement that existed at any time during the period, including the general terms and conditions of each arrangement.

- The **number and weighted average exercise prices** of share options for each of the following groups of options.

    - Outstanding at the beginning of the period.
    - Granted during the period.
    - Forfeited during the period.
    - Exercised during the period.
    - Expired during the period.
    - Outstanding at the end of the period.
    - Exercisable at the end of the period.

- For share options **exercised** during the period, the **weighted average share price** at the date of exercise.

- For share options outstanding at the end of the period, the range of exercise prices and weighted average remaining contractual life.

In addition, IFRS 2 requires disclosure of information that enables users of the financial statements to **understand how the fair value** of the goods or services received, or the fair value of the equity instruments granted, during the period **was determined**.

Entities should also disclose information that enables users of the financial statements to understand the effect of share-based payment transactions on the entity's **profit or loss for the period** and on its **financial position**.

- The **total expense recognised for the period** arising from share-based payment transactions, including separate disclosure of that portion of the total expense that arises from transactions accounted for as equity-settled share-based payment transactions.

- For **liabilities** arising from share-based payment transactions

    - The **total carrying amount** at the end of the period.

    - The **total intrinsic value** at the end of the period of liabilities for which the counterparty's right to cash or other assets had vested by the end of the period.

CHAPTER ROUNDUP

You need to be familiar with and able to describe

- IAS 19 *Employee Benefits*

  - Definitions.

  - Treatment of short-term benefits.

  - Treatment of post-employment benefits.

    - Defined contribution pension schemes.

    - Defines benefit pension schemes – the problems for the business of such schemes and how scheme assets and liabilities are accounted for.

- IFRS 2 *Share-Based Payments*

  - When they should be recognised.

  - How they should be measured.

TEST YOUR KNOWLEDGE

Check your knowledge of the chapter here, without referring back to the text.

1.   Retirement benefits

(a)   Accounting for retirement benefits remains one of the most challenging areas in financial reporting. The values being reported can be significant, and the estimation of these values is complex and subjective. Standard-setters and preparers of financial statements find it difficult to achieve a measure of consensus on the appropriate way to deal with the assets and costs involved.

(i)   Describe four key issues in the determination of the method of accounting for retirement benefits in respect of defined benefit plans.

(ii)   Discuss how IAS 19 *Employee Benefits* deals with these key issues and to what extent it provides solutions to the problems of accounting for retirement benefits.

TEST YOUR KNOWLEDGE: ANSWER

1. Retirement benefits

    (a)   (i)   There are many key issues in determining how accounting for retirement benefits is carried out in respect of a defined benefit plan.

        (1)   The two main alternative approaches are what might be called the **income statement approach** or the **statement of financial position approach**. Under the income statement approach, the pension cost is seen as an operating cost and under the accruals or matching concept, the attempt is made to spread the total pension cost over the service lives of the employees. The statement of financial position approach however concentrates on the valuation of the assets and liabilities of the plan, and the cost to the profit and loss account is the change in value of the plan net assets or liabilities.

        (2)   Regarding the assets of the defined benefit plan, there are two issues: **whether or not they should be included** on the statement of financial position of the company and **how** they would be **valued**. Alternative valuation methods such as cost, market value and fair value are available.

        (3)   How should scheme liabilities be valued? Should they be valued using an **actuarial valuation or a market value**? Usually, actuarial techniques will have to be used, as there is no market value for such liabilities but then, there is an issue over which actuarial method should be used – accrued benefits or prospective benefits.

        (4)   Should **discounting** be used when valuing the scheme liabilities in order to take account of the time value of money?

        (5)   If **actuarial gains and losses** occur, where should they be **recognised** – in the income statement or in the Statement of Total Recognised Income and expense? Should such gains and losses be recognised immediately or spread over the remaining service lives of the employees? Or should the actuarial gains and losses only be recognised in the income statement if they exceed a predetermined amount? The problem that faces standard-setters is how to deal with the volatility of actuarial gains and losses.

        (6)   **How often** should **actuarial valuations** take place? In theory, they should take place at each year end, but the costs and practicalities of this makes it difficult and onerous.

        (7)   If there are **changes to the defined benefit plan** such as improvement of benefits or addition of new benefits in relation to past service how should these be accounted for? The alternatives are to recognise the cost immediately in the income statement, spread it over the remaining service lives of employees or to offset it against any surplus in the scheme.

        NB: Candidates are only required to describe **four** of the above.

(ii)   IAS 19 *Employee Benefits* follows a **statement of financial position approach** to accounting for defined benefit schemes. The assets of the scheme are to be valued on an actuarial basis using the **projected unit credit method** and the liabilities should be discounted to reflect the time value of money and the particular characteristics of the liability. The discount rate to be used is the rate of return on high quality corporate bonds of equivalent currency and term as the scheme liabilities being valued.

IAS 19 does not prescribe the frequency of full actuarial valuations. It states that the assets and liabilities of the plan must be determined with sufficient regularity that the amounts recognised in the financial statements do not differ materially from the amounts that would be determined at the statement of financial position date. IAS 19 does not require that the surplus or deficit in the scheme is recognised in the statement of financial position as an asset or liability. If the company chooses the option in IAS 19 of immediately recognising actuarial gains and losses direct to reserves, the surplus or deficit will appear on the statement of financial position as the pension asset or liability; however, if any of the alternative treatments involving smoothing of actuarial gains and losses through the income statement are chosen, the statement of financial position will not recognise the actual surplus or deficit.

Past service costs for active employees are recognised in the income statement over the period in which the increases in benefits vest (immediately if the benefits vest immediately).

14

Taxation

INTRODUCTION

If a company generates profits it is liable to wind up paying tax. Tax can be a highly significant cost for any business but it is not simply calculated based on business profits. We have seen in earlier sections that the choice of accounting treatment can impact on reported profits. Revenue authorities do not want companies to be able to influence tax payable through such selections and therefore apply their own tax rules to the determination of taxable profits.

This chapter examines this idea and the knock-on impact it has in the form of deferred tax.

CHAPTER LEARNING OBJECTIVES

The syllabus areas covered by this chapter are

Interpretation of Financial Information

- The effect of accounting practices

    - Understanding of the effect of accounting practices on the numbers most significant for investment decisions (profit, earnings per share, asset value etc).

Accounting Terminology and Concepts

- Accounting terminology and a knowledge of accounting concepts and conventions to include the statement of financial position, income statement, statement of cash flows and notes to the accounts. An understanding of the distinction between capital and revenue, the valuation of assets for accounting purposes and the determination of profit and earnings share on the nil, net and full distribution bases. An understanding of significance of the statement of accounting policies in relation to the concept of a true and fair view.

Presentation of Financial Statements

- Impact of statutory and non-statutory regulation on UK financial statements.

- An understanding of the effect on the presentation of financial statements of the Companies Act and non-statutory regulations, including standards and other guidance issued by IASB and stock exchange requirements.

In the respect of taxation:

It is emphasised that the intention of the examination is to assess student's analytical and interpretative skills rather than their technical accounting ability. It is also expected that they should have an understanding of standard accounting practices and an awareness of matters currently under discussion.

1 INTRODUCTION

1.1 Corporation tax

Since 1 April 1964, all UK resident companies have been subject to a single tax, corporation tax, on all their profits (income and chargeable gains) wherever generated (either in the UK or overseas). Any income generated abroad may also be subject to overseas tax.

In calculating the corporation tax payable, Her Majesty's Revenue and Customs (HMRC) work on a strict legal basis, i.e. individual companies (separate legal entities) are assessed separately for tax purposes. In a group situation, tax is *not* levied on group profits (though some concessions may ultimately be available from group membership). Tax is levied on the individual group members based on their individual profits, the group tax charge being an accumulation of these separate amounts. Hence, with reference to group tax situations

- UK subsidiaries are subject to UK corporation tax based on their own profits.

- Overseas subsidiaries are subject to their own relevant country's corporate taxes based on their individual profits, these profits will not automatically be subject to UK corporation tax as we discuss later.

- The overall group tax charge is an accumulation of UK and overseas taxes, as all other figures, e.g. turnover, are an accumulation of UK and overseas figures.

1.2 Basic accounting

Exam tip | You may be asked why the charge and cash payment differ, e.g. Summer 2005, Question 11.

1.2.1 Accounting for tax charge

Tax accrues through the accounting period as the company generates taxable profits. However, for accounting purposes the tax is only formally calculated at the end of the accounting period. The estimated charge is accounted for as follows.

- Tax charge is increased in the income statement (profit and shareholders' funds reduced).
- Tax liability is increased on the year-end statement of financial position (liabilities increased).

1.2.2 Accounting for tax payment

Corporation tax is paid over four instalments, two within the current accounting period and two after the end of the accounting period.

When tax is paid, the following accounting entry will be made.

- Cash balance decreased (CREDIT: Cash).
- Tax liability decreased (DEBIT: Corporation tax payable).

In practice, the company will be paying some of its tax charge before providing for the full year tax charge at year end. However, the year-end statement of financial position will show the net tax liability, being the total estimated charge for the year minus the two instalments paid to date.

1.3 Accounting regulations

The accounting regulations are governed by IAS 12 *Income Taxes*.

1.4 Corporation tax regime

The payment rules are summarised as follows.

- Companies with taxable profits of £1.5m or more will be required to pay tax on a quarterly basis.

- The payments will be due on the 14th day of months 7, 10, 13 and 16, following the start of the accounting period.

- Payment will be made based on the **estimated** tax bill of the company for the current year, with any final adjustment to tax payable for the full year being paid once the taxable profits for the year have been agreed with HMRC.

Any balance payable under these arrangements is due nine months and one day after the end of the accounting period.

For companies with annual taxable profits of less than £1.5m, the payment rules will not change. They will pay tax nine months and one day after the end of the accounting period. The payment would therefore be for an agreed amount of tax, based upon the tax-adjusted profits for the accounting period.

Example

A company has an accounting period ending on 31 December 2007. The estimated taxable profits for the year will be £2m and the tax will be paid according to the quarterly rules. The final taxable profit for the year, agreed after the year end with HMRC, is £2.4m.

Assuming a corporation tax rate of 30%, what payments will the company make and when?

On the basis of the original estimated taxable profits of £2m, the total estimated tax bill will be £600,000 (£2m × 30%).

The actual amounts paid on a quarterly basis will be based on the estimated taxable profits. However, the amount paid nine months after the year-end will be the balance based on the final, agreed tax charge of £720,000 (£2.4m × 30%).

Date of Payment	Amount Paid (£)
14 July 2007	150,000
14 October 2007	150,000
14 January 2008	150,000
14 April 2008	150,000
1 October 2008	120,000
Total (in £)	**720,000**

1.5 Composition of the tax charge

The tax charge in the income statement for a particular year will probably just be one figure, though this will be analysed in the notes. The headings that may be included in this note are

	(£)
UK corporation tax at X%	X
Less: Relief for overseas tax	(X)
	X
Overseas tax	X
Deferred tax	X
Adjustments related to prior years	X
Total income statement tax charge	X

We will look at each of these items in the following sections, discussing the basis of the charge and how it will impact on the statement of financial position.

2 UK CORPORATION TAX

2.1 Introduction

The corporation tax charge is a percentage rate applied to the taxable profits. Corporation tax rates are determined at each budget for the coming Financial Year (FY), a period running from 1 April to 31 March of the following year, which takes its name from the calendar year in which it starts. For example, the financial year starting 1 April 2008 and ending 31 March 2009 would be referred to as FY 2008.

2.2 Rates of corporation tax

Three rates are announced each year.

- The full corporation tax rate for companies whose profits fall above a certain limit.

- A smaller company tax rate for companies whose profits fall below a certain limit.

In recent years, these rates have been as follows.

Financial Years	Main Rate/Limit		Small Companies' Rate/Limit	
	%	£'000	%	£'000
2002–2006	30	1,500	19	300
2007	30	1,500	20	300
2008	28	1,500	21	300

The small companies' rate will rise to 22% for the 2009 financial year. For companies whose profits are between £300,000 and £1,500,000, a graduated tax rate applies.

For the sake of simplicity, a rate of 30% has been used for all illustrative examples in this chapter.

If a company's year end is 31 March, then its accounting year falls completely within one financial year and it will simply apply the relevant rate for that year. If, however, a company's year end falls on some other date (i.e. its accounting period straddles two financial years) the profits are time apportioned between the two financial years with each part taxed at the appropriate rate.

2.3 Adjustments to profits

We noted above that the corporation tax charge is a percentage applied to the **taxable profits**. These taxable profits are not necessarily the same as accounting profits.

Accounting profits can, to a very large extent, be dependent on the accounting policies adopted by the company (e.g. depreciation rates, etc.). HMRC does not want companies to be able to manipulate their tax charge by use of creative accounting policies, hence profits are recalculated based on HMRC's own standards to arrive at the taxable profits figure. This recalculation is done by taking the original profit as reported by the company and adjusting it to apply tax rules.

There are two types of difference between taxable and accounting profits.

2.3.1 Permanent differences

Permanent differences are one of the following.

- Income which is never subject to corporation tax, e.g. dividends from UK companies. As a result, a company may have reported profits but no tax charge.

- Expenses which are never allowed, e.g. entertaining, fines, etc. Expenses are deducted from revenue to calculate profit, however, HMRC does not allow the deduction of these particular expenses and hence, the taxable profits are higher.

As a result of these items, the corporation tax charge will seldom simply be the financial accounting profits multiplied by the prevailing tax rate.

2.3.2 Timing differences

Items where the

- Profit effect is in one period when the revenue or cost is recognised on the basis of the fundamental accounting concepts.

- Tax effect is in another period based on tax legislation.

The result being that the items are taxed, but the tax charged does not match against the profits for the year to which they relate. Examples of such items include

- Royalties payable and receivable (short-term timing differences).
- Capital allowance and depreciation.
- Revaluations of non-current assets.
- Losses.

Example

This is an example of an adjustment to profits calculation.

	P/T	£'000
Profit before tax per the financial statements		2,400
Less: Income not subject to corporation tax		
– Dividends received from UK companies	P	(500)
Add: Expenditure not allowed for tax		
– Entertaining	P	60
– Fines	P	40
– Depreciation	T	500
		2,500
Less: Capital allowances	T	(1,000)
Profits chargeable to corporation tax		£1,500
Corporation tax at 30% (1,500 × 30%)		£450

The P/T column indicates Permanent/Timing difference.

As we can see from this example, the effective tax rate has turned out to be 18.8%, (450 ÷ 2,400), significantly less than the nominal or statutory tax rate for that financial year of 30%.

2.4 Adjustments for prior years

Companies are in a catch-22 situation. They must make a corporation tax provision at the year end to complete their audited accounts, but HMRC will not agree the tax charge until they have received these audited accounts. As a result, it is quite likely that there will be a slight mismatch between the figure originally put in the accounts and that finally agreed by HMRC.

Example

The Example from earlier in this chapter showed a company estimating its tax bill for the year to be £600,000 and paying quarterly instalments based on that estimate. After publishing the financial statements for that year, the company finally agreed the tax bill as £660,000. The remaining balance was duly paid nine months after the year end. What is to be done with the extra £60,000?

The standard accounting treatment adopted is the latter, being that any shortfalls or overcharges in previous years are made up for this year.

2.5 Corporation tax on dividends and interest

2.5.1 Dividends paid and payable

Dividends are a means by which the company distributes profits to the shareholders. As such, they do not represent a tax-allowable expense and are therefore paid out of profits after the tax charge for the accounting period has been deducted.

2.5.2 Dividends received

If dividends have been received from another UK company, the profits out of which they are being paid will already have been taxed. Therefore, the recipient company is not required to pay any further tax to HMRC.

It is required that companies show dividends received as being the net cash amount received above the tax line, with no tax implications for the income statement tax charge.

2.5.3 Interest receivable

Interest receivable is treated as investment income in the income statement and is chargeable to tax. It is shown as a gross figure in the income statement, with the tax charge thus being higher as a result of the additional taxable income.

2.5.4 Interest received net of withholding tax

It is, however, often the case that interest income is paid net of a withholding tax, with the recipient therefore in a similar position to having received a dividend net of the 'tax credit'. Although these situations appear similar, interest income is required to be grossed up in the income statement to include the tax withheld. This treatment is disallowed for dividend income, which should be included in the income statement as a net amount received, as detailed above.

The tax charge must include the tax withheld on the interest income, although, as this tax has already been deducted by the paying company, it will never actually be paid by the recipient company.

3 OVERSEAS TAX

3.1 How overseas tax arises

A UK company may become subject to overseas tax when it conducts part of its operations abroad, e.g. through the operations of an overseas branch.

In a group situation, the profits of any overseas subsidiaries will be subject to overseas tax, i.e. the corporate tax regime of the country in which it is incorporated and operates, not UK corporation tax.

Remember that tax is calculated on a strict legal basis, i.e. individual companies profits are taxed separately, we do not tax group profit.

For these reasons, the tax charge in both individual company or group accounts may include an element of overseas tax.

3.2 Double tax relief

You will recall that UK companies are subject to corporation tax on *all* their profits wherever generated in the world. As a result, if we have set up a branch in, say, France, the UK tax authorities will wish to subject the profits of that branch to UK corporation tax. We may also find, however, that the French authorities wish to tax the profits that have been generated on their soil. Hence, these profits are taxable twice.

In a group situation, the profits of the overseas subsidiaries will have been subject to overseas taxes when earned. If a dividend is paid from these subsidiaries out of their after-tax profits to the UK holding company, then this income received by the UK holding company will be subject to UK corporation tax. Hence, effectively the income from which the dividend that has been paid has been taxed twice: once overseas and once when remitted as a dividend to the UK parent.

This problem is not just confined to the UK, but is quite common internationally. Clearly, such double taxation, were it to stand, would be a distinct disincentive to overseas investment. As a concession in these situations, HMRC authorities of most countries have developed tax treaties alleviating this problem and ensuring that the income is only taxed once.

In the UK, the effect is that the income will be subject to UK corporation tax, but then double tax relief will be given. The tax charge and corresponding liability will be reduced by the lower of

- The overseas tax paid.
- UK corporation tax on the same profits.

If the figures are material then the tax note will then disclose three items.

- Corporation tax charge.
- Overseas tax charge.
- Overseas or double tax relief as a reduction against the corporation tax charge.

4   DEFERRED TAX

> Deferred tax is an accounts measure, used to match the tax effects of transactions with their accounting impact.

4.1 What is deferred tax?

Exam tip

> Questions on deferred tax are the most common from the material in this section and may involve small calculations e.g. Winter 2004 Question 9, Summer 2004 Question 7.

When a company recognises an asset or liability, it expects to **recover or settle the carrying amount** of that asset or liability. In other words, it expects to sell or use up assets, and to pay off liabilities. What happens if that recovery or settlement is likely to make future tax payments larger (or smaller) than they would otherwise have been if the recovery or settlement had no tax consequences? In these circumstances, IAS 12 requires companies to recognise a **deferred tax liability** (or **deferred tax asset**).

4.2 Definitions

Do not worry too much if you do not understand the concept of deferred tax yet; it should become clearer as you work through this section. First of all, here are the definitions relating to deferred tax given in IAS 12.

> - **Deferred tax liabilities** are the amounts of income taxes payable in future periods in respect of taxable temporary differences.
>
> - **Deferred tax assets** are the amounts of income taxes recoverable in future periods in respect of
>   - Deductible temporary differences.
>   - The carryforward of unused tax losses.
>   - The carryforward of unused tax credits.
>
> - **Temporary differences** are differences between the carrying amount of an asset or liability in the statement of financial position and its tax base. Temporary differences may be either
>   - **Taxable temporary differences**, which are temporary differences that will result in taxable amounts in determining taxable profit (tax loss) of future periods when the carrying amount of the asset or liability is recovered or settled.
>
>   - **Deductible temporary differences**, which are temporary differences that will result in amounts that are deductible in determining taxable profit (tax loss) of future periods when the carrying amount of the asset or liability is recovered or settled.
>
> - The **tax base** of an asset or liability is the amount attributed to that asset or liability for tax purposes.
>
> *(IAS 12)*

We need to look at some of these definitions in more detail.

4.3 Tax base

We can expand on the definition given above by stating that the **tax base of an asset** is the amount that will be deductible for tax purposes against any taxable economic benefits that will flow to the entity when it recovers the carrying value of the asset. Where those economic benefits are not taxable, the tax base of the asset is the same as its carrying amount.

Example

State the tax base of each of the following assets.

(a) A machine cost £10,000. For tax purposes, depreciation of £3,000 has already been deducted in the current and prior periods and the remaining cost will be deductible in future periods, either as depreciation or through a deduction on disposal. Revenue generated by using the machine is taxable, any gain on disposal of the machine will be taxable and any loss on disposal will be deductible for tax purposes.

(b) Interest receivable has a carrying amount of £1,000. The related interest revenue will be taxed on a cash basis.

(c) Trade receivables have a carrying amount of £10,000. The related revenue has already been included in taxable profit (tax loss).

(d) A loan receivable has a carrying amount of £1m. The repayment of the loan will have no tax consequences.

Solution

(a)   The tax base of the machine is £7,000.
(b)   The tax base of the interest receivable is nil.
(c)   The tax base of the trade receivables is £10,000.
(d)   The tax base of the loan is £1m.

In the case of a **liability**, the tax base will be its carrying amount, less any amount that will be deducted for tax purposes in relation to the liability in future periods. For revenue received in advance, the tax base of the resulting liability is its carrying amount, less any amount of the revenue that will *not* be taxable in future periods.

Example

State the tax base of each of the following liabilities.

(a)   Current liabilities include accrued expenses with a carrying amount of £1,000. The related expense will be deducted for tax purposes on a cash basis.

(b)   Current liabilities include interest revenue received in advance, with a carrying amount of £10,000. The related interest revenue was taxed on a cash basis.

(c)   Current liabilities include accrued expenses with a carrying amount of £2,000. The related expense has already been deducted for tax purposes.

(d)   Current liabilities include accrued fines and penalties with a carrying amount of £100. Fines and penalties are not deductible for tax purposes.

(e)   A loan payable has a carrying amount of £1m. The repayment of the loan will have no tax consequences.

Solution

(a)   The tax base of the accrued expenses is nil.
(b)   The tax base of the interest received in advance is nil.
(c)   The tax base of the accrued expenses is £2,000.
(d)   The tax base of the accrued fines and penalties is £100.
(e)   The tax base of the loan is £1m.

IAS 12 gives the following examples of circumstances in which the carrying amount of an asset or liability will be **equal to its tax base**.

-    **Accrued expenses** have already been deducted in determining an entity's current tax liability for the current or earlier periods.

-    A **loan payable** is measured at the amount originally received and this amount is the same as the amount repayable on final maturity of the loan.

-    **Accrued expenses** will never be deductible for tax purposes.

-    **Accrued income** will never be taxable.

4.4 Temporary differences

You may have found the definition of temporary differences somewhat confusing. Remember that accounting profits form the basis for computing **taxable profits**, on which the tax liability for the year is calculated; however, accounting profits and taxable profits are different. There are two reasons for the differences.

- **Permanent differences**. These occur when certain items of revenue or expense are excluded from the computation of taxable profits (for example, entertainment expenses may not be allowable for tax purposes).

- **Temporary differences**. These occur when items of revenue or expense are included in both accounting profits and taxable profits, but not for the same accounting period. For example, an expense which is allowable as a deduction in arriving at taxable profits for 20X7 might not be included in the financial accounts until 20X8 or later. In the long run, the total taxable profits and total accounting profits will be the same (except for permanent differences) so that temporary differences originate in one period and are capable of reversal in one or more subsequent periods. Deferred tax is the tax attributable to **temporary differences**.

Temporary differences are known as timing differences in the UK.

Example

A company buys a machine for £160,000, which it expects to last for three years and then have a residual value of £70,000.

What will be the reported profits and statement of financial position position at the end of each of the three years both without and with deferred tax? Assume that profits before tax are £100,000 in each year. Ignore the small companies' rate.

Solution

Without deferred tax

The corporation tax charge will be based on taxable profits (an adjustment to accounting profits) and will result in the following.

	Year 1 (£)	Year 2 (£)	Year 3 (£)	Total (£)
Income statement				
Profit before tax	100,000	100,000	100,000	300,000
Corporation tax	(27,000)	(30,000)	(33,000)	(90,000)
Profit after tax	73,000	70,000	67,000	210,000
Statement of financial position extract				
Corporation tax liability	27,000	30,000	33,000	

The corporation tax charge has been based on the following adjustment to profits.

Adjustment to Profit & Tax	Year 1 (£)	Year 2 (£)	Year 3 (£)	Total (£)
Profit before tax	100,000	100,000	100,000	300,000
Add: Depreciation	30,000	30,000	30,000	90,000
Less: Capital allowances	(40,000)	(30,000)	(20,000)	(90,000)
Profit chargeable to tax	90,000	100,000	110,000	300,000
Tax at 30%	27,000	30,000	33,000	90,000

We can see that in total the tax charge of £90,000 represents 30% of the total profits of £300,000. Ideally, therefore, to apply the matching concept the tax charge for each year would be £100,000 × 30% = £30,000, i.e.

Tax Charge

	Year 1 (£)	Year 2 (£)	Year 3 (£)
Ideal wanted	30,000	30,000	30,000
Corporation tax charge	(27,000)	(30,000)	(33,000)
Difference	3,000	0	(3,000)

Hence, the tax charge is £3,000 too low in Year 1 but correspondingly £3,000 too high in Year 2.

With deferred tax

We can use deferred tax to recognise an extra £3,000 in Year 1.

- Deferred tax charge up £3,000 (Debit).
- Deferred tax liability up £3,000 (Credit).

Resulting in a lower profit after tax and a deferred tax liability on the statement of financial position.

In Year 2, no change is made to the deferred tax provision as this year the actual tax charge is the same as the ideal charge wanted.

In Year 3, we take a deferred tax credit, the effect on the accounting equation being

- Deferred tax charge down £3,000 (profits, hence shareholders' funds up – CREDIT).
- Deferred tax liability down £3,000 (liabilities down – DEBIT).

Thus cancelling the deferred tax liability established in Year 1 down to zero and giving the following income statement and statement of financial position figures.

	Year 1 (£)	Year 2 (£)	Year 3 (£)	Total (£)
Income statement				
Profit before tax	100,000	100,000	100,000	300,000
Corporation tax	(27,000)	(30,000)	(33,000)	(90,000)
Deferred tax	(3,000)	–	3,000	–
Total tax charge	(30,000)	(30,000)	(30,000)	(90,000)
Profit after tax	70,000	70,000	70,000	210,000
Statement of financial position extract				
Corporation tax liability	27,000	30,000	33,000	
Deferred tax liability	3,000	3,000	–	

We can see that now the total tax charge each year is the same at £30,000. Likewise, the corresponding profits after tax are identical each year at £70,000 as could reasonably be expected when the business has performed the same each year.

Once more, this Example shows that the deferred tax charge or credit is based on any timing differences that arise. In Year 1 of this Example, we have accounting profits of £100,000 and taxable profits of £90,000 – a £10,000 timing difference has arisen and hence a £3,000 (£10,000 × 30%) deferred tax charge results.

Example

Given below is an example from Roche Group of the extensive tax disclosures required.

Roche Group
Extract from Notes to the Financial Statement, Year Ended 31 December 2004

Income tax expenses in millions of CHF	2004	2003
Current income taxes	2,167	1,794
Adjustments recognised for current tax of prior periods	25	39
Deferred income taxes	153	(388)
Total charge for income taxes	2,345	1,445

Since the Group operates across the world, it is subject to income taxes in many different tax jurisdictions. The Group calculates its average expected tax rate as a weighted average of the tax rates in the tax jurisdictions in which the Group operates. Within the Group's average expected tax rate, the increasing significance of Genentech and Chugai causes an increase in the rate which has been offset by ongoing improvement of the Group's structures.

The Group effective tax rate can be reconciled to the Group's average expected tax rate as follows.

Reconciliation of the Group's effective tax rate in millions of CHF	2004	2003
Group's average expected tax rate	24.1%	24.3%
Tax effect of		
– Unrecognised tax losses	–1.5%	–0.1%
– Non-taxable income/non-deductible expenses	+0.3%	–0.1%
– Impairment of financial assets	+0.0%	+1.2%
– Other differences	+2.1%	+0.5%
Continuing businesses before exceptional items effective tax rate	25.0%	25.8%

	Profit before tax	Income taxes	2004 Tax rate	Profit before tax	Income taxes	2003 Tax rate
Continuing businesses before exceptional items effective tax rate	6,568	(1,645)	25.0%	5,119	(1,319)	25.8%
Amortisation of goodwill	(572)	–		(489)	–	
Major legal cases	–	–		216	(87)	
Changes in Group organisation in continuing businesses	(199)	33		–	–	
Exceptional income from bond conversion and redemption	908	(290)		–	–	
Continuing businesses effective tax rate	6,705	(1,902)	28.4%	4,846	(1,406)	29%
Discontinuing businesses	277	(75)		430	(80)	
Changes in Group organisation in discontinuing businesses	2,503	(368)		(395)	41	
Group's effective tax rate	9,485	(2,345)	24.7%	4,881	(1,445)	29.6%

Income tax assets (liabilities) in millions of CHF	2004	2003
Current income taxes		
Current income tax assets	159	238
Current income tax liabilities	(947)	(714)
Net current income tax asset (liability)	(788)	(476)
Deferred income taxes		
Deferred income tax assets	1,047	900
Deferred income tax liabilities	(3,564)	(3,133)
Net deferred income tax asset (liability)	(2,517)	(2,233)

Deferred income tax assets are recognised for tax loss carry forwards only to the extent that realisation of the related tax benefit is probable. The Group has unrecognised tax losses, including valuation allowance, of 172 million Swiss francs (2003: 594 million Swiss francs), of which 88 million Swiss francs expire within four years and 40 million Swiss francs expire within six years. The remaining 44 million Swiss francs of losses expire after fifteen years or more. Deferred income tax liabilities have not been established for the withholding tax and other taxes that would be payable on the unremitted earnings of certain foreign subsidiaries, as such amounts are currently regarded as permanently reinvested. These unremitted earnings totalled 27.6 billion Swiss francs at 31 December 2004 (2003: 22.8 billion Swiss francs).

5 TAXABLE TEMPORARY DIFFERENCES

> The rule to remember here is that: 'All taxable temporary differences give rise to a deferred tax liability.'

5.1 Examples

The following are examples of circumstances that give rise to taxable temporary differences.

5.2 Transactions that affect the income statement

- **Interest revenue** received in arrears and included in accounting profit on the basis of time apportionment. It is included in taxable profit, however, on a cash basis.

- **Depreciation** of an asset is accelerated for tax purposes. When new assets are purchased, allowances may be available against taxable profits which exceed the amount of depreciation chargeable on the assets in the financial accounts for the year of purchase.

- **Development costs** which have been capitalised will be amortised in the income statement, but they were deducted in full from taxable profit in the period in which they were incurred.

- **Prepaid expenses** have already been deducted on a cash basis in determining the taxable profit of the current or previous periods.

5.3 Transactions that affect the statement of financial position

- **Depreciation of an asset** is not deductible for tax purposes. No deduction will be available for tax purposes when the asset is sold/scrapped.

- A borrower records a **loan** at proceeds received (amount due at maturity) less transaction costs.

The carrying amount of the loan is subsequently increased by amortisation of the transaction costs against accounting profit. The transaction costs were, however, deducted for tax purposes in the period when the loan was first recognised.

5.4 Fair value adjustments and revaluations

- **Financial assets or investment property** are carried at fair value. This exceeds cost, but no equivalent adjustment is made for tax purposes.

- Property, plant and equipment is **revalued** by an entity (under IAS 16), but no equivalent adjustment is made for tax purposes.

5.5 Reasoning

Try to **understand the reasoning** behind the recognition of deferred tax liabilities on taxable temporary differences.

- When an **asset is recognised**, it is expected that its carrying amount will be recovered in the form of economic benefits that flow to the entity in future periods.

- If the carrying amount of the asset is **greater than** its tax base, then taxable economic benefits will also be greater than the amount that will be allowed as a deduction for tax purposes.

- The difference is therefore a **taxable temporary difference** and the obligation to pay the resulting income taxes in future periods is a **deferred tax liability**.

- As the entity recovers the carrying amount of the asset, the taxable temporary difference will **reverse** and the entity will have taxable profit.

- It is then probable that economic benefits will flow from the entity in the form of **tax payments**, and so the recognition of all deferred tax liabilities (except those excluded above) is required by IAS 12.

Example

A company purchased an asset costing £1,500. At the end of 20X8 the carrying amount is £1,000. The cumulative depreciation for tax purposes is £900 and the current tax rate is 25%.

Requirement

Calculate the deferred tax liability for the asset.

Solution

Firstly, what is the tax base of the asset? It is £1,500 – £900 = £600 (its tax written down value).

The entity must therefore recognise a deferred tax liability of £400 × 25% = £100, recognising the difference between the carrying amount of £1,000 and the tax base of £600 as a taxable temporary difference.

5.6 Revalued assets

Under IAS 16 assets may be revalued. This does *not* affect current taxable profits so the tax base of the asset is not adjusted. The difference between the carrying amount of a revalued asset in the statement of financial position and its tax base is a temporary difference and gives rise to a **deferred tax liability or asset**.

6 DEDUCTIBLE TEMPORARY DIFFERENCES

> The rule to remember here is that: 'All deductible temporary differences give rise to a deferred tax asset.'

6.1 Examples

The deferred tax asset must also satisfy the **recognition criteria** given in IAS 12. These state that a deferred tax asset should be recognised for all deductible temporary differences to the extent that it is **probable that taxable profit will be available** against which it can be utilised. This is an application of prudence. Before we look at this issue in more detail, let us consider the examples of deductible temporary differences given in the Standard.

6.2 Transactions that affect the income statement

- **Retirement benefit costs** (pension costs) are deducted from accounting profit as service is provided by the employee. They are not deducted in determining taxable profit until the entity pays either retirement benefits or contributions to a fund. (This may also apply to similar expenses.)

- **Accumulated depreciation** of an asset in the financial statements is greater than the accumulated depreciation allowed for tax purposes up to the statement of financial position date.

- The **cost of inventories** sold before the statement of financial position date is deducted from accounting profit when goods/services are delivered, but is deducted from taxable profit when the cash is received.
  (*Note.* There is also a taxable temporary difference associated with the related trade receivable.)

- The **NRV** of inventory, or the **recoverable amount** of an item of property, plant and equipment falls and the carrying value is therefore **reduced**, but that reduction is ignored for tax purposes until the asset is sold.

- **Research costs** (or organisation/other start-up costs) are recognised as an expense for accounting purposes but are not deductible against taxable profits until a later period.

- Income is **deferred** in the statement of financial position, but has already been included in taxable profit in current/prior periods.

- A **government grant** is included in the statement of financial position as deferred income, but it will not be taxable in future periods.
  (*Note.* A deferred tax asset may *not* be recognised here according to the Standard.)

6.3 Reasoning

Let us lay out the reasoning behind the recognition of deferred tax assets arising from deductible temporary differences.

- When a **liability is recognised**, it is assumed that its carrying amount will be settled in the form of outflows of economic benefits from the entity in future periods.

- When these resources flow from the entity, part or all may be deductible in determining taxable profits of a **period later** than that in which the liability is recognised.

- A **temporary tax difference** then exists between the carrying amount of the liability and its tax base.

- A **deferred tax asset** therefore arises, representing the income taxes that will be recoverable in future periods when that part of the liability is allowed as a deduction from taxable profit.

- Similarly, when the carrying amount of an asset is **less than its tax base**, the difference gives rise to a deferred tax asset in respect of the income taxes that will be recoverable in future periods.

Example

Pargatha Co recognises a liability of £10,000 for accrued product warranty costs on 31 December 2007. These product warranty costs will not be deductible for tax purposes until the entity pays claims. The tax rate is 25%.

Requirement

State the deferred tax implications of this situation.

Solution

What is the tax base of the liability? It is nil (carrying amount of £10,000 less the amount that will be deductible for tax purposes in respect of the liability in future periods).

When the liability is settled for its carrying amount, the entity's future taxable profit will be reduced by £10,000 and so its future tax payments will be reduced by £10,000 × 25% = £2,500.

The difference of £10,000 between the carrying amount (£10,000) and the tax base (nil) is a deductible temporary difference. The entity should therefore recognise a deferred tax asset of £10,000 × 25% = £2,500 **provided that** it is probable that the entity will earn sufficient taxable profits in future periods to benefit from a reduction in tax payments.

6.4 Taxable profits in future periods

When can we be sure that sufficient taxable profit will be available against which a deductible temporary difference can be utilised? IAS 12 states that this will be assumed when sufficient **taxable temporary differences** exist which relate to the same taxation authority and the same taxable entity. These should be expected to reverse in either of

- The same period as the expected reversal of the deductible temporary difference.
- Periods into which a tax loss arising from the deferred tax asset can be carried back or forward.

Only in these circumstances is the deferred tax asset **recognised**, in the period in which the deductible temporary differences arise.

6.5 Unused tax losses and unused tax credits

An entity may have unused tax losses or credits (i.e. which it can offset against taxable profits) at the end of a period. Should a deferred tax asset be recognised in relation to such amounts? IAS 12 states that a deferred tax asset may be recognised in such circumstances **to the extent that it is probable future taxable profit will be available against which the unused tax losses/credits can be utilised**.

7 MEASUREMENT AND RECOGNITION OF DEFERRED TAX

7.1 Basis of provision of deferred tax

There are various methods of accounting for deferred tax, only one of which is adopted by IAS 12.

- **Flow-through method**.
- **Full provision method** (as under IAS 12).
- **Partial provision method** (as adopted in some countries, e.g. formerly the UK).

7.2 Flow-through method

Under the **flow-through method**, the tax liability recognised is the expected current tax liability for the period (i.e. no provision is made for deferred tax). The main **advantages** of the method are that it is straightforward to apply and the tax liability recognised is closer to many people's idea of a 'real' liability than that recognised under either full or partial provision. The main **disadvantages** of flow-through are that it can lead to large fluctuations in the tax charge and that it does not allow tax relief for non-current liabilities to be recognised until those liabilities are settled. In addition, profits may be overstated because there is no deferred tax charge leading to excessive dividend payments, distortion of earnings per share and of results in the eyes of shareholders.

7.3 Full provision method

The **full provision method** has the **advantage** that it recognises that each temporary difference at the statement of financial position date has an effect on future tax payments. If a company claims an accelerated tax allowance on an item of plant, future tax assessments will be bigger than they would have been otherwise. Future transactions may well affect those assessments still further, but that is not relevant in assessing the position at the statement of financial position date. The **disadvantage** of full provision is that, under certain types of tax system, it gives rise to large liabilities that may fall due only far in the future, if at all. Furthermore, it may be said to be less realistic than the partial provision method, if more objective. IAS 12 requires full provision.

7.4 Partial provision method

The **partial provision method** addresses this disadvantage by providing for deferred tax only to the extent that it is expected to be paid in the foreseeable future. This has an obvious intuitive appeal, but its effect is that deferred tax recognised at the statement of financial position date includes the tax effects of future transactions that have not been recognised in the financial statements, and which the reporting company has neither undertaken nor even committed to undertake at that date. It is difficult to reconcile this with the IASB's *Framework* document, which defines assets and liabilities as arising from past events. Where partial provision is required, the difference between the amount provided and the maximum (i.e. under the full provision method) should usually be disclosed.

7.5 Recognition

As with current tax, deferred tax should normally be recognised as income or an expense and included in the profit or loss for the period in the **income statement**. The exception is where the tax arises from a transaction or event which is recognised (in the same or a different period) **directly in equity**.

The figures shown for deferred tax in the income statement will consist of **two components**.

(a)   Deferred tax relating to **temporary differences**.

(b)   Adjustments relating to **changes in the carrying amount of deferred tax assets/ liabilities** (where there is no change in temporary differences), e.g. changes in tax rates/ laws, reassessment of the recoverability of deferred tax assets, or a change in the expected recovery of an asset.

Items in (b) will be recognised in the income statement, *unless* they relate to items previously charged/credited to equity.

Deferred tax (and current tax) should be **charged/credited directly to equity** if the tax relates to items also charged/credited directly to equity (in the same or a different period).

Examples of International Accounting Standards which allow certain items to be credited/charged directly to equity include

■   **Revaluations** of property, plant and equipment (IAS 16).

■   The effect of a **change in accounting policy** (applied retrospectively) or correction of a **prior period error** (IAS 8).

8   PRESENTATION AND DISCLOSURE OF TAXATION

> IAS 12 contains rules for comprehensive presentation and disclosure of taxation items, which are summarised here.

8.1 Presentation of tax assets and liabilities

These should be **presented separately** from other assets and liabilities in the statement of financial position. Deferred tax assets and liabilities should be distinguished from current tax assets and liabilities.

In addition, deferred tax assets/liabilities should *not* be classified as current assets/ liabilities, where an entity makes such a distinction.

8.2 Presentation of tax expense

The tax expense or income related to the profit or loss from ordinary activities should be presented on the **face of the income statement**.

8.3 Disclosure

As you would expect, the major components of tax expense or income should be disclosed separately. These will generally include the following.

■   **Current tax expense** (income).

■   Any adjustments recognised in the period for **current tax of prior periods** (i.e. for over/under statement in prior years).

■   Amount of **deferred tax expense (income)** relating to the origination and reversal of **temporary differences**.

■   Amount of the benefit arising from a previously unrecognised tax loss, tax credit or temporary difference of a prior period that is used to **reduce current tax expense**.

- Amount of the benefit from a previously unrecognised tax loss, tax credit or temporary difference of a prior period that is used to **reduce deferred tax expense**.

- Deferred tax expense arising from the **write-down**, or reversal of a previous write-down, of a deferred tax asset.

- Amount of tax expense (income) relating to those **changes in accounting policies** and **errors** which are included in the determination of net profit or loss for the period in accordance with IAS 8, because they cannot be accounted for retrospectively.

There are substantial additional disclosures required by the Standard. All these items should be shown separately.

- Aggregate current and deferred tax relating to items that are charged or credited to **equity**.

- An explanation of the relationship between **tax expense (income)** and **accounting profit** in either or both of the following forms.

    - A numerical reconciliation between tax expense (income) and the product of accounting profit multiplied by the applicable tax rate(s), disclosing also the basis on which the applicable tax rate(s) is (are) computed.

    - A numerical reconciliation between the average effective tax rate and the applicable tax rate, disclosing also the basis on which the applicable tax rate is computed.

- An explanation of **changes in the applicable tax rate(s)** compared to the previous accounting period.

- The amount (and expiry date, if any) of **deductible temporary differences**, unused tax losses, and unused tax credits for which no deferred tax is recognised in the statement of financial position.

- In respect of each type of **temporary difference**, and in respect of each type of **unused tax loss** and **unused tax credit**

    - The amount of the deferred tax assets and liabilities recognised in the statement of financial position for each period presented.

    - The amount of the deferred tax income or expense recognised in the income statement, if this is not apparent from the changes in the amounts recognised in the statement of financial position.

- In respect of **discontinued operations**, the tax expense relating to

    - The gain or loss on discontinuance.

    - The profit or loss from the ordinary activities of the discontinued operation for the period, together with the corresponding amounts for each prior period presented.

In addition, an entity should disclose the amount of a deferred tax asset and the nature of the evidence supporting its recognition, when

- The utilisation of the deferred tax asset is dependent on future taxable profits in excess of the profits arising from the reversal of existing taxable temporary differences; and

- The entity has suffered a loss in either the current or preceding period in the tax jurisdiction to which the deferred tax asset relates.

CHAPTER ROUNDUP

You need to be familiar with, able to describe and perform basic calculations on

- Corporation tax

  - Adjustments to profits
  - Adjustments for prior years

- Overseas tax and double tax relief

- Deferred tax and IAS 12

  - **Deferred tax liabilities** are the amounts of income taxes payable in future periods in respect of taxable temporary differences.

  - **Deferred tax assets** are the amounts of income taxes recoverable in future periods in respect of

    - Deductible temporary differences.
    - The carryforward of unused tax losses.
    - The carryforward of unused tax credits.

  - **Temporary differences** are differences between the carrying amount of an asset or liability in the statement of financial position and its tax base. Temporary differences may be either

    - **Taxable temporary differences**, which are temporary differences that will result in taxable amounts in determining taxable profit (tax loss) of future periods when the carrying amount of the asset or liability is recovered or settled.

    - **Deductible temporary differences**, which are temporary differences that will result in amounts that are deductible in determining taxable profit (tax loss) of future periods when the carrying amount of the asset or liability is recovered or settled.

  - The **tax base** of an asset or liability is the amount attributed to that asset or liability for tax purposes.

  - There are various methods of accounting for deferred tax, only one of which is adopted by IAS 12.

    - **Flow-through method**.
    - **Full provision method** (as under IAS 12).
    - **Partial provision method** (as adopted in some countries, e.g. formerly the UK).

TEST YOUR KNOWLEDGE

Check your knowledge of the Chapter here, without referring back to the text.

1   Taxing matters

NB: Assume that the relevant corporation tax rate is 30%.

(a)   C plc's accounting profits before tax in its first year of existence were £1,000,000. Non-current assets purchased in the year cost £50,000 and are being depreciated straight-line over five years. Capital allowances are at a rate of 25% calculated on the reducing balance of expenditure. C plc charged bad debts of £10,000 and made a provision for doubtful debts of £12,000. Provisions for repair costs of £60,000 were set up in the year but only £20,000 was actually paid. Entertainment of UK customers cost £4,000, while entertainment of overseas customers cost £2,000. Royalties receivable of £45,000 have been recognised in the accounts but not yet received. Royalties payable of £10,000 have been charged in the accounts, but not yet paid.

What are C plc's profits chargeable to corporation tax in the year?

(b)   In the year ended November 30 2006, D plc recognised income from royalties of £60,000 in its income statement. Of this, only £20,000 was received in cash during the year. It has also recognised a charge for patent royalties payable of £10,000, none of which had been paid in cash by the end of the period.

The carrying value of property, plant and equipment in D plc's statement of financial position at November 30 was £360,000 and its written down value for tax purposes at that date was £270,000.

What amounts will appear in D plc's statement of financial position at November 30 2006 relating to deferred tax.

2   Deferred tax Part 1

(a)   Grant Ltd had taxable temporary differences of £100,000 at 31 March 20X1. During the year ended 31 March 20X2, depreciation exceeded capital allowances by £10,000 and in the year ended 31 March 20X3, capital allowances exceeded depreciation by £25,000. Given a tax rate of 30%, calculate the deferred tax provision at 31 March 20X2 and 20X3. Show the deferred tax movements recognised in the income statements of both years.

(b)   Haven Ltd had a liability for deferred tax of £60,000 in its statement of financial position at 31 December 20X1. During the year ended 31 December 20X2, depreciation was £100,000 and capital allowances were £125,000. Given a tax rate of 25%, calculate the deferred tax movement in the income statement of 20X2 and the liability for deferred tax at 31 December 20X2.

3.   Deferred tax Part 2

Explain, with examples, the nature and purpose of deferred tax.

TEST YOUR KNOWLEDGE: ANSWERS

1. Taxing matters

   (a)

	(£)	(£)
Accounting profit before tax		1,000,000
Add: back Disallowed expenditure		
Depreciation (50,000 × $\frac{1}{5}$)	10,000	
Doubtful debts	12,000	
Provision for repairs not paid in the year	40,000	
Royalties charge not yet paid	10,000	
Entertainment	6,000	
		78,000
Less: Expenditure not charged but tax allowable Capital		
allowances (25% × 50,000)		(12,500)
Less: Income credited not yet taxable		
Royalties accrued not yet received		(45,000)
Profits chargeable to corporation tax		1,020,500

   (b)

	(£)
Deferred tax liability	
Royalties receivable (40,000 × 30%)	12,000
Property plant and equipment (90,000 × 30%)	27,000
	39,000
Deferred tax asset	
Patent royalties (10,000 × 30%)	3,000

   Workings

		Carrying Amount £'000	Tax Base £'000	Temporary Difference £'000
1.	Asset – royalties receivable	40	0	40
	Taxable temporary difference: deferred tax liability @ 30%			
2.	Asset – property plant etc	360	270	90
	Taxable temporary difference: deferred tax liability @ 30%			
3.	Liability – royalties payable	(10)	0	(10)
	Deductible temporary difference: deferred tax asset @ 30%			

   Note

   The tax base of an **asset** is the amount that will be deductible for tax purposes from any taxable economic benefits that will flow to the entity when it uses or sells the asset. The tax base of the royalties receivable asset is £nil because the full amount of the cash received will be liable to tax. When the property plant and equipment is used (and disposed of at the end of its useful life), cash inflows will be taxed after deducting £270,000 of allowable expenditure (its tax written down value).

Taxable temporary differences arise when the carrying amount of an asset exceeds its tax base. These create deferred tax liabilities in the statement of financial position.

The tax base of a **liability** is its carrying amount (here £10,000) less any amount that will be deductible for tax purposes in future periods when the liability is settled/paid (here £10,000 because when D pays the royalties, it will reduce its taxable profits of that period by £10,000). The tax base is therefore £nil.

Deductible temporary differences arise when the carrying amount of a liability exceeds its tax base. In principle, these create deferred tax assets; deferred tax assets can only be recognised to the extent that it is probable that there will be sufficient future taxable profits against which to offset the deductions.

2.   Deferred tax

(a)   **Grant Ltd**

	(£'000)
Taxable temporarydifferences at 31 March 20X1	100
Depreciation exceeds capital allowances	(10)
Taxable temporary differences at 31 March 20X2	90
Capital allowances exceed depreciation	25
Taxable temporary differences at 31 March 20x3	115

Deferred taxliability

	(£'000)
At 1 April 20X1 (£100,000 @ 30%)	30.0
To income statement (£10,000 @ 30%)	(3.0)
At 31 March 20X2	27.0
At 1 April 20X2	27.0
To income statement (£25,000 @ 30%)	7.5
At 31 March 20X3	34.5

Income statement

31.03.20X2: Reduction in deferred tax charge – £3,000

31.03.20X3: Increase in deferred tax charge – £7,500

(b)   **Haven Ltd**

Deferred tax liability

	(£'000)
At 1 January 20X2	60
Increase in charge (W)	6
At 31 December 20X2	66

WORKING

	(£'000)
Capital allowances	124
Depreciation	(100)
Increase in taxable temporary differences	24
Transfer to income statement (24 @ 25%)	6

3.   Deferred tax Part 2

IAS 12 *Income Taxes* deals with accounting for current and deferred tax. Current tax is the amount of income taxes payable (or recoverable) in respect of the taxable profit (or loss) for the period. Current tax is essentially short-term in nature and results in current liabilities (and assets) and cash flows.

Deferred tax is a method of accounting for the future tax effects of transactions that have taken place prior to the statement of financial position date. It can result in recognising both deferred tax liabilities and assets. The approach adopted in IAS 12 is based on the concept of **temporary differences** which are identified in the statement of financial position; these are differences between the **carrying amount** of an asset or liability in the statement of financial position at its **tax base**.

(a)   **Carrying amount** is the amount at which an asset or liability is recognised in the statement of financial position under IFRS. The net book value of property plant and equipment is its carrying amount.

(b)   **Tax base** is the amount attributed to an asset or liability for tax purposes. The tax base of an asset represents the extent to which there are future tax deductions available to offset against taxable profits generated by using or selling that asset. Asset and liabilities can have nil tax bases.

The concept of deferred tax in IAS 12 is that there are unavoidable future tax consequences of recovering assets and settling liabilities carried in the statement of financial position and these tax consequences should be accounted for in the current statement of financial position as deferred tax assets or liabilities.

Deferred tax liabilities arise from **taxable** temporary differences and deferred tax assets result from **deductible** temporary differences. Deferred tax assets can also result from **carrying forward unused tax losses** to be relieved against future taxable profits.

The following examples illustrate the application of the concept of deferred tax in IAS 12.

(a)   **Property plant and equipment.** Where an item of property plant and equipment is depreciated in the financial statements and the expenditure is deductible for tax purposes more rapidly, its carrying amount in the statement of financial position will exceed its tax base. The difference between the net book value in the balance and the tax written down value represents a taxable temporary difference on which a deferred tax liability must be recognised.

(b)   **Income/receivables taxable in later periods.** When income is recognised as receivable in the income statement but is not taxable until received in cash in a later period, there is a taxable temporary difference, being the excess of the receivable asset in the statement of financial position at the nil tax base of the asset. Deferred tax on the difference must be provided

(c)   **Expenditure/payables deductible in later periods.** When costs are charged in the income statement of the current period but are not deductible for tax until paid in cash in a later period, there is a deductible temporary difference. To the extent that it is probable that there will be sufficient taxable profits in future against which the tax deduction can be offset, a deferred tax asset will be recognised

(d)   **Asset revalued to fair value.** If an asset, say land and buildings or a financial asset, is measured in the statement of financial position at fair value, a taxable temporary difference arises on the excess of carrying amount (fair value) over its tax base (say, historic cost). A deferred tax liability must be recognised, irrespective of the probability of selling the asset in the foreseeable future.

15

Foreign Currency

INTRODUCTION

Most businesses will be influenced in some way by exchange rates, perhaps as an importer or exporter paying and receiving in a foreign currency, perhaps through an investment in an overseas subsidiary.

This chapter examines how foreign currency items should be dealt with in the account and how changes in exchange rates may distort our analysis of those accounts.

CHAPTER CONTENTS

CHAPTER LEARNING OBJECTIVES

The syllabus areas covered by this section are

Interpretation of Financial Information

The effect of accounting practices

Understanding of the effect of accounting practices on the numbers most significant for investment decisions (profit, earnings per share, asset value etc).

Accounting Terminology and Concepts

Accounting terminology and a knowledge of accounting concepts and conventions to include the statement of financial position, income statement, statement of cash flows and notes to the accounts. An understanding of the distinction between capital and revenue, the valuation of assets for accounting purposes and the determination of profit and earnings share on the nil, net and full distribution bases. An understanding of significance of the statement of accounting policies in relation to the concept of a true and fair view.

Presentation of Financial Statements

Impact of statutory and non-statutory regulation on UK financial statements

An understanding of the effect on the presentation of financial statements of the Companies Act and non-statutory regulations, including standards and other guidance issued by IASB and Stock Exchange requirements.

In the respect of foreign currency:

It is emphasised that the intention of the examination is to assess student's analytical and interpretative skills rather than their technical accounting ability. It is also expected that they should have an understanding of standard accounting practices and an awareness of matters currently under discussion.

1 IAS 21 THE EFFECTS OF CHANGES IN FOREIGN EXCHANGE RATES

Exam tip

Questions rarely arise on this area in Section B or C questions, though the impact of exchange rate movements may well be significant within any Section A analysis.

1.1 Introduction

If a company trades overseas, it will buy or sell assets in **foreign currencies**. For example, an Indian company might buy materials from the US, and pay for them in US dollars, and then sell its finished goods in Germany, receiving payment in Euros, or perhaps in some other currency. If the company owes money in a foreign currency at the end of the accounting year, or holds assets which were bought in a foreign currency, those liabilities or assets must be translated into the local currency (in this text £), in order to be shown in the books of account.

A company might have a subsidiary abroad (i.e. a foreign entity that it owns), and the subsidiary will trade in its own local currency. The subsidiary will keep books of account and prepare its annual accounts in its own currency. However, at the year end, the holding company must 'consolidate' the results of the overseas subsidiary into its group accounts, so that somehow, the assets and liabilities and the **annual profits of the subsidiary must be translated from the foreign currency into £**.

If foreign currency exchange rates remained constant, there would be no accounting problem. As you will be aware, however, foreign exchange rates are continually changing, and it is not inconceivable for example, that the rate of exchange between the Polish zlotych and sterling might be Z6.2 to £1 at the start of the accounting year, and Z5.6 to £1 at the end of the year (in this example, a 10% increase in the relative strength of the zlotych).

1.2 Definitions

These are some of the definitions given by IAS 21 *The Effects of Changes in Foreign Exchange Rates*.

- **Foreign currency**. A currency other than the functional currency of the entity.

- **Functional currency**. The currency of the primary economic environment in which the entity operates.

- **Presentation currency**. The currency in which the financial statements are presented.

- **Exchange rate**. The ratio of exchange for two currencies.

- **Exchange difference**. The difference resulting from translating a given number of units of one currency into another currency at different exchange rates.

- **Closing rate**. The spot exchange rate at the statement of financial position date.

- **Spot exchange rate**. The exchange rate for immediate delivery.

- **Monetary items**. Units of currency held and assets and liabilities to be received or paid in a fixed or determinable number of units of currency. *(IAS 21)*

1.3 Functional currency

Each entity – whether an individual company, a parent of a group, or an operation within a group (such as a subsidiary, associate or branch) – should determine its **functional currency** and **measure its results and financial position in that currency**.

For most individual companies the functional currency will be the currency of the country in which they are located and in which they carry out most of their transactions. Determining the functional currency is much more likely to be an issue where an entity operates as part of a group.

An entity can **present** its financial statements in any currency (or currencies) it chooses. IAS 21 deals with the situation in which financial statements are presented in a currency other than the functional currency.

Again, this is unlikely to be an issue for most individual companies. Their presentation currency will normally be the same as their functional currency (the currency of the country in which they operate).

1.4 Foreign currency transactions: Initial recognition

IAS 21 states that a foreign currency transaction should be recorded, on initial recognition in the functional currency, by applying the exchange rate between the reporting currency and the foreign currency **at the date of the transaction** to the foreign currency amount.

An **average rate** for a period may be used if exchange rates do not fluctuate significantly.

1.5 Reporting at subsequent statement of financial position dates

The following rules apply at each subsequent statement of financial position date.

- Report foreign currency **monetary items** using the **closing rate**. Examples of monetary items include payables and receivables, debt securities, cash and bank balances.

- Report **non-monetary items** (e.g. non-current assets, inventories) which are carried at **historical cost** in a foreign currency using the **exchange rate at the date of the transaction** (historical rate).

- Report **non-monetary items** which are carried at **fair value** in a foreign currency using the exchange rates that existed **when the values were determined**.

1.6 Recognition of exchange differences

Exchange differences occur when there is a **change in the exchange rate** between the transaction date and the date of settlement of monetary items arising from a foreign currency transaction.

Exchange differences arising on the settlement of monetary items (receivables, payables, loans, cash in a foreign currency) or on translating an entity's monetary items at rates different from those at which they were translated initially, or reported in previous financial statements, should be **recognised in profit or loss** in the period in which they arise.

There are two situations to consider.

- The transaction is **settled in the same period** as that in which it occurred: all the exchange difference is recognised in that period.

- The transaction is **settled in a subsequent accounting period**: the exchange difference recognised in each intervening period up to the period of settlement is determined by the change in exchange rates during that period.

In other words, where a monetary item has not been settled at the end of a period, it should be **restated using the closing exchange rate** and any gain or loss taken to the income statement.

Example

A company makes a sale to a US customer for $1,500 dollars when the rate of exchange is $1.50:£1.00. The sale is settled with a payment of $1,500 cash, which is still held at year end. At the statement of financial position date the rate of exchange has moved to $1.40:£1.00.

At what rate should the sale be recorded and at what rate should the cash be evaluated in the statement of financial position?

Solution

Applying the above rules, this transaction should be denominated at the historical rate, i.e.

- Cash up £1,000 ($1,500 ÷ 1.5) (DEBIT: Cash)
- Sales up £1,000 ($1,500 ÷ 1.5) (CREDIT: Retained profits – revenue)

Thus, we have recorded a sale of £1,000 and are showing cash of £1,000.

At the year end, however, we still hold this cash as $1,500 in dollar bills. The question is how should we evaluate this asset on the statement of financial position. What is the value of $1,500 at the statement of financial position date?

Clearly, at the statement of financial position date we could exchange each of these dollars at the rate of $1.40:£1.00 and obtain a total of £1,071 ($1,500 ÷ 1.4). This, therefore, represents a fair value of the asset to be placed on the statement of financial position. However, we have this cash evaluated at just £1,000 from recording the original transaction. The question is, how do we deal with this change in value?

This change in value is an example of an exchange difference arising from a foreign exchange transaction. In this case, we have made a gain of £71 by holding on to a foreign currency asset arising from our trading activities, which appreciated as the US dollar strengthened. This £71 gain should, therefore, be treated as part of our trading profit for the year.

The impact on our accounting equation of taking account of this exchange difference is

- Cash up £71 (DEBIT: Cash).
- Exchange gain (profit) up £71 (shareholders' funds up) (CREDIT: Retained earnings).

Hence, we have the following recorded in the income statement.

Income statement	(£)
Sales	1,000
Exchange gain	71
Total	1,071

Matching the total value of our cash asset with a value of £1,071 within total assets. Similarly, if we had not been paid cash but instead had a receivable, this receivable would be evaluated at £1,071 – its worth to the business at the year end.

Conclusion

All **monetary** foreign currency assets and liabilities (cash, receivables, payables, loans) should be evaluated on the statement of financial position at the **closing rate**. This evaluation will give rise to exchange differences if the exchange rate has fluctuated.

Example

On 31 October, a company buys some inventory from an overseas supplier for 10,000 Hong Kong dollars when the exchange rate is HK$10:£1.00. This inventory is still held at the year end (31 December).

What will be the impact on the accounting equation of recording the various transactions, what would appear on the year-end statement of financial position and what exchange gains or losses arise if the goods are paid for

- Immediately?
- 30 November at a rate of HK$9:£1?
- 8 February of the following year at the rate of HK$11:£1?

NB: The year-end rate is HK$9.5:£1.

Solution

Pay immediately

If we pay this liability immediately we will pay HK$10,000, which will cost us £1,000 at the current rate of HK$10:£1.

Purchase transaction

The impact of the purchase on the accounting equation will be

- Inventory up (net assets up) £1,000 (HK$10,000 ÷ 10).(DEBIT: Inventory)
- Cash down (assets down) £1,000 (HK$10,000 ÷ 10). (CREDIT: Cash)

Recording the transaction at the historic rate as required by IAS 21.

Statement of financial position assets/liabilities

No other entries would be recorded in the books, we would simply replace the £1,000 cash asset by a £1,000 inventory asset and hold nothing denominated in Hong Kong dollars.

Inventory still held at the year end must be valued in accordance with the rules laid out in IAS 2, i.e. it should be valued at the lower of **cost** and net realisable value.

Assuming there is no net realisable value problem in this case, the inventory should be valued at its cost (i.e. the purchase price) of £1,000, irrespective of how the exchange rate may have moved in the intervening period.

Per IAS 21, all **non-monetary** assets (i.e. inventory and non-current assets) should be left at their **historical rates**, i.e. their original costs at the statement of financial position date.

Pay on 30 November

Purchase transaction

The impact of the purchase on the accounting equation will be

- Inventory up (assets up) £1,000 (HK$10,000 ÷ 10). (DEBIT: Inventory).
- Payables up (liabilities up) £1,000 (HK$10,000 ÷ 10). (CREDIT: Payables).

Again recording the transaction at the historic rate.

Cash payment – 30 November

If we delay payment until 30 November, by which time the exchange rate has moved to HK$9:£1, then to fully clear the liability we will need to buy HK$10,000, which will cost us £1,111 (HK$10,000 ÷ 9) even though the liability is recorded as £1,000. This is because the Hong Kong dollar has been appreciating against sterling, hence our liability, though fixed in Hong Kong dollar terms, has risen in sterling terms – we have made a loss.

The impact of this transaction on the accounting equation will be

- Cash down £1,111 (assets down). (CREDIT: Cash)
- Payables down £1,000 (liabilities down). (DEBIT: Payables)
- Exchange loss up (profit down) £111 (shareholders' funds down). (DEBIT: Retained earnings)

Statement of financial position

This transaction is now settled, hence there would be no foreign currency liability to record. We still hold the inventory, however, and this would still be valued at £1,000, its original cost, as above.

Pay on 8 February

Purchase transaction

The impact of the purchase on the accounting equation will be

- Inventory up (assets up) £1,000 (HK$10,000 ÷ 10). (DEBIT: Inventory)
- Payables up (liabilities up) £1,000 (HK$10,000 ÷ 10). (CREDIT: Payables)

As in the two previous examples, the original transaction is recorded at the historical rate.

Statement of financial position

At the year end, the exchange rate has moved to 9.5 Hong Kong dollars to the pound and at that date, we have the inventory on the statement of financial position and we still owe the Hong Kong supplier. How are these two items recorded?

The inventory, as a non-monetary asset, should be left at its historical rate (its cost) of £1,000, i.e. no retranslation or revaluation is carried out.

This time we also have a foreign currency payable of HK$10,000. This payable, as a monetary liability, should be retranslated (per SSAP 20) at the closing rate of HK$9.5:£1. We should, therefore, recognise £1,052 (HK$10,000 ÷ 9.5) as our full liability rather than the £1,000 at which we originally recorded it. After all, if we were to pay it now we would have to pay £1,052, hence surely this is the fairest reflection of the true position.

We, therefore, need to increase the value of the payable by £52 to bring it up to its fair value of £1,052. The impact on our accounting equation of reflecting this increase in the value of the payable would be

- Payables up £52 (liabilities up). (CREDIT: Payables)
- Exchange loss up (profits down) £52 (shareholders' funds down). (DEBIT: Retained earnings)

Hence, we recognise a loss this year as the currency has moved against us.

Cash payment – 8 February

On 8 February, when this liability is subsequently paid, the exchange rate has moved to HK$11:£1, hence to clear our HK$10,000 liability, which is currently in the books at £1,052 following our year-end retranslation, we will need to pay £909 (HK$10,000 ÷ 11).

In this instance, we are paying less than we had anticipated. We have made an exchange gain of £143 (£1,052 – £909), which would become part of the profits for this next year.

The impact on the accounting equation for this would be

- Cash down (assets down) £909. (CREDIT: Cash)
- Payables down (liabilities down) £1,052. (DEBIT: Payables)
- Exchange gain (profits up) £143. (DEBIT: Retained earnings)

Example

White Cliffs Co, whose year end is 31 December, buys some goods from Rinka SA of France on 30 September. The invoice value is €40,000 and is due for settlement in equal instalments on 30 November and 31 January.

The exchange rate moved as follows.

	€ = £1
30 September	1.60
30 November	1.80
31 December	1.90
31 January	1.85

Requirement

State the accounting entries in the books of White Cliffs Co.

Solution

The purchase will be recorded in the books of White Cliffs Co using the rate of exchange ruling on 30 September.

DEBIT	Purchases	£25,000
CREDIT	Trade payables	£25,000

Being the £ cost of goods purchased for €40,000 (€40,000 ÷ €1.60/£1)

On 30 November, White Cliffs must pay €20,000. This will cost €20,000 ÷ €1.80/£1 = £11,111 and the company has therefore made an exchange gain of £12,500 − £11,111 = £1,389.

DEBIT	Trade payables	£12,500
CREDIT	Retained profits	£1,389
CREDIT	Cash	£11,111

On 31 December, the statement of financial position date, the outstanding liability will be recalculated using the rate applicable to that date: €20,000 ÷ €1.90/£1 = £10,526. A further exchange gain of £1,974 has been made and will be recorded as follows.

DEBIT	Trade payables	£1,974
CREDIT	Retained profits	£1,974

The total exchange gain of £3,363 will be included in the operating profit for the year ending 31 December.

On 31 January, White Cliffs must pay the second instalment of €20,000. This will cost them £10,811 (€20,000 ÷ €1.85/£1).

DEBIT	Trade payables	£10,526
	Retained profits	£285
CREDIT	Cash	£10,811

2 IAS 21 CONSOLIDATED FINANCIAL STATEMENTS STAGE

2.1 Definitions

The following definitions are relevant here.

> **Foreign operation.** A subsidiary, associate, joint venture or branch of a reporting entity, the activities of which are based or conducted in a country or currency other than those of the reporting entity.
>
> **Net investment in a foreign operation.** The amount of the reporting entity's interest in the net assets of that operation.
>
> *(IAS 21)*

2.2 Determining functional currency

In order to determine the functional currency of a foreign operation it is necessary to consider the **relationship** between the foreign operation and its parent.

- If the foreign operation carries out its business as though it were an **extension of the parent's operations**, it almost certainly has the **same functional currency** as the parent.

- If the foreign operation is **semi-autonomous** it almost certainly has **a different functional currency** from the parent.

The translation method used has to reflect the economic reality of the relationship between the reporting entity (the parent) and the foreign operation.

2.3 Accounting treatment: same functional currency as the reporting entity

The same standards and procedures identified in Section 1 above for individual company accounts should be applied to the financial statements of a foreign operation, **as if the transactions of the foreign operation had been those of the parent**.

We can summarise the treatment here.

- **Income statement**: translate using actual rates. An average for a period may be used, but not where there is significant fluctuation and the average is therefore unreliable.

- **Non-monetary items**: translate using an historical rate at the date of purchase (or revaluation to fair value, or reduction to realisable/recoverable amount). This includes inventories and non-current assets (and their depreciation).

- **Monetary items**: translate at the closing rate.

- **Exchange differences**: report as part of profit for the year.

2.4 Accounting treatment: different functional currency from the reporting entity

The financial statements of the foreign operation must be translated to the functional currency of the parent. Different procedures must be followed here, because the functional currency of the parent is the **presentation currency** of the foreign operation.

- The **assets and liabilities** shown in the foreign operation's statement of financial position are translated at the **closing rate** at the statement of financial position date, regardless of the date on which those items originated. The balancing figure on the translated statement of financial position represents the reporting entity's net investment in the foreign operation.

- Amounts in the **income statement** should be translated at the rate ruling at the date of the transaction (an **average rate** will usually be used for practical purposes).

- **Exchange differences** arising from the re-translation at the end of each year of the parent's net investment should be **taken to equity**, not through the income statement for the year, until the disposal of the net investment.

Example

The abridged statement of financial positions and income statements of Darius Co and its foreign subsidiary, Xerxes Inc, appear below.

Draft statement of financial position as at 31 December 2007	Darius Co (£)	(£)	Xerxes Inc (€)	(€)
Assets				
Non-Current Assets				
Plant at cost	600		500	
Less Depreciation	(250)		(200)	
		350		300
Investment in Xerxes				
100 €1 shares		25		–
		375		300
Current Assets				
Inventories	225		200	
Receivables	150		100	
		375		300
		750		600
Equity and Liabilities				
Equity				
Ordinary £1/€1 shares	300		100	
Retained Earnings	300		280	
		600		380
Long-Term Loans		50		110
Current Liabilities		100		110
		750		600

Income statements for the year ended 31 December 2007	Darius Co (£)	Xerxes Inc (€)
Profit before tax	200	160
Tax	100	80
Profit after tax, retained	100	80

The following further information is given.

- Darius Co has had its interest in Xerxes Inc since the incorporation of the company.

- Depreciation is 8% per annum on cost.

- There have been no loan repayments or movements in non-current assets during the year. The opening inventory of Xerxes Inc was €120. Assume that inventory turnover times are very short.

- Exchange rates: €4 to £1 when Xerxes Inc was incorporated
€2.5 to £1 when Xerxes Inc acquired its non-current assets
€2 to £1 on 31 December 2006
€1.6 to £1 average rate of exchange year ending 31 December 2007
€1 to £1 on 31 December 2007.

Requirement

Prepare the summarised consolidated financial statements of Darius Co using

(a) The presentation currency method.
(b) The functional currency method.

Solution

Presentation currency method

Step 1 The statement of financial position of Xerxes Inc at 31 December 2007, other than share capital and retained earnings, should be translated at €1 = £1, the closing ratio. The shareholders' funds are then the balancing figure.

Summarised statement of financial position at 31 December 2007	(£)	(£)
Non-Current Assets (NBV)		300
Current Assets		
Inventories	200	
Receivables	100	
		300
		600
Non-Current Liabilities		110
Current Liabilities		110

∴ Shareholders' funds = 600 − 110 − 110 = £380

Since Darius Co acquired the whole of the issued share capital on incorporation, the post-acquisition retained earnings including exchange differences will be the value of shareholders' funds arrived at above, less the original cost to Darius Co of £25. Post-acquisition retained earnings = £380 − £25 = £355.

Summarised consolidated statement of financial position as at 31 December 2007	(£)	(£)	(£)
Assets			
Non-Current Assets (NBV)	(350 + 300)		650
Current Assets			
Inventories	(225 + 200)	425	
Receivables	(150 + 100)	250	
			675
			1,325
Equity and Liabilities			
Equity			
Ordinary £1 shares (Darius only)			300
Retained Earnings	(300 + 355)		655
			955
Non-Current Liabilities: loans	(50 + 110)		160
Current Liabilities	(100 + 110)		210
			1,325

NB: It is quite unnecessary to know the amount of the exchange differences when preparing the consolidated statement of financial position.

Step 2 The income statement should be translated at average rate (€1.6 = £1).

Summarised income statement of Xerxes inc for the year ended 31 December 2007	(£)
Profit before tax	100
Tax	50
Profit after tax, retained	50

Summarised consolidated income statement for the year ended 31 December 2007

	(£)	(£)
Profit before tax	(200 + 100)	300
Tax	(100 + 50)	150
Profit after tax, retained	(100 + 50)	150

Step 3 The equity interest at the beginning of the year can be found as follows.

	(€)
Equity value at 31 December 2007	380
Retained profit for year	80
Equity value at 31 December 2006	300
Translated at €2 = £1, this gives	£150

Step 4 The exchange difference can now be calculated.

	(£)
Equity interest at 31 December 2007 (stage 1)	380
Equity interest at 1 January 2007 (stage 3)	150
	230
Less retained profit (stage 2)	50
Exchange gain	180

Consolidated statement of movements on reserves for the year ended 31 December 2005

	(£)
Consolidated reserves at 31 December 2006	325
Exchange gains arising on consolidation	180
Retained profit for the year	150
Consolidated reserves at 31 December 2007	655

NB: The post-acquisition reserves of Xerxes Inc at the beginning of the year must have been £150 – £25 = £125 and the reserves of Darius Co must have been £300 – £100 = £200. The consolidated reserves must therefore have been £325.

Functional currency method

Step 1

Summarised statement of financial position of Xerxes inc as at 31 December 2007

	Rate	(£)	(£)
Non-Current Assets at NBV	€2.5 = £1		120
Current Assets			
Inventories	(Assumed) €1 = £1	200	
Receivables	€1 = £1	100	
			300
			420
Non-Current Liabilities	€1 = £1		110
Current Liabilities	€1 = £1		110

Shareholders' funds = (420 – 110 – 110) = £200

In arriving at the consolidated statement of financial position the same comments apply as in Step 1 for the presentation currency method. The post-acquisition reserves of Xerxes Inc will be £200 − £25 = £175.

Summarised Consolidated statement of financial position as at 31 December 2007

	(£)	(£)	(£)
Assets			
Non-Current Assets at NBV	(350 + 120)		470
Current Assets			
Inventories	(225 + 200)	425	
Receivables	(150 + 100)	250	
			675
			1,145
Equity and Liabilities			
Equity			
Ordinary £1 shares			300
Retained Earnings	(300 + 175)		475
			775
Non-Current Liabilities: loans	(50 + 110)		160
Current Liabilities	(100 + 110)		210
			1,145

Note. As with the presentation currency method, it has been quite unnecessary to know the amount of the exchange differences when preparing the consolidated statement of financial position.

Step 2 The following rates should be used for the income statement.

	Rate
Depreciation	€2.5 = £1
Opening inventories	€2.0 = £1
Closing inventories	€1.0 = £1
All other items	€1.6 = £1

Summarised income statement for the year ended 31 December 2007

	(€)	(€)	Rate	(£)	(£)
Profit before tax, depreciation and increase in inventory value		120	€1.6 = £1		75
Opening inventory	120		€2.0 = £1	60	
Closing inventory	200		€1.0 = £1	200	
Increase in inventory value		80			140
		200			215
Depreciation (8% × € 500)		40	€2.5 = £1		16
Profit before tax		160			199
Tax		80	€1.6 = £1		50
Profit after tax, retained		80			149

Step 3 Since there were no movements in non-current assets or loan repayments, the opening statement of financial position in euros can be summarised as shown below. This has been translated at €2.5 = £1 for non-current assets and at €2.0 = £1 for monetary items and inventories.

Summarised statement of financial position as at 31 December 2006	(€)	Rate	(£)
Non-Current Assets NBV €(300 + 40)	340	€2.5 = £1	136
Inventories	120	€2.0 = £1	60
Net Current Monetary Liabilities (balancing figure)	50	€2.0 = £1	25
	410		171
Shareholders' Funds €(380 – 80)	300	Balancing figure	116
Loans	110	€2.0 = £1	55
	410		171

Step 4   The exchange difference can be calculated.

	(£)
Shareholders' Funds at 31 December 2007	200
Less Shareholders' Funds at 31 December 2006	116
	84
Less retained profit before exchange differences	149
Exchange loss	(65)

Summarised consolidated income statement for the year ended 31 December 2007	(£)
Profit before tax £(200 + 199 – 65)	334
Tax £(100 + 50)	150
Profit after tax, retained	184
Shareholders' funds at 31 December 2006	116
Less cost of shares	25
Post-acquisition reserves in Xerxes Inc at 31 December 2006	91
Reserves of Darius Co at 31 December 2006	200
Consolidated reserves at 31 December 2006	291

Consolidated statement of movements on reserves for the year ended 31 December 2007	
	(£)
Consolidated reserves at 31 December 2006	291
Retained profit for the year	184
Consolidated reserves at 31 December 2007	475

3   IMPACT ON ANALYSIS

The following should be borne in mind when trying to analyse the results or financial position of a company where foreign exchange is involved.

3.1 Impact on ratios

The presentation currency method does not really distort any of the relationships inherent in the foreign companies accounts, i.e. gearing ratios, current ratios, return on capital employed, etc. will be maintained in the sterling accounts. There will be some slight distortions as the income statement has been translated at the average rate. However, these are unlikely to be significant.

Under the functional currency method however, there are likely to be significant distortions in these relationships. Non-current assets will be evaluated at a historical rate that may be a rate that was prevailing several years ago and bears little similarity to the current rate.

3.2 Selective reporting

The presentation currency method advocates reserve accounting, i.e. gains and losses are taken to equity and not reported as part of the profit for the year.

When a foreign currency appreciates resulting in a profit in equity it is very common for there to be no comment on this fact in the directors' reports. Rather, the directors simply report that the financial position is looking particularly good in an attempt to lead the user of the accounts to believe that this is down to the effectiveness of management and trade.

Where the foreign currency is declining against sterling and a loss is taken to equity, directors tend to be very quick to report that the change in the financial position is poorer than expected as a result of an exchange loss.

With the foreign currency movement in equity being reported in the statement of total changes in equity, which is a primary financial statement, exchange gains and losses should be easily identified and thus tied back to management comment (or lack of comment) on this area.

3.3 Foreign exchange mismatching

A foreign exchange mismatch arises where money is borrowed in a hard currency that has low interest rates and invested in a soft currency that has high interest rates. We will consider firstly the reasons why this may be done and secondly, the consequences that are likely to arise.

3.4 Reasons

The reason for undertaking such a transaction is to boost reported profits. The investment in the soft currency with high interest rates will result in a high value of interest income. The borrowings in the hard currency with low interest rates will result in a low interest expense. The end result is a net interest income figure boosting reported profit.

3.5 Likely consequences

The likely result of undertaking this, however, is that the soft currency will decline in value against the hard currency. That loss in value is likely to more than cancel the net profits that have been generated. It is impossible to generate a risk-free profit by such transactions.

When we retranslate the cash deposits and the borrowings using the presentation currency method, we are liable to see a net loss that will be taken direct to equity.

The company has, therefore, achieved a boost in reported profits but it has certainly not boosted its financial position in any way, in all probability it will have deteriorated.

4 ANALYSING FOREIGN EXCHANGE RISK

4.1 Introduction

The risks a company may face with respect to foreign currency may be categorised under one of three headings.

- Transaction risk.
- Translation risk.
- Operating or economic risk.

4.2 Transaction risk

4.2.1 Definition

Transaction risk is the risk that the sterling value of any foreign currency receipts or payments may vary as a result of exchange rate fluctuations, resulting in a change in the anticipated operating cash flows.

Example

A company buys goods for $5m to be paid for in three months' time. The current (spot) exchange rate is $1.60:£1.

How much will be paid in three months' time if the exchange rate at that date is

- $1.60:£1
- $1.50:£1
- $1.70:£1

Solution

$1.60:£1

At this rate, the sterling amount payable would be $\dfrac{\$5,000,000}{1.60}$ = £3,125,000.

$1.50:£1

At this exchange rate, the sterling amount payable would be $\dfrac{\$5,000,000}{1.50}$ = £3,333,333.

$1.70:£1

At this exchange rate, the sterling amount payable would be $\dfrac{\$5,000,000}{1.70}$ = £2,941,176.

Conclusion

We can see that as a result of a relatively minor fluctuation in exchange rates, the sterling amount payable has moved dramatically. Clearly, there will be a problem here in, say, determining the level of overdraft needed to buy the equipment or even whether the purchase is viable at all if the exchange rate moves in the wrong direction.

4.3 Analysis of transaction risk

To analyse the extent of any transaction risk faced by a company, we need to determine the level of exports and imports undertaken. We also need to identify whether there are any monetary assets or liabilities in foreign currency (e.g. deposits, borrowings) on which the interest flows give rise to transaction risk.

4.3.1 Sales

The segmental analysis required by IAS 14 must give a geographical analysis of revenue.

If the sourced sales for any country exceed the destination sales then, clearly, some of that country's produce has been exported. These differences should help us to identify where we are producing and exporting from and where we are selling and importing into.

We would then need to consider two further factors.

- How exchange rates have varied against each other between the exporting and importing countries.
- The credit period taken, i.e. the delay between the transaction occurring and the cash flow taking place.

These factors, when considered together, should give us an indication of the likely extent of exchange gains or losses resulting from sales transactions.

4.3.2 Purchases

Little information is available here so it is very difficult, unless we are given the information in the financial and operating review, to determine the level of transaction risk that a company or group faces as a result of its imports. It will, therefore, be necessary to consider the type of business and its likely source of raw materials to get an indication of this risk.

4.4 Treasury Department hedging activities

The methods by which treasury departments attempt to avoid this transaction risk involve one of two ideas.

- Fixing the sterling value of the amount to be paid or received by one of
    - Invoicing or being invoiced in sterling.
    - The use of forward exchange contracts or futures.
    - The use of currency swaps.

- Matching foreign currency amounts payable and receivable, which may be possible where we are both importing and exporting, with the result that any loss made on one (the payable or receivable) is matched by a profit from the other.

4.5 Translation risk

4.5.1 Definition

Translation risk is the risk that the sterling value of any foreign denominated assets, liabilities, profits and losses will vary from one year to the next as a result of changes in exchange rates, which will impact on the reported results and position when

- Consolidating the results of overseas subsidiaries.
- Evaluating overseas loans raised by a UK company.

NB: This type of risk has no direct cash flow implications. Rather, what we have is variability of reported net assets and profits in sterling that may be caused purely by exchange rate fluctuations, with the net assets and profits in local currency terms being fairly stable. As a result, trends and ratios in the accounts may be distorted.

Example

A UK holding company (H) has a US subsidiary (S), both of which have the following assets and liabilities in local currency terms.

	H	S
	£m	$m
Assets	50	100
Liabilities	–	(70)

What will be the sterling value of the overseas subsidiary's assets and liabilities and the group's assets and liabilities if the exchange rate is

- $2:£1?
- $1:£1?

Solution

	$2:£1		$1:£1	
	S	Group	S	Group
	£m	£m	£m	£m
Assets	50	100	100	150
Liabilities	(35)	(35)	(70)	(70)
Gearing		53.8%		87.5%

If we imagine that the assets and liabilities of both the holding company and the subsidiary have not changed throughout the year and that the exchange rate started the year at $2:£1 and ended the year at $1:£1, then a number of accounting anomalies arise including

- Group debt is up £35m but no new loans have been raised and consequently the group gearing position has deteriorated, although this is purely the result of exchange rate movements.

- Group assets have risen by £50m and consequently group shareholders' funds (in the form of retained earnings) must also be up by £15m (£50 – 35) to ensure that the statement of financial position balances. Clearly, the group has not generated any profits during the year. This difference arises purely as a result of exchange rate movement (it is an exchange gain).

- Similarly, if we delved into any current ratios or quick ratios or any other ratios, we are likely to find similar distortions.

4.6 Analysis

Since translation risk results from the potential change in value of any foreign denominated assets or liabilities held either at the start of the year or as a result of profits for the year, the analysis of the extent of any translation risk depends on the ability to determine the net value of any overseas assets, liabilities or profits.

In addition, to enable us to determine the impact on gearing and liquidity ratios of the group, we would need to be able to determine a breakdown of the assets and liabilities denominated in foreign currencies. Clearly, this will not be possible from a set of group accounts and could only be determined by looking to the accounts of the overseas subsidiaries concerned.

BPP
LEARNING MEDIA

In conclusion, it will probably be difficult to exactly evaluate the translation risk that a company or group faces, however, it is important to appreciate that it does exist and to bear it in mind when analysing the performance or position of a group with overseas subsidiaries or a company with overseas loans or assets.

4.7 Treasury department hedging activities

Some companies or groups are less concerned by this form of exchange risk, since it does not result in any direct cash flow. It does, however, result in fluctuating profits that other companies view as intolerable.

The primary means of hedging involves the matching of overseas denominated assets and liabilities to give the minimal net accounting exposure to that particular currency. This may be achieved by taking out foreign denominated loans to the same value as the net assets of the overseas subsidiaries and immediately converting the cash raised into sterling, leaving the foreign subsidiaries net assets matched by the new liability and hence zero net currency exposure.

4.8 Operating or economic risk

Operating or economic risk is the risk that the sterling value of a company's cash flow may vary as a result of foreign exchange fluctuations regardless of whether

- There is no overseas trade/transactions/assets and liabilities.
- All overseas trade/transactions are fully hedged.

Example

A UK tour operator specialises in providing guided tours to overseas visitors. Since operations are conducted in the UK, he bills all of his customers in sterling. His revenue will, therefore, depend on two things.

- The sterling charge per tour sold.
- The number of tours sold.

If sterling were to strengthen, then the tours would appear significantly more expensive to the foreign visitors and hence, the number of tours sold (and consequently revenue) would fall.

In this example, there is no exporting or importing involved, but the revenues and profits of the company will be impacted upon by exchange rate fluctuations.

Example

A UK importer of French wine hedges all imports to fix their sterling value and hence avoid transaction risk. If sterling strengthens against the euro, then

- This importer's costs are fixed in sterling terms as a result of the hedging activities.

- A competitor who did not hedge will find that his sterling costs are reduced and hence he can reduce his prices and increase his market share at the expense of the importer who did hedge his purchases.

As a result, despite hedging and fixing the sterling value of the imports, the importer's revenue and profits will be reduced.

Example

Jaguar export to the US where they compete primarily against Mercedes and BMW. As a result, the relative demands for their products depend on the relative strength of the dollar against sterling and euro respectively.

Jaguar's US performance is, therefore, influenced by any relative movement between sterling and euro, even though none of these transactions are being denominated in euros.

4.9 Analysis

This type of risk is perhaps the hardest to analyse as it is determined by factors that may not directly impact on the company. Successful analysis requires a thorough appreciation of

- Competitors and the currency of their costs and pricing.

- The elasticity of demand for the product, i.e. can a cost increase easily be passed on to the customer or not?

4.10 Treasury department hedging activities

It is unlikely that companies or groups try to hedge against this type of risk since the factors involved may be too complex to determine exactly. An approach that could be utilised would be to, say, vary pricing policy to suit the demand elasticity and currency in order to maintain volumes and use currency derivatives (options and futures) in order to maintain values.

CHAPTER ROUNDUP

You need to be familiar with the provisions of IAS 21 with respect to

- Definitions

    - **Foreign currency**. A currency other than the functional currency of the entity.

    - **Functional currency**. The currency of the primary economic environment in which the entity operates.

    - **Presentation currency**. The currency in which the financial statements are presented.

    - **Exchange rate**. The ratio of exchange for two currencies.

    - **Exchange difference**. The difference resulting from translating a given number of units of one currency into another currency at different exchange rates.

    - **Closing rate**. The spot exchange rate at the statement of financial position date.

    - **Spot exchange rate**. The exchange rate for immediate delivery.

    - **Monetary items**. Units of currency held and assets and liabilities to be received or paid in a fixed or determinable number of units of currency. *(IAS 21)*

- Accounting treatment

    - Transactions (Historical rate/average).

    - Statement of financial position items

        - Report foreign currency **monetary items** using the **closing rate**. Examples of monetary items include payables and receivables, debt securities, cash and bank balances.

        - Report **non-monetary items** (eg non-current assets, inventories) which are carried at **historical cost** in a foreign currency using the **exchange rate at the date of the transaction** (historical rate).

        - Report **non-monetary items** which are carried at **fair value** in a foreign currency using the exchange rates that existed **when the values were determined**.

    - Exchange gains/losses

- Accounting treatment for subsidiaries

    - Same functional currency as reporting entity.

        - **Income statement**: translate using actual rates. An average for a period may be used, but not where there is significant fluctuation and the average is therefore unreliable.

        - **Non-monetary items**: translate using an historical rate at the date of purchase (or revaluation to fair value, or reduction to realisable/recoverable amount). This includes inventories and non-current assets (and their depreciation).

        - **Monetary items**: translate at the closing rate.

        - **Exchange differences**: report as part of profit for the year.

- Different functional currency from the reporting entity.

    - The **assets and liabilities** shown in the foreign operation's statement of financial position are translated at the **closing rate** at the statement of financial position date, regardless of the date on which those items originated. The balancing figure on the translated statement of financial position represents the reporting entity's net investment in the foreign operation.

    - Amounts in the **income statement** should be translated at the rate ruling at the date of the transaction (an **average rate** will usually be used for practical purposes).

    - **Exchange differences** arising from the re-translation at the end of each year of the parent's net investment should be **taken to equity**, not through the income statement for the year, until the disposal of the net investment.

- Analysis implications

    - Transaction risk.
    - Translation risk.
    - Economic risk.

TEST YOUR KNOWLEDGE

Check your knowledge of the chapter here, without referring back to the text.

1.   **Net investment plc**

The accounts of US Inc, a subsidiary of UK plc since June 30 2007, for the year ended June 30 2008, are as follows. US Inc's functional currency is the US dollar.

Income Statement

	(US$)
Revenue	9,000
Cost of sales	(4,000)
Gross profit	5,000
Other operating expenses	(2,000)
Profit before taxation	3,000
Taxation	(1,000)
Profit for the period	2,000

Statement of financial position

		(US$)
Non-current assets		3,000
Current assets		
Inventories	1,000	
Receivables	2,000	
Cash	3,000	
		6,000
		9,000
Current liabilities		(4,000)
Net assets		**5,000**
Share capital		1,000
Retained earnings		4,000
Equity		5,000

Exchange rate details are as follows.

June 30 2007	1.8
June 30 2008	1.5
Average for the year	1.7

Requirements

(a)   Translate the accounts into sterling in a form ready for consolidation assuming that the group has chosen to present its financial statements in £ sterling.

(b)   Prepare a schedule reconciling the movement between net assets as at June 30 2007 and June 30 2008.

2.   **Foreign currency discussion**

A company may carry on foreign activities in two ways. It may have transactions in foreign currencies or it may have overseas branches and subsidiaries. Such companies need to include foreign currency transactions and foreign operations in their financial statements.

Requirement

Explain the two alternative methods of foreign currency translation used by IAS 21.

TEST YOUR KNOWLEDGE: ANSWERS

1. **Net investment plc**

Income statement	(US$)	X rate	(£)
Revenue	**9,000**	1.7	5,294
Cost of sales	(4,000)	1.7	(2,353)
Gross profit	**5,000**	1.7	**2,941**
Other operating expenses	(2,000)	1.7	(1,176)
Profit before taxation	**3,000**	1.7	**1,765**
Taxation	(1,000)	1.7	(588)
Profit for the period	**2,000**	1.7	**1,177**

Statement of financial position		(US$)	X rate		(£)
Non-current assets		3,000	1.5		2,000
Current assets					
Inventories	1,000		1.5	667	
Receivables	2,000		1.5	1,333	
Cash	3,000		1.5	2,000	
		6,000	1.5		4,000
		9,000	1.5		6,000
Current liabilities		(4,000)	1.5		(2,667)
Net assets		**5,000**	1.5		**3,333**
Share capital		1,000	1.8		556
Retained earnings		4,000	n/a		2,777
Equity		**5,000**			**3,333**

Reconciliation of movement in net assets	($'000)	X rate	(£'000)
Net assets at June 30 2007	3,000	1.8	1,667
Profit for the year	2,000	1.7	1,177
Exchange differences *(see below)*	–	n/a	489
Net assets at June 30 2008	5,000	1.5	3,333

NB: Net assets in dollars at June 30 2008 have been calculated by working backwards from closing dollar net assets and deducting the income statement profit for the year.

2. **Foreign currency discussion**

IAS 21 uses the terms 'functional currency' and 'presentation currency'. An entity's functional currency is the currency of the primary economic environment in which it operates. An entity's presentation currency is the currency in which its financial statements are presented. IAS 21 states that each entity must determine its functional currency, which is a matter of fact, and that it must measure its results and financial position in that currency. However, an entity can present its financial statements in any currency that it chooses.

There are two methods of foreign currency translation.

■   The '**functional currency**' method used to translate foreign currency transactions into the entity's functional currency.

■   The '**presentation currency**' method used to translate the financial statements of an entity from its functional currency to a different presentation currency.

Translating foreign currency transactions into the functional currency

Under this method, non-monetary items are translated at the exchange rates ruling at the time the relevant transactions occurred. Where non-monetary items, such as property, have been revalued (i.e. are measured at fair value), they are translated at the exchange rates applicable at the time the revaluation occurred. Monetary items are translated at the closing rate; theoretically, they should also be translated at the rate applicable at the time the transaction occurred but, for practical purposes, the transactions giving rise to monetary assets are assumed to have occurred at the end of the period. The theoretical exchange rate for monetary liabilities would be the future exchange rate when the liability would be settled. Since this is unknown, the year-end rate is used as a reasonable surrogate. All exchange gains and losses are recognised in profit and loss for the period taken to the consolidated income statement (note that there is an allowed alternative to deal with hyperinflation).

This translation method is also used where an entity keeps its books and records in a currency other than its functional currency. In theory, this situation might arise where an entity has a foreign operation with the same functional currency as its own. A foreign operation has the same functional currency as its parent where the **trade** of the **foreign operation** is more dependent on the **economic environment** of the **parent's currency** than on that of the local currency, for example, when the foreign operation is essentially merely an extension of the business of the parent. However, the IASB has taken the view that this situation will not arise in practice because such integral foreign operations must always measure their results and financial position in the functional currency of the parent (and therefore will keep their books and records in the same functional currency as the parent).

Translation to a presentation currency

Where an entity presents its financial statements in a **different currency from its functional currency**, all **assets and liabilities** (both monetary and non-monetary) are translated at the **closing rate**. **Income and expenses** are translated at the **exchange rates at the date of the transactions**. In practice, an **average rate** for the period is normally used. **Exchange differences** are not taken to the income statement, but instead are **taken to equity** and recognised in a separate translation reserve.

This method is used where an entity has a foreign operation with a different functional currency from its own. This is the case where the foreign operation is regarded as being separate from the operations of the parent and not dependent on the economic environment of the parent's currency. This is the **typical situation** in which the branches and subsidiary companies of most **major industrial and commercial companies** operate. The financial statements of the foreign operation must be translated from its functional currency into the currency in which the parent presents its financial statements (normally the parent's functional currency) so that consolidated financial statements can be prepared.

16

Associates and Joint Ventures

INTRODUCTION

An investment in the shares of another company may be held for long-term purposes. If it is a small investment giving little or no influence in the operations of the company concerned, then it is being held for its income and gain generating capacity and its accounting treatment reflects that. If it is a controlling interest then it will be consolidated into group accounts.

The question examined in this chapter is how a significant but non-controlling interest should be accounted for.

CHAPTER LEARNING OBJECTIVES

The syllabus areas covered by this section are

Interpretation of Financial Information

The effect of accounting practices

Understanding of the effect of accounting practices on the numbers most significant for investment decisions (profit, earnings per share, asset value etc).

Accounting Terminology and Concepts

Accounting terminology and a knowledge of accounting concepts and conventions to include the statement of financial position, income statement, statement of cash flows and notes to the accounts. An understanding of the distinction between capital and revenue, the valuation of assets for accounting purposes and the determination of profit and earnings share on the nil, net and full distribution bases. An understanding of significance of the statement of accounting policies in relation to the concept of a true and fair view.

Presentation of Financial Statements

Impact of statutory and non-statutory regulation on UK financial statements.

An understanding of the effect on the presentation of financial statements of the Companies Act and non-statutory regulations, including standards and other guidance issued by IASB and stock exchange requirements.

In the context of associates and joint ventures:

It is emphasised that the intention of the examination is to assess student's analytical and interpretative skills rather than their technical accounting ability. It is also expected that they should have an understanding of standard accounting practices and an awareness of matters currently under discussion.

1 ACCOUNTING FOR INVESTMENTS

It has already been noted in Chapter 9 *Investment and Group Accounting*, that the accounting treatment accorded to an investment in the financial statements of an investing company will be determined by the level of control or influence, if any, that the investor derives from the investment. However, it is worth briefly reviewing this area again to provide a logical introduction for a discussion of the accounting treatment accorded to associates and joint ventures.

1.1 Trade investment (0%–20%)

Where our holding is so small as to confer no influence over the other company, then that investment should be treated as a trade investment.

1.1.1 Accounting treatment

The accounting treatment would be as follows.

- Statement of financial position at cost, less provision for any diminution in value.
- The income statement should record dividends received as income.

1.2 Significant influence (20%–50%)

If the level of voting influence fell in the above range, then the investing company would normally have significant influence over the other company and hence that other company would normally be treated as an associated undertaking of the investing company.

If the level of votes held was exactly 50%, then the investing company would probably be sharing control jointly with another investor and the company being invested in would be known as a joint venture.

1.2.1 Accounting treatment

The accounting treatment for associated undertakings is to apply equity accounting, i.e.

- Record the investment as an asset on the group statement of financial position at the group's share of the net assets of the associated undertaking.
- In the group income statement, record the group's share of the profits of the associated undertaking.

Rather than bringing in simply cost in the statement of financial position and dividends in the income statement, we are bringing in the group's share of net assets and profits into those two statements. Hence, if we owned 40% of an associated undertaking our share of its net assets and profits would be calculated as its net assets or profits $\times$ 40%.

Joint ventures are accounted for either using the equity method or proportionate consolidation.

Neither associates nor joint ventures are group companies and their accounting treatment is governed by an entirely separate set of rules contained in IAS 28 *Investments in Associates* and IAS 31 *Interests in Joint Ventures*.

1.3 Control (more than 50%)

Where one company controls another, that second company is a subsidiary undertaking of the first.

1.3.1 Accounting treatment

The accounting aim for dealing with subsidiaries is identical to that for dealing with associated undertakings, however the mechanics involved and what will ultimately be seen on the statement of financial position are very different. As regards to the accounting aim

- The statement of financial position should record net assets of the subsidiary on an individual line-by-line basis, including them as part of the net assets controlled by the single economic group.

- The income statement should record the profit of the subsidiary also on a line-by-line basis, as part of the net profits generated by the group.

1.4 Scope of this chapter

The accounting treatment of trade investments and the process of producing group accounts incorporating subsidiaries have already been covered in the chapter on *Investment and Group Accounting*. This chapter looks at the accounting treatment of companies in which our investments give us either significant influence (i.e. associates) or control jointly with another investor (i.e. joint ventures).

2 ACCOUNTING FOR ASSOCIATES

2.1 Definitions

- **Associate**. An entity, including an unincorporated entity such as a partnership, over which an investor has significant influence and which is neither a subsidiary nor a joint venture of the investor.

- **Significant influence** is the power to participate in the financial and operating policy decisions of an economic entity but is not control or joint control over those policies.

- **Joint control** is the contractually agreed sharing of control over an economic activity.

- **Equity method**. A method of accounting whereby the investment is initially recorded at cost and adjusted thereafter for the post acquisition change in the investor's share of net assets of the investee. The profit or loss of the investor includes the investor's share of the profit or loss of the investee.

The key to associate status is significant influence.

2.2 IAS 28 Investments in Associates

IAS 28 requires all investments in associates to be accounted for in the consolidated accounts using the equity method, *unless* the investment is classified as 'held for sale' in accordance with IFRS 5 in which case it should be accounted for under IFRS 5.

The use of the equity method should be **discontinued** from the date that the investor **ceases to have significant influence**.

From that date, the investor shall account for the investment in accordance with IAS 39 *Financial Instruments: Recognition and Measurement.* The carrying amount of the investment at the date that it ceases to be an associate shall be regarded as its cost on initial measurement as a financial asset under IAS 39.

2.3 Separate financial statements of the investor

In the investor's individual accounts the interest is the associate should be treated as follows.

- Accounted for at **cost**; or
- In accordance with **IAS 39**.

2.4 Application of the equity method: consolidated accounts

Many of the procedures required to apply the equity method are the same as are required for full consolidation. In particular, **intra-group unrealised profits** must be excluded.

Goodwill is calculated as the difference (positive or negative) between the cost of acquisition and the investor's share of the fair values of the net identifiable assets of the associate. This should be treated as required by IFRS 3. Appropriate adjustments should be made to the investor's share of the profits or losses after acquisition, to account for depreciation.

2.5 Consolidated income statement

The basic principle is that the investing company (X Co) should take account of its **share of the earnings** of the associate, Y Co, whether or not Y Co distributes the earnings as dividends. X Co achieves this by adding to consolidated profit the group's share of Y Co's profit after tax.

Under equity accounting, the associated company's sales revenue, cost of sales and so on are *not amalgamated* with those of the group. Instead the group share only of the associate's profit before tax and tax charge for the year is added to the corresponding lines of the parent company and its subsidiaries.

2.6 Consolidated statement of financial position

A figure for **investment in associates** is shown which at the time of the acquisition must be stated at cost. This amount will increase (decrease) each year by the amount of the group's share of the associated company's profit (loss) for the year.

Example

P Co, a company with subsidiaries, acquires 25,000 of the 100,000 £1 ordinary shares in A Co for £60,000 on 1 January 2007. In the year to 31 December 2007, A Co earns profits after tax of £24,000, from which it pays a dividend of £6,000.

How will A Co's results be accounted for in the individual and consolidated accounts of P Co for the year ended 31 December 2007?

Solution

In the **individual accounts** of P Co, the investment will be recorded on 1 January 2007 at cost. Unless there is an impairment in the value of the investment, this amount will remain in the individual statement of financial position of P Co permanently. The only entry in P Co's individual income statement will be to record dividends received. For the year ended 31 December 2007, P Co will be

Double Entry	(£)
DEBIT: Cash	1,500
CREDIT: Retained Earnings – income	1,500

In the **consolidated accounts** of P Co equity accounting principles will be used to account for the investment in A Co. Consolidated profit after tax will include the group's share of A Co's profit after tax (25% × £24,000 = £6,000). To the extent that this has been distributed as dividend, it is already included in P Co's individual accounts and will automatically be brought into the consolidated results. That part of the group's profit share which has not been distributed as dividend (£4,500) will be brought into consolidation by the following adjustment.

Double Entry	(£)
DEBIT: Investment in associates	4,500
CREDIT: Retained Profits – income from shares in associates	4,500

The asset 'Investment in associates' is then stated at £64,500, being cost plus the group share of post-acquisition retained profits.

2.7 Pro-forma consolidated income statement

The following is a **suggested layout** for the consolidated income statement for a company having subsidiaries as well as associated companies.

	($'000)	($'000)
Revenue		1,400
Cost of Sales		770
Gross Profit		630
Distribution Costs and Administrative Expenses		290
		340
Share of Profit of Associates		17
		357
Finance Income		(30)
		387
Finance Costs		20
Profit before Taxation		367
Tax		145
Profit for the year		222
Attributable to:		
Equity holders of the parent		200
Minority Interest		22
		222

2.8 Consolidated statement of financial position

As explained earlier, the consolidated statement of financial position will contain an **asset 'Investment in associate'**.

The amount at which this asset is stated will be its original cost plus the group's share of any **profits earned since acquisition** which have not been distributed as dividends.

Example

On 1 January 2007 the net tangible assets of A Co amount to £220,000, financed by 100,000 £1 ordinary shares and revenue reserves of £120,000. P Co, a company with subsidiaries, acquires 30,000 of the shares in A Co for £75,000. During the year ended 31 December 2007 A Co's profit after tax is £30,000, from which dividends of £12,000 are paid.

Show how P Co's investment in A Co would appear in the consolidated statement of financial position at 31 December 2007.

Solution

Consolidated statement of financial position as at 31 December 2007 (extract)	(£)
Non-current assets	
Investment in associate	
Cost	75,000
Group share of post-acquisition retained profits	
(30% × £18,000)	5,400
	80,400

An important point to note is that this figure of £80,400 can be arrived at in a completely different way. It is the sum of

(a)   The group's share of A Co's net assets at 31 December 2007, and

(b)   The premium paid over fair value for the shares acquired.

This can be shown as follows.

		(£)	(£)
(a)	A Co's net assets at 31 December 2007		
	Net assets at 1 January 2007	220,000	
	Retained profit for year	18,000	
	Net assets at 31 December 2007	238,000	
	Group share (30%)		71,400
(b)	Premium on acquisition		
	Net assets acquired by group on 1 Jan 2007 (30% × £220,000)	66,000	
	Price paid for shares	75,000	
	Premium on acquisition		9,000
	Investment in associated company per statement of financial position		80,400

Example

Set out below are the draft accounts of Parent Co and its subsidiaries and of Associate Co. Parent Co acquired 40% of the equity capital of Associate Co three years ago when the latter's reserves stood at £40,000.

Summarised statement of financial positions	Parent Co & Subsidiaries (£'000)	Associate Co (£'000)
Tangible non-current assets	220	170
Investment in associate, at cost	60	–
Loan to associate	20	–
Current assets	100	50
Loan from parent	–	(20)
	400	200
Share capital (£1 shares)	250	100
Reserves	150	100
	400	200

Summarised income statements	Parent Co & Subsidiaries (£'000)	Associate Co (£'000)
Operating profit	95	80
Tax	35	30
	60	50

You are required to prepare the summarised consolidated accounts of Parent Co.

Notes

(1)   Assume that the associate's assets/liabilities are stated at fair value.

(2)   Assume that there are no minority interests in the subsidiary companies.

Solution

Parent Co consolidated income statement	(£'000)
Net profit	95
Share of profit of associated company (50 × 40%)	20
Profit before tax	105
Tax	35
Profit attributable to the members of Parent Co	80

Parent Co Consolidated statement of financial position	(£'000)
Assets	
Tangible non-current assets	220
Investment in associate (see note)	104
Current assets	100
Total assets	424
Equity and liabilities	
Share capital	250
Reserves (W1)	174
Total equity and liabilities	424

Note	(£'000)
Investment in associate	
Group's share of net assets (40% × 200)	80
Premium on acquisition (W2)	4
	84
Loan to associate	20
	104

Workings

1.   **Reserves**

	Parent & subsidiaries (£'000)	Associate (£'000)
Per question	150	100
Pre-acquisition		40
Post-acquisition		60
Group share in associate (£60 x 40%)	24	
Group reserves	174	

2.   **Premium on acquisition**

	(£'000)
Share capital	100
Reserves at date of acquisition	40
	140
Net assets acquired (40% × 140)	56
Cost	60
Premium on acquisition (goodwill)	4

3   JOINT VENTURES AND JOINTLY CONTROLLED ENTITIES

3.1 Introduction

IAS 31 *Interests in Joint Ventures* covers all types of joint ventures. It is not concerned with the accounts of the joint venture itself (if separate accounts are maintained), but rather **how the interest in a joint venture is accounted for by each joint venturer** (i.e. each 'partner' in the joint venture).

The assets and liabilities, income and expenses of the joint venture must be reported in the financial statements of the venturers and investors, whatever the form of the joint venture.

IAS 31 looks at the various forms of joint venture which may be undertaken and then looks at how joint ventures are dealt with in the **individual financial statements** of the venturer *and* the **group financial statements**.

3.2 Definitions

The IAS begins by listing some important definitions.

- **Joint venture**. A contractual arrangement whereby two or more parties undertake an economic activity which is subject to joint control.

- **Control**. The power to govern the financial and operating policies of an economic activity so as to obtain benefits from its activities.

- **Joint control**. The contractually agreed sharing of control over an economic activity.

- **Significant influence**. The power to participate in the financial and operating policy decisions of an economic activity but is not control or joint control over those policies.

- **Venturer.** A party to a joint venture that has joint control over that joint venture.

- **Proportionate consolidation**. A method of accounting whereby a venturer's share of each of the assets, liabilities, income and expenses of a jointly controlled entity is combined line-by-line with similar items in the venturer's financial statements or reported as separate line items in the venturer's financial statements.

- **Equity method**. A method of accounting whereby an interest in a jointly controlled entity is initially recorded at cost and adjusted thereafter for the post acquisition change in the venturer's share of net assets of the jointly controlled entity. The income statement reflects the venturer's share of the profit or loss of the jointly controlled entity.

(IAS 31)

3.3 Forms of joint venture

The **form and structure** of joint ventures can vary enormously. There are, however, three main types identified by the Standard.

- **Jointly controlled operations**.
- **Jointly controlled assets**.
- **Jointly controlled entities**.

We will look at each of these below. They are all usually described as joint ventures and fulfil the definition of a joint venture given above.

Whatever the form and structure, every joint venture will have **two characteristics**.

- Two (or more) venturers are bound by a **contractual arrangement**.
- The contractual relationship establishes **joint control**.

3.4 Jointly controlled operations

In this type of joint venture, there is no separate entity set up to deal with the joint venture, whether in the form of a corporation, partnership or other entity. Instead, the venturers **use their own assets and resources** for the joint venture, i.e. their own property, plant and equipment is used and they carry their own inventories.

The venturers also incur their own expenses and liabilities, and raise their own finance which then represents their own obligations. In these situations, the activities of the joint venture will often be performed by the venturers' staff alongside the venturers' **other similar activities**. The way that income and expenses are shared between the venturers is usually laid out in the joint venture agreement.

IAS 31 uses the example of building an aircraft to illustrate this situation. Say that Boeing is to build the body of the aircraft and the engines are to be built by Rolls Royce as specified by the airline customer for the aircraft. You can see that different parts of the manufacturing process are carried out by each of the venturers. In the Rolls Royce factory, workers will work on the engines for the Boeing plane alongside others working on engines for different aircraft.

Each venturer, Boeing and Rolls Royce, bears its own costs and takes a share of revenue from the aircraft sale. That share is decided in the contractual arrangement between the venturers.

3.5 Accounting treatment of jointly controlled operations

When a joint venture in the nature of jointly controlled operations exists, IAS 31 requires a venturer to recognise the following in its financial statements.

- The **assets** it controls and the **liabilities** it incurs.

- The **expenses** it incurs and the **income** it earns from the sale of goods or services by the joint venture.

Separate accounts for the joint venture are not required, although the venturers may prepare management accounts for the joint venture, in order to assess its performance.

3.6 Jointly controlled assets

In this type of joint venture, the venturers have **joint control**, and often **joint ownership** of some or all of the assets in the joint venture. These assets may have been contributed to the joint venture or purchased for the purpose of the joint venture, but in any case they are **dedicated to the activities of the joint venture**. These assets are used to produce benefits for the venturers; each venturer takes a share of the output and bears a share of the incurred expenses.

As with jointly controlled operations, this type of joint venture does *not* involve setting up a corporation, partnership or any other kind of entity. The venturers **control their share of future economic benefits** through their share in the jointly controlled asset.

IAS 31 gives examples in the oil, gas and mineral extraction industries. In such industries companies may, say, jointly control and operate an oil or gas pipeline. Each company transports its own products down the pipeline and pays an agreed proportion of the expenses of operating the pipeline (perhaps based on volume).

A further example is a property which is jointly controlled, each venturer taking a share of the rental income and bearing a portion of the expense.

3.7 Accounting treatment of jointly controlled assets

IAS 31 requires each venturer to recognise (i.e. include in their financial statements) the following in respect of its interest in jointly controlled assets.

- Its **share of the jointly controlled assets**, classified by their nature, e.g. a share of a jointly controlled oil pipeline should be classified as property, plant and equipment.

- Any **liabilities** it has incurred, e.g. in financing its share of the assets.

- Its share of any **liabilities incurred jointly** with the other venturers which relate to the joint venture.

- Any **income** from the sale or use of its share of the joint venture's output, together with its share of any **expenses** incurred by the joint venture.

- Any **expenses** which it has incurred in respect of its interest in the joint venture, e.g. those relating to financing the venturer's interest in the assets and selling its share of the output.

This treatment of jointly controlled assets reflects the **substance and economic reality,** and (usually) the legal form of the joint venture. Separate accounting records need not be kept for the joint venture and financial statements for the joint venture need not be prepared. Management accounts may be produced, however, in order to monitor the performance of the joint venture.

4 JOINTLY CONTROLLED ENTITIES

Exam tip

> The most frequently asked question in this area is the distinction between equity accounting and proportional consolidation, e.g. Winter 2006 Question 9, Summer 2006 Question 5.

4.1 Introduction

This type of joint venture involves the setting up of a corporation, partnership or other entity. This **operates in the same way as any other entity**, except that the venturers have a contractual arrangement establishing their joint control over the economic activity of the entity.

A jointly controlled entity effectively operates as a **separate entity**: it controls the joint venture's assets, incurs liabilities and expenses and earns income. It can, as a separate entity, enter into contracts in its own name and raise finance to fund the activities of the joint venture. The venturers share the results of the jointly controlled entity, and in some cases they may also share the output of the joint venture.

The **substance** of jointly controlled entities are often similar in substance to the joint ventures discussed above (jointly controlled assets/operations). In the case of the oil/gas pipeline mentioned earlier, the asset might be transferred to a jointly controlled entity for tax or similar reasons. In other circumstances, a jointly controlled entity may be set up to deal with only certain aspects of the jointly controlled operations, e.g. marketing or after-sales service, design or distribution.

As a separate entity, the jointly controlled entity must maintain its **own accounting records** and will **prepare financial statements** according to national requirements and IASs.

4.2 Accounting treatment – separate financial statements of venturer

IAS 31 states that where a venturer prepares separate financial statements (as a single company), investments in jointly controlled entities should be either

- Accounted for at **cost**; or
- In accordance with **IAS 39**.

The same accounting treatment must be applied consistently to all jointly controlled entities.

4.3 Accounting treatment – consolidated financial statements of venturer

IAS 31 requires all interests in jointly controlled entities to be accounted for using *either* proportionate consolidation *or* the equity method. There is an exception that where an interest is classified as held for sale it should be accounted for in accordance with IFRS 5.

4.4 The proportionate consolidation method

A venturer can report its interest in a jointly controlled entity in its consolidated financial statements using one of the two reporting formats for **proportionate consolidation**.

IAS 31 maintains that this treatment reflects the **substance and economic reality** of the arrangement, i.e. the control the venturer has over its share of future economic benefits through its share of the assets and liabilities of the venture.

The proportionate consolidation method differs from normal consolidation in that only the group share of assets and liabilities, income and expenses are brought into account. There is therefore **no minority interest**.

There are **two different formats** with which the proportionate consolidation method can be used.

- **Combine on a line-by-line basis** the venturer's share of each of the assets, liabilities, income and expenses of the jointly controlled entity with the similar items in the venturer's consolidated financial statements.

- Include in the venturer's consolidated financial statements **separate line items** for the venturer's share of the assets and liabilities, income and expenses of the jointly controlled entity.

Example

Both of the above methods produce exactly the same net results and they are demonstrated in this Example.

Set out below are the draft accounts of Parent Co and its subsidiaries and of Joint Venture Co. Parent Co acquired 50% of the equity capital of Joint Venture Co three years ago when the latter's reserves stood at £40,000.

Summarised statement of financial positions	Parent Co & Subsidiaries (£'000)	Joint Venture Co (£'000)
Tangible non-current assets	220	170
Investment in joint venture	75	–
Current assets	100	50
Loan to Joint Venture	20	–
	415	220
Share capital (£1 shares)	250	100
Reserves	165	100
Loan from Parent Co	–	20
	415	220

Summarised income statements	Parent Co & Subsidiaries (£'000)	Joint Venture Co (£'000)
Net profit	95	80
Taxation	35	30
	60	50
Dividends	50	10

Parent Co has taken credit for the dividend received from Joint Venture Co.

You are required to prepare the summarised consolidated statement of financial position of Parent Co, under each of the formats of proportionate consolidation described by IAS 31.

4.4.1 Solution: line-by-line format

Parent Co consolidated statement of financial position	(£'000)
Goodwill (W1)	5
Tangible non-current assets (220 + (50% × 170))	305
Current assets (100 + (50% × 50))	125
Loan to joint venturer (note)	10
	445
Share capital	250
Reserves (W2)	195
	445

NB: The loan is the proportion of the £20,000 lent to the other venturer.

Workings

1. **Goodwill**

	(£'000)
Cost of investment	75
Share of net assets acquired (50% × 140)	70
Premium on acquisition	5

2. **Reserves**

	Parent Co & Subsidiaries (£'000)	Joint Venture Co (£'000)
Per question	165	100
Pre-acquisition		(40)
Post-acquisition		60
Group share in joint venture		
(£60 × 50%)	30	
Group reserves	195	

Solution: separate line method

Parent Co consolidated statement of financial position	(£'000)	(£'000)
Goodwill (as above)		5
Tangible non-current assets		
Group	220	
Joint venture (170 × 50%)	85	
		305
Current assets		
Group	100	
Joint venture (50% × 50)	25	
		125
Loan to joint venturer		10
		445
Share capital		250
Reserves (as above)		195
		445

In both these cases the **consolidated income statements** would be shown in the same way.

4.5 Allowed alternative: equity method

A venturer can report its interest in a jointly controlled entity in its consolidated financial statements under the **equity method**, as discussed in Section 2. The argument for this method is that it is misleading to combine controlled items with jointly controlled items. It is also felt by some that venturers have significant influence over the entity, not merely joint control.

Example

Shown below are the supporting notes for Roche regarding the treatment of associates and joint venturers.

Roche Group
Extract from Notes to the Financial Statement, Year Ended 31 December 2004

Associated companies

The Group's investments in associated companies have been accounted for using the equity method. The goodwill arising from investments in associated companies is classified as part of the investments in associated companies.

Investments in associated companies in millions of CHF	Share of net income		Statement of financial position value	
	2004	2003	2004	2003
Basilea Pharmaceutica (Switzerland)	(31)	(28)	–	31
Other investments in associated companies	(12)	(16)	55	79
Total investments in associated companies	(43)	(44)	55	110

Basilea Pharmaceutica: The Group owns a non-controlling interest of 33% (2003: 46%) in Basilea.

Pharmaceutica Ltd ('Basilea'): Basilea is a Swiss biotechnology company in the anti-bacterial, anti-fungal and dermatology fields.

The Group's other major investments in associates are Tripath Inc, and Antisoma. Additional information about these companies is given in Note 41. Transactions between the Group and its associated companies are given in Note 38. On 20 April 2004 the Group announced that it would no longer continue the joint development of the renal transplantation drug ISA(TX)247 with Isotechnika. As a result the Group no longer has the potential to exercise significant influence over Isotechnika and accordingly Isotechnika is no longer reported as an associated company. An impairment loss of 10 million Swiss francs (2003: none) was recorded on the Group's investments in associates.

Joint ventures

The Group's interests in joint ventures are reported in the financial statements using the proportionate consolidation method. The significant joint ventures are detailed below.

Bayer joint venture: As part of the disposal of the Roche Consumer Health business (see also Note 7) the Group sold to Bayer its 50% stake in Bayer Roche LLC, a joint venture with Bayer in the over-the-counter (OTC) field to market and distribute the product Aleve and certain other OTC products in the United States.

Joint ventures: recognised income statement and statement of financial position amounts in millions of CHF	2004	2003
Income statement		
Sales	230	249
Expenses	(159)	(190)
Net income after taxes	71	59
Statement of financial position		
Long-term assets	–	235
Current assets	14	173
Non-current liabilities	–	(88)
Current liabilities	(3)	(187)
Net assets	11	133

4.6 Proposed changes to accounting for joint ventures

In September 2007 the IASB, as part of its convergence agenda with the US FASB, published ED 9 *Joint Arrangements*. The most significant changes proposed are

- To shift the focus in accounting for joint arrangements (formerly known as joint ventures) from their legal form to the contractual rights and obligations agreed between the parties.

- To remove the choice of accounting for jointly controlled entities (equity method or proportionate consolidation). If the parties only have a right to a share of the outcome of the activities of a jointly controlled entity, their net interest in the arrangement would be accounted for under the equity method. If these proposals are adopted proportionate consolidation of jointly controlled entities will be prohibited. This will remove one of the differences between IFRS and US GAAP as US GAAP only permits the equity method of accounting in these circumstances.

5 ANALYSIS POINTS

5.1 Equity accounting

Equity accounting for associates advocates a one-line consolidation that provides very little information about the assets or profits of the associates.

In the statement of financial position the one-line approach for associates gives no indication of the breakdown of the assets and liabilities. It is quite conceivable that the associate could be in a desperate liquidity or gearing position but this would not be revealed in the group financial statements.

The treatment in the income statement is very similar in that the group share of the associate's profit is shown separately from group amounts. The group share of the associate's tax is added to the other elements of the group tax charge. This provides very little breakdown of how the profit has been generated by the associate.

5.2 Proportionate consolidation

Utilising the proportionate consolidation method for joint ventures requires the group to directly incorporate its share of each individual asset and liability and its share of each individual element of income or expense within the group accounts.

As a result, any factors impacting on the performance or position of the joint venture will, to an extent, be reflected in the group accounts. Clearly, the impact will depend on the significance of the joint arrangement to the group.

CHAPTER ROUNDUP

You need to be familiar with and able to define

- **Associate**. An entity, including an unincorporated entity such as a partnership, over which an investor has significant influence and which is neither a subsidiary nor a joint venture of the investor.

- **Significant influence** is the power to participate in the financial and operating policy decisions of an economic entity but is not control or joint control over those policies.

- **Joint control** is the contractually agreed sharing of control over an economic activity.

- **Equity method**. A method of accounting whereby the investment is initially recorded at cost and adjusted thereafter for the post acquisition change in the investor's share of net assets of the investee. The profit or loss of the investor includes the investor's share of the profit or loss of the investee.

- IAS 28 *Investments in Associates*

    - IAS 28 requires all investments in associates to be accounted for in the consolidated accounts using the equity method, *unless* the investment is classified as 'held for sale' in accordance with IFRS 5 in which case it should be accounted for under IFRS 5.

- IAS 31 *Interests in Joint Ventures*

    - **Joint venture**. A contractual arrangement whereby two or more parties undertake an economic activity which is subject to joint control.

    - **Control**. The power to govern the financial and operating policies of an economic activity so as to obtain benefits from its activities.

    - **Joint control**. The contractually agreed sharing of control over an economic activity.

    - **Significant influence**. The power to participate in the financial and operating policy decisions of an economic activity but is not control or joint control over those policies.

    - **Venturer**. A party to a joint venture that has joint control over that joint venture.

    - **Proportionate consolidation**. A method of accounting whereby a venturer's share of each of the assets, liabilities, income and expenses of a jointly controlled entity is combined line-by-line with similar items in the venturer's financial statements or reported as separate line items in the venturer's financial statements.

    - **Equity method**. A method of accounting whereby an interest in a jointly controlled entity is initially recorded at cost and adjusted thereafter for the post acquisition change in the venturer's share of net assets of the jointly controlled entity. The income statement reflects the venturer's share of the profit or loss of the jointly controlled entity. *(IAS 31)*

- Jointly controlled operations, venturer recognises in its financial statements

    - The **assets** it controls and the **liabilities** it incurs.

    - The **expenses** it incurs and the **income** it earns from the sale of goods or services by the joint venture.

- ■ Jointly controlled assets, venturer recognises

    - – Its **share of the jointly controlled assets**, classified by their nature, e.g. a share of a jointly controlled oil pipeline should be classified as property, plant and equipment.

    - – Any **liabilities** it has incurred, e.g. in financing its share of the assets.

    - – Its share of any **liabilities incurred jointly** with the other venturers which relate to the joint venture.

    - – Any **income** from the sale or use of its share of the joint venture's output, together with its share of any **expenses** incurred by the joint venture.

    - – Any **expenses** which it has incurred in respect of its interest in the joint venture, e.g. those relating to financing the venturer's interest in the assets and selling its share of the output.

- ■ Jointly controlled entity, venturer uses either

    - – Proportional consolidation.
    - – Equity method.

- ■ Analysis issues

    - – Very little information in group accounts.

TEST YOUR KNOWLEDGE

Check your knowledge of the chapter here, without referring back to the text.

1. Hartlepool plc

    The statement of financial position of Hartlepool plc and Accrington plc as at May 31 2007 are as follows.

	Hartlepool (£'000)	Accrington (£'000)
Other non-current assets	5,000	2,000
Investment in Accrington plc	600	–
	5,600	2,000
Current assets	2,900	2,300
Total assets	**8,500**	**4,300**
Current liabilities	(1,000)	(2,000)
Non-current liabilities		
	(4,100)	(1,300)
Total liabilities	**(5,100)**	**(3,300)**
Net assets	**3,400**	**1,000**
Share capital	700	100
Retained earnings	2,700	900
Equity	**3,400**	**1,000**

    Hartlepool plc has just acquired 40% of Accrington plc's shares for £600,000. Assume that the assets and liabilities of Accrington plc are recorded in the above balance at their fair values.

    Requirement

    Prepare the statement of financial position of Hartlepool plc as at May 31 2007 accounting for Accrington plc under the equity method.

2.   Hartlepool plc Part 2

The statement of financial positions of Hartlepool plc and Accrington plc as at May 31 2007 are as follows.

	Hartlepool (£'000)	Accrington (£'000)
Other non-current assets	5,000	2,300
Investment in Accrington plc	600	–
	5,600	2,300
Current assets	2,900	2,900
Total assets	**8,500**	**5,200**
Current liabilities	(1,000)	(2,000)
Non-current liabilities		
	(4,100)	(1,100)
Total liabilities	**(5,100)**	**(3,100)**
Net assets	**3,400**	**2,100**
Share capital	700	100
Retained earnings	2,700	2,000
Equity	**3,400**	**2,100**

Hartlepool plc acquired 40% of Accrington plc's shares for £600,000 on May 31 2006.

At the date of the acquisition, Accrington plc's retained earnings were £900,000. Assume that the assets and liabilities of Accrington were recognised at their fair values at the date of acquisition. The group does not amortise goodwill and no impairment has been identified.

Requirement

Prepare the statement of financial position of Hartlepool plc as at May 31 2007 accounting for Accrington plc under the equity method.

3.   Horribilis plc

Horribilis plc has owned 30% of the shares of Annus plc for many years. The income statement for the year ended March 31 2007 for each company are as follows.

	Horribilis (£000)	Annus (£000)
Revenue	4,500	3,000
Cost of sales and operating expenses	(2,000)	(1,000)
Operating profit	2,500	2,000
Finance costs	(500)	(100)
Profit before taxation	2,000	1,900
Taxation	(800)	(600)
Profit for the period	1,200	1,300

Requirement

Prepare the income statement for Horribilis plc for the year ended March 31 2007, accounting for Annus plc using the equity method of accounting.

TEST YOUR KNOWLEDGE: ANSWERS

1   Hartlepool plc

Consolidated statement of financial position as at May 31 2007	(£'000)	(£'000)
Other non-current assets		5,000
Investment in associate		
Share of net assets (40% × 1000)	400	
Goodwill on acquisition	200	
		600
		5,600
Current assets		2,900
Total assets		**8,500**
Current liabilities	(1,000)	
Non-current liabilities	(4,100)	
Total liabilities		**(5,100)**
Net assets		**3,400**
Share capital		700
Retained earnings		2,700
		3,400

2.   Hartlepool plc Part 2

Consolidated statement of financial position as at May 31 2007	(£'000)	(£'000)
Other non-current assets		5,000
Investment in associate		
Share of net assets (40% × 2100)	840	
Goodwill	200	
		1,040
		6,040
Current assets		2,900
Total assets		**8,940**
Current liabilities	(1,000)	
Non-current liabilities	(4,100)	
Total liabilities		
		(5,100)
Net assets		**3,840**
Share capital		700
Retained earnings *(see below)*		3,140
Equity		**3,840**

Working

	(£'000)	(£'000)
Hartlepool		2,700
Accrington	2,000	
Less: retained earnings at acquisition	(900)	
Increase since acquisition	1,100	
Hartlepool's share	× 40%	440
		3,140

3. Horribilis plc

Consolidated income statement for the year ended March 31 2007	(£'000)	(£'000)
Revenue		**4,500**
Cost of sales and operating expenses		(2,000)
Operating profit		**2,500**
Share of associated company's profit (30% ×1,300)		390
Finance costs		(500)
Profit before taxation		2,390
Taxation		(800)
Profit for the period		**1,590**

17

US GAAP Reconciliation

INTRODUCTION

Most major companies now operate on an international basis and have both UK and overseas investors. With many key investors being based in the US or familiar with US accounting conventions, it is considered appropriate to reconcile from IFRSs to US GAAP. In this chapter we examine the major areas of difference. You are unlikely to be asked to undertake such a reconciliation, but you may be asked to explain the items within one.

CHAPTER CONTENTS

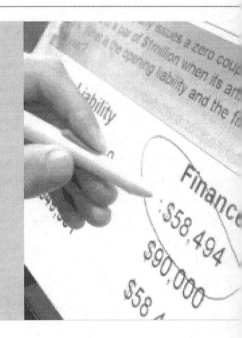

CHAPTER LEARNING OBJECTIVES

The syllabus area covered by this chapter is

Overseas Accounting Practices

An elementary understanding of the effect of the differences in corporate accounting practices, international accounting standards and practices and taxation practices in the USA, EU and other main international markets in interpreting earnings per share, asset value and gearing.

1 INTRODUCTION

Exam tip

> Questions occasionally arise from this area involving a discussion of the contrasting approaches, e.g. Winter 2005 Question 4, Summer 2005 Question 2

There are some non-US listed companies that also have their shares publicly traded in the United States via ADRs (American Depository Receipts). ADRs are formed by packaging together a number of a company's shares which, once registered with the Securities and Exchange Commission (SEC), can be traded on the US stock market and will pay a US dollar dividend. Both of these features are attractive to a US investor wishing to invest and receive returns in dollars. SEC requirements include the filing of financial statements. Registrants therefore file an annual report on a **Form 20-F**. They can prepare financial statements either using US Generally Accepted Accounting Principles (GAAP) or using non-US accounting principles.

If the financial statements are based on non-US GAAP, the entity must prepare and file a reconciliation statement itemising the adjustments required to convert net income (profit attributable to ordinary shareholders) and shareholders' equity to US GAAP. The reconciliation must be accompanied by a discussion of the differences in the principles and methods used. A quantified description of the differences between the statement of cash flows filed and the numbers and classification under US GAAP is also required.

Since 2007 the SEC has removed the requirement for foreign companies to reconcile financial information to US GAAP if their accounts are prepared using IFRS as promulgated by the IASB. This new rule came into force in March 2008. For filings with the SEC from that date the US GAAP reconciliation was no longer required.

The SEC has also been consulting about the potential use of IFRS in filings by US domestic corporations. In August 2008, the SEC announced the planned issuance of an IFRS "road map" leading to 5 standards for US corporations by 2014. As the convergence process between the IASB and FASB develops, it is likely that in due course the differences are reduced to insignificant areas.

2 REVIEW OF FORM 20-F

Reviewing extracts from a Form 20-F provides a useful way of understanding some of the key differences between IFRS and US GAAP. The following sets out some of the key differences included in a UK company's Form 20-F (**Appendix – Extract from Novartis Form 20-F 2004**). You should refer to this as you read through the rest of this chapter. All references refer to the page numbers and section numbers in the extract.

For the examination, it is possible that one or more of the three company accounts that form the basis for Section A questions will include a Form 20-F. An understanding of US GAAP and the contrast with IFRS reporting will therefore be required.

Broadly, the differences between IFRS and US reporting have been split into the following three categories:

- Income statement.
- Statement of financial position.
- Statement of cash flows.

Overall IFRS is "principle-based" whereas US GAAP is "rules based" and has more industry specific requirements.

3 INCOME STATEMENT DIFFERENCES

The following are examples of income statement differences that arise under US GAAP.

3.1 Extraordinary items

Under IFRS extraordinary items are prohibited. Under US GAAP extraordinary items are permitted, but are restricted to items that are both infrequent in occurrence and unusual in nature.

3.2 Accounting for joint ventures

Under US GAAP only the equity method is permitted in accounting for joint ventures (i.e. including the share of joint venture net income as one line in the income statement and inclusion of the share of net assets in the statement of financial position investment heading). IFRS permits both the equity method and proportionate consolidation of joint ventures (where the share of joint venture results are incorporated into every line within the income statement and statement of financial position).

As stated in Chapter 16 the IASB proposes to remove the option of accounting for jointly controlled entities by means of proportionate consolidation.

3.3 Earnings per share

Both US GAAP and IFRS require the disclosure of basic and diluted EPS from continuing operations and net profit or loss per share. However, US GAAP also requires additional disclosure of results from discontinued operations, extraordinary items and the cumulative effect of changes in accounting policies on a per share basis.

3.4 Presentation of discontinued operations

IFRS requires the disclosure of post-tax income or loss from discontinued operations on the face of the income statement. US GAAP requires the presentation of both pre- and post-tax results from discontinued operations to be shown on the face of the income statement.

4 STATEMENT OF FINANCIAL POSITION DIFFERENCES

4.1 Inventory (Extract page 7, I)

IFRS does not permit LIFO (Last In, First Out) inventory costing allocation. However, LIFO inventory costing is both permitted and the most common method used by companies preparing accounts under US GAAP. Such companies are, however, required to disclose the LIFO reserve (being the difference between the cost of inventory determined under LIFO and FIFO – the usual method used by IFRS companies) in the notes to the financial statements.

4.2 Deferred tax presentation and measurement

Under IFRS, deferred tax assets and liabilities are always classified as non-current. US GAAP requires the deferred tax asset or liability to be split between current and non-current in line with the underlying asset or liability to which it relates.

Differences may also occur since US GAAP requires that deferred tax assets are always recognised, with a valuation allowance made against the asset unless realisation is 'more likely than not' to occur. The approach under IFRS is to only recognise deferred tax assets where it is 'probable' that realisation will occur.

4.3 Revaluation

Under IFRS, property plant and equipment may be carried at historic cost or revalued amount (measured as fair value at the revaluation date), net of accumulated depreciation and impairment losses. Under US GAAP, revaluation is not generally permitted.

IFRS also permits revaluation of intangible assets where an active market exists which may be referred to in order to ascertain a value. Revaluation of intangible assets is not permitted under US GAAP.

4.4 Operating lease commitment disclosure

IFRS requires that the total commitments to pay rentals under operating leases must be disclosed in a financial commitments note. IAS 17 only requires disclosure of the operating lease rentals analysed between those amounts due in the next year, with a breakdown of when such lease commitments are due to expire. This does not reveal the total amount due over the whole life of the leases.

US GAAP requires this information to be disclosed both for operating and for finance/capital leases. This helps analysts who wish to capitalise operating leases. To do so, they must also make assumptions about the exact timing of operating lease rentals and an appropriate interest/discount rate.

4.5 Pensions (Extract pages 3, 4 and 7, e and k)

While IAS 19 permits either immediate recognition in full or the 'corridor method' for actuarial gains and losses, US GAAP only permits the corridor method. In addition, US GAAP requires the recognition of a minimum liability equal to the unfunded accumulated benefit obligation. No such requirement exists under IFRS.

The full recognition of pension surpluses and deficits on statement of financial position also requires the recognition of actuarial gains and losses directly in the statement of equity in the period in which they arise. Under US GAAP, the actuarial gains and losses are passed through the income statement over the expected remaining service life of the employees.

4.6 Presentation of minority interest

IFRS requires the presentation of a minority interest within equity. Note that under US GAAP, a minority interest is shown between equity and liabilities.

4.7 Derivatives and compound capital instruments

4.7.1 Convertible bonds

Under IAS 32, a convertible corporate bond is treated as a compound capital instrument, and the issue proceeds are split between an equity portion and debt portion and are accounted for separately. However, under US GAAP, the entire proceeds of the convertible bond are treated as a liability until conversion takes place or the debt is redeemed.

Note that a similar difference exists under IAS 39 with respect to multiple derivatives embedded in a single hybrid instrument, whereby the components may be separated under IFRS, but will be treated as a single instrument under US GAAP.

4.7.2 Freedom of classification for financial instruments

IAS 39 was amended in December 2003 to permit any financial instrument to be designated to the 'fair value' category, and marked to market through the income statement. IAS 39 was also amended to permit loans and receivables to be designated as 'available for sale' and marked to market through equity. US GAAP requires loans and receivables to be accounted for at amortised cost, and does not allow freedom in the usage of the fair value classification.

4.7.3 Reclassification of financial instruments

Whereas transfer out of the 'trading' category is permitted under US GAAP (although they should be rare), such transfers are prohibited under IAS 39.

Both US GAAP and IFRS employ the concept of 'tainting' the held-to-maturity category where a sale occurs, only IFRS is explicit in setting a two-year time limit for use of the 'held-to-maturity' classification. US GAAP also prohibits the use of the classification following a sale, but offers no explicit guidance on a time period.

4.8 Measurement of provisions

Under IFRS, provisions are measured as the best estimate of the amount required to settle the obligation (typically using an expected value approach) and must be discounted to a present value. US GAAP is informed by 'conservativism', and provisions are therefore measured at the low end of the range of possible amounts. In addition, there is no requirement to discount certain provisions to fair value.

4.9 Research and development (Extract page 7, i)

IAS 38 requires the capitalisation of all types of research and development expenditure where capitalisation requirements are met. Under US GAAP, almost all research and development expenditure must be expensed as incurred (save website development and software development in certain circumstances).

Note that purchased research and development assets within a business acquisition may be capitalised in order to determine goodwill under US GAAP, but the asset will be immediately written off through the income statement following the acquisition. IFRS 3 permits acquired research and development assets to be recognised as a finite life intangible (and subsequently amortised), or may be included within goodwill where it is not separately measurable (and subsequently subjected to impairment reviews).

4.10 Presentation of offsetting amounts

Whereas US GAAP requires offsetting amounts to be disclosed separately regardless of the circumstances, IFRS requires net presentation where a legal right of set-off exists and the entity intends to settle net.

4.11 Impairment

US GAAP requires the company to compare the carrying amount of a long-lived asset with its **undiscounted** cash flows to determine whether an impairment has arisen.

5 STATEMENT OF CASH FLOWS

5.1 Classification of interest

Under IAS 17, interest paid or received may be treated as an operating, investing or financing cash flow. US GAAP is entirely prescriptive, requiring interest to be treated as an operating cash flow only.

5.2 Inclusion of bank overdrafts in cash

IAS 1 permits bank overdrafts to be treated as cash if the overdraft forms an integral part of the entity's cash management. US GAAP does not permit this treatment.

Appendix – Extract from Novartis Group Form 20-F 2004

Significant differences between IFRS and United States Generally Accepted Accounting Principles (US GAAP)

The Group's consolidated financial statements have been prepared in accordance with IFRS, which as applied by the Group, differs in certain significant respects from US GAAP. The effects of the application of US GAAP to net income and equity are set out in the tables below.

	Notes	2004 $ (millions)	2003 $ (millions)
Net income under IFRS		5,767	5,016
US GAAP adjustments:			
Purchase accounting: Ciba-Geigy	a	−366	−339
Purchase accounting: other acquisitions	b	17	−175
Purchase accounting: IFRS goodwill amortization	c	170	172
Available-for-sale securities and derivative financial instruments	d	−183	−240
Pension provisions	e	−6	−18
Share-based compensation	f	−326	−273
Consolidation of share-based employee compensation foundation	g	−4	−3
Deferred taxes	h	100	−63
In-process research and development	I	−55	−260
Reversal of currency translation gain	j	−301	
Other	I	13	−20
Deferred tax effect on US GAAP adjustments		163	−9
Net income under US GAAP		4,989	3,788
Basic earnings per share under US GAAP (USD)		2.12	1.59
Diluted earnings per share under US GAAP (USD)		2.11	1.57

	Notes	Dec 31, 2004 $ (millions)	Dec 31, 2003 $ (millions)
Equity under IFRS		33,783	30,429
US GAAP adjustments:			
Purchase accounting: Ciba-Geigy	a	3,049	3,131
Purchase accounting: other acquisitions	b	2,803	2,808
Purchase accounting: IFRS goodwill amortization	c	554	327
Available-for-sale securities and derivative financial instruments	d	−64	
Pension provisions	e	1,346	1,209
Share-based compensation	f	−129	−96
Consolidation of share-based employee compensation foundation	g	−864	−728
Deferred taxes	h	−510	−609
In-process research and development	I	−1,489	−1,338
Minimum pension liability	k	−501	−37
Other	I	−45	−56
Deferred tax effect on US GAAP adjustments		168	−162
Total US GAAP adjustments		4,318	4,449
Equity under US GAAP		38,101	34,878

Components of Equity in Accordance with US GAAP

	Dec 31, 2004 $ (millions)	Dec 31, 2003 $ (millions)
Share capital	1,008	1,017
Treasury shares, at nominal value	−154	−151
Share premium	1,103	743
Retained earnings	32,178	31,069
Accumulated other comprehensive income:		
Currency translation adjustment	3,561	1,940
Unrealized market value adjustment on available-for-sale securities, net of taxes of USD −78 million (2003: USD −62 million)	725	275
Unrealized market value adjustment on cash-flow hedges, net of taxes of USD 5 million (2003: USD 7 million)	−20	7
Minimum pension liability, net of taxes of USD 201 million (2003: USD 15 million)	−300	−22
December 31	38,101	34,878

	2004 $ (millions)	2003 $ (millions)
January 1	34,878	33,225
Net unrealised market value adjustment	397	381
Increase in share premium related to share-based compensation	334	373
Minimum pension liability	−278	−22
Associated companies' equity movement	50	10
Foreign currency translation adjustment	1,621	2,735
Net income for the year under US GAAP	4,989	3,788
Dividends paid	−1,888	−1,654
Acquisition of treasury shares	−2,002	−500
Redemption of call and put options on Novartis shares		−3,458
December 31	38,101	34,878

Notes to the US GAAP Reconciliation

(a) **Purchase accounting**: The accounting treatment for the 1996 merger of Sandoz and Ciba-Geigy under IFRS is different from the accounting treatment under US GAAP. For IFRS purposes the merger was accounted for under the uniting of interests method (no longer allowed by IFRS), however, for US GAAP the merger did not meet all of the required conditions of Accounting Principles Board Opinion No. 16 for a pooling of interests and therefore is accounted for as a purchase under US GAAP. Under US GAAP, Sandoz would be deemed to be the acquirer with the assets and liabilities of Ciba-Geigy being recorded at their estimated fair values and the results of Ciba-Geigy being included from December 20, 1996. Under US GAAP, the cost of Ciba-Geigy to Sandoz was approximately USD 28.5 billion. All of the purchase price was allocated to identified property, plant & equipment and intangible assets with a definite useful life. There was therefore no residual goodwill arising from accounting for this transaction.

The components of equity and the income statement adjustments related to the US GAAP purchase accounting adjustment for 2004 and 2003 are as follows:

2004 Components to reconcile	Net income $ (millions)	Foreign currency translation adjustments $ (millions)	Equity $ (millions)
Intangible assets related to marketed products	−518	369	3,972
Property, plant & equipment	55	−67	−726
Inventory		58	627
Other identifiable intangibles	−25	5	53
Investments		14	149
Deferred taxes	122	−95	−1,026
Total adjustments	−366	284	3,049

2003 Components to reconcile	Net income $ (millions)	Foreign currency translation adjustments $ (millions)	Equity $ (millions)
Intangible assets related to marketed products	−478	472	4,121
Property, plant & equipment	51	−81	−714
Inventory		62	569
Other identifiable intangibles	−25	9	73
Investments		15	135
Deferred taxes	113	−120	−1,053
Total adjustments	−339	357	3,131

The intangible assets related to marketed products and other identifiable intangibles are being amortized over 15 and 10 years, respectively.

(b) **Purchase accounting: other acquisitions**: Prior to January 1, 1995, the Group wrote off all goodwill, being the difference between the purchase price and the aggregate fair value of property, plant & equipment and intangible assets and liabilities acquired in a business combination, directly to equity, in accordance with IFRS existing at that time. The adoption of IAS 22 (revised 1993) required that goodwill was capitalized and amortized, however, did not require prior period restatement. The material component of goodwill recorded directly to equity, under IFRS prior to January 1, 1995, related to the acquisition of Gerber Products in 1994. The net book value of goodwill under US GAAP attributable to Gerber Products was USD 2 870 million as of December 31, 2004 and 2003. In accordance with IAS 22, the difference between the purchase price and the aggregate fair value of property, plant & equipment and intangible assets and liabilities acquired in a business combination is capitalized as goodwill and amortized over its useful life, not to exceed 20 years. Under US GAAP, the difference between the purchase price and fair value of net assets acquired as part of a pre-1995 business combination is also capitalized as goodwill. Effective January 1, 2002, the Group adopted Statement of Financial Accounting Standards No. 142 (SFAS 142), *Goodwill and other Intangible Assets*. SFAS 142 requires that all goodwill and other intangible assets existing on implementation on January 1, 2002 are tested for impairment and thereafter are assessed for impairment on an annual basis. From January 1, 2002 goodwill and intangible assets deemed to have an indefinite useful life are no longer amortized on a regular basis. For the purpose of the reconciliation to US GAAP, goodwill was generally amortized through the income statement over an estimated useful life of 20 years up to December 31, 2001. Therefore, there is no amortization charge since 2002 under US GAAP.

BPP LEARNING MEDIA

In 2004, as a result of adverse changes in the operating environment of certain businesses, or of the decision to divest certain products, in accordance with SFAS 142, non-cash charges of USD 42 million were recorded (2003: USD 119 million) for impairments of goodwill and divestments. Gerber goodwill was also reviewed for potential impairments in 2004 however, this did not result in the Group needing to record a charge. The process of evaluating goodwill involves making judgments and estimates relating to the projection and discounting of future cash flows. This evaluation is sensitive to changes in the discount rate. An increase to discount rates is likely to result in a significant impairment charge under US GAAP.

Also included are US GAAP adjustments to the equity method accounting results of Roche and Chiron totaling USD 12 million income (2003: USD 56 million expense). The impact of the additional impairment charges, the Roche and Chiron adjustments and other adjustments totaling a net income of USD 47 million resulted in a USD 17 million income in 2004 (2003: USD 175 million expense). Note m (ix) provides further disclosure regarding impairment under US GAAP.

(c) **Purchase accounting**: **IFRS goodwill amortization:** As described above, as of January 1, 2002, goodwill is no longer amortized but only subject to impairment testing under US GAAP. The corresponding reversal of the regular goodwill amortization under IFRS resulted in an additional income in the US GAAP reconciliation of USD 170 million (2003: USD 172 million).

(d) **Available-for-sale marketable securities and derivative financial instruments**: Under IFRS, fair value changes which relate to the underlying movement in exchange rates on available-for-sale debt securities have to be recognized in the income statement. Under US GAAP, SFAS 133 requires the entire movement in the fair value of the securities to be recognized in equity, including any part that relates to foreign exchange movements. This resulted in US GAAP income being reduced by USD 181 million (2003: USD 228 million).

Prior to the adoption of IAS 39 from January 1, 2001 in the IFRS consolidated financial statements, investments were stated at the lower of cost or market value on an individual basis. This results in a different amount of unrealized gains or losses being recorded in the separate component of equity under US GAAP compared to IFRS and an additional expense under US GAAP on disposal of available-for-sale securities during 2004 and 2003. This resulted in an additional expense of USD 2 million (2003: USD 12 million).

The above differences result in an additional US GAAP expense of USD 183 million in 2004 (2003: USD 240 million).

In 2004, the Group recorded a revaluation to fair value in its equity on privately held companies under IFRS. Under US GAAP such investments have to be accounted for at cost. Accordingly, USD 64 million booked in the IFRS equity was reversed.

(e) **Pension provisions**: Under IFRS, pension costs and similar obligations are accounted for in accordance with IAS 19, *Employee Benefits*. For purposes of US GAAP, pension costs for defined benefit plans are accounted for in accordance with SFAS 87 *Employers' Accounting for Pensions* and the disclosures are presented in accordance with SFAS 132 *Employers' Disclosures about Pensions and Other Post-retirement Benefits*. Differences in the amounts of net periodic benefit costs and the prepaid benefit cost exist due to different transition date rules, pre-1999 accounting rule differences and different provisions for recognition of a prepaid pension asset. Under IFRS the recognition of a prepaid asset is subject to certain limitations, and any unrecognised prepaid pension asset is recorded as pension expense. US GAAP does not allow a limitation on the recognition of prepaid pension assets recorded in the statement of financial position.

The following is a reconciliation of the statement of financial position and income statement amounts recognized for IFRS and US GAAP for both pension and post-employment benefit plans.

	2004 $ (millions)	2003 $ (millions)
Pension plans:		
Net asset recognised for IFRS	3,349	3,046
Difference in unrecognised amounts	1,446	1,314
Net asset recognised for US GAAP	4,795	4,360
Net periodic pension (cost)/income recognized in IFRS	−198	−54
Difference in recognition of actuarial and past service amounts	−9	−35
Net periodic pension (cost)/income recognised for US GAAP	−207	−89
Other post-employment benefit plans:		
Liability recognised for IFRS	−495	−460
Difference in unrecognised amounts	−100	−105
Liability recognised for US GAAP	−595	−565
Net periodic post-employment benefit cost recognized for IFRS	−75	−63
Difference in recognition of actuarial and past service amounts	3	17
Net periodic post-employment benefit cost recognized for US GAAP	−72	−46
Total US GAAP income statement difference on pensions and other post-employment benefits	−6	−18

The disclosures required by US GAAP are different from those provided under IFRS. On December 23, 2003, the Financial Accounting Standards Board ('FASB') issued *Statement of Financial Accounting Standards* No. 132 (revised 2003), *Employers' Disclosures about Pensions and Other Post-retirement Benefits*, an amendment of FASB Statements No. 87, 88 and 106, and a revision of FASB Statement No. 132. The following provides the required separate presentation for Swiss and foreign plans under US GAAP:

	Swiss pension plans		Foreign pension plans	
	2004 $ (millions)	2003 $ (millions)	2004 $ (millions)	2003 $ (millions)
Benefit obligation at beginning of the year	9,793	8,569	4,072	3,276
Service cost	179	137	172	148
Interest cost	366	358	214	201
Actuarial losses	1,193	240	208	455
Plan amendments			−41	15
Foreign currency translation	1,048	1,093	156	163
Benefit payments	−659	−604	−213	−186
Benefit obligation at end of the year	11,920	9,793	4,568	4,072
Fair value of plan assets at beginning of the year	13,218	11,771	2,910	2,594
Actual return on plan assets	484	571	254	345
Foreign currency translation	1,348	1,451	69	55
Employer contributions			207	92
Employee contributions	45	29	7	10
Plan amendments			−7	
Benefit payments	−659	−604	−213	−186
Fair value of plan assets at end of the year	14,436	13,218	3,227	2,910
Funded status	2,516	3,425	−1,341	−1,162
Unrecognized past service cost			−35	−49
Unrecognized net actuarial losses	2,699	1,285	956	861
Net asset/(liability) in the statement of financial position	5,215	4,710	−420	−350
Components of net periodic benefit cost				
Service cost	179	137	172	148
Interest cost	366	358	214	201
Expected returns on plan assets	−520	−613	−195	−183

	Swiss pension plans		Foreign pension plans	
	2004 $ (millions)	2003 $ (millions)	2004 $ (millions)	2003 $ (millions)
Employee contributions	−45	−29	−7	−10
Recognized actuarial losses			75	53
Recognized past service cost			−32	27
Net periodic benefit cost/(income)	−20	−147	227	236
Accumulated benefit obligation	11,217	8,248	4,209	3,565

Principle actuarial assumptions used	%	%	%	%
Weighted average assumptions used to determine benefit obligations at the end of the year				
Discount rate	3.3	3.8	5.2	5.7
Expected rate of salary increase	1.5	2.5	3.6	3.7
Weighted average assumptions used to determine net periodic pension cost of the year ended				
Discount rate	3.8	4.0	5.5	6.2
Expected return on plan assets	4.0	5.0	6.7	8.2
Expected rate of salary increase	2.5	2.5	3.6	3.7

(f) **Share-based compensation**: The Group does not account for share-based compensation, as it is not required under IFRS (although this is now required by IFRS 2). Under US GAAP, the Group applies Accounting Principles Board Opinion No. 25 (APB 25) *Accounting for Stock Issued to Employees* and related interpretations in accounting for its plans. As described in Note 26, the Group has several plans that are subject to measurement under APB 25. These include the Long-Term Performance Plan, the Leveraged Share Savings Plan, the Swiss Employee Share Ownership Plan (ESOP), the Restricted Share Plan and the US Management ADS Appreciation Cash Plan.

Compensation expense recognized under the Long-Term Performance Plan was USD 27 million for 2004 (2003: USD 29 million).

The Leveraged Share Savings Plan is considered to be compensatory based on the fair value of the allocated Novartis AG shares. The shares are blocked for a five year period, at which time the bonus taken in shares are matched on a one-for-one basis. Compensation expense recognized under this plan was USD 27 million for 2004 (2003: USD 16 million).

The Swiss Employee Share Ownership Plan (ESOP) is considered to be compensatory based on the fair value of Novartis AG shares at a fixed date. Compensation expense recognized under this plan was USD 219 million for 2004 (2003: USD 176 million).

The Restricted Share Plan is considered to be compensatory based on the strike price for the underlying instruments, which is zero at the date of grant. Compensation expense is recorded at the grant date and is calculated as the number of instruments granted, multiplied by the share price on that date. Compensation expense recognized under this Plan was USD 5 million for 2004 (2003: USD 5 million).

The US Management ADS Appreciation Cash Plan is considered to be variable because the final benefit to employees depends on the Group's share price at the exercise date. Compensation expense is recorded at each statement of financial position date by estimating the number of rights outstanding multiplied by the spread between the share price on the statement of financial position date and the strike price. Compensation expense for this plan was USD 21 million for 2004 (2003: USD 47 million).

This plan was supplemented in 2001 by the US ADS Incentive Plan which grants options on Novartis ADSs.

In 2004, employees were given the choice of converting their option grants to share grants at the ratio of 4:1. Under US GAAP such share grants are considered to be compensatory based on the fair value of Novartis AG shares or ADS at the grant date. In 2004 this expense amounted to USD 27 million.

The total US GAAP expense of the above items is as follows:

	2004 $ (millions)	2003 $ (millions)
Long-Term Performance Plan	27	29
Leveraged Share Savings Plan	27	16
Swiss ESOP Plan	219	176
Restricted Share Plan	5	5
ADS Appreciation Cash Plan	21	47
Option grants converted to share grants	27	
Total US GAAP additional compensation expense	326	273

(g) **Consolidation of share-based employee compensation Foundation**: The Group has an employee share participation Foundation that settles the obligations of the Group's share-based compensation plans that is not required to be consolidated for IFRS. However, this Foundation is consolidated under US GAAP.

The consolidation of this Foundation reduces net income by USD 4 million (2003: USD 3 million) and US GAAP equity by USD 864 million (2003: USD 728 million).

(h) **Deferred taxes**: Under IAS 12 (revised) *Income Taxes* and US GAAP, unrealized profits resulting from intercompany transactions are eliminated from the carrying amount of assets, such as inventory. In accordance with IAS 12 (revised) the Group calculates the tax effect with reference to the local tax rate of the company that holds the inventory (the buyer) at period-end. However, US GAAP requires that the tax effect is calculated with reference to the local tax rate in the seller's or manufacturer's jurisdiction. The effect of this difference increased US GAAP income in 2004 by USD 100 million (2003: USD 63 million reduction) and reduced equity by USD 510 million (2003: USD 609 million).

(i) **In-process research and development (IPR&D)**: Under US GAAP, IPR&D is considered to be a separate asset that needs to be written-off immediately following the acquisition as the feasibility of the acquired research and development has not been fully tested and the technology has no alternative future use. Up to March 31, 2004, IFRS did not consider that IPR&D was an intangible asset that could be separately recognized, accordingly it was included in goodwill for IFRS purposes. Under IAS 38 (revised) for all post-March 31, 2004 acquisitions IPR&D is now separately identified and recorded as an intangible asset subject to annual impairment tests.

During 2004, IPR&D arose on the acquisition of 100% of the shares of Sabex (USD 132 million) and Durascan (USD 8 million).

During 2003, IPR&D has been identified for US GAAP purposes in connection with acquisitions, principally the acquisition of 51% of the shares of Idenix. All projects of Idenix are under research or development, therefore the full goodwill recorded under IFRS amounting to USD 297 million was considered as IPR&D under US GAAP. IPR&D recognized on other acquisitions amounted to USD 39 million in 2003. The income booked for the reversal of the amortization of IPR&D recorded under IFRS as a component of goodwill amortization amounted to USD 85 million (2003: USD 76 million). The total net IPR&D expense for 2004 was USD 55 million (2003: USD 260 million). The impact of IPR&D reduced US GAAP equity by USD 1,489 million (2003: USD 1,338 million).

(j)   **Reversal of currency translation gain**: During 2004, under IFRS the Group recorded a recycling gain from cumulative translation differences of USD 301 million arising from the partial repayment of capital of a subsidiary. US GAAP does not recognize this concept so this gain has been eliminated for US GAAP purposes.

(k)   **Minimum pension liability**: The additional minimum pension liability required under US GAAP reduced equity by USD 501 million (2003: USD 37 million).

(l)   **Other**: There are also differences between IFRS and US GAAP in relation to (1) capitalized interest and capitalized software, (2) LIFO inventory, (3) reversals of inventory provisions. None of these differences are individually significant and they are therefore shown as a combined total.

(m)   **Additional US GAAP disclosures**:

    (i)   **Financial assets and liabilities**: Apart from the following exceptions, the US GAAP carrying value of financial assets and liabilities is equal to the IFRS carrying values.

    (ii)   **Cash, cash equivalents and time deposits**

	2004 $ (millions)	2003 $ (millions)
Carrying value of cash and cash equivalents under IFRS	6,083	5,646
Carrying values of time deposits under IFRS	1,353	651
Change due to consolidation of share-based compensation foundation under US GAAP	−712	−650
Total under US GAAP	6,724	5,647

    (iii)   **Marketable securities**

	2004 $ (millions)	2003 $ (millions)
Carrying values of marketable securities under IFRS	6,623	6,134
Carrying values of other investments under IFRS	1,286	1,076
Marketable securities in share-based compensation foundation consolidated under US GAAP	13	16
Total under US GAAP	7,922	7,226

The components of available-for-sale marketable securities under US GAAP at December 31, 2004 and 2003 are the following:

	Cost$ (millions)	Gross unrealised gains $ (millions)	Gross unrealised losses $ (millions)	Carrying value and estimated fair value $ (millions)
As at December 31, 2004				
Available-for-sale-securities:				
Equity securities	681	201	−10	872
Debt securities	6,587	494	−31	7,050
Total	7,268	695	−41	7,922
As at December 31, 2003				
Available-for-sale-securities:				
Equity securities	1,744	209	−293	1,660
Debt securities	5,299	270	−3	5,566
Total	7,043	479	−296	7,226

Proceeds from sales of available-for-sale securities were USD 5 915 million and USD 6 293 million in 2004 and 2003 respectively. Gross realized gains were USD 75 million and USD 199 million on those sales in 2004 and 2003 respectively. Gross realized losses were USD 228 million and USD 115 million on those sales in 2004 and 2003 respectively. The cost used to determine the gain or loss on these sales was calculated using the weighted average method. As at December 31, 2004 there were no (2003: USD 258 million) unrealized losses on equity securities that existed for more than 12 months.

The maturities of the available-for-sale debt securities included above at December 31, 2004 are as follows:

	2003 $ (millions)
Within one year	325
Over one year through five years	5,145
Over five years through ten years	918
Over ten years	662
Total	7,050

(iv) **Non-derivative financial instruments**: The US GAAP carrying values are equivalent to the IFRS carrying values for all non-derivative financial assets and liabilities with the exception of privately held companies that are valued at cost under US GAAP. Non-derivative financial assets consist of cash and cash equivalents, time deposits, and marketable securities. Non-derivative liabilities consist of commercial paper, bank or other short-term financial debts, and long-term debt.

The carrying amount of cash and cash equivalents, time deposits, commercial paper, and bank and other short-term financial debts approximates their estimated fair values due to the short-term nature of these instruments. The fair values of marketable securities are estimated based on listed market prices or broker or dealer price quotes. The fair value of long-term debt is estimated based on the current quoted market rates available for debt with similar terms and maturities.

The estimated fair values of the long and short-term financial debt are provided in notes 18 and 20 to the IFRS consolidated financial statements.

(v) **Earnings per share**: As discussed in item (g) above, in the past, the Group established the Novartis Foundation for Employee Participation to assist the Group in meeting its obligations under various employee benefit plans and programs. This Foundation supports existing, previously approved employee benefit plans.

For US GAAP purposes, the Group consolidates this Foundation. The cost of Novartis AG shares held by the Foundation is shown as a reduction of shareholders' equity in the Group's US GAAP statement of financial position.

Any dividend transactions between the Group and the Foundation are eliminated, and the difference between the fair value of the shares on the date of contribution to the Foundation and the fair values of the shares at December 31, is included in consolidated retained earnings. Shares held in the Foundation are not considered outstanding in the computation of US GAAP earnings per share.

The consolidation of this entity had the following impact on basic and diluted earnings per share:

Basic earnings per share	2004	2003
Net income under US GAAP (USD millions)	4,989	3,788
Weighted average number of shares in issue under IFRS	2,447,954,717	2,473,522,565
Weighted average number of treasury shares due to consolidation of the employee share participation foundation under US GAAP	−92,464,445	−93,430,809
Weighted average number of shares in issue under US GAAP	2,355,490,272	2,380,091,756
Basic earnings per share under US GAAP (USD)	2.12	1.59

Diluted earnings per share	2004	2003
Net income under US GAAP (USD millions)	4,989	3,788
Weighted average number of shares in issue under IFRS	2,447,954,717	2,473,522,565
Call options on Novartis shares		27,446,092
Weighted average number of treasury shares due to consolidation of the employee share participation foundation under US GAAP	−92,464,445	−93,430,809
Weighted average number of shares for diluted earnings per share under US GAAP	2,355,490,272	2,380,091,756
Basic earnings per share under US GAAP (USD)	2.11	1.57

(vi)   **Pro forma earnings per share**: Statement of Financial Accounting Standards No. 123 (SFAS 123) *Accounting for Stock-Based Compensation* established accounting and disclosure requirements using a fair-value based method of accounting for share-based employee compensation. Had the Group accounted for share options in accordance with SFAS 123, net income and earnings per share would have been the pro forma amounts indicated below:

	2004	2003
Net income under US GAAP (USD millions):		
As reported	4,989	3,788
Stock-based employee compensation cost included in the determination of net income	326	273
Stock-based employee compensation cost that would have been included in the determination of net income if the fair value based method has been applied to all awards	−542	−459
Pro forma	4,773	3,602
Earnings per share (USD):		
As reported:		
Basic	2.12	1.59
Diluted	2.11	1.57
Pro forma:		
Basic	2.03	1.51
Diluted	2.02	1.49

The weighted average assumptions used in determining the fair value of option grants were as follows:

	2004	2003
Dividend yield	1.8%	1.8%
Expected volatility	23.1%	24.0%
Discount rate	3.6%	4.0%
Expected life	10 yrs	9 yrs

These pro forma effects may not be representative of future amounts since the estimated fair value of share options on the date of grant is amortized to expense over the vesting period and additional options may be granted in future years.

(vii) **Deferred tax**: The deferred tax asset less valuation allowance at December 31, 2004 and 2003 comprises USD 1 265 million and USD 1 590 million of current assets and USD 1 456 million and USD 987 million of non-current assets respectively. The deferred tax liability at December 31, 2004 and 2003 comprises USD 1 289 million and USD 1 202 million of current liabilities and USD 3 993 million and USD 3 935 million of non-current liabilities respectively.

(viii) **Foreign currency translation**: The Group has accounted for operations in highly inflationary economies in accordance with IAS 21 (revised) and IAS 29. The accounting under IAS 21 (revised) and IAS 29 complies with Item 18 of Form 20-F and is different from that required by US GAAP.

(ix) **US GAAP goodwill**: Goodwill is the only intangible asset within the Group which is not subject to amortization under US GAAP. All goodwill components were tested for impairment during 2004. The fair values of the businesses were determined using the expected present values of future cash flows.

The Group estimates that the aggregate amortization expense for intangibles subject to amortization for each of the five succeeding financial years will not materially differ from the current aggregate amortization expense.

The changes in the carrying amount of goodwill for the years ended December 31, 2004 and 2003 are as follows:

	Pharmaceuticals Division $ (millions)	Consumer Health Division $ (millions)	Total $ (millions)
January 1, 2003	67	4,399	4,466
Additions		7	7
Impairment losses	−12	−179	−191
Goodwill written off related to disposal of businesses	−35	−5	−40
Reclassification to separately identified intangibles		−423	−423
Translation effects	2	116	118
December 31, 2003	22	3,915	3,937
Additions		535	535
Impairment losses		−106	−106
Goodwill written off related to disposal of businesses		−13	−13
Reclassification from separately identified intangibles		6	6
Translation effects	1	80	81
December 31, 2004	23	4,417	4,440

(x)   **Details to significant capitalized trademarks and product rights:**

	Gross carrying value Dec 31, 2004 $ (millions)	Accumulated amortization Dec 31, 2004 $ (millions)	Net carrying value Dec 31, 2004 $ (millions)	Net carrying value Dec 31, 2003 $ (millions)
Famvir	1,860	−559	1,301	1,360
Voltaren	2,011	−955	1,056	1,095
Tegretol	653	−261	392	385
Other pharmaceutical products	4,255	−2,131	2,124	2,777
Total Pharmaceuticals Division	8,779	−3,906	4,873	5,617
Sandoz	864	−142	722	561
OTC	155	−55	100	100
Animal Health	500	−238	262	274
Medical Nutrition	25	−23	2	7
CIBA Vision	540	−223	317	336
Total Consumer Health Division	2,084	−681	1,403	1,278
Total	10,863	−4,587	6,276	6,895

Novartis usually applies the straight-line amortization method although there can be exceptions as indicated below. For Pharmaceutical Division products the patent life generally reflects the useful life although in certain circumstances a value is also given to the non-patent protected period.

For other segments the maximum useful life used is 20 years.

Famvir

The value of Famvir has been bifurcated, with the majority of the value assigned to its sales under patent protection. This portion is amortized over the remaining patent life until 2010.

The remainder is amortized over an additional 10-year period representing its value as a branded non-patent protected product. This amortization charge is half of the amount during the patent period.

Voltaren

Voltaren is off-patent in the US and many other countries. Novartis applies a straight-line amortization period and the useful life ends in 2011.

Tegretol

Tegretol is off-patent. Novartis applies a straight-line amortization period and the useful life ends in 2011.

(xi)   **Effect of New Accounting Pronouncements: International Financial Reporting Standards:**
In December 2003, International Accounting Standards (IAS) were amended as the IASB released revised IAS 32, *Financial Instruments: Presentation* and IAS 39, *Financial Instruments: Recognition and Measurement*. These Standards replace IAS 32 (revised 2000), and supersedes IAS 39 (revised 2000), and must be applied for annual periods beginning on or after January 1, 2005.

In December 2003, as a part of the IASB's project to improve International Accounting Standards, the IASB released revisions to the following Standards that supersede the previously released versions of those Standards: IAS 1, *Presentation of Financial Statements*; IAS 2, *Inventories*; IAS 8, *Accounting Policies, Changes in Accounting Estimates and Errors*; IAS 10, *Events after the Statement of financial position Date*; IAS 16, *Property, Plant and Equipment*; IAS 17, *Leases*; IAS 21, *The Effects of Changes in Foreign*

Exchange Rates, IAS 24, *Related Party Disclosures*; IAS 27, *Consolidated and Separate Financial Statements*; IAS 28, *Investments in Associates*; IAS 31, *Interests in Joint Ventures*; IAS 33, *Earnings per Share* and IAS 40, *Investment Property*. The revised Standards must be applied for annual periods beginning on or after January 1, 2005. During 2004 the following International Financial Reporting Standards (IFRS) were issued: IFRS 2, *Share-Based Payments*; IFRS 3, *Business Combinations*; IFRS 4, *Insurance Contracts*; IFRS 5, *Non-Current Assets Held for Sale and Discontinued Operations* and IFRS 6, *Exploration for and Evaluation of Mineral Resources*. The following is a summary of the material impact on the Group's consolidated financial statements expected from applying these revised Standards.

(a) **IAS 39 on financial instruments: cash flow hedges for forecast intragroup transactions**

Under IAS 39 (revised) no cash flow hedge accounting is available on forecast intragroup transactions. Any deferral of hedging gains or losses that were included in the 2004 and 2003 consolidated financial statements needs to be reversed.

(b) **Presentation of minority interests to be changed**

IAS 1 (revised) requires that minority interests are included in the Group's equity in the consolidated statement of financial position and not be shown as a separate category and that it is no longer deducted in arriving at the Group's net income. The effect of this is to increase the Group's equity at January 1, 2005 by USD 138 million. Earnings per share will continue to be calculated on the net income attributable solely to the equity holders of Novartis AG.

(c) **Presentation of the tax related to associated companies to be changed**

IAS 1 (revised) requires that the tax related to the result of associated companies is no longer included in the Group's tax expense. From January 1, 2005 the Group's share in the results of its associated companies will be included on one income statement line and will be calculated after deduction of their taxes and minority interests.

(d) **IFRS 2 on share-based payments**

IFRS 2 comes into force on January 1, 2005 and requires that the fair value of any equity instruments granted to employees or other parties is recognized as an expense. Novartis only uses grants of its equity instruments to compensate its employees. Up to December 31, 2004 the approximate fair value of these equity instruments has been charged to the business operations in the segment reporting but has been off-set by a matching income in Corporate other income & expense. Therefore, no pre-tax operating income charge was ultimately recognized in the Group's IFRS consolidated financial statements.

From January 1, 2005 Novartis will calculate the fair value of the granted options using a variant of the lattice binominal approach. The amounts will be charged to income over the relevant vesting periods, adjusted to reflect actual and expected levels of vesting. As permitted by IFRS 2, Novartis will restate in 2005 its prior year audited historical consolidated financial statements to reflect the cost of grants awarded since the effective date of IFRS 2 on November 7, 2002.

The Group does not anticipate that there will be any material additional tax benefit from this change in accounting policy.

(e) **SIC-12 change relating to consolidation of equity compensation plans**

Changes to the Standing Interpretations Committee SIC-12 come into force on January 1, 2005 which require the consolidation of equity compensation plans. Prior to this change there was no requirement under IFRS to consolidate these plans.

The effect of consolidation of these plans from January 1, 2005 will be to reduce the Group's financial assets and equity by USD 864 million and to increase its treasury shares by 87.3 million.

This change will have a corresponding impact on the Group's earnings per share (EPS) calculation prepared under IFRS. The equity compensation plan is already consolidated under US GAAP and the additional treasury shares are included in the US GAAP EPS calculation.

(f)   **IFRS 3 on business combinations and related goodwill amortization**

Under IFRS 3, with effect from January 1, 2005, goodwill is considered to have an indefinite life and is not amortized, but is subject to annual impairment testing. This relates not only to goodwill that has been separately identified and recorded in the Divisions' operating statement of financial positions but also to the goodwill that is embedded in the equity accounting of associated companies. Additional goodwill of USD 352 million recognized on transactions consummated after March 31, 2004 is already subject to the new accounting policy and has not been amortized.

(g)   **IAS 38 revised on intangible assets**

Under IAS 38 (revised), Novartis is required to adopt changes to accounting for intangible assets at the same time as it adopts IFRS 3. The following are the principal accounting policy changes.

–   A cost needs to be allocated to In-Process Research & Development (IPR&D) as part of the process of allocating the purchase price of a newly acquired business combination. This amount needs to be recorded separately from goodwill and must be assessed for impairment on an annual basis. Once a project included in IPR&D has been successfully developed and is available for use it needs to be amortized over its useful life. Previously, IPR&D was included under goodwill for IFRS purposes but not for US GAAP accounting purposes, where it was separately recognized and immediately expensed. As required by the transitional rules, IPR&D has already been separately capitalized for IFRS purposes for all post-March 31, 2004 acquisitions.

–   Acquired R&D assets, such as those related to up-front and milestone payments also need to be capitalized as intangible assets, even if it is uncertain as to whether the R&D will ultimately be successful in producing a saleable product. Previously intangible assets were only recognized if they were acquired after FDA or similar regulatory body approval. Under US GAAP acquired R&D assets that have not received regulatory approval will continue to be immediately expensed.

(xii)   **Effect of New Accounting Pronouncements: US GAAP**: In December 2003, the Medicare Prescription Drug, Improvements and Modernization Act of 2003 (the Medicare Act) was approved in the United States. The Medicare Act provides for two new prescription drug benefit features under Medicare. The Group provides post-retirement benefits to its United States employees so the benefits provided are impacted by the Medicare Act. SFAS 106, *Employers' Accounting for Post-retirement Benefits other than Pensions*, requires that enacted changes in the law that take effect in future periods and that will affect the future level of benefit coverage be considered in the current period measurements for benefits expected to be provided in those future periods. The Medicare Act reduced the cost of medical benefits to be borne by the Group by USD 7 million in 2004. The effect of this change in estimate is included in the December 31, 2004 liability for other post-employment benefits.

FIN 46 *Consolidation of Variable Interest Entities* was effective for Novartis starting January 1, 2004. The Group has concluded that this had no impact on the consolidated financial statements.

In March 2004, the EITF reached consensus on Issue No. 03-1, *The Meaning of Other-Than-Temporary Impairment and its Application to Certain Investments* ("EITF 03-01"). EITF 03.01 provides guidance on other-than-temporary impairment models for marketable debt and equity securities and non-marketable securities accounted for under the cost method. On September 30, 2004, the FASB issued FSP 03-01-1, *Effective Date of Paragraphs* 10-20 of EITF Issue 03-01, *The Meaning of Other-Than-Temporary Impairment and its Application to Certain Investments*, delaying the effective date for the recognition and measurement guidance in EITF 03-01, until certain implementation issues are addressed and a final FSP is issued. The disclosure requirements in EITF 03-01 remain effective. In light of the deliberations on EITF 03-01, the Group changed its policy for the accounting for other-than temporary impairments, such that all available-for-sale equity securities with unrealized losses at the statement of financial position date are assessed for impairment (previously when the fair value was 50% of cost for a sustained period of six months). The effect of the change in estimate, which has also been adopted in the Group's IFRS consolidated financial statements, has been to record additional impairment charges on the available-for-sale equity securities of USD 101 million. Please also refer to Note 1 "Accounting Policies".

In November 2004, the FASB issued FASB Statement No. 151, *Inventory Costs*, an amendment of ARB No. 43, Chapter 4, clarifying the existing requirements in ARB No. 43 by adopting language similar to that used in IAS 2.

The guidance is effective for inventory costs incurred during fiscal years beginning after June 15, 2003. The adoption of FAS 151 will not have an impact on the Group's consolidated results of operation or financial position, since the key elements are already utilized in the Group's IFRS and US GAAP consolidated financial statements.

In December 2004, the FASB published FASB Statement No. 123 (revised 2004), *Share-Based Payments*. This provides guidance on how companies must recognize the compensation cost relating to share-based payment transactions in their financial statements. It will require companies to recognize a compensation cost for the value of options granted in exchange for employee services, based on the grant date fair value of those instruments. FAS No. 123 (revised) is effective for public entities as of the beginning of the first interim or annual reporting period that begins after June 15, 2005, however early application is possible. Novartis intends to adopt this revised Standard from January 1, 2005.

CHAPTER ROUNDUP

ITEM	IFRS	US GAAP
INCOME STATEMENT ITEMS		
Extraordinary items	Not permitted	Permitted but restricted
Segmental reporting	Business area and geographical area	Components used internally for reporting to top management
Interest charges	Capitalisation of interest permitted	Capitalisation of interest mandatory
Joint ventures	Equity method or proportional consolidation	Equity method only
EPS	No requirement for discontinued activities	Requires disclosure of discontinued activities and extraordinary items
Discontinues operations	Post-tax income/loss on income statement	Pre- and post-tax income/loss on income statement
STATEMENT OF FINANCIAL POSITION ITEMS		
Inventory	LIFO not permitted	LIFO permitted
Deferred tax	Non-current asset/liability	Split between current and non-current
Revaluation	Permitted	Not permitted
Operating leases	Total commitments disclosed for operating leases	Full disclosure for both operating and finance leases
Pensions	Full recognition or corridor method	Corridor method only
Minority interest	Within equity	Between equity and liabilities
Derivatives		
– Convertible bond	Split between equity and debt	Treated debt until converted
– Financial instruments	May use fair values	No freedom to use fair value
– Reclassification	Reclassification from trading not permitted	Reclassification from trading permitted
Provisions	Best estimate	Conservatism
R&D	Must capitalise if requirements met	Expensed as incurred
Offsetting amounts	Netted where legal right of set-off exists	No netting
STATEMENT OF CASH FLOWS		
Interest	Maybe in – operating cash flow – investing cash flow – financing cash flow	Operating cash flow only
Bank overdrafts	Part of cash	Not part of cash

TEST YOUR KNOWLEDGE

There are no Test Your Knowledge questions for this chapter, it is simply summarising information from earlier chapters.

BPP
LEARNING MEDIA

INDEX